ACCLAIM FOR COLLEEN COBLE

"Coble's atmospheric and suspenseful series launch should appeal to fans of Tracie Peterson and other authors of Christian romantic suspense."

—*LIBRARY JOURNAL*
REVIEW OF *TIDEWATER INN*

"Romantically tense, but with just the right touch of danger, this cowboy love story is surprisingly clever—and pleasingly sweet."

—USATODAY.COM
REVIEW OF *BLUE MOON PROMISE*

"Colleen Coble will keep you glued to each page as she shows you the beauty of God's most primitive land and the dangers it hides."

—WWW.ROMANCEJUNKIES.COM

"[An] outstanding, completely engaging tale that will have you on the edge of your seat . . . A must-have for all fans of romantic suspense!"

—THEROMANCEREADERSCONNECTION.COM
REVIEW OF *ANATHEMA*

"Colleen Coble lays an intricate trail in *Without a Trace* and draws the reader on like a hound with a scent."

—*ROMANTIC TIMES*, 4½ STARS

"Coble's historical series just keeps getting better with each entry."

—*LIBRARY JOURNAL* STARRED
REVIEW OF *THE LIGHTKEEPER'S BALL*

"Don't ever mistake [Coble's] for the fluffy romances with a little bit of suspense. She writes solid suspense, and she ties it all together beautifully with a wonderful message."

—LifeinReviewBlog.com
review of *Lonestar Angel*

"This book has everything I enjoy: mystery, romance, and suspense. The characters are likable, understandable, and I can relate to them."

—TheFriendlyBookNook.com

"[M]ystery, danger, and intrigue as well as romance, love, and subtle inspiration. *The Lightkeeper's Daughter* is a 'keeper.'"

—OnceUponaRomance.com

"Colleen is a master storyteller."

—Karen Kingsbury,
best-selling author of
Unlocked and *Learning*

Seagrass Pier

ALSO BY COLLEEN COBLE

HOPE BEACH NOVELS
Tidewater Inn
Rosemary Cottage

UNDER TEXAS STARS NOVELS
Blue Moon Promise
Safe in His Arms

THE MERCY FALLS SERIES
The Lightkeeper's Daughter
The Lightkeeper's Bride
The Lightkeeper's Ball

LONESTAR NOVELS
Lonestar Sanctuary
Lonestar Secrets
Lonestar Homecoming
Lonestar Angel

THE ROCK HARBOR SERIES
Without a Trace
Beyond a Doubt
Into the Deep
Cry in the Night
Silent Night: A Rock Harbor
Christmas Novella (e-book only)

THE ALOHA REEF SERIES
Distant Echoes
Black Sands
Dangerous Depths
Midnight Sea
Holy Night: An Aloha Reef
Christmas Novella (e-book only)

Alaska Twilight
Fire Dancer
Abomination
Anathema
Butterfly Palace

NOVELLAS INCLUDED IN:
Smitten
Secretly Smitten
Smitten Book Club

OTHER NOVELLAS
Bluebonnet Bride

SEAGRASS PIER

A
HOPE BEACH
NOVEL

By Colleen Coble

THOMAS NELSON
Since 1798

NASHVILLE   MEXICO CITY   RIO DE JANEIRO

Published in Nashville, Tennessee, by Thomas Nelson. Thomas Nelson is a registered trademark of HarperCollins Christian Publishing, Inc.

Thomas Nelson, Inc., titles may be purchased in bulk for educational, business, fund-raising, or sales promotional use. For information, please e-mail SpecialMarkets@ThomasNelson.com.

Publisher's Note: This novel is a work of fiction. Names, characters, places, and incidents are either products of the author's imagination or used fictitiously. All characters are fictional, and any similarity to people living or dead is purely coincidental.

Unless otherwise noted, Scripture quotations are taken from the King James Version.

ISBN 978-0-7180-1173-4 (Library Edition)

Library of Congress Cataloging-in-Publication Data

Coble, Colleen.
  Seagrass pier : a Hope Beach novel / Colleen Coble.
      pages cm
  ISBN 978-1-59554-784-2 (trade paper)
  I. Title.
  PS3553.O2285S43 2014
  813'.54--dc23
                                        2014002835

Printed in the United States of America

14 15 16 17 RRD 6 5 4 3 2 1

*For my brother-in-law Harvey, whose plot
suggestions were invaluable for this book.
Love you, brother!*

ONE

The constriction around her neck tightened, and she tried to get her fingers under it to snatch a breath. She was losing consciousness. A large wave came over the bow of the boat, and the sea spray struck her in the face, reviving her struggle. She had to fight or he would kill her. She could smell his cologne, something spicy and strong. His ring flashed in the moonlight, and she dug the fingers of her right hand into his red sweater. The pressure on her neck was unrelenting. She was going to die.

Elin Summerall bolted upright in the bed. Her heart pounded, and she touched her throat and found it smooth and unharmed. It was just that dream again. She was safe, right here in her own house on the outskirts of Virginia Beach, Virginia. Her slick skin glistened in the moonlight streaming through the window.

The incision over her breastbone pulsed with pain, and she grabbed some pills from the bedside and swallowed them. *In and out.* Concentrating on breathing helped ease both her pain and her panic. She pulled in a breath, sweetly laden with the scent of roses blooming outside her window, then lay back against the pillow.

Her eyes drifted shut, then opened when she heard the tinkle of broken glass. Was it still the dream? Then the cool rush of air from the open window struck her face, and she heard a foot crunch on broken glass.

She leaped from the bed and threw open her door. Her heart pounded in her throat. Was an intruder in the house? In her bare feet, she sidled down the hall toward the sound she'd heard. She paused to peek in on her four-year-old daughter. One arm grasping a stuffed bear, Josie lay in a tangle of princess blankets.

Elin relaxed a bit. Maybe she hadn't heard glass break. It might still have been part of the nightmare. She peered around the hall corner toward the kitchen. A faint light glimmered as if the refrigerator stood open. A cool breeze wafted from the kitchen, and she detected the scent of dew. She was sure she'd shut and locked the window. The hair stood on the back of her neck, and she backed away.

Then a familiar voice called out. "Elin? I need you."

Relief left her limp. Elin rushed down the hall to the kitchen where her mother stood in front of the back door with broken glass all around her feet. The refrigerator stood open as well. Her mom's blue eyes were cloudy with confusion, and she wrung her hands as she looked at the drops of blood on the floor.

Elin grabbed a paper towel. "Don't move, Mom. You've cut yourself." She knelt and scooped the bits of glass away from her mother's bleeding feet. Her mother obediently sat in the chair Elin pulled toward her, and she inspected the small cuts. Nothing major, thank goodness. She put peroxide on her mother's cuts and ushered her back to bed, all the while praying that when morning came, her mother's bout with dementia would have passed. For now.

It was only when she went back to the hall that she smelled a man's cologne. She rushed to the kitchen and glanced around. The glass in the back door was shattered. *Inwardly.*

He's been in the house.

The neat plantation-style cottage looked much the same as the last time Marc Everton had been here. Seeing Elin Summerall again hadn't even been on his radar when he pulled on his shoes this morning, but his investigation had pulled up her name, and he needed to find out what she knew.

He put the SUV in Park and shut off the engine. Blue flowers of some kind grew along the brick path to the front door. A white swing swayed in the breeze on the porch.

He mounted the steps and pressed the doorbell. He heard rapid footsteps come his way. The door swung open, and he was face-to-face with Elin again after all this time. She was just as beautiful as he remembered. Her red hair curled in ringlets down her back, and those amazing aqua eyes widened when she saw him.

She leaned against the doorjamb. "Marc, what a surprise." Her husky voice squeaked out as if she didn't have enough air. Her gaze darted behind her, then back to him. "W-What are you doing here?"

"I needed to talk to you. Can I come in?"

She swallowed hard and looked behind her again. "I'll come out." She slipped out the door and went to the swing, where she curled up with one leg under her, a familiar pose.

He perched on the porch railing. "I-I was sorry to hear about Tim. A heart attack, I heard. Strange for someone so young."

She nodded. "His lack of mobility caused all kinds of health problems." She glanced toward the house again and bit her lip.

The last time he'd seen her she was pregnant. And Tim had thrown him off the premises. While Marc understood the jealousy, it had been a little extreme.

His jaw tightened. "I'll get right to the point. I'm investigating Laura Watson's murder. I saw a news story this morning about you receiving her heart."

She gulped and clutched her hands in her lap. "That's right. What do you mean 'investigating'?"

"I'm with the FBI."

"I thought . . ." She bit her lip and looked away. "I mean, you used to be in the Air Force."

"I was ready for something new."

"Sara never told me you'd left the military."

He lifted a brow but said nothing. He doubted he'd often been the topic of conversation between his cousin and Elin. Eyeing her, he decided to lay his cards on the table. "My best friend was murdered while investigating this case. My supervisor thinks I can't be objective now and wouldn't assign me to the case, but he's wrong. I took some leave, and I'm going to find his killer."

She gulped. "Oh, Marc, I'm so sorry."

He brushed off her condolences. "The article said you received Laura's heart, that you've been having some kind of memories of the murder."

Her face paled, but her gaze stayed fixed on him. "Yes, it's been a little scary."

"Sorry to hear you've been sick. You all right now?"

When she nodded, a long curl fell forward, spiraling down her long neck to rest near her waist. He yanked his gaze back from that perfect, shining lock. Her hair was unlike any other woman's he'd ever met. Thick and lustrous with a color somewhere between red and auburn and lit from within by gold highlights.

Her hand went to the center of her chest. "I had a virus that damaged my heart. I'm still recovering from surgery, but the doctors are pleased with my progress."

"That's good." He pushed away the stab of compassion. The only reason he was here was to find out what she knew about the murder. "So tell me about these visions or whatever they are."

⌒

Elin exhaled and forced her tense shoulder muscles to relax. She had to do this. But what if she told him everything and he didn't believe her? No one else had listened. Was it because she didn't know herself anymore and it came across to others?

His dark good looks, only enhanced by a nose that had been broken several times, had always drawn female attention. She'd vowed they would never turn her head, but she was wrong. So wrong. He'd haunted her dreams for nearly five years, and she thought she'd finally put the guilt to rest. But one look at his face had brought it surging back. The scent of his cologne, Polo Red, wafted to her, instantly taking her back to that one night of passion.

She'd been so young and stupid. They hadn't even liked each other, and to this day, she wondered what had gotten into her.

Marc opened the iPad in his hand and launched a program. "How did you find out she was your donor?"

"I have access to the records, and no one thought to lock me out." She twisted her hands together. "To explain this, I need to give you some background, so bear with me." She plunged in before he could object. "I've worked matching up donors with recipients for five years. I love my job."

"I know."

Those two words told her a lot. "Anyone who works with organ donation has heard the stories. They've even hit the news on occasion. Accounts of things the recipient knew about the donor. Things they should have had no way of knowing."

He nodded. "Cell memory."

At least he knew the term. "That's right. Within hours of receiving my new heart, I started having flashbacks of Laura's murder." She touched her throat. "I'm choking, fighting for my life. I remember things like the color of the murderer's hair. I keep smelling a man's cologne. I went to the department store to identify it. It's Encounter." She saw doubt gathering on his face and hurried on. "He was wearing a sweater the night he killed her. It was red."

He lifted a brow. "A sweater? On a Caribbean cruise?"

She bit her lip. "Maybe he put it on to prevent being scratched. I fought—I mean, Laura fought—very hard."

He didn't believe her. He hadn't taken a single note on his iPad. She had to convince him or Josie would be orphaned. Mom would have to go to a nursing home. "He's stalking me."

His somber gaze didn't change. "What's happened?"

"Someone broke into my house the other night. I'd just had a nightmare about the murder, and I heard the glass break. At first I thought it was an intruder, then Mom called for me. I found her in the kitchen in the middle of broken glass. I cleaned her up and got her to bed before I looked around more." She shuddered and hugged herself. "The glass in the back door had been broken from outside. He'd been here."

"What makes you think it's the man who killed Laura?"

"Who else could it be? He knows I'm remembering things because it was in the newspaper. He has to silence me before I remember everything."

He closed the cover on his tablet. "Well, thank you for answering my questions, Elin. I'll look into your claims. I've heard about cell memory, but most doctors consider it part of the psychological trauma from organ transplants. Have you been to a doctor? Maybe the intruder the other night was a nightmare. You said you'd been dreaming. And he wasn't actually *in* the house, was he?"

She stayed put in the swing. "You have to believe me. I know I sound like I'm crazy, but it's all too real."

His mouth twisted. "The police didn't believe you either, did they?"

She shook her head. "But they don't know me. You do."

His eyes went distant. "I'm not sure I do either. You seem— different somehow."

Her eyes burned. Everyone said that, but she didn't *feel* any different. Okay, maybe some of her likes and dislikes had changed, but it meant nothing. She was still Elin Summerall, Josie's mommy and Ruby's daughter.

The front door opened, and she saw her daughter's small hand on the doorknob. *No, no, Josie, don't come out.* Her daughter emerged with a bright smile. The red top and white pants she wore enhanced her dark coloring. Her distinctive hazel eyes were exactly like the man's in front of her. Maybe he wouldn't notice. A futile hope. Marc was a good detective, the best. Tenacious too.

"Hi, honey. Mommy is busy. Go back inside with Grandma."

Josie's eyes clouded. "She's sleeping. I want to go to the park."

Marc's gaze swept over Josie and lingered on her widow's peak. "This is Josie?"

There was no escaping this reckoning. "Yes. Josie, say hello to Mr. Everton."

"Hi, Mr. Everton. You want to come to my birthday party? I'll be five next month."

His smile was indulgent. "What's the date?"

"July 10."

His eyes widened, and Elin could almost hear the wheels spinning in his head, see him calculating the time. Tim hadn't come back for a month after that night.

He bolted upright, and his hands curled into fists. "I'd love to, Josie." His voice was controlled, but the look he shot Elin was full of fury and disbelief.

Elin forced a smile. "Go inside, honey. We'll go to the park in a little while. I need to talk to Mr. Everton for a few minutes."

Her daughter gave a final pout, then turned and went back

inside. The door banged behind her as a final punctuation of her displeasure.

The silence stretched between Elin and Marc as their gazes locked. How on earth did she begin?

He paced to the door and back, then dug into his pocket and popped a mint from its package. He popped it into his mouth. "She's my daughter and you never told me." He spat out the tight words, and a muscle in his jaw jumped.

⸺

Marc struggled to control his anger. He'd instantly recognized Josie's resemblance to him instead of her red-haired mother. And Tim had been blond. Josie's hazel eyes were flecked with green and gold, just like his. The dimple in her right cheek matched his. So did the shape of her face and her dark curls. And her widow's peak.

He paced the porch and looked at Elin. Her figure was enough to stop traffic, but their personalities had never really meshed. Except for that one night after her father died. Ravaged by grief, she'd shown up at his house looking for Sara, and he gave her a drink to calm her down. One drink led to another and another until they crossed a line of no return. A night they both regretted.

He saw hope and fear warring in her beautiful face. "Why?" His voice was hoarse, and he cleared his throat. "Why didn't you tell me?"

She bit her lip. "As far as I was concerned, Tim was her father. That was one of the conditions he made before we were married, that he wanted her to be *his* daughter."

"He's been gone for two years. You could have come to me as soon as he died." His gaze swung back to the door. Elin had deprived him of two years he could have had with his daughter. His fists clenched again, and his throat ached from clenching his jaw.

Her eyes shimmered with moisture. "The last thing he asked me before he died was to never tell you. H-He was jealous. I'm sure you realized that when you came here with Sara that day and he went into a rage."

He gave a curt nod. "So you never planned to tell me?"

Her chin came up. "No. I'd betrayed Tim once. I didn't want to do it again."

The fact he had a child still floored him. What did he do with this? "I'll talk to my attorney and draw up some support papers."

A flush ran up her pale skin. "I don't want your money, Marc! Josie is *my* daughter. Tim is her daddy, and we don't need another one. The only thing I need from you is for you to find that man and put him behind bars before he hurts me."

"I intend to." Surely she wouldn't keep his daughter away from him? He wasn't going to be one of those deadbeat dads, no way. "But I'm not so sure about that cell-memory stuff."

She wrung her hands. "I see your skepticism. Don't you think I know it's crazy? Everyone just says, 'There, there, Elin. You've been through so much. This will pass.' But it's getting worse! The dreams come nearly every night. You have to help me."

Against his will, he saw the conviction in her face. So what if it was some kind of hallucination from the heart transplant? Josie was still his daughter. He owed it to her to see if there was any truth to this. And his lack of control that night still haunted him. Her grief for her father had been a poor excuse for what they'd done.

He went back to his perch on the porch railing and picked up his pen. "Start over from the beginning."

TWO

Elin rolled over and looked at the clock. It was nearly two in the morning, and she hadn't fallen asleep yet. She massaged the pain between her breasts. The discomfort had lessened substantially this week, but the twinges reminded her every day of how fragile her life was.

What if Marc tried to take her daughter? Even trying to be part of Josie's life would be a complication Elin didn't have the emotional energy to handle. She flipped on her light since she wasn't sleeping anyway and reached for her MacBook.

She called up the real-estate listing again and stared at the house on Hope Island she'd purchased. Her father had been stationed on the quaint little island for three years during her teens, and she treasured the memories of time spent with her parents and sister. Maybe she could recapture that peace and learn something about Laura in the process. She felt well enough to handle the move now.

She heard a sound and raised her head. Was Mom up again? Or maybe Josie? She closed her computer and got up. After opening her door, she listened a moment but the sound didn't come again. Still, it wouldn't hurt to check. She moved on to her daughter's room, then relaxed when she saw Josie curled up with her stuffed bear. Elin went to the tiny room her mother occupied, barely bigger than a closet. She slept as well.

Though the sound must have been her imagination, she couldn't shake off the sense of unease. She stood in the hallway outside Josie's room and listened to the hall clock ticking. Nothing. Turning toward her bedroom door, she mentally shrugged at her nerves.

Something thudded as if someone had bumped into a wall. In an instant, she was in Josie's room and had her daughter in her arms. Josie barely stirred and only turned her face into Elin's chest. Elin clutched her and listened again. There was no phone in here.

A gleeful whistle echoed down the hall. Someone was in the house, between her and the outside door. There was only one room in the house with a lock, and it also had a phone. To get there, she would have to go closer to the intruder, but she had no choice. She practically flew down the hall and into her office. As she slammed the door shut and locked it, she glimpsed a shadow rounding the corner.

A man laughed, a low chuckle from the other side of the door. Terror climbed in her throat. She backed up until her thighs struck her desk, then whirled and grabbed the phone. No dial tone, but her cell phone was charging on the other side of the desk. She shifted Josie to the other shoulder and snatched for her mobile and dialed 911. Thank goodness her little girl hadn't awakened.

"Someone's in the house." She whispered her address to the dispatcher. "Please hurry."

"There's a squad car two blocks from your location." The woman on the other end sounded calm. "Officers will be there in just a couple of minutes. Stay on the line until they arrive."

The doorknob rattled almost playfully, and the man's whistle came again. It vaguely sounded like a tune from *The Phantom of the Opera*. "The police will be here in a minute!" Elin shouted.

His fingernails raked against the door. "You shouldn't have told the police, Elin." His voice sounded distorted as if he'd deliberately masked it. "Everything I do is for you, you know. You should have kept quiet." A police siren wailed in the distance. His footsteps faded as he ran out the back door still whistling that same chilling tune.

He was the murderer, the man who choked her in her dreams. Cradling Josie, she sank onto the chair. No one believed her. She gazed down into her daughter's sweet face. He would kill her, and then what would become of Josie and her mom?

—

The salt-laden wind lifted Elin's long red hair off her neck as she dangled her legs above the ocean. Seagrass Pier seemed to go on forever and ever into the misty morning, and she wished she could walk out into those clouds and leave her problems behind.

She forced a smile as Marc's cousin, Sara Kavanagh, dropped to the weathered boards beside her. "You can't even see the horizon." Elin had fled to Sara's after the break-in a week ago, and the movers had brought her things two days ago.

Sara tucked a strand of honey-colored hair behind her ears. "It's like that a lot in the morning."

"I love it." One of her coworkers had told her this was where Laura spent the last year of her life, and Elin had fallen in love with it in a heartbeat. "It was built by a sea captain in 1905." She studied the grand old structure with its parapet walkway around the top. "His wife probably watched for him from the widow's walk."

Sara smiled. "Enough small talk. How are you doing, really? Was it hard telling Marc?"

Elin shuddered. "You should have seen his expression when I told him about the flashbacks. He really thought I was a crazy woman."

Sara hugged her, a firm embrace that brooked no nonsense. "You're not crazy." She waggled a brow. "At least not in the traditional sense. You'll be fine."

Sara was an EMT with the Coast Guard. She knew about medical things. Elin desperately wanted reassurance, but she feared there was none. Not for this. She still felt the dream's chill and power. "You believe me, don't you, Sara?"

"You know I do. That's why I was glad when you said you wanted to come here. To get to Hope Beach, the killer will have to come by ferry, and he'll be recognized as a stranger. This house is remote too. Not many know about it, and it's easiest to take a boat to get here. The dirt road takes forever." She turned her head and studied the lines of the house. "How did Kerri hear about this place?"

"We did some research on Laura after I started having the dreams. She worked here as a nursing aide all last year until the owner went to an assisted-living place. Then she went to work for the cruise line. When Kerri was searching for information, she ran across the listing. We'd just sold Mom's house before I got sick, and I really needed a bigger one if she was going to live with me long term. I thought we could move here and maybe learn more about Laura. I hope it doesn't take long for my cottage to sell."

"And you're close to me. Coffee dates, surfing, sunbathing. I love it!"

Elin studied Sara's dear face. They'd been friends since high school. She knew everything about Elin except one important fact. She swallowed hard. "I had to admit something else to him, Sara. He guessed, and I couldn't lie. You're going to be upset with me for not telling you before now, but I'd made Tim a promise. I couldn't break it."

Sara's smile vanished. "I already know, Elin. Marc is Josie's father."

Elin's gut clenched. "How did you know?"

"I grew up with Marc. He's more like a brother than a cousin. I know what he looked like as a kid. Exactly like Josie. And you both acted totally weird at your father's funeral. Wouldn't look at one another. When Marc saw you coming, he went the other way."

That stung. Especially because it was true. "You never said anything."

"I knew you had a good reason for keeping the truth from me." Sara leaned over and hugged her. "I could give you a little space for love's sake."

Elin returned her hug. "You're the best friend ever." The truth should be told even if it was uncomfortable. "I went to his house looking for you the day Dad died. I was a wreck. He gave me a drink to calm me down." She rubbed her head. "We both drank too much. He'd just gotten word he was shipping off to Afghanistan, and I was nearly hysterical. The next thing I remembered was waking up in his bed. I was so mortified. It was wrong. We both knew it too. I mean, I never so much as looked at him that way."

"Don't I know it. He always called you the ice princess."

Elin shrugged. "Oil and water, that was always us. It was so out of character. He tried to talk to me that morning, but I grabbed my clothes and ran. To this day, it haunts me. I disappointed God and hurt Tim."

"Tim was injured shortly after that, right?"

Elin nodded. "As soon as he came home, I confessed. I couldn't marry him without telling him the truth."

"I bet he was mad."

Elin didn't like remembering the pain in his eyes. "He forgave me and said he understood. But I don't think he ever really got over it."

Sara leaned back on her palms. "What did Marc say when he realized he was Josie's father?"

"I think he could have murdered me." Elin examined the ends

of her hair. She needed a trim. "I'm afraid he's going to want to tell Josie the truth. He didn't ask yet, but he will."

"Marc has always loved kids. What will you do?"

"I don't know yet."

Sara hugged her knees to her chest. "He deserves to have a relationship with Josie."

Elin shook her head. "I wish I could forget what I did. God took me to the woodshed over my betrayal, and I still suffer a thousand deaths from guilt. But all that doesn't matter now. Laura deserves justice."

"I know. Marc will get him."

"I'm not sure he really believes me. I think he's just humoring me."

"What did the police say after the break-in? Didn't that make them pay more attention?"

"By that time they'd already categorized me as a crackpot. I believe they think I broke the window myself to convince them. And by the time they got there after he actually broke in, he was gone. I had no proof."

The sun had burned away the morning clouds, and she squinted in the glare to see two figures out front. "Mom and Josie are up. I'd better get them breakfast." She gulped the last of her cold coffee and got to her feet.

Sara rose too. "Since when did you start drinking coffee?"

Elin looked at the cup in her hand. "I guess about six weeks ago. It smelled so good one morning and I had some. I don't know why I hated it before."

They started for the house, and she realized she was happy for the first time in weeks. Something about this place spoke to her soul. The wind grabbed her fears and buried them in the sand dunes. She could breathe here, could see a future again. Marc and Sara would help her. She wasn't facing this alone any longer.

They reached the wide porch, and she stopped at the screen door. "What about you and Josh?"

Sara made a face. "There is no me and Josh. It's hopeless. He's determined not to let me past that guard he has up."

"Have you tried, I mean, *really* tried?"

Sara stared at her, then shook her head. "I guess not. I want him to realize he can trust me. I've tried to show him my character for the past two years, but I don't know if he will ever put down his resistance."

"What if you tell him how you feel? What's the worst that could happen?"

"You mean like how would I deal with the ridicule at the base when he runs the other way?" Sara grinned, but her eyes were sad. "I'm going to let God work on him. He'll do a much better job than I will."

"He always does." Elin opened the screen door and entered the house with Sara on her heels.

Josie ran to grab her leg. "Mommy, Grammy burned the bacon."

She smelled it then, the acrid smoke swirling from the kitchen. She rushed to the kitchen and found her mother scrubbing at a saucepan. "Are you all right, Mom?"

Her mother wore a white housedress over jeans. She teetered on red high heels, and three pink curlers peeked from underneath several spots in her blond hair, badly in need of a fresh dye treatment.

Her expression was vague as she glanced up. "There you are, Elin. I have breakfast ready."

The familiar sense of helplessness erased Elin's optimistic mood. Her mother's dementia had worsened recently, in spite of the medicine that was supposed to prevent the ministrokes that took her mother further and further away from her. How was she going to handle this too?

When Marc saw the name on his cell phone, he nearly didn't answer it. But his boss would just call back. "Hey, Harry. Sorry, I've got to run in five minutes. What's up?"

The man's gruff voice bellowed in his ear. "What the devil do you think you're doing? Did I or did I not specifically tell you to keep your nose out of this case? The next thing I know, you've taken leave and are poking around."

He set his jaw. "What I do on my own time is my business."

"If you compromise the integrity of this investigation, you'll be out. Do I make myself clear?"

"Perfectly." Marc couldn't keep the bite out of his voice.

Harry heaved a sigh. "Look, Marc, I know how you feel. But I don't even believe Will's death is related to this case. It was an organized crime hit. This wasn't the only case you two were investigating."

"I told you he called me and said he had a new lead he was sure would lead us to the killer. Will got cut off before he could tell me where to meet him. Two hours later he was dead. I find that a little too coincidental."

"It was a shot to the head. See, this is why I want you off the case. You have no objectivity right now. Take your time off, but use it to get your head back in the game. Work on restoring that car. Go play beach volleyball. Find a pretty girl and go surfing. You've been through the fire lately. You could use some distraction."

Marc gritted his teeth but said nothing. Harry would not dissuade him from doing what he knew was right.

"If I find out you're still poking around, I'm going to personally come down there and kick your butt. Got it?"

"Got it."

Marc was just going to have to be careful with his poking around.

THREE

The scent of burned bacon still lingered in the air as Elin fitted several skeleton keys in the lock to the third floor. "One of these has to fit."

Her mother had fallen asleep on the sofa, and this seemed like a good time to explore. Sara held Josie, all arms and legs like a monkey, as they stood at the end of the second-floor hallway. They were both eager to see the rest of the house.

The lock finally clicked. Elin twisted the old black knob, and the door creaked open. Stale air rushed past her face, and she sneezed at the dust. "I don't think anyone has been up here in ages."

Sara wrinkled her nose. "I think we'll need that broom you brought."

Wielding the broom like a samurai sword, Elin ascended the wooden stairs, creaking underfoot like a leaky ship. "I love poking around old houses. You never know what you'll find. And the history of this place is fascinating. Dad always wanted a chance to explore here."

"I think I could do without finding anything that moves." Sara shuddered and climbed the steps behind her.

They emerged into a third-floor attic space. The rafters obstructed the headroom in a few places. Light streamed through the windows and illuminated dust motes thrown into the air by their movement across the wide plank boards. Boxes and crates crammed the space as well as old furniture, some of it shrouded by sheets and some if it gathering dust.

"Look at all this stuff." Sara set Josie down and lifted a corner of the closest sheet to reveal an old desk.

Josie giggled and crawled under it.

"Come back here, you little scamp." Sara pulled her out. "There might be spiders under there." She shivered and brushed a cobweb from Josie's curls.

Elin's adrenaline surged at all the great stuff to explore. The people who had put these things here were dead and buried, but what a wealth of stories she might find in all their belongings. "Construction started in 1905 by Captain Joshua Hurley for his new bride, Georgina. He didn't live here long because he never came back from a sea voyage in 1907. The house stayed in his family until the owner put it up for sale, and I bought it. She was the last of the Hurleys and had no children. She was born here in 1930. Laura took care of her until she went into an assisted living place."

Sara hadn't moved from the center of the room. "So Joshua had a child?"

Elin nodded. "Twins, from what I've heard. A boy and a girl. At least that's what the previous owner told me. She said the family has always looked for Georgina's diary collection, but it's never been found. There are all kinds of secret rooms in the place, I guess. I'd love to find her diaries. I'd give them to the family, of course. But I'd love to read them first."

"Did she remarry?"

"I don't know." She couldn't put her finger on why the history intrigued her so much. Maybe it was because Georgina had been a widow too. Elin still found the mantle of *widow* hard to wear. Every time she laughed or let herself forget about Tim for a few minutes, the guilt surged back as soon as she realized she was letting go of him.

"If generations of Hurleys haven't found it, then I doubt we will." Sara moved toward the biggest window and peered out. "Hey, what a great view! I wonder how we get to the widow's walk?"

Elin glanced around. There were probably some stairs up into the ceiling. She flipped on her flashlight and shone it around the space. A small closed-in area in the north corner caught her eye, and she walked over to check it out. A doorway opened on one side.

"Found it!" She put down her light and swept out the stairs with her broom. "There's a door at the top. I'm going up."

"Wait, Elin, it may not be safe!"

"The owner had a contractor fix everything on this place before she listed it. It's fine according to the home inspection." Elin mounted the stairs and struggled with the door of the cupola for several minutes until she found the right key to unlock it. It opened easily, and she peered into the sky. Over the wrought-iron railing, she saw the whitecaps rolling into the sand and smelled the fresh scent of the sea. Bird droppings marred the walk around the top of the roofline, and two gulls squawked when she put her right foot onto the balcony. She tested it before resting her full weight on it. It seemed solid, and she saw several areas of new wood the contractor had probably installed.

Sara was still muttering dire warnings below her, but Elin ignored her and put her other foot outside. The sea breeze lifted her hair, and she moved to the railing and looked out at the whitecaps. She could stay up here for hours. She shook the railing, and it didn't wobble. "The home inspector said it was sturdy. I could even put some deck chairs up here and come up to enjoy the view."

"Or just go down to the water, you silly girl," Sara called up.

Elin sighed and took one last look at the incredible panorama of sea, sand, and sky. A figure on the beach caught her eye. Who could be out here? No one walked this area. It was too far from the inhabited part of the island. She shaded her eyes but could only make out a general sense of size. Probably a man. He seemed to be walking slowly and looking for something. She watched him until he disappeared over a sand dune.

She retraced her footsteps and left the balcony to the gulls. "I love it up there. Go check it out." She scooped up her daughter. "Here, lock it when you're done." She handed Sara the ring of skeleton keys.

Muttering about the insanity, Sara went up the stairs. "Wow, you're right. It's pretty amazing. Almost like being in my helicopter."

"You see anyone? I saw some guy walking along the water."

Sara's footsteps came back to the door, and she stepped back onto the stairs. "I didn't see anyone. Maybe it was a fisherman."

"Maybe." But a sense of unease nagged Elin as they went back downstairs.

———

A bit of smoke still hung in the air in spite of all the open windows as Elin put away the last of the dinner dishes. Her mother sat on the back deck and pointed out birds to Josie. The clouds in Mom's eyes had rolled out and left her chattering like her usual self.

The doorbell rang, and Elin wiped her hands on a dish towel and went to open the door. Her brother-in-law stood smiling at her from the other side of the door, and she tensed. "Ben, what on earth are you doing here?"

His blond hair had been moussed and styled to stand up in a surfer style, and he wore khaki shorts and a blue shirt that intensified the color of his eyes. "I got stationed here a month ago and heard you had just come to the island. I thought I'd stop by and welcome you." He lifted a basket of fruit. "Josie loves pears."

"She does indeed." She took the basket from him. "Thanks so much. She'll be glad to see you. She and Mom are on the back deck."

He'd been married to her friend Kerri for a while, but they'd divorced about four years ago. He was Tim's half brother and had been to the house on occasion when Tim was in town. She could overcome her dislike for Josie's sake. The man had an ego the size of a whale.

She took him through the house and out the back door. "Look who's here."

"Uncle Ben!" Josie squealed and ran to him.

He swung her up into his arms. "You can't possibly be Josie. You're much too tall."

She giggled. "I *am* Josie. I'm going to go to school next year. Did you bring me a present?"

"Would I come to see you empty-handed?" He put her down and reached into his pocket. "What do you think it is?"

"A puppy?"

"In my pocket?" He rolled his eyes. "I don't hear any barking."

"It's candy!"

"Your mother would throw me off the pier." He slowly withdrew his hand, then handed her a small box.

She squealed and opened it. "It's a necklace! Look, Mommy, a dolphin necklace."

The blue and silver necklace sparkled in the sunlight. Elin smiled and fastened it around her daughter's small neck. "Very nice. Ben, you're spoiling her."

"I like to. I don't want her to forget Tim."

"Me neither." Not that Ben looked much like Tim, but it was still nice of him to think of Josie. Her frosty feelings began to thaw a little.

This move might be a good thing in more ways than one. Family was here. Sara was like her sister, and now Ben would be able to stop by on occasion.

FOUR

It was utterly ridiculous to live this far from civilization. Kalianne Adanete knocked at the front door of the only house on this point looking out on the Atlantic. The old house had good bones, but if she owned it, she'd tear this place down and build a fancy new house with an entire wall of windows that would take advantage of the spectacular view.

She smiled at the woman who answered the door. "Good morning. I'm here about the job helping the dementia patient."

She gave her name and looked her prospective employer over. Gorgeous skin that made her aqua eyes stand out even more. In her late twenties with legs that probably got her a lot of attention from men. And that hair. Most men could only dream of having a woman with hair like that. That red wasn't from a bottle. And Kalianne knew fake color better than most since her first career had been as a hairdresser.

The woman smiled back. "Come in. I'm Elin Summerall. I appreciate you coming all this way. I know it's not an easy spot to get to. Did you drive or bring a boat?"

"I drove. Took me an hour though, so I think I'll bring a boat next time."

Kalianne followed her inside to a pleasant room. Painted

pale blue, the gleaming wood floors and comfortable furnishings of overstuffed blue and white furniture made the large room feel cozier. Nautical touches adorned the lamps, tables, and walls. It was a room meant for relaxing with a glass of wine and an adoring lover. Not that she'd ever have that opportunity since this would never be her place. And the owner looked more like the kind of person into green smoothies and vegetable plates instead of parties.

Kalianne glanced around at the windows. They would be easy enough to leave unlocked. But she might not need to get back in when Elin was gone. There might be an opportunity to look around when she was watching the old lady.

"Nice room," she said.

"Thanks, I thought so too the first time I saw it. I can't claim to have done anything with it myself." Elin gestured to the sofa. "Have a seat. My mother and my daughter are having tea and cookies on the back deck. Let me go get them. I don't like leaving them alone."

Kalianne glanced around. The woman had spent a tidy sum on decoration. This sofa wasn't cheap. She dropped onto the sofa, then cleared her throat. This job would be hers, or she'd know the reason why. "About the job. How old is your mother?"

Elin stopped on her way to the door. "Fifty-five."

"Young for dementia." How awful to be senile so young. She pushed away the unwanted stab of sentiment.

Sorrow shadowed Elin's eyes and flattened her lips. "She started having ministrokes two years ago. We had her stable, then the strokes started up again a couple of months ago. She'd been insisting on living alone, but I made her move in with me just before we came here. She's starting to do dangerous things like leaving the stove on."

Kalianne noticed the dark circles under Elin's eyes. "And you need some respite care?"

Elin glanced toward the door. "I–I have some business I need to attend to, and I can't be here all the time. I'd like for you to come every day from nine to three. There might be times I need you to stay longer." She named a generous salary. "You brought references?"

Hiding her elation, Kalianne nodded. "Of course. Feel free to call them."

"I'll do that, and you'll hear from me in the next couple of days. But let me go check on Mom and Josie." She started toward the door.

An older woman, her hair awry, came through the door. She wore mismatched clothing and two different shoes. Her blue eyes seemed fixed on something only she could see. She looked younger than fifty-five with that fragility blondes could have. Kalianne suspected she might be a handful though.

"Where's Josie?" Elin's voice held more alarm than Kalianne would have thought. She started past her mother, but a little girl holding a cookie trailed after her grandmother into the living room. "There you are, Josie." The relief in her voice was palpable. "Mom, I'd like to introduce you to a–a new friend." She touched her mother's arm. "This is Kalianne. Kalianne, this is my mother, Ruby Whiteford."

Ruby held out her hand. "Hello."

Kalianne rose and took the older woman's limp hand. "Glad to meet you, Ruby. I hope to see you more often. We can do some interesting things. Do you like to garden?"

Ruby looked at Elin. "I–I think so."

Elin picked up her daughter. "She loves gardening. She'd like nothing better than to have a small plot out back with tomatoes."

"I love gardening too. And walks along the beach. Knitting too." As the woman brightened, Kalianne knew she'd hit the right notes with both mother and daughter. She'd get the job.

They chatted a few more minutes before she shook hands with

Elin and headed back to the car she'd brought out from Kill Devil Hills. There was no cell service out here, so she'd have to wait until she got back to civilization before she called her brother to report on a successful day.

———

Marc drove his SUV off the ferry at the Hope Beach dock and headed down the narrow two-lane road to town. There was a good team assembled here, and he'd need their help if he was going to get to the bottom of what was happening to Elin. If it was even real. He still wasn't convinced her so-called visions weren't the by-product of the antirejection drugs she was on or the trauma of her surgery.

And she could have told him she was moving out here. Had she deliberately kept him in the dark to keep him away from Josie? He wouldn't put it past her.

A daughter. I have a daughter. The news kept surprising him. The anger at Elin had only intensified since he heard the news a week ago. How did he assimilate this into his life? Josie deserved a father, a real father. Not someone on the sidelines, but someone who cheered on every accomplishment and celebrated every lost tooth. Elin had to agree to let him be part of his daughter's life. They could do that and be civil, couldn't they? If she didn't agree to his demands, he'd take matters into his own hands.

He parked in front of the Coast Guard station and walked in to ask for the team who had responded to the distress call out on the *Seawind.* He would have to handle this with delicacy, because if someone from the Coast Guard called Harry, the heat from his boss would only intensify.

He found the three men and Sara in a conference room down the nondescript tan hallway. Nodding, he shut the door and went to the head of the long table. "You all know why I'm here. I realize you wrote up a report on what you saw when you landed on the ship, but I want to go over it all with you personally in case there's some small detail you remember as we talk about it."

The guy in the Dodgers cap was the first to speak. "No problem. I'm Josh Holman, and this is Curtis Ireland. Sara you know, and the fellow across the table is Alec Bourne."

Marc gave Josh a hard look. He'd heard about the guy Sara was so crazy about. He shook their hands, then flipped open his iPad and navigated to his notes about the murder. "You found the deceased, Laura Watson, on the aft deck level five under a pile of PFDs, correct?"

Sara answered first. "That's right. Only her hand showed from under the life jackets. Alec removed everything, and I checked her pulse. There was none. I noted the ligature marks on her neck and concluded she'd been strangled with a thin wire or cord of some kind."

"Most likely a guitar string, according to forensics." He turned to Josh. "You were aboard the ship as a passenger, correct?"

The other man nodded. "Just a vacation."

"Did you offer assistance when you heard about it?"

"I did. I placed the call for the team to come and help."

Marc watched Josh and noticed he seemed uncomfortable at the line of questioning. Was he hiding something? "So you filed a distress call indicating there had been a murder?"

"I did."

"The crew specifically told you it was a murder?"

Josh nodded. "The woman who summoned me said the deceased had been strangled."

Marc turned his attention to the other crew members. "Did you notice anyone with a particular interest in the crime? Anyone taking pictures or hanging around?"

The other three Coasties shook their heads. He would have to talk to the ship employees. He thanked them, and the men filed out. Sara lingered until they were alone.

She walked to the coffee service and poured two cups. "You look like you could use something stronger." She handed him a cup. "You doing okay?"

"You knew about Josie."

She flinched at his accusation. "Elin told me this morning, though I wasn't surprised. I'd suspected it ever since Josie was about a year old."

That stung. "Why didn't you tell me?"

Her gray eyes were grave. "What good would it do, Marc? She was married to Tim at that point. Your interference would have caused them more problems."

He tamped down the rage roiling in his belly and took a sip of the coffee, then grimaced. It had been on the burner too long. "I want to see Josie."

"I'm sure you do." Sara bit her lip. "Would it do any good to tell you to take it easy on Elin? She's been through a lot, and these flashbacks, or whatever they are, have her really scared. I know you're angry—and you have every right to be—but think about what she's been going through."

"You think there's anything to that whole cell-memory thing? Sounds pretty sketchy."

She sipped her coffee before answering. "She's changed since the transplant. She drinks coffee for one thing, and she's always hated it. Even the smell."

He blinked. "Maybe her tastes changed."

"She started drinking it right after she got a new heart."

He grinned and set the coffee down. "Maybe she saw the light."

Sara's frown didn't ease. "It's more than that. She has always been a huge oldies fan."

He nodded. "Go on."

"She hasn't listened to her favorite *Forrest Gump* soundtrack in weeks. Now she listens to country music, especially Alan Jackson."

"That doesn't mean much." Though he shrugged it off, he frowned. "Anything else?"

"You're not taking this seriously."

"I'm helping her, aren't I? How much more seriously do you want me to take it?"

Sara pressed her lips together and shook her head. "She's always worn browns and tans. I've tried to get her to wear more color for years, and she always says her hair is enough of an accent color. But she had on a bright-green top yesterday. *Bright green.* She has always hated green."

He tried to recall if he'd ever seen her in a bright color but failed to remember a single time. She favored a caramel color.

"It's not just the colors though. She's totally changed her style. When was the last time you saw her in a dress or skirt with heels?"

"A few days ago." And her long legs had looked terrific in that skirt. But try as he might, he couldn't remember seeing her in a dress before that. Or heels. He hadn't gone to her wedding, but Sara had told him Elin wore tennis shoes under her dress, a fact that hadn't surprised him.

Maybe there was more to this than he thought. Or maybe nearly dying had messed with her head.

FIVE

"Woman, you are living in the outback!" Small suitcase in her left hand, Kerri Summerall stepped out of the boat and hugged Elin with her other arm. "But I have to say it's gorgeous out here. Look at that house!" She stared with awestruck eyes at the big house on the hill.

Elin had helped Kerri get the job with the organ procurement organization, or OPO for short, about three years ago after her divorce from Ben, and it had been fun working together. The two of them had even been mistaken for sisters, though Kerri's hair wasn't as vivid a red as Elin's, and she was three inches shorter than Elin.

Elin linked her arm with Kerri's and guided her up the path to the house. "I love it here, and Josie is thriving in all the sea air."

"And your mother?"

Elin's smile faded. "Slipping by the day."

"I'm so sorry." Kerri hugged her. "I'm here to cheer you up though. We're not going to work all day, are we? I brought my swimsuit."

"I've missed you. It's been hard to get used to working from home when I like office interaction."

Kerri laughed. "You mean office drama? Is that a subtle way of asking if I've murdered Jean yet? And to answer that, no. She is still looking over my shoulder and questioning every organ I award. Without you there to act as a buffer, I've been keeping Walgreens in business buying antacids."

Elin laughed. "It's *so* good to see you! Why don't you tell her you're going to work from home too, and you can move right into my office."

Kerri groaned. "I don't have a good excuse like you did. Besides, you're the golden child who can do no wrong."

There was some truth to Kerri's statement. Elin had gone to work at the OPO when her father died. He'd been a cop and had been injured while apprehending drug dealers. He died before he could get the new liver he needed. Her uncle was the HR manager, and he'd encouraged Elin's interest in organ donation. He'd helped her get the job, and she knew she got a few perks no one else received. Right now she was so thankful for them. Without her uncle's intervention, she would be without a job instead of happily working from home.

They reached the house, and she opened the screen door for her friend. "I don't have it completely furnished yet, but it's looking pretty good."

Kerri gaped when she stepped inside. "Nice digs. On second thought, I'll see if Jean will put in for me to work from home. You've got a spare room?"

"Lots of them. Let me show you to your room. When you're done freshening up, the office is there." She pointed out the large room with big windows that looked out onto the ocean. "I'll be in here with iced tea."

"A siren song if I ever heard one. I don't really need to freshen up. Let's get our work over so we can play." She set her suitcase down by the door, then extracted her MacBook from the top zippered compartment. "We could have done this by phone, but I wanted to see you. I don't know what got into Dragon Lady, but she agreed."

Elin lifted the lid of her laptop and navigated to the OPO website. "You went to the hospital to check out the donor?"

"Just came from there. So sad. The family was happy to know his organs could be used though. He was fifteen and dove into a shallow pool. Broke his neck just above C4. They pulled him out and did CPR until the ambulance arrived, but brain death was declared a few hours later."

Elin winced. Nasty break. An injury above C4 would have required a ventilator for the victim to breathe. "We have such a large amount of organs to find homes for, this might take awhile. It depends on who we can reach."

Kerri's smile faded. "They are such a nice family too. Three kids. The dad is a pediatrician and the mom is a nurse. They are Christians too, which was a comfort. They immediately knew the scope of the injury when they saw the MRI. They'd like the organs to go to recipients as young as we can find. I think that's a reasonable request, but you know what Jean would say."

Elin nodded. "Follow the list. Maybe we'll get lucky and the first ones up will be children."

"Maybe." Kerri didn't sound convinced. She moved a chair around so they could share the desk and she could see Elin's computer screen. "What do we have?"

"Let me run a search for tissue matching." Elin executed a few keystrokes and let the computer do its thing. She noticed Kerri staring at her. "What?"

Kerri's smile was embarrassed. "I promised Isaac I'd say hello for him."

Elin's cheeks heated. "That's nice."

"I did my duty. The guy needs to learn to speak up for himself. Not that it would make any difference. You're not ready for a new relationship anyway."

Their coworker was nice enough. Early thirties with a kind

manner and smile. He'd tried to get Kerri to set them up a few times. What would Kerri think if she knew Josie's father was in the picture now? She should tell Kerri and get it over with.

"You have a strange expression, Elin. Is something wrong?"

Kerri had been a huge help to her when the dreams started. She'd assisted her in finding the donor's name and what had happened to her. She deserved to know the truth.

Elin shook her head. "Not really wrong, but things are a little different in my life right now. You'll probably hear about it sooner or later."

"You're dating someone?" Kerri looked a little crestfallen.

"No, no, nothing like that. Um, most people don't know this, but Tim was not Josie's biological father. I introduced Josie to her father a couple of days ago."

"What? B-But you've never said a thing." She studied Elin's face. "That explains why Ben used to make snide comments about you."

"About me?"

"He thought Josie didn't belong to Tim." She studied her fingernails. "I'm sorry, I shouldn't have brought it up."

"He's here on the island, by the way. He stopped by the other day."

Kerri rolled her eyes. "We have better things to talk about than my ex. So you told Josie's father about her? Who is he?"

"Marc Everton."

Her eyes widened. "Marc Everton?"

"You know him?"

Kerri shook her head. "Not personally, but I know the name. He's heading up that homicide investigation." Her expression cleared. "Thanks for telling me. I'll try to let Isaac down easy."

Elin didn't bother trying to explain her relationship with Marc wasn't like that.

Her cell phone rang, and she looked at the screen. *Unknown.* Maybe she shouldn't answer it.

"What's wrong?"

Elin stared at the screen a moment longer. "I don't know who's calling. It might be that guy. But it could be an important call that isn't picking up right." She slid her finger across the screen to answer the call. "Hello?"

No answer. Only the faint sound of "Music of the Night." Nausea roiled in her stomach, and she quickly disconnected the call. "It was him."

Kerri touched her arm. "Get your number changed. Now. At least he doesn't know where you live now. Once you get that changed, he can't contact you."

Elin nodded and called up her phone server. "I hope you're right."

———

The sea spray struck Marc in the face as his speedboat sliced through the rolling waves out to Seagrass Pier. It was a pretty spot on the north side of Hope Island. The widow's walk around the top was a lacy white that sparkled in the sun. The three-story structure looked like it had grown up out of the rocky knoll that looked out to sea.

A long fishing pier stretched out into the horizon. The pier looked like it could withstand about anything the sea threw at it. He motored past it into the small harbor where he anchored at a short dock. He tied up his boat, then strode up the pathway cut out of the rock. Maybe he should have called her first, but he didn't want her to throw a roadblock in his way. In the last ten days, all he'd thought about was his daughter. He didn't intend to go one more day without seeing Josie.

He reached the big front porch and saw the front door was open. Before he got to the steps, he heard giggling from the side of the house. He changed directions and headed that way. When he rounded the corner of the house, he saw Josie dressed in white shorts and a pink top.

She crouched beside an oleander bush and giggled behind her hand. "You can't find me, Mommy."

Marc's heart squeezed when he saw her dark curls and the shape of her face. *My daughter.* He wasn't sure he could ever forgive Elin for keeping Josie from him. For cheating him out of these years. Josie still hadn't seen him, and he let his gaze wander over her sturdy legs and feet encased in white sandals. Pink polish tipped her small toes, and a pink bracelet circled her left wrist. She was all girl. His parents would adore her, but he couldn't quite put his head around telling them yet. There was so much to figure out about the future.

He knew the moment she spotted him because her eyes went wide before she leaped to her feet and raced for the backyard. "Wait!" He went after her, but she'd already thrown herself at her mother's legs by the time he reached the patio.

Elin scooped up Josie and turned to face him. Her frosty gaze skewered him. "What are you doing here?"

"I came to see you. And Josie." He added the last in a firm tone. She looked beautiful this morning in a short khaki skirt that showed off her tanned legs. The bright-green top was an unexpected splash of color. Like Sara had said, he'd never seen Elin in bright colors.

"You should have called first."

"And you shouldn't have moved without telling me. Were you hoping I wouldn't find you?"

"Of course not."

He took a step closer, hating that his first meeting with his daughter was going so badly. Elin's tone hadn't helped. "Hello, Josie."

The little girl buried her face in her mother's neck and didn't look at him. Elin shifted her to the other arm. "She's a little shy. This is Mr. Everton, Josie. Remember him? Can you say hello?"

"No." Her refusal was muffled.

Elin's lips twitched. "I suppose you might as well come in since you're here. I was about to fix lunch. Would you like to join us?"

"Sure. Is your mom here?"

"She's inside knitting. I tried to coax her to the beach, but she didn't feel like coming outside." Elin put her daughter down and led her to the back door.

Marc followed her inside the back-porch area. A white washer and dryer were the only furnishings in the space, and the herbal scent of fabric softener wafted in the air. Through the whitewashed pine utility room was the kitchen. White cabinets lined one wall, and a vase of blue flowers atop the pine table added a welcoming touch in the dining area.

"Mom," Elin called.

Marc stood with his hands in his pockets. Elin's mother had always liked him, but would she still if she knew he was Josie's father?

Elin washed her hands, then poked her head through the door into the other room. "Mom, you want to help me fix lunch? We have a visitor."

When her mother didn't answer, Elin stepped through into the living room, and Marc followed her. The pleasant room was empty. A skein of yarn and knitting needles lay on the floor by the sofa. The front door was open to the porch.

A worried frown crouched between Elin's eyes. "The door was locked when I went outside."

"It was open when I got here."

"Did you see Mom?"

He shook his head. "I heard Josie giggling and went that direction."

"Wait here with Josie." Elin transferred her daughter's hand to his, then raced up the oak stairs to the second floor.

Josie's hand was so small in his. He liked the way her fingers curled around his before she snatched her hand back. "I'm not going to hurt you, honey. I'd like to be friends."

She stared up at him. "You're too big."

He crouched beside her. "Now I'm not so big. But it's good to have big friends. I can protect you."

"Mommy protects me." Her glare softened. "Mommy wants you to go away."

"What makes you say that? She was going to feed me lunch, remember?"

Her hazel eyes clouded. "Maybe you just scared her because you're so big. She yelled at you."

"She wasn't expecting me, but I'm Sara's cousin. You know Sara, Mommy's friend?"

Her expression brightened. "Sara takes me for ice cream."

"I'd like to do that too. And we can go for a boat ride. I can teach you to surf." There were so many things he wanted to say to his daughter, so many things he wanted to know about her too. It would take time to be part of her life, but in spite of his impatience, he had the sense the journey would be worth it. He handed her the pink gift bag in his hand. "I brought you something."

Her sudden smile made his heart surge. "What is it?"

"You'll have to open it and see."

She dug into the sparkly tissue and pulled out a box. "It's an iPad! My friend Mina has one. She plays games on it."

"A mini. I loaded some games for you too." He helped her open the box and pull out the tablet. "There are some princess games and a Mickey Mouse one."

She clutched it to her chest. "Can I play it now?"

"You sure can."

She clambered into a chair at the table and pushed an icon. She acted like she was an expert with it already. Kids took to technology so quickly.

Elin came back down the stairs at a gallop. "She's not in the house." Her panicked gaze went to the door. "She can't swim."

He rose and went toward the door. "She probably just went for a walk. I'll find her." Why was Elin so worried? Ruby was a grown woman. She was allowed to go for a walk by herself.

Six

It has to be here somewhere." Ruby struggled through the waves lapping at her knees. Her husband had told her he'd hidden the ring in the water. If she could just find it, the discovery would erase the worry from the face of the young woman in the house. What was her name? It was on the tip of Ruby's tongue. All she knew for sure was she loved the pretty redhead and her little girl. But where was Owen? He'd been here just a few minutes ago.

She sat on a rock and rubbed her head. Why couldn't she think right? There were so many things she couldn't remember, and she didn't like it. It made her feel out of control and lost. But she wasn't lost. She was right here on the shore with Owen. He'd be back in a minute. They'd always been together, and he never left her for long.

Then she heard his voice calling her name. She turned around and saw him jogging toward her with the redhead and her little girl right behind him. She rose and waved. "Owen, I'm here."

He reached her, and she flung her arms around him. "Where have you been? I've been calling and calling for you." She pulled away and gazed up into his face. Had his hair always been so dark? And weren't his eyes more turquoise rather than hazel? He was taller than she remembered too. How could she forget what her own husband looked like?

She clutched his arm. "I can't find it. You said it was here, but I've looked and looked."

"What are you looking for?"

"The ring you hid for me. My engagement ring." The redhead's brow was furrowed. Didn't she know frowning aged a woman? She wanted to tell the pretty woman to always smile. Owen said he treasured her laugh lines. Her fingers found the tiny furrows at the edges of her eyes. Where was this place?

The redhead picked up her left hand. "Your ring is right here, Mom. It's safe and sound."

Ruby stared at the tiny diamond sparkling on her finger. It was worn, and the hand was wrinkled like that of an old woman. A twenty-year-old shouldn't have wrinkly hands. She pulled away from the woman's grip and put her hands in the pockets of her capris. The sun did funny things to her vision.

Owen put his arm around her and turned her toward the woman and girl. "It's time for lunch now, Ruby. Elin and Josie missed you. Elin can't remember how to make your chicken salad, and she needs your help."

"My daughter's name is Elin." Her thoughts began to clear a bit, and she looked past him to her daughter. It had been so long since she'd seen her, and she was all grown up. Someone had kept Elin from her. What enemy would do that? "There you are, Elin. I couldn't find you." Relief coursed through her, and she reached to gather her granddaughter up. "Josie, you've grown two inches since I saw you last."

"Grammy, you saw me at breakfast. I did eat a lot of cereal though."

Ruby started to shake her head, then bit her lip and said nothing. The little girl didn't need to be reminded of how little she understood the passage of time. She turned to stare at the woman again. "Wait, you're not Elin. Elin hates green. Who are you?"

The woman's eyes filled with tears. "Let's go fix lunch, and we can talk about it." She took Ruby's arm. "You can take a nap, and everything will be fine when you wake up."

"Oh, I hope so. I'm very tired. It will all be better after my nap." She clung to the young woman's hand and followed her to the big house on the hill.

Her mother and daughter were both down for a nap. Seated at the pine table, Elin sipped her coffee laced with lots of cream and looked at Marc over the rim of her cup. Her pulse still raced, but no amount of self-talk convinced her it was still a reaction from seeing her mother with the waves up to her knees. It was not knowing what Marc expected from her. And she really didn't want to share Josie.

"Your mom has Alzheimer's?" Marc's voice held sorrow.

She shook her head. "Her dementia is from ministrokes, but the end result is the same."

"I'm sorry. Can anything be done to help her?"

The words tried to stick in her throat, but she forced them out. "No. I've taken her to every type of doctor, and the damage is permanent."

He looked down at his coffee. "That has to be hard on you. The two of you have been so close since your father died."

"I'm losing her. She isn't the same person she used to be."

"The real Ruby is still there, Elin. Even if she wears her hair in an odd way or her clothes don't match. That fierce love she's always had for you is still there. I saw it in her face when she looked past me and saw you."

"She doesn't know who I am." The anguished admission burst past her restraints. "Losing her to death would be easier than this."

He nodded, his hazel eyes grave. "I can understand that. If there's anything I can do to help, let me know."

"She thought you were Dad today. You look nothing like him, not beyond brown hair. And yours is darker than his."

"I was who she needed me to be today. That should show you she hasn't changed inside. She's just a little confused."

A little? How could he dismiss it so easily? She gritted her teeth. "What do you want, Marc?"

The softness in his eyes vanished, and he fixed her with a glare. "I would think the answer is obvious. I want to get to know my daughter."

She fell silent for a moment. How did she even answer that? She'd known the repercussions of telling him the truth would come, but she'd thought she would have a little more time. "It's too soon. And while we're talking about Josie, let's clear up the gift thing. I try not to spoil her too much. You should have asked before getting her that iPad. It was too much."

"Technology makes the world run, Elin. Every kid should know her way around an iPad."

She couldn't squelch the faint smile that lifted her lips. "Yours is never far away, I see."

"Never." He looked down and a muscle in his jaw twitched. "You should have told me about this a long time ago. The more I've thought about it, the madder I've gotten, Elin. You had no right to shut me out. Josie deserves better than that from you, and so do I." He put his coffee cup on the table and leaned forward. "I intend to be part of her life. If you try to prevent it, I'll take you to court."

His threat squeezed the air from her lungs. "You wouldn't do that."

His mouth flattened. "Just try me."

The intensity in his words made her stand and pace the wood floor. "It was the right thing to do. Tim deserved a chance at a happy family."

"You really think it was the right thing to live a lie all those years? To let him raise *my* child?" He shoved back from the table so hard that the chair fell back when he stood. "What kind of woman would be okay with that?"

Her fingers curled into her palms, and she wanted to hit him. "I told him about you, about the night Josie was conceived. He understood it was just a reaction to hearing about Dad's death. I-I had too much to drink—we both did. It never should have happened." She raked a hand through her red curls. "I've been tormented by guilt. Haven't you been?"

He pressed his lips together. "Yeah, I've had guilt, but that shouldn't stop you from doing what's right. And keeping it from me was *wrong*."

She looked down at her hands. "It was right for Josie, me, and Tim. He was happy with me and Josie by his side. He adored her." Her voice thickened, but she wouldn't cry. Not in front of him. Nothing she could do would ever really make up for her lapse that one night, her very great sin.

Marc stared at her as if he couldn't believe what he heard. "Play it any way you want, Elin, but make no mistake. I *will* be part of my daughter's life. I want her every weekend. I'll pick her up on Saturday morning and bring her home after dinner on Sunday."

"It's too soon, Marc! She doesn't know you. Besides, I want her to go to church with me."

He raised a brow. "I want her to get to know my parents too, and we can do Sunday dinner together in Norfolk. You have to share her, Elin. You have no choice."

What right did he think he had to come in here and dictate how things would be? She rubbed her forehead where pain began to pulse. "This is more than I can deal with right now, Marc. How about Saturday afternoons for now? She needs time to get to know you."

His strong jaw flexed, and his eyes were like flint. "Fine. But eventually I will want her every other weekend. I'm entitled to that. Any court will award me that right."

He was right. She saw a dismal future stretched out ahead of her—a future of bickering and stress. She never should have told him the truth. What if she lost Josie to him?

SEVEN

Sunday dawned with overcast skies, but there was no rain in the forecast. Elin got the skiff out of the boathouse, then loaded up her mother and daughter for the trip around the west side of the island to town. After a week at Seagrass Pier, she craved human companionship. Would Marc be at church? She hoped he'd gone back to Norfolk. Surely he wouldn't stay at Hope Island until her stalker was caught. Not that he even seemed focused on her problem. He just wanted justice for his murdered partner.

She docked the boat, then walked down the street to the church. Josie whined and wanted to be carried, but Elin couldn't heft her far in these heels. Her ankles wouldn't take the stress.

"There's the church," she told her mother.

A steeple crowned the white clapboard structure, and the wooden double doors stood open in welcome. She entered and blinked in the room's dim light. Sara saw her and pointed to the pew where she sat. Several other people smiled her way, and her unease began to ebb.

"Honey, those heels are high enough to cause nosebleeds." Sara moved to the middle of the pew. "I hoped you'd make it. There's a church picnic following the service, and I brought extra food so you wouldn't feel funny about staying." Her honey-colored hair was in an updo, and her red dress made her gray eyes sparkle.

A smiling brunette with a toddler on her lap turned around and smiled her way. "I'm Amy Ireland. Sara has told me so much about you. Welcome to Hope Beach. We should get together for lunch this week. The kids could play together."

"I'd love that." *Ireland.* The unusual name struck a chord. "Is your husband Curtis?"

Amy nodded. "Do you know Curtis?"

It was too soon to explain why she was here. "I've heard his name from Sara. They're on the same team."

"You'll meet him soon enough. He's checking out some equipment today, but he'll be along in time for the picnic."

"You're a midwife, right? And know about herbal remedies?"

Amy brightened. "Oh yes. Sara told me about your heart transplant. If you're interested, I'd love to help you find the right remedies to keep your heart working at its best."

"I was about to ask that." Elin's biggest fear was her body would reject her new heart. She'd try anything to keep that from happening.

Sara introduced her to another friend, Libby Bourne, and the women chatted a few minutes. Elin began to relax. If Marc were coming, he'd be here by now. She could enjoy the day. The praise team took the stage, and Josie's hand crept into hers. Then Marc's broad shoulders blocked her vision as he moved into the pew and sat beside her. He wasn't smiling as he settled beside her and turned on his iPad.

She glanced at Sara. "Did you know he was coming?" she whispered.

Sara shrugged. "I invited him. He will be on the island a few weeks while he's investigating."

He called up his Bible app, then turned to her mother. "Good morning, Mrs. Whiteford. You look very nice this morning."

And her mother *did* look attractive in her navy slacks and

white blouse. It had been all Elin could do to get her mother not to wear the red capris and the orange tank top she'd put on first thing this morning.

Her mother simpered and took Marc's hand. "There you are, Owen. Elin wanted me to wear my red capris, but I told her you'd like these better."

Elin watched him smile and let her mother hold his hand. Should she intervene and explain to her mother that he wasn't her dead husband? She'd tried to tell Mom that Dad was in heaven, but it always upset her. The grief would strike all over again as if he'd just died. Church wasn't the place to cause a scene like the one that would blow up if she tried to explain.

She leaned over and whispered in his ear, "We're having a picnic on the beach after church today. You're welcome to come with us so Josie has a chance to get to know you better."

His lips flattened. "Fine."

She rose with the rest of the congregation to sing. Her mother let go of Marc's hand and reached for the songbook. Her clear soprano voice sang out with gusto, and Elin's eyes filled. Such a contradiction. Though she forgot her husband was dead, she never seemed to forget her love for Jesus. Did that mean her mother was still in there somewhere?

With his hand freed up, Marc moved closer to Josie. Elin's heart constricted at the longing in his face as he gazed down at their daughter. He stroked their little girl's soft curls, and she looked up at him. A wary smile made its way to Josie's face, and he scooped her up before she could protest. She leaned away from Marc a few inches, and her gaze examined his face. Then she relaxed in his arms and curled one arm around his neck. He grinned and chimed in with the song service.

He had a good voice, deep and resonant. Josie nestled against him in an even more trusting manner, and Elin resisted the urge to grab her daughter out of his arms. What if he grew bored with playing daddy and vanished back to Norfolk? Josie would be hurt. She wasn't one to quickly give her affection, but Marc's concentrated attention on her had quickly melted her reserve.

Elin's gaze fell on a slip of paper sticking out of her Bible, and she leaned down to retrieve it. It looked like it had been torn from a yellow legal pad. A single sentence slashed its way across the paper.

I found you.

⸺

"You're staring." Elin shook some pills into her palm and took them with a sip of water, then leaned back on the beach blanket.

She had grown more beautiful in the last few years. Maturity had brought new angles to the planes of her face. The shadows behind her eyes worried him though. "What's that? Headache?" He spared a glance toward his daughter who was building a sand castle with Ruby.

She shook her head. "Antirejection meds. And I'll need to take a nap here in the sun soon. I hate not being 100 percent."

"I thought you looked like something was wrong. You're just tired?"

She reached into her beach bag and brought out a yellow slip of torn paper. "It's more than that."

He took the paper and read it. "Where'd you get it?"

"It was stuck in my Bible this morning. I think he's found me." Her voice wobbled, and she bit her lip.

"I think you're reading too much into it. Look at the crude printing. Don't you think it looks like a kid wrote it? Maybe some children were playing hide-and-seek in the sanctuary. Or maybe it's been there awhile, and you just now found it."

"I read it every day. I would have seen it. And one of those

kids today just happened to put it in my Bible? I don't think so."
She regarded him steadily, her aqua eyes sad. "Why don't you
believe me, Marc? You know I wouldn't lie about something like
this. If I'm in danger, Josie is too. You need to take this seriously."

He fell silent at her question. No, she wouldn't lie about something like this, but her perception might be off from all she'd gone
through. "I'm not saying the guy isn't after you, but I don't think
this proves he's here on the island."

"You're not even going to check it out, are you?"

The disappointment in her voice stabbed him. "I didn't say
I wouldn't check it out. I'll poke around and see if there are any
new residents or visitors who have reserved a room for more than
a week."

Her eyes lit with relief. "I have to live for Josie's sake. And for
my mom."

The thought of someone harming her made his gut clench. He
looked toward Ruby. "She seems okay today." The older woman
patted sand into place without any sign of confusion.

She followed his gaze. "It comes and goes. Church seemed to
ground her. She's been fine ever since the opening song."

"I'm really sorry. I wish I could help. You're hiring an aide?"

She nodded and reached over to pick up a handful of sand,
then let it trickle through her fingers. "Every day I see her slipping
away just like this sand. Memory after memory is just gone."

"I'm sorry." His gaze lingered on his daughter. The thought of
fathering a little girl left him floundering. He knew nothing about
being a father.

When he looked back at Elin, her expression betrayed no
emotion. "If you hurt my daughter, I–I . . ."

He held up his hand. "Chill. She's not just your daughter."

The words hung between them, and color ran up her neck and
splotched her cheeks. "You sound like you're still mad."

"I guess I am. Wouldn't you be mad if the tables were turned?"

She exhaled. "Fine. And I'm okay with you spending Saturday afternoons with her, but you need to give it some time. She doesn't warm up easily."

"Don't give me that, Elin. She warmed right up to me. I'm going to have my parents come to the island. It's time they met their grandchild."

"I–I have my mom to contend with. The new aide won't be working on the weekend. I think it's too soon for you to take her anywhere without me. She's not used to going with strangers. Invite them to come here. I have plenty of room."

He gritted his teeth. "I'm not a stranger. I'm her father. My mother was a nurse. She's used to dealing with dementia. You'll have to let me take her eventually."

Her eyes sparked. "Eventually, but not now."

"Fine. I'll have them come here."

Her slow nod finally came. "I hope you tell your parents before they arrive. It's going to be a shock."

Not nearly as shocking as the day he learned about his daughter.

EIGHT

The clock finally ticked over to three, and Elin swung her legs over the side of the bed. She hated the enforced rest time the doctor had prescribed. It make her feel weak and not in control.

She found Marc playing with Josie on the living room floor. He looked up when she entered. "Josie was telling me about a wonderful play area in the attic." He grinned. "She wants to show me something up there."

So he'd quickly won Josie's affection. Elin wasn't sure how she felt about that. "I can show you. This way." She turned toward the stairs, and he lifted Josie into his arms and followed.

Elin led him to the attic door, where she fitted the key into the lock to the third floor.

Josie seemed attached to Marc's hip. She'd never seen Josie take to someone so quickly, especially a man. She flipped on the light and led the way up the stairs.

Standing in the center of the space, she frowned as she looked around. Something was different. She couldn't put her finger on it, not at first. Then she saw that someone had taken all the sheets off the furniture. On one side, she saw an old gold sofa that had to be nine feet long. And a fine, old high-backed chair. There was a pile of rolled-up rugs against one wall, and jumbled against the wall on the other side, she saw an open chest with old toys and dolls spilling from it.

"Someone's been up here." She moved to the trunk and put the toys and dolls back into the wooden box.

Marc set Josie on the floor, and she ran to look at the toys with her mother. "Where do you keep the key to this floor?"

"In the dresser beside my bed." She handed Josie a small china doll. "Be careful, honey. It's very old."

"She has a cute smile, Mommy. Do I smile like that?" Josie looked up at her and smiled, exposing only her front teeth.

Elin had to laugh at the cheesy smile. "Just like that." Her gaze locked with Marc's amused one.

She turned away quickly. What was she doing exchanging a moment of such intimacy with him? It was like he had really segued into being Josie's dad, and Elin wasn't ready for that. What about Tim? How did she even hope to keep his memory alive in Josie when Marc's strong personality would run roughshod over Tim's quiet ways?

"These are really old toys. I bet they're worth some money." He bent over and picked up a bear. "This looks like a Steiff. It's in really good shape."

She took the stuffed animal from him. When she turned back to the box, she discovered Josie had emptied it and was standing in it. "Josie, I was picking them up."

"I fit in here. It can be my house. Close the lid!" She sat down and hugged her knees to her chest. "I can pop up and surprise you like my jack-in-the-box."

"Okay, for just a second." Elin lowered the lid, holding it about an inch off the bottom from closing. "One, two, three!" She helped Josie push the lid up, and the little girl leaped to her feet giggling.

"Boo, Mommy!" She made a face, something between the doll's smile and a grimace.

Elin gasped and stepped back a step. "You scared me! My goodness. But let's pick all this up."

She smiled and lifted her daughter out of the box. The lace of Josie's shoe caught on something, and Elin paused to untangle it. The lace wound around a small curvature in the corner of the chest. She freed it, then lifted Josie out of the way and bent over to examine the bottom better.

Marc knelt beside her. "What's wrong?"

"There's a weird latch or something here." She tugged on it but nothing happened.

"Let me try."

His warm fingers brushed hers, and she pulled her hands back and moved away a few inches. He ran his hands over the bottom, then looked at the chest from the side. "I think there's a false bottom."

Her pulse leaped. "Maybe the diaries are in there. These toys are old. Look at that Tinkertoy set. They might have belonged to the Hurley twins." She told him about the missing diaries. "I mean, it's not a big deal, but I love history, and it would be fun to read about her life. I'd love to find them."

He nodded. "Let me see if I can figure out how to raise it without ruining the chest. It looks quite valuable."

He bent to his task and pulled on the latch. Nothing happened. "Got a screwdriver handy?"

"No, but try this." She handed him her key chain.

He took one of the skeleton keys and slipped it under the latch, then pried gently. There was a clicking sound, and one edge of the bottom popped up. He moved to the other side and did the same to the nearly invisible latch there. In moments, the bottom was loose.

He handed the keys back to her. "Let me lift it out of the way."

Josie clambered onto her lap and watched with interest. "It's a secret place?"

"It is indeed." Elin was afraid to hope there might be something important under there.

Marc slid his fingers under each end of the bottom and lifted. The material appeared fragile, and she prayed it didn't break. His hands caught on one side, and he paused to go more slowly, lifting first one end out of the way, then the other.

When he laid the false bottom on the floor, she leaned over the chest to peer inside. A gauzy material covered the contents, and it looked like it might tear at the slightest touch. She gently peeled back the layers to reveal three bound leather books.

"It's just books, Mommy. Dusty old books." Josie sounded disgusted. She scooted off Elin's lap and picked up the round box of Tinkertoys. "Can I play with these?"

"Sure." Elin couldn't take her eyes off the books. They had to be the diaries.

She picked up the first one and opened the cover. The fine leather was soft in her hands. The inside pages were yellow and a little brittle. She turned to the next page.

Georgina Hurley 1907

Elin closed the book. She would read it during her resting times. It might help her stay awake. She hated sleeping because of the nightmares.

———

She yanked on the bedroom door, but it wouldn't budge. He'd locked her in with that music blaring. He knew she hated the song "The Cold Hard Facts of Life." She shuddered as the Porter Wagoner lyrics about murder twanged their way down her spine.

She kicked the door, and pain shot up her leg. "Let me out of here!"

A knife blade slid under the door. "Sure you want me to open the door?" His voice sounded gleeful and way too happy about the fear in her voice.

She stepped back and looked around for a weapon. The heavy lamp would have to do. "You don't scare me." The thump of her heart told a different story. She grabbed her phone. "I'm calling the police!"

The knife disappeared. "You'd better not, Laura." His voice was cold. "I might just turn my attention to Sammie."

The blood froze in her veins. She stepped closer and pressed her forehead against the door. "You wouldn't."

But he would. She knew what he was capable of. The cell phone fell from her fingers and thumped onto the carpeted floor. "I won't call. Just go away and leave me alone."

The lock clicked, and she heard his footsteps clack rapidly away along the wood floor. The front door banged. She waited until she heard his truck engine rev up and pull out of the drive before she grabbed her cell phone and called her sister.

———

Sweat slicked Elin's skin, and she bolted upright in bed. Another nightmare. She rubbed her throat and swallowed. Just to be on the safe side, she padded down the hall and checked on her daughter and mother. Both slept, unaware of the storm rolling in off the ocean. She went back to her bed, unwilling to sleep again. Her gaze went to the diaries.

Flashes of lightning lit her bedroom as she snuggled under the sheet and opened the first diary. She'd been dying to read it, and she wasn't about to go back to sleep and fall into that nightmare again.

Written in my hand, February 3, 1907. Georgina Hurley

The February wind blew through Georgina's thin coat as she stepped off the ship onto Seagrass Pier and surveyed her new home for the first time. Her blood wasn't used to such dampness and cold, though Joshua had assured her it was nearly forty-five here today.

Joshua saw her shiver and wrapped his greatcoat around her. "We'll soon be inside, love."

She thanked him with a smile. He towered above her five-two height by at least a foot, and his dark good looks attracted every lady in his sphere. She'd been astonished when he began to call after dining at one of her father's soirees. When he'd asked her to marry him, she quickly accepted, and their marriage of six months had been quite harmonious. Most of the time.

But she didn't like the way her life was about to change. Joshua hadn't listened to her pleas either.

He dropped a kiss on her forehead. "It's a far cry from Cambodia, isn't it?"

"Very different." Her eyes took in the magnificent house towering over the sand dunes that seemed to go on forever. Three stories high, it was crowned with a lacy black railing and a cupola. The grand porch wrapped around one side, and the soft gray-green color seemed to blend into the hillside. The shutters could be closed to typhoon winds and storms. It had been built to withstand anything nature could throw its way.

She sent an appealing glance up at her handsome husband. "It's beautiful, Joshua, but I don't want to stay here. I want to go with you."

Impatience flickered in his eyes. "I know, I know." He offered her his arm and escorted her up the boardwalk to the house. "A ship is no place for a woman in a delicate condition. We both know that, Georgina."

He rarely used her name, preferring instead to call her *love* or *darling*. He must be displeased at her complaint. What would it take to get him to see she wasn't some shrinking violet of a woman but one used to making her own way in the world? She'd discovered new plants and had been places most women would be much too timid to venture. When was the last time she'd even been in the States? Ten years ago, perhaps?

She stepped into the house. A grand hall led to a large room on one side and a dining space on the other. A huge walnut staircase gleamed in the afternoon light. A fire coaxed her into the large parlor, and she shed her coat and approached the fireplace. "It's quite beautiful."

His expression was pleased as he surveyed the house. "The builder did a fine job. This is the first I've seen the completed structure myself."

She turned at a commotion in the entry. Four men lugged in her chests and luggage. "I should find our room so they can stow my belongings."

He put his hand on her shoulder. "The housekeeper will do that. You're a lady of leisure now, my dear. You must not infringe on the duties of our staff." He motioned to the unsmiling, middle-aged woman who appeared in the doorway. "Mrs. Winston, our belongings have arrived. Please get them unpacked. Oh, and we're ready for tea and some sandwiches."

Georgina pressed her lips together at his tone and moved so his hand fell away. She liked this less and less.

"Of course, Captain Hurley." She curtsied and turned to speak to someone in the room behind her, then scurried to lead the sailors up the large staircase.

A few minutes later a housemaid in a white apron and cap carried in a tray of tea and sandwiches. Georgina made sure to give her an extra-warm smile. "Thank you. What's your name?"

The maid, about seventeen with ruddy cheeks and bright-blue eyes, bobbed. "I'm Susan, Mrs. Hurley."

"I'm sure we will get along very well, Susan." Georgina removed her hat and placed it on the table by the sofa. "Is there sugar?" She'd developed quite a sweet tooth since her pregnancy.

"Yes, ma'am." Susan set the tray on the table in front of the sofa.

"I'll pour myself." Georgina moved to the table.

"Of course." Susan bobbed again, then practically ran for the kitchen.

She frowned at her husband. "Have you been terrorizing the servants? They seem quite timid."

"I made it clear when I hired them that I expect nothing but the best service. It's as it should be. I don't want you making friends of them either. They need to keep to their place, and you need to keep to yours. No fraternizing like you did aboard ship."

She curled her fingers into the palms of her hands and took a deep breath. "Joshua, you need to understand who I am. I'm not like your mother or your sister. I'm quite competent to do things for myself. I refuse to be some kind of matriarch who throws her weight around. I simply won't do it."

He blinked at her vehemence, and his mustache quivered, a sure sign of his displeasure. "You have a new role to fulfill, Georgina. You're my wife now. You'll soon be the mother of my child as well. I realize it will take some time for you to adjust to your new position, but there will be plenty of time here in the house to figure it out."

He wasn't listening to her. She fought the rising sense of

frustration. His expectations were something she couldn't meet. She didn't *want* to be anyone other than herself. Her father had allowed her to travel with him all over the world, and she didn't take kindly to being relegated to such a constricted life.

But what were her options? She loved Joshua. Did that mean she needed to change herself, become some other person? Why couldn't he accept her for who she was?

NINE

T he diary's cover was smooth and worn in Elin's fingers when she closed it. How many years had Georgina written in it? How many times had she picked it up and flipped through its pages? Elin glanced around the bedroom. It had been built with its own indoor bathroom right from the beginning, though bathrooms weren't that common back in 1907. This had likely been Georgina's room too. Had she sat by herself on her bed while the thunder rattled the windows and the wind threw whitecaps onto the sand? Had she ever been frightened living out here without her husband?

"What are you reading, honey?" Her mother stood in the doorway to Elin's bedroom. She wore pink curlers in her hair and a black nightgown. Her eyes were bright and alert. It was a good night.

"The storm woke you?" Elin patted the bed beside her. "This diary belonged to the original owner of the house. It's very interesting."

Her mother crawled onto the bed. "Who was she?"

Elin told her about Georgina and her adjustment to her new role. "I sympathize with what she was going through. I don't know who I am anymore either. I'm a widow, but I don't feel my life is over. I love my job, but lately I feel adrift from it, ever since my heart transplant." Her chest felt heavy.

Her mother's blue eyes softened. "I remember when I married your father. I'd had all these dreams of going to medical school and becoming a doctor. There were times after you and Abby were born when I wondered where that dreamy-eyed girl had gone. What had happened to all those plans?"

Elin had never heard her talk about that big of a dream. "Did you talk to Dad about it? You could have gone back to school."

Her mom nodded. "He didn't understand why I wasn't content with raising our two girls and being a mom. We grew up in the era of *Leave It to Beaver.* Your dad thought that should be enough, but I wanted more than washing dishes and taking cupcakes to school parties. I wanted to make a difference."

"You made a difference in my life and in Abby's." Elin took her mother's hand. "You volunteered a lot. And you got a job when I was ten or eleven."

"As a receptionist. Quite a comedown from my dream of being a doctor."

"I never knew you were unhappy."

"I never said I was unhappy." Her mother settled back against the pillow. "That's not what I meant. Contentment is found in your heart, Elin. It's not in a profession or in a relationship. Your roles don't define who you are. You define your roles. How you approach the different roles in your life is something you figure out for yourself. They don't make you someone different from who you are at your core. I realized when you were about eleven that no one else could be your mom but me. No one else could teach you values but me. I was glad I'd stuck it out."

Elin contemplated her mother's words. They held a lot of wisdom, but they didn't answer the questions she had about how she'd changed since her heart transplant. Did Laura's memories change her? Did having different tastes mean she was more like Laura and less like herself? She didn't know anymore.

"Didn't you regret your decision?"

Her mother shook her head. "Not in the least. I could have gone to school when you went off to college, but by then I found my interests had changed. We evolve as women. Let yourself grow, honey. It's okay."

The phone on the bedside table rang, and she picked up the handset and looked at it. *Unknown.* That could mean a telemarketer, or it could mean her office was calling. She was tempted to let it go to voice mail, but it might be important. There might be a new donor she needed to find recipients for.

She clicked it on. "Hello." There was only silence on the other end. "Hello?" She pulled the handset away from her ear and looked at it. She appeared to still be connected. She put it back to her ear and said hello again. This time she heard the faint strain of music playing.

Her throat tightened. Was that a *Phantom of the Opera* tune? She couldn't tell for sure. Maybe it was her imagination. Before she could freak out, she clicked the phone off and practically threw it back onto its base.

"Who was that?"

Thunder rattled the windows, and Elin jumped. "No one was there."

"Then why are your eyes so big? And your mouth is trembling like you're scared."

"The storm has made me jumpy. That's all." That had to be all it was. It was likely her imagination that the music was the same. She'd heard it over and over in her head ever since he'd broken in. She was seeing danger around every corner, just like that silly note.

She was perfectly safe here.

The next morning Elin felt heavy and slow from lack of sleep. She sat on a beach towel under a dome of blue sky and watched Josie build a sand castle with her grandmother. Mom's eyes were as clear as the sky above, and she chattered with Josie as if she'd never called her by the wrong name. If Elin could only freeze this moment for all time. The scent of the sea, the squawk of the seagulls, and the warmth of the sun would be poignant reminders of a perfect day free from worry.

Mom squinted in the sun, then rose and dusted the sand from her hands. "We have a visitor."

Elin twisted to see Kalianne Adanete climb out of a dinghy at the dock in the tiny crescent of harbor. Elin got up and pulled on her cover-up as the nurse's aide approached with a smile. The woman had an air of competence in spite of her youth and attractiveness. Her denim skirt showed off shapely legs, and she wore her blond hair in a French knot.

Why did she feel such relief at the thought of help? This was her dear mother. Caring for her shouldn't feel like such a burden. The problem was, she was so afraid of failing her.

As the woman neared, Elin held out her hand. "Thanks for coming right away. I hope I didn't interrupt anything important."

"I was thrilled to get the call." Kalianne shook her hand, then turned to smile at Elin's mom. "Hello, Ruby. You look like you're having a good time."

"Josie and I are making a sand castle." The older woman's hand swept over the sand turrets and moat. "I remember you. You're one of Elin's friends from high school. Mary, isn't it?" She frowned disapprovingly. "You were always a bad influence on Elin. I'm sorry I had to forbid her from running around with you."

Elin's throat tightened. She should have known the clouds in her mother's eyes wouldn't stay gone for long. "You remember Kalianne, Mom. She's going to spend some time here and help us find fun things to do."

Her mother's nod was uncertain, and she turned her back to rejoin Josie at the sand castle.

Elin motioned for the aide to join her a few feet away where they couldn't be overheard. "She was doing really well all day until now."

Kalianne patted her arm. "It's all right. May I call you Elin, or would you prefer Mrs. Summerall?"

She so liked this young woman. Her confidence strengthened Elin's courage. "Oh yes, please call me Elin. We're going to be seeing quite a lot of one another."

Kalianne glanced toward her new charge. "So where do you want me to start with your mom?"

Elin shaded her eyes as she looked into the afternoon sun to the west. She pointed toward the house. "She loves gardening. There's a plot in the backyard that just needs to be tilled. I found a tiller in the garden shed, but I'm not sure how to work it."

"There isn't a tiller made I don't know how to operate."

"I can get whatever plants or seeds you want too." Elin led her back to rejoin her mother and Josie. "Mom, would you like to have a garden?"

Her mother looked up. "A garden? Can I have tomatoes?"

"If we can keep the sea spray from wilting them," Kalianne said. "I think they'll be sheltered behind the house."

Josie jumped up and tugged on the new aide's hand. "Can I help too?"

Kalianne picked her up. "You sure can. I'll teach you how to weed and everything."

Josie pulled back and studied the woman's face. "I don't know. Will there be bugs? I hate bugs, especially centipedes." She shuddered. "They have too many legs."

"No centipedes allowed in my garden," Kalianne assured her.

"What about cats? Mommy hates cats." Josie looked to Elin for confirmation.

"That's right." She shivered. "You'll protect me from the kitties, won't you?"

"I'll shoo them away." Josie seemed in no hurry to get out of Kalianne's embrace.

Watching them, Elin smiled. They could be very happy here with some support from Kalianne.

Josie finally wiggled to be let down. "I'll find my sand shovel." When her feet hit the ground, she ran for the house and disappeared inside.

Elin picked up the beach towel and her *Superman* comic book to follow her daughter. "We'd better see what she's up to. Who knows where the shovel is. She'll have the entire contents of her closet in the middle of her bedroom."

Kalianne smiled and pointed to the comic book. "*Superman*? I have nearly all of them from the seventies. My dad collected them, and he gave them to me."

"You lucky girl. I pick them up whenever I run into them. I don't have anything near a complete collection."

"Wouldn't it be nice to find a real man like that?"

It bothered Elin that her thoughts immediately went to Marc at the phrase *real man*. She had no interest in him that way. She glanced at her mom, who already looked more engaged and interested in life. It would be great to have Kalianne around.

TEN

The ice-cream shop wasn't busy on this Monday afternoon. Sara glanced around the room and didn't see Elin and Josie, but then, she was about ten minutes early. As she moved toward a corner table to wait, she heard her name.

"Sara." Ben's blue eyes warmed when he smiled up at her. Assigned here from Florida, he hadn't been in his new position long. He was the new head of IT. She hadn't had much contact with him yet and didn't even know his last name. In his late thirties, his blond hair had a casual cut. He was out of uniform and in khaki shorts and a light blue polo.

"Have a seat." He indicated the chair at his table.

"I'm waiting for a friend, but I'm a little early." She glanced at the door before she sat down.

"Good work on that rescue last week. When I heard there were two kids aboard the sinking boat, I feared we'd have a fatality or two. The youngest was only two, right?"

She nodded. "It was pretty tense. Seas were running at twenty feet. The parents stayed calm though, and that helped."

His smile made her feel like she was in a spotlight. Was he *flirting* with her? Her cheeks warmed, and she couldn't force herself to look away. It had been awhile since such a handsome guy showed interest.

"Can I get you some ice cream? Or you can share my banana split."

"I'd better wait for my friend."

He leaned forward, his gaze intent on her face. "You're good at your job. I like that. I hope you don't think I'm being too forward, but I wondered if you'd want to go to dinner with me. Maybe take in a movie or something on Saturday. If you're free, that is."

Feeling tongue-tied, she glanced down at her hands. Josh wasn't making any moves in her direction. Wasn't it time she moved on from a hopeless relationship? Not that there had ever been a real relationship between them. She didn't owe him anything.

Ben's eager smile dimmed. "Earth to Sara."

"Sorry, you took me by surprise. I'd like that, Ben. There's a new *Star Trek* movie hitting the theater in Kill Devil Hills."

His grin returned full force. "I'm a Trekkie myself. You're the local here, so you pick where we go. You have a favorite restaurant there?"

"Do you like Mexican? Bad Bean Baja Grill is good in spite of the unfortunate name."

He laughed, a nice sound that warmed her heart just a little. The bell above the door jingled, and she waved to Elin and Josie. "My friends are here. I'll see you Saturday."

He rose and stared toward Elin and Josie. "Elin, I didn't expect to run into you today."

Josie rushed to hug him, and Elin took her turn receiving a hug. "Ben, how great to see you again." She turned to Sara. "Ben is Tim's half brother. He introduced me to Tim actually. I didn't realize you two knew each other."

Ben sent an amused smile Sara's direction. "We just met since I moved to the island."

A warm feeling settled in Sara's chest. It felt good to know Elin approved of this new guy in her life.

Ben rested his hand on Sara's shoulder and gave it a little squeeze. "I wish I could stay and chat, but I need to get back to work."

The three of them stepped to the counter to order their ice cream. Elin studied Sara's face. "I sensed some chemistry between the two of you."

Sara's smile felt too big, and her pulse still thumped against her ribs as if she'd just run two miles. "Maybe a little." She shut up until they had their order and were seated at a table in the far corner.

Elin scooped up pecan and caramel with her ice cream. "Okay, what's the deal? You are smiling like you just won the lottery."

Sara frowned at her. "Since when do you get something other than a hot fudge sundae?"

Elin looked down at her sundae. "Hot fudge didn't sound good today." Her brow furrowed, then cleared. "Don't try to change the subject. What's going on with Ben?"

A giggle tried to bubble up in Sara's chest, but she stuffed it back down. "He asked me out."

Elin reached over to wipe up a dribble of ice cream down Josie's front. "Did you say yes?"

"Um, I did." Sara took another bite so she didn't have to say more. She'd never been good at hiding anything, and Elin knew her too well.

Elin's eyes widened. "Seriously, you're going out with him? What about Josh?"

"That ship sailed a long time ago. If it was ever in the dock. Josh is never going to get over his fear of commitment, and my birthday is coming in two weeks. Do you know how hard it is to think about turning thirty without a prospect in sight?"

"You don't need a man to be complete. You're the most self-sufficient person I know."

Sara gave a heavy sigh. "Maybe that's the problem. Josh doesn't think I need him. Is it too much to hope he might be jealous if he sees me with another guy?"

Elin took another bite of her sundae. "Josh strikes me as the type to use it as verification he was right and all women are fickle."

Sara slumped back in her chair. "You're probably right. Maybe I should cancel." She straightened. "No, I will *not*. I deserve a life, a family. I'm not waiting around on Josh any longer. It's amazing you know Ben. What can you tell me about him?"

Elin looked down at her ice cream. "Well, I dated him for a little while. Then he introduced me to Tim, and it was all over. I always felt a little guilty about that. You've heard me talk about Kerri?"

Sara nodded. "Your coworker friend."

"She was married to him for about a year, but it didn't work out. So be cautious, okay? Ben doesn't seem the type to settle down. At least he didn't with Kerri."

Sara's bubble of happiness deflated. "It's just a movie and dinner. Now let's talk about something else. How did Sunday go with Marc? He came over after church, right?"

"Yes." She glanced down at Josie, who was nearly finished with her ice cream. "Honey, you can play with the toys in the corner for a little while if you like."

"Yay!" Josie scrambled down from her chair and raced over to the small table and chairs that held crayons and toys.

"I didn't get a chance to tell you what I found in my Bible at church. Marc thinks kids were playing. I'm worried it's more sinister." She pulled a scrap of yellow paper out of her purse.

Sara stared at the words. "'I found you.' That does sort of sound like kids playing hide-and-seek, but under the circumstances, it still feels off. Have you seen anyone out at Seagrass?"

Elin shook her head. "I'm having a security system installed though. I've been jittery ever since I got this." She glanced at her watch. "I'd better go. Mom should be done at the doctor's by now.

That new aide is such a big blessing. She came early enough to fix breakfast."

"You can use the help." Sara watched Elin gather her belongings and her daughter, then head for the door. It was only when her friend was gone that she realized she still held the scrap of paper.

It wouldn't hurt to get it analyzed. She knew someone who could tell if a child wrote it.

———

Elin got her mother and daughter settled for the night. After the day in town, they were all tired, so she didn't even have to read Josie a story. Leaving the door cracked a bit, she headed to the living room where she took the herbal remedy she'd gotten from Amy. Maybe it was her imagination, but she was feeling better since she started it. She curled up with a suspense novel, maybe not the best choice of reading material with her current state of mind.

The evening held a bit of a chill, so she pulled a red chenille throw over her legs and opened her book. Something creaked and she looked up. Just the house settling or the wind. She turned the page of her book. Another sound came to her ears, a scratching sound as though someone was running his fingernail along the chalkboard in the kitchen.

A shiver ran down her spine, and she kicked off the throw. Even though she told herself it was nothing, the hair on her arms stood at attention. She got to her feet and grabbed a poker from the set at the fireplace. Wielding it like a baseball bat, she tip-toed toward the kitchen and winced when a floorboard squeaked under her feet.

The scratching in the kitchen stopped, and she heard the screen door slap against the doorjamb. At least that's what it sounded like. She froze, then retreated, reaching for the phone on the end table. There was no 911 on the island, and would the police even believe her? Without thinking, she dialed Marc's number.

He answered on the first ring. "Elin?"

"I think there's someone in the house," she whispered.

"Lock yourself in the bedroom with your mom and Josie. I'm on my way. Go now. I'll stay on the line." A door slammed and an engine started.

She took comfort from the fact he was coming. She tucked the poker under her arm, then rushed up the stairs to Josie's room. Holding the phone to her ear with her shoulder, she scooped Josie up. Her daughter didn't stir as she carried her down the hall to where her mother slept.

"I'm in my mother's room," she whispered. She shut the door and locked it, then slid to the wood floor and sat with her back to the door. She cradled Josie to her chest.

"I'm nearly to the harbor." His voice was urgent. "I'll lose you out over the water, but I'm coming. Do you have a weapon?"

"Just the fireplace poker."

"Better than nothing."

She heard his feet slapping something solid, and his breath was labored. A thud sounded. "Are you on the boat?"

"Yes. I won't be able to hear you in a minute, and I have to navigate out of the harbor. I'll be there in twenty minutes." His voice began to cut out.

Twenty minutes. That seemed so long. She didn't hear the rest of what he said because his voice was too garbled. She ended the call and pressed her ear against the door. Nothing.

She had difficulty regaining her feet with Josie in her arms, so she grabbed a blanket off the end of her mother's bed and laid her daughter on it. She tiptoed to the window and gazed down into the yard. The tiny back-porch light pushed back the edges of darkness by only a few feet. Darkness shrouded the rest of the yard, and she saw no movement. Maybe the intruder had left.

She hadn't heard a boat approach her remote point, but maybe he'd cut the motor out in the bay, then rowed to shore. Or maybe he'd taken the longer dirt road. Was that the distant rumble of an engine? It was too soon for Marc to be here. A yellow glow of a boat light showed the craft moving away from shore.

He was gone.

She sagged against the wall, then went to take Josie back onto her lap. The little girl hadn't stirred, and Elin's mother still slept soundly. At least they wouldn't be awake the rest of the night the way she would. What had the man been doing in the kitchen, and why hadn't he come after her in the living room? Did he just intend to scare her to death?

Or maybe it was just a thief looking to steal something. It might have nothing to do with Laura's murder.

She wanted to explore the kitchen and see if he'd left anything behind, but she wasn't about to do so by herself. There was no reason to be stupid. The man could have left a booby trap behind. Or a bomb. Who knew?

It seemed an eternity before she heard the sound of another boat engine. She laid Josie on the blanket again, then rushed to the window and looked out to see Marc tying up to the pier. He ran toward the house, and when he reached the back-porch light, she saw he had a gun in his hand. The tightness in her chest eased. She opened the bedroom door and rushed down the stairs, where she threw open the door and launched herself against his chest.

He stiffened, then his arms came around her and his hand smoothed the back of her hair. "Hey, it's all right. Did you see anyone?"

His male scent was like armor around her, and his embrace was a shield. She told him about the boat she'd seen. "I've been afraid to go into the kitchen."

"Good. I told you to stay out of there just before we got cut off." With his arm around her, he steered her toward the sofa. "You stay here while I check it out."

She shook her head. "I want to see. It sounded like he was scratching his nails on the chalkboard."

She clung to his arm as they advanced to the kitchen. He reached over and flipped on the light. Scrabble tiles lay on the kitchen table. They spelled out a chilling message.

Death.

ELEVEN

Marc couldn't tear his gaze from the ominous word on the table. He pulled out his phone and snapped a picture for proof. "I'm going to take this with me. You don't want your mother to see it. Josie can't read so she wouldn't know what it said, but it might upset your mom. I don't think you should stay out here alone."

When her chin jutted out, he knew he was in trouble. Her aqua eyes flashed and she shook her head, then moved to the cabinet where she took down a jar of Jif. She opened the lid and grabbed a spoon, then began to lick it off the spoon.

He took a step closer to her. "Look, I know it's upsetting to think about moving when you just got here, but I don't think it's safe."

"You believe me now. Or do you think I did this myself to get sympathy?"

He hadn't even considered the thought, but he allowed it to linger a moment before he rejected it. Elin wasn't the kind for histrionics. Her ice-princess persona liked control, and her first impulse had been to grab a fireplace poker and attack. Whoever had spelled out the word on the table was dangerous.

"You could stay at Tidewater Inn. That's a nice place, and we met Libby at church on Sunday."

The last of the peanut butter disappeared, and her spoon clattered into the sink. "I am so tired of running. If he can find me here, he can find me anywhere. I don't know what to do or where to go to get away from him."

He nodded. "It took me twenty minutes to get here. I could have found all of you murdered in your beds. At least in town or out at Tidewater Inn, you'll have other people around. People who could help if you screamed. I'm calling Libby."

"All right."

Libby answered right away, and he explained the problem.

"I wish I could help, but we're full for the next month. Could someone stay with her? Maybe some of the Coasties? Or a friend? There are five bedrooms in that house, and she's surely only using three. Tell her I'm praying for her."

"I will." He hung up the phone and turned to face Elin. "No room. You have a spare room?"

She nodded. "There is one upstairs and another one down the hall, both with their own bathrooms. I'd thought about taking the downstairs one for my master, but I wanted to be near Josie in case she cried in the night."

"I'm moving in."

She gasped. "You can't do that. I-It would cause talk."

"Rumors won't kill you. That man might. I don't want anything to happen to my daughter. Besides, your mother is here. It will be perfectly respectable."

All the way out here on the boat, he'd been tormented by what he might find. What if the guy had murdered them all? He kept seeing visions of Elin's red hair splayed out on the floor and an even redder slash across her neck. Of finding his daughter dead. "I'll move my stuff in tomorrow, but in the meantime, you can show me the room." When she opened her mouth, he shot her a look. "I mean it, Elin. Nothing you say could make me leave here tonight."

"All right."

Her sudden capitulation shocked him, but he followed her when she turned and headed to the living room.

She went to the hall by the entry and flipped on the light. "This way."

His feet thudded on the gleaming wood floors as he went down the hall behind her. He peeked into the room. A king bed covered in a blue-and-white quilt dominated the large room. The pale blue walls made him think of a perfect day at sea. Seascapes hung on the walls, and a thick white rug anchored the bed. He nearly whistled at how beautiful it was. "Nice."

A soft smile lifted her lips. "I love this house."

"I hope your room is as nice as this. Pretty spectacular." When he turned back around, he nearly knocked Elin over. He grabbed her by the shoulders and steadied her. "Sorry." She didn't step back and neither did he.

She looked up at him. "Thanks for coming. I didn't know who else to call."

"I'm Josie's father. Of course you should call me." He cleared his throat, which had gone dry. Why was he suddenly seeing her from a different perspective? She'd always been too icy and controlled for him. The elder of the two girls, she had always been too focused on herself and what she wanted. When he settled down, he wanted someone with empathy and a carefree spirit.

He stared down at her. She seemed different now though. The air thickened between them. Her eyes were huge in her pale face, and it took all his restraint not to lower his lips to hers, just to see how she would react.

He dropped his hands from her shoulders and stepped around her. "This will be just fine. I'll see you in the morning." Stopping at the door, he waited until she exited, then closed it before he lost his last bit of self-control.

Elin wrapped her wet hair atop her head and secured it with a clip. Swathed in a white terry robe, she stared at herself in the mirror. Who was she? The heart that pumped under her ribs was changing her, forming her into someone she didn't know anymore. Fear suffocated her daily, and though she'd struggled to push it aside, it still bubbled up every time she caught a glimpse of herself.

In her mind's eye, she had short dark hair, not long red hair. When she looked in the mirror, she expected to see dark brown eyes, not the aqua ones staring back at her. She swayed, suddenly dizzy, then sat on the toilet lid and closed her eyes. Her throat tightened, and she could feel something against her windpipe as he squeezed the life from her. His face was blurry, so blurry, but his hair was blond. And that cloyingly strong cologne he wore added to her lack of air.

"Look at me."

Had he really said that to Laura as she died, or was Elin jumbling it all up? She rubbed her throbbing head. She wasn't Laura, she was *Elin*. She loved oldies, not country music. Her favorite color was tan, not green. She liked chocolate, not caramel.

"Mommy?"

She opened her eyes and smiled at Josie, who stood in the doorway. "You're still in your nightgown. Get your bathing suit on, and we'll go swimming today."

"There's a man in the kitchen. Mr. Marc. He's cooking breakfast." Confusion filled Josie's hazel eyes.

"He's going to be staying here awhile."

And he's going to want to tell Josie he is her father.

She didn't know how long she could stall him. The thought of telling Josie made her shudder. She was too young to really understand, but she would still ask why she'd never seen him before they came here. She would ask questions.

Elin was beginning to question the wisdom of involving Marc in her life like this. She hadn't known whom to turn to, and he'd always seemed so strong. Strong in character, strong in faith, and strong in courage. She hadn't stopped to think of the complications involving him would bring. Had he been about to kiss her last night? She would have let him, and she didn't know where that urge came from. Maybe it was just the longing to feel a man's arms around her. Widowhood was lonely.

Josie tugged on her arm. "Come see, Mommy."

She let Josie pull her out of the room and down the stairs. The aroma of bacon made her tummy rumble, and she realized how hungry she was. When they reached the kitchen, Marc turned with a spatula in his hand. His gaze warmed when he saw her, and she realized she was still in her robe with her hair piled atop her head.

"You're quite domestic." She winced at the banality of her comment. "I mean, thanks for cooking breakfast. Josie was very excited about it. She usually gets a boiled egg and a bagel."

"Every growing girl needs bacon." He turned back to the stove. "Nice kitchen, by the way. All stainless, granite. Someone spent some money in here."

"I have found myself enjoying cooking here even though I always thought I wasn't much of a cook." She released Josie's hand, then opened the cupboard and took down blue-and-white plates. "Is coffee on?"

He nodded. "It's ready."

Josie helped her set the table, and Marc carried a bowl of scrambled eggs and a plate of bacon to the table. He pulled out a chair at the head of the table, the place where Elin usually sat.

She turned toward the doorway. "I'll get Mom."

"She went for a walk on the beach."

"What? You let her go by herself?" She sprang for the door.

He grabbed her arm. "You can't smother her, Elin. Where's she going to go? This point is pretty self-contained. She can't wander far. Besides, she was very bright this morning."

"Her mental state can change in an instant." She yanked her arm out of his grip. "She could drown, or she could wander in the woods and get lost. We haven't lived here very long, and she might not remember how to get back. And I'm *not* smothering her. I'm just concerned for her safety."

He frowned. "Suit yourself."

She started for the door again, but it opened and her mother stepped into the kitchen. Her cheeks were pink and her eyes bright with excitement.

"Mom, I was about to go looking for you." Elin bit her lip when her mother frowned. "I mean, it's time for breakfast."

Her mother's expression cleared, and she stepped to the sink to wash her hands. "I worked up quite an appetite. And I saw a whale blowing off the point. It was quite an exciting morning. I wished you were with me."

"I'd like to have seen that. I'm sure Josie would have been excited too."

Her mother came to the table and sat in the chair across from Marc's. "Maybe it will still be there after breakfast."

Elin pressed her lips together and sat down. Marc was already causing total upheaval in the household.

TWELVE

Sara strained to hear over the roar of the helicopter as she leaned out the window at the boat in distress below them. "They're taking on water fast." Her medical-supply kit was fully stocked and ready.

In the cockpit, Josh nodded and maneuvered the craft lower until the powerful winds off the rotors kicked the waves even higher. On the boat deck below, Alec waved to let them know he'd arrived. He unclipped himself and motioned to the three men on the boat.

Sara frowned when one of them tossed two boxes overboard before rushing to where Alec was preparing to airlift them. Could this be a drug boat?

She spoke into the mic in her helmet. "Josh, did you see that guy throw something overboard? Looked like a couple of crates. Might be drugs."

"I noticed and sent a message to headquarters. A cutter is nearly here anyway, and they'll see if they can retrieve it."

He'd been impersonal and remote with her for two weeks. No flirting, no joking around. Even Curtis had noticed and tried to pry out any problems. One thing about Josh, he kept his real thoughts to himself. It was a good thing she'd given up. Nothing would ever get through that thick skull of his.

The Coast Guard cutter came into view below and zoomed toward the sinking boat. When the three men aboard saw the vessel, one of them dove overboard and started swimming for shore. Seagrass Pier was barely visible in the distance, but the swimmer struck out for it.

"One's escaping!" She pointed out the dark head, barely visible in the waves.

"They see him. No one is in danger, and my engine is cutting out. I'm radioing Alec to ride back on the cutter. Something is wrong with this thing."

She nodded and sat back in her seat. Curtis exchanged a commiserating glance with her. It took only ten minutes to get back to the airfield. She yanked off her helmet and hopped out of the chopper. Let him be alone the rest of his life. She stalked toward the building to change out of her flight suit and head for home, but Josh called her name.

He jogged toward her. "Sara, wait up. Want to go get coffee?"

She put her hands on her hips as he neared. "What is with you, Josh?" When he blinked, she remembered Elin's advice and took a step closer, then jabbed her forefinger in his chest. "It's no secret how I feel about you. I've been in love with you for two years. One minute you flirt with me, and the next you act like we're strangers. I'm sick of the way you blow hot and cold. If you want to be with me, then say so. If not, I'm moving on. I'm not wasting my life waiting on you to make up your mind."

His blue eyes widened, and his smile faded. Nothing like drawing a line in the sand. Was she ready for him to totally walk away? She tipped her chin up and stared him down.

He took a step back. "Where is this hostility coming from? I thought we were friends."

"Friends. Is that what you call our relationship? Do you flirt with friends?"

His strong jaw flexed. "You know I care about you, Sara. We're good friends."

"Fine, if that's how you feel." She turned to go.

He caught her by the forearm. "Don't be like that."

"You mean don't expect anything to change? Don't expect you to finally tell me how you feel? Don't put any demands on you? What is broken in you, Josh? It's perfectly normal for a woman to want a man to show her how he feels. Most people want commitment and a love that will last."

"Love never lasts. I don't know anyone who has a perfect marriage."

"Marriage or any other kind of relationship takes hard work. Of course there are ups and downs. That doesn't mean it isn't worth it or that you're better off staying alone. Is that what you want? To die alone and unloved? Never to feel your child's arms around your neck or to wake up next to someone you love every morning? I don't want that kind of aimless existence."

He stared down at her with what looked like longing. "What makes you so sure that kind of thing is worth the risk? What if you roll over and hate the face next to you one morning? What about regrets?"

She wished he'd open up and tell her where all these fears came from. His parents had a nasty, contentious divorce, but surely it was more than that. "The only thing I would regret is if I had a chance at happiness and threw it away. Some things are gone for good once the opportunity passes. You can't go back."

"What are you trying to say, Sara?" His voice was quiet.

At least he wasn't angry. She took a step closer. "I've always believed we could have something special, something that would last a lifetime. I think you believe it too, but you've been afraid. Now is the time to make a move."

Should she tell him she had a date? Would it push him the other way or make him realize he was about to lose her?

"What if things don't work out? What if our friendship is ruined by trying to bring romance into it? Don't those things worry you at all?"

"Life is always a gamble. The best things are worth fighting for. I think you're worth fighting for. I hope you feel the same about me. Do you love me, Josh?"

She held her breath after her question. Where was all this boldness coming from?

Something flickered in his eyes, a tamped-down passion she'd glimpsed a time or two over the past two years, and joy bubbled up.

She touched his face. "Say it."

His throat worked. "I-I care about you, Sara. You know that." He backed away, and her hand fell to her side. "I'd better get back to work."

Her elation deflated, and she watched him retreat. It was over.

⌣

"So what have you found out so far in the diaries?" Marc adjusted a cushion and leaned back on the sofa.

He'd been here two days now, and he already seemed like a fixture in the house. Her mother catered to him, and Josie was never far from his leg. In shorts with his feet bare and his brown hair tousled from an ocean swim, he was entirely too male and too handsome for Elin's peace of mind. She didn't want this pull of attraction.

She averted her gaze and picked up the diary. "She was quite an adventurer. Have you ever heard of Isabella Bird?"

"Sure. A Victorian lady who traveled to the outer reaches of the world—Japan, Hawaii, Tibet. She was a naturalist, I think."

Elin tucked her feet under her and opened the leather-bound book. "Georgina was like that. She traveled with her father who went out looking for exotic species of orchids and other plants for Victorian gardens. His specialties came from Cambodia, a place she loved. So she didn't take to the conventions of married life. She wasn't used to being told what to do by a man."

"Sounds like a spitfire."

"I like her. I've just gotten to the part where one of her friends from Cambodia has come to see her."

APRIL 24, 1907

Chann hung back until Georgina rushed to hug him. He looked so different without his conical hat and his krama, a scarf the Khmer people used for everything from carrying babies to protection from the sun. About thirty, Chann was tall for a Cambodian with shiny dark hair and a ready smile that warmed her from the inside out. His gray suit fit him perfectly.

She flung her arms around him. "I wasn't expecting you until next week." He held himself stiffly, and she realized she'd embarrassed him. Stepping back hastily, she gestured for him to follow her to the parlor.

"Please be seated. I'll ring for tea. Joshua should be home soon." She quaked a bit at the thought of his reaction. He'd been quite upset when she told him Chann would be stopping by for a visit. It was only by threatening to leave herself that she got his agreement to let her friend stay.

Her husband's jealousy was growing old.

Chann didn't smile. "I can only stay a moment. I've been followed."

She studied his face after his surprising announcement. That explained his somber appearance. "By whom?"

Instead of answering, he rummaged in his valise and withdrew a folder. The handsome leather tooling depicted a Cambodian couple in traditional dress. "Can you keep this for me?" His fingers stroked the leather as if it contained something very dear to him.

"Of course." She didn't ask what it was. It was none of her business.

"Tell no one you have it, Miss Georgina. Not even your husband. Hide it somewhere safe. I'll be back for it when I can." His voice was a whisper, and he glanced through the open window behind her before thrusting the leather folder into her hands.

"Are you in danger, Chann? What can I do to help?"

He held her gaze. "Nothing and no one can help me. I must help myself."

She looked down at the pouch. "What's in it?"

"It is best if you do not know, Miss Georgina. Keep it well hidden. As far as you know, I came for a short visit, nothing more."

Before she could ask any more questions, she heard Joshua's heavy tread on the porch. Without stopping to think, she flew to the door and down the hall to the kitchen, then up the back stairway. Luckily no one was in the kitchen. She had the leather pouch tucked into her skirts in case she ran into one of the servants.

The stairs to the third floor stood open, so she rushed up them and looked around wildly for a place to stash the leather folder. There. She tucked it away, then returned downstairs. The coast was still clear, so she ducked into her room and smoothed her hair while she waited for her high color to subside. When she heard Joshua's unmistakable footsteps in the hall, she sat on the edge of the bed and pasted on a smile.

He rapped at the door, then opened it. "Georgina, are you all right? You have a guest in the parlor." His grim tone told of his displeasure.

"I'm being a terrible hostess, but I needed a moment." She fanned herself, and his frown eased. "I knew you would be along soon to make him welcome."

"Of course, of course. And quite right that you should wait for me. We don't want any wagging tongues." He held out his hand. "I told your friend I'd fetch you."

She put her hand on his arm and rose. "Thank you."

He stared down at her as if trying to see into her thoughts. "Did you know he was coming today?"

"I did not. The last word I had was he would arrive next week. I was surprised to hear he had arrived."

"I quite dislike how free you are with other men, Georgina. You must behave more decorously. Men can get the wrong idea."

How quickly he had discontinued the use of his pet names for her. They'd been here nearly three months, yet his high standards had become more exacting and his disapproval harder to bear. What had he ever seen in her? She hadn't changed, but his view of her had soured.

"Chann is my friend, Joshua. He's like a brother to me, but nothing more. If I had wanted to marry him, I would have. Father would not have prevented me."

His lips twisted. "Your father gave you too much license."

She wanted to fly to her father's defense, but she pressed her lips together and turned toward the door. Nothing she could say would change her husband's mind.

———

Elin closed the book. "Can't you just picture her life here? And what an exotic existence she lived before coming here. I would like to travel like that, see strange and wonderful places."

"Sounds like her husband was a jerk."

She couldn't think with his gaze on her. "It was a different time back then. I think she would have fit in this era much better."

"And you would have fit there."

She frowned, unsure how to take his comment. "Are you saying I'm timid and easily manipulated?"

"You like to keep the peace whatever the cost." His gaze sharpened. "Though maybe not so much anymore. The old Elin wouldn't be searching for the murderer so tenaciously. She would have tried to block out the problem by suggesting the killer just get along before she went back to following all the rules and being the perfect daughter."

She should have been offended, but a bubble of laughter in her throat surprised her. And Marc too from his expression. "Was I really that bad?"

He grinned. "Only worse. You seem different now. I think losing your dad made you grow up some."

"It did." That was a better answer than saying getting a new heart had changed her.

Marc found himself watching Elin over the next couple of days as he looked online for clues and made calls in his covert investigation. The gentle care she showed her mother and Josie touched him and made him watch her even more. She laughed more, in spite of the circumstances, and didn't obsess about the small things.

On Wednesday morning, he met her and Josie at the bottom of the stairs. "Things have been stressful lately. I recommend a little R & R for all of us."

She wore a cute tan sundress splashed with orange flowers. Her curly hair was caught up on top of her head, and she looked about twenty. Her eyes brightened. "What did you have in mind?"

"It's a surprise." He put his hand atop Josie's head and looked at Elin. The real surprise was she didn't shoot him down. "I guarantee you'll all like it."

She tipped her head to one side. "Do I dare trust you?"

Josie danced around her. "Yes, Mommy, yes! I love surprises."

"Your mommy does too. She just doesn't know it yet."

A hint of color stained her cheeks. "Give me a hint."

"It involves wind and sand."

Josie antics grew more energetic. "Yay! A day at the beach!"

"Not exactly. Grab your flip-flops and let's go."

For the first time, a hint of worry swam in Elin's eyes. "What about Mom?"

"She'll love it too. She's already down by the boat."

"You left her alone? Marc, you have to learn you can't do that." Elin brushed past him and hurried to the window where she peered out. "I can't see her."

"That's only because you can't see the harbor well. She's standing guard over the sunscreen and sunglasses." He opened the front door. "Come on, we're wasting daylight."

The smile started to return to her face. "Okay." Taking Josie by the hand, she exited and hurried down the walk toward the harbor.

Marc locked the door behind them, then jogged to catch up with her. "There's Ruby, right where I left her."

"Gramma!" Josie tore her hand from Elin's and raced to join the older woman standing beside the boat.

Ruby's eyes were bright when she turned to face them, and Marc saw the way Elin relaxed. What must it be like to always be conscious of danger lurking around the corner? Not just for her but for her mother and Josie.

He picked Ruby up in his arms. "Let's get you onboard."

She giggled like a girl as he splashed through the water with her, then set her on the middle seat before going back to shore for

Josie. His daughter practically climbed his leg like a tree when he reached for her. He set her atop his shoulders and gave her a ride to the boat. Reaching under the seat, he extracted her flotation vest and cinched it around her.

"Don't forget Mommy." She settled into the seat beside her grandmother.

"Oh, I won't." Smiling, he waded back through the knee-high waves to Elin, who was staring at her sequined sandals with dismay.

"I'm going to ruin my new shoes."

"We can't have that." Before she could protest, he scooped her up too.

Her arms came around his neck, and he caught the scent of her perfume, a light and sweet smell that made him want to hold her closer. Her hands touching his skin felt soft and tentative as if she couldn't believe she was in this situation. Her eyes widened as she stared up at him. The moment seemed to stretch out forever as he stared back. Something changed inside him as he studied the faint blush on her cheeks. Awareness flickered to life in the depths of her clear aqua eyes. Something indefinable shifted between them, and he had to force himself to set her in the boat when he reached her seat.

Her long lashes swept down and obscured her expression when he set her down. "Thank you." Her voice went husky.

"No problem." He vaulted into the motorboat and settled at the helm, then fished his key out of his pocket and started the engine.

He reached for his water and took a gulp to quench his suddenly dry mouth. Turning back around, he gazed at his three passengers and pointed. "We'll be there in five minutes."

He couldn't turn back around fast enough after finding Elin's gaze on him. The engine responded to the throttle and zoomed quickly toward the stretch of beach in the distance. At the time when he'd come up with this idea, a beach all to themselves seemed a fun idea.

———

"Kite flying?" Elin wound her fingers around the ball of string and couldn't hold back the incredulous laugh that burst nervously from her throat. "I haven't flown a kite in years."

"I thought so." Marc looked entirely too smug and handsome as he helped Josie get her kite up in the air. "I'm going to teach you to be spontaneous."

Her cheeks heated. His statement indicated he planned to be around for a while, that they were going to have some kind of relationship. And what had happened between them when he carried her to the boat? The frisson of awareness she'd felt had shown in his eyes too, and his arms had tightened around her.

The wind yanked at her kite, and she ran out some string to let the breeze carry it up toward the puffy clouds scuttling by. Her kite was a Wonder Woman one in red, white, and blue. He'd brought Josie a princess one, and her mother ran along the lapping waves like a kid with her dolphin kite. Elin's worries slipped away like the tide.

Josie's kite was in the air, and Marc let her handle it by herself after showing her how to keep it floating. He jogged to the top of a sand dune with Elin. "Looks like you need help."

His warm hands closed over hers, and her knees went weak. She lost her balance on the soft sand and sat on her rump. The wind yanked the kite up, and she lost her grip on the string. She and Marc grabbed for it at the same time, and he fell onto her.

The air rushed out of her lungs, but it wasn't as much from his weight as from the feel of his skin against hers. She hadn't been this close to a man since Tim died, and the sensation felt . . .

nice. Too nice, in fact. She snatched her escaping breath back and jumped to her feet.

He got up too, brushing the sand from his bare legs. Her gaze followed his big hands to the muscular curve of his thighs and calves. She turned away quickly. What on earth was wrong with her? This was *Marc*. Not some new suitor who would welcome her unruly thoughts.

THIRTEEN

So he just turned and walked off?" Elin couldn't believe Josh was so pigheaded. "What did you do?" The sand was warm on her bare feet. A gull fixed its black eyes on her and stared, probably waiting to see if she would drop a crumb for it.

Sara stooped and picked up a perfect shell, then dropped it in her bag. "Came here for sympathy." Her laugh was forced.

The scent of rain hung in the air from the dark, low clouds overhead. The women walked along the cove just north of the pier where driftwood and shells collected. Elin had been glad to leave Marc's suffocating presence at the cottage. Ever since their kite outing yesterday, she'd found herself uncomfortable around him. What if he noticed the way she looked at him? She'd die of embarrassment.

"I have a feeling this was the final straw." Elin couldn't blame her. Sara had been more than patient.

Sara's eyes glistened, and she nodded without saying anything. She probably couldn't discuss it without letting the tears fall. Elin wished she could talk some sense into Josh. "I'm sorry, Sara."

"I'm okay." She sighed and reached for her purse. "Oh, and that note you got at church? I had it analyzed. It was likely written by a male in his thirties or forties."

Elin swallowed. "So it wasn't a kid."

"I'd hoped it was. Try not to worry."

"Let's talk about something else." Elin forced a smile. "You have your big date on Saturday. Have you run into Ben any more?"

Sara shook her head. "I saw him from a distance yesterday, but he didn't see me. I'm trying to look forward to it, but right now I wish I could cancel it and stay home. I'm not sure I'm ready. I don't want to get into any kind of rebound relationship. Talking to Josh today, I realize it may be a long while before I'm over him."

"I think you should go. Maybe he'll see you or hear about it, and it will make him jealous."

"You said you were worried it would prove to him that women are fickle."

"It doesn't sound like you have anything to lose though."

Sara picked up another shell. "That wouldn't be fair to Ben. Besides, I don't think Josh cares enough to be jealous. He was able to walk away today after I told him I loved him. That tells me every-thing I need to know." Her throat was choked.

"I guess so." A crate scraped against the rocks just offshore. "Hey, look at that. What do you suppose it is?" She waded into the water toward it before the current carried it back out to sea.

Sara waded out with her. "We had a rescue earlier this week, and I saw one of the men aboard throw a couple of boxes over. It was right out there." Sara pointed offshore. "This might be one of them." The two women steered the crate to shore, then dragged it onto the sand. "We'll need a crowbar to get it open."

Elin turned toward the house. "I'll go ask Marc to bring one."

Sara frowned. "Wait, he's here? You didn't say anything about it when I called for you to meet me. I wouldn't have pulled you away."

"There was a break-in Monday night." Elin told her friend about the scare. "So he insisted on moving in."

"He's *staying* with you?" Sara's expression turned worried. "He thinks the threat is that serious?"

"I was going to go to Tidewater Inn, but Libby had no open rooms. Full-on tourist season."

Sara stopped tugging on the top of the crate. "So you think it was the same guy who killed your donor?"

"Yes. It's creepy the way he's playing with me."

"Could it be someone else? Someone who gets his kicks out of scaring women? That's all he's done so far."

That gave Elin pause, and she shrugged. "It could be anyone. An article ran in the newspaper about my cell memories, remember? Someone could have read it and decided to start scaring me. I would love to believe it wasn't the murderer, and this guy is just some sick jokester." She remembered the Scrabble letters and shuddered. "It doesn't feel that way though. I'm sure it's him."

"That was in the article too. He could be playing to everything he knows about your memories."

"It feels like the same man though. What if he decides silencing me isn't enough and goes after Josie or Mom? I have to help find him and put him behind bars where he can't hurt anyone else."

"Have you tried pulling up even more memories?"

Elin shivered at the thought. "I don't know how to do that. I try to remember more, but it's all blank."

"What if you got some of that cologne and maybe a man's red sweater? You could go out on a boat with them and see if they trigger anything else. I'll help you. It's worth a try."

Elin found it hard to breathe. "It's terrifying when the memories come. I hate them. But I don't want to just wait around for him to try again either. I guess I'm game to try it. I'll have to go to Virginia Beach or a bigger city to find the cologne. It's uncommon. I ought to check on my house too. A college student is housesitting, and I haven't heard from her for a few days. I have visions of the place being trashed during a party. She's supposed to be keeping it clean for real-estate showings."

"I'm ready to get away for a day. I'm off tomorrow. We could run over to Virginia Beach, check on your house, then shop a bit."

"Okay. I'll see if Kalianne can keep Mom. She's not a good traveler. And my sister, Abby, wants Josie for a couple of days."

"Let's leave about nine. I'll meet you at the dock with my car." Sara squinted toward the house. "Your knight in shining armor is outside."

"I stopped believing in fairy tales a long time ago. Life never seems to turn out the way we expect." She started for the house. "I'll see if we can find a crowbar."

Marc waved at her, and she wished she could stop her pulse from galloping every time she was around him. Why was that happening when she'd never looked at him that way before?

The two women stood close together as though they were talking about something personal. Sara's smile seemed forced as he stopped in front of them.

Marc held up the crowbar. "Took me a minute to dig it out of the garage. This the box?"

He eyed the crate at their feet. It bore no distinguishing marks and seemed a typical storage unit. At first the top resisted his attempts to open it, but the crowbar finally slid under the lid and popped it loose. He pried it off the rest of the way with his hands. The inside seemed to be filled with only shredded rubber, but he flung the wet packing material out of the way to reveal plastic-covered, white, oblong packages.

"Heroin," Sara said. "I thought they were drug smugglers. I should see if they caught the one who jumped overboard. I can identify him." She pulled out her cell phone. "Oh wait, this doesn't work here."

"Go closer to the house so it logs on to the Wi-Fi. Then you can use it."

Sara nodded at Elin and walked toward the house to deal with her call.

Marc shoved his hands into his pockets. "I checked into your break-in. The police located the skiff used to come out here—at least they think they did. It was the same type as one stolen from the dock in Hope Beach, and it showed up onshore down the sand from Tidewater Inn."

"Did Libby or Alec see anything?"

He shook his head. "Alec is the one who found the boat, and he called it in."

"Why do they think it's the same one?"

He didn't want to have to tell her, but someone would spill it to her anyway. "They found your name carved in the side of the boat with a skull and crossbones beside it. Your full name."

She shuddered and took a step back. "Sara had an idea about trying to jog my memory. She wants us to go out on a boat with the killer's cologne and a red sweater." She hugged herself. "It scares me though. What if she takes over more and more?"

He didn't like the way the color drained from her face. "'She'? Who do you mean, Elin?"

"Laura. I'm becoming Laura." She rubbed her forehead. "I see things she saw, like things she liked. Sara thinks I haven't noticed how much I've changed, but it terrifies me. What if I lose who I really am?" She swallowed hard and turned to look out to sea.

He followed her gaze out over the whitecaps. There was a boat, just barely visible at the horizon. He put his hand on her shoulder. "Traits can change like the sea, Elin. You might like coffee now or hate oldies, but you're still you down inside. Your daughter is the most important thing to you. You would do anything to help your mom. You love your job of matching organ donors with recipients because you feel such purpose in helping others. Quit worrying about extraneous things, honey."

Something flickered in her eyes at the endearment that slipped out, but she turned toward Sara before he could identify if it was irritation or warmth.

"Did they catch the smuggler?" she asked Sara.

Sara shook her head. "And they think he might be dangerous. The drug boat is registered to Devi Long, a known drug smuggler on the run from the authorities in Florida. He is believed to have killed at least three men so far, but he's eluded the authorities at every turn. Here's his picture."

She turned her phone around to show them a good-looking Asian man in his forties.

"He leaped overboard just offshore here and swam this way," Sara said. "You both need to be careful. He could still be lurking about."

"It's possible, but I'd guess it's far more likely he had someone pick him up. Did the Coasties find any sign of him when they searched here?" He'd seen them picking through the seagrass and brush for a couple of hours before getting back on their cutter and cruising off.

Sara shook her head. "No sign at all."

The wind lifted Elin's long red hair and blew it across her face. She swiped it out of her eyes. "Could this Long have been the man who broke in the other night?"

"No. He swam ashore yesterday. The break-in was on Monday night." He understood where Elin was coming from. Any other intruder wouldn't be nearly as terrifying as Laura's murderer finding her.

"Oh, right."

She looked so small and scared standing there on the beach in her bare feet. The sundress she wore showed off tanned arms that looked eminently touchable. He averted his gaze.

"We'll find the guy, Elin. I won't let him hurt you or Josie." He glanced at his cousin. "Elin says you have an idea about helping her remember more details about the killer. Smart. I could wear the red sweater and cologne."

Sara tucked a honey-colored lock behind her ear. "That's a little too threatening, I think. Let's just try having her smell the cologne and touch the sweater. We don't want to scare her to death. We could go out tomorrow night after we get the cologne. It was nighttime, right?"

Marc had studied the file over and over. "About midnight. Moonless night, too, so really dark." He glanced overhead. "Should be a good night for it. It's supposed to be like this for the next three days."

Elin's face showed she was anything but excited about it. "Just stay close to me, okay? If I start having an intense flashback, I'll need you two to bring me out of it." She swallowed hard. "Sometimes they're pretty scary."

He wished they didn't have to put her through it, but they had to find this guy. Sooner or later he was bound to find a soft spot in their defense.

Fourteen

Finally the house was empty. Kalianne would be undisturbed for the entire day since Elin had gone to Virginia Beach. Once Kalianne was sure Ruby was sleeping soundly in her chair, she headed to the hall bedroom with a flashlight. Where on earth should she look first? The house was old. Were there even any guarantees it was still here?

She wanted to check Marc's room first, mostly because he intrigued her. Though she'd put on her most seductive smile and tried her best, he hadn't noticed her as more than a fixture. He had eyes only for Elin, which peeved Kalianne a bit since the woman was at least eight years older than her.

His room was set up like a master. About fifteen feet square, it held only a sleigh bed and matching dresser with nickel pulls. He'd put out no pictures or decorations, not that she expected it of him. Most guys didn't think about the niceties like that. She opened his closet and found only four pairs of jeans, a pair of khakis, and six shirts. The dresser held underwear and socks, nothing personal. Disappointed, she shut the top drawer and checked out each one in turn, only to find them empty.

She went to the attached bathroom next, pausing to sniff his cologne and sigh. His toothbrush and deodorant were in the cabinet with his comb. She plucked a dark hair from the comb and rolled it around in her fingers before dusting it off in the wastebasket.

So impersonal. She didn't know him any better than she did this morning.

Next she checked out the office. Nothing. Then she headed upstairs to the old lady's room. It was one of those rooms that appeared not to have been used much over the years. It still had the original plaster walls, unlike the other bedrooms that were covered in newer drywall. She tested the wide floorboards for movement, but they all appeared solid. After opening the closet door, she removed the shoe boxes and other storage boxes from the shelves and pressed around on the back of the closet walls. When she found nothing, she flipped on the flashlight and shone it around the ceiling area and floor.

Was that the outline of a hidden panel? Kalianne grabbed the chair from the corner and dragged it into the closet, then mounted it and moved her hands around the panel. It didn't move, but there had to be a way to open it. She began to press each corner. When she touched the third corner, she felt it shift. With renewed interest, she pressed harder, and the opposite corner popped loose, allowing her to pry the panel off.

She shone her light into the space. The illumination revealed only dusty rafters at first. She stood on her tiptoes and poked her head cautiously into the space. There. What was that brown thing? Her fingers barely reached to the far rafter, and she snagged the leather tie around it. Once it was safely in her hands, she stepped down from the chair and turned, eager to take a look at the hidden stash.

"What are you doing in my room?" Ruby's voice sounded bewildered.

Kalianne spun around. "Um, I was looking for your new shoes. I thought you might like to wear them."

Ruby swayed a bit on her feet, and her hair stuck up in places from the way she'd been sleeping. "I have new shoes?"

"Red ones," Kalianne improvised. "You said something about them before you fell asleep."

"I love red." Ruby came toward her. "That's mine."

Before Kalianne could react, the old woman grabbed the leather pouch from her hands. Kalianne tried to grab it back, but Ruby turned and rushed away. Kalianne followed, but Ruby was up the stairs to the third floor before she could blink. As she yanked on the door, she heard a click.

She rattled the knob. "Ruby, unlock this door!"

Ruby giggled from the other side like a child playing hide-and-seek, then her footsteps went up the stairs. Gritting her teeth, Kalianne rushed down the hall to the stairway to the first floor. There were keys around here somewhere, but she wasn't sure where Elin kept them. Rummaging through the drawers in the kitchen, she found nothing. Next she checked the drawers in the side tables in the living room, but the keys weren't there either. Maybe they were in Elin's bedroom.

She raced back upstairs and down the hall to the master bedroom. She hit the jackpot when she yanked out the top drawer on the bedside table. Her fingers closed around the ring of keys, and she turned to hurry to the third-floor stairwell. It took another few minutes to figure out the right key, and she fumed the entire time.

She unlocked the door and threw it open, then stomped up the narrow staircase in an angry staccato. Her brother owed her big-time for this.

With great effort, she pitched her voice low and soft. "Ruby, where are you?"

A giggle to her left answered her, and she turned but didn't see the old woman. "Come out, come out, wherever you are. Olly, olly, oxen free."

Ruby burst out from behind an old piano with a delighted grin on her face. "I fooled you!" She did an awkward dance under the eaves.

"You sure did. Now where is the leather pouch you took from me?"

Ruby's grin faded. "Pouch? I don't have a pouch."

Kalianne gritted her teeth. "I had it in your room. You took it and ran."

Ruby took a step back at Kalianne's sharp tone. "I don't have a pouch."

"A leather folder. It had a leather tie wrapped around it. This big." Kalianne measured it out with her hands.

Ruby shook her head. "I don't have it. I'm hungry. I think I'll make some soup."

She turned and hurried down the stairs. Kalianne stomped after her. She would get that pouch no matter what it took.

———

Josie kicked her feet against the back of the seat. "I want to see Aunt Abby. *Now.*"

"We're almost there, honey." Elin could see the red metal roof of her cottage from here as she turned the corner into the cul-de-sac. "Quit kicking the seat." Josie had been impatient when they stopped at the mall to buy the cologne, and Abby had texted her several times as well. "There's Aunt Abby's car." She pulled in beside her sister's blue Camry and shut off the car.

Sara hopped out on her side. "I'll get Josie out."

Elin climbed out and hugged her sister. "You look great, Abby. I've missed you."

Abby returned her hug. She smoothed the pink sweater over her curves. "I've lost five pounds."

Her sister was on a perpetual diet, even though her generous curves looked good on her. In her late thirties, she wore her blond hair in a perky style with the ends flipped up. Her husband was a dermatologist and didn't want her to work, so she spent her time perusing fashion magazines and volunteering at a local senior center. They had no children, though not for lack of trying, and Abby liked to take Josie for the weekend every chance she got since they lived only twenty minutes apart.

"Aunt Abby!" Josie pelted toward her aunt. "You haven't been to see my new room."

"Not yet, bug, but I'll see it when I bring you home." She turned and looked at Elin. "I should be there by dinner tomorrow. We can go out for seafood. Charles is out of town at a seminar so I can stay the weekend."

"Perfect." Elin opened the back door and grabbed Josie's small case, then stowed it in her sister's backseat. "Have fun."

"We will." Abby buckled Josie into the car seat she always had in the car for her niece, then went around to the driver's side. "I knocked on the door, but Lacy didn't answer. Her car is in the garage though. Maybe she's sleeping in."

"I've got my key. See you tomorrow." Elin waved as they pulled away, then turned toward the house. "I don't like it that she isn't answering the door. I have a feeling the house is going to be trashed."

The house looked normal. Still the same neat and clean cottage she'd taken such pride in. The grass hadn't been mowed in a few days, but it would be two or three more before it needed a trim. The flower bed had no weeds.

Sara followed her to the front door. "Have you talked to her since you left?"

Elin shook her head. "I've tried to call her a few times this week but just left messages. She hasn't called me back. She has finals though. I suppose she could be neck-deep in studying with no time for reassuring me that she's taking care of my house."

She mounted the big front porch and stepped to the red door. There was no sound from inside. She pressed her finger firmly on the doorbell. A dog barked and she frowned. "She's not supposed to have pets. She assured me she would have someone else take care of Max."

Sara glanced at her. "You love dogs. I've never known you to complain about a dog's presence in your house."

Elin's irritation faded, and she remembered nuzzling her golden retriever when she was growing up. "I don't know why I said that." She pressed the doorbell again, and the barking grew more frantic. "I'm going to use my key."

She inserted her key in the lock and opened the door. "Lacy? It's Elin." The dog, a tiny Yorkie, leaped against her leg. "Hey, Max." She leaned down and picked up the dog. "What's that smell? It's like rotten meat."

The women ventured farther into the house. The living room seemed fine at first until Sara pointed out an upended table. Pieces of a broken blue vase lay scattered around it. Something didn't feel right. The house was too still, almost waiting. And that smell . . .

Still carrying Max, she moved to the kitchen. Two saucers were in the sink along with a coffee cup and a red glass. Max's food dish held only two pieces of food, and his water dish looked murky as though it hadn't been freshened for several days. The strong odor came from the overflowing trash can.

"I'm not sure she's here, but I'm surprised she'd leave Max all alone." There had been a doggy door in the kitchen when she moved in. She nudged it with her foot and it opened, so Max had been able to use it.

Sara turned back toward the door to the living room. "Let's check the bedrooms."

They went back through the living room to the entry and headed up the open stairway to the second floor. "Lacy? Are you all right?" Elin had no sense that anyone else was in the house. The silly girl had likely gone off with friends without a care for little Max. Some people didn't deserve to have a pet.

Lacy's room was the first one on the right, and it was empty. The bed was made, and the room appeared as though it wasn't being used. Lacy's things weren't on the dresser. Sara opened the closet. Empty.

"It looks like she left."

"And didn't take Max?" Elin shook her head. "Let's check the other rooms."

Elin's bedroom door hung partway open, and she saw a pale hand on the carpet. She gasped and flung the door fully open. "Lacy!"

Lacy, dressed in Elin's blue negligee, lay on the beige carpet. She wore a long red wig, and it lay spread out around her head.

Sara leaped to her side and placed her hand on her carotid artery. "It's barely pulsing."

"She's dead, isn't she?" Elin asked.

"She's been strangled with a wire, but her heart is still beating."

Sara pulled out her phone. "I'm calling for an ambulance and then the police."

Looking at her young friend, Elin knew the ambulance would be too late.

Fifteen

Police cars lined the street around Elin's house. Marc showed his ID, then pushed his way through the throng of neighbors and officers to get to Elin. This had to have been a huge shock to her. She'd been nearly incoherent when she called him.

He found her seated in the pale-blue living room with Josh beside her. Marc surveyed her shocked white face, then moved to sit beside her. "You okay?"

Her lips trembled and she nodded. "I can't believe it."

He glanced at Josh. "How'd you hear about this?"

"Scanner." Josh pressed a glass of water into her hand.

Marc should have been glad someone was caring for Elin, but he didn't like that Josh had gotten here so fast. What was he doing in Virginia Beach anyway? Marc popped a mint into his mouth.

He took Elin's hand. "What happened?" He listened to her describe what they'd found.

"She died shortly after she got to the hospital, but at least they saved her organs."

The fact the dead woman had been dressed like Elin disturbed him. Had she been the intended target, or had the killer forced her to dress up like Elin as a warning? Either way, the killer was escalating.

She turned her head to whisper to him. "The responding officer is the one who came after he broke in the first time. I think he believes me now. If he'd only listened the first time. None of the detectives believed I knew anything about this guy." She rubbed her head. "I wish I could remember more. He has to be stopped. He's killed two women now."

"That we know of."

She sucked in her breath. "Could it be a serial killer?"

"Maybe. The method of killing is the same."

Sara came through the kitchen door with a coffee cup in her hand. "It's fresh with cream."

"Thanks." Elin wrapped her fingers around the cup and took a sip. "My stomach is in knots. I just want to get out of here. Do you think we could go?"

"I'll check with the officers. They already interrogated you both, I assume?"

Sara nodded. "At great length."

It had taken Marc three hours to get here by the time he caught the ferry and drove through the traffic. He didn't doubt the police had hammered them with questions. He found the detective in charge who told him they could leave, but that someone would be out to ask more questions tomorrow.

"Let's go," he told the women.

Elin rose. "Let me rinse out my cup first."

He followed her into the kitchen, away from the hubbub going on in the rest of the house. "Do you know how he got in?"

She shook her head. "The police are checking all that out. They asked for permission to get my phone records to see when I last spoke to her. I think it was a week ago." She shuddered and hugged herself. "I should call Lacy's parents. They don't know yet."

His gaze roved over her pale face and trembling mouth, her shadowed eyes. She was much too fragile to be the one to deliver such horrific news. "The police will do that. You can stop by once the shock has worn off and offer your condolences. Where do they live?"

"In Charlotte. She was their only child." Tears welled in her eyes. "I feel like it's my fault. He wanted to punish me, didn't he? I think he forced her to dress that way. She saw my negligee once and laughed at it, saying she wouldn't be caught dead in something so matronly on her wedding night. She wouldn't have tried it on for fun. And where did she get that wig? She was a college student. There was no money in the budget for something that expensive. The police said it was human hair."

Seeing her cry tore him up. He started to embrace her, then realized he didn't have that right. She wouldn't welcome such familiarity from him. "You need to take some medicine or anything?"

She shook her head. "I'm fine."

He popped another mint, then stuffed his hands in the pockets of his jeans. "The police will get a lot of clues from here. They can track down where he bought that wig, and I'm sure they'll find some forensic evidence. They'll be combing the place for hair and fiber."

She brushed the tears away. "I'm going to stop him. Lacy was my friend, and I loved her. Seeing her like that made me realize just what a monster he is. I'm going to do what Sara said and go out on the boat tonight to see what I can pull up from Laura's memories."

At least she was saying *Laura* and not *me*. "I'd like to come along."

She rinsed out her cup and turned it upside down in the dish rack. "All right."

"Did you call your sister and tell her about this?"

She shook her head. "Not yet. I don't want to worry her. Josie will pick up on it."

He pulled out his phone. "She should be warned. What if this guy decides to go after her too?"

Elin's eyes grew enormous in her white face. "Why would he do that?"

"He's sending you some kind of message. We have to figure out what that is. And keep everyone you love safe while we do it. Give me her number."

She rattled off the number, and he punched it into his phone. "Abby? It's Marc Everton."

"Why, Marc, I haven't spoken to you in years. Elin's all right, isn't she?" Her voice sharpened from curiosity to worry.

"She's all right, but the house sitter isn't." He briefly explained the situation and heard her gasp softly on the other end of the phone. "Is there anyone there with you besides Josie?"

"No, Charles is out of town. Why?"

"This guy seems to have a vendetta against Elin, and he's taking it out on people she cares about. Engage your security system. I'll tell the police to have an officer sit outside tonight."

"You're scaring me. Are you sure that's necessary?"

"No, but I don't want to take any chances. Not with you and not with Josie." His little girl had already wound him around her little finger. He'd kill anyone who threatened her. "On second thought, let's all stay together tonight. We'll come get you both. Then I'll be able to watch all of you."

When he ended the call, he found Elin staring at him. "Thank you for watching out for us." She shivered and hugged herself.

He wasn't sure how long he'd be able to protect them. Killers were good at finding a weak link in their targets' defenses.

———

Elin rubbed her burning eyes and turned on a desk lamp. Dusk was falling, and she was tired after the events of the day. She'd go to bed early, but Lacy deserved worthy recipients of her organs.

She took a dose of her herbals and opened her laptop. From the living room, she heard Josie's excited squeal and Abby's measured tones. At least they were all here together.

She picked up the phone and rang Kerri.

"I was just about to call you," Kerri said. "You working on Lacy's donation? I'm so sorry, Elin. Are you okay?"

"As good as I can be, knowing he was after me." She told her friend about Lacy's attire.

"I'm at the hospital and I noticed her dress. That's just freaky. Do the police have any leads?"

"They had a bunch of forensics people there, so I hope so." Elin opened her list of recipients and sorted them by blood type B, then by tissue type. "Ready to get to work?"

"Ready." A volley of key clicks came from Kerri's end. "You want to take heart and lungs? I'll call the rest."

"Okay." This was her favorite part of the job—calling the recipient's doctors and letting them know they had an organ. "I'll call you when I'm done on my end. Good luck." She ended the call with Kerri, then placed the first call to the doctor of the recipient who needed the heart.

She was smiling when she got off the phone from the final call. A sixteen-year-old boy was about to get a new heart. Elin's smile faded when she thought of the pain Lacy's family was going through right now.

A soft knock sounded behind her, and she turned to see Marc in the doorway. Her heart always seemed to hiccup when she spied him. His sleeveless T-shirt showed off muscular arms and a flat stomach. His dark hair curled a little at the nape of his neck, and when he turned those hazel eyes her way, any thoughts in her head dried up and blew away.

He leaned against the doorjamb. "About ready for the boat trip?"

Dread curled in her belly. She didn't want to immerse herself in the night Laura died.

She forced a smile. "I'm ready. Let me close out of here."

"Did you find recipients?"

"Yes."

He frowned. "You don't sound all that excited."

"I-It's the thing we're doing on the boat." She clasped herself. "You have no idea what it's like to have memories that aren't mine. It's like I'm dreaming with everything distorted and frightening."

His gaze softened. "I'm sorry. We don't have to do this if you don't want to. The day has been stressful enough."

Shaking her head, she shut the lid of her MacBook and rose. "I can't sit back and do nothing. He was in my house, Marc! He's not going to hurt those I love. I don't trust what he might do next. We have to figure out who he is and get him behind bars."

"You don't have to convince me." He took her arm. "I've got two guards walking the perimeter, and we won't be gone long."

The heat from his fingers warmed her skin. If she leaned in closer, she'd be able to smell his cologne.

"Elin?"

She blinked. "Sorry, I was woolgathering. I'm ready."

His grip on her tightened. "You're sure? Maybe this isn't the best evening to do this. I don't think he'll try anything with me here. Having a man in the house is likely to scare him off."

A man in the house. What an appealing thought. She liked walking into the kitchen in the morning and seeing him there, coffee already brewing. She'd never dreamed how quickly she would acclimate to having him around. Or how quickly their hostility would turn to . . . something else. She couldn't quite name it yet. Attraction for sure. But maybe more than that.

Smiling to reassure him, she led the way out of the office

and nearly mowed down Kalianne, who was hovering outside. "Is everything all right, Kalianne? Where's Mom?"

"Oh fine, fine. But she won't eat. I fixed her some supper, and she thinks she ate already. She hasn't eaten enough today to keep a bird alive."

How sweet of Kalianne to be so concerned. "What did you fix her? She's gotten to be a picky eater, though she used to be willing to try just about anything."

"I fixed beef and noodles with mashed potatoes. And I brought brownies I made last night. She looked at them, then turned away. I thought she loved chocolate."

"She does. Let me check on her. She's in the kitchen?" When Kalianne nodded, Elin went down the hall to the kitchen.

Her mother had already put on her pajamas and fuzzy slippers. She wore a terry robe too even though it was eighty degrees outside and not that cool inside even with the air-conditioning. She sat at the large white table staring blankly at her plate of food. Her fork had fallen to the floor beside her napkin.

Elin stooped and picked them up. "That looks good, Mom. Enough for us too? I'm a little hungry, and I'm sure Marc is starved."

He followed her to the table. "I'm famished. Noodles. There's never been a better food invented. Did you make these, Ruby? I've lusted after your noodles for years. No one makes them like you."

Mom brightened a little and smiled up at at Elin. "I made them, I think. Didn't I, Elin?"

She went around to the other side of the table. "He's right— you make the best noodles in the world, Mom. You roll them out by hand and cut them nice and thin." She pulled the bowl to her and ladled some onto her plate. "Yum, it smells wonderful. Do you have enough salt?"

Her mother hesitated, then picked up the clean fork Elin had placed beside the plate. She scooped up a forkful and placed it in her mouth. Chewing reflectively, she finally smiled and nodded. "They are pretty good, if I do say so myself. What do you think, Owen?" She looked expectantly at Marc.

He glanced at Elin but moved to an empty chair and got some noodles. "They're great, Ruby. Thanks for making them for me."

Tears glistened in her eyes, and she put down her fork. "I'm confused. You're not Owen." She rubbed her hand. "What's happening to me? I am losing myself." She pushed back from the table and ran from the room.

Kalianne hurried after her, calling her name.

Elin knew the feeling her mother was experiencing. There were times she wanted to run crying from the room too. In another few months, would either of them be the women they were a year ago?

Sixteen

The motorboat rocked in the waves offshore. Pinpricks of light from the house's windows looked like fireflies on the hillside. The wind tangled Elin's curls, and she wished she'd thought to tie back her hair before coming out here tonight. Was this really a good idea? Nervousness rippled over her spine and heightened every sense: the smell of the sea, the roar of the engine, the taste of the salt on her lips.

Abby hadn't wanted her to do this, and she was likely watching out the window at the boat's lights offshore. She would be praying for Elin too, a thought that comforted her.

Marc's figure loomed in front of her, and he sat beside her. "You look like you're about to jump overboard. We don't have to go through with it."

"I can do this." The words bolstered her flagging courage. "I have to figure out who he is. He might have done this before, and he might do it again."

"It's a brave thing to try. Sara and I will be right here with you. If it gets too scary, we won't press you." He reached over and took her hand.

She clung to his strong fingers, then forced herself to release them. "I don't want to have to do this more than once, so let's find out all we can."

She looked around the boat. It was a forty-five-foot vessel with a large deck area. Not at all like the cruise ship where Laura died. Would this even work? Maybe they should have tried to get aboard the same kind of boat.

The engine cut off, then Sara stepped toward them. "Ready? Let's go around to the other side of the boat. Laura was found on the aft deck. I've got the cologne."

"And I have the red sweater." Marc rose and held out his hand.

Her fingers curled around his, and his strength gave her courage to stand. If she could hold his hand the entire time, she might make it through this. She dreaded the memories, the dreams. This was the first time she'd ever consciously tried to re-create what happened that night. What if she wasn't Elin Summerall when this was over? What if Laura's memories crushed out her own?

She forced herself to walk with Marc to the other side of the craft. At the first sight of the life jackets, she stumbled. Those bright-orange flotation devices brought a hazy memory floating to her. And the smell of the canvas, moldy and pungent, made her feel as though she had no air.

Marc steadied her. "You okay?"

She managed to smile and nod. "Fine." His skeptical gaze remained on her face, and she lifted her head. "I'll be okay. Let's get this over with."

"Okay, I've tried to re-create as much of that day as I can remember." Sara pointed to the life preservers. "She was under a pile of PFDs. Her feet were here." She moved to the end of a bench just to the left of the orange pile.

Elin edged closer, though the stronger scent of mold made her want to retch. "What was I—she—wearing?"

"White shorts and a red tank top. Her hair was up in a ponytail, and her feet were bare."

Elin's hand went to her throat. She could almost see a woman's outline under the pile of life jackets. Her breathing came hard and labored in her chest. She couldn't breathe, and she took a step back.

Marc's warm hand touched her back. "Ready to try this?"

She nodded, unable to speak, wishing she could change her mind. But Josie was counting on her. She had to protect her daughter.

Marc pulled out a length of piano wire. "He used something like this to choke her." He opened the bag in his hand. "Here's the sweater. I doused it with the cologne."

Elin's fingertips had no feeling in them as she closed her hand around the sweater Sara thrust at her. She stepped to the railing and looked out over the dark water . . .

She'd seen Theo kissing another woman, and all she wanted to do right now was cry. Laura staggered to the railing and rubbed her damp eyes. When a footfall sounded behind her, she thought it might be him following her to apologize. Well, let him try. If he thought she would forget it, he was very wrong. Then she caught a whiff of the cologne. It wasn't Theo. She stiffened and turned to go, but strong fingers gripped her arm.

A voice as smooth as a calm sea whispered against her neck, "Don't go. I was looking for you. Just for you." His hand touched her upper arm, then moved to the back of her neck. "I could kill her for you. Theo would never kiss her again. You don't deserve that kind of treatment. Or do you?" His fingers brushed her neck before the tweak of a hard pinch made her flinch.

Her limbs turned to ice. She pulled away and started for the inside deck. He snatched her back before she'd gone two feet. His breath hissed through his teeth, and he slammed her back against his chest. She struggled to get away, but the alcohol she'd had left her dizzy and unsteady.

His breath smelled of wintergreen, and he pressed his lips against the side of her neck. She caught a glimpse of a red sweater. His strong cologne made her gag, and she felt light-headed. He must have practically bathed in the stuff. He kept her pinned, and she couldn't move her head more than a few inches. His hand was clamped around her arm, and a signet ring with the letter R glittered in the bit of deck lighting.

He released her, and she fell to her knees. She caught a glimpse of something shiny as he whipped it over her head. Then something choked off her air. She brought both hands to her neck, but she couldn't get even a finger under the thin wire around her skin. Her eyes fluttered, and she sagged to the deck.

She was drowning, drowning. Her lungs burned, and she struggled harder, then crashed into a pile of orange life vests. The musty scent was the last thing she remembered.

Through a fog, Elin heard Marc say her name, felt Sara touch her arm, but it was as if she were numb and couldn't move. She tried to speak, but she couldn't form her lips into words. Who was she? Where was she? Where was Theo? Was she dead?

Her vision faded to a pinprick, and the musty scent of the life preservers grew stronger as she sank into their embrace.

———

The boat rocked in the waves as Marc leaped forward to catch Elin before she could hit the deck. He hadn't liked the look on her face before she went limp. If this re-creation had harmed her, he didn't know how he could live with himself. He shouldn't have let her do it.

He eased down with her in his arms and pulled her onto his lap. He brushed her long red hair out of her face. "Elin, it's all right. It's over." Her long lashes didn't move. Her face had lost all color. He looked up at Sara. "Any ideas on bringing her around?"

She knelt beside them. "Let me get some water from the galley." She rose and hurried to the port side, flipping on the deck lights as she went.

His anxiety heightened a notch as he studied Elin's face in the brighter light. Sara returned with a glass of water. He glanced up at her. "What just happened in her memories?"

Sara's mouth trembled. "Even her movements weren't her own. She never tosses her hair the way she did while remembering Laura's murder. She walked differently too."

"You think it really is possible she could become someone else?"

"I think so, Marc. There's something going on we don't understand."

He didn't want to believe it, but Elin clearly knew something she would have no way of knowing without picking up some of Laura's memories.

Her lids fluttered, and she began to stir. A bit of color came back to her cheeks. "Don't touch me, Theo."

Theo? Marc raised her head a bit. "Elin, can you open your eyes?"

She grimaced, then flung up her hand. She blinked and opened her lids. "Marc? What happened?" Her expression changed, and her hand went to her throat.

Relief flooded him. Elin's voice, Elin's expressive face. "You're fine. We're on the boat, remember? You were trying to remember what happened the night Laura died."

Her eyes widened. "I remember. I *was* Laura. I smelled the cologne, and I saw everything just like it happened."

She seemed to realize she was on his lap and struggled to sit up. He eased her into a seated position but didn't let go of her in case she fainted again. She seemed in no hurry to stand.

Sara knelt beside them on the deck. "Here, drink this. How do you feel?" She uncapped the water and handed it to Elin.

Elin gulped down half the water. "I feel a little shaky. But I remember so much more. There was an *R* on his ring." She began to recount what she'd seen when she smelled the cologne.

"Who is Theo?" Marc asked.

Her face fell. "I don't remember. Laura was mad at him, though, when she caught him kissing another woman. He was drunk. Maybe he was a shipboard romantic interest." She inhaled and shook her head. "The man offered to kill the woman Theo was kissing. I think he likes killing."

She shuddered, and he knew she was remembering finding Lacy. She made no effort yet to pull out of his arms, and Marc was content to keep her right where she was. Her softness was just as he remembered it. That night had been etched into his memory for all time.

"Anything else you remember?" he asked.

"His breath smelled of wintergreen, like the pink candy. Or wintergreen gum." She touched her throat again.

"Do you remember what Theo looks like? Any memory of him?" Sara asked.

She shook her head. "Nothing, sorry."

He realized he was enjoying the feel of her in his arms, a dangerous position. He shifted her a bit. "I think I'd better find this Theo and talk to him. I can look at the passenger manifest. Full name might be Theodore. That's not a common name, so we might hit pay dirt."

She finally made a move to get up, and he released her. Sara helped her to her feet, then held out her hand to him. He took it and got up.

Sara hugged Elin. "I'm sorry we put you through this. It's over. You want more water?"

Elin shook her head. "It's okay. At least some good has come of it. If we find this Theo, maybe we'll get some answers." She looked to Marc as if searching for confirmation.

He nodded. "I have a copy of the manifest on my computer. Let's see what we can find out." He walked back to the helm where he'd stashed his laptop. Sara flipped on the light in the small room, then she and Elin settled on the bench seat behind him while he opened the file.

He swiveled in the pilot's chair to face them. "There are two Theodores. Theodore Jensen and Theodore Farmer. Either one ring a bell?"

The tiny lines between her brows furrowed, then Elin shook her head. "I just remember Theo, no last name."

He jotted down the phone numbers and addresses of the two men. "There's a guy with a last name of Theobold. That might be him too. One of them lives in California and one lives in Florida. This other guy lives in Virginia Beach. Let's call him first." He pulled out his phone and punched in the Virginia number first.

The call rang three times before a male voice answered. "If you're selling something, I'm hanging up."

Marc put on a stern tone. The guy's attitude really bugged him. "This is Marc Everton with the FBI. I'm investigating the murder aboard the *Seawind*. Is this Theo?"

"Yeah." His voice was more respectful. "I didn't see anything. And besides, someone already interrogated me."

So he *did* go by Theo. "Right, but I'm trying to discover if you knew the deceased, Laura Watson, at all."

"I don't think so." His voice held a wary note.

"What does that mean? You either knew her or you didn't." Something about this guy put his hackles up.

"Look, you know how it is aboard ship. Love 'em and leave 'em. I played around with a few women. It was a long cruise—two weeks. Plenty of time to play the field. I didn't get all their last names, but yeah, there was one Laura. It could have been her."

"Did anyone ever show you a picture of the deceased?"

"Nope."

He is lying. Maybe shock would loosen his tongue. "Did she cause a scene when she caught you kissing another woman?"

"Who told you that?" Theo snapped.

"Is it true?"

"Look, it was totally uncalled for. We'd spent one night together, and all of a sudden she thinks she owns me. There was no reason for her to go off like that." His voice rose. "She slapped me and stalked off."

"What happened next? Did you go after Laura? Maybe you wanted to teach her a lesson." Could this be the killer? Every instinct told him the guy was hiding something.

"Get real, man. Why would I do that when a pretty woman was all ready to offer condolences, if you know what I mean."

Marc could almost hear the man's smirk in his voice. He gritted his teeth and tried to get past his dislike. "So you didn't see her after she slapped you?"

"Not for even a second."

"Can anyone corroborate your whereabouts after the incident?"

"If I knew the chick's name and number, I'd give it to you. Her first name was Bambi. Can't be too many of them on the list."

Marc ran his gaze over the manifest. "Try again. There was no Bambi aboard."

"Maybe it was a fake name. Look, I have to go. If you have anything else to say, you can talk to my attorney."

Marc heaved a sigh. How did he go about finding this Bambi? He'd bet a hundred bucks this guy wasn't as innocent as he claimed.

SEVENTEEN

The seat cushion was hard under her thighs, a comforting sensation that proved she was Elin, not Laura. She was here aboard the boat with Sara and Marc. The vision or whatever it was when she'd smelled the cologne and had a surge of Laura's memories wasn't real. This was real. Sitting here under the stars with the boat rocking in the waves.

Marc ended his phone call. "The guy is hiding something."

"Like what?" Sara asked.

Marc's gaze went to Elin, and she felt the intensity of it. He must have disliked that Theo because his hazel eyes were blazing. "The name Bambi mean anything to you?"

She started to shake her head, then stopped. An image of a woman floated in her memory. "I–I don't know. Maybe. Theo was kissing a woman with big blond hair. Obviously dyed and the ends were tipped with hot pink. I think that might be her name."

Sara lifted a brow. "Fake name?"

He shrugged. "Got to be."

"I think her real name was Barbara. She was older than Theo. Maybe forty." Where were all these details coming from? Elin couldn't consciously recall them. What if they were made up by her desire to get answers? But no, she could swear she'd actually seen the woman.

Marc leaned over his computer and perused the list again. "Seven Barbaras. I'll get some records pulled so we can check the birth dates. Maybe we can find the right one. She might have seen Theo go off to confront Laura."

Had there been a confrontation? Elin couldn't remember, but it didn't feel right. She couldn't remember ever speaking with this Bambi either. Maybe it was all a dead end.

Sara put her arm around her. "I think we'd better get her home. She still looks like she might keel over any minute."

"Yeah." Marc swiveled back around and started the engine. The boat putted slowly toward the boathouse in the harbor.

"I need some air." Elin rose and went toward the door to the deck. When Sara started to follow her, Elin shook her head. "I'll be fine. I want a minute by myself. Maybe something else will come to me."

Sara sank back onto the cushions, but the worry didn't leave her eyes. Marc glanced at Elin with a lifted brow but then nodded. She escaped into the damp night air. The waves lapped against the bow of the boat, and the stars twinkled down as if it were any other night. And maybe it was. Most people would look up into the sky and revel in the gorgeous sight. But this night was just like the one when Laura gasped her last, and Elin felt the young woman's presence keenly in this moment.

Was she here, inside her? Or just her memories? Elin didn't even know if Laura had been a Christian, though she hoped so. It might be comforting to know for sure of her final destination. One thing she knew for sure—what she felt wasn't a spirit. Wherever Laura had gone, the journey was a permanent one, just like the Bible said.

The chugging of the engine lulled her thoughts for a few minutes. The shore drew nearer, and she could make out the outline of the house in the moonlight.

A shadow flitted by the front porch, and she put her hand

to her throat and leaned in closer to see. Someone was out there. Abby? Maybe her mother had slipped outside without being seen? But something about the figure seemed to be male, and Elin remembered the other night when she thought she'd seen someone walking along the beach.

Her throat tightened, and she wanted to call out a warning as the man paused in front of the large front window. The light filtering through the curtains revealed his shape a bit better, and something in the slant of his neck terrified her.

It's him!

She pressed down the fear as illogical, but her terror only escalated. What if he was watching Abby and Josie, trying to decide how to break in and harm them? She whirled and ran for the wheelhouse to tell Marc to hurry. As she reached the door, she looked behind for one last glimpse. No one was there. Only a tree moving in the stiff wind.

Had that been all she'd seen? Or was there more?

———

Every nerve was strung tight enough to twang. Marc strode the grounds looking for a possible intruder, even though Elin hadn't been certain of what she'd seen. The night breeze blew the scent of the sea into his nostrils, and the recent rain left the ground mushy under his Nike flip-flops.

He swept the beam of his flashlight over the flower bed by the front window. It revealed no one lurking in the shadows, just the small tree with its branches moving in the wind. His high alert status began to ebb a bit. Maybe no one had been here.

"See anything?" Elin exited the front door and came down the steps to join him by the plantings. She wore a white robe over green pajamas and was barefoot.

He gestured. "It might have been that tree."

"Oh, I pray so!"

The delicate scent of her perfume teased his nose, and he shifted to take in the sweetness a bit better. Though the vastness of the landscape surrounded them, it felt very intimate to be out here alone with her with the stars overhead and the sound of the surf in the background.

"Everyone else in bed?" He trained his flashlight on the ground again before moving on to the end of the house.

She followed closely. "I put Josie in my bed. I just couldn't face the thought of having her alone in a room in case someone is out here."

"And your mom and Abby?" As long as she continued to follow him around, he could ask questions all night. What did that say about his level of attraction?

Elin grabbed his arm. "Marc, look at that."

He saw where she was pointing. Footprints. He focused the beam of light on the outline. "Looks like a man's sandal. Size twelve or thirteen. Big guy. And it's fresh." He knelt beside it. "Look here. No insect tracks through it, no collection of dew. The guy was past here in the last hour."

"I *did* see someone then."

He rose and stared down at her. "You sound relieved."

"Not relieved, exactly, but at least I know I'm not crazy. I–I was beginning to wonder. So many things have been happening to me."

He took her by the shoulders. "Elin, you are *not* crazy. I admit I had my doubts about cell memory, but you know details there's no other way to know."

The moonlight illuminated her face, and the relief there made his heart clench. She must have been worried about this more than he'd realized. He hadn't stopped to think of the stress she was under. How would he feel if he was experiencing things that had happened to another man? It would be hard to live with.

Her gaze, lit with vulnerability, searched his. "Do I seem different to you, Marc?"

What would she say if he told her he found her immensely appealing? Being around her was messing with his peace of mind. He could conquer it, though, with a little willpower.

"Those are Laura's memories, not yours. Things will settle down once we have that guy behind bars." He forced himself to let go of her and sweep his flashlight over the ground again. "Looks like he went this way. Go on back inside and call the sheriff in Hope Beach. We probably ought to have him take a look out here since it's clear someone was trespassing."

"I think you should come back inside too. You don't have backup, and the guy could get the jump on you."

"I'll just poke around a little, then come in. I'll be careful."

She nodded, then retreated to the front door. "I'll be back out in a minute."

He watched her through the large window as she went to the portable phone and dialed. Her hair glimmered in the overhead light as she twirled a long curl of it around her finger and paced the floor while she spoke to the sheriff. Her translucent skin held a flush of color, and it sounded as though she had raised her voice.

If he didn't move, she would come back out and find him gawking. He pointed his flashlight into the darkness and moved around the side of the house toward the back. His light illuminated the back deck and the fire pit in the yard. A small animal dashed across the grass and he flinched, then relaxed.

Then something pierced his arm, and sharp pain radiated up to his shoulder. He dropped to his knees—an arrow was in the fleshy part of his forearm. A warm trickle ran down his arm. He touched the sticky fluid. Blood. Someone had shot him with an arrow. His fingers closed around the arrow, but he didn't pull it out. Might cause more bleeding.

Gritting his teeth against the pain, he peered into the darkness near the edge of the tree line. The shadows made it too dark to see. Where was the guy? Adrenaline surged through him, and he breathed hard and fast through his mouth. He lifted his head, but there was no renewed attack.

An engine roared, and he staggered to his feet and looked toward the water. The lights of a small boat exited the small cove just down the beach, and the craft zoomed away.

The front door slammed, and Elin joined him a few seconds later.

"Did you hear the boat?" She inhaled sharply. "Marc, you're hurt."

"Yeah. The guy shot me with an arrow." The pain had ramped up, and he felt a little dizzy. "I think I'd better sit down."

She grabbed his arm and guided him to a chair on the deck near the porch light. She knelt and looked at his arm. "Sara, come quick!"

The back door banged, and his cousin came flying out of the house. Her eyes went to his arm. "Oh my gosh, is that an arrow?"

"Yeah," he said through gritted teeth. "I think I'm blacking out." That was all he knew as darkness rose to claim him.

When he came to, Elin was kneeling on one side of him and Sara on the other. Both women had wet cheeks. His gaze fastened on Elin, and he reached up to touch the tears on her face. "Don't cry." His voice sounded so weak, he closed his eyes a moment and tried to muster more strength.

"Don't talk." Sara put a blood pressure cuff on his arm. "I think you're in shock."

His vision swam and he tried to focus. Something white attached to the arrow fluttered in the breeze. "There's a paper attached to the arrow."

Elin leaned in close and studied the paper. "It's a note."

Her cologne wafted up his nose, and he struggled to speak. "A note? Can you read it?"

Her face was stricken when she raised her gaze to meet his. "It says, 'She's mine. And you're a dead man.'"

EIGHTEEN

S heriff Tom Bourne looked harried when Elin opened the door about ten that night. Her call had interrupted his investigation of a break-in at the school. "Thanks for coming out so quickly."

"Attempted murder is more serious than a little graffiti on a school fence." A big man, Tom's dark brown hair showed a few strands of gray at the temples. "Where is the arrow?" He carried a duffel bag in one hand and a flashlight in the other.

"This way." She led the sheriff to the living room, where Marc lay on the sofa.

Sara had managed to extricate the arrow and stop the bleeding. It had barely missed an artery. He would have some pain for a few days, but it could have been so much worse.

Marc's head lolled toward them. "Glad you could join the party, Sheriff." Pain strained his voice.

The sheriff walked a few feet and stared at the arrow on the coffee table in a plastic bag. "You use a latex glove to remove that?"

"I did," Sara said.

"Tell me what happened."

Elin shivered as she listened to Marc relay the events of the attack.

"There's a note here." Bourne peered closer. "'She's mine. And you're a dead man.'" The sheriff shook his head. "Sounds like an irate boyfriend, Ms. Summerall. You have a messy breakup recently?"

She tensed. "Not at all. I'm a widow, and I haven't dated in five years." Was Marc remembering their one and only "date" when Josie was conceived?

Tom's brow furrowed. "Any recent admirers ask you out maybe?"

She started to shake her head, then remembered Isaac. Biting her lip, she tried to decide if she should mention him. It seemed a shame to pull him into something so messy.

"There is?" Tom probed.

She sighed and nodded. "There's a coworker who has asked me out a few times, but I've never dated him." She told him Isaac's name. "He's harmless though. Really, this is connected to Laura, not me. I'm just getting the fallout from whoever was after her. Maybe he's after me because he thinks part of Laura is in me, and he wants to eradicate everything about her."

Bourne didn't react for a moment, then he took off his hat and wiped his forehead. "Sounds right. So we should look into anyone Laura threw over. See if she had a disgruntled boyfriend."

"There's another wrinkle too." Marc told the sheriff about Lacy's death and how she was dressed.

Bourne's frown deepened the more he listened. "It sounds like the guy is really fixated on you, Ms. Summerall. I'm not so sure this is about Laura. If he was focused on her, wouldn't he have dressed Lacy up to resemble her, not you? I think we need to keep an open mind about it and look at all the different angles."

He picked up the plastic bag containing the arrow and note. "I'll send this to the state boys and have them go over it. It might take some time for them to check for fingerprints and DNA. One of the disadvantages of living on an island with little resources."

"You might alert the police about this," Marc said. "It's probably tied in with their murder investigation of Lacy's death."

"I'd planned to do just that." Tom's tone implied his displeasure at being told how to do his job. He went down the steps into the yard with his bright flashlight. "I'll make a cast of the footprints. Can you show me where they are?"

Elin took a step toward the kitchen door. "Of course."

Marc held out a hand toward her. "You're looking a little stressed, Elin. You've been through a lot in the last few months. That virus, a heart transplant, and then the constant worry of a killer after you. You should get to bed. Sara can show the sheriff the crime scene."

His concern warmed her. "I'm no shrinking violet, Marc. If he's watching me, I don't want him to think he's terrorizing me. I won't let that happen."

He struggled to sit up, his face contorted with the pain. "You don't have to be a pit bull all the time. There's no shame in getting some rest."

She tilted up her chin. "I'll rest later. Sara, watch him. I'll show the sheriff around."

She led the sheriff out the back door, although everything in her didn't want to venture into the darkness. An owl hooted in the woods, and a few moments later something shrieked.

"An owl got something, I think," Bourne said.

His impersonal tone made her shiver. Predator and prey, was that what the world was all about? Sometimes it seemed that way, but she was determined to get back to waking up every morning with anticipation for whatever blessing God might bring her way. She was tired of flinching at every shadow. In fact, she refused to let the stress affect her. If Marc had noticed, Josie probably had too.

Shouldn't every day be lived with anticipation? That maniac might succeed in taking her life someday, but he had no right to steal her joy. She'd let him until now, but no more.

Her head high, she marched around the side of the house. Only when the sheriff left did she head for bed, a place she was reluctant to go. The nightmares would be sure to come tonight, so she reached for Georgina's diary.

It just might keep the nightmares at bay. *For a while.*

AUGUST 21, 1907

Georgina ran her hands over her swollen stomach. This baby kicked so much that sometimes she didn't get a wink of sleep. A smile curved her lips. But she didn't mind. Another week or two and she would hold this little one in her arms. She fanned her face. The heat and humidity had grown unbearable in this past month, even though the servants opened every window.

She packed the last of Joshua's trunk and turned to find him staring at her. "What's wrong?"

He wore his captain's uniform and looked the picture of the handsome officer who had swept her off her feet a year ago. He planned to make a trip to Hope Beach to check on his ship. It would sail in another three weeks. They'd both prayed their baby would arrive before he had to leave.

He took a step closer to her. "Someone was outside last night."

Her gaze darted to the window, and she put her hand to her throat. "Someone was watching us?"

"Maybe. I was gone all evening." His eyes narrowed. "Did you have a visitor?"

She stared back at him, refusing to show any sign of guilt. "Of course not. I would have told you." She started to turn, but he caught at her arm and swung her around. "Let go of me. You're hurting my arm." She tore her arm from his grasp and rubbed it. "Your jealousy is ridiculous, Joshua."

"Oh, so now I'm ridiculous?" He raised his hand as if to strike her.

She tipped her chin up and stared him down. "You would *dare* lift your hand to me, your pregnant wife? Do not think I will cower inside and hide any bruises. The day you strike me is the day I leave. My father will welcome me back at a moment's notice."

He lowered his hand. "You have no money to leave."

She struggled to keep her tone level. "He would send me money as soon as I asked. I'm not your slave, Joshua."

He sank to the edge of the bed. "It maddens me to think of you with another man."

Pity stirred and she banished it. It did no good to sympathize with him. Another rage would strike him again. "Look at me." When he lifted red eyes her direction, she touched her belly again. "What man would look at me like this? I lumber like a beached whale, and I'm as fat as a toad. Your imagination takes you on ridiculous flights of fancy, Joshua. I am your wife. I would never betray you. Never."

They'd had this conversation before, and it never went anywhere, but she always hoped he would listen. She'd be able to breathe again out of his constant scrutiny. And she would have her baby to occupy her time.

"This isn't the first time you've seen tracks around the house. I must say, I'm rather worried. Who could be peering in our windows and checking out our property?"

At her question, his contrition vanished and he focused on the problem. "A thief perhaps?"

"Your money is safely stowed at the bank. We have nothing of real value here. Food, furniture. Nothing worth going to prison for."

He rose from the side of the bed. "I don't wish to make it seem an accusation, Georgina, but I found something in the yard."

He walked to his bureau and opened the bottom drawer. Under his socks he pulled out a krama. He held the scarf out to her. "Can you explain this?"

She picked it up in her hands, and the scent of curry permeating the fabric wafted to her nose. "It's Khmer."

"I know. Has Chann been in touch with you?"

She held his gaze. "He has not. I haven't heard from him since he was here four months ago."

Then who had left this outside if not Chann? Her thoughts flew to the leather pouch she'd hidden. Her friend had been panicked that it remain safe. Could someone be after that? Or was Chann back to reclaim his property?

"So you have kept track of the time since you saw him last."

She sighed. "Everything relates to my baby. I was about four months along. That is all, Joshua." She threw down the cloth and moved toward the door. "I'm quite tired of trying to reassure you. Believe what you like."

As she opened the bedroom door, a trickle of water between her legs became a sudden torrent. She stood staring at the puddle on the floor until she realized what it meant.

"The baby," she whispered. "The baby is coming. Fetch the midwife."

Nineteen

Elin shut the diary and smiled at her mother, who had curled up on the bed with her again. She'd been listening with rapt attention to Georgina's tale.

"I saw that pouch thing," her mother said. "It was folded and wrapped with leather ties."

Elin's smile faded. "That's not possible, Mom. I'm sure it's long gone. She hid it over a hundred years ago."

"I saw it. It's about this size." She measured about four inches by nine out with her hands. "I can't remember where I found it though. Or what I did with it. I think it's in the attic."

Hallucinations were common, and maybe listening to the graphic story in the diary had made it seem real to Mom. Elin's eyes burned, and she wished she could bring her mother back from the fog.

Her mother's blue pajamas flapped when she leaped from the bed. "Let's go look upstairs. Maybe I'll remember where I hid it."

No amount of persuasion dissuaded her mother when she wore that expression of obstinacy. "All right." Elin dug the keys out of her bedside drawer.

Marc nearly mowed her down when she exited her room. His injured arm was in a sling, and his right hand shot out to steady her. The warm touch of his hand on her arm sent shivers up her back.

She didn't move away. "Sorry. I wasn't watching where I was going."

Her mother barely glanced at him and continued on down the hall to the stairway door. "Hurry up, Elin."

He finally dropped his hand. "Where's the fire?"

"Mom says she's seen the leather folder Georgina describes in the diary. She says she found it and hid it again, even though she doesn't remember where she found it or where she hid it. We were just going upstairs to look around." She shook her head. "I shouldn't have read her that diary."

"I'll help." He continued to look down at her with an amused expression.

"Bored, huh?"

He grinned. "Nothing to watch on TV except home-improvement shows and a movie I've seen three times."

"You should rest. You lost a lot of blood."

"I'm fine. Knocked back three Advil and I'm good to go."

He touched her on the shoulder as they turned to join her mother. It was crazy how she felt around him. Where were these feelings coming from? Maybe she was going crazy. With all she had going on, the last thing she needed was a romantic entanglement, especially with Marc, who was a complication in her life in so many ways.

She went upstairs first. "There are some halogen lights over there." She pointed to the corner.

Marc went to drag them to the center of the space. The long cords reached the outlets, and Elin blinked when the bright lights flooded the room and pushed back the night shadows. The large room looked even bigger with the light reaching to all the corners.

She eyed him a moment. "I wanted to ask you something.

Why didn't you tell the sheriff you'd take care of forensics? I bet you could get results faster than he could."

He hunched his shoulders. "It's kind of a problem right now. I, uh, I'm not supposed to be investigating this. My supervisor thinks I'm haring off on a wild-goose chase."

Her stomach plunged. "What do you mean? They don't believe me?"

He straightened and his gaze held hers. "I'm positive Laura's killer murdered my partner, but my boss thinks it was a mob hit. He told me to take some leave and let it alone."

"So you could get in trouble for poking into this?" Warmth spread through her when she realized how much he'd put on the line to help her. "Thank you."

His firm lips twisted into a wry grin. "Don't thank me yet. He's still out there."

"You'll find him."

"I will."

His confident tone gave her courage. "Thank you for telling me." She pointed out closed doors in two different walls. "There are more rooms than just this big room too. I hadn't realized. When I was up here before, I was looking for the way up to the widow's walk."

Her mother wore a faraway expression. Holding out her arms as though embracing someone, she began to dance to imaginary music. Elin remembered her dancing with Dad when she was a child. They would turn on "Unchained Melody" by The Righteous Brothers and slow dance on the living room rug. Did Mom hear that old tune in her head now?

Elin touched her arm. "Mom?"

Her mother danced on, oblivious to her daughter's presence.

Marc's eyes were warm with compassion, and he touched Elin's arm again. "Let's look in the other rooms since you haven't seen them yet." He grabbed a halogen light in his good hand and carried it with him toward the first room.

She opened the door and flipped on the overhead light. The weak glow barely showed the floor right under it. Marc plugged in the halogen light and flipped it on. The bright light showed what was likely once a servant's room. About fifteen feet square, it held an old iron bed and a battered chest of drawers. A small closet held dresses draped on hooks.

"It's like a peek into another time." Elin touched a gray flapper-style dress in the closet and gazed at the T-strap shoes with their chunky heels so reminiscent of the early twenties. "The days of live-in help were pretty much over after World War I. I wonder who these belonged to?"

"And why didn't the family get rid of all these old things?" He moved to the dresser and pulled open one drawer after the other. "Old pictures in here. Doilies too and some old teacups. Doesn't look to be anything of value."

In slim-fitting jeans and a black T-shirt, Marc stood with his hands on his hips and surveyed the rest of the room. "What makes you think the pouch your mother has been talking about is the same Georgina mentions in her diary?"

"I don't, not really. I think the diary has become vivid in her mind, but there is no way to distract her when she gets so obsessed with something. It's easier to just play along until she loses interest."

He nodded at the door to where the older woman still danced with an imaginary partner. "Like now. We could talk her into going to bed now, I think."

"Probably." Elin burrowed into the closet and began to pull out the long-dead servant's belongings. "I'll take her down in a minute."

"I think you're as obsessed as she is." Marc's voice revealed his amusement. "Here, hand some of that stuff to me."

She dumped shoes into his outstretched hand. "What if something is worth finding up here?"

"You mean like the leather-pouch thing?"

"No, I think that's long gone. But maybe there's an old Van Gogh or Rembrandt up here. Or some fabulously valuable jewelry. Hidden treasure of some kind." She shot him an impish grin to show she was only joking. But was she? The bigger treasure to her mind was finding out about the people who had lived in Seagrass Pier.

She stumbled as she exited the closet. Marc caught her with his one arm and snatched her to his chest to steady her.

"Thanks," she mumbled through a mouth suddenly too dry.

His enticing masculine scent overpowered her reserve, and her hand stole up his chest. She stared into his face and willed him to kiss her. His hands held her tight against him. His eyes darkened, and his head started a downward trajectory before he jerked back and released her as if her skin had burned him.

Her cheeks went hot, and she turned her back on him. "I think I'd better get Mom to bed."

⌒

The good scent of freshly turned dirt filled Marc's nostrils on Saturday morning, and he stretched out his back, then dusted off his hands. He'd taken off the sling this morning, though Elin had protested. His arm was a little sore, but not that bad. The roar of the sea was muffled here behind the house. "I think we're done. All the seeds are planted, and I'll water the tomatoes and peppers."

"You're a good son," Ruby said, her blue eyes vacant and watery.

His gaze locked with Elin's, and he wished he could erase the pain he saw in her face. He'd nearly kissed her last night. It would be stupid to go there, but he could at least look. The wind lifted her long curls and swirled them around her head like a halo. His fingers itched to plunge into that red hair.

Josie tugged at the hem of his knee-length shorts. "Look, Mr. Marc, I have my own tomato plant."

He touched her soft hair, marveling again at how much she looked like him. "I'm sure it will give you lots of tomatoes."

When was Elin going to agree to tell her who he was? He glanced at her and saw from her expression she'd read his mind. Her eyes narrowed, and she shook her head.

The screen door on the back entry banged, and he glanced over to see Kalianne heading their way with a tray of lemonade. She sent a smile his way that made him tense. He was decidedly *not* available to someone like her when he had a daughter to raise.

His gaze went back to Elin. And Kalianne definitely wasn't his type. He preferred the tall, willowy type with legs that went on forever and a giggle that made him smile.

Kalianne reached him. "Thirsty?" Her smile insinuated something other than lemonade.

"I could use a cold drink." He kept his tone light and avoided looking her in the face.

She moved to Elin and Ruby, and they both took a sweating glass of lemonade. There was a kid's cup with a straw for Josie. Kalianne set the tray down on a tree stump at the edge of the garden and took the last glass for herself.

"I noticed the third-floor stairway was unlocked," Kalianne said. "Tell me where to find the key, and I'll lock it up for you. We wouldn't want Ruby or Josie going up there by themselves."

Elin took a sip of her drink. "We were looking around up there last night. I'll lock it when I go back in. I've got the keys in my purse. I think Josie must have found them in my drawer because it was unlocked the other day."

"Looking around?" Kalianne's eyes still flirted with Marc.

"Mom was talking about having seen an old leather folder that rolls up. She insisted on going to the attic to look for it."

Kalianne straightened. "How interesting. Maybe she was just dreaming it."

"Probably, but we went up to explore."

"So you don't think she's actually seen something like that? She mentioned it to me too, and I told her I'd help her find it."

Elin lowered her voice. "Try to distract her. I'm sure there's nothing to her story."

"I'll do that, and if she won't be distracted, it won't hurt to look around with her like you did last night. Could you put the key somewhere I can find it?"

"I'd rather you didn't go up there at all if I'm not here. I'm happy to unlock it for you and go along if she wants up there. I'm just afraid she'll wander off and climb the stairs to the widow's walk. It's not safe for her. Or for Josie."

A look of displeasure flitted across Kalianne's face. She turned away to look at the garden. "Whatever you say."

Ruby moved closer to Marc. "My son here is a good gardener. Have you met him?"

Kalianne looked over and smiled. "I sure have. Though he's not your son."

Confusion filled Ruby's eyes, and Marc sent Kalianne a warning frown. "She's just teasing you, Ruby." He patted the older lady's shoulder, then moved closer to Kalianne and spoke in an undertone. "Don't argue with her."

"I don't believe in lying to patients."

"She doesn't understand. You don't need to correct her when she's confused." When Kalianne shook her head and started to reply, he held up his hand. "Just do what you're told, Miss Adanete."

Her brows drew together. "I don't believe you're my employer."

Elin joined them. "Is there a problem?"

"I was just explaining to Kalianne that she shouldn't argue with your mother when she's confused. You don't do it. She doesn't think I have the authority to give her an order."

"No, the doctor said not to." Elin looked hard at Kalianne. "And Marc can give any orders he pleases. He's only looking out for Mom's best interests."

Kalianne's cheeks flushed, and her eyes sparked fire. "Whatever you say." She grabbed up the empty tray and stalked back toward the house.

"Sorry if I was out of line." Marc wasn't sure if she'd stood up for him because she believed it or because she wanted to save face in front of Kalianne.

"You weren't. I trust you, Marc."

Her words warmed him until he remembered she hadn't trusted him enough to tell him about Josie.

TWENTY

"Mommy, we're home!" Josie's voice carried over the water as the boat docked. Abby had taken her and Mom to a festival at Kill Devil Hills right after they'd planted the garden.

Elin waved from the shore as her sister took Josie's hand and disembarked the ferry. Josie smiled hugely as she ran to her mother. Elin scooped up her daughter. "I missed you! Did you have a good time with Aunt Abby?"

Her daughter nodded and planted a kiss on her cheek. "We had a pedicure. I got five different colors." She pointed at her toes peeking from the ends of her sandals.

"Very nice." Elin put her down, and Josie ran to hug her grandmother, who was having a pretty good day from the clarity of her blue eyes.

Elin let her gaze sweep the passengers hurrying down the plank to shore. Could any of them be responsible for Lacy's death? Most seemed to be with families, but there were one or two men who ambled off by themselves.

She shivered and turned her attention back to her sister. "Thanks for taking her. She was very eager, and I just wasn't up to it."

Abby studied her. "You look a little pale. Have you heard anything else about the murder?"

Josie had dragged her grandmother over to the water to peer at a tide pool. They would be busy for at least a few minutes.

Abby looked over to where their mother crouched over the pool with Josie. "I think I should keep Josie for now. It's dangerous for her, Elin. Surely you can see that. Let me take her with me."

"I don't dare let her out of my sight. I know you love her, Abby, but I'd die before I'd let anything happen to her."

"So would I." Abby looked fierce.

Elin hadn't expected to be arguing with Abby over Josie. "Listen, let's not fight about this. We're safe. Marc is here. You have to admit he's quite capable of protecting all of us."

Abby's fists unclenched, and she gave a reluctant nod. "I always thought there was something between the two of you. You could cut the chemistry with a knife. Are you dating him?"

"What? Of course not." She would have to tell Abby the truth. "But he does have a vested interest in keeping Josie safe."

"I don't get it."

"He's Josie's father."

Abby's eyes went wide, then filled with certainty. "I knew it! Why on earth didn't you marry him? Did he leave you when he found out about Josie?"

"I never told him."

Abby gasped, and she shook her head. "I don't understand. You never looked at another man but Tim."

Elin looked down. "It's not something I'm proud of. The night Dad died, I kind of lost it. Drank too much. We both did. One thing led to another." Her face burned. "I ran out of there and wanted to forget it. He tried to talk to me a few times afterward, but I was so ashamed." The memory of that night still brought a lump to her throat.

Abby frowned. "You cried for days after the call came in about Tim's injury, and I thought it was because you were worried about him. It was because you were pregnant? Did you tell Tim?"

"Yes. He wanted to marry me anyway. I think he wanted to prove he could beat Marc. He never had a good thing to say about him after that." She shook her head. "I'm sorry if I sound critical of Tim. I don't mean to. He was good to Josie and me."

Abby's brow furrowed, and she shook her head. "I would disagree with that, Elin. You live in a rose-colored world, honey. Tim was demanding and short with you. He was often impatient with Josie. It was hard to bite my tongue."

Elin looked at her in surprise. "You've never said anything."

"Would it have done any good? I didn't want to make your life any harder than it was. You were Tim's drudge. It was guilt, wasn't it? You let him treat you like that because you thought you deserved to be punished."

Elin couldn't hold her sister's gaze, and she looked down at the ground. "Maybe."

"I shouldn't say this, but I was glad when Tim died, Elin. I thought that finally you'd be free to be happy."

Elin bit her lip. She wasn't ready to admit she'd had a stab of relief herself. It wasn't something she was proud of. Her tears had mostly been for Josie, who would grow up fatherless. She hadn't minded the way Tim treated her. At least most of the time.

Abby took her arm and steered her to join their mother and Josie. "I bet Marc was livid. Most men would be."

"He was taken aback."

Abby studied her. "He's strong and driven. It's clear he wants to protect you and Josie."

"I wish he didn't have to." She rubbed her head. "If only I could remember that man's face. I get bits and pieces, then it fades into mist. I did remember the name Theo. Marc is checking it out."

"Don't wait on Marc to find it out. You're good at that kind of thing. I don't want you waiting around while the killer gets closer."

"Fair enough. I'll do some digging." She hugged her sister. "You're always good for me, Abby. Now let's get home."

———

The sunset threw gold and red colors over the sand. Marc leaped for the volleyball and spiked it over the net for the winning point. He raised a victorious fist at Curtis and Ben, who returned the gesture. They shook hands with the other team, all other Coasties.

Curtis slapped him on the back as they turned toward the parking lot. "You're a good player, Everton. It's all or nothing with you, isn't it?"

Marc grinned. "I don't like to lose. Ben didn't seem to either. Did you see how ripped that guy is? He must work out every day." He rubbed the towel over his perspiring face.

"He's big into martial arts. I wouldn't want to take him on in a dark alley."

"I'm pretty rusty with my training. I should get back to it." They reached the parking lot. "Thanks for inviting me. I needed to decompress."

"How's the investigation going? Learn anything new?"

"Not enough." Marc leaned on the hood of his Tahoe and told Curtis about trying to get Elin to remember the night of the murder.

"Man, that was extreme."

"Yeah. If my boss gets wind that the guy shot me with an arrow, he'll have my hide."

"Sara said your partner died while investigating this. I'm sorry, man."

"Me too. He was a good man. Left two little kids. I have to find his killer."

"Yeah, you're tenacious, Everton. I could see that just watching you play volleyball. That guy doesn't have a chance. But, dude, you seriously think your boss won't hear about this?"

"You're right. I probably ought to call and tell him." Marc didn't relish the reaming he was going to get. "It might actually convince him my partner's death wasn't an organized-crime hit." Or it might get him fired.

"Anything I can do?"

Marc shook his head. "Just have Amy keep feeding Elin those herbs. She has more color in her cheeks and more energy. She can't reject that heart. We need it to work a long, long time. Josie needs her."

He hadn't voiced his worry about that heart to anyone, especially not Elin. She had enough worries, but he bet this was one of the reasons for her nightmares too.

"Amy is confident she can keep it ticking along. She's a marvel."

Marc raised a hand. "See you next week, same time, same place."

"Tell Elin we're praying for her."

"Will do." Marc slid under the wheel and dug for his keys. As he slid it into the ignition, he spotted a yellow sticky note on the steering wheel.

The block letters screamed at him. *IF YOU DON'T STAY AWAY, I WILL KILL YOU.* Marc jumped from the SUV and looked around. The parking lot was deserted.

———

The glow of the computer lit the dark office. Elin had been so engrossed in her research she hadn't turned on the light. She rose and stretched out the cramps in her muscles, then went to open her window and smell the night scent of the sea on the breeze.

The moon glimmered on the peaks of the whitecaps. The only sound she heard was the lull of the waves. Nothing moved in the house either, so Marc had probably gone to bed too. The green glow of the clock blinked to midnight.

She turned and stared at the glowing computer through bleary eyes. She'd gotten a copy of the ship manifest and had looked up all the Barbaras. Only one was the right age, and she lived in Virginia Beach, close enough for her to pay a call. But Theo's face still eluded her. Was he the same as the killer? She wished she knew for sure.

Her cell phone chirped, and she picked it up, realizing it was connected to the wireless network in the house that allowed the text to come through. She swiped it to look at the message.

I can smell your fear. Shall I take Josie first?

The very thought that he knew her daughter's name took her breath away. She nearly dropped the phone, then tightened her grip on it. No, she wouldn't let him terrify her. He fed off her fear. The text had no cell number associated with it, so he must have used an online messaging service. Could she text him back? Would it go through?

She texted the message: *You're smelling your own fear of being caught. And you will be.*

With a defiant stab of her finger, she sent it on its way, but it bounced back almost immediately. Fueled by anger, she hunched over her laptop again and began to search. She would find him and bring him to justice. But a niggling of fear lifted the hair on the back of her neck. She couldn't let him hurt Josie. Would he really? Surely he was just trying to terrify her.

When a tap came on the door to her office, she straightened with a gasp, then curled her fingers into her palms. "Who is it?"

"It's just me." Marc's deep voice came from the other side of the door. "I saw the glow under the door when I got home and thought maybe you forgot to shut off the computer."

She threw open the door and flipped on the light, then blinked in the sudden glare. "I was just doing some research." He brushed past her close enough for her to smell the scent of sun and surf on him. She resisted the urge to reach out and touch him. "You've got Max."

He rubbed the little dog's head as he approached her laptop. "He was whining like a banshee at the back door." He must have felt her tense because he shook his head. "He heard a bunny or some other animal. I checked. All is quiet on the home front." He put Max on the floor, and the dog went to curl up under her desk. "See, he's not worried."

She smiled. "That's a relief."

He frowned. "What's wrong?"

"What makes you think something's wrong?"

"Your eyes are shadowed, and your lips are trembling a little."

She pressed her lips together to show him she was fine before giving up and reaching for her phone. "I got a text." She showed him the message. "I tried to text him back but it bounced." She lifted her chin. "But I'm not letting him terrify me. I'm going to track him down."

His jaw flexed, and a fire burned in his gaze. "I won't let him hurt you, Elin. Or Josie or Abby either. We'll find him." He reached out and gripped her arm.

The warmth in his touch brought heat to her cheeks. She could feel every whorl of his fingertips against her skin, and it took all her strength to keep from rushing into his arms. This unwanted emotion had to stop. The only reason he was here was because of Josie.

She shook off his grip and turned back to the computer. "I think I found our Bambi. The only Barbara young enough lives in Virginia Beach. She's thirty."

"Let me get into a confidential database." He logged out of her screen and went to another site where he entered a username and password. "Here she is. Look familiar?"

He turned the laptop around to show her a young woman with blond hair. There was no other color on the tips in this picture, but she might have done the dye job just before the cruise.

Something lurched in Elin's chest. "That's her!" She leaned in closer. "I remember that birthmark by her eye too, now that I see it."

What were these emotions churning in her when she looked at Bambi's picture? It felt very much like jealousy. Elin rubbed her forehead. Oh, why couldn't she remember Theo's face? If only she could bring it into focus, it might help her know if he was the killer.

"Mommy?"

She turned to see Josie looking a little pale as she swayed in the doorway. "What's wrong, sweet girl?"

Josie clutched her midsection. "My tummy hurts." She folded over and vomited all over the gleaming wood floor.

Elin leaped forward, but Marc got there before she did. He scooped up Josie out of the mess and soothed her as she broke into noisy sobs. She vomited again, all down the front of him.

"I'll clean her up." He took her across the hall to the bathroom. "Can you grab her some other clothes?"

She rushed up the steps to her daughter's bedroom and yanked open her pajama drawer. When she got back to the bathroom, Josie had quit crying and was lying quietly on his bare shoulder with her eyes closed. Her soiled pajamas were at his feet along with his shirt. When he saw her, he sat on the toilet seat, and she helped him pull on the clean pjs.

"I think she's asleep." His hazel eyes held a shadow of worry. "Do we need to take her to the ER?"

"Children often get intestinal upsets." She touched her daughter's head. "She doesn't have a fever. I think she's fine. Just put her back to bed, if you would. I'll clean up the mess in the office."

"I'll do it when I come back down. I think I need to learn father-type things."

She gaped after him as he carried her daughter back to bed. She'd known he was a good man, but this was above and beyond the call of duty.

TWENTY-ONE

After his shower on Saturday morning, Marc finally got the last trace of vomit odor out of his nose. He popped a mint as he poked his head into Josie's bedroom and saw Elin slipping flip-flops on Josie's small feet. The little Yorkie lay stretched out beside them. Beautiful mother, sweet daughter, and dog. All that was needed was the father to complete the picture of a perfect family.

"Mr. Marc!" Josie escaped her mother and ran to cling to his leg.

He hugged her tightly, her tiny form already so familiar. She'd taken complete possession of his heart. He picked her up, and she hugged his neck. "You feeling okay?" He looked to Elin for confirmation too.

She smiled and nodded, looking downright alluring in her close-fitting denim capris and green tee. Her feet were bare, the toes tipped in pale orange. "I slept with her, and there was nary a peep all night. Just a tummy upset."

He averted his gaze from the V where her T-shirt plunged. "Glad to hear it." She was too darned cute for his peace of mind. If he wasn't needed to protect his daughter, he'd be out of here so fast, he'd leave a wake behind the boat.

Josie wiggled to be put down, and he set her small feet on the floor. She ran for the door calling Abby. He started to follow her, but Elin spoke his name, and he turned with a lifted brow.

She took a step closer. "I just wanted to thank you for last night. Most people can't stomach cleaning up a sick kid, especially if they aren't used to it. You didn't even retch once."

He grinned. "I held it in, but I admit the stench about brought me to my knees."

She inhaled, and her gaze locked with his. "I think I'm about ready to tell her the truth."

He felt the impact deep in his gut. His little girl would know he was her father. How would she react? Was he even ready for it himself? The thought of disappointing his daughter caused him pain.

Elin's aqua eyes took on a shadow. "You have a funny expression. You don't want to tell her?"

He straightened. "Of course I do. I just hope she's not upset. She loved Tim."

"She doesn't really remember much about him. Only what she's been told. And she knows his picture, of course. She loves you already, Marc. You don't need to worry."

Abby's voice called down the hall. "Hey, you two, I could use some help out here."

Marc's pulse kicked. Was Josie throwing up again? He rushed down the stairs with Elin on his heels. In the kitchen, he found Abby with her hands in bread dough. Josie held out dough-coated hands to Max, who eagerly licked at them.

Elin scooped up the little dog. "He shouldn't be eating flour."

"Tell me about it." Abby swiped a lock of hair out of her eyes with her forearm. "After you get her cleaned up, could one of you get started on putting potatoes in the oven?"

When Abby looked at him, Marc realized this was going to be up to him. When was the last time he had more than pizza and takeout? It was about time he learned his way around the kitchen.

When Josie came to stay with him, she needed more than breaded chicken strips and French fries.

He hooked Josie's waist with his arm and carted her toward the half bath off the entry. She smiled up at him, her dimple flashing, then planted a doughy hand on his cheek. "Hey, you did that on purpose."

She giggled and nodded. "I can make you look like a ghost." Her hand went toward his face again, and he flinched back. His instinctive movement made her giggle harder, and he had to grin. "You little scamp. I should dunk you in the bathtub."

"What's a scamp?"

"It's a playful little girl." He set her on the bathroom floor and turned on the water, then put her hands under the stream.

By the time they were done, he had more water on him and on the floor than he'd expected. He backed into the opposite wall and knocked off a vase sitting on a wall shelf behind him. It shattered on the tile floor, and he bent to pick up the pieces.

"Mr. Marc, what's that say?" Josie pointed to a decorative mirror above the shelf.

The smile on his face vanished when he saw words written in lipstick. The garish shade of red added to the ominous tone.

It's cold in the grave. He will soon find out.

Another threat, this one directed at him. Had the killer left it there Thursday night when he shot the arrow? This bathroom wasn't used often, and the vase might have covered up the message. "It's just lipstick." He dried her hands and hustled her out of the room.

When he headed through the living room, he saw Ruby knitting in her chair. "There's Grandma. Why don't you keep her company a little while? She could probably use some help holding the yarn."

Josie ran to her grandma and climbed onto the sofa beside her. Marc left them and went back to the kitchen. "Have either of you used the half bath under the stairs lately?"

"What's wrong? Is it a mess?" Elin started for the door, but he grabbed her arm. She stared at him with wide eyes. "What is it?"

"I broke a vase. The one on the shelf."

Relief lit her eyes. "That's fine. I'll get the broom and dustpan."

He released her arm and shook his head. "There was something written in lipstick on the mirror." He told her about the message.

Her eyes widened, and she gulped. "He was in here?"

"Looks like it. I'm praying he hasn't been here since the other night, that this isn't a new message."

"Max heard something last night," she reminded him.

He nodded. "I didn't see anything though. Unless one of you moved that vase when you dusted, I think it's safe to assume he was here on Thursday night and wrote that note."

"I haven't even been in that bathroom," Abby said. "This is scary though, Elin. I still think you should come stay with me when I leave this afternoon. I don't like you being out here alone."

"I'm not alone. And this threat seems to be against Marc, not me."

The concern in her eyes made his pulse stutter. But maybe Abby was right. What if he couldn't protect Elin and Josie? Being in town might be better, though home invasions happened even more often in cities. Still, someone might respond to a cry for help.

Or not.

He pulled out his cell phone. "I think I'll call and get some alarms on the doors and windows."

⌒

This skirt wouldn't do. It was much too short. Sara changed for the third time, this time pulling on a pair of black slacks that weren't too tight. The pink-and-white sleeveless top showed just a hint of cleavage, so maybe it should go too. She flung open her closet and surveyed her options. The white jacket over the top would hide her curves a little better.

She yanked it on and turned to survey herself in the full-length mirror on the door. Just the right touch in the nick of time since she heard footsteps on the walk outside. She quickly slashed on a bit of pink lip gloss and hurried to the living room as the doorbell pealed.

Ben smiled through the screen when she opened the entry door. "I'm five minutes early, but I couldn't wait any longer." He held up a bouquet of daisies. "These seemed the kind of flower you'd like. Not pretentious but with a beauty all their own."

Smooth, very smooth. She hid a smile as she pushed open the door. "Come in and let me put them in water." She took the flowers from him.

"You look very nice. I like your hair loose."

Maybe she should have put it up. "Thanks." He was eyeing her like he might lunge at any minute. "You look nice too." And he did. His khakis appeared new, and the light-blue shirt he wore was a good foil for his blond hair and blue eyes.

She led him down the entry hall to the living room on the right. "I'll be right back. There are chocolate-chip cookies on the coffee table."

"My favorite." He looked around. "Nice room. I like sea cottages. They make it feel like summer all the time. And this peach lets me know we're at the beach."

"This place was a wreck when I bought it. It's been fun to fix up." The old plantation cottage had been in bad disrepair. She'd refinished the maple floors and repaired the plaster walls. The last bathroom had just been redone too. "I'll be right back." She went down the hall to the kitchen, painted a pale yellow.

She put down the flowers and leaned against the counter, then inhaled. What was she doing? How could she blithely date another man when her heart still wanted only Josh? It wasn't really fair to Ben to get his hopes up. She could see this would end in heartache for him. He liked her way too much already. Could she ever feel anything for him? He was handsome enough.

But he wasn't Josh.

She was tempted to call Elin and ask her to call with an emergency. Shaking her head, she found a vase and filled it with water. She could handle one evening. Only time would tell if anything could come of this. She'd never expected to fall for Josh either. It just happened out of the blue. Lightning could strike again, couldn't it?

Carrying the vase of flowers, she went back to the living room where Ben perused the pictures on her shelves. He had a picture of her with the Coastie team in his hands. Josh had his arm draped casually around her shoulders in the photo. That had been a fun day. They went windsurfing and sat around a fire on the beach. An eternity ago when Josh hadn't been avoiding her like she was a man-o'-war who might sting at any moment.

He turned when she put the vase on the coffee table. His gaze was warm as it swept over her. "You've been with this team awhile?"

She nodded. "Three years. We work well together."

"You and Josh look pretty cozy. You ever date him?" His tone was too casual.

She bristled, then realized he had a right to wonder if she had any kind of relationship going on. What could she say, really? In spite of all her hopes and dreams, nothing had developed with Josh. She needed to accept the fact that nothing ever would.

She shrugged. "I'm good friends with all my team. We hang out, watch movies, and joke around. You know how it is."

"Yes, I sure do." He put the picture down.

Two could pry. She might as well find out about him too. "How about you? Any serious relationships?"

"I'm sure Elin filled you in. I was her brother-in-law once upon a time. And married to her friend Kerri." His grin widened. "You know how it is when you're in the military. You get shifted around too often to build a relationship if the spouse doesn't understand."

"Is that what happened with you and Kerri?"

He shrugged. "We just had different goals in life. She hated traveling, and I took every assignment I could. But I'm tired now, ready to settle down."

She inhaled and turned away at his admission he was ready to settle down. She'd thought she was too, but not with just anyone.

He came up behind her, and his breath stirred her hair. "Good job on that boat interception the other day. I hear one of the guys threw something overboard."

She turned to face him, then stepped back. He was a little too far into her personal space. "My friend and I found one of the boxes on the beach near her home. Heroin."

"No kidding. Our job of keeping out the drugs gets harder and harder. I heard we're looking for a drug lord out of Miami. I've been looking for him, but no luck so far."

"We haven't seen him either. He's pretty elusive from what I hear." She was bored with the conversation, but it was better than talking about Josh. Poor Ben's small talk proved he was just as nervous as she was.

She grabbed her purse. "I'm ready if you are."

His ready smile came back. "Sure thing. I'm ready for some seafood and Spock."

She smiled and followed him to the door. Maybe this evening wouldn't be so bad. He was a nice enough guy, right out there with how he felt. She didn't see him taking one step forward and two steps back in a relationship.

TWENTY-TWO

The SUV sped through the labyrinth of streets in Virginia Beach. Once Sunday lunch was over, they'd decided to make a quick run to try to catch Bambi. Abby and Josie had gone to town with them and would spend the afternoon at the festival again. Her mom and Kalianne were working in the garden.

Elin just *had* to figure this out. Then maybe the dreams would stop. Maybe then she could get her life back. She consulted her phone's GPS and pointed for Marc to turn right. He whipped the vehicle around the corner and slowed to stare at the numbers on the houses. "There it is."

The house was a neat beach bungalow with weathered gray shake shingles and white shutters. Honeysuckle rambled up the porch railing and spilled over the rock rim of the garden. The plant climbed so high, she could only see the movement of the swing and the dim outline of the people in it as it lazily swung back and forth.

Marc turned off the SUV. "Ready?"

She inhaled and nodded, then swung open her door. Would the woman recognize her from the newspaper article? And what about the man with her? Her head high, she walked up the flag-stone path and mounted the front steps with Marc close on her heels. When she spied the woman's face, her flip-flops seemed rooted to the painted porch boards.

I know the woman staring at me from the swing.

She gulped and forced a smile. "Bambi. I hope we're not interrupting."

Bambi shot the man beside her a panicked glance, then rose and smiled. "I think you must have the wrong person. My name is Barbara." Her low, husky voice was the type that would attract men like bees to an empty soda bottle.

The man rose also. Dressed in a suit and tie, he appeared to be a wealthy businessman. Every blond hair was in order, and his shoes gleamed. "Who are you anyway? What a ridiculous name to call my wife." He gripped her waist protectively.

Elin glanced at Marc. Now what? Barbara's demeanor left no doubt she didn't want her husband to know anything about the cruise and what had gone on there.

Marc clasped Elin's arm and took a step back. "Sorry we disturbed you." He sent her a warning glance and led her down the steps to his SUV. She slid in, and he shut the door behind her.

When he got in the driver's side, she frowned and shook her head. "I wanted to talk to her."

"We will. I got the feeling her husband was about to leave. We'll drive down the street and wait a few minutes." He started the engine and pulled his vehicle away from the curb.

She glanced in the rearview mirror and saw the man kiss Bambi, then stride to the silver Corvette in the drive. "You're right. He's leaving."

Marc drove around the block. When they pulled up to the curb again, the sports car was nowhere in sight. Bambi wasn't on the porch any longer either.

"I hope she didn't leave too," Elin said.

Marc turned off the key and slid it into his pocket. "She wasn't dressed to go anywhere. She didn't even have shoes on. A woman like her would have on makeup before she even went to the grocery store."

Good insight. She swung open her door and waited for him to join her before heading back to the porch. They didn't even have to ring the doorbell. Bambi opened the bright-blue door before they could press the button.

"What do you want? Why are you tormenting me?" Tears hung on her lashes.

"May we come in? I'm sure you'd rather the neighbors didn't hear our questions." Marc's tone dared her to disagree.

Bambi bit her lip, then shoved open the screen door. "My husband will be back in an hour. I can't have you here."

"Our questions won't take long." Marc held open the door for Elin.

Inside, the cool gray walls mingled with yellow accents and gave a welcoming feel. The white linen furniture in the living room looked new. Whitewashed floors and white trim gave the room a modern look. It all appeared newly redecorated.

Bambi indicated the sofa before settling into an overstuffed yellow chair. "Have a seat and let's get this over with."

Elin perched on the edge of the sofa. "I want to know what happened on the cruise between you and Laura Watson."

Bambi folded her arms across her ample breasts. "I don't know what you're talking about."

"We can wait until your husband comes back to answer these questions if you'd rather." Marc's mild voice contrasted with his steely expression.

Bambi flushed. "Look, it was nothing, okay? She was all bent out of shape because we had a simple dance."

An image flashed into Elin's head. "You went back to his room, didn't you? And spent the night." She didn't know how she knew it, but when Bambi bit her lip and looked away, Elin knew the knowledge was true.

"It was just a shipboard fling. It meant nothing. It was only one night, but my husband wouldn't understand. You can't tell him!"

Marc leaned forward. "Your marriage is none of our business. But we need to know what Laura said to you. And how she acted."

"She was like a crazy woman! She caught us in the hall outside his room the next morning. She flew at me and would have scratched my face if Theo hadn't grabbed her. It made no sense. I mean, didn't she know he was just fooling around with her? That kind of man isn't the type to stay around more than a night or two."

"This Theo. What can you tell me about him?" Marc asked.

Her forehead furrowed. "Not much. I don't know his first name."

Elin felt a kick in her gut. "His first name is Ron." Marc hadn't told her that, but she somehow knew it.

"Do you think he could have murdered Laura Watson?"

Bambi laughed. "You've never met him, have you? He'd have to actually care about a woman to get mad enough to harm her. He had a bevy of women on that trip. Laura and I weren't the only ones." She twisted her wedding ring on her hand. "And don't tell my husband, but Theo was with me when the Watson woman died. He couldn't possibly be the murderer."

Now what? The death clearly had nothing to do with this love triangle. She glanced at Marc and recognized the furrow in his brow. The problem he was working out in his head was unpleasant.

⌒

"I'm in the kitchen," Sara called through the open window when Marc pressed the doorbell of her cottage. "The door's unlocked."

He stepped through the screen door and walked on the

gleaming wood floors to the kitchen. "I smell coffee." The rich aroma teased his nose.

She was dressed in khaki shorts and a pink top that showed off her toned arms. "I put it on as soon as you called. You sounded serious. What's up?"

He accepted the cup of coffee she pressed into his hand. "Just some more questions."

She gestured for him to follow her to the back deck. "About Laura or Lacy?"

Hummingbirds fluttered at a feeder a few feet away from the chair he dropped into. "A little of both."

She frowned as she leaned back in her chair. "I'm not sure what that means."

Sara wasn't going to like the things he had to ask. He took a sip of his coffee. "How well do you know Josh? You've worked with him for three years, and I know you hoped a relationship would develop that hasn't."

She put down her coffee cup. "Why are you asking about Josh? I thought you wanted to talk about Laura and Lacy."

"He was there when both women died. I find that a little strange."

Her eyes widened, and she leaned forward. "That's ridiculous, Marc! Just because Josh is skittish about relationships doesn't mean he's some kind of killer."

"No, but it makes me wonder about him. I looked up his IQ. It's in the genius range. His father died in prison, and his mother was an alcoholic. Those are all characteristics on the list of things serial killers have in common." He inhaled. "And Josh and Laura went to the same high school. He even dated her a couple of times when he was a senior. Will's wife found some notes and scanned them for me last night. Will was looking at Josh too."

Her color high, she rose and paced the deck. "I can't believe you would even entertain a thought like this. Josh is a good man. He's had a hard life, yes, but that should be cause for compassion from you, not condemnation."

Her reaction almost made him question his suspicions. Almost. "When did he get to Elin's house in Virginia Beach?"

She stared at him. "Fine. I'll answer your questions, and you'll see how far off base you are. He got there about an hour after I called the police. He said he heard it on the scanner in his car."

"Many killers like to go back to the scene and see what's happening. Don't you find it odd he was so close? Clearly he was already in town."

She dropped back into her chair. "And that's a crime? Everyone on the island goes to Virginia Beach to shop. His mother lives here. I'm sure he was checking on her. As you said, she's an alcoholic. He worries about her. He often comes over on his days off."

"How did he seem when he came in?"

Her gray eyes held sorrow. "Elin and I both needed him. He came right in and made sure we were okay. The police seemed glad to have him too since we were both so upset. He helped calm us down enough to answer questions coherently."

He took a sip of his coffee, then set it on the patio table. "Does he play the guitar?"

She nodded slowly. "He has an old guitar that was his dad's that he strums on sometimes. He taught himself the chords. But anyone has access to a guitar string."

He gritted his teeth at her stubborn refusal to look at facts. "These things all add up, Sara. You are around him a lot. I'd like you to watch him, see if he reveals anything he shouldn't know about those murders."

She set her coffee down so hard it sloshed over the top of the cup. "I won't spy on him! You can't ask that of me. You know how I feel about him."

He looked at her steadily. "What if you're wrong about him, Sara?"

She didn't flinch away from his gaze. "What if *you* are? And then he finds out you suspected him of such a thing—and even worse—that I helped you? He would never forgive me."

"What about Elin? Are you willing to look the other way when she's in danger?"

Her color got even higher. "I'm not doing anything to harm her. And don't you dare suggest to her that she should distrust Josh. You have no evidence to base this on. It's not fair, Marc. I can't believe you could even entertain any suspicions toward a fine man like Josh. I mean, he puts his life on the line for other people all the time."

"Just because he's a Coastie doesn't mean he's incapable of murder."

"Well, I know Josh. You're on the wrong path here."

He shrugged. "No harm, no foul from looking into it."

"There's harm, all right! When you're looking at him, you're ignoring finding the real killer."

Darkness often hid inside the most innocuous face. She hadn't seen it as often as he had.

"Just keep your eyes open, okay? You can do that much for your best friend."

She stared at him. "Look somewhere else, okay? It's not Josh." She rose and scooped up their coffee cups. "You can let yourself out."

TWENTY-THREE

The old lady was driving her crazy. Kalianne wiped her muddy hands on her jeans. "We planted plenty of beans, Ruby. We don't need any more."

Dressed in red capris and an orange blouse, Ruby looked the picture of a crazy old lady. She wore two different sandals, one brown and one white. Her graying blond hair hung limply under a straw hat.

When Ruby looked at her with a blank expression, Kalianne snatched the seeds out of her hands. "No more planting. We have enough."

Ruby whimpered and reached for the seeds. "But I want to plant more."

Kalianne slapped her hand away. "I said no more!" She tried to ignore the twinge of sympathy at the way Ruby's blue eyes filled with tears. "How about you water the seeds? There's a hose on the side of the house."

Ruby's expression cleared. "I'll get the hose." She trotted toward the house, moving fast for someone her age.

At last a bit of respite. Kalianne sat on a stone wall at the end of the garden and inhaled a breath of fresh air. She dug out her cell phone from the pocket of her cutoffs and called her brother. "Hey, it's me. They found a crate of heroin. Is there more for me to find?"

"I told you I'd call you tonight. I can't talk now."

"Just say yes or no. I've got a window of about an hour to look for more. Is one crate all there is?"

"Hang on a minute. Hey, guys, I need to run to my car a minute. I'll be right back."

She heard male voices in the background, then his footsteps sounded on tile. Traffic noise rumbled in the distance, and a door slammed.

"I'm here," he said. "They found just one crate? Who found it?"

"Coasties. They identified it as heroin and called the cops."

He swore. "Just what I didn't need."

"How many boxes?"

"One more. It's about a foot square brown box. Sealed up too and locked. Don't open it."

More drugs. How boring. "Okay. Anything else you want from me?"

"Have you found the pouch yet?"

She rolled her eyes. "No, but I've only started looking."

"Any way you can get those people out of the house for good?"

"Well, I could burn the house down, I guess." She was only half kidding. A constant dream of hers since childhood had been to burn down a house. She could only imagine the thrill of watching a consuming fire flare into the night.

"Don't be stupid."

She crossed her legs and glanced around for Ruby, who had been gone longer than she expected. "So I'll look for that box this afternoon. Anything you want from inside the house?" Maybe she could burn it down once she found that pouch.

"Just that pouch! I can't believe you let that old bat get the best of you."

The tension in his voice told her she'd pushed him as far as she should. "I'd better go check on that old lady. I'll let you know if I find anything."

"Okay, I'll call you tonight around nine. Thanks for doing this, Kalianne. You won't regret it. You'll be a Cambodian princess when this is all over."

The comment made her smile. "You'd better come through for me. I'm already sick of being buried out here. I'm not too keen on the thought of having to work here for even another day."

"Then find that pouch and that box and you can get out of there." A male voice shouted something indistinguishable in the distance. "Listen, I have to go. Keep me posted."

"I will." She ended the call. "Ruby?" Walking toward the side of the house, she wanted to scream with frustration. If there was one thing she hated, it was not knowing fully what was going on. She'd bet money her brother had only told her half the truth of all of this.

She rounded the corner. No Ruby. The hose lay uncoiled in the dirt with water running out the end. She shut off the faucet, then went to the front of the house calling her name. Elin was still gone, so she wouldn't have distracted Ruby. Kalianne looked over the landscape. A movement at the top of the cliff caught her eye.

Ruby stood at the very edge looking down into the waves crashing on the rocks below. She swayed as she stood. Kalianne's voice caught in her throat. She didn't dare shout for fear Ruby would be so startled she'd fall. She ran for the path and climbed the rocks. When she reached the top, she saw the old woman still standing at the edge. Taking care to move as noiselessly as possible, she hurried toward Ruby and grabbed her arm.

Ruby tried to pull her arm free to go back to the edge. "Owen is calling for me. I want to go to him."

"Elin and Josie need you. Let's go find them." When the woman continued to struggle, Kalianne slipped her hand into her pocket and grabbed a syringe. She uncapped it and plunged the needle into Ruby's arm, then pressed the plunger.

That should keep her under control for a while.

———

Elin pushed her windswept hair out of her eyes and crossed her legs. The Hope Beach sheriff's office was quiet, but then it was dinnertime. She jiggled her leg and looked out the window. Across the street Abby helped Josie with her ice-cream cone. Marc had picked them up in Kill Devil Hills on their way back from Virginia Beach.

"Nervous?" Marc went to the coffee service on a table along one wall. "I think this is probably coffee from yesterday." He felt the pot. "Yep, it's cold."

"I don't want any, thanks." She spared a peek at him.

Dressed in jeans and a pale-yellow shirt, he looked all male. His hair curled a bit at the collar, and his eyes were shadowed. His presence in her house had grown more disturbing with every passing day. She didn't want to feel this pull toward him.

The sheriff breezed in. Tom Bourne seemed to fill the room with his presence. He went to his desk and wasted no time in pleasantries. "I heard from the Virginia Beach police. I told them what you said about Josh Holman, and they're looking into his whereabouts during the time of the murder."

Elin gasped. "Josh? He couldn't be involved. He's a Coastie."

Both men stared at her. "Any profession has a few bad apples, Elin," Marc said.

She had to convince them. "You can't seriously be suspicious of him. He's a great guy. Just ask Sara."

"Sara is a little biased. I'm surprised to see you taking up for him though. You don't even know him that well."

"I know him through Sara. She's a good judge of people. If she loves him, he's worth it." She glanced at the sheriff. "What else did they say? Did they find any forensic evidence?"

He shrugged. "They found hair samples, but those might belong to you or Lacy. They're checking out everything, but it's too soon to tell. And since you brought up forensics, I heard back from the state boys about the arrow. It was clean. They are heading this way to question Josh though. I'm supposed to have him here in a couple of hours."

"I think it's ridiculous. Whoever killed Lacy murdered Laura too. That couldn't have been Josh."

"He was onboard that ship too, Elin. And he dated Laura in high school."

At Marc's words, Elin sank back in her chair. Was it possible the killer could be Josh? She shook her head. "I have those memories, Marc. He doesn't have that signet ring. His build is all wrong too. Don't waste time looking at him. I'd be frightened of Josh if he were the killer."

"You don't know that for sure," Marc said. "Those memories might not be as accurate as we think. You might be experiencing emotions about him because of hearing Sara talk about him. There are lots of reasons why he might not cause alarm bells to go off for you. It could have been anyone on that ship, Elin."

She was getting nowhere with him. Maybe she would have to figure this out by herself. No one seemed to be listening. "Is that all?"

Tom nodded. "Not much to go on at the moment. The Virginia Beach police would like to talk to you again after they speak with Josh. You'll be around?"

She nodded. "I've told them all I know though. We didn't see anything that might tell them who did this."

"I'll send them your way." Tom rose and went around to open the door for them. "I'll let you know if I hear anything."

Elin strode down the hall, her heels clicking on the tile floor. She wanted to get far away from Marc. He was supposed to be helping her find the killer, not derailing law enforcement onto a useless rabbit trail.

"Wait up, Elin." Marc's steps sounded behind her.

She ignored his call and increased her steps until she burst through the exit door and out into the sunshine where she could breathe. His hand on her arm brought her up short. She jerked out of his grip and turned to face him.

"Don't shoot the messenger. We have to examine every possibility."

She pointed her finger at him. "No, we need to hone in on the real killer. Your obsession with Josh is going to get me murdered." She broke off, her voice choked.

"I'm going to protect you."

"Don't delude yourself. A determined killer can get to me unless we find him first. And it's *not* Josh."

He blinked at her vehemence. "You seem to feel strongly about this."

She put her hand to her heart. "I *know* it here, Marc. Josh isn't a killer. That murderer may be watching us even now, toying with us and waiting for his chance. We can't afford to get sidetracked."

His hazel eyes narrowed. "Okay. I'll look at the rest of the passenger manifest."

"What about that Theo guy? You didn't have a good feeling about him. I'd like to hear his voice myself and see if I have any reaction to it."

"Barbara cleared him. Or don't you believe her?"

"I'd rather doubt her word than suspect Josh." The tightness in her chest loosened. He was listening.

He finally nodded. "We'll see who else we can find. But there's something else I want to talk to you about."

She didn't like his somber expression. "What's wrong?"

"My parents are coming tomorrow to meet Josie. We need to tell her tonight who I am."

She bit her lip. She'd told him she was nearly ready, but now that the moment was here, she wasn't sure. "It's too soon, Marc. She needs time to get to know you."

"She already loves me, Elin. You know it as well as I do. We have to tell her."

She wanted to object again, but he was right. She glanced across the street at her daughter, happily licking her Superman cone. "Let me think about how to do it."

A homeless man shuffled by with his shopping cart piled high. He looked at them as if he knew no one would help him. Marc pulled a twenty out of his pocket. "Would you like some dinner?"

The man blinked, and a bit of hope crept into his eyes. His dirty fingers closed around the bill Marc offered. "Thank you, sir. I haven't eaten in two days. You have a good heart." He turned toward the hot dog stand.

Elin gazed up at him. How many men noticed the homeless? "Why'd you do that?"

"I saw the way he looked at Josie's ice cream. He was hungry."

She couldn't look away from his earnest expression.

"What? You're looking at me funny."

"You're not all macho man, are you? You have a lovely soul, Marc."

A hint of color came to his face. "I'm nothing special that way, Elin."

She clamped her lips shut. She was liking everything about him these days. This was dangerous ground she treaded.

He crossed the street to join Abby and Josie, and she stared after him. She pressed her hand against her breastbone. Maybe she should lie down. Her lonely heart was yearning for him way too much.

TWENTY-FOUR

Elin put the glasses of lemonade on the coffee table and smiled as she watched Marc frolic on the floor with Josie on his back. She loved horsey rides, and she clung to his shirt with both hands as she shrieked with delight. Max ran around them barking frantically. The little Yorkie had already become part of the family.

Josie kicked her small bare heels into Marc's ribs. "Again!"

He groaned and rolled over, snatching her off his back as he did. He cradled his daughter to his chest and breathed heavily. "You're making an old man out of me, kiddo."

Josie lay in his embrace for a few moments before she struggled to sit up. She straddled his chest, then bounced up and down, grinning when he let out a moan with every thump.

He finally sat up and ran his hand through his wild hair. "Your mommy and I want to talk to you." He thumbed a mint out of the roll in his hand.

Elin's smile vanished. Her pulse throbbed in her throat. How on earth did she explain something like this to a four-year-old? She needed to take the lead, though, or Marc would. And this should come from her. What did he know about small children?

She cleared her throat. "Sit up here by Mommy a minute, Josie. I have something very exciting to tell you."

Josie scrambled to her feet. "Are we going to the zoo?"

"No, it's even better than the zoo."

Josie climbed onto the sofa beside her. "Nothing is better than the zoo. Unless I'm getting a baby brother. Is that the special news?"

Elin couldn't meet Marc's amused gaze. "No, it's not a baby either. This is even better."

Josie frowned as if the very idea of something better than a baby was silly. "Did you buy me something?"

"No, it's not that. Just listen to me for a minute, honey." She glanced around for a prop. She spied Josie's picture on the end table and scooped it up. In the photo, Tim had her on his lap. They were both smiling into the camera. "This was you when you were one. See your dark hair?"

Josie touched her brown curls. "It's still dark. Not red like yours." Her tone indicated she was very displeased by that.

"No, it's not red like mine. It's not blond either. It's a beautiful shade of brown, the prettiest color there is. And your eyes are such a pretty color, part green and part gold. You look exactly like yourself, and I love everything about you."

Josie smiled and leaned in for a hug. "I love everything about you too, Mommy."

Elin held her close and pressed a kiss onto her daughter's soft hair, smelling of sunshine and coconut shampoo. This wasn't going to be easy. "Sometimes a little girl is lucky enough to have two daddies."

Josie pulled away and her brow furrowed. "Two daddies?"

"Uh-huh. One daddy brings her home and loves her, and the other daddy is where she gets her hair and eyes. He loves her too." Elin felt mired in topics too complex to explain to a small child. "You like Mr. Marc, don't you?"

Josie looked over at Marc. "I don't want him to ever go away."

His mouth softened into a smile. "I'm not planning on ever leaving you, Josie. I will always be around to help you."

Pain squeezed Elin's chest as she watched the two exchange a tender glance of devotion. What had she done? No wonder Marc had been enraged. If ever a man was meant to be a father, he was. The attachment between them could almost be touched.

Elin managed a smile. "Well, there is something special about Mr. Marc. He's the kind of daddy who gives a little girl her dark hair and pretty eyes. In fact, he's *your* daddy."

Josie had no reaction at first except to stare at him. Then she slid off the sofa and went to where he still sat on the floor. She fingered his hair, then ran a finger over his eyelid. "My hair is like yours. Your eyes have yellow spots in them too."

"That's right. I'm your daddy. I would have been with you before now, but I didn't know about you."

Elin tried not to feel hurt at his remark. Marc wouldn't try to turn Josie against her. At least she didn't think he would. She'd always thought him an honorable man. "There's another surprise, honey. Your daddy has a mommy and daddy too. They are your grandma and grandpa."

"I already have Grandma Ruby. And Grandma and Grandpa Summerall."

Though Josie hadn't seen Tim's parents much, she looked at their picture often and asked about them. They lived in California, and she'd only seen them twice in her lifetime. "I know, but you're a lucky little girl because Mr. Marc's parents are really nice. They don't live very far away, and they are going to come here tomorrow."

Josie absorbed the information. "They're nice?" She looked to Marc for confirmation.

"They are very nice."

"Should I still call you Mr. Marc? I'd rather call you Daddy."

Marc swallowed and his throat clicked. "I would like it very much if you wanted to call me Daddy."

"Okay. Can I go find Grandma Ruby and tell her?"

"She's napping," Elin said quickly. This news needed to come from her. She'd hoped to tell her mother when she got back from town, but Mom had been strangely sleepy all day and hadn't woken from her nap. "I'll go see if she's ready to wake up."

Heaven only knew how her mother would take this news. Or even if she could totally comprehend it.

———

Tuesday morning dawned with overcast skies. Rain showers should arrive by lunch. Marc threw a ball to little Max and kept an eye on the pier. His parents should be arriving anytime, hopefully ahead of the storm. Elin had been unable to rouse her mother last night, so Ruby still didn't know she would have to share Josie with another set of grandparents.

He gulped at the thought of telling his parents this news. He should have told them on the phone about Josie, but he wanted to break it to them in person. How would they react? They'd always been so proud of him, often telling their friends what a good Christian he was. Oh, he was a moral, upstanding citizen, all right. He hated disappointing them, but he'd wrestled his guilt to the ground with God, and that was all that really mattered. His parents would get over it.

The putter of a motor came to his ears. He tossed the ball one last time, then went down to the harbor dock to meet them. They thought they were just coming for a nice week at the island. He lifted a hand in greeting as the boat neared.

His father wore his old fishing hat, stained and floppy from many years of use. Lures circled the crown. No one would guess he'd been a well-known attorney with clients from all over the world. His grin appeared, and he rose to toss a line to Marc.

His mother waved gaily. She wore a pink sundress that strained a bit at the seams. She'd refused to go up the one size necessary since she'd hit menopause. Christine and Frank Everton had met in high school and married at nineteen. They were still the most loving couple Marc had ever seen. He'd always wanted to have a marriage like theirs someday, but that seemed a more and more unlikely dream.

Marc tied off the boat, then helped his mother step onto the dock. They looked younger than their early sixties. They'd stayed active over the years with golf and tennis. His father had recently retired from his law practice, and they both kept busy with charities and friends.

He hugged his mother and inhaled the familiar scent of her perfume, Chanel No. 5. "Glad you could come."

His father clapped a hand on his shoulder and squinted toward the house. "Nice place here, son. Where's Elin? We're looking forward to seeing her. And she has a little girl. Your mom will be in her glory spoiling her."

Marc managed a grin. "Yeah, well, I have something to tell you before we go find the others."

His mother hugged him. "You're getting married. I *knew* it." She released him and patted his arm. "You don't need to worry, son. We'll be happy to welcome any woman you choose into the family. You have good judgment."

Marc's neck heated, and he shook his head. "It's not that, Mom." He cleared his throat. "I shouldn't throw this at you so fast, but I didn't want to drop a bombshell on the phone." He gestured to the fishing pier to his right. "Let's sit down a minute." He led them along the shore to the pier, then sat on the edge of the boards and dangled his legs over the side. His mother joined him quickly, but it took his dad a minute to maneuver down with his bad knee.

"What's this all about, Marc?" His dad frowned. The frown that said, "Get to the point and make it quick." His attorney face.

"It's about Josie."

"Is something wrong with her? Oh, that poor little baby. Where is she?" His mother started to get up.

Marc stopped her with a hand on her arm. "She's perfect in every way, Mom. I'm sure you'll agree because . . . sh-she's my daughter."

An explosion couldn't have caused more of a reaction. His mother blanched, and his father nearly fell into the ocean. Marc steadied his dad and kept his hand on his mom's arm. The situation could go either way, though he was betting on his mother's desire for grandchildren.

She stared into his face. She must have seen the truth in his eyes because she nodded. "She's four, right?"

"Yeah." He could see the wheels turning as she did the math, since she'd attended Elin's wedding. "I didn't know when she married Tim. You know me well enough to realize I would never have abandoned my baby. Elin had a bad time when her dad died and . . ." He looked away. "Anyway, I don't want you to think badly of her. She told Tim, and he wanted to marry her anyway. He never wanted me to know."

His mother shook off his grip and got up with difficulty in her tight dress and high-heeled sandals. "I think it's scandalous she never told you. And us. We had a right to know. I've longed for grandchildren forever, Marc. *Forever!* And you. You've missed years of your daughter's life. How dare she deny us the knowledge we had a little granddaughter?"

Marc scrambled to his feet too and stopped her before she could march toward the house. "Calm down, Mom. Tim made her promise to keep it to herself. He loved Josie and was good to her. I'm grateful for that." No reason to tell them about the killer just yet. They had enough to absorb with the news about Josie.

His dad struggled to his feet. "How are you handling this, son? Did she just tell you because she wants child support?"

Trust his dad to look at the legalities. "I was shocked. And Elin hasn't mentioned support." He made a mental note to start writing her a check every week. And there was no reason to tell them she wouldn't have admitted Josie was his if he hadn't guessed. It would make them think even more poorly of her. "I already love Josie. You will too. She looks just like me."

His mother's face crumbled at his words. "Like you?"

"Brown curls, hazel eyes. She has your chin, Mom." He offered her his roll of mints. "Here, have a mint."

She thrust them away. "A mint won't calm me like it does you." Her eyes swam with tears, and she clasped her hands together. "I can't wait to see her. What does she know?"

"She's only four, so all she knows is I'm the kind of daddy who gives a little girl her hair and eyes. It was hard to explain it to her last night. She's excited about having another grandma and grandpa though." He told them about Ruby's dementia.

"Poor little mite. We want to help in any way we can," his mother said. "Can we meet her now?"

He nodded toward the house as Elin and Josie headed their direction. "Here they come now. Take it easy on Elin. She's had a rough time."

But he was speaking to the wind because his mom was already flying toward her granddaughter.

TWENTY-FIVE

The sound of the chopper rotors faded into the distance as Sara walked toward her car. The bright-blue bowl of sky overhead did nothing to lift her mood. She hadn't been able to keep her gaze from Josh all day. Her cousin's insinuations—no, downright *accusations*—kept poking themselves into her thoughts.

But this was *Josh*, not some stranger lurking in the shadows. She knew him, knew his dedication to saving people, his concern for other people.

"Hey, Sara," Josh called from behind her.

She turned to wait for him and Curtis. They'd both changed into jeans and T-shirts. Josh wore a Dodgers one and his well-worn matching ball cap. They fell into step together and walked toward the parking lot. "I was just heading over for ice cream. Want to come?"

Curtis grinned. "Not today. Amy and I are meeting with the adoption agency. We got a call last night. They've got a little girl, two days old. I think we're going to get her today."

"Seriously?" Sara squealed and hugged him. "That is awesome news!"

"Amy couldn't sleep, and I found her painting the nursery this morning when I woke up. I told her she should have awakened me, and I would have gotten up to help."

"It was yellow, wasn't it? I bet she painted it pink."

Curtis grinned. "You're close. Lavender. I didn't even know we had lavender paint. She's been out gathering supplies all day. Stuff like diapers, powder, sleepers. I think she's texted me twenty times today with pictures."

"I don't blame her. It's super exciting. I want to meet the new baby as soon as you get her all settled."

"Libby plans to have a baby shower next week too. She arrived at the house this morning before I left."

They reached the parking lot, and Curtis headed for his truck. "Talk to you all later."

Josh leaned against her car. "I heard you had a date the other night."

She pressed her key fob to unlock the door. "Well, dinner at least. Just getting to know Ben a bit."

Was he jealous? She eyed his placid expression. He didn't seem upset or anything. Maybe he really didn't care. Or maybe he was relieved there wouldn't be any pressure on him to commit to something.

"Gonna go out again?"

Now there was an edge in the question. She considered her answer. While it might be telling to see if she could make him jealous, she didn't want to play games. Maybe it was a little naive of her to think their relationship was better than that.

"I don't know," she said finally. "He hasn't asked me, but we had a nice time. How did you know about it?"

"I overheard him telling someone he was going to marry you."

She blinked. "Whoa, that's a little extreme. We barely know each other."

"Sometimes a woman comes along who makes a guy reconsider his decisions in life."

Was he talking about himself? He'd never really responded to her confession the other day. She'd hoped he would tell her he loved her too, but that hadn't happened. Was this as close as she was going to get?

She put her hand on his arm. "What does that mean, Josh?"

He took off his Dodgers cap and raked his hand through his brown hair. "I don't know myself, Sara. I don't deserve a woman like you. I'm afraid I would fail you in the end. I want you to be happy. I'm not sure I could make you happy."

His expression tugged at her heart. "I don't know why you would say that. You're the first one to volunteer for dangerous missions. You do things for other people and never tell them about it. If I hear about someone finding a basket of food on her front porch or his lapsing insurance miraculously paid, I know you're the one who has done it. What has caused you to be so mistrusting of your own worth? You never talk about your past or your childhood. Something has hurt you, but you can let it go and move on if you want to."

He lifted tormented blue eyes to meet hers. "It's not that easy. I'm afraid of being like my father."

"You're not your father, Josh. I know the man inside you. You're a good man, the best. You can't look at your father's failings and take them on yourself."

"It's more than that."

At least he was opening up. "What do you mean?"

"He beat my mother and me. And I stood back and let him beat my brother to death." His face paled, and he dropped his gaze to the ground. "So much for being a good guy, huh?"

"How old were you?"

"Twelve."

182

She couldn't help stepping closer to hug him. He stood stiffly in her embrace, then sighed and dropped his head into the crook of her neck. His arms came around her, and he crushed her to his chest. She lifted her head, and he looked into her eyes. Her lids fluttered shut of their own accord. His lips came down on hers, and she tasted him outside of her dreams for the first time. Or maybe this *was* a dream. But no, her fingertips rested on the hard muscles of his chest. His hands fanned across her back as he pressed her closer.

If this was a dream, she wanted never to awaken.

He kissed her like a starving man, and she wrapped her arms around his neck and kissed him back with all the love welling in her heart, an emotion she'd never been able to express before. When he finally pulled away, she made a mewl of protest and tried to pull his head back down for another kiss.

His hands fell away and he stepped back. "I was trying to say good-bye, but you make it really hard, Sara."

"Good-bye?" She tried to clear her fuzzy thoughts.

"I told you—I can never make you happy. I know that about myself. And you deserve so much more." He turned and ran off toward his truck.

She didn't even try to go after him.

———

"Are those people my grandma and grandpa?" Josie asked in a loud whisper. She clung to her mother's hand.

Elin squeezed her daughter's small fingers. She was nervous too. Marc's mother had always terrified her. Christine Everton was one of those people with a personality bigger than life. She'd always been kind to Elin when she'd been at their house with Sara, but whenever Elin looked into her hazel eyes, she felt so inadequate. Christine did everything well.

She swallowed hard and pasted on a smile as Marc and his parents neared. "Welcome to Seagrass Cottage. It's a little remote, but your suite is very nice, and I think you'll like it."

Christine seemed not to hear. Her attention was fixed on Josie. Were those tears in her eyes? Elin felt horrible as she recognized the overwhelming love on the older woman's face. She'd thought she was doing the right thing in honoring Tim's wishes, but it seemed she was wrong about so many things.

Christine knelt in front of Josie. Her smile wobbled a bit. "You must be Josie. You look just like your daddy did when he was your age."

Josie looked from Christine to Marc. "My hair is brown."

"I know. And curly. You're beautiful." Her voice was choked.

In that moment, Elin opened her heart to Christine. Any woman who would show such unfettered love for her daughter was worthy of friendship and love. She looked up and met Marc's gaze of approval. Something fluttered in her chest.

Josie hung on to Elin's leg, but she began to smile as Christine coaxed her forward with a piece of bubble gum she dug out of her purse. The older woman scooped up Josie as soon as she stepped forward. Surprisingly, the little girl didn't struggle. She stared at her new grandmother with wide eyes.

Frank stood close as well, and his big smile seemed to calm Josie. She hadn't been around a grandfather very often.

"Want to go find some seashells?" Frank suggested.

Josie looked uncertainly at her mother, then nodded. "Are you coming too, Mommy?"

"I'll be right here. Your new grammy and grandpa will take good care of you."

Josie's expression said she wasn't so sure about that, but she let Christine carry her toward the sand dunes. Elin exhaled. "That went better than I expected."

"I was afraid Mom might tear you limb from limb for depriving her of her granddaughter." Though he smiled, Marc's voice held a serious edge.

"Josie could use some extra loving. She doesn't understand the way Mom can change and ignore her."

"Where is Ruby today?"

"Napping. She's been extra tired the last few days. I probably ought to get her in to see the doctor. Something might be wrong." Elin didn't want to think about one more problem though. What if her mother had something seriously wrong? Though the time would come sooner or later, she wasn't ready to lose her mother. The dementia was bad enough.

"Is Kalianne with her?"

She shook her head. "I gave her the day off. I knew I'd be home all day." There was something in his manner she couldn't put her finger on. "Is something bothering you?" The breeze blew a long strand of hair into her eyes, and she swiped it away.

"They will want to see her often, Elin. Are you ready for that?"

At least he was being direct. "I think so. It did me a world of good to see the love on your mom's face. There's never too much love in a child's life."

"No." He continued to look at her with an unfathomable expression.

"What?"

"Elin, she needs a father in her life too."

"You're here, aren't you?" Her pulse sped up at his expression. Surely he wasn't going to ask for custody.

He took a step closer. "She needs two parents. All the time."

"That's not possible though. At some point we'll have that maniac behind bars. You'll go back to Norfolk to your job, and I'll go back to mine. But at least she can see you often. And your parents. I know it's not ideal, but it's how lots of kids live."

On one hand, his presence made her feel more secure, but it also left her unsettled. She couldn't decide if she was looking forward to him moving out or not.

"I don't want my daughter to live like that." He took a deep breath, then exhaled. "I think we should get married."

The breath left her lungs. She gaped but no words came. Studying his face, she saw he was serious. Or crazy. Or maybe she was the crazy one because her mind was conjuring up lovely images of a life spent with Marc. She couldn't love him, could she? Love didn't strike so fast, surely.

When she didn't answer, he rushed on. "Hear me out. I wouldn't expect anything from you, not a real marriage, of course. Too much water under the bridge for that. But we could buy a big place together where we each had our own space. Then we'd be there for Josie. Both of us." He turned and gestured at the big cottage. "Maybe even live in this place. I could get transferred out here maybe. You work from home anyway, so it doesn't matter where you live."

"B-But don't you think that's a little extreme?" She couldn't breathe, couldn't look away from his penetrating gaze. "Josie will be fine. She'll know she's loved. It warms my heart that you already care about her so much, but I think you're going a little overboard."

"I don't think so. Can you at least think about it, Elin? Josie deserves to be put first."

"I always put her first!"

He nodded. "I'm not saying you don't. But I'm willing to change my life for her. Can't you do the same?"

She turned her back on him and ran for the house. Because the one thing his proposal had shown her was that she was developing feelings for the infuriating man, and the thought of a loveless marriage left her cold.

TWENTY-SIX

Elin didn't know how she got through the rest of the day. All she wanted to do was think about Marc's proposal. It was like probing a toothache with her tongue. She couldn't seem to think about anything else. She got her guests situated for the night, then went to her bedroom.

The light was on, and she paused to take in the scene in her light-blue bedroom. Dressed in a light-blue nightgown, her mother lay curled up on her bed. "Mom, what are you doing in here?"

Her mother's blue eyes sharpened as she sat up and put down her book. "Elin, there you are. You should have been in bed at nine. I came to tuck you in. You should have sent your friends home long ago. Their parents will be worried."

If only she were ten again and could crawl into her mother's lap and tell her all her woes. Even if her mother understood what she was saying, she couldn't help. "They are Marc's parents, remember? They're here to see him." She'd tried to tell her mother Marc was Josie's father but had been unable to make her understand. "You should get to bed yourself, Mom. It's nearly midnight."

"Is it? I'm wide-awake."

And her mother did look a little brighter and more alert than she'd seen her in a while, even if she did think Elin was a child.

Elin joined her on the bed. It almost felt like when she was a teenager and would lie on her mother's bed and tell her about her day. Maybe her mother would understand tonight. She so needed someone to bounce around her thoughts with her. Just smelling the scent of her mother's cologne, a sandalwood she'd worn forever, took her back to her teen years.

Her mother brushed the long hair from Elin's face. "You look troubled, honey. What's wrong?"

Elin's eyes burned at the compassion in her voice. Every day it seemed she lost more of both herself and her mother. Why did life have to be so hard?

She swallowed the lump in her throat. "It's boy trouble."

The tips of her mother's mouth turned up into not quite a smile but an expression of commiseration. "Tell your mama all about it."

The familiar entreaty brought tears surging back to her eyes. "It's Marc. He wants to marry me."

"But isn't that a good thing?" Her mother caressed her cheek. "He *is* Josie's father."

Elin gasped. "You knew?" She hadn't thought her mother had understood.

"I'm not in my dotage yet, Elin." Her mother shook her head. "I knew the first time I saw Josie that Tim wasn't her father. You couldn't hide something that big from me. I know you too well. So what's the problem? Surely you told him yes."

"I ran away." Her voice wobbled. "All he wants is to be with Josie. I don't want to be just Josie's mother. What kind of marriage would that be?"

"You love him." Her mother smiled.

Did she? "I–I don't think it's love. Maybe it could be, but it's mostly that I realize now that I want a real family someday. Not some kind of sterile arrangement."

Her mom patted her hand. "Honey, it only takes seeing how

he watches you to know he cares about you. He might have his guard up and not know it yet, but he'll figure it out."

"You really think so? I don't see it. Tim feared this would happen, you know. He hated Marc."

Even now, she could see the determination on Tim's face when he threw Marc out of the house that day. His jealousy had grown into downright hatred.

Her mother cupped her face in her hands. "Tim is dead, Elin. You're still a young woman. I would hate to see you lock yourself away from love and happiness because of a dead man's jealousy. That's just silly. You're more alive and fully yourself when you're around Marc. I see the old Elin then."

She blinked. "W-What do you mean, the old Elin?"

Her mother dropped her hands away. "You haven't been as open and transparent as usual for a while. Coming so close to dying did something, I think. It made you more serious, more guarded. He's good for you. And you're good for him."

Elin relaxed a bit. Her mother wasn't talking about personality changes, just the trauma of the illness. She looked her mother fully in the eyes. "What makes up who we are, really? What we like or dislike? How we walk, talk?"

"It's how we love, honey. And you love with your whole heart. God shines through you. Don't ever let that change."

"How do I stop it?" she whispered.

But her mother's blue eyes were clouding up, obscuring the loving woman who had guided Elin for all her thirty years. Where did Mom go when she left? And was there any way to bring her back, or would she go away forever? This was worse than losing her to death, and it mirrored what Elin felt was happening to her.

She helped her mother to bed. When she got back to her room, she looked out at the dark night. The nightmares seemed close tonight. She picked up Georgina's diary.

—

DECEMBER 5, 1907

The three-month-old twins slept peacefully in their cradles in Georgina's lavish bedroom. *Twins.* She still couldn't believe it. A son and a daughter. Joshua had paid little attention to his daughter, but he nearly burst with pride when he saw his son. He'd almost delayed his departure at their early arrival, but he'd had little choice. Two months had stretched into three, and he was overdue by a good month now.

She left her children in the care of the nurse while she went up to the widow's walk. Joshua was due in anytime, and he would be quite tiresome if he didn't see her wave from the parapet. She'd been watching for him for weeks, and though it was too soon to worry, she had felt dread curling in the pit of her stomach with each passing day.

Some sailors never came home.

She couldn't imagine Joshua allowing anything to keep him from his destination. He wrapped his power and determination around him like an impenetrable cloak. Not even the sea would dare to contradict his will.

She reached the parapet and rested her hands on the iron railing. Black storm clouds roiled on the horizon, and the wind freshened. She lifted her face and inhaled the scent of the approaching rain. The heavy surf pounded the sand dunes and rolled back for a fresh attack.

No white sail marred the sea's blue perfection. Tension uncoiled in her neck. Maybe she had a few hours before he arrived. She lived with the constant hope he would return and be the man she'd thought she married. One who cared more about her than about his image in society.

A sound startled her and she whirled. A man exited the door to the walkway around the top of the house. She'd never seen him before, but she instantly recognized him as Khmer. About her own height, he had glossy black hair and almond-shaped eyes that reminded her of Chann. He wore a bright-red krama around his neck.

Even as a smile formed on her lips, the menacing expression on his face penetrated. She took a step back, but the railing prevented her from moving more than a few inches. "Who are you?"

"It is where?" His heavily accented English was difficult to make out.

"What is it you want?"

He stopped a foot away and glared at her. "The pouch, woman. Given to you by Chann. I want it."

How did she get rid of him without lying? "My husband will be here anytime. You need to leave."

In a movement as quick as a mongoose after a snake, he grabbed her by the shoulders and shook her so hard, her head flopped back and forth. His roughness left her dizzy. He didn't release her, and she winced as his fingers tightened, then he thrust her back until she was hanging partially over the railing.

The sound of the sea mingled with the roar of the blood in her ears. She fought to get away from him before he could throw her off the parapet. He bent her back so far, she was nearly upside down. The spikes on the railing bit into her waist. Her hands flailed, then she dug her fingernails into his face. He winced, but his expression grew more determined.

He intended to throw her over the side with as little thought as a fisherman tossing a fish back into the sea.

Then he reeled away, and the pressure on her shoulders was gone. She staggered to an upright position and realized Chann had pulled the man off her. The two struggled in a deadly two-step near the edge of the railing. One wrong move, and they'd both go over the end.

Gusts of wind shook the house as the storm intensified. Chann's face twisted in fierce determination, and the other man growled and fought back. He was bigger and heavier than Chann and had nearly pushed her friend over the railing. Georgina twisted her hands together in a futile desire to do something to help. If only she had a weapon.

Her hair! She dove her fingers into her updo. The wind teased her hair loose when she extracted a hairpin. She quickly rushed to the struggling men and plunged the point of her hairpin into the back of the assailant's neck. It wouldn't kill him, but it would distract him like a bee sting.

He released his grip on Chann and slapped his hand on his neck. Chann launched forward and seized his arm, then hurled him over the side of the railing. The man plummeted to the ground without a sound. Nausea roiled in Georgina's stomach, and she bent over, retching.

Instantly, Chann was by her side. He didn't touch her but stood back respectfully and offered his hanky when she finally lifted her head. "I am so sorry, little sister. You are hurt?"

She pressed his hanky against her lips and shook her head. "No, no, I am unharmed. Who was he?"

"A very bad man. I cannot stay. Others will come for what you have hidden. Do not let anyone take it. Someday the world will be ready to see this treasure, but not now. Not when greedy men would seek it for their own gain."

"I don't understand."

His gentle smile came. "You will do what I ask?" When she nodded, his face grew more sober. "Even if you hear of my death, do not tell anyone, little sister. What you hide is a map to a great treasure, an ancient city of wonder in Cambodia. It must not be discovered in my lifetime. Maybe never. Guard it well."

"I do not wish to keep this from my husband. May I tell him?"

His dark eyes grew shadowed. "I am sorry to tell you this news. I heard in town that his ship sank. All aboard were lost."

Spots danced in front of Georgina's eyes, and she swayed where she stood. "H-He's dead? Joshua is dead?" Chann caught her as she crumpled.

What did she care about hidden cities? She would have to raise her children alone.

TWENTY-SEVEN

Marc kept glancing at Elin from the corner of his eye as they drove to Norfolk on Thursday morning. She hadn't said much the entire trip. Ignoring his proposal wouldn't fix anything, but every time he opened his mouth to bring it up, he shut it again. What more could he say to convince her? He didn't know what her problem was. Any logical look at their conundrum would arrive at the same answer: marriage.

"Anything new in the diary?" he asked.

She straightened, and a hint of color came to her cheeks. "I know what it was she hid. Her friend had discovered an ancient city full of treasure somewhere in Cambodia. Others were after the map to its location, but he said she was never to turn it over. So it might actually still be in the house."

"You think your mother found it?"

"Maybe." Then she shook her head. "I think it's all a little far-fetched to think it could still be there. I mean, that was over a hundred years ago. Surely someone would have found it."

"Has any Cambodian city been discovered in the past hundred years?"

"Well, there was Angkor Wat. But I don't think that was the one from her description in the diary."

"Maybe there really was no city. We have all those satellites now to find missing structures."

"Maybe. But if I find the pouch, I'm going to hide it again."

They entered the city limits, and he slowed the vehicle.

"Josie has taken to your parents," she said, still staring out the window as they entered the Norfolk traffic. "We should pick up a little gift to thank them for keeping her while we investigate."

"Spending time with her is all they need. They're eating it up." Maybe this was his opening. "Have you thought about what I said Tuesday night?"

"There hasn't been much time."

"Surely you can see how much sense it makes, Elin. Josie will thrive in a stable home."

Her jaw set, she shook her head. "You would regret it some-day, Marc. What if you found another woman you could love? Then where would we be? Right now you're a novelty to her. If you become an integral part of her life and then leave, it would crush her. She's lost one father. I don't want her to lose another."

"I'm not going anywhere. It's not like I'm going to date if we're married. What kind of man do you think I am?" Maybe he didn't want to know because the thought she believed him capable of such a lack of integrity stung.

Something stirred in his heart as he looked at her. Her face was set and strained. What was holding her back?

She looked at the paper in her hand. "We can talk about it once we get the killer behind bars." She gestured to the stop sign at the next street. "We turn here. The Watson house is the third one on the left. It has red shutters and a red front door."

"You've been here before?"

"No." She turned to look at him. "I don't know how I know it, but I do."

This whole cell-memory thing had him a little off center. "Okay." He saw her slight shudder and realized she was as disori-ented by this as he was. Probably more.

He turned and drove down the street slowly. There it was, just as she had described it. A two-story with neat shutters and a red door. The yard was well kept, and the grass freshly mowed. A swing set sat in the backyard. "There it is."

He pulled the SUV into the driveway and opened his door to the pungent odor of asphalt. "Smells like the driveway was just resealed. Maybe I shouldn't park here."

As if on cue, a man exited the house waving his hands. "Park in the street!"

Marc spared a glance at the guy. Tall and thin with a balding head and small, neat ears. He wore khakis and a T-shirt proclaiming him the best dad in the world. Starting the car, Marc backed into the street and parked at the curb. "Is that her dad?"

Elin hadn't taken her eyes off the man. "Yes." Her voice was barely audible. "I-I'm frightened of him, Marc. I don't want to get out of the car."

"Sit here. I can handle questioning him."

She turned a pale face toward him. "No, I want to go too. Just stay close to me."

He nodded, and they got out of the car. He took her arm at the curb and approached the house.

The man didn't return his smile but stared at them with obvious suspicion. "If you're selling something, just get back in your fancy Tahoe and head on out of here."

"We're not selling anything. I'm a special agent with the FBI. We have a few questions about your daughter." He'd thought mentioning Laura would cause the man to put down his guard, but Mr. Watson continued to glare at them. With Watson's obvious hostility, Marc didn't want to reveal Elin's identity.

"What do you want? I already answered a ton of questions." He turned back toward the house.

A woman stepped through the screen door. In her fifties like the man, her hunched shoulders and downcast eyes told a story of submission. Were those bruises on her arms? She wore cutoffs and a red V-neck top. Her feet were bare.

"I need to talk to you both. I'm investigating your daughter's death." Marc's fingers curled into his palms. A man who would hurt a woman was pure scum. He hadn't liked Watson's attitude, but now he actively disliked the man.

"Is everything okay, Jerry?" The woman's voice was timid. "This man is with the FBI. Maybe they've found Laura's killer."

"Get back in the house, Judy. This doesn't concern you."

She cowered back against the door and turned to go back inside.

"You'll answer more questions for me here, or I'll haul you in for questioning." Marc didn't rein in his sharp tone. "You can answer them in your living room or in a locked room of my choosing. Your choice."

The man glared at him, then shrugged. "Suit yourself." He turned and stomped back toward the house.

Marc raised his brows at Elin, then took her arm and followed Watson inside. It took a moment for his eyes to adjust to the dim interior. Foil covered every window, and only a few lamps illuminated the interior. The place was neat, but a pungent odor permeated the air. Marijuana.

He didn't like how white Elin looked, and the way she pressed against his side told him she'd rather be anywhere but here.

<hr/>

She couldn't stop shivering. Elin sat beside Marc on a sofa that was much too familiar. The house reeked of pot, just like usual. Her father—no, *Laura's father*—had been smoking it most of the day, evidenced by his red-rimmed eyes and dilated pupils. Had Marc noticed? She glanced up at him. He'd noticed all right. If his jaw got any harder, it would crack.

"Let's get this over with." Watson plopped into his worn leather recliner. "Judy, get started on lunch. I'll handle this."

When Mrs. Watson turned toward the kitchen door, Marc shook his head. "You can eat later. I need to speak to both of you."

To Elin's surprise, Watson scowled and allowed his wife to sidle over to the rocking chair where her knitting lay on the floor. She eased into the chair and picked up her yarn. The material appeared to be a pink baby blanket. Who was having a baby? Laura's little sister? Her name hovered on the edge of Elin's memory. Sammie. And she was sixteen.

"Where's Sammie?" she blurted out. "We need to talk to her too."

Watson scowled again. "Samantha isn't feeling well. She doesn't know anything anyway."

"Not well?" Elin rose and turned toward the stairs when she heard a creak. "Sammie, are you up there?"

A figure moved down the steps. A young brunette stood on the bottom step. Dressed in pink capris and a sleeveless white top that stretched over a bulging belly, she stared at Marc and Elin.

"Samantha, this is none of your concern. Go on up to your room," her father barked.

Samantha didn't budge, though her hand drifted along the smooth surface of the oak banister. "I–I thought I heard Laura's voice. Just now." She rubbed her eyes. "Maybe I was dreaming, but I heard her say, 'Sammie.' No one else ever calls me Sammie anymore."

Heat flooded Elin's face. What would this family do if she revealed she had Laura's heart? That she heard things, saw things that only Laura could know? She thought Sammie would rush to embrace her, but Watson might just throw her out the door.

A lock of hair fell into her face, and she brushed it back without thinking. Sammie's eyes widened. She stepped down the final step and came toward Elin as if in a trance. When the young girl stopped in front of her and continued to stare, Elin couldn't look away. What did Sammie see in her face? Was Laura in there somewhere looking back?

"Who are you?" Sammie whispered.

"They're here to ask questions about your sister," Watson said. "That's all you need to know. Get on back upstairs."

"I'd like to speak to the whole family," Marc said. "Do you have any other children? Any other members of the family who live with you, like a grandparent?"

"We just had the two girls. No one else. Look, what's all this about? And Samantha, you will make them think you are some kind of weirdo with the way you're staring. Sit down. You're making a fool of yourself."

"Who are you?" Sammie asked again. "You remind me of Laura somehow. Did you know my sister?" Her voice broke. "I miss her every day. I told her he'd kill her."

Marc shot to his feet. "Who? Do you know who might have targeted your sister?"

Watson jumped up too. "Now you've done it, you stupid girl. I told you never to talk about that. He had nothing to do with Laura's murder."

Elin felt such pity for the young woman. A terrible grief crouched in Sammie's eyes. The two sisters had been close, and her heart clenched with a reciprocal love. How could she not give Laura's sister some assurance? Yet she wasn't convinced it would help the situation.

Sammie didn't move. "You knew her, didn't you? That's why you called me Sammie with her same inflection."

Elin nodded. "I knew her a little." A confession hovered behind her lips, but she managed to hold it back when Marc's hand slid across the sofa and covered hers with a warming squeeze.

The tension in Sammie's shoulders eased, and she moved to lower herself awkwardly by her mother's feet. Judy put down her knitting and rested her hand on her younger daughter's shoulder as if to bring a measure of comfort.

Elin could almost feel that touch on her own shoulder. She knew the weight of it, the touch of the work-roughened hands on her skin. The scent of the woman's shampoo and lotion. This was like some kind of time warp, and she needed to get away. To breathe fresh air and not look into the grief-ravaged faces of the other two women.

But with Marc's hand on hers, she managed to compose herself. They had to know whom Sammie referred to. Whom her father wanted to protect.

Marc leaned forward. "Samantha, who frightened Laura?" He held up a warning hand to Watson, who was practically snarling from his recliner.

Sammie leaned her head against her mother's knee. "Dad's business partner, Ryan Mosely." She shot a defiant glare at her father. "He was obsessed with her. Always asking her out and stuff. And he was *old*. In his forties. He should have known she was too young for him. Dad encouraged it though. He wanted Laura to marry the pervert. And when she finally told Ryan she didn't ever want him to even call her, he went ballistic."

"In what way?" Marc asked.

"He sent her nasty e-mails and stuff. He even left a dead rat at the back door." Sammie shuddered. "Laura asked Dad to call him off, but he wouldn't. He said she should wake up and realize what side her bread was buttered on. So Laura decided to work for the cruise line to get away for a while. She hoped Ryan would move on to someone else."

"But he didn't?"

Sammie shook her head. "He booked a cabin on her first

cruise. I tried to get Laura to quit her new job and stay home, but she thought he wouldn't be able to do much onboard the ship. She was wrong. He killed her. I know it." She burst into tears, then turned and buried her face against her mother.

"D-Did he frighten her with music from *The Phantom of the Opera*?" Elin asked.

Sammie rolled her eyes. "He wouldn't be caught dead listening to something like that. He's a redneck all the way."

Something in what she said rang true to Elin. Chills skittered down her spine. Laura had been afraid of this Ryan Mosely.

TWENTY-EIGHT

Marc exhaled and put the SUV in gear. The vehicle rolled away from the Watson residence. He couldn't get out of there fast enough as Watson had hustled them out. Marc had asked Samantha if she wanted him to find her a shelter, but she refused. He feared she was in for a tongue-lashing with her father. Or worse. What a family. He braked at the stoplight, then turned to head back to Hope Beach.

"You okay?" he asked Elin, who hadn't said a word since they got in the Tahoe.

When she didn't answer, he glanced over at her and saw sobs shuddering through her. He pulled the Tahoe to the side of the road and unbuckled his seat belt so he could slide across the bench seat and embrace her. He slipped his arm around her and pulled her close. The faint scent of her sweet perfume slipped up his nose. Having her in his arms again felt like coming home. Resting his chin on her hair, he patted her back while she sobbed against his shirt. She fit exactly right in his arms.

He pressed a kiss on her hair. "Hey, you did great. I know it had to be hard, but you held it together. We got some good information today."

She stiffened and pulled back. "You don't know what it cost me."

His hand stilled on her back. "The memories were bad in there."

She nodded. "They're so vivid, Marc. I knew just how Judy Watson's hands would feel. I knew that odor in there was marijuana. You smelled it too, didn't you?"

He nodded. "He smoked pot a lot?"

"Every night, I think. And did you see the bruises on Judy's arms? He hits her all the time. I hate him, and I don't even know him."

"I saw the bruises. I'd call the cops, but I think she would say they happened in another way. It's sad. But I saw enough today to hate him myself. It's not just what you remember from Laura."

"It *is*. I just felt the hate rising up. And I don't like to feel that way. I want to like people and extend them the benefit of the doubt. I was unable to do that with him. He's an evil, evil man."

"I could feel that too." How did he even go about reassuring her? "In this case, it was a good thing you knew Sammie's nickname. I don't think we would have gotten anything out of them if she hadn't heard you call her that."

She pulled out of his embrace. "Marc, you don't get it!" She thumped her chest. "I even said Sammie's name the way her sister did. I'm afraid, so afraid. I don't want to be someone else. I want to be me. What if someday I wake up and look in the mirror and Elin Summerall isn't there anymore? What if I forget who I am?"

He heard the desperation in her voice, but he didn't know how to alleviate it. "I've seen some changes in you, Elin, but they aren't important to the core of who you are. I mean, identity changes all the time. You've been a daughter, a wife, a mother. You've been an employee. Now you're a somewhat-notorious figure in the news with your memories of the murder." He grinned but she didn't smile back. "You're still you."

"In what way?" She was listening now, the tears in her eyes drying up.

"Tastes aren't who you are. Memories aren't who you are. Roles aren't either, for that matter. Your personality is made up of how you think and react. How you treat people. How you interact with strangers and family. Those things haven't changed, Elin. You always think of other people before yourself. Was Laura like that? With a father like Watson, I doubt it. I bet all she thought about was escape, no matter who it hurt."

She bit her lip and pushed her hair behind her ears. She scrubbed the last traces of tears from her cheeks with the back of her hand. "I'm afraid of suddenly not loving Josie. Or Mom or . . ." She looked away.

Who else was she afraid of not loving? Tim? But he was gone. Something stirred in Marc. Jealousy? Ridiculous. Tim was never coming back from the grave. Marc examined her face, the sweet curve of her cheek and her large, expressive eyes. She had no idea how beautiful she was. Exactly how did he plan to live with her and not feel the desire welling even now? Not want to touch her petal-soft skin? Not remember the way her lips tasted and how she felt in his arms?

He jerked his thoughts away from the danger zone. Maybe his idea of a marriage of convenience between them really *was* a pipe dream. He might not be able to keep his hands off her.

———

His office was quiet as Marc navigated around the computer screen. Elin could have been beside him, but she feared getting too close to him would cause her to give away her feelings. He could tell her what he found.

She walked to the window and looked down onto the busy

street. The virus hadn't killed her. This problem could be overcome too. God had made her who she was, and she intended to keep herself. But how? How did she protect herself from Laura's influence?

Marc glanced at her. "Shut the door, would you? If my boss sees us poking around, I'm in trouble. He's not supposed to be in today, but you never know."

She stepped across the room and shut the door. "Lock it?"

"Yeah, good idea." He leaned back in the office chair. "Aha."

She turned and went to look at the computer with him. "What did you find?"

"First off, Josh is in the clear. He got a delivery of food about the time Laura was murdered. And he called to complain about a noisy party in the next room fifteen minutes later. I think we can rule him out."

"Oh, good! Sara will be so relieved. What else?"

He popped a mint. "Ryan Mosely and Jerry Watson own a mechanic's shop. They've been in business together for twenty years. Mosely must have started working there in his twenties. And they are solvent. Not raking in a ton of money but a nice, steady income."

"Has he ever been arrested?"

"That's the interesting thing. Look here." He clicked to another screen. "When he was eighteen, he was arrested for peeping in windows. Got probation. Then when he was twenty, he was arrested for battery. A girlfriend claimed he was stalking her, and when she ordered him to leave, he hit her with his fist. Spent a night in jail, then she dropped the charges. We should talk to her." He pulled his iPad toward him and jotted down her name and address, then rose and took her arm.

She fell into step beside him, and they headed for the exit. "Do you think we should go see Mosely too?"

"Let's get some evidence first about his past behavior. We can bring it up to him and see how he reacts."

She blinked in the bright sunshine as they headed to the Tahoe. "Do you remember seeing his name on the passenger manifest?"

"He's there. I'm going to take a look at the logs and see if she registered a complaint about harassment."

He slid under the steering wheel, and she went around to the passenger side. The traffic was heavy on the street, so she waited a moment before opening the door. Before she could slide in, she heard the squeal of tires. Her head jerked up to see a dirty brown car speeding right at her. She stood frozen as the vehicle seemed to deliberately take aim at her.

She felt a tug on her arm as Marc yanked her inside. The car crashed into the door and tore it partially from its hinges. She sat stunned as the vehicle raced away and disappeared around the corner. Her pulse thudded in her chest. If Marc hadn't intervened, the driver would have hit her.

"That appeared deliberate." His breath was harsh in her ear, and his hand, still on her arm, trembled a little.

Elin nodded. "And he didn't stop. I didn't see the license number, did you?" She should move away, but his presence helped still the tremors rippling along her skin.

He shook his head. "It all happened so fast." He finally dropped his hand away and scooted back under the steering wheel. "I didn't even see the driver, did you?"

"I caught a glimpse of a figure wearing a fedora. I couldn't tell if it was male or female. Or any details, really." Her hands trembled as she fastened her seat belt. "Marc, could it have been Mosely? What if Watson called him and told him we'd been informed of his unwanted attention to Laura?"

"Maybe." His lips flattened. "But it might have been Laura's killer too."

She shuddered. "It didn't seem his style. He seems much more inclined to terrorize me before he strikes."

"Maybe. Or he could just be done playing cat and mouse. Maybe we're getting too close so he planned to finish it." He started the Tahoe and pulled out into traffic. "It could have been Mosely. That makes a lot of sense." He turned at the light.

"How far to the old girlfriend's house? What's her name?"

"Kimberly Bussey. She's on this side of Norfolk, about ten minutes away."

Elin twisted in her seat and looked behind them. No sign of the brown car. She wanted all this to be over. What if he'd killed her today? She had no provisions for Josie other than her sister taking custody. Marc would not want Abby to have his daughter. He would want to raise her himself. And really, he should. He was her father. Josie was growing to love him more and more every day.

Was she being selfish by refusing to consider his proposal? She wanted only the best for her daughter, and there wasn't a finer man around than Marc Everton.

He glanced at her, then flipped on the turn signal. "You're awfully quiet. You okay?"

What would he say if she told him she was actually considering his offer? She exhaled. "Fine. I–I was just thinking about what would have happened to Josie if that car had hit me."

He braked, then turned left. "I would take care of her. I don't want you worrying about that. You're thinking about marrying me?"

She wasn't quite ready to go that far. "Well, at least you should probably adopt her legally. Right now she's Tim's daughter by law."

"I'm willing to do that." He sounded eager. "What about Tim's parents? Will you have to tell them?"

"Yes, but I don't think they'll care. They haven't shown that much interest in her. I suspect Tim may have told them Josie wasn't his biological child."

He braked. "Here we are. Let's pray she's home and will talk."

Twenty-Nine

The search for the missing contraband hadn't turned up anything. Sara redid her ponytail and surveyed the landscape off the point at Seagrass Pier. She turned to Josh and shrugged. "I think this is a waste of time."

They'd been instructed to make one more pass looking for the other crate thrown overboard in the rescue two weeks ago. It seemed a lost cause. She didn't think there were more drugs to find.

"Yeah, I think so too," Josh said.

Since their discussion on Tuesday, he hadn't strung more than two sentences together to her. Two could play that game though, and Sara was trying to act as though he meant nothing to her. Her attempt to be honest hadn't gotten her anywhere. Maybe because it was hopeless.

"I think I'll check over on the other side of the forest. There's an area behind the house we haven't searched. You guys go on back to Hope Beach, and I'll talk to you tomorrow. I promised Elin I'd hang around tonight at the house and make sure there were no problems with her mother."

"Fine." He turned to go.

She couldn't bear another minute of his distance. "Josh, your brother's death wasn't your fault. Besides, you were only twelve years old! What could you have done to stop it? Don't you think he would want you to be happy? He wouldn't want you punishing yourself for your whole life."

He stilled. "I don't know. You deserve someone better than me. I wouldn't want to disappoint you."

"What do you think your rejection is doing?" She took a step closer and touched his arm. "I know you love me. Why can't you just say it?"

"Once I say it, I–I . . ." He gulped and took a step back so her hand fell from his arm. "I'm an all-or-nothing guy."

"So give it your all," she said softly. "That's all any of us can do."

He shook his head. "I don't know. I love you too much to . . ." His eyes widened as he realized what he'd said.

The words were like a balm to her sore heart. Her smile burst out, and she threw her arms around his neck. "That's all I wanted to hear."

His arms came around her, then just as quickly released. He grabbed her wrists and tugged them down from his neck. "I'm sorry I said that, Sara. It solves nothing. I'd better go search. Talk to you later." He turned and ran in the opposite direction.

Her smile faded as she watched him rush down the sand dunes toward the other boat. This time it was one step closer and five steps back. But at least he'd *said* it. She had no idea how to get through his fear of failure, but she would figure it out. Now that she knew he loved her. Maybe Marc could throw some light on a guy's thinking with this problem. She'd ask him.

The last place for her to search lay through a thick maritime forest of gum trees and loblolly pine interspersed with grasses and holly bushes. A glimpse of southern twayblade drew her deeper into the cool woods. She decided to relax and enjoy the walk even if she found nothing. It was a beautiful July day, and the sound of birds twittering in the trees drained all her tension away. She inhaled the fragrant scent of forest. Maybe she could even forget about Josh's hurtful behavior for a few minutes.

She wound through the trees and stood at the edge of a small clearing. A movement on the other side caught her eye. The figure was half hidden in the shadows, but something about the other person struck her as furtive.

Sara moved as quietly as she could to the left to circle around to see what was going on. The glimpse of a red top kept her oriented as to where to head. Twenty feet away, she stopped behind a large oak tree and peered around.

Kalianne. What was Elin's new aide doing out here alone? Sara stepped a bit closer and saw her bending over a crate. One very much like the one tossed overboard in the drug boat rescue. Kalianne lugged it toward a small cave in a rock face. She shoved it into the space, then heaped leaves in front of it.

Why would she be hiding it? Sara watched her a moment longer, then stepped out from the shelter of the trees. "Looks like you found what we were looking for."

Kalianne whirled around and stepped in front of the opening. "What are you talking about? I was just out for a walk." Her walking shoes were worn and caked with mud.

Really? Did she think Sara hadn't seen what she'd just hidden? She pointed to the cave. "That crate. The Coast Guard is combing the area looking for it. It's probably drugs from a boat we rescued last week. We knew there was another one out here."

Kalianne shook her head. "It's just some stuff Ruby asked me to hide for her. You know how old people can be."

"Let me just take a look, okay?" Sara walked toward her.

Kalianne stayed put in front of the crate. "I can't let you look at it. It would be a breach of Ruby's privacy."

"I know Ruby much better than you do, and I know she wouldn't mind." Sara tried to walk around the other woman, but

Kalianne stepped to the left to block her again. "Kalianne, you will not stop me from looking at that crate. If you resist, I'll call for assistance. I'm not the only Coastie out here looking for this evidence. Now let me pass."

Kalianne's eyes were desperate, but she stepped aside. "Suit yourself."

Sara was bending toward the crate when something in the woman's deceptively mild tone warned her. She turned and started to stand, but she was too late. Kalianne brought up a large rock in her hand and smashed it into the side of Sara's head.

Bright flashes of color and light exploded in Sara's vision, and she crumpled to the ground, smelling the scent of mud and leaves as darkness claimed her.

———

Kimberly Bussey's house sat in the middle of a block of well-manicured lawns and stately, sweeping driveways. Marc parked in front of a porch with massive white pillars. "I don't know what I was expecting, but I hadn't thought she came from money."

Elin released her seat belt. "I guess it's because the Watsons are middle class so we assumed Ryan was as well." She opened her door and got out.

Marc did the same and joined her at the bottom of the wide stone steps to the front porch. "There's a Corvette in front of the garage. A new one. Wonder if it's hers."

"She might live here with her parents."

"I doubt it. She has to be forty by now or near there. You wouldn't think she'd be living with her parents at that age." He mounted the steps and pressed the doorbell. Elin stood close enough behind him he could feel her breath stir the back of his neck. He moved a fraction of an inch closer to the door. He refused to let his thoughts wander.

The door opened, and a woman in her late thirties or early forties peered at them. Her blond hair, cut in a stylish bob, looked freshly highlighted. She wore a short white skirt and a sleeveless pink top. Pretty in a way that looked like any enhancements had cost the earth. "Can I help you?"

"Are you Kimberly Bussey?"

She frowned. "I am. Who are you two?"

"I'm a special agent with the FBI and am investigating a murder aboard a ship a couple of months ago. Could we come in and speak with you?"

"I haven't been on a cruise in years. What's this all about?" She didn't wait for his answer but opened the door wider and stepped out of the way. "This way."

Her high-heeled sandals clicked on the polished wood floors as she led them to a large living room dominated by a massive stone fireplace. The white leather furniture was so pristine, he was half afraid to sit on it.

She gestured to two upholstered chairs flanking the fireplace. "Have a seat and tell me what you want." She went to the sofa and sat gingerly on the edge of the cushion.

Elin held out her hand. "I'm Elin Summerall."

Kimberly looked startled, but she shook her hand. "Pleased to meet you." Her expression sharpened. "Elin Summerall. The woman with the memories of a murder? I saw the article in the newspaper a few weeks ago. I thought you were a crackpot, but you seem to be sane."

The woman was outspoken, so maybe she would be just as candid about Ryan Mosely. Marc settled into the comfortable chair and waited until Elin sat down. "In our investigation, we ran across a complaint you made against an old boyfriend, Ryan Mosely."

Her gray eyes widened. "You think Ryan might have something

to do with this murder? Honestly, it wouldn't surprise me. He's a scary, scary guy."

Marc took out his iPad. "In what way? What was your relationship with him?"

"We went out a few times. He seemed to think it was more than that when I told him I didn't think we were compatible."

"How did you meet him?"

"I took my car in for repair. I was young and impressionable, and he was a handsome devil who had a way with words. That proverbial bad boy who is always irresistible to women." Her bark of laughter held no levity. "Luckily for me, I caught him peeping in my bedroom window and realized what a sleazeball he was. The problem was, he wouldn't leave me alone. I came home one night and found him in my kitchen." She gave a delicate shudder.

"What happened?"

"He tried to kiss me, but I wrenched away and grabbed a knife. I told him to leave. He knocked the knife from my hand, then smashed his fist into my face." She fingered her jaw. "Right here. I had a bruise for weeks. I'm lucky he didn't break it."

"He didn't . . . harm you?" Elin put in.

Kimberly wrinkled her nose. "Not in the way you mean. I screamed at him, then grabbed a pan and threw it at him. He finally left, and I called the police, who took a statement."

"Why did you drop the charges?"

She swallowed hard. "He told me if I didn't, my little sister would be next."

"You believed him?" Marc asked.

"Not at first. But a week later my sister came home bubbling about this really gorgeous guy named Ryan who walked her home from school. I had a sick feeling in the pit of my stomach. I knew it was him."

"And it was?"

She nodded, her face pale. "I parked by school the next day, and he was there waiting for her. He saw me and saluted with a smirk that turned my stomach. I drove straight to the police station and dropped the charges."

"Did he bother you or your sister again?" Elin asked.

"No. And you can be sure I went to another place for auto repair." She shivered and hugged herself.

"Have you ever run into him?"

"I saw him once in a department store. He grinned and started my way, but I boogied out of there before he could get to me. I hope never to hear his voice again. Why are you looking at him for this murder?"

Marc itched to get his hands on this Mosely. "He was stalking the young woman who died. She was the daughter of his partner. Even though she told him she didn't want to date him, he booked a cabin on a ship she worked on. Do you think he's capable of murder?"

"Absolutely. I think he's capable of anything. I hope you throw his butt in jail. I'd be happy to know I'd never run into him again."

Marc rose and closed the cover of his iPad. "We'll check him out. Thanks for your cooperation."

Thirty

They were stalled in traffic, and the stink of exhaust made Elin feel half sick. Her tummy rumbled, and she realized they hadn't eaten lunch. She glanced at her watch. Nearly five. They had a three-hour drive ahead of them, plus a ferry ride out to the island. The last ferry left at seven. "We aren't going to make the ferry. I had no idea it was so late."

Marc braked to miss a car cutting in front of him. "I didn't either. Sorry, I should have paid better attention. We can drive to Nags Head and charter a boat home, then come back tomorrow to get my Tahoe, or we can stay here and talk to Mosely. What do you want to do?"

She considered it. "Your parents are there with Josie. Do you think they'd mind if we don't come back tonight? And I could call Sara and have her make sure Mom is doing okay. Kalianne is off tomorrow. We can stay in a hotel."

"My parents are in their element. They won't mind at all." He frowned. "I have a spare room at my place if you don't mind staying there. And Sara left some things in the spare room. I think you're about the same size."

"We are." The thought of being alone with him made her pulse race. She wasn't sure how she could handle it, but she didn't want to spend the night in a hotel either. "Okay." Surely she could keep her distance. She'd be mortified if he figured out how she was beginning to feel about him. He'd made it clear he had no romantic interest in her.

She hadn't been at his place since *that night*. And she wasn't sure she was up to it tonight, but it was the logical choice. They were only friends, focused on the common goals of finding a killer and raising their daughter. That was all.

"Let's grab some food, then track down Mosely." He glanced at her. "Let's go to Los Fiesta."

"Okay." He'd gone after food from there that night, but she'd never been there.

She shut up and looked out the window. Traffic was finally moving again. A car followed very close on their bumper. She moved in her seat so she could see better. "What's that car behind us? It kind of looks like the car that hit us."

He looked into the rearview mirror and frowned. "It's a brown Chevy just like that one. Let's see what he does."

He looked to the right and left, then whipped the car into the right lane and made a quick exit off the interstate. The other car tried to follow them but missed the exit and rolled to a stop along the side of the highway. The car started to roll backward, but the vehicle approaching in the closest lane honked.

She clenched her fingers in her palms. "I think it was him!"

"Looks like it. Let's see if we can follow him." Marc gunned the Tahoe onto the freeway entrance. "There it is in the right lane."

"Don't get too close. We don't want him to see us."

Marc nodded. Two cars were between them and the brown car. "Write down the plate number."

She grabbed her phone and notated the number. The car ahead of them moved to the left lane, and Marc eased the vehicle a little closer to the brown car. The red pickup between them and the brown car rolled off the freeway at the next exit.

"I think I'd better hang back," Marc said.

But the driver must have realized he'd been spotted. Black smoke roiled from the tailpipe, and the brown car darted into the left lane.

Elin leaned forward. "Don't let him get away!"

Marc whipped the steering wheel to the left and jammed the Tahoe in between a white Honda and a black SUV, but the brown car accelerated again and zoomed around the three cars in front of it, then darted into the right lane and exited the freeway.

Marc smacked the steering wheel. "I can't get over."

Elin watched the brown car race to the stop sign, then make a left. It disappeared over the hill. "We tried. We can call in the license-plate number."

Marc reached for his phone and nodded. Elin turned her head and looked out the window at the passing buildings. It looked like he was heading toward the restaurant now. Her pulse still raced from the chase, and she didn't feel like eating anymore.

He put his phone on the console. "The plate was reported stolen."

She groaned. "Great. So we have no idea who it was."

"Nope. Let's go eat and forget this for a while." He pulled into the parking lot of the restaurant.

Marc parked the Tahoe, and she quickly climbed out and stood looking at the bright-blue building with its garish orange lettering.

Marc came around the front of the vehicle and touched her arm. "Looks like it pays to be a bit on the early side for dinner. We might even get a table."

They walked inside, and some of Elin's discomfort faded at the rich scent of spicy tacos and fajitas. The orange walls and comfy booths made her smile. They placed their order for chipotle chicken tacos with an order of guacamole to share.

Elin glanced across the table at him. "Nice place."

"Yeah." He stared at her intently. "I don't bring people here much. I don't like to share it. I've only been here with Sara and my partner."

His words left her tongue-tied. Was it some kind of tacit admission that he felt something for her? "Will. Have you checked in with his wife lately?"

He nodded. "She requested Will's cell phone records for me. I've been looking through them for any unusual numbers. I asked her if he ever mentioned the mechanic shop or Ryan. She thought he took his vehicle in for work there a couple of days before he was killed."

"So we might be on the right track."

"Maybe."

The server brought their chips, dip, and guacamole. Marc thanked her and salted the chips. His gaze collided with hers in a way that made her cheeks warm. She searched for some hint of how he was feeling. His mouth was relaxed, and his hazel eyes stared straight into hers. She might have seen a flicker of heat in their depths, but she wasn't quite sure.

Sara's head pulsed and throbbed with a pain that seemed to be centered above her left ear. She struggled to open her eyes, knowing the agony would intensify once she was fully awake. Her shoulders hurt, and something chafed at her wrists.

She moaned and realized a rag prevented her from speaking. She forced her lids open to a mere slit. Instead of brilliant sunlight, she found darkness had fallen while she was out. Her hands were tied behind her, which was why her shoulders felt out of joint. Leaves covered her legs, and the darkness above her was complete. She saw only a glimmer of light in front of her. She struggled to a sitting position but could not get any leverage to stand. Her head bumped something.

A cave, she was in a cave.

It all came back to her then. Kalianne and the crate. The rock in her hand and the crushing blow. Where was the woman? And why had she left her here?

Panic struggled to gain control, but she fought it back. *Breathe.* In and out, in and out. The tightness in her chest eased, and she rolled to her stomach, then wriggled toward the mouth of the cave where the small amount of light beckoned. Leaves crunched under her, and the strong, damp odor of detritus and mud filled her nose.

When she reached the exit of the cave, a pair of boots blocked the opening. Someone walked back and forth. She couldn't reach out, couldn't speak. Grunts and moans came from behind the gag, but she wasn't sure she was being heard. Her gaze traveled up the bare legs extending from shorts as the person strode past.

Kalianne.

What was the woman up to? She paced the front of the opening, waving her hands and muttering to herself. Sara struggled to hear past her own harsh breathing.

"Sends me out here and leaves me to figure out what to do by myself!" A kick at a shrub nearly sent Kalianne sprawling. "How dare he leave me to handle this by myself? He should have been here over an hour ago. I'm tempted to get in my boat and head out of the country. I don't know what I'm supposed to do about this." Another kick.

Kalianne whirled, and the moonlight struck her face. Her eyes widened. "You're awake." She offered up an uneasy smile. "Sorry I had to do that. Your head hurt?"

It hurt so badly Sara was afraid she was going to be sick. She swallowed down the bile in her throat and managed to nod.

Kalianne knelt beside her. "I'll remove the gag if you promise not to yell. The Coasties were all over this place looking for you. They're gone now, so yelling won't do you a bit of good. Promise?"

A wave of dizziness assaulted Sara when she nodded again. All she wanted was a sip of water.

Kalianne reached around and untied the cloth. "I've got a canteen of water. Here you go." She held the cold metal lip up to Sara's lips.

Sara sipped greedily, then coughed. The nausea passed more quickly with the brackish water calming her roughened throat. "Thanks." Her voice was a hoarse croak. "Can you untie me?"

Kalianne stepped back and shook her head. "Sorry, I can't go that far. My brother should be here any minute, and he'll figure out what to do with you."

"W-Who's your brother? Devi Long?"

Kalianne inhaled sharply. "How'd you know? Do you know Devi?"

"No, but I heard he was behind this drug shipment." Dread curled in her stomach. The man wasn't known for his mercy. He was likely to dump her overboard for the sharks. "He's going to kill me, Kalianne. You know that. Then where will you be? An accessory to murder. Do you want that on your conscience? Let me go. Please."

Kalianne stared down at her. "H-He wouldn't kill you."

Sara flexed her arms against her bonds. Were they just a trifle looser? "He's murdered other people."

"That's just what the news says. It's not true. Yeah, he's a drug smuggler. I wish he weren't, but it pays the bills." She must have seen Sara's wince because she shrugged. "You'd be surprised at how many people don't really care how he makes his money. He spends it freely on others, and he's quite popular with people whose names you would know."

Sara turned her head when a twig snapped. More rustling noises came from her right. Whoever headed this way walked with assurance as though he knew where he was going. The breeze lifted her hair, and the faint aroma of a cigar came to her.

Kalianne sniffed. "Here he comes now. He's never without his cigar." She looked down at Sara. "I'm really sorry you got messed up with this. You should have left it alone." She moved away in the darkness, and her thrashing through the underbrush grew fainter.

Sara heard her greet someone, then she made out the deeper tones of a male voice. Her pulse ratcheted up, and she strained harder at her bonds. There was no question they had to kill her. If they let her go, they knew she'd go straight to the authorities. She had to get away.

The rope at her wrists gave a bit, and she felt something wet run along the skin. A coppery scent wafted to her, but she didn't care if she was bleeding. He'd do a lot worse to her than rub the skin off in a small place. She worked the knots until finally her left hand slipped free. Bringing both arms around in front of her, she tore the remaining piece of rope from her right hand, then untied her ankles. She couldn't feel her feet, but she stumbled up anyway.

Her legs wouldn't hold her, and she fell to her knees just as a dark figure loomed in the moonlight.

THIRTY-ONE

Marc rested his hand on Elin's shoulder as he escorted her back to his SUV. "I shouldn't have eaten so much." He patted his belly. This had been almost like a real date.

"You might have to roll me to the Tahoe." She moved so his hand fell away.

Had she done it deliberately? She'd been skittish all day, probably from his proposal. Yet he could have sworn she was thinking about it. The thought of living with her and Josie forever made him want to push harder, but he didn't want to scare her.

"Mosely doesn't live far from my place, only about five minutes." He started the engine and pulled into the street. She still hadn't spoken, so he glanced at her from the corner of his eye. "You're quiet."

"Just contented." She leaned her head against the seat. "It's been a crazy day, and I'm tired."

He wanted to ask what she was thinking, but she'd already let him know she didn't want to talk about his proposal. "There's his place." He pulled to the curb and turned off the car.

The house was a ranch, probably about twenty years old, with tan vinyl siding and a small porch. The weeds and grass were a good eight inches tall. The shingles showed some wear and would need to be replaced in the next year.

He glanced at her in the dim twilight. "Wait here. I'll just check and see if he's home. It kind of looks deserted. I bet the yard hasn't been mowed in three weeks."

She shoved open her door. "I'm coming too. I don't trust that guy. He might be waiting to ambush you."

Though he appreciated the way she sprang to his defense, he didn't need protection. He came around the front of the vehicle and caught her arm. "Let me go first in case he's the one who's after you."

He stepped in front of her and advanced to the front porch. Spiderwebs clung to the siding around the door. Another web sparkled in a corner between a porch railing and the ceiling. Several newspapers, their print blurry from rain, lay piled near the door.

A cat darted from under the swing and leaped down toward them. Elin gave a startled scream, then leaped to his other side. "Keep that thing away from me."

He grinned and pushed the cat away with his foot. "Shoo, cat. I forgot you were so afraid of them."

She shuddered, her eyes fixed on the cat as it sprang into the overgrown bushes. "They're so sneaky."

"I think we should get Josie a kitty." It was all he could do not to grin.

"Over my dead body." She peered up at the darkened window. "I don't think anyone is here."

"Doesn't look like it." He mounted the steps, then pressed the doorbell.

It echoed eerily inside. There was no other sound, so he went to the picture window and cupped his hands around his eyes to look inside. The furnishings consisted of a sofa and love seat plus a couple of chairs. There was no movement in the shadowy interior.

"Let's look in the garage," Elin said.

He followed her down the steps and around to the attached garage. The grimy windows obscured much of the view, but he rubbed at the glass, then peered inside. "There's only a lawn mower and tools inside. No vehicle."

A male voice spoke behind them. "You looking for Mosely?"

He turned to see a white-haired man in shorts holding a pit bull by a leash. The man's skinny legs ended in white socks and black shoes. "We are. You a neighbor?"

The man waved to his left. "I live next door. Haven't seen him in a while. I called the police a couple of days ago to have them check inside. I was afraid he'd fallen or something."

"There's no vehicle. You know what he drives?"

The man's eyes narrowed. "Seems a personal question. Who are you?"

"FBI. I have a few questions for him."

The man's frown eased. "He in trouble?"

Marc ignored the question. "He didn't mention any trips to you?"

"Nope. Which is why I called the cops. They checked in at the mechanic shop he owns. They hadn't seen him either, but according to the other owner, Mosely takes off like this on occasion. I don't know though. I've been living here five years, and this is the first time he's vanished."

It sounded like Watson knew more than he'd let on. They might need to pay him another visit.

"About that vehicle?" Marc prompted.

"He drives a brown Chevy to work."

Mosely *had* been driving the brown car. Watson had to have warned him he was being investigated. "Thanks for your help." Marc took Elin's arm and led her toward the Tahoe. He could feel the older man's gaze on them until they pulled away from the curb.

Elin twisted in her seat to stare at him. "So it was Mosely who tried to hit us?"

"Looks like it. Let's go back over there and talk to Watson." Marc glanced through the window. It was after eight and would be dark soon. "I think that guy is a powder keg waiting to go off. I'd rather not have you around when he does, so I think we'd better wait until morning."

"I'm not afraid of him." Her quivering voice betrayed her true feelings.

"We're almost home. We can stop by in the morning. Hopefully he won't have started smoking his pot by the time we get there."

"Okay."

He pulled into his driveway and shut off the engine. Marc's house was on a quiet cul-de-sac. Painted in a cool blue-gray, its white shutters and red door gave it a restful air he'd always loved. What would Elin think about his remodel inside? He hadn't been able to figure her out ever since he'd suggested marriage.

———

Marc flipped on the lights, and the soft glow of the lamps illuminated the interior of gleaming wood floors, white trim, and warm gray walls. He tried to dispel his grumpy mood and forced a smile when she joined him in the kitchen, which thankfully was clean. He'd put all the dishes in the stainless steel dishwasher before he left.

He gestured toward the island. "I redid the kitchen two months ago. Granite counters, cherry cabinets. Cost the earth, but I like it."

"I do too." She was a little pale, and her voice seemed strained.

"I could use something to drink. How about you?" He moved past her to the fridge. "I've got Pepsi, iced tea, and bottled water. Or I could make coffee."

"Toomers?" Her tone picked up.

"Of course. My favorite Hope Beach blend."

"I'll have some of that."

He moved to the Cuisinart coffeepot. "It won't keep you awake?" He ground the coffee and made a full pot. The aroma began to fill the kitchen.

"It might, but it will be worth it. Besides, I'm not sleepy. We need to go over what we know so far."

The unspoken question hung between them, and he turned to pull down cups from the cupboard. She reached past him for a cup.

He resisted the urge to draw in her scent. Being alone here screamed danger. "Mosely's probably getting notices from the city about his grass. Looks like he's been gone awhile."

"Or too busy to cut his grass. Should we ask the police to help track him down?"

"Maybe. But they didn't seem concerned enough when the neighbor called them in. I'd guess Watson dispelled any worries when they questioned him about his partner." The coffee was done, so he poured two cups of it. "Heavy whipping cream?" He handed her the cup, and their fingers touched. The jolt of electricity made him pull his hand back hastily. When she nodded at his question, he went to the fridge and got out the carton of cream.

"Thanks."

She poured a liberal amount into her coffee. The tension between them was palpable, and he swallowed. Maybe this hadn't been such a good idea. His mind kept returning to that other night. He was honest enough to admit to himself he felt a powerful attraction to her. She seemed different now. So warm and caring. Or maybe he was just getting to know the real person.

She carried her coffee back to the living room, then curled up on his tan leather sofa. "What next?"

He dropped into his favorite chair and set down his coffee.

"This is maybe a crazy thought, but let's verify that he owns a brown Chevy."

"Good idea."

He leaned over and grabbed his laptop from the tabletop. He navigated to the DMV site and entered his authorization code. "Hmm, he owns a pickup truck. A 2013 Ford. And a '95 brown Chevy Lumina. Bingo."

He closed the lid of his laptop and put it back on the table. An awkward silence filled the room. He grabbed his coffee and swallowed down the tepid drink, then set down his cup. "Well, I might as well show you to your room. We can watch a movie or something, if you like. It's only nine fifteen. Unless you'd like some alone time. There are girl books Sara has left."

She smiled. "Girl books?"

"Romance." He grinned back at her, relieved the tension seemed to be easing.

"And guys aren't into romance?"

"Well, not that kind of starry-eyed stuff. It pays to be practical when you think about who you're spending your life with." He leaned forward. "Like us raising Josie together. It makes sense. We're friends and we get along. There shouldn't be any real surprises. We like a lot of the same things, and we know each other pretty well."

"You're pushing again." Her voice was quiet.

"I'm just passing the pressure along that I'm going to get when we get back to Seagrass Pier." He sent a cajoling smile her way. "My parents will want to know what I'm going to do about providing for their granddaughter. That reminds me. I have a check for you." He dug into his wallet and pulled out a check for two thousand dollars. "Here you go."

She didn't smile back, and she didn't take the check from him. "I don't need any help in providing for her. As long as I'm alive. That's not why I told you about her, Marc."

What was her beef? Why couldn't she see past their troubled history to the logical answer? "I know that, but she *is* my daughter. Don't you feel even a little guilty you deprived me of her for five years? I had a right to know."

The edge of anger in his voice shocked him. He'd thought he'd moved beyond recriminations. Getting angry about it wouldn't change the past. "Sorry."

"And I'm sorry for what happened too." Her voice was nearly inaudible. "Don't you think I've agonized over it all this time? If I could change it, I would."

Getting up, he gestured to the hall. "Let me show you your room."

THIRTY-TWO

The house felt close and airless, but Elin knew it was just her mental state. The realization she had feelings for Marc threw her. She wasn't ready for something like that, not after Tim. What if Marc changed like Tim had? Tim had been loving and supportive too, in the beginning.

Marc gestured to the first bedroom on the right of the hall. "This is where Sara stays when she visits. There's an attached bathroom, and it's already stocked with bubble bath, toothpaste, and everything else she uses."

The large room felt even bigger with the cathedral ceiling and the pale lavender paint. Crisp white linens covered an enormous four-poster bed. Brightly colored pillows added a punch of color. The white carpet was spotless.

She stepped into the room. "Nice. I think I even catch a scent of her perfume." She stepped to the dressing table and picked up a spray bottle of violet water. "That reminds me, she was supposed to call tonight after she checked on Mom and Josie."

A sense of unease gripped her. Sara was the most responsible person she knew, and she'd promised to stop by after work. "I hope everything is okay."

"Maybe her phone died, and she had to wait to get back home

to call. She might still be there. My parents love her, and they'd make it hard for her to leave."

"Maybe. I think I'll call." She dug her phone out of her bag and called her friend. The call rang four times, then went to voice mail. "No answer. Maybe you're right. Her phone won't work on the point unless she's in the house."

"I'm sure it's nothing to worry about. Want me to call Mom at the house?"

"I hate to bother her. She'll think I'm neurotic." She managed a smile. "And maybe I am. I'm not used to being away from Josie so much, but I know we have to find the killer before he comes back."

A horrible thought assailed her. Maybe he'd already come back—and murdered everyone in the house. "Actually, yes. I do want you to call and make sure everything is okay. She logs on to the Wi-Fi, right?"

He nodded and dug his phone out from his pocket. After a few punches on the phone, he put it to his ear. "Hey, Mom. Just checking in. Everything okay?" He listened a moment, then gave Elin a thumbs-up. "No sign of anyone hanging around the place, right? Okay, great. Listen, have you seen Sara? Hello? Are you there? I seem to have lost you."

He pulled the phone back from his ear and looked at it. "I have full bars."

"Wi-Fi service comes and goes out there, especially in a storm." She pointed to the window where flashes of lightning lit up the western sky. "It might have taken out the power, even temporarily, and the Wi-Fi would have gone down."

He put away his phone. "Maybe she'll call back when she gets a signal again. But she said all was well. She and Dad are playing Candy Land with Josie. I could hear her giggling in the background."

"That's great. What about Mom? Did Christine mention how she'd been today?"

He shook his head. "I didn't get a chance to ask her." He stepped past her and pulled open the top drawer. "Sara left nightgowns and some other clothing in here. There's a dress or two in the closet too. If you can think of anything you need, just let me know. I'll let you get settled. I think I'll shower, then go watch a movie. Feel free to join me or stay here. Your call."

He closed the door behind him, and she stared at it. Her presence here seemed to cause him no discomfort, but it had given her a taste of the torture she would experience if they were married in name only. How could she even think about it? And yet she *was* thinking about it. A lot.

She went to the bathroom and turned on the shower, then disrobed and stepped into the steaming spray. He was right—it made a lot of sense for Josie's sake. Elin had mourned the thought of her daughter being raised by a single mother. A child needed a father around too, and seeing him only on the weekends wasn't the same thing at all. Plus, Marc's parents would be doting grandparents. Mom tried, but she was retreating further and further into the mists of time.

She sudsed her hair, then rinsed it. Marc would be a dutiful husband. He'd be home on time and would let her know where he was. He'd take Josie to the park and out to dinner on a father-daughter "date." At every school function, he'd be there with her cheering on their daughter. If she played volleyball or ran in track, he'd be out there coaching her. When the boys started calling, he'd vet every male who walked through the door.

Maybe that would be enough. It was more than Tim had done.

What would happen once Josie went off to college? It would be just the two of them then. Divorce? She didn't believe in divorce, and neither did he. They were both believers, and they would take marriage vows seriously. The long, lonely years of an empty bed stretched ahead of her. What kind of life would that be? And did

God expect her to bury all the longings of her heart for Josie's happiness?

She wasn't the first mother to wrestle with these questions. Maybe Marc had the answers she didn't. She turned off the tap and wrapped a fluffy white towel around her, then padded into the bedroom where she found blue cotton pajamas. There would be no seduction in these baggy things.

Not that she intended there to be. She'd wrestled with enough guilt over the first time, and she wasn't about to repeat it. She dried her hair, then left it down on her shoulders and went to find Marc.

———

Standing in the moonlight, the man in front of Sara was as sleek and muscular as a sea otter with hair just as black and shiny. He wore close-fitting designer jeans and a green polo. With a pencil-thin cigar clenched between his teeth, he stared at her without speaking. He appeared to be in his late forties and was at least part Asian. Women would find his magnetism attractive.

Sara swallowed and rubbed her tingling legs. She wobbled to her feet and stood to face him. There was no emotion in his eyes. He could kill her as easily as he'd stomp on a bug.

Kalianne plucked at his shirtsleeve. "She didn't really see anything. I say we just take her out to one of the outer islands and leave her. A passing ship will find her in a few days, and we'll be long gone."

Sara cast a furtive glance into the shadows. This man would have no mercy. She needed to get away from him and find help.

He never looked away from Sara. "Don't be ridiculous, Kalianne. She's seen you and me. She can identify both of us. I'll handle this. You go on back to town."

His dark eyes were mesmerizing, and it took great effort for Sara to pull away her gaze and send an imploring glance at Kalianne. "Don't let him pull you into murder, Kalianne. I don't think you want my death on your conscience."

He took a step closer. "Shut up."

Something glittered as his hand came up. A gun. Sara stared down the deadly bore. If she could just leap into the shadows and escape him. Seagrass Cottage was not that far. But if she headed to the house, she'd be putting everyone there in danger. What should she do?

Kalianne stepped between her brother and Sara. "I don't like it, Devi. Smuggling drugs is one thing, but I won't be a party to murder. Sara has been good to me."

"Get out of the way, you idiot," he snarled.

Sara took advantage of Kalianne's distraction to dive for the cave. There might not be a way out in there, but at least it was dark, and he'd be at a disadvantage too. His gun barked, and a bullet spit rock shards inches from her face. She felt along the cave face for the small opening she'd noticed earlier. It might only be an indentation, but it might also be a way out of here.

There it was! She moved farther into the darkness, feeling her way. The tunnel widened until she was able to stand up. She stood and turned the other direction, listening to him swear and order Kalianne to find a flashlight. Sara heard a slap and winced. He was taking out his rage on Kalianne, but she couldn't worry about that. She had to get out of here.

She moved deeper into the cave, keeping her fingertips in contact with the rock surface to orient herself. What if she ended up lost in here? She had a tiny flashlight attached to her keys, but she didn't dare use it. Not when she could still hear the two arguing outside.

Pressure seemed to build in her ears, but she wasn't sure if it was because she was descending or if it was panic building from the claustrophobic darkness. She paused and concentrated on her breathing. In and out, in and out. The pressure around her eased, and she listened to Devi and Kalianne again. Their voices were fainter now, barely distinguishable. Were they moving away? She strained to make out what they were saying.

"I'll stay here and guard the entrance. Go back to my boat and get a flashlight." His voice was faint.

Sara stared behind her. There was not even a glimmer of moonlight. Maybe he wouldn't be able to see her flashlight if she flipped it on. For good measure, she shuffled another ten steps into the cave, then turned and looked and listened. Nothing. Her hand dove for the keys in her pocket, and she pulled them out, fumbling for the tiny flashlight. Her trembling hand found the switch, and she turned it on.

Nothing.

Panic closed her throat. She would be stuck in here forever waiting for him to come find her and shoot her. She fought down the fear and felt along the length of her tiny light. The end seemed a little loose. She tightened it, and a small beam of light rewarded her. Even though the illumination was minute, it comforted her. She listened to determine if Devi had seen it, but no sound was behind her. Shining the light ahead of her, she moved deeper into the cave.

It branched in two different directions, and she stared at her options. Which way should she go? Instinct told her the one on the right might lead back to the main cave, and she started to the left, then heard running water. She stopped and shone her light into the distance. A trickle of water ran from the ceiling. Would it take her to the ocean? She might get into a dangerous spot that way too.

Which way, Lord? Something still nudged her to the left, so she listened and walked toward the sound of the dripping water. It was cooler and danker here. She almost turned back then, but an imperceptible nudge moved her forward.

She walked on until she came to a passage that turned back to the right again. It was beginning to feel like a labyrinth. She would need to remember which way she went at every branch of the passage. She went right, though it felt less out of true knowledge than panic.

She wanted to put as much distance between her and her pursuers as possible. But she was beginning to feel there might not be an end to this cave.

Thirty-Three

Marc turned at a soft footfall and saw Elin with her damp hair on her shoulders. The soft blue pajamas intensified the color of her eyes. She had no idea how beautiful she looked in those shapeless pajamas with her feet bare.

He averted his eyes and gestured to the chair. "Have a seat." Best to have her as far away as possible. He fast-forwarded the movie through the beginning credits and paused it. "Want to play Trivia instead?"

She groaned. "You're still playing that? Sara and I always thought you had the cards memorized. I'm no challenge for you." She padded across the gleaming wood floor and settled beside him. "But before you get it out, could we talk?"

He put down the remote. "Sure." Her serious tone made him wonder what she was thinking.

She pulled her knees to her chest. "It's about this whole marriage thing."

"Okay." Was she going to say no? Her eyes seemed to indicate her answer wasn't going to be the one he wanted.

"Have you really thought about what this would mean? Neither of us believes in divorce. What kind of life are we going to have if we get married only for Josie's sake? In fifteen years she'll be off to college, and it will be just the two of us. Then what?"

He stumbled over the question. "I hadn't thought about that."

"Do you want a loveless life?"

Her soft question made him blink. Loveless? "Was that what you had with Tim?" When she winced, he knew he'd struck a nerve. "Tell me."

She swallowed hard. "Tim was so different before he was injured. Kind, strong, a take-charge kind of guy."

"I figured that never changed. The injury changed him?"

She shook her head. "My sin changed him." She focused on her hands. "He *said* it wouldn't matter, that he could love the child because she was mine. And he tried, but I broke his trust. He grew suspicious, hostile if I came home late from work. By the time he died, he was a bitter, angry man. At least he tried to love Josie. He gave up on me."

"It wasn't your fault, Elin. He chose to let the bitterness grow. You asked for his forgiveness, right?"

She gave the barest nod of her head. "More than once."

"Yet he never let go of it. That was a sin he chose."

"Maybe." She raised anguished eyes to his. "You might change too, Marc. I a-admire you now. I have no doubts you want to take care of Josie and me, that you want to do what's right. But you might grow bitter at being denied a real marriage."

He examined his heart, then shook his head. "I'm not that kind of man. I don't hold on to slights. I deal with them and move on."

She stared at him, then nodded. "I can see that about you. But what about Josie? Is it fair to make her grow up without any siblings? I'd always thought I'd have more children, a houseful, really."

"So you're saying you want to remarry and have kids with someone else?" The thought of that left him feeling like he'd just been hit by a tank. The thought of her with another man made him curl his fingers into his palms.

She shook her head. "Maybe you want to marry someone and

have kids with her. Josie would have siblings that way. We need to think this through carefully."

He frowned. "I thought about it before I asked you, Elin. I want to do what's best for Josie. I know you do too. A-And I think it's best for us too. I'll be a good husband to you."

She wet her lips and looked down. Something was going on in her head that he couldn't figure out.

She finally lifted her head and looked him in the eye. "What's best for Josie is to grow up in a happy home. For her to feel loved and treasured. For her to know her home won't be torn apart by divorce or bickering."

"I don't intend to bicker with you. Or to ever divorce. I put high regard on my word, and I won't break it." Did she think he would enter into marriage lightly? He thought she knew him better than that.

She nodded. "I feel the same, but have you thought about the day-to-day business of being married?"

"You think I'll make it hard on you? I won't. We can have separate suites, and you can do what you like. I won't make any demands on you. I'll even do my share of the cooking and cleaning." He grinned to try to defuse the tension.

She wet her lips again. "We can't just ignore the chemistry between us. Can you deny it still exists? I feel it every time you look at me."

He'd thought he was doing a better job of hiding his attraction. "What difference does it make? I won't act on it."

"Why not?" she asked, her voice soft. "Because you don't trust me? Trust is pretty important in a marriage."

He exhaled and leaned back, unsure where she was going with this. Did he trust her? Maybe not.

"What are you thinking? Your silence is making me nervous," she said. "Talk to me."

"Thought that's what I was doing. I'm thinking about trust

and what it means. You didn't tell me about Josie, and that was wrong. Part of me understands why you did it, but maybe I'm afraid you won't be honest with me."

She winced, and her eyes grew luminous. "You don't understand the pressure I was under."

"He's been dead for two years."

"I didn't want to open a can of worms. And I wanted to forget that night. I assumed you did too. It was so out of character for us."

"We have to quit beating ourselves up over it."

She nodded. "I haven't forgiven myself even now. And I'm sure Tim never did." Her voice lowered to a whisper and wobbled on the last two words.

"God has and that's all that matters." Against his will, he saw where her decision had come from.

She inhaled. "What do you want from a marriage, Marc? Can you tell me honestly?"

He stared into her face, seeing the vulnerability she laid bare. How did he feel? He hadn't let himself look too deeply for fear of what he'd see. He wasn't aware he'd reached for her until his fingertips traced the curve of her cheek and sank into her thick, damp hair. He stared into her eyes and felt something rising in his chest, a powerful emotion he'd never thought to experience.

Her eyes fluttered shut as she drifted toward him. His gaze went to her lips, so soft and kissable. He leaned closer, nearly dying for the taste of her, the feel of her in his arms. He brushed his lips across hers. The sweet scent of her breath made him pull her closer and sink in for a deeper kiss. He'd forgotten how wonderful it felt to hold her.

His cell phone rang, and he blinked. He didn't want to open his eyes, didn't want to let the world intrude on this moment.

"Marc?" she muttered against his lips. "Your phone. It might be important."

He opened his eyes and smiled down into her face. "Slave driver." He reached for his phone. The screen read *Josh Holman*. Why would he be calling? He thumbed it on. "Marc here."

"Have you heard from Sara?" Josh's voice was worried. "She never came back from Seagrass Pier. I called the house, and they haven't seen her. I'm there now, and her boat is still here, but there's no sign of her."

"We haven't heard from her." Marc glanced at the clock above the fireplace. It was ten. She should have been back hours ago. "On our way."

———

The moon illuminated her brother as he knelt over his bag. Kalianne didn't like his quick, furtive movements or the way he flexed his jaw and muttered under his breath. She inhaled when she caught sight of the long cylinder in his hand. "What are you doing?"

He glanced up. "Thanks to your ineptitude, I must ensure the Coastie never talks."

He puffed on his cigar, then held the tip to the stick of dynamite in his hand. The fuse began to sputter, and he tossed it into the cave, then turned and walked away.

Her chest burning with the desire to stop this, Kalianne followed him, and they stopped a safe distance away. The *whump* that came a few seconds later made her cry out and clap her hands over her ears. A cascade of rocks and debris rained into the space that had once been the opening. She sank to her knees and moaned.

She'd participated in a murder. Her stomach revolted and she fought nausea.

Her brother jerked on her arm. "You are weak, Kalianne. We did what had to be done."

She didn't resist as he dragged her to her feet. "You mean, *you* did what you wanted." Tears coated her lashes and blurred her vision. She was just as guilty as he was.

"Now you must get back into the house and find the pouch. It is most unfortunate you let the old woman take it away from you. We were so close."

"At least we know it's there. Are you *sure* it's the map?"

"I'm positive. Chann Seng never gave up its hiding place, and that golden city still exists somewhere in the jungles of Cambodia. I mean to find it. We will be kings and queens, Kalianne. There are riches there beyond imagination."

"Why do you care so much? You don't need the money."

His teeth gleamed in the moonlight. "Power, Kalianne. The money I have now is but a drop in the bucket to what I will have. Plus, I can shed the persona of a smuggler and take my rightful place as an explorer. The world will open at my feet. No one would dare seek to arrest me."

He propelled her away from the murder site. She tried not to think about poor Sara, crushed and buried under tons of rock. Really, it was the woman's own fault. She shouldn't have interfered. To distract herself, Kalianne imagined finding that ancient Khmer Empire city. Gold, precious jewels, vast statues worth millions. Such wealth was beyond her imagination, though Devi had expounded on it at great length for years. He'd sought that pouch for over ten years, and when he'd found Chann's diary in a shack in Cambodia, he'd known it would soon be in his hands.

He'd sent her in here with the promise of all the money she could imagine. If only she could find that pouch with the map. That stupid old lady.

They exited the forest, and she looked toward the house. Lights shone from several of the windows. "I'll find it if I have to shake the truth out of her."

"There will be a great search for the woman tomorrow. Go tonight. Find it now while there is still time."

"People are in the house. An attorney and his wife. Also the old woman and the little girl."

"Drug them." He reached into his bag and handed over a vial of pale liquid. "One drop of this in their drinks, and not even a hurricane will wake them."

"Okay." Her fingers closed around the vial. She wasn't about to drug the little girl. The old lady, yeah. And the other couple. But not the kid.

"Don't leave until you have the map. I want it found tonight." He took the path toward the pier.

She took a deep breath, squared her shoulders, then walked briskly to the back of the house. The Evertons sat at the table on the deck.

Mr. Everton waved when she got nearer. "I thought you were gone for the day. What brings you back?"

"I forgot to give Ruby some medicine."

Mrs. Everton lifted a brow. "You could have called. We would have done it."

"I tried, but the phone was out. It's probably not a big deal since it doesn't seem to be helping her memory, but I want to do everything I can for her. Is Ruby in the living room?"

Mrs. Everton nodded. "She's reading Josie a story."

"I brought some new tea I found and thought I'd make some before I go. You want some too?"

"That would be lovely. You're a sweet girl, Kalianne. I'm so glad you're taking such good care of Ruby."

Kalianne smiled and thanked her. Inside the kitchen, she shut the door behind her and exhaled. This was working out better than she'd hoped. When she peeked into the living room, she saw Ruby holding Josie. The little girl was already asleep.

"Here, Ruby, let me take her to bed. She's out."

Ruby's eyes were vague, but she didn't protest when Kalianne lifted Josie out of her lap and carried her toward the stairs. "This kid is heavy."

It was all she could do to carry Josie up the stairs and deposit her in bed. She pulled the covers over her, then went back to the living room. "Ruby, do you remember where you put my leather pouch? You know, the tan one? It's old and about this big." She measured the width with her hands. "I want you to help me look for it."

"Okay." Ruby started to get up.

"Not now. I'm going to fix some tea, but I'll be back. Maybe you can show me where the pouch is, okay?" She waited a moment, but Ruby didn't respond.

Kalianne pressed her lips together and went to make the tea. Checking to make sure the Evertons weren't looking through the window, she put a drop of the pale liquid into each cup. When the water was hot, she brewed the tea, then carried out a tray of cups and the teapot.

"Here we go." She placed it on the table, then poured the tea, taking care they got the right cups.

In fifteen minutes, they yawned and excused themselves for bed. Now to find the map.

THIRTY-FOUR

Elin glanced at the house as they hovered in for a landing on the front of the beach by the pier. The windows were dark, so everyone was asleep. It was nearly midnight. The moon, bright and golden above them, lit the scene as well as a streetlight.

Marc took her arm, and they bent over and ran under the rotating blades to meet Josh and Curtis on the beach.

"Any sign of her?" Marc asked when they reached the two men.

Josh shook his head. "Just her boat." He pointed out the dinghy bobbing at the pier. "We were searching for another crate that had been tossed overboard from that drug-boat rescue a couple of weeks ago. We'd searched most of the area, but she was going to look over there." He pointed to the area behind the house that backed up to the maritime forest. "Then she planned to hang out at the house."

"How did you know there was a problem?" Elin wanted to grab a flashlight and go looking now herself.

"I tried to call her a bunch of times, thinking she was at her house." His voice was pinched. "When I kept getting voice mail, I found Mr. Everton's cell number and called him. He said they hadn't seen Sara. I had him come down to see if her boat was still here. When he called back and said it was, I knew something was wrong. I shouldn't have left her to search alone."

"Has anyone gone into the forest to look for her?" Marc asked.

Curtis nodded. "Your dad went back there with a flashlight, but he didn't see any sign of her." He gestured toward the pile of equipment on the sand. "So we gathered lights and com units, then took the chopper to Kill Devil Hills to get you so we could do an organized search by grids."

"Let's go."

From Marc's clipped tone, Elin knew he was worried about his cousin. She was too. This wasn't like Sara. She could have fallen down a hole or something. Or she'd run into the drug smugglers, and they'd shot her.

She shuddered and turned toward the path to the forest. "Let's get going. We have to find her." She grabbed a bright halogen light and headed away from the ocean. The others seized equipment and followed her.

Marc jogged to catch up with her. "I tried to call her too, and it dumped me right into voice mail."

"If she's here, there is no cell service. It's going to be hard looking in the forest at night, even with lights."

"I know."

Elin reached the tree line and flipped on the light. She cupped her other hand to her mouth. "Sara!" She paused and listened. Nothing but the rustle of the wind in the trees.

Josh moved off to her left. "I'm going this way. Curtis, you fan out to the east."

The halogen lights put out more light than Elin had imagined. With four lights glaring into the darkness, it was almost as bright as dusk.

Marc shone his light along the path. "I want to see if she's dropped anything, or if there's a sign of other people tracking through here. You ever been back here?"

"No. We always go to the beach."

The smell of the forest, fecund and earthy, added to her sense of unease. She stopped and called often for Sara, but there was no response.

Shining his light on the ground, Marc strode a couple of feet ahead of her. She kept her light glaring higher, at face level, hoping to catch a glimpse of Sara running to meet them.

They reached a small clearing and walked through it to an area where rocks protruded from the earth. Stopping, Elin called again. The search felt hopeless.

"Whoa, what's this?" Marc stooped and picked up something. "Is this Sara's cell phone?" He held up a white iPhone.

She stepped closer to see. "Looks like it. Turn it on."

"You found her cell phone?" Josh spoke from behind them.

"I think it's hers." Marc turned it on, then went to recent calls. "Yep, there's a call from me last night. And a couple from you, Josh. She has to have been here." His beam scanned the area slowly, lingering on every bit of ground.

"Is that rope?" Josh stepped close to the rock face and knelt, then turned with a hank of rope in his hands. "Looks like it was tied. Could she have been restrained with this?" His voice held an edge of fear.

Elin swallowed and touched the rope. "Maybe." She didn't want to believe some criminal might be doing harm to her best friend. Turning away, she shone her light around the area. "Looks like something was dragged here."

Marc stooped. "I see it. That crate maybe."

She swept her light up the rock face. A tiny sliver of an opening peeked out at the top of a pile of rocks. "Do you think this is a recent cave-in?" She prodded the rock pile with her foot and small pebbles rolled off. "Look up there. Could this have been a cave?"

Josh began to climb the rocks, but he kept sliding back down. "I think it's recent. Call Curtis, and let's try to remove the rocks."

"You don't think she's in there, do you?" The thought of finding Sara's crushed and broken body under this pile made her shake.

Marc grunted. "I hope not, but there's evidence she's been here. I think we have to consider that she might be inside."

Her hands shook as she tried to raise Curtis on the walkie-talkie. When he answered, she spoke quickly. "Curtis, it's Elin. We need you right away. We have clues to Sara." She told him where they were.

"On my way," he said.

———

Marc paused to wipe the dust and sweat from his face. The same dust coated his throat and mouth. They'd made little headway on the cave-in. Had it been done deliberately? He didn't want to find Sara's body on the other side.

The moon had gone behind some clouds, but their lights lit up the place and illuminated the graffiti on the rocks.

Josh worked tirelessly at the pile, not pausing or even showing any signs of weariness. Marc took his arm. "Have some water, Josh."

"Sara has none." He didn't look up and renewed his efforts.

"I think we need to regroup and think about this. It might take days to get through this by hand. Maybe we should call for some equipment."

Josh finally paused and wiped the back of his hand across his forehead. He looked from Marc to the rock pile. "Maybe. This thing seems to go on forever. We have to find her. She has to be all right." His shoulders slumped as he joined the rest of them by the backpack of water and snacks.

"We'll find her. I'm sure she's fine." Marc wished he felt as confident as he sounded.

Elin came from the other side of the pile. Her face and hands were black with dirt. "I'll take some water." Her voice was hoarse.

He handed her a bottle of water, and their hands touched. If only she didn't have to be working out here so hard. She appeared so fragile in the glare of the halogen lights. He wanted to protect her from what they might find in that cave. With every minute that passed, he grew more concerned.

Josh accepted the bottle of water Curtis offered. "Let's mobilize some assistance."

"I'll call it in." Curtis walked a few feet away, out from under the tree cover. His low voice echoed back to them.

Josh glanced around. "I used to come out here when I was a kid with my dad. He liked hunting deer. Something keeps bugging me. I have this memory of playing in a cave, but it wasn't here." He gestured to the north. "It was that way, I think. I wish he were still alive so I could ask him about it."

Marc capped his water. "Think, Josh. It might be a branch off this one. If you can find it, we might be able to use the lights and wind through the passages to find her." He couldn't help the leap of hope he felt, even though it was a long shot.

Josh rubbed his head. "I'm thinking. It was a long time ago, and it's hard to remember."

Curtis jogged back to join them. "Ben is sending out some equipment, but it will be daylight before they get here. I say we keep working in the meantime. We might get through."

"Yeah, I agree." Marc set down the bottle of water and started for the rock pile.

"Wait a second." Josh turned and looked to the north. "I seem to remember it being by a waterfall. Anyone know of a waterfall around here?"

Elin frowned. "I haven't explored this area, but Sara said something about a waterfall. She said it was at the head of Larson Creek."

"I know where that is!" Josh ran off to the north, his light bobbing ahead of him.

"Wait for me!" Marc grabbed his light. "You two want to come or stay here and keep working on moving the rocks?"

Elin grabbed a light and stepped toward him. "I'm going with you."

"Let's split up and maximize our chances," Curtis said. "I'll keep working here. Ben was going to see about sending out some manual labor in the meantime too, and I'll need to guide them here."

Marc took Elin's hand. "Stay close. Curtis, call us if you break through."

"Will do." He bent over the rocks again.

Marc kept hold of Elin's hand as they chased the bobbing, weaving light ahead of them. "Josh seems to know where he's going."

"I just pray it's a passageway that will lead us to Sara." She sounded out of breath.

The chances of that were slim. Marc was beginning to lose hope altogether. They crossed a stream and climbed up a hillside covered with clover that filled his nose with its scent when they stepped on it. Josh's light had stopped at the top of it, and they found him bending over a small opening.

Marc stooped and stared. "That's it? It hardly looks big enough to crawl though."

Josh kicked a clump of dirt out of the way. "It's bigger inside than it looks out here. Of course, I was a kid then, so even this opening seemed bigger than what I'm seeing now."

"I think I can fit through if you men can't," Elin said.

Josh laid on his belly and shoved the light through, then poked his head in. "The room is still there. Looks to be about five feet high, and it branches off to the south. I'm going in." His voice was muffled.

"I'll be right behind you."

Josh's head emerged, and he looked up at Marc. "I don't know what we'll find in there. It may be very unsafe. No sense in both of us getting killed. Let me go, and you stay here and guard this entrance. Whoever caved in the other opening might try to do the same here."

The man made sense. Marc nodded. "If you haven't found anything in an hour, come back. We need to get those rocks moved if this doesn't lead to her."

"I'm not coming back without her. This is the answer. I just know it." Josh wriggled through the opening and was gone.

Marc glanced down and saw tears in Elin's eyes. "You okay?"

She nodded. "We have to find her."

—

The leather pouch was important. Ruby clutched it to her chest and huddled in the corner of the attic. The darkness outside frightened her, but she had to do this. Elin had told her the story of Georgina's pouch. It must never be found. She must guard it with her life.

For a moment, she saw a girl with long brown hair standing on the parapet with this pouch in her hands. Where would Georgina want her to hide this? Ruby didn't like her new aide anymore. She'd been so insistent on having this treasure, but it was not for her. Not ever.

Ruby's gaze fell on a space under the stairs to the roof. Would there be a hiding place under there? She rose and examined the wall encased in oak paneling. There was a screwdriver around here somewhere. She put down the leather pouch, then found it in an old toolbox. She used the tool to pry a corner of the paneling loose to reveal the cavity under the stairs, then she opened the pouch and withdrew the old map inside.

It didn't look that important. Hand drawn, it looked old and faded. She stuffed the map behind the paneling, then tapped the nail back into place. No one would ever find it unless she told them where it was.

This secret would go to the grave with her. Owen would be so proud of her. Smiling, she carried the pouch to the chest and put it in the hidden compartment in the bottom.

THIRTY-FIVE

Kalianne checked on the guests, but they didn't stir when she spoke their names loudly. Mr. Everton's breathing was loud and labored, so she hoped she hadn't harmed him. She didn't want another murder on her conscience.

Maybe she should search this room while they slept so soundly. She hurried to the living room and took Ruby by the hand. "Let's go find my pouch now, okay? It wasn't very nice of you to hide it. It's mine, Ruby."

Ruby blinked, and tears filled her eyes. "I didn't take anything, Kalianne. I'm sleepy. I want to go to bed now."

"You can't go to bed until we find my pouch." She jerked on Ruby's arm and led her up the stairs. "Let's look here first."

Ruby dug in her heels. "That's Christine's room. I'm not supposed to go in there."

"They're sleeping and won't notice." Kalianne opened the door and dragged Ruby inside the bedroom.

The old woman huddled in the corner and wouldn't budge. She was going to be more trouble than she was worth. Gritting her teeth, Kalianne went to the closet and flipped on the light, then went through every bit of the closet. Nothing. She pressed and tugged on anything that might be a hidden panel, but she didn't find the pouch. She checked every inch of the room and attached bathroom.

When she came out of the bathroom, she saw Ruby sitting in the corner with her eyes closed. Kalianne shook her, then pulled her up. "Let's go to the attic, Ruby. Maybe you'll remember where you hid it."

She'd been certain the old woman had put it up there initially, but after searching when she could, she'd thought maybe Ruby had moved it. But it was likely still up there. She flipped off the light, then urged the old woman up the steep stairway to the third floor. Even with the light on, there were too many shadows to be able to perform a good search. This was never going to work.

And she was tired, emotionally exhausted from what had happened in the forest. Maybe she should just go home tonight.

"I remember where it is."

Kalianne whirled and saw her heading to a chest against the wall. Joining the old woman, she watched as Ruby lifted everything out of the chest, then opened a hidden compartment in the bottom.

"The pouch!" She snatched it from Ruby's hands and clutched it to her chest. Finally.

"What are you doing?" said a tiny voice to her right.

She turned to see Josie standing near the top stair. Dressed in white pjs, she held her pink bunny in one arm. "What are you doing out of bed, honey?"

"I heard Grandma crying. Why is she crying?"

"She just cries sometimes. You know that."

Josie nodded and climbed the last step. "Why are you up here? It's dark."

Kalianne did her best to hide the leather pouch behind her. "I like to come up here and imagine watching for a ship." She needed to get that kid out of here and back to bed. Maybe she should drug her after all.

"Mommy likes to read the diary up here."

Diary.

"What diary?"

"You know, the lady who used to live here a long, long time ago. Mommy likes to read about her. She had twins. Mommy read it to me." Josie lowered her voice and leaned forward. "She hid a leather pouch here."

"Your mother did?"

"No, silly. The lady who lived here. Mommy read me that part the other day. A friend asked her to hide it forever, to never let anyone find it. I think she hid it really, really good."

Kalianne gave her best smile. "Where did your mommy put the diary?" Maybe it would be helpful for Devi as well.

Josie shook her head. "I don't know where it is."

All she had to do was come back when Elin was here and grab the diary. Kalianne took Josie's hand. "We'd better get to bed. Your mommy will be upset that you're still up."

Josie's fingers curled around Kalianne's. "Where is Mommy? She always tucks me in. And I want a horsey ride with my daddy. I'm not sleepy." Her lower lip trembled.

"How about if I read you a story? Then when Mommy and Daddy come, I'll send them to tuck you in. Okay?"

She breathed a sigh when Josie nodded and didn't object to moving toward the stairs. Finding the pouch was a jolt of adrenaline. Devi would be so happy with her.

"Come along, Ruby." When she turned to look, Kalianne felt a cool breeze on her face. Ruby had opened the door to the outside. "Josie, I'll be along in a minute. You go pick out the book you want, okay?"

"'Kay." Holding on to the railing, Josie went back down the stairs.

Kalianne hurried up the steep rooftop access. When she

stepped out into the sea breeze, she saw Ruby with one foot half over the railing. Kalianne rushed to grab the old woman's arm and got there as the other leg swung toward the railing. If she hadn't been here, Ruby would have fallen from the parapet.

Kalianne dragged her back to safety. "Ruby, what were you doing up here?"

The old woman cried noiselessly, the tears leaving tracks on her face that gleamed in the moonlight. "I want to be with Owen. I miss him."

"It's not time yet. Come to bed." She led Ruby toward safety.

That had been a close call. The last thing she needed was to get the police out here.

———

Sara's light was beginning to flicker, and she fought back the rising panic. She was going to die in this inky blackness. No one would ever find her bones. She slid to the ground and turned off her light, plunging the cramped space into utter darkness.

She pulled her knees to her chest and buried her face as she tried to pray. The words wouldn't come, but she felt God's presence, and her panic began to edge into peace. She and Josh were not to be. She'd never hear him finally tell her he loved her. She'd never rest in his arms.

The hard rock bit into her head as she leaned back and tried to think of what to do. Her flashlight wouldn't last much longer. Should she try to go back the way she'd come and see if she could dig out of the cave-in, or would that be futile? Should she press on, hoping she'd find another tunnel out? There was no easy answer. She sat in the inky blackness and listened to her shallow breathing. It was the only sound.

She couldn't curl into a ball and die here. If she was about to step into eternity, she would do it on her feet, still fighting. Her fingers curled around the tiny flashlight, but she resisted the impulse to flip it on. She would turn it on every few minutes, just to orient herself. Sidling along the cold rock face, she shuffled forward a few feet. Her feet struck something in the way, and she flipped on her flashlight.

It was another branch in the trail. Which way now?

She stared to the right, but it was too dark beyond three feet. The left passageway went only two feet, then stopped at an impassable wall. Or was it? The wall was only six feet high. Was that a glimmer of light from above it? She shut off her flashlight to make sure. Yes, it was! She moved to the wall in her path and ran her fingers along its surface to see if she could find indentations to use to climb it. The dim light gave her courage.

She found several likely spots and fitted her right foot in the first one, then reached above her head for the tiny sliver of a grip she'd found. Grunting, she hoisted herself off the floor, then reached for the next hold. Her fingers began to cramp, and she paused a moment to try to fit her toe into a better spot. There it was. Little by little, she crept up the wall until she could peek over it. The faint light didn't show her much, just more rock.

Her fingers lost their purchase, and she slid down a few inches below the top of the wall. Resting a moment, she leaned her head against the cold rock, then tipped her head at a sound she couldn't place. It seemed to emanate from the other side of the wall. A kind of shuffling sound. Her heart seemed to stop as she realized it was probably Devi coming to kill her.

Where could she hide? Or would he even look on this side of the passage? Maybe he would come to the wall and stop. The opening at the top might be too small for a man. She didn't want to slide down the wall for fear he would hear her, so she waited with her face pressed against the rock.

Someone coughed, a short bark, then more shuffling came to her ears. She waited, barely breathing, to see what he might do.

"Great, just great," came a barely discernible mutter.

Her eyes widened. It sounded like Josh, but it couldn't be. Could it? The Coasties would have put up a hue and cry when she didn't return, but why would any of them be in this cave? Cautiously, she stretched onto her toes so she could peek over the top of the wall.

A familiar Dodgers ball cap was right below her. Josh leaned against the wall and wiped his forehead with his forearm.

"Josh?" Her voice was barely a squeak.

His head jerked up, and he brought up the flashlight. The beam hit her full in the face and blinded her after being in the dark so long.

"Sara!" He dropped the flashlight and began to climb the wall.

She reached for the top and pulled herself up, her toes scrambling for purchase in her urgency to reach him. His fingers touched hers as she struggled up the final few inches. Both panting from exertion, they faced one another at the top.

"Josh, I can't believe you're here. How did you find me?"

He leaned forward, and his lips found hers. She struggled to stay glued to the wall as the press of his lips brought tears coursing down her cheeks. She thought she'd never see him again, never smell his cologne or feel the roughness of his evening whiskers. Her fingers itched to plunge into his hair, but all she could do was hang on to the wall for dear life.

He lifted his head. "I thought you were dead." His voice was choked. "We saw the cave-in, and we thought we'd find your broken body inside. I couldn't stand it." His gaze bored into hers. "I love you, Sara. I've always loved you. My life has no meaning without you. Forget everything I said earlier. It was fear talking."

"I know." She could barely whisper past the lump in her throat. "I'm going to try to get through this opening."

"I'll catch you." His feet thudded back onto the cave floor.

She sought another toehold and found it, then pushed with her left leg and swung her right onto the top of the wall. With her last bit of strength, she hoisted herself atop the wall. It wasn't as wide as she expected, and she couldn't stop herself from hurtling right on over. Then she was falling.

A pair of strong arms caught her and held her close. She looked into Josh's blue eyes. Safe.

THIRTY-SIX

Elin wrapped a blanket around her friend, who looked a little shocky with pale skin and blue lips. Sara's teeth chattered, even though it was seventy-five outside and about the same here in the living room. The big windows showed the sun beginning to peek over the water.

Elin thrust a cup of hot tea in her hands. "Here, drink this."

Sara wrapped both hands around the cup. "I d-don't know why I'm s-so cold."

Josh sat close to her on the sofa. "You're having a reaction. Are you hurt at all?"

Sara sipped the tea, then shook her head. "I don't think so."

"What happened?" Marc sat in an armchair on the other side of the area rug. His hazel eyes were alert, and he didn't look like a man who had been up all night.

Sara stared up at Elin. "You're not going to like this, Elin. Kalianne was part of this."

Elin lowered herself to the chair. "K-Kalianne? Mom's aide? I don't understand."

"She's Devi Long's sister. I came upon her with a crate, and when I insisted on seeing inside, she knocked me out." Sara shook her head. "I'm ashamed I let her get the upper hand."

Josh took her hand. "She didn't seem the type to get violent." He laced his fingers with hers.

Elin looked at their linked hands. Something good had come out of this awful night. "She tried to kill you?"

"No, that was Devi, I'm sure. She called him, and he came to take care of their 'little problem.' She objected and tried to protect me. When she stepped in front of me, I ran into the cave. I found the deeper passage, and the next thing I knew, I heard the cave-in."

Elin shuddered. "I have always thought I was a good judge of character. I guess that's not true." She looked at Marc. "Can we get her picked up?"

"We can try, but I'd guess Devi took her away before she could give away any more information about him." He pulled out his cell phone and placed a call.

A sense of dread curled in Elin's belly. "Mom's been sleeping a lot. I thought it was part of her dementia. What if it wasn't? What if Kalianne's been drugging her so she could go out and search for those drugs?" Her fingers curled into fists. "I've been so stupid!"

"We all trusted her. I gave her those tops and capris. I liked her." Sara took another sip of her tea. "She was good at her masquerade."

Marc ended his call. "I think they have a lead on her and her brother. A Coast Guard cutter stopped a speedboat offshore a few hours ago. There was a couple aboard who sounds like those two. The Coasties didn't find anything amiss, so they let them go, but they told the patrol they were headed to Kill Devil Hills. We've got the description of the boat and its identification number. A patrol boat is headed that way to see if their boat is in the harbor."

"I doubt they'll be there." Josh still hadn't let go of Sara.

"I should check on Mom." Elin started to get up, but Marc shook his head.

"Let her sleep. I don't think Kalianne did her any real harm."

"I'm so glad I never had her watch Josie." She glanced at Josh and Sara. "There must have been a lot of money in the drugs for them to go so far."

"A crate that size could contain millions of dollars in heroin," Sara said. "I wish I'd gotten a chance to see inside it."

Marc yawned. "There's time for a little shut-eye if you all want to head to bed. Everyone will be up in a couple of hours."

A secret smile hovering on her lips, Sara glanced at Josh. "I'm not really tired. I think I'd like a walk along the beach."

"I'm game." Still holding on to her hand, he rose and helped her up. "We'll be back in time for breakfast."

Elin watched them go. "Something happened between them."

Marc grinned. "You think?" His smiled faded when their gazes locked. "We got a little interrupted in our own discussion. Want to go back to it, or are you too tired?"

What was he saying? That kiss had shattered her last bit of resistance. She loved him so much. Had he been about to admit he had feelings for her? She'd asked him how he felt, and he hadn't answered.

She feigned a yawn. "We can talk about it another time. I'm pretty tired." She rose and headed for the stairs.

———

Elin had gone off to rest awhile ago, and Marc sat with his parents on the back deck with the birds singing from the trees lining the back of the property. Saturday morning cartoons playing on TV would keep Josie and Ruby occupied for a few minutes while he discussed things with them.

His mother looked about to burst. She still wore her blue robe, but his father was dressed in jeans and a red T-shirt. His fishing hat perched on one side of his chair. They both looked tired, probably from keeping up with a four-year-old.

Marc stirred nuts into his oatmeal. "What do you think of your granddaughter?"

His mother handed him the cinnamon. "Oh, Marc, she is darling! But I'm so worried Elin is going to yank her away from us."

"Elin wouldn't do that."

His mother shifted in her chair. "We have no rights to her. I'm sure her birth certificate lists Tim as her father. What if you and Elin get into a spat, and she refuses to let us see her? We'll have no recourse."

"Elin wouldn't do that."

His father gave a slow nod. "She doesn't seem the vindictive type."

"What are you going to do to ensure you get to see Josie? That we all do?"

His mother would worry that bone into shards. "I'm working on it."

"What does that mean? Have you gotten a lawyer? Your father could help with that. I think we should get Elin to agree to give us grandparent rights."

"Things are fragile right now, Mom. Don't rock the boat. Let me handle this. I don't need a lawyer." It took everything in him to keep his voice from rising. He wasn't four.

She bit her lip. "I'm just worried, honey. We love Josie already."

"So do I. And Elin is thankful we love her daughter. A child never has too much love."

"You know how your father and I feel about a child growing up without a father. You'll need to take extra steps to ensure Josie always knows you'll be there for her."

"I intend to." He choked down another bite of oatmeal.

Feeling so helpless in this situation wasn't something he relished. Elin held all the cards. He had to dance to her tune. For the first time, he wondered if he *should* talk to his dad about the legalities. How many fathers had found themselves standing on the outside of their children's lives? He didn't want to be one of them. And the killer closing in made things even more difficult.

"You know exactly what you want to do," his father observed. "Let's hear your plan."

Trust his father to recognize the intent on his face. "I want to marry Elin."

His mother gasped and half rose until his father grabbed her arm. "I knew you had feelings for her! I can see it whenever you look at her." She toyed with her spoon, twirling it around on the table. "I was beginning to think you didn't believe in a lasting love and marriage."

He had to shake his head and look away from his mother's penetrating gaze. "I only have to look at you and Dad to know real love exists. That kind of love is hard to find."

"Does she love you?"

He made a face. "I doubt it." Though that kiss last night had shattered his certainty about a marriage of convenience only. But if she loved him, why was she avoiding talking more about marriage?

His father leaned forward. "Marriage takes work. It's not about luck or just love either. It's about commitment. When you're in the thick of the battle with raising kids, juggling busy careers, and finding time to mow the grass, a couple can look at each other and wonder where love went. It's still there though, if you look for it and nurture it. You don't enter into a commitment like that for convenience sake."

"You against it, Dad?"

His father shook his head. "I didn't say that. You are not the kind of man who makes a promise lightly. How do you feel about Elin? You skirted your mom's question pretty well, but that speaks volumes too. You love her."

Marc exhaled and sat back in his chair. The bald statement

was a stone pressing against his heart. It was so much easier to convince himself he only wanted this for Josie. The truth was so much more complex.

"No rebuttal?" His father was in full attorney mode now as if he were arguing a case.

Marc shook his head. "I don't want to love her."

His mother's eyes softened. "Love isn't something you can turn off and on like a water spigot."

He exhaled. "Yeah. Kind of inconvenient though. I don't think she feels the same."

"You're afraid to talk to her about it?"

"She'd run away if she knew I loved her, and things would be strained between us. I don't want that. I thought it was better if we had a common goal. We could at least be friends, and maybe in time she'd come to feel something for me."

His dad gave that sound he often made in court—something between a chuckle and a clearing of his throat. "Son, you need to take a good look at her. Love is written all over her face."

"I've only seen distance and wariness." But that was a lie. There had been something she wanted to say last night, but he'd been too afraid to let her close.

THIRTY-SEVEN

Sunday morning Elin slept in until eight, and by the time she showered, Christine had everyone fed and ready to head out for church, followed by an afternoon at the beach. Elin hated that she'd overslept and would miss church.

Christine hailed her when she came down the stairs. "I can't get your mother out of the garden. She thinks she has to pull every weed before church."

"I'll see what I can do." Christine followed her out the back door. Mom was standing in the mud in her bare feet, and she didn't stop when Elin called to her.

Her mother plunged the hoe into the dirt, displacing a tomato plant. "I need to find it."

Elin touched her arm. "What are you looking for, Mom?"

"The pouch. That leather pouch. It has to be here. Kalianne took it."

Elin frowned and looked at Christine. "What's Kalianne got to do with this? Have you seen her lately?" She hadn't told them about Kalianne's involvement. There hadn't been time.

Christine frowned. "I don't know. We haven't seen her since late Friday night."

"Friday night?" Elin's pulse sped up. "I thought she left early."

"She did, but she came back, saying she forgot to give your mother her medicine. She fixed us some tea, and we went off to bed while she was still here." Christine rubbed her eyes. "Neither of us have felt very well this weekend. I'm tempted to stay home from church today myself, but I don't want to disappoint Josie."

"She'll be fine if you don't feel up to going." She studied the circles under Christine's eyes. "But about Kalianne. What time was this?"

"Oh, after dark. Maybe nine?"

After her attack on Sara. "Did she give Mom her medicine then?"

"I think so. I didn't watch her. She went inside for a little while, then came out with some new tea. It had a funny taste, and I wondered if I was allergic to it. Maybe that's why I haven't felt well." Christine shook her head. "But Frank feels the same. Maybe it's a bug."

"Maybe she drugged you." Elin launched into what Kalianne had done. Christine's eyes got bigger and bigger. "So she came here after she thought Sara was dead. What does she want here? That's what I don't understand." She glanced at her mother again, who was still digging in the dirt.

That leather pouch. Could her mother have mentioned the diary to Kalianne? Maybe that's what she was looking for. Elin kicked off her flip-flops and stepped into the garden. "Mom, come with me for a minute. I need to talk to you."

"I can't find it." Tears hung on her mother's lashes. "It's not here."

"I don't think you put the leather pouch in the garden. You went to the attic, remember?"

The clouds in her mother's eyes lifted, and she nodded. "We found it though, me and Kalianne. I told her to leave it here, but I can't find it."

"Kalianne wants the leather pouch?"

Her mother nodded again. "It belongs to her."

"It doesn't belong to her. If she comes here asking for it again, tell me, okay?" Though her mother nodded, Elin knew she'd never remember. "Did Kalianne give you tea the other night? Or did she give Josie anything?"

"Josie." Her mother looked toward the house. "Josie couldn't find it either. Kalianne made her go to bed." Tears ran down her cheeks. "I don't like Kalianne anymore. She yells at me."

"She's not coming back," Elin assured her. "Let's get you cleaned up."

She led her mother out of the mud and over to the hose where she washed the mud from her bare feet. "You're going to miss church if you don't hurry."

Her mother brightened. "I like the songs." She shuffled toward the house at a slightly faster pace.

Christine leaned down and turned off the spigot. "I think we should take Josie and your mother back to our house, Elin. Surely you can't want them here with so much danger."

"You're right." Elin hadn't wanted to let go of her little girl, but the danger wasn't over. And there wasn't anyone to watch Mom either. Kalianne and her brother would be back. Laura's killer too. "Take them home with you after church. Call me every day though, okay?"

Christine embraced her, and Elin clung to her solid figure. "I'll take good care of her, honey. We already love her. Frank knows a lot of policemen. We'll hire someone to watch the house too, just in case."

"Thank you," she choked out. "We'll get through this. Thank you for loving my little girl in spite of everything."

"Thank you for letting us into her life. And yours." Christine released her with a final pat.

Elin watched her go. What would Marc think of this turn of events?

With the house quiet, Elin went to her office to do a little work. She heard the shower running in Marc's bedroom, so he was up too. She rubbed bleary eyes as she fired up her program. She'd gotten a text message a few minutes ago about a new donor she needed to work on ASAP. She studied the middle-aged woman's stats. Good lungs, bad heart, good corneas, kidneys, and liver. The work would get her mind off what was happening here.

She pulled up her list of recipients and began running through her matching procedure. She pulled out her phone and scrolled to the first recipient, a man in his midthirties who needed a liver transplant. Before she could place the call, a bar filled the screen of her computer.

YOU WILL NEVER MARRY HIM. YOU LOOK GOOD IN BLACK.

She gasped and rocked back in her chair. Looking around wildly, she tried to think of how someone could have taken over her computer. This was a highly secure website. It would be no easy matter to hack into it.

Marc appeared in the doorway with no shirt and his hair still wet. "What's wrong?"

She pointed to the screen. "Look."

He moved around behind her, and she caught a whiff of his clean-smelling skin. She handed the laptop to him so she could move to a safer distance.

"He knows a lot about computers. And I think he's obsessed with you, wants you for himself. It would explain why he hasn't just killed you the way he did Laura."

She shuddered and clasped her arms around herself. "I'm beginning to think so too."

He stared at the screen a moment. "What if he's another OPO representative?"

Her eyes widened. "Oh, I hope not. That seems wrong—that someone who is dedicated to bringing life from death would parcel out such pain to people."

"Evil can lurk in any heart. Let me get my computer too." He handed her the laptop, then headed for the door. "Can you get me a list of all the OPO representatives in this area?"

She nodded and went into an even more secure area where she downloaded a list of names. The thought of one of her coworkers being involved made her shudder. "Before you go, I need to tell you something. I told your mom she could take Josie home with her today. I'm worried about her being in the middle of this mess." She told him about Kalianne coming over after the attack on Sara.

"I was going to do my best to convince you to do that today. My parents will take good care of her. I want her out of here too. Glad you agreed." He stepped into the hall. "I'll be right back with my computer."

That had gone better than expected. Now to get this mess figured out.

Marc returned and sat in a chair with his computer on his lap. "I'm going to export the manifest. Send me the list, and I'll run a comparison to see if there were any OPO representatives on that boat the night Laura died."

She nodded. "Give me your e-mail address." She typed it in as he rattled it off, then attached the file to it. "You realize I'm not supposed to share this information?"

"You can trust me with anything." He bent over his computer keyboard. "It's here. Let's see what I can find out."

Warmth spread through her at his words. She knew she could trust him.

The ominous message on her screen vanished, and she eased back into her chair and exhaled. The doorbell rang, and she glanced out the front window of the office to see Sara standing outside. "I'll be right back."

She went to the door and hugged her friend. "You're okay?"

"Yep." Her smile was brilliant. She wore a sleeveless white top over a full skirt that swirled around her knees.

"I want to hear everything." She gestured to the hall. "Marc is in the office. We might be on to something." She led Sara to the office and pulled a chair up for her beside the desk.

Marc barely looked up. "Hey, Sara."

She smiled. "Is that the best you can do when I nearly died Friday night?"

He looked up then, and his slow smile emphasized the dimple in his right cheek. "Sorry. Distracted. Did Elin tell you what happened?"

"No, just that you might be on to something. What's up?"

"I had a threatening message come up on my computer. It was when I was in a secure OPO website, so Marc thought maybe the killer is another representative."

Sara's levity vanished. "How bizarre. I hope he's wrong."

Marc looked up. "I'm not. There was one on the ship."

"You're kidding! Who was it?" This wasn't something Elin really wanted to hear. Work would never be the same again.

"Kerri Summerall. Know her?"

Elin nodded. "Quite well. But she's the nicest person you'd ever meet." She turned to Sara. "You know Kerri. She was instrumental in getting me the new heart."

"And we know the killer is a man, so this is a dead end," Sara said.

"It wouldn't hurt to at least talk to her," Marc said. "Maybe she saw something." But his voice held little enthusiasm.

"I'll talk to her." Elin looked at her computer screen. "So we're back to a master hacker. Can we research the people on the manifest and see if there are any computer experts on it?"

"It will take time, but yeah, I can work on that. I'll get my assistant to start running checks."

Sara rose and walked to the window. "I wondered if the two

of you would like to have a celebratory dinner with Josh and me tonight." When she turned back toward them, her smile beamed.

"Only if you tell me what you're celebrating." Elin wanted to hear the whole story from her friend. "I bet I can guess though. The idiot finally came to his senses."

"Hey, that's my future husband you're talking about." Sara's smile grew wider. "We're getting married in a month."

Elin leaped up to hug her. "A month! Isn't that a little fast?"

Sara's smile was bright enough to light the room. "Neither of us want a big wedding, and I've waited on him for way too long as it is. I want to nab him before he changes his mind."

Marc hugged her too. "I hope I get to give you away."

She clung to him. "I wouldn't have it any other way. And Elin will be my maid of honor."

At least the horrible evening had brought something good with it.

THIRTY-EIGHT

The moon glimmered on the waves as they rolled to shore. Elin's flip-flops smacked on the old boards as she and Marc walked out to the end of the pier. Marc kicked off his flip-flops and dangled his feet off the end of the pier. She lifted her face to the fresh sea scent as she settled beside him. A dolphin leaped out of the water and splashed back down a few feet to their west.

A good omen for what she intended to tell Marc.

Her heart thumped in her chest. Maybe it was too soon for this decision. Maybe it was the wrong decision, and she would regret it.

She turned her head and looked at the lights gleaming out through the house. "I wonder what this place looked like in Georgina's day. I think it was about the same size. I haven't seen any obvious additions. Of course, she probably didn't have electric lights out here for a long time. Maybe when she was older, electricity made its way this far."

"Still no sign of the leather pouch you're looking for?"

She shook her head. "I wanted to hope Mom really found it, but I think it was just a hallucination. I'm sure it's long gone."

"She said Kalianne found it. When the police pick them up, hopefully we can get it back. If it even exists. The city hasn't been found though, so maybe it does."

"True." She lay back on the grayed boards with her legs still dangling over the edge of the pier and stared into the night sky. A million stars twinkled down on her, and the moon looked as big as a hot-air balloon.

"Gorgeous night."

"It is." What was she doing making small talk when she'd suggested this walk for a specific purpose? Her cowardice disgusted her.

Marc lay back too, then rolled on his side to stare at her. "Okay, Elin, what gives? It's not like you to suggest a romantic walk on the beach, so you must have something up your sleeve. You remembered something about the killer?"

She rolled to her side too, and they lay nose to nose about a foot apart on the cool boards. His spicy cologne mingled with the salt air. It felt way too intimate for what she wanted to say, but she wasn't backing out now.

She propped her head on her hand. "It's not about the murderer. I've been thinking about what you said about raising Josie together."

His eyes widened, and he propped his head on his hand too. "You've made a decision?"

"Sort of." She wet her lips. "I'll accept your suggestion."

"That's great!"

A little stunned at the light in his eyes, she shook her head. "Don't agree too quickly. I have one caveat."

"Name it." No regret lingered in his eyes, no trepidation.

Now came the difficult part. She could already feel the heat building in her cheeks. What kind of woman said what she intended to say?

"You look frightened." His words were soft. "You can tell me anything."

He was much too close and much too enticing. Unable to look into his eyes, she sat up and drew her knees to her chest. "What do you think of me, Marc?"

He sat up too. "I think you're strong and courageous. You see a glass half full no matter what is going on in your life. I love the way you think about other people first."

"I didn't phrase that right. How do you *feel* about me?" She wasn't sure she'd even be able to hear his answer over the pulsing blood in her veins. Surely that kiss meant something. Marc wasn't like some men. He wouldn't have kissed her like that unless he felt something.

The moonlight illuminated his face as he turned toward her. "I don't want to tell you because it might change your mind."

Her chest hitched, and pressure built behind her eyes. She would *not* cry. "I see. You feel nothing for me but friendship?"

He frowned. "I didn't say that. Heck, I might as well get it all out in the open." Reaching over, he twisted a long lock of her red hair around his finger. "I love you, Elin. I didn't want to, but when I'm around you, I feel somehow bigger and more capable. More whole."

Her throat closed, and her mouth went dry. Was he saying what she thought he was? She was afraid to look away in case the warm light in his eyes would disappear when she looked again.

"Nothing to say?" His rueful smile wobbled a little. "You going to change your mind now that you know I'm crazy about you?"

Moisture gathered on her lashes, and she shook her head. "I love you, Marc. Everything about you—your tenderness for Josie—did me in. When I saw how much love you were capable of, I began to want a piece for myself. My caveat was that I wanted us to at least have a date once a week and see if there was any spark left on your side."

His hand plunged into her hair, and he pulled her into his arms. His familiar male scent made her burrow closer. She could feel his heart thudding under her ear.

He touched her chin and tipped her face up, then his lips claimed hers. Warm and persuasive, the sweet pressure of his mouth made her wrap her arms around his neck. He loved her! Wonder filled her, and she returned the passion in his kiss with all the pent-up loneliness of the last five years.

He ran his thumb over the tears on her cheek and then passed the back of his hand over the other side of her face. "Why are you crying?" A shadow hunkered in his eyes.

"I'm happy, so happy," she whispered. "I never thought you would say you loved me. I never dared hope for it."

"I looked up that verse last night, the one in Corinthians about love." He fumbled in his pocket with one hand. "I wrote it out and was going to give it to you when I proposed with a ring, but you derailed my plans." He pressed the paper into her hand. "Love is always supposed to protect, trust, hope, and persevere. I want to show that kind of love to you and Josie."

More tears spilled from her eyes. "What do you think Josie will say?"

His tender smile beamed. "She'll ask if she can be the flower girl. But enough of Josie. Kiss me again, woman."

So she obliged. The taste of him wasn't anything she was going to get tired of.

⌒

Marc put down his suspense novel and wished he could go to sleep. He kept replaying the evening with Elin. They were going to be a family. He wanted to shout it from the rooftop.

He wasn't a warm milk kind of guy, but maybe a bowl of cereal would help. The kitchen was quiet, and he fixed his cereal, then carried it to the table by the window. He glanced down on the moonlit backyard. Silvery light bathed the flowers and trees all the way to the line of live oaks. He sat down and lifted the spoon to his mouth.

The glass shattered, and wood splinters flew from the chair he was sitting in. That was a gunshot. He dove under the table as things exploded around him again. His gun was in his room. He had to get his gun before Elin became a target. Reaching up, he flipped off the light and crawled into the living room and down the hall to his room. He grabbed his Glock from the top shelf in the closet and raced to Elin's room.

She was in the doorway when he got there. "I thought I heard gunshots." Her eyes were wide and frightened.

"You did. Go to your room and lock the door. Call the sheriff too. I'll go after the shooter."

She grabbed his arm. "Be careful, Marc. If he hurts you . . ." Her eyes swam with tears.

He squeezed her hand. "I will. You won't get rid of me so easily."

He raced down the stairs, then paused at the bottom and listened. The only sound that came to his ears was the wind. He dropped to his knees, crawled to the living room window, and looked out toward the water. Nothing moved but the waves and the trees.

After checking to make sure the front door was secure, he crawled to the dining area. The breeze came through the broken glass and lifted his hair. The hammock on the deck creaked in the wind too. He went to the kitchen and cautiously peered out the window. Nothing out of order.

The roar of a motor caught his attention, and he went to the living room again in time to see boat lights heading away from shore.

On Tuesday morning Elin hurried along to Oyster Café in Hope Beach. Kerri waved to her from a table in the courtyard. She wore her auburn hair up in a ponytail, and the turquoise top she wore enhanced the green in her hazel eyes.

Elin hugged her. "You got here early."

Kerri released her and sat back down. "You're buying. And besides, I could hear the excitement in your voice when you called. You're really going to marry Marc?"

Elin couldn't hold back the smile. "I am. I still can't believe it. I can't even tell you how happy I am."

"Where is the bridegroom today?"

Elin told her about the attack the night before. "He took the bullets to the FBI office to check ballistics." She rubbed her head. "I just want this over so we can get on with our lives."

"Me too. This is so scary. I'm glad you have Marc. But you said you had something else to talk to me about. What's up?"

Elin held up one finger as the server, a middle-aged woman dressed in shorts and a tank top, approached. They ordered coffee and she-crab soup. Once they were alone again, she pulled her chair closer to her friend. "Were you on the *Seawind* cruise? You never mentioned it."

Kerri went red, then white. She nodded. "I should have told you, but I didn't want you to know how stupid I was."

"I don't understand."

Her friend slumped back in her chair. "Ben had been calling, asking if we might stand a chance of getting back together. At first I told him no, but he told me he'd booked us on that cruise. I thought, what the heck? It's worth a try, especially if I got a free cruise out of it. Boy, was I wrong."

"What happened?"

"He'd gotten us two separate cabins, but I found it almost impossible to get him out of mine. But not for the reason you might think. He only wanted to talk about you. He asked how you were since the transplant, if you were seeing anyone. I think he only wanted me to go so he could grill me about you. He never so much as tried to kiss me." She blinked rapidly.

"I'm sorry, Kerri."

She nodded and twisted the napkin in her fingers. "I should have known better. And it's not your fault. He's just a freak."

The server brought their coffee. Elin thanked her and stirred in the cream as her thoughts raced. Could Ben still be attracted to her? But no, he'd gone out with Sara and seemed very interested. And he hadn't been by to see her, though she'd suspected he would.

"Did you meet Laura at all? She worked in the medical facility. You probably wouldn't have needed that, but I thought she might have been around for meals or something."

"I didn't, no. I would have told you I was there if there'd been the least bit of contact."

"I thought so, but I wanted to ask." Had Ben met Laura? Elin doubted Kerri would know.

"I didn't mean to upset you," Kerri said. "It's not a big deal. We tried and it didn't work. End of story."

"Ben is here, on Hope Island. Did you know that?"

Kerri shook her head. "But you know how he puts in for every fun assignment out there." She stopped and bit her lip. "Wait, are you saying he arrived after you did?"

When had he arrived on the island? Elin remembered back to what he had told her. "Actually, I think he got here before I did." The realization eased her trepidation. "A month or so before."

"Well, um, I think I might have mentioned to him that you were moving here. You put the offer on your house two months before you moved in. He called after we got home from the cruise. I think I might have said something."

She pushed away her unease. "At least he hasn't bothered me. It's no big deal."

"I hope not."

Elin stared at her friend. "What aren't you telling me, Kerri?"

"Haven't you ever wondered if he was a little obsessed with you?"

"Obsession seems a little strong."

"What happened when he showed up after Tim died? You didn't say."

Elin sipped her coffee to take away the chill she felt thinking about it. "He said in the Bible, the surviving brother took care of the widow, and he'd give me the children Tim couldn't."

Kerri shuddered. "Okay, that's seriously creepy. He tried to jump you?"

"Well, he tried to kiss me, but I shoved him away. He got really mad. I thought he was going to hit me, and I locked myself in the bathroom with my cell phone. I told him to leave or I'd call the police."

"And he did?"

She nodded. "I heard the door slam, then his truck started. I watched out the bathroom window until he pulled out of the driveway, then I ran to the front door and locked it."

"Did you see him after that?"

She put her coffee cup down. "I saw him a couple of times at his mother's. He acted like nothing had happened, so I did too. I chalked it up to distress over Tim's death. I think it was just grief talking. And when I saw him here, things weren't tense."

"That's probably it." Kerri looked unconvinced.

"Enough about this. All I have to do is stay out of his way. I think I need to warn Sara though. He may have transferred his obsession to her. Someone said he'd told him he intended to marry her. He won't be happy when he hears she's marrying Josh."

"Definitely warn her."

The server brought their soup, and Elin tucked into it. Sara was smart enough to handle someone like Ben.

—

Marc was getting coffee when his phone rang. He winced when he saw Harry's name on the display. His boss had already gotten wind of the bullets he'd brought in for analysis. His gut tightened at the thought of being fired.

He thumbed it on. "Everton."

"Well, you did it again, Marc."

Harry didn't sound mad. "Did what?"

"Ballistics of the bullets you brought in match the one that killed Will."

Marc's heart leaped. "Same gun?"

"Looks like it." Harry cleared his throat. "Looks like I owe you an apology. But you still disobeyed a direct order. I should fire you."

"But you won't."

"I'd be pretty stupid to fire my best agent. Find that guy, Marc. He murdered one of our own."

"I intend to. Thanks for letting me know personally, Harry."

"Least I could do. I'll send a couple more agents your way tomorrow. There will be nowhere for him to hide."

"Thanks. I'll touch base with you in the morning." He'd barely disconnected the call when his phone rang again. A Norfolk number. "Everton," he barked, expecting a sales call.

"Mr. Everton?" a female voice quavered, then gulped.

"Samantha?"

"Yes. I hope you don't mind me calling you."

He immediately remembered how pregnant she was. "Are you all right?"

"I'm fine." She inhaled. "I know where Ryan is. He just called Dad, and I overheard him say he was at the cabin."

"Cabin?"

"Yes, it's near Roanoke, out in the woods." She told him how to get there. "His family has owned it forever, and he's been holed up there. I forgot about it."

"Thank you for calling. I'm sure it wasn't easy."

"Don't tell my dad. He'd hit me if he knew."

"I won't. And if you ever want to get out of that house, I'll help you." He swung his Tahoe around to head toward the Outer Banks.

"I'm going to get out of here. I'm leaving with my boyfriend in the morning. Find Laura's killer, Mr. Everton."

"I'll do my best, Samantha."

"What about the woman who was with you? I can't get her out of my mind. The way she said my name, the way she tucked her hair behind her ear."

The hopeful tone in her voice tugged at his heart. Didn't he owe her the truth? "She has Laura's heart, Sammie. And she has some of Laura's memories with it." Her quick inhalation echoed in his ear. "But she's not Laura, honey. Her memories of Laura's death are helping us track down the murderer."

"W-Will you call me when you arrest him? I just want to see justice for Laura."

"I'll do that. Will you still have this number?"

"I'll keep it. Thank you, Mr. Everton. For everything."

He ended the call and saved her number to his phone. Following Samantha's directions, he drove straight to the cabin. The drive was a narrow dirt track back to a small cabin with a green metal roof. A porch extended across the front of the structure. A green Ford pickup, only its bed showing, sat along the side of the cabin. Must be Mosely's. Assuming the man wouldn't answer the front door, Marc went around to the back door and tried the handle. It opened easily, and he stepped into a dimly lit kitchen smelling of bacon.

On the other side of the wall, someone hammered. A radio

played country music in the distance, and he caught a whiff of strong male cologne. The same one they'd doused the red sweater with. The door opened noiselessly, and he peered into a square living room.

A man with shaggy blond hair appeared to be building book-cases. He sang in a low baritone along with the music, an old Willy Nelson tune.

"Ryan Mosely?"

The man jerked around and faced him with the hammer held up as if to strike. Marc tried a smile and held up his hand in a placating gesture. "Hey, I'm not a robber. I'm investigating the murder of Laura Watson."

Mosely's eyes went empty. "I don't know a thing about it. And you're trespassing. You didn't even knock."

"If you don't know anything about it, why did you follow us in your brown car and try to hit us?"

Mosely's face went red.

"I don't warn off easily." Marc advanced into the room. "You were aboard that ship too. I have the manifest. And I know you were stalking her. What happened? She rejected you one time too many and you strangled her?"

The man gripped the hammer hard, but at least he lowered it. "It wasn't me." His smile was way too easy and practiced.

Marc took another step toward him. "Then who did? You were stalking her. Don't tell me you didn't see something." Marc studied the man's demeanor, the way he held his gaze, the way he didn't blink. "Was anyone else hanging around her?"

Mosely's mouth flattened. "Yeah, that loser Theo. But she soon figured out his game. He didn't care enough to hurt her. And when I went back inside, I saw him reeling off with another woman to his cabin."

He thought back to the memories Elin had. "Let me see your hands."

Mosely stared at him, then extended his hands. "No scratches."

"Like that's what I'm looking for this far out from the attack. What about that ring, Mosely? You wear it all the time?" The ring had an *R* on it, and Marc dropped his hand a few inches closer to his gun. "My partner Will came to see you, didn't he? You knew you had to get rid of him, didn't you?"

Mosely took a step back, then the hand holding the hammer rose again, and he sprang toward Marc.

Marc sidestepped the blow and drew his gun, but Mosely's arm came down too fast. The hammer smacked into the side of Marc's head, and as he sank into darkness, he heard the man laugh before his footsteps faded into nothingness.

THIRTY-NINE

The rest of the afternoon stretched luxuriously in front of Elin. She'd dropped the car off to be serviced, and it wouldn't be ready until three. She didn't feel like shopping, even though the thought of planning the wedding enticed her. What she really wanted was an ice-cream cone and to visit with friends. Her call to Sara dumped her into voice mail.

With no choice, she bought a cone and ate it by herself at the picnic table by the road. Her phone rang, and she dug it out of her purse. Marc's mother's name came up on her screen. "Hey, Christine."

"Elin, thank goodness I got you. I didn't want to worry you, but it's your mother."

"What's wrong?"

"She seems to have forgotten who I am and where she is. She's locked herself in her bedroom and is wailing like a banshee."

Elin's stomach plunged. "My car is in the shop." She noticed the bike-rental shop right next door. "But I can rent a bike and get to the ferry. I'll be there as quickly as I can."

"I'll let you know if things change."

Minutes later, Elin pedaled out of town toward the ferry dock. There wasn't much traffic today since it was the middle of the week with the next ferry not due in for two hours. The breeze lifted her hair and filled her nose with the scent of wildflowers. Her leg muscles burned with the unfamiliar task of riding a bike, but in a good way. She'd spent way too much time at a desk.

She eased up on the speed a bit when her heart began to thump in her chest. The doctor had given her the go-ahead for a normal life, but it wouldn't pay to rush into exercise too quickly. Several cars passed, slowing down as they came abreast of her. The road entered a stretch of no houses, only maritime forest on one side and seagrass mixed into sand dunes on the other. The roar of the waves and the sound of the birds lulled her as she rode along.

Her phone rang, and she stopped to answer it. Christine again. "Josie coaxed Ruby out. She seems fine now. I hope I didn't worry you too much."

"Oh, good. Would it help if I talked to her?"

"I think it's better if we don't rock the boat. I'll call you again if I need you."

Elin ended the call and exhaled. Thank goodness. She wheeled the bike around in the other direction and headed back toward town.

Something thumped, and she thought she'd run over a rock, but then the front of the bike wobbled, and she realized the tire was flat. Great. Several miles from town without a car in sight. She dismounted and knelt by the tire. A nail gleamed in the side of the tire. She pulled out her phone and tried to decide who to call. Maybe the bike shop?

A truck slowed, and she glanced over to see a man smiling as he ran his window down. She smiled back, relieved she wouldn't have to walk this thing back to town. But a prickle of unease settled along her spine at the sight of his blond hair, which was stupid. Lots of guys had blond hair.

He parked the truck. "Got a flat?"

The sound of his voice made her take a step back, though she couldn't put her finger on why. "A bad one." She pointed out the nail.

He opened his door and got out. "I'll throw it in the back of the truck and take you to town. I was heading in for groceries anyway."

"Uh, no thanks. My friend is coming this way shortly. I'll just wait."

"You mean Marc?" An easy smile lifted his mouth. "I don't think you'll see him for a long time, and if he survives the fire, he'll have a pretty nasty headache from that hammer I hit him with. Though I don't think he'll survive the fire."

It took a moment for his words to soak in. She had to find Marc, save him. She whirled to run into the maritime forest, but his hand clamped down on her arm as she went for her cell phone. She tore at his strong fingers, but he propelled her toward the truck as if she weighed no more than a child.

"You're Ryan Mosely," she gasped.

"You're too smart for your own good." His fingers tightened on her arm. "You're even prettier up close."

Before she could react, his other hand came up, and she caught a whiff of chloroform on the cloth he moved toward her face. She went limp as if she'd fainted and shut her eyes, hoping he wouldn't dope her. His grip loosened, and she dropped to her knees and rolled under the truck.

He made a grab at her but missed, and she scooted into the center where he'd have to crawl to reach her. She could see his boots, then he dropped to his knees and peered at her.

His face contorted with rage. "I'm going to make you very sorry you gave me so much trouble."

He stood back up, and she watched his boots go around to the back. The tailgate scraped and banged as he opened it. Did he have a gun or something back there? She quickly sidled to the same side she came in under, hoping he'd think she would try another exit.

In a flash, she was on her feet and running for the forest. A shot whizzed over her head, and she hit the knee-high grass on her belly.

Then a shout came to her ears, a different male voice. She peeked up over the top of the weeds and saw Ben's truck parked behind the green one. The rifle in his hands barked twice, and Mosely crumpled to the ground.

Elin jumped to her feet and swayed as the blood rushed from her head. Ben had saved her. She hurried toward him. "Mosely was going to kill me!"

"I know." He put the gun down to his side. "I saw him aim the rifle at you. I was going hunting and had my rifle with me." He raked his blond hair back with a hand that appeared a little shaky. "Are you all right? Did the bullet hit you?"

"No, no, I'm fine. Just scared." When he put his arm around her, she let him lead her to his truck and seat her in the passenger seat. "Sorry to be so shaky. I–I didn't think I'd be able to get away."

"Let me get you to town and have the doctor look at you. You're white and shaking." He went around to the driver's side and got in.

"What about Mosely?"

"He's dead. I'll have the sheriff come out and collect the scum."

She exhaled and leaned back against the headrest. "Thank you, Ben."

"You're welcome."

Several sandwich wrappers lay crumpled on the floor, and she banged her foot against a pipe wrench.

"Sorry it's such a mess." He ran up his window and cranked up the air-conditioning. He started the truck and accelerated away.

She grabbed her seat belt and reached down to lock it into

place. A folder lay on the floor with pictures spilling out of it. Photos of her. Standing in the window at Seagrass Cottage, one even in her nightgown. Something squeezed in her chest, and she glanced up to see Ben staring back.

His gaze went from her to the pictures and back. Without expression, he reached to his door and clicked the lock on the doors, then flipped the child-protection switch before she could unlock her door.

"You killed Laura." She couldn't wrap her head around it. Not Ben, her own brother-in-law. "Why?"

"That was Mosely, not me." His voice betrayed no emotion. "But I'd finally had enough of your rejection. I thought all the stink you made about remembering Laura's death would be the perfect diversion. I could kill you and everyone would assume it was the same man who murdered Laura."

Elin could barely force the words out. The darkness in his eyes sapped all the heat from her body. "And Lacy? Was that Mosely too?" When he shook his head, her knees nearly gave out. "You?"

"It was her fault. I stopped by thinking you were there, and she slapped me when she found me in the kitchen."

"I don't believe you. You had a red wig with you and made her put it on. You planned it all along."

His eyes were fathomless, cold and emotionless. "Shut up, Elin."

She tried to yank up the lock on her door, but it wouldn't budge. Even her window wouldn't roll down. "Let me out of here."

"I can't do that. You never should have broken up with me to go with my brother. That *ruined* everything, Elin. Everything."

He terrified her. "You don't want to hurt me, Ben. You're my brother. You and I only went out a few times. It was a long time ago." She wished she'd said nothing when he shot a look of such venom her way. She cringed back against the door.

"You've always been mine, and you always will be. My brother had no right to take you away. I made sure he paid though."

Elin couldn't breathe as she thought through what he'd said. Tim had suffered a heart attack and died within hours of Ben's visit. "Did you kill Tim?"

The truck bounced over ruts, and he gripped the wheel and wrenched it back into the middle of the path. "He didn't deserve to live with what he was putting you through."

She remembered how Tim had shouted at her the day Ben was there. She'd buried so much of Tim's treatment, thinking she deserved it, accepting the penance. "Oh, Ben, I don't know what to say. He was your brother."

"Half brother. Once he came along, Dad never bothered much with me. First Tim took my father, then he took you. He deserved what he got."

"H-How did you kill him?"

"An injection of adrenaline. He was sleeping and I shot it between his toes, then left. I bet you never even saw the puncture mark."

"I didn't." Her mouth felt like cotton. "Neither did the coroner, evidently. Where are you taking me?"

"Where we can be together forever." The corner of his mouth twisted into a sinister smile. "They'll find us sooner or later, you know. But it will be too late. We can be together in eternity."

"Y-You're going to kill me?"

He shot a glance her way, a softer one filled with pleading. "I'll make it painless, my darling. You'll fall asleep in my arms and we will go together. Just like Romeo and Juliet."

If she could just get to her phone. She glanced at her purse on the floor where her phone peeked from a side pocket. Maybe once he got out of the truck, she could grab it and dial 911.

He must have seen her glance, because he reached down and

slipped her phone loose. Rolling down his window, he tossed it out into the weeds. "No one can be allowed into our final time together."

A scream built in her throat, but there would be no one around to hear. She didn't want him to see her terror. "I'll explain everything to them, Ben. Just let me go."

Shadows gathered in the truck as it entered a patch of trees. When he didn't answer, she yanked again on the door handle. Bushes scratched at the sides of the truck as it rolled deeper into the forest. Up ahead, the sunshine sparkled on grass.

A small seaplane sat in the clearing. An old metal hangar sat at the side of the road. He grabbed a garage-door opener and pressed the button. The door rose and he drove inside, where he parked the truck and grinned. "It's go time."

———

Something thick choked Marc's throat, and he coughed. His head pounded like someone had used it for a punching bag, but he managed to open his eyes. Thick smoke roiled at the ceiling, and flames shot up the drapes at the windows.

Fire.

He staggered to his feet, then fell back to his knees as the smoke stole his breath. He had to get out of here. It all flooded back to him—Mosely, the attack. He must have set the fire and left Marc to die.

He crab-crawled back toward the kitchen where he'd entered. The smoke lessened a bit once he got through the kitchen door. He got to the front door and threw it open. The fire roared louder behind him at the fresh influx of air, and he rushed outside. Drawing in a fresh lungful of oxygen, he stumbled twenty feet away, then turned to watch flames licking around the edges of the metal roof and bursting out the windows. There was a final roar as the flames ate up the logs.

Mosely would go after Elin. He knew it. Fumbling for his keys, he paused long enough to throw up in the bushes, then hurried toward his Tahoe. He had to get to her.

———

Sara felt as though she could float along the walk to Seagrass Pier without touching the ground. The ring on her hand already felt part of her. She wanted to share her joy with Elin. With her bare toes in the sand and the sun on her face, she walked along the sand toward the house. Gulls squawked overhead, and the salty spray swirled around her ankles with every incoming wave.

Life couldn't get much better than this.

She saw no activity at the house, and no one came to the door when she pressed the bell. Cupping her hands around her eyes, she peered into the window and saw only an empty living room. She probably should have called. She walked to the top of a dune and looked into the harbor where she'd docked her boat. The boat she'd thought was Elin's was one she didn't recognize. Someone was here then, but who? And why was the door locked and everything so quiet?

Unease stirred, and she fished her key out of her purse, then went to the back door and unlocked it. Stepping inside the kitchen, she opened her mouth to call out, then stopped. Wait, maybe that wasn't a good idea. If there was an intruder, he would be alerted to her presence.

A sound upstairs caught her attention. A sliding, scraping noise as if someone had opened a drawer. She pulled out her phone, then dialed the sheriff's office. She told the dispatcher she'd discovered an intruder.

"Tom is out on a call right now, Sara, but I'll send him along as soon as I can. You're sure it's an intruder?" Mindy Stewart asked.

"I heard someone upstairs, and I don't recognize the boat. I think it should be checked out."

"Okay, I'll tell Tom. Let me know if it ends up being nothing." Her tone indicated she thought that was likely.

"I will." Sara hung up. Putting her phone on vibrate, she went back to the living room and tiptoed to the bottom of the stairs. Wisdom would tell her to leave, but what if Elin was in danger upstairs? Marc or his parents could have taken all the boats. Elin might still be here.

Sara looked around for a weapon, but before she found anything, she heard steps coming toward her. Spinning on her heel, she darted for the closet in the hall and left the door open just a crack.

Kalianne came into view. Sara held her breath and watched the woman pull out her cell phone and make a call. She strained to hear, but Kalianne's back was to her, and her voice was muffled. Opening the door a bit more, she leaned forward.

"I can't find it, Devi, and Elin is gone. I'd hoped to find her here with Marc and his parents gone, but there's not a soul here. I need to get out of here. Our faces are plastered all over town. Someone is bound to see me. What if the map doesn't exist any longer? There's no guarantee the old woman found it and hid it. I can't believe it wasn't in that stupid pouch!"

What map could she be talking about? Thank the Lord Elin wasn't here.

Kalianne listened a few moments. "Who is this Ben Summerall and why would he have taken Elin?"

Sara's eyes widened. *Ben* had Elin? She couldn't quite wrap her head around that.

"Where does he have her?" Kalianne stared at herself in a wall mirror and used her free hand to fiddle with her hair. "Okay, I'll meet you there. Where's the turnoff to the old airstrip?" She listened a few more moments. "It'll take me half an hour. If you can get there first, do it. I think the diary is in her purse. If we can just get that, maybe it will be enough. There might be details from the map."

The diary. Sara had been a little bored with the old history, so she hadn't paid much attention. What would Devi want with it? Surely he didn't think the map led to anything real.

Kalianne clicked off her phone, then went down the hall to the powder room. Sara waited until the door closed, then eased out of the closet and exited the house as quietly as she'd entered. She called the sheriff's office again and told Mindy what she'd overheard.

"The sheriff will apprehend Devi on the road. Can you stop Kalianne there?" Mindy asked.

"I'll see what I can do." Sara ended the call and turned back toward the house.

It would do no good to call Josh since he was out on patrol. She eased through the back door and pulled a small pistol from her purse. The door to the powder room was still closed. When the sound of water running stopped, Sara raised the barrel of her gun and waited.

Kalianne's eyes widened when she opened the door and saw her. She attempted a smile. "Sara."

"Alive and well, no thanks to you. Put your hands up."

FORTY

The ferry docked with Marc first in line to drive off. He pulled out his phone to call Elin for the fifteenth time. Why wasn't she answering? Had Mosely already gotten to her? His phone rang, and he glanced at the screen, praying it was Elin since she'd had so many missed calls, but the display showed Sara's name.

He thumbed it on. "Sara, have you seen Elin?"

"Where are you?" Her voice rose to a nearly hysterical decibel.

"Just leaving the ferry. What's wrong?"

"Ben's got Elin!"

Ben? Not Mosely? His breath hitched in his chest. "Tell me."

Sara launched into what she'd heard. "The sheriff should be there soon. He's looking for Devi too."

"I'm close to the old airfield, I think. Tell me where to turn off." He scanned the landscape as she told him to look for a nearly overgrown path. "I think this is it. There's an old gray fence post on the right side."

"That's it! Call me if you find her."

Marc dropped his phone into the passenger seat and gunned his Tahoe down the road. On the way to his destination, he saw several cars parked behind a familiar green pickup. Mosely's. A body lay sprawled in the ditch, a red patch spreading from his chest. Marc recognized the shirt on the victim even though he couldn't see his face. It was Mosely.

He accelerated past another two miles, then whipped his Tahoe into the narrow, overgrown cow path that headed toward the trees. It didn't appear like any kind of airfield, but maybe there was a big clearing on the other side. The weeds lay beaten down in wheel tracks ahead of him, so it looked like another vehicle had been through here recently.

Something white gleamed in the path ahead of him. An iPhone? He stopped the SUV and jumped out to retrieve it. When he turned on the screen, a picture of Josie popped up as the background. This had to be Elin's! He leaped back into the Tahoe and floored the accelerator. The vehicle's back tires spun in the sand, then gripped and shot the SUV forward.

As he entered the trees, he scanned the area hoping to see a house or cabin. Or even another vehicle, but only stands of live oak lined the path. The road was so narrow through here he had to let up on the accelerator. The shrubs brushed against his big vehicle as he rolled through.

Where was Elin?

FORTY-ONE

The gloomy interior of the hangar made it hard to make out more than the looming shapes of workbenches and tools scattered around the perimeter of the large building. Elin sat on a carpet square in the corner with her hands tied behind her. She worked at loosening her bonds, but all she'd managed to do was bloody her wrists.

Ben worked at something in the corner, but she couldn't see what. He'd tied her up before he unlocked the truck, and she hadn't had a chance to try to escape or grab a metal tool as a weapon. She prayed for God to help her, but no great inspiration came to her. There seemed to be no way out.

Ben stepped away from the corner, then exited the cabin without a glance her way. Where was he going? When he disappeared from view, she staggered to her feet and raced to the workbench. There had to be a knife or something she could use to cut the rope. Was that a drywall knife under a piece of wood? She turned around and felt along the workbench until she felt the cool outline of the knife.

It took a few moments to expose the blade and several more to figure out how to press the blade against the rope without cutting her skin. Keeping an eye on the door, she sawed furiously at her bonds. It seemed an eternity before the rope fell away.

She looked for a place to hide near the door. Once he came in, maybe she could make a run for it. An old airplane wing sat perched on its end near the door. She slid behind it and waited.

When she heard his footsteps again, Elin shrank back into the shadows behind the plane wing. She had to get out of here before Ben carried out his plan. His form blocked the tiny bit of light as he entered. She prayed the shadows would make him wait for his eyes to adjust before he realized she wasn't in the corner.

He moved her direction. She shoved the wing out of the way, and it toppled forward. As she darted toward the door, the wing crashed to the floor. Elin slammed the door behind her as she ran for the trees.

Behind her, Ben shouted, and she dared a glance back. The door was still shut so she prayed the airplane part blocked the passage for a few more seconds until she could melt into the shadows of the forest.

The glass in the door rattled, and she put on an extra burst of speed and plunged into the coolness of the shade. Ben yelled behind her, but she didn't waste any time looking back this time. Running faster than she thought possible, she darted around trees and leaped over shrubs in her way. Where could she hide? A low-hanging live-oak branch beckoned her, and she leaped atop it and shimmied up into the leaves.

She climbed as high as she could, until the branch began to thin enough she feared it might not hold her. Then she scooted against the main trunk and held her breath, praying all the while he hadn't seen her mad scramble into the tree.

She pressed her face into a covering of moss and waited. Some scuffing came below, and she peered down to see Ben standing with his hands on his hips as he looked around.

"Elin? It won't do any good to hide. I'll find you sooner or later. You can't escape."

Don't look up. She barely dared to breathe. The thick leaves should obscure her from view, but she wore a bright orange top that might be seen.

"This is all your fault, you know. I couldn't let you marry Marc, now could I? His death is on your conscience, not mine."

She squeezed her eyes shut. Could Marc be dead? Wouldn't she know it, feel it somehow? *Please, God, let him be all right.* She opened her eyes and pulled in oxygen.

"I was surprised you didn't guess it was me. I gave you so many clues. Especially the song 'Music of the Night.' Remember when we went to see *The Phantom of the Opera*?"

Had they? She didn't really remember it.

Ben's gaze went to the base of the tree. Even from here, she could see the scuffed-up dirt where her foot had found purchase. His head went back, and he stared into her face.

"Come out, come out, wherever you are." Then he put his foot on the lowest branch and began to climb.

———

Marc's headache had abated some, and he fought with the wheel as his Tahoe hit the potholes. Through the trees, Marc glimpsed an old airplane hangar and an airfield beyond it. Could Elin be inside? He stopped his vehicle and got out.

A woman's scream echoed from the woods, and he whipped around. It sounded like Elin.

He ran in the direction of the scream and entered the coolness of the shade from the big trees. Did he dare call out for Elin, or would it alert Summerall? Though Marc didn't want her in danger, he willed her to make some kind of sound. Scanning the underbrush, he looked for prints or a trail of some kind. Anything that would tell him which direction to move.

Cocking his head, he listened for thrashing or breathing. Nothing but birdsong and the wind in the leaves came to his ears. He saw some crushed weeds by a bramble bush and walked in that direction. There was matted grass on the other side of the bushes, so someone had come this way recently. Following his instincts, he hurried farther east.

"Stay away from me!" Elin's voice came from his left this time.

He got a better bead on the direction and set off toward her. She'd sounded high up, so he scanned the trees. Most were too small to climb, but a large live oak with low-spreading branches was about thirty feet ahead. His gaze touched on the big branch that almost reached the ground, then traveled up the tree. He caught a glimpse of orange, then saw Elin scrambling back from another figure that crawled toward her.

Summerall. He had a syringe in his hand and a smile on his face that could freeze someone's blood.

"Ben!" Marc leaped onto the first branch. "It's all over. Come down from there."

Summerall didn't even look in his direction. He continued to advance on Elin with the syringe. "It's not too late, Elin. Come to me. We can be in eternity together. I love you. I know you love me too."

He was going to reach Elin before Marc could stop him. He reached for his gun, only to realize he'd left it on the seat of the Tahoe. He glanced around for some kind of weapon and grabbed a stout branch.

"Ben!"

At Marc's shout, the man stopped and glanced at the ground. His cold gaze swept over him, and he smiled. "I really wanted to kill you myself. I'm glad I get the chance."

He released the branch he clung to and dropped to the ground like a cat. He set the syringe on a rock. His smile widened as he flexed his hands and leaped toward Marc.

Marc feinted back, but Summerall came right after him. A hard blow to his neck with the side of Ben's hand left him gasping for breath. Ben darted back, then swung around with a back kick that struck Marc in the stomach and drove him to his knees.

His vision dimmed, and he fought to draw in enough breath. Could he even beat this guy? Marc struggled to his feet. Summerall's smile never faded as he danced around Marc.

Elin dropped to the ground, and he shook his head when she started toward Ben. She paused and glanced around. Before either of them could find a weapon, Summerall made another move, and Marc found himself on the ground with the guy's knees on his chest and his forearm across his neck.

Marc strained to find the leverage to throw Summerall off. His lungs cried out for air, and his vision was already starting to cloud.

"No!" Elin grabbed a stick and walloped Summerall on the back with it.

The distraction rattled the guy enough that the pressure on Marc's throat eased. He flung out his hands and touched a rock. With the last of his strength, he gripped it and smashed it into the side of Summerall's head.

He fell off Marc and hit the ground with his eyes closed and his mouth slack. Marc got up as Elin rushed into his arms.

"I thought Mosely had killed you," she muttered into his chest.

He pulled her tight and pressed a kiss against her hair. "You can't get rid of me that easily."

FORTY-TWO

Twilight cast gold and yellow highlights over the darkening water. Gulls swooped over the water looking for a last-minute meal. The tranquility eased the tension from Elin's neck and shoulders as she sat with Marc on the edge of the pier looking out into a sea that seemed to go on forever. What a day it had been.

She leaned her head against Marc's shoulder. "I can't believe it's over."

He pressed a kiss against her temple. "You're safe."

"I keep seeing Ben's expression as he crawled toward me with that needle in his hand." She pressed her face against his chest for a moment, then looked up. "He killed Lacy too."

"I know." His arm tightened around her.

"What about Mosely? He strangled Laura." She shuddered, remembering her struggle with him.

"I think he'd done it before. The guy was a psychopath. No regret at all." He kissed her forehead. "He can't hurt you anymore."

"Ben said he was dead, but I wasn't sure."

"One shot through the heart and one through the head. Mosely's not going to hurt another woman."

"Let's get our daughter home with us."

The light in his eyes intensified. "I like the sound of that. 'Our daughter.' And we'll be a family." When she didn't smile back, he frowned. "What's wrong, honey? I thought you'd be so relieved to have this over."

"Is it over, really? Or am I always going to have some of Laura's memories? Will I ever go back to hating coffee? Or watching my favorite movies?" She searched his gaze. "Am I even the person you think you love?"

His warm hand circled her cheek, and he rubbed his finger over her lips. "You're talking about unimportant things, Elin. Tastes come and go. The places we find our identities can vary depending on what part of our lives we're in. Look at my parents. For years, my dad's identity was in his job. Now he's content to be a grandpa, and the law isn't nearly as important. You've been a mom and a wife. You've been a single mom struggling to do it all on your own. You're your mother's caretaker. All those responsibilities change us and shape us, but you're still *you*. You have the same giggle. You still rescue stray animals and give whatever you have to help others. Your heart is as big as the ocean and just as clear."

His words caused warmth to spread from her heart down to the toes she dangled above the water. "You're not afraid to marry me? What if I change even more?"

"What if I do? We all change as we go through life. It's part of what makes living interesting. The trick with loving someone is to nurture those changes and encourage one another to be better people. I think the Elin-and-Marc team will be unstoppable."

His lips came down on hers, and she lost herself in the swirling sensation of want and need his kiss elicited. She wound her fingers into his hair and poured herself into showing him how much she loved him.

He broke the kiss with a sharp exhale. "Mercy, you'll be the death of me. Let's get this wedding planned and soon."

"How soon?" Her smile felt as though it would split her face.

"I'm not doing anything tomorrow. How about you?"

"I haven't even begun to look for a dress. Or a caterer or flowers."

"You want all that stuff?" He slapped his forehead. "How long will it take to plan?"

"I think Josie will be disappointed if she doesn't get to be a flower girl. And this will be fun for your parents. You're their only boy. They will want to make a big deal of it for Josie's sake."

"You have them pegged pretty well."

"And there's Sara. I don't want our wedding to overshadow hers."

"Don't tell me you're going to make me wait until they get married?"

She chuckled at the alarm in his voice. "No, but I don't want ours to be so big that Sara feels left out."

"You want a double wedding?"

She shook her head. "I want Sara to bask in the glow of her *own* day."

His eyes darkened and he cupped her cheek. "See, that's exactly what I mean. You always think of others. Who you are hasn't changed, Elin."

When he kissed her again, she knew he was right. The way she felt inside was still uniquely *her*. The way God had made her. The good and the bad. If Marc could love her, warts and all, she would be content with that.

She wrapped her arms around his neck. "Let's call your parents and tell Josie."

"In just a minute. I'm not ready to let the world in just yet."

A Note from the Author

Dear Reader,

I think we women get too focused on trying to be everything to the people we love. We get tied up in how we look, what we wear, how we decorate, and our various roles in life. I know my roles have morphed through the years. But the cool thing I've come to realize is that they are *supposed* to. How boring it would be never to grow and evolve as a woman and as a Christian.

As I've gotten older, those things I mentioned have become less important (though I still don't like to be seen without my makeup!), but one thing I know—my real identity is in Christ who teaches us how to love others. When I go on to heaven, I want my legacy to be one of shining out love.

I've had a great example of that in my life. Diann Hunt recently lost her battle with ovarian cancer. But even as her body grew weaker, her spirit grew stronger. The lens shining out Jesus became so highly polished and brilliant that it was nearly blinding.

So I'm resolving to work on my real identity, a daughter of God. How about you? E-mail me and let me know what you're working on. I love to hear from you!

Love,
Colleen
colleen@colleencoble.com

READING GROUP GUIDE

1. Elin and Marc made a poor choice the night Josie was conceived. When Sara found out she was pregnant, do you think she did the right thing?

2. Do you know anyone who has had an organ transplant? Have you ever seen any evidence of cell memory?

3. Sara tried to forget about Josh by dating another man. What did you think of that?

4. Sara and Elin didn't believe Josh was guilty of the murder based on how they felt about him. Do you ever make judgments that way? If so, have you ever been wrong?

5. Having a loved one with dementia is hard. Have you ever experienced it? if so, what was the hardest part for you?

6. Scents can be very evocative of feeling. Is there any scent in your past that brings a specific time and feeling to mind?

7. Marc wanted to be part of Josie's life enough to marry to protect her. Why would that be a tough plan to follow?

8. Why do you think women can be attracted to bad boys like Ryan Mosely?

9. The book's theme is about identity. What do you think identity is?

ACKNOWLEDGMENTS

I'm so blessed to be a part of the terrific Thomas Nelson dream team! Through their tireless hard work and commitment, *Rosemary Cottage* hit the *USA Today* bestseller list, which was a super exciting day. They really are my dream team!

I can't imagine writing without my editor, Ami McConnell. I crave her analytical eye and love her heart. Ames, you are truly like a daughter to me. Our fiction publisher, Daisy Hutton, is a gale-force wind of fresh air. She thinks outside the box, and I love the way she empowers me and my team. Marketing director Katie Bond is always willing to listen to my harebrained ideas and has been completely supportive for years. Fabulous cover guru Kristen Vasgaard works hard to create the perfect cover—and does. You rock, Kristen! And, of course, I can't forget my other friends who are all part of my amazing fiction family: Amanda Bostic, Becky Monds, Jodi Hughes, Kerri Potts, Heather McCulloch, Laura Dickerson, Elizabeth Hudson, and Karli Cajka. You are all such a big part of my life. I wish I could name all the great folks at Thomas Nelson who work on selling my books through different venues. I'm truly blessed!

Julee Schwarzburg is a dream editor to work with. She totally gets romantic suspense, and our partnership is a joy. She brought some terrific ideas to the table with this book—as always!

My agent, Karen Solem, has helped shape my career in many ways, and that includes kicking an idea to the curb when necessary. Thanks, Karen, you're the best!

I'm so grateful for my husband, Dave, who carts me around from city to city, washes towels, and chases down dinner without complaint. My kids—Dave and Kara (and now Donna and Mark)—and my grandsons, James and Jorden Packer, love and support me in every way possible, and my little Alexa makes every day a joy. She's talking like a grown-up now, and having her spend the night is more fun than I can tell you.

Most important, I give my thanks to God, who has opened such amazing doors for me and makes the journey a golden one.

AN EXCERPT FROM
DANCING WITH FIREFLIES
BY DENISE HUNTER

S ee ya," Jade told Daniel as she got out of his car. "Thanks
for dinner."

"No problem."

Daniel waited for Jade to enter the rear storeroom door, then
continued through the alley. He hated leaving her there. She
couldn't even turn on the showroom lights. He'd moved the old
fridge for her and loaned her the office microwave. She was all set
up. He still didn't like it.

Something buzzed nearby. He stopped at the end of the alley
and leaned over the passenger seat. Jade's phone. Must've fallen
from her pocket. It lit up with an incoming text.

APPOINTMENT REMINDER: DR. KLINE MON JUNE 23 9
AM, DOWNTOWN OFFICE

He set the phone aside and backed down the alley. Moments
later, he knocked on the solid metal door.

"It's me, Jade," he called.

He gave it ten seconds and knocked louder. "Jade. Open up."

He could try the office phone, but she'd probably let it ring
through to voice mail.

He knocked again. "Jade!"

He couldn't imagine it taking this long to get to the door. Maybe she'd gone next door for a shower. But she hadn't had time to gather her things and leave.

He was about ready to kick the door in when it opened. "All right already. What's the—"

Her eyes widened, and her lips pressed together. She dashed down the hall. The bathroom door swung shut behind her. The sounds of her vomiting propelled his feet forward.

She was leaning over the toilet when he entered, shaking. He pulled her hair back, holding it until she finished. A slick sheen of sweat had broken out on her forehead. He wet a paper towel and set it on the back of her neck.

The text message tickled the frayed edges of his mind. His mind flashed back to the wedding two weeks earlier. Something she'd eaten, she'd said.

A few minutes later she straightened and flushed, wiping her mouth with the towel. Her pallor frightened him as he connected all the dots. The wedding episode, the doctor's appointment, and now again.

"Better?"

She nodded.

"Come on." He wrapped his arm around her waist and helped her to the office, stopping at the fountain where she rinsed her mouth.

Once there, she sank onto the antique sofa, giving him a wobbly smile. "Better watch out—you had the brisket too."

"Don't even, Jade." He set her cell on the desk. "You left this in my car. I saw a text about a doctor's appointment, and now I find you like this, just like at the wedding. What's going on?"

She folded her arms, hunching her shoulders. Her eyes studied the floor.

"Jade?"

She met his gaze. "You can't tell anyone."

His gut twisted hard at the fear in her eyes. He swallowed hard. "Are you sick?"

She breathed a laugh, tucked her bare feet under her.

"You're scaring me."

"I'm not sick, Daniel. I'm—I'm pregnant."

"Pregnant?" The word rung in his ears like an echo at Riverbend Gorge. He stood and walked away. He needed to move. Needed to hide a minute while he collected his thoughts.

He should be thinking about her health, her emotional well-being, her financial situation. But instead all he could think of was Jade with another man. Jade smiling at someone else. Jade in love with someone else. Jade making a baby with someone else. A fiery coal burned deep in his gut.

"Three and a half months."

Three and a half months ago she was with another man. Did she love him still? Where was he? Why wasn't he here, holding her hair while she vomited, helping her find a job, finding a flipping place to live?

"You can't tell anyone."

"You're just full of secrets, aren't you?" He hadn't meant to sound so harsh.

"I keep dumping my stuff on you."

He had to pull it together. She didn't need this right now. Didn't need him to be selfish and jealous. He schooled his features, then faced her. "What about the father?" he asked, careful to keep a neutral tone.

She no longer looked so pale. Blood had rushed north, blotching her cheeks. "He's—he's out of the picture."

He shouldn't feel so relieved. It was pure selfishness. She needed support, financial and emotional. Not jealousy. "You need to tell the family."

"I can't."

"Jade—"

"I was going to. I was going to tell them after Madison and Beckett got back, then Mom had her heart attack and Dad said—"

"No stress."

"You know Nana's second heart attack killed her. I couldn't live with myself if something happened to Mom because of me. I just have to wait awhile, until she's stronger."

"You should tell someone. Madison or Ryan."

"I'm telling *you*." Her eyes met his and held. He felt heady with the knowledge that he was her confidante. It had been an accident, but still. She'd told him. Now she was his responsibility. He had to make sure she was taking care of herself.

"Do you have insurance? Are you seeing a doctor?"

She nodded. "Yes and yes."

Of course. The text. He wasn't thinking straight. She looked so little on that old sofa. Had her face thinned out? Were those hollows under her eyes?

"Have you told your doctor you're getting sick so much? It can't be good for you. Or the baby."

Baby. The word made it seem so real. Jade was having someone else's baby.

"She knows. It's not uncommon, you know. Otherwise I feel fine, and I have an ultrasound on Monday just to make sure everything's good."

"I'm going with you." Where had that come from?

"What?"

"You need support. If you're not telling anyone else, I'm it."

She tilted her head. "You don't have to do that, Daniel. It's only a couple months. Or as long as I can hide it."

He wanted to know about the father. He wanted to know who he was, if she'd loved him. But of course she had. Jade wouldn't have made love to him otherwise. Not Jade. The thought sliced him wide open.

"It's a relief, actually, telling someone." Then she met his eyes, soothing the ache in him. "I'm glad it's you."

His breath left his body. "Me too."

AN EXCERPT FROM
DANGEROUS DEPTHS
BY COLLEEN COBLE

ONE

Leia Kahale rubbed an aromatic salve of crushed ginger, aloe, and other natural ingredients gently into the deformed hand of the old woman seated in front of her. Hansen's disease was manageable these days, but the scars were not so easily erased. The sight of her grandmother's missing fingers and toes had ceased to make Leia flinch long ago. To her, Ipo Kahale was the most beautiful woman to ever grace Moloka'i's shores.

"That feels much better, Leia," her grandmother said in a hoarse voice. Leprosy had taken her vocal cords as well as her lips and nose, and her words had a flat, toneless quality. "You should have been a doctor."

"My mother agrees with you, Tūtū. I thought you had a pact to always take up different sides of the fence." Leia put the salve down and stood. She was nearly a head taller than her grandmother's five feet, and Tūtū was practically skin and bones. Leia stepped out from under the shade of the coconut tree to test the pulp of the mulberry bark she was fermenting in wooden tubs of seawater. The odor of fermentation had been the most distasteful part of learning the ancient art of making bark cloth, but now she barely noticed the sour tang. She stirred the mess, then eyed the strips of *tapa*, or *kapa* as the Hawaiian version was called, she'd laid out for the sun's rays to bleach. They could stand some more time in the strong sunshine.

"*Kapa* obsesses you," her grandmother observed when Leia joined her on the garden bench again. "I was never so driven."

"I wish I had your talent for the painting of it."

"Already, you're better than I was, *keiki*, but you try too hard." She nodded toward the pots of fermenting bark. "You're like the unformed cloth, Leia. There is much beauty and power hidden inside you. I grow tired of seeing you shrink back when you should be taking your place in the world. Look forward, *keiki*, not backward." Ipo put her deformed right hand over Leia's smooth brown one.

"I'm finding my way, *Tūtū*. I'm finally doing something I love. No more inhaling antiseptic for me." Leia gave her grandmother a coaxing smile. "I love it here—the quiet that's so profound it's almost a sound, the scent of the sea, the strobe of the lighthouse on the point." Kalaupapa, a small peninsula that jutted off the northern coast of Moloka'i, could be reached only by plane, mule, boat, or a long, strenuous hike down the mountain, but Leia liked it that way. She wasn't hiding here at all, not really. "Besides, I'm needed here. The residents are eager to try my natural remedies."

"It's a good place for those of us who don't want to face the stares of curious strangers. But you deserve more than a dying town filled with aging lepers." Her grandmother caressed Leia's hand with gnarled fingers.

"Like what—breathing smog in San Francisco? Besides, you're wise, not old. Old is just a state of mind. When I watch you, I see the young girl inside," Leia said. Today was going to be a good day. There was no sign of the dementia that often rolled in and took her grandmother away from her. Leia touched the tiny scar on her own lip. "I just want to learn more about making *kapa* from you. I like feeling an important part of this little community."

She turned and looked toward the sea. Her nose twitched as the aroma of the ocean blew in to shore. Smells ministered to her soul—the scent of brine, the rich perfume of the mass of ginger and plumeria outside her clinic, the sharp bite of the ink for the *kapa* she made. Sometimes she wished she could guide herself through life by scent alone. Her garden had been taken over by her hobby. Lengths of *kapa* covered the rocks and tree stumps in the yard, and the wooden shelves attached to the back of the building bowed under the weight of supplies.

She stood and stretched. Usually by this time, her friend Pete Kone had arrived with a dozen teenagers to learn the process of making the bark cloth from her. The art had recently been revived in the Hawaiian community, and Leia taught a cultural class to eager young Hawaiians. "Where is everyone? It's nearly eleven, and no one has come in."

"Pete must be running late again." Her grandmother stood and went to the corner of the cottage, where she peered across the street to the beach. "Just look at your sister. Your mother is going to have a fit when she sees her clothes. She'll have sand all through them."

Leia's cat, Hina, entwined herself around her ankles, then nipped at the speckled polish on her toes. Completely black except for a white spot at her throat, Hina was named after a Hawaiian goddess of the moon, and she carried the attitude of her namesake—she thought she ruled the family. She roamed the Kalaupapa Peninsula like a small panther. Leia moved her feet out of temptation's way and picked up the cat. She joined her grandmother at the side of the building.

On the beach, Eva lay on her stomach on the sand with her nose nearly touching a *honu*, the Hawaiian green sea turtle. Leia watched her sister mimic the turtle's slow blink and neck roll. Twenty-year-old Eva often took Leia's breath away with her sheer beauty. Her blonde hair, bleached almost white by the sun, topped a face that looked at the world through the almond-shaped eyes of Down syndrome.

"I'll get her." Leia stepped around the side of the building and hurried across the hot sand. Hina clutched her shoulder hard enough to hurt. "Time to come in, Eva." She touched her sister's silky blonde hair. Lost in a world where she was one with the turtle, Eva didn't respond until Leia took her hand. Her lopsided smile radiated a charm that few could resist. Leia didn't even try.

She helped Eva to her feet, then linked arms with her and turned toward the cottage. The noise of a plane's engines overhead rose over the sound of the surf. Leia squinted against the brilliant sunshine. Shading her eyes with her hand, she gazed at the plane. It surged and rose, then fell once more before rising on the wind again. The engine made a laboring sound, sputtered and whined. A plume of smoke trailed from the engines, then a flash of light superimposed itself on Leia's eyes, and she flinched. Eva shrieked and clapped her hands over her eyes. She began to moan.

"It's okay, sweetie," Leia said, patting her arm. Hina yowled, dug her claws into Leia's arm, and shivered. Leia, riveted, watched the plane.

The aircraft began to spiral in a death dance toward the sea. The silver bird separated from a small form that jettisoned from the cockpit. The puff of a parachute and the sight of the lone survivor floating toward the water galvanized Leia into action. She raced to her shop and picked up the phone. Dead again. The phone service in this part of the island was spotty. She stepped outside again and ran toward the boat.

"I'm coming too!" Eva ran after her.

"Stay here," Leia told her sister, but Eva thrust out her chin and clambered aboard the boat. There was no time to argue with her. She started the engine of the *Eva II*, a twenty-eight-foot Chris-Craft her mother anchored in the bay. Scrambling over the deck, she got Eva into her seat then handed her sister the cat to distract her. She flung herself under the wheel and turned on the engines.

Leaving Kalaupapa behind, she opened the throttle to full speed and urged the boat in the direction she'd seen the plane fall.

A sea rescue was always difficult. The reflection of the sun on the water made it hard to see a person in the waves, and she wasn't quite sure where the plane had gone in. A craft might slip under the waves without leaving any wreckage behind as evidence. She stared into the rolling waves. Several times she thought she saw the pilot, but it was only a whitecap bobbing. The Coast Guard might soon appear if there was a boat in the area, but she couldn't count on that.

"Do you see anything, Eva?" Eva could see an ant climbing a monkeypod tree at fifty paces. Her sister had calmed down and was staring across the water.

Eva shook her head. "Did he drown, Leia?" She pushed a wisp of hair from her eyes.

"I hope not." Leia squinted against the glare of sun. A movement caught her attention, and she grabbed a pair of binoculars from where they were stowed in a cabinet. The waves parted, and she caught a glimpse of a face bobbing in the waves. Clad in an orange flight suit and helmet, the man thrashed in the lines of his parachute. He managed to free himself, then ripped off his helmet.

"I see him," Eva said in a singsong voice. She stood and leaned over the side.

"Sit down," Leia said, reaching toward her sister. Eva was leaning over so far that a rogue wave could pull her overboard. With the cat draped around her neck like a shawl, Eva sat on the seat but leaned forward with an eager smile. Leia turned to scan the sea again. Anxiety gnawed at her stomach. She'd lost the pilot in the swells. He had to be close. She cut the engine, and the craft slowed, then slewed to the right. A large swell lifted the boat then dropped it in a trough. A dark head popped up. "There he is." She grabbed the life preserver and heaved it toward the man. "Grab hold!" she shouted.

The pilot turned toward her and moved feebly toward the floating preserver. He looped one arm through the hole, and she began to pull him toward the boat. When he was five feet from the side, Eva screeched.

"It's Bane!" Eva reached over the side toward him.

Leia's pull on the rope slackened at the familiar name, then her gaze traveled to the man in the water. Thick black hair in a military cut framed a Hawaiian face marked by strong bones and a firm, determined chin. The facial hair around his mouth hadn't been there when she'd seen him last, and it gave him the look of a pirate. Exertion had leached some color from his dark complexion, but the eyes above the prominent nose had haunted her sleep for months. The lump that formed in her throat had nothing to do with the danger he was in and everything to do with the threat to her peace of mind he'd caused in the past year.

Bane Oana blinked salt water out of his eyes and flailed in the water. Eva screeched Bane's name again, then Leia found her wits and resumed pulling on the wet rope. Bane helped her by swimming with one hand while hanging on to the life preserver. Within minutes he was alongside the boat. Leia leaned over the side. A wave slapped her in the face, and the warm water soaked her hair. She flinched when he grabbed her wrist but continued to haul him aboard. He collapsed on the deck of the boat.

Eva moved to kneel beside him, but Leia stopped her. "Eva, get my emergency kit," she said, dropping to her knees beside him. "It's in the cabinet." She picked up his hand, and her fingers found the pulse at his wrist. It was too fast, but steady and true. Kind of like the man himself.

He tugged his hand away gently and propped himself on his elbows. "I'm fine. Mind if I borrow your radio? I need to call in the accident." He frowned and glanced around the open water.

Leia pushed him back against the deck. "Just lie still a minute.

The plane isn't going anywhere, and neither are you until I check you out." Hina leaped from Eva's shoulders and landed on Bane's chest. He jerked and pushed at the cat, who began to lick his face. Her purr was loud enough for Leia to hear over the boat engine. "She's glad to see you. You're the only one she treats like that."

"How did I get so lucky?" Bane flinched away from Hina's pink tongue. "She's weird all the way around. I know no other cat that will come out on a boat."

"She remembers you," Eva said. She stared at Bane while she twisted a lock of her hair. "Where did you go? I missed you."

Leia busied herself in her first-aid kit so she didn't have to look in Bane's face. How was he going to explain his absence to Eva? Her sister had pestered her with questions since Bane quit coming around. Leia hadn't been able to tell her she'd sent him away with a lie and an attitude that hurt him. Still, the truth would have hurt him more in the end.

"Where did you go?" Eva said again.

Bane cleared his throat, and Leia decided to take pity on him. There would be time for questions later. She plucked Hina from his chest and handed the cat to her sister. "Take care of Hina for me, Eva." She opened Bane's flight suit and slipped the stethoscope inside to listen to his heart. Her finger touched the warm flesh of his chest, and she nearly jerked her hand back. Her cheeks burned, and she avoided his gaze. Her own pulse shot up. The *thump-thump* of his heartbeat in her ears rattled her.

Checking his reflexes, she finally stood and held out her hand to help him to his feet. "You seem to be okay. Other than smelling like a fish."

"I could have told you that ten minutes ago," he grumbled. He stood but continued to hang on to her hand. His gaze examined every inch of her face. "How have you been, Leia?"

"What are you doing here?" Bane had the power to disrupt her life. Even now, she could almost sense the vibrations around her, a warning that her life was about to change.

"It sounds like you're not glad to see me. I thought when I took this assignment—" He dropped her hand and straightened his shoulders.

She didn't answer. Even Eva seemed to sense the tension between them, because she backed away and began to hum to the cat. Leia pointed. "The radio is over there. You'd better call in your accident."

"If it was an accident. I'd say there's something screwy going on." Bane stalked to the VHP radio and grabbed the mic.

She listened as he called the Coast Guard, who patched him through to his boss. Bane had been with the Coast Guard, and she'd heard he resigned his commission and was doing civilian research as an oceanographer. She hoped he hadn't come here planning a reconciliation, because it wasn't going to happen. It couldn't, no matter how much she might want it.

"The controls just weren't responding, Ron," Bane was saying into the mic. "There was a bang like a small bomb, and the plane wallowed like a whale. We need to recover it and see if it was sabotaged." He listened then nodded. "I'll get right on it." When he hung up the radio, his eyes were shadowed with fatigue. "I don't suppose you've overcome your dislike for cell phones?"

She shook her head. "Nope."

He grinned. "I didn't think so. I need to call Kaia and see if she and her dolphin can come sooner than she planned."

"Her dolphin?"

"Yeah, Nani. I've got to recover that plane. I didn't work for months on that equipment to lose it now."

"What are you working on?"

He grinned. "Tony talked me into his pet project. He found a financial backer and roped me into it. So I'm working for his investor, Ron Pimental. He's got a small fleet of research and salvage vessels. I was ready to do something a little different. The thought of seeing you again sweetened the offer."

Tony Romero and Bane had been tight for years. Bane worked at Tony's dive shop before joining the Coast Guard, and the two men were more like brothers than friends. She'd been their younger "sister" until the first time Bane kissed her. She dropped her gaze and began to put her medical kit away. "It doesn't seem your type of job. I never expected you to resign your commission."

"Why? I get to continue mapping the ocean floor, plus I get to dive sunken ships and see the new coral forming. Life doesn't get much better than that."

Life had been better for her before he came back to disrupt it. She looked back at the water half expecting to see his dog's shaggy head. "Where's Ajax? You two are usually joined at the hip."

"He's coming on the ship with Ron."

"Tony has been obsessed with finding that Spanish galleon for years. Who was fool enough to put up good money on this project?"

He grinned. "Your cynicism is showing. I think we have a shot at it. Pimental Salvage has state-of-the-art equipment, and he's got a knack for finding ships. It's a good combo. He should be here in a few hours." He stretched his long legs out in front of him and folded his arms over his chest. "How's your 'ohana?"

"They're good. I was just visiting with Tûtû when I saw your plane go down." She didn't want to make small talk with him. The boat suddenly seemed claustrophobic. "I'm living there now, treating the residents with natural meds."

His dark eyes raked her. "Still hiding?"

"I like it there," she shot back.

"Can we go diving?" Eva asked. "You promised to take me to see the honu." She grabbed her sketch pad from the floor. "I drew a picture of one. See?" She thrust the picture under Bane's nose.

Bane studied the sea turtle picture. "You're really talented, Eva. You should go to art school."

The sea turtle looked exactly like the one Eva had been imitating on shore. Eva had a rare talent that often awed Leia. "Great job, Eva. But Bane is too busy to take you diving."

"He said he's never too busy for me!" Eva protested.

"I did, didn't I?" Bane aimed a challenging look at Leia. "When we go diving is up to your sister, Eva. She could have called me months ago and hasn't."

"And I wasn't going to," she muttered.

"Afraid?"

She met his gaze. "You can take her diving any time you like. Just name the day." The last thing she wanted to do was chart the dangerous depths with Bane again, but no one dared call her a coward.

"When are you free?"

Bane knew how much she loved diving—they'd spent years exploring the underwater world. Their love of the wonders in the sea had been their first bond. "Who said anything about me? She's the one who wants to go." She knew he wouldn't be taken in by her bluff. She watched out for Eva in all circumstances.

His smile faded, and he examined her face. He let out a huff, and his lips tightened. "How about tomorrow evening, Eva?"

His gaze told Leia she'd won this round, but the war wasn't over. She felt a tingle down to her toe ring. She had to stay out of his way. He'd forget about her soon enough. Sooner than she'd forget him, unfortunately. She loved him enough to make sure she didn't give in to his charms.

His gaze wandered to the dive boat in the distance moving toward shore, and his gaze sharpened. "Hey, I should go see Tony."

"That's not his boat, but I'll take you to Kaunakakai," she blurted before she thought.

Amusement lifted his lips. "I'm game. I can call Kaia from the shop."

She was always a sucker for Bane's smile.

D0030287

Help Your Teenager Beat an Eating Disorder

- Learn why you need to act now
- Find out what the research says about which treatments work
- Take charge of changes in eating habits and exercise
- Put up a united family front to prevent relapse

James Lock, MD, PhD | Daniel Le Grange, PhD

Praise for *Help Your Teenager Beat an Eating Disorder*

"In the fall of 2005 our daughter was confined to a hospital bed. Her doctor recommended *Help Your Teenager Beat an Eating Disorder*. I recognized my daughter's anorexic behaviors in the very first paragraph of Chapter 1, but didn't realize then how invaluable the book would be in the months to follow. This book has been one oasis of sanity that I've revisited many times, and each time I've found hope and help. I'll continue to recommend it as required reading for any parent who's fighting for their child's life."

—Ann, member of *www.maudsleyparents.org*

"The book is of high quality and would be of help to any family facing this difficult situation."

—*Doody's Review Service*

"Eating disorders can creep into your family life and take you by surprise. This book, written by two of the foremost clinicians in the field, illustrates the multifaceted nature of the problem and allows you to expand your resources based on their wisdom."

—Janet Treasure, PhD, FRCP, FRCPsych,
Director, Eating Disorders Research Unit,
Kings College London, United Kingdom

"This book is essential reading for any parent or family member of a teen with an eating disorder. It's especially useful for those who have been told to 'not be the food police' or that they have no role in helping support a loved one with an eating disorder. It offers practical advice for how to help, along with something just as important: hope."

—Harriet Brown, author of *Brave Girl Eating:
A Family's Struggle with Anorexia*

"Parents facing their son or daughter's eating disorder are caught in a stormy night of fear and confusion. This second edition is a welcome lighthouse. Like the authors' family-based treatment model, the book empowers parents with the information and direction needed to ride out the storm and find safety."

—Laura Collins Lyster-Mensh, MS, founder
of Families Empowered and Supporting
Treatment of Eating Disorders (F.E.A.S.T.)

"There are many red flags that parents should recognize when it comes to their adolescent daughter or son's eating habits, and this intelligent book points them out clearly and concisely."

—Publishers Weekly

"The second edition has been fully updated to incorporate current diagnostic classifications for feeding and eating disorders and the latest research evidence. Lock and Le Grange use their wealth of academic expertise and clinical wisdom to offer parents empathy, understanding, and practical advice. Written in accessible language, the book is filled with realistic scenarios aimed at affirming and mobilizing parents to take action. Lock and Le Grange address many of the pervasive myths about eating disorders, assuage guilt, and offer hope to parents in the frightening early stages of the illness. Highly recommended."

—Dasha Nicholls, MBBS, MD,
Feeding and Eating Disorders Service,
Great Ormond Street Hospital and Institute
of Child Health, London, United Kingdom

"From two renowned clinician-researchers, this book offers plenty of useful information. Throughout, vignettes offer clear-cut advice on how to respond to the many issues parents encounter before, during, and after treatment."

—W. Stewart Agras, MD,
Department of Psychiatry,
Stanford University

HELP YOUR TEENAGER BEAT AN EATING DISORDER

Also from James Lock and Daniel Le Grange

FOR PROFESSIONALS

Eating Disorders in Children and Adolescents:
A Clinical Handbook
Edited by Daniel Le Grange and James Lock

Treating Bulimia in Adolescents: A Family-Based Approach
Daniel Le Grange and James Lock

Treatment Manual for Anorexia Nervosa, Second Edition:
A Family-Based Approach
James Lock and Daniel Le Grange

Help Your Teenager Beat an Eating Disorder

SECOND EDITION

James Lock, MD, PhD
Daniel Le Grange, PhD

THE GUILFORD PRESS
New York   London

© 2015 The Guilford Press
A Division of Guilford Publications, Inc.
370 Seventh Avenue, Suite 1200, New York, NY 10001
www.guilford.com

The information in this volume is not intended as a substitute for consultation with healthcare professionals. Each individual's health concerns should be evaluated by a qualified professional.

Printed in the United States of America

This book is printed on acid-free paper.

Last digit is print number: 9   8   7   6   5   4   3   2   1

Library of Congress Cataloging-in-Publication Data

Lock, James.
   Help your teenager beat an eating disorder / James Lock, Daniel Le Grange.
— Second edition.
      pages cm
   ISBN 978-1-4625-1748-0 (paperback) — ISBN 978-1-4625-1796-1 (hardcover)
   1. Eating disorders in adolescence—Popular works.   2. Parent and
teenager.   I. Le Grange, Daniel.   II. Title.
   RJ506.E18L63 2015
   616.85′2600835—dc23
                                                                2014034977

To my children
—JDL

To my mother and late father
—DLG

*We would like to thank
all the many patients and families
with whom we have worked over the years
for helping us learn how best to help them.*

Contents

Introduction   1

PART I   GETTING STARTED
First Steps toward Helping Your Child
with an Eating Disorder

Chapter 1   Act Now   13

Chapter 2   Get Together   35

Chapter 3   Don't Waste Time on "Why?"   57

PART II   UNDERSTANDING EATING DISORDERS

Chapter 4   Know What You're Dealing With   79
The Complexity of Eating Disorders

Chapter 5   Get Into Your Child's Head   101
*The Distorted Thinking Behind
Your Teenager's Behavior*

Chapter 6 Understand Your Options   124

*What the Research Says about the Best Ways
to Treat Anorexia, Bulimia, Binge-Eating Disorder,
and Avoidant/Restrictive Food Intake Disorder*

PART III MAKING TREATMENT WORK
How to Solve Everyday Problems
to Help Your Child Recover

Chapter 7 Taking Charge of Change   145

*How to Apply Family-Based Treatment
to Help with Eating Disorders*

Chapter 8 Playing a Supporting Role   187

*Other Ways You Can Be a Part
of Your Child's Recovery*

Chapter 9 Harnessing the Power of Unity   214

*How to Stay on the Same Page in Your Fight
against Eating Disorders*

Chapter 10 Staying Empowered and Informed   236

*How to Work with Professionals
Who Are Trying to Help Your Child*

Resources   253

Further Reading   281

Index   297

About the Authors   310

Introduction

When your children are sick, you don't just bring them home from the doctor's office or hospital and leave them to their own defenses. If it's the flu, the child needs fluids and rest and medicine to bring the fever down. If it's an allergy, someone needs to check package labels to make sure the allergen isn't included in a food. If your child has asthma, you make sure the inhaler is available and watch vigilantly for signs of an attack. And if your child has a very serious illness, like cancer or heart disease, you don't just expect it to get better on its own.

Someone needs to be there when the doctor isn't. That person is you. Parents are an integral part of the treatment of their children for every illness you can think of. Why, then, should it be different for eating disorders?

It shouldn't. Eating disorders are extremely serious illnesses that can threaten your child's very survival. By their nature, they are self-perpetuating and insidious. That's why a significant proportion of teenagers and adults who have eating disorders end up in the hospital at some point during the course of their illness: They need the constant, consistent vigilance of a team of professionals to ensure that they return to normal weight and normal eating habits.

The trouble is what happens when they get home. Many treatment programs for eating disorders still advocate keeping parents

1

out of their teenager's care for a variety of reasons that we explain in this book. The consequence is often a relapse. When an eating disorder still has a hold on a teenager, leaving the child to manage it on her own once she's at home just gives the eating disorder a chance to slip through the flimsy defenses of self-care and send her on a downward spiral toward physical and psychological damage once more.

For more than two decades we have watched adolescents and their parents struggle with this horrible cycle of getting better and then getting worse again. Most of those who come to our offices arrive feeling anxious about their child's bewildering condition and overwhelmed or even defeated by this strange illness. Numerous parents have already been told by other professionals to stay on the sidelines or they will "make things worse." Many are confused in general, not quite knowing whether their child really has an eating disorder, or what precisely an eating disorder is, or what they should do about it.

We wrote this book to clear up misconceptions that we have found—and that the research is beginning to reveal—only make it harder for adolescents to recover from eating disorders: that you are to blame for the problem, that your child needs to be treated without any input or involvement (aka "interference") by you, that you need to leave diagnosis and treatment to the professionals in a way you would never agree to if your child had cancer or a heart problem, or even a broken bone. This book therefore has one simple purpose: to help you understand eating disorders and their insidious nature and to show you how you can help your child in "plugging those tiny cracks" where the eating disorder keeps slipping into her or his life.

That doesn't mean this book is a "self-help" manual. Eating disorders are very serious illnesses, and we have no evidence that self-help approaches are sufficient by themselves for adolescents and their families. Instead, this book is intended to provide straight answers and hard facts about eating disorders based on the available research evidence and our own extensive clinical experience. Its goal is to offer you a perspective that is only beginning to emerge: that you have an important role to play in helping your

child recover. We believe, in fact, that you are key to your teenager's return to health. This applies whether you are just considering having your child evaluated by a doctor or your child has undergone several other treatments in the past and has not yet conquered this illness. You are certainly in the best possible position to take action fast, before an eating disorder has an opportunity to do serious damage to your child's health. The research shows that when anorexia and bulimia are treated early, there is a good chance of full recovery. So, if nothing else, we hope this book moves you to take your child's problem seriously and get help *now*. Ideally, the book will help you go further than that: It should help you establish a foundation on which you and the clinicians you work with can build a successful partnership in defeating the disorder that has overtaken your child. We hope to demystify eating disorders, and at the same time we encourage you to consider how you can help with the problems that such an illness is causing for your child and family.

The parents who come to our offices usually arrive believing they *shouldn't* be involved in helping with their child's eating disorder. This message typically comes from an external source, because few parents would subscribe instinctively to "staying out of it" if their child had any other life-threatening illness. Therefore, this book may appear at first to be taking a radical stance. We hope you'll realize that is not the case when you read the data in Chapter 6 and elsewhere, which show that parents' participation in treatment can make an enormous positive contribution to the recovery of an adolescent with an eating disorder. Regardless of the cause or treatment type, we will argue in this book that you not only can but should be involved. This book will help you figure out how.

The approach we mostly use in our own treatment centers is called *family-based treatment*. The concept behind this treatment is derived from decades of family work involving anorexia nervosa at the Maudsley Hospital in London. This work illustrates the importance of parents' involvement and support in finding solutions to the dilemmas faced by their adolescents with eating disorders. This perspective stands in stark contrast to approaches that blame parents and exclude them from treatment.

The fact that this book is for parents in the first place sets it apart from many books on eating disorders. When this book was first published, most of these books in print were directed at adults or teenagers themselves who were ill, which left a big gap in sources of information for parents. That's why we crafted this book to answer the questions that parents had brought to us over many years of practice and still bring to us—everything from "Am I to blame?" to "What do I do when he disappears after a meal and I know he is going to throw it all up?," "Just how do we get her to eat a healthy meal again when she won't let us?," "Shouldn't she be on some medication as well?," and "I don't understand this illness; isn't the solution straightforward—you eat, and that's that?"

We have been gathering answers to these questions, separately and together, for a combined total of more than 40 years as clinician–researchers (meaning that we see patients and we also conduct research studies) treating adolescents with eating disorders at academic medical centers. Eating disorders are relatively rare, yet each of us has seen hundreds of patients and their parents during this time. We have treated patients in inpatient settings, group programs, and individual and family therapies. We have spent our academic careers exploring how better to help adolescents with eating disorders, and this book is an important part of that effort.

Each chapter in this new edition has been substantially revised, providing updates on clinical factors and treatment research related to eating disorders in youth. We've streamlined the examples and added new ones related to key interventions and concepts discussed. Happily, since the publication of the original book, research on the treatment of eating disorders in children and adolescents has made advances, particularly in documenting the effectiveness and efficiency of family interventions for these disorders. Other exciting developments include discoveries related to cognitive process and interventions related to cognitive process in eating disorders, which we discuss in this new edition. We also describe the impact, which is mostly positive, of the revisions in the diagnostic system used to categorize mental disorders on child and adolescent eating disorders. The new (fifth) edition of the American Psychiatric Association's *Diagnostic and Statistical Manual of Mental Disorders* (DSM-5) better

takes into account developmental issues related to eating disorders, including making the requirements for the diagnosis of bulimia nervosa and anorexia nervosa less stringent and adding new eating disorder diagnoses, including binge-eating disorder and avoidant/restrictive food intake disorder. While we have added substantial new material on binge-eating disorder, we have provided only limited information about avoidant/restrictive food intake disorder because so little is known about that disorder at this time.

A particular issue that has struck us in a very meaningful way is just how resourceful parents usually are and what a great resource they are when they are brought into the treatment process. We strongly believe that if parents can be helped to get a better understanding of eating disorders and to take definite early steps to intervene in these problems in a constructive way, many lives will be improved and some lives actually saved.

Both of us have worked as clinicians and researchers in academic medical settings for the past two decades. Although we have worked in different parts of the world, our mutual interest in the treatment of adolescents with eating disorders has brought us together in our thinking about how best to do what we do on a daily basis in our respective practices. This has led to a rich and productive collaboration that started in 1998 when we jointly wrote our first book, a manual for clinicians who treat adolescents with anorexia. Since then we have conducted workshops about this treatment throughout the world. We discuss our difficult cases with each other, we present our research findings at professional meetings, and we continue to collaborate on ongoing and new clinical treatment studies. Since the publication of the first edition of this volume, we are pleased that increased attention to the role of parents in helping their children with eating disorders has led to the founding of several parent organizations (see the Resources at the end of this book) who are strong advocates for increased awareness of their role in helping their children, demanding better clinical services for eating disorders, and promoting new research efforts to learn more about how to help children and adolescents with eating disorders. Further, we are told daily that eating disorder treatment programs from around the world use this book to educate families about

their role in helping their children with these problems. The book has been translated into Portuguese, Japanese, Dutch, and Polish. Throughout all this work with adolescents and their parents, we are reminded every day of the real value of parents' contributions to the treatment process. It is this collective experience of treating teenagers with eating disorders, engaging their parents in this process, and researching and writing about these experiences in academic journals that continues to inspire us to involve parents in the process through writing this book.

HOW TO USE THIS BOOK

This book is divided into three parts. The titles for the chapters were chosen carefully to draw your attention to the urgency of the matter, to highlight the most salient aspects of eating disorders, and then, with this knowledge, to help you respond to your child's illness in the best possible way. If our use of imperatives such as "Act Now," "Get Together," and "Don't Waste Time" seems aggressive, it's intended to get your attention. It's human nature to hope that a health problem will go away on its own, but to postpone seeking help for your son or daughter can be extremely dangerous. Sadly, treatment approaches that rob you of your rightful role as guardian of your child's health only encourage you to let others make critical decisions about what to do and when.

In Part I of this book, we focus on *why* you need to take action now if your child has symptoms of an eating disorder. We discuss why eating disorders are serious problems, why you must act together as parents to get treatment started and worry less about "why" this problem developed and more about "how" to get it eradicated. Dealing with eating disorders effectively always requires you to perceive your child's anorexia or bulimia as an urgent matter that needs your prompt attention. In fact, "urgent" is the byword for Part I. It's worth repeating what we said earlier: If your child has signs of an eating disorder, it's urgent that she or he get help, and it's you, the parents, who are in the best possible position to see that your child gets this help.

Part II provides you with more "nuts and bolts" about eating disorders. Eating disorders can be very confusing to doctors, parents, and sufferers alike. Therefore, it's important for you to know what you're up against, perhaps more so than with many other types of illness. The purpose of this section of the book is to make sure you appreciate the complexities of these illnesses. We discuss the various types of eating disorders, particularly anorexia nervosa, bulimia nervosa, binge-eating disorder, and avoidant/restrictive food intake disorder, as well as how starvation and binge eating and purging can lead to severe medical problems. You will find that we often discuss eating disorders as if they were entities independent of your child. We do this to stress our view that eating disorders are illnesses and not willful choices being made by your child to oppose you. Next we illustrate how a teenager with an eating disorder thinks. The distortions common to such thought processes are illustrated to underscore the need for treatment. They can also help you separate the illness from the child so that you can remain supportive of your son or daughter, who is, after all, suffering from real distortions in how he or she experiences his or her body, and in his or her thoughts and beliefs about food and weight. We end this section with information about the main treatment approaches for eating disorders and the evidence available for their effectiveness so that you'll have a good scientific understanding of what may help your child and what may not.

Part III is designed to help you tackle the practical problems you will face in trying to get and use help for your child's eating disorder. We illustrate various ways that parents can be involved in each of the known major treatments for eating disorders, even if the form of treatment discourages parental involvement. We also offer tips to help you confront the cultural forces that contribute to disordered thinking about food and weight. Most important, though, is the partnership that we mentioned earlier. To seal up those cracks that your child's eating disorder will do its best to slip through, the entire treatment team needs to establish a united front to fight the illness. This means that both parents—or you and any other adults who are invested in helping your child recover—need to be "on the same page" in dealing with the illness at all times. It means that you

also need to find a way to form a fruitful alliance with the professionals on your treatment team. So this section includes chapters that help you stave off the eating disorder's efforts to "divide and conquer" and help you stand your ground constructively when you have disagreements with the experts who are trying to cure your teenage son or daughter.

WHAT YOU WILL LEARN FROM THIS BOOK

After you have read this book, we hope you will feel confident that you have a role in helping your adolescent in her recovery from an eating disorder. You should know the ways in which eating disorders develop and when to get worried as normal adolescents' concerns with their bodies become more serious. You will know the medical problems that can and will develop if your child's eating disorder isn't treated effectively. You will know what to expect when you have your child evaluated and what kinds of treatments are likely to be offered. You will learn that parental involvement can take many forms, such as actually helping your starved child to eat at home, supporting individual therapy for your child, monitoring binge-eating and purging episodes, and participating in treatments that enhance your adolescent's interpersonal capacities and roles.

We also hope that after reading this book you will be certain that there is help for your adolescent with an eating disorder and that the resources we provide at the conclusion will be helpful to you in determining where to go for this assistance.

A NOTE FROM THE AUTHORS

This book is not intended as a self-help guide, nor is it intended in any way to substitute for the advice of a physician or therapist. Moreover, research into eating disorders, their causes, and the best treatments is ongoing; to stay abreast of advances in the field, consult reliable sources such as those listed in the Resources and Further Reading sections.

This book is aimed at helping parents with older children and adolescents, not young children or adult children.

Eating disorders increasingly affect both teenage girls and teenage boys, although they are still more common in girls. That said, all statements in this book, unless otherwise noted, apply to both adolescent boys and adolescent girls. To emphasize this point, we alternate pronouns in examples throughout the text. We also include many examples of adolescents with eating disorders, which are thoroughly disguised to protect privacy or presented as composites of real clinical cases.

GETTING STARTED

First Steps toward Helping
Your Child with an Eating Disorder

CHAPTER 1

Act Now

You don't know what to do.

Thirteen-year-old Sheila has been losing weight for 6 months. At first you thought it was normal teenage dieting. But she's too thin now. She has stopped eating with you but insists on cooking everything for the whole household. Last week she made four desserts but wouldn't eat any of them. She has a book with a list of the calories in everything most of us eat, but she doesn't need it anymore because she knows it by heart. Besides, at present, she eats only three things: raw vegetables, tofu, and dry cereal. She's still doing well in school. Her straight As, though, seem more of a burden than a source of accomplishment to her. When she isn't studying, she's going for a run or doing sit-ups. She ignores calls from her friends and seems more and more depressed. When you try to encourage her to eat, she fumes and says it's none of your business. She insists she's fine.

You don't know what to do.

You caught 17-year-old Donna throwing up. She said she was sick. But it wasn't the first time. You have heard her before. Always heading off to the bathroom after every meal. She says it was nothing—she only had an upset stomach. You've noticed she hardly eats breakfast or lunch, but when you come home

in the evening, lots of food is gone from the pantry, especially cookies, potato chips, and bread. You've had to go to the store midweek to restock. One of her friends told you she was worried about Donna. You are too.

You don't know what to do.

Tom used to be a great high school diver. He's too weak now to perform his toughest dives. He eats only protein bars and fruit drinks. He is constantly exercising to get perfect abdominal muscles, but you can see his ribs. He says he's still too fat. Where there used to be muscle, there's mostly bone and skin now. At first his coach complimented Tom on his weight loss because it had improved his dive entries. Now the coach has called you and suggested Tom take a leave from the team. Tom's best friend called him "skeleton" to tease him, but you know he's worried too.

You don't know what to do. *Should* you do something?

This is the first problem you face if you're concerned that your son or daughter may have an eating disorder. You know most eating problems in children are transient. You remember lots of struggles over junk food and sweets with your other children, or you've seen it in other families. Many children commonly go through periods of being picky eaters, eating more than usual, eating less than usual, and even complaining about upset stomachs or having periods of mild digestive problems and constipation. You've asked other parents and relatives about these types of behaviors and learned that, although usually short-lived, eating problems are nearly universal. As children enter puberty, many, especially girls, are very much interested in their appearance and weight and may try dieting or other weight-loss strategies. You expect this because you know it's normal to become more concerned about appearance in the teenage years and because you've known your son's or daughter's friends to express similar thoughts and engage in the same types of behavior. You don't want to create a problem where there isn't one.

How do you know if there's a real problem?

If you think your child's thoughts and behaviors resemble those of Sheila, Donna, or Tom, however, it's time to take action to help. Left untreated, eating disorders can lead to chronic health problems, depression, and even death. With the severe weight loss associated with anorexia nervosa, for example, starvation leads to lower body temperatures, decreased blood pressure, and decreased heart rate, as well as rough and dry skin, loss of hair, cessation of menstruation in young women, and osteoporosis. Because the body isn't being fed, it turns to muscle for fuel. This causes weakness, fatigue, and, in particular, decreased cardiac mass (the heart being a large muscle in the body), which can prompt dangerous changes in heart rhythm and may thereby cause cardiac failure and death. Over time, the risk of death as a result of the complications of anorexia is estimated at 6–15%. This mortality rate is the highest for any psychiatric disease.

For bulimia nervosa, the risk for death appears to be lower, but there still are risks of severe medical complications. One of the most common of these complications is depletion of potassium (hypokalemia), which results from loss of body stores of this essential electrolyte due to purging stomach contents. Without potassium, which is required for many basic physical processes but is very important for muscle contraction, cardiac arrhythmias are possible, leading to cardiac arrest and death. In addition, with chronic vomiting, the linings of the esophagus and stomach can become eroded, causing bleeding, ulcers, erosion of tooth enamel, and even death if the bleeding cannot be stopped. Chronic use of laxatives and purgatives leads to intestinal problems, including pain and severe and unremitting constipation. Both vomiting and the use of laxatives lead to severe depletion of water from the body (dehydration), which can cause low and changing blood pressure, increasing the likelihood of fainting and falls. For binge-eating disorder, the medical risks include obesity, hypertension, and diabetes. The specific medical risks associated with avoidant/restrictive food intake disorder are not known, but in cases of severe weight loss accompanying this disorder, the risks of malnutrition are similar to those found in anorexia nervosa.

We discuss these complications in more detail in Chapter 4. By now, though, you can undoubtedly see that eating disorders have serious health consequences. To be complacent in the face of a possible eating disorder is the greatest risk a parent can take in the battle to prevent such serious problems from developing.

WHAT DOES AN EATING DISORDER LOOK LIKE AS IT DEVELOPS?

If you're to catch a problem before it becomes an eating disorder, you have to know what to look for over time. Sheila, Donna, and Tom's problems did not develop in a day. Like most eating disorders, their problems developed gradually and sometimes in secret. If you understand the path by which more typical, temporary eating problems and weight concerns can become real eating disorders, you can get a sense of where your own child is on that trajectory.

Extreme Dieting: The Path to Anorexia Nervosa

Fourteen-year-old Rosa has always been a terrific child. Her parents said she had spoiled them because she was always so easy, independent, reliable, and mature. That's why they were so shocked by her recent weight loss. She had never shown the slightest sign of emotional problems. She was an honor student, swim team champ, and popular at school. She had never been overweight; in fact, she'd always been on the thin side.

The problems seemed to begin during the summer before ninth grade. Rosa had been on the summer swim team. It was the first time her parents noticed that she wanted to stay longer to swim after practice. She wanted to get fitter, she said, so she could be a starter on both the breaststroke and freestyle teams. At the same time, she started a vegetarian diet. She felt it was cruel to eat animals, and besides, she didn't need fat in her diet when she was trying to be healthier. At first her parents understood and supported her efforts at self-improvement as Rosa seemed happy and confident.

Then Rosa attended the special 3-week swim camp for the summer team located in another part of the state. She left in

the middle of July and returned at the end of the first week of August. When her parents picked her up at the bus, they were startled, almost frightened by how thin Rosa had become. They didn't say anything right away. They were just glad to have their daughter home. They surmised that the food hadn't been too good at the camp, and Rosa implied as much. They didn't have good vegetarian choices, she said, and she was very active. She had made both teams as a starter.

And then school began. The ninth grade was a transitional year for Rosa. Students from three middle schools were combined in a single high school, so there were many new kids in her class. Her parents noticed that Rosa seemed more preoccupied and worried about schoolwork, but they thought this was to be expected when starting high school. Rosa's day began at 5:00 A.M. with swim practice for 2 hours before school. She then attended classes for the day and reported for another swim practice from 5:00 to 7:00 P.M. Rosa arrived home after the family had already eaten. She studied until 11:00 P.M.

Out of sight of her parents, Rosa had developed a highly limited eating pattern. She allowed herself one cup of orange juice before morning practice. She told her mother she had a bagel and cream cheese at school with milk after practice, but in reality, she ate half a dry bagel and water. The lunch her mother carefully prepared for her was thrown away each day. Again before afternoon practice, she would drink a glass of orange juice. Because she came home after the family had eaten, her parents didn't know how much she had for dinner. Usually she had a carefully weighed slice of tofu, a few carrots, and an apple.

Her parents grew increasingly alarmed at Rosa's continued weight loss. The coach of the swim team called to ask what was wrong with Rosa. She was afraid that Rosa might have an eating disorder. Her parents made an appointment with her pediatrician, which took some time to set up. When they arrived, the pediatrician said that Rosa was too thin, and Rosa promised to eat more. Unfortunately, she did not. Her parents tried to intervene, but she easily became angry when they talked to her about eating, and they hated to confront her.

Although anorexia nervosa usually starts in early adolescence, typically at 13–14 years, it is not uncommon to see children between

the ages of 8 and 11 develop this eating disorder. Anorexia usually begins with an episode of dieting that gradually leads to life-threatening starvation. At times some identifiable precipitating event triggers the dieting process. Maybe the child is teased about her weight, or her friends start dieting. Or perhaps she sees her parents dieting. Some girls start dieting at the onset of menses, when they make the transition to a new school or level in school, or when they begin dating. The illness of a parent may also trigger dieting. It's important to understand that these events often start the dieting process, but that does not mean these triggers are the causes of anorexia nervosa. It is dieting that usually appears to be the starting point for anorexia nervosa.

Teens diet for a number of reasons. Sheila says she began dieting to become a healthier person, whereas Tom's dieting was initially designed to improve his diving. Most teenagers report that dieting began because of a wish to lose weight, eat healthier, or improve performance in a sport. A few adolescents begin consuming fewer calories in the service of being "good," as they define it, using an ascetic formulation along the lines of "The less you consume, the better you are."

All of these motivations to diet share some features. For example, each implies some notion of self-improvement, in particular improvements that are concrete and outward and thus noticeable by others—to look better, perform better, be healthier. However, there are differences among these motivations for dieting as well. The emphasis on a thin appearance suggests a connection with social norms of beauty, whereas improvement in performance of a sport, in health, or in morality is related more directly to perfectionism, drive, and ambition. These latter qualities appear to be common personality features in children who develop eating disorders.

Regardless of motivation, dieting usually begins informally. The child may start by cutting out desserts and snacks, but over time, meats and other proteins, fats, and sugars are eliminated too. Once food choices are narrowed, dieting efforts are typically focused on lowering the quantities of food consumed even within this limited range of options. Often detailed calorie counting, exact

measuring, and elaborate preparation of foods become the rule. At this point, adolescents may attempt to remove themselves from the company of others while eating, prepare meals independently of others, and sometimes cook elaborate meals and desserts for others without eating the food themselves.

Alongside this extreme food restriction, a schedule of increased exercise is often employed to ensure continued weight loss. At this point, whatever weight goals might have been set initially have typically been long surpassed, and the goal of weight loss in itself is firmly established. Sometimes self-induced vomiting or diet pill and laxative use may begin in an attempt to purge the small portions consumed.

For a child on the path to an eating disorder, on the one hand, eating is often associated with guilt, anxiety, and anger. Not eating, on the other hand, is associated with feelings of accomplishment, power, and strength. Paradoxically, with increased weight loss, hunger cues are diminished, making the process of continued food restriction easier. Nonetheless, most teens with anorexia are still extraordinarily preoccupied with food. Some will visit supermarkets and bakeries to look at and smell the food, but abstain from eating it. Parents may notice unusual food rituals beginning to develop, such as eating only out of certain bowls or plates, weighing and measuring foods precisely, using chopsticks, and so forth. The period of time over which this cascade of events takes place is variable, but it can be as short as 4–6 weeks or as long as a year or more. At some point during this process, in girls who have begun menses, menstruation likely ceases.

> Rosa became too weak to swim and was taken off the swim team. At school, she was more and more isolated, and her friends stopped talking to her because they were afraid to ask her what was wrong. She became tearful and moody at home. She was so thin now that none of her clothes fit, even though they had been purchased only a month before, when school began. She was always cold; she wore sweaters and was constantly turning up the heat while the rest of the family sweltered. Her worried parents thought she was depressed and sought help from a psychiatrist.

Failed Dieting and Overeating:
The Path to Bulimia Nervosa

Sixteen-year-old Jasmine had always set high standards for herself. She wanted to be the best at everything. She worked hard at school and got good grades. She was generally well liked, though she always worried about who her friends were. She had worried about her weight for as long as she could remember and first began trying to lose weight when she went on a liquid diet with her mother when she was in fifth grade. She herself was never teased for being overweight, but she had seen other girls and boys teased when she was a child and was worried that she too would be teased. The diets she tried never made any difference. She lost a few pounds but then gained the weight back.

For the junior prom Jasmine decided she wanted to look great. She had a boyfriend, her first, and she wanted him to find her beautiful. That meant *thin*. Her boyfriend had never commented on her weight, but Jasmine was sure it was just because he was too nice to say anything. She knew she was too fat. She was determined to lose 15 pounds before the prom.

She began skipping breakfast altogether, and lunch as well. She would then go to the gym after school and exercise for 2 hours. She found some over-the-counter diet pills and drank lots of coffee, all in an effort to keep herself from being so hungry. Still, she woke up at night feeling hungry. But she stuck with her routine and lost 15 pounds for the prom. Everyone told her how wonderful she looked, and her boyfriend seemed happy with her appearance too. All of her friends congratulated her on her diet and wanted to know how she did it.

After the prom Jasmine tried to keep her diet plan going, but it became harder and harder to do. She would come home from school and be too tired to go to the gym. When she missed her workout, she was certain she would gain weight, so she tried to eat even less the next day. However, she began to be so hungry that she couldn't stop herself from eating. One day after school when no one else was home, Jasmine was so hungry that she ate a box of cookies. She went to the gym and tried to "exercise the calories away," but there were too many and she was too tired. The same thing happened the next day. This time Jasmine was so upset she decided to try to throw up the cookies. She had promised herself that she would never do

this, but she couldn't stand the worry about gaining weight. She would throw up just this once.

Jasmine tried to follow her own injunction, and sometimes she succeeded, but at least once or twice a week she failed and overate so much that she felt she had to purge. Slowly, week by week, she got into a pattern of eating very little and then binge eating in the afternoon, followed by purging. On days she found she couldn't vomit, she took some of her mother's laxatives to relieve her fears about gaining weight.

During this time, Jasmine's weight had gradually increased despite her efforts to diet, using diet pills and laxatives, and vomiting. Jasmine was increasingly despondent. Her boyfriend broke up with her because she stopped wanting to get together with him. She felt too ashamed of her weight to see him. In addition, she was afraid to go out with him because she might have to eat something and that would start her overeating.

Jasmine's mother hadn't suspected anything until one day she heard Jasmine throwing up in the shower. She asked her what was wrong, and Jasmine confessed to throwing up purposely, but only that one time. Still, her mother remained concerned and noticed that Jasmine had taken some laxatives from the medicine cabinet. Again, Jasmine denied she used them to lose weight, claiming she had done so because she was constipated. Finally, the mother of one of Jasmine's girlfriends called Jasmine's mother to tell her that her daughter had caught Jasmine throwing up at school. Jasmine's mother now tried to find help.

Binge-eating episodes and purging usually begin a little later than the extreme dieting of anorexia nervosa. Still, adolescents who binge eat and purge often report long histories of preoccupation with weight. Some say they remember worrying about their weight as early as kindergarten. Some were mildly to moderately obese during early childhood and remember being teased. Often these adolescents have experimented with a variety of diets for brief periods, only to abandon such efforts. Many report that in response to severe dieting and fasting behaviors, they develop an urge to overeat and feel increasingly out of control when eating. Once they've overeaten, they feel guilty and anxious and, as a result, seek ways

to relieve themselves of their fear of gaining weight. This leads to purging in its various forms. Most often purging is accomplished through vomiting, but it can also include the use of laxatives, diuretics, and compensatory exercise.

Adolescents with bulimia nervosa, like their adult counterparts, report that to a great degree their self-worth depends on feeling satisfied with their weight and appearance. Often these adolescents report that they eat very little breakfast or lunch, but that upon returning to their homes after school, they binge. This is a time when there is usually little parental supervision and the binge eating can occur secretly. In addition, binge eating can become a way to cope with feelings of loneliness, boredom, and anxiety. Alternately, some adolescents report nighttime binge eating, another time when they are less likely to be observed.

Most adolescents, like adults, with bulimia nervosa report intense feelings of shame about these behaviors. As the disorder becomes more entrenched, teens begin to organize their lives around the management of binge eating and the compensatory activities related to it. They become more irritable and withdraw from friends and families. Often their schoolwork declines. They also report increasingly depressed moods. Once these altered patterns of eating are firmly established and extend their hold on the adolescent, binge eating and purging become a convenient way to avoid other problems and may be increasingly incorporated into the adolescent's coping strategies. These factors combine to make bulimia nervosa surprisingly resistant to change, even when someone is motivated to make such an effort. In addition, sometimes adolescents with bulimia nervosa report a history of other impulsive behaviors such as alcohol use and shoplifting.

Jasmine's mother took her to see a psychologist, who diagnosed her with bulimia nervosa, but Jasmine refused to return for therapy. Her mother tried to persuade her to go, but she said she could stop the behavior on her own. It appeared that this was the case, as Jasmine's mother saw no evidence of continued purging or binge eating for several months. However, her hopes were dashed when she discovered several bags of vomit and food containers in the garage. She called the psychologist

again, who suggested they come in as a family to discuss how to proceed.

Using Food to Manage Emotions and Social Difficulties: The Path to Binge-Eating Disorder

> Sheiko is 18 years old and lives with her mother and younger sister. Sheiko has been worrying about her weight since she was 12 years old. In the last year or so she began to binge eat, especially when she was alone at home or late at night. Sheiko says she often feels sad or depressed because of a fight with a friend or rejection by a potential romantic partner. She tries to eat to make herself feel better. "Guys won't like me unless I'm skinny," she says, which then makes her sad, and she thinks if she eats she will feel better. She also binges when she is lonely: "People don't like me anyway—what's the point of losing weight?" Unfortunately, after she binges she feels like a failure: "I'm weak; I don't have any self-control," she says. Sheiko is a senior in high school and hopes to go to college. She is a good student with excellent grades.

Like many adolescents with binge-eating disorder, Sheiko began having emotional difficulties some time before the onset of binge eating. She had tried to diet, but this led to overeating in response to emotional and social crises. As in Sheiko's case, the symptoms of adolescents with binge-eating disorder intensify over time and are complicated by depression, social anxiety, shame, and feelings of failure. Most adolescents with binge-eating disorder describe using food to help with their emotions, mostly negative ones like depression and anger. Sheiko's mother took her to the pediatric clinic. The pediatrician there told Sheiko she was overweight and needed to lose weight or risk developing high blood pressure or diabetes.

DOES YOUR CHILD HAVE AN EATING DISORDER?

The first of the following lists contains items that you should be on the lookout for if you think it's possible your child is developing

or has an eating disorder. If they are present, then you'll want to exercise additional vigilance to see if these warning signs are really indications that your child is developing an eating disorder that needs evaluation and treatment. The second list includes items that, if present, suggest that you need to take immediate action to have your child evaluated and treated.

Warning Signs of the Development of an Eating Disorder
- Diet books
- Evidence of visiting pro-anorexia or eating disorder websites
- Dieting behavior
- Sudden decision to become a vegetarian
- Increased picky eating, especially eating only "healthy foods"
- Always going to the bathroom immediately after eating
- Multiple showers in a day (to purge in the shower), especially directly following eating
- Unusual number of stomach flu episodes
- Skipping meals
- Large amounts of food missing

Act-Now Signs and Symptoms
- Fasting and skipping meals regularly
- Refusing to eat with the family
- Two skipped periods (in girls) in conjunction with weight loss
- Any binge-eating episodes
- Any purging episodes
- Discovery of diet pills or laxatives
- Excessive exercise (more than an hour a day) and weight loss
- Persistent and unremitting refusal to eat nondiet foods
- Refusing to allow others to prepare foods
- Extreme calorie counting or portion control (weighing and measuring food amounts)
- Refusing to eat with friends

If at this point you've determined you need to have your child evaluated for an eating disorder, you'll want to consult someone

who is an expert in these problems. This usually means someone besides a pediatrician or family physician, most of whom have had little training or experience with eating disorders. Certainly all of these professionals will have heard of eating disorders, and many will have had some limited experience, but most are not sure when an expert is needed, and they can unintentionally reassure parents, beyond the point at which they should, about not needing help.

This does not mean you should bypass your pediatrician or family physician on the way to an expert in eating disorders—quite the contrary. A physician can rule out other causes of your child's problems, which should get you closer to knowing whether an eating disorder is likely. Your pediatrician should be able to get an accurate weight and height for your child and perform a physical exam, including ordering basic laboratory work, that will uncover readily identifiable medical conditions that might be causing the problems you're observing—unexplained weight loss, loss of menstruation, or other physical symptoms such as lightheadedness or fainting. This examination may also reveal evidence that your child's problem is more urgent than you thought. If, for example, it turns out that your child has low blood pressure, a low heart rate, or signs of severe purging (erosion of tooth enamel, inexplicable swollen salivary glands, inexplicable weight loss), you'll know that you were right to act now. In some cases, when a teenager has developed such problems, hospitalization is necessary.

A basic medical workup for an adolescent with an eating disorder would include the following: a complete physical to check for signs of severe starvation (e.g., assessment of weight relative to height, low blood pressure, low heart rate, dry skin, low body temperature), as well as tests for liver, kidney, and thyroid functioning. These examinations help to assess the degree of illness and its chronicity, as well as to rule out other possible organic reasons for weight loss including diabetes, thyroid disease, or cancers. Common laboratory tests include a complete blood count; an electrocardiogram; studies of electrolytes, BUN (blood urea nitrogen), and creatinine; thyroid studies; and a test for urine specific gravity. Your pediatrician should be able to discuss the purpose of each of these tests, help you to understand any unusual laboratory results,

and alert you if there is any cause for immediate medical intervention.

Assuming that your child is not too sick and that another medical problem is not clearly causing the problems with eating, you will
need to proceed to an evaluation by an expert in eating disorders
in children and adolescents. That's why you should take advantage
of this appointment with the pediatrician to find out what kind of
experience he or she has had with eating disorders. It may require
a little tact and skill, but if you know the doctor fairly well, you will
probably find a way to ask these important questions:

"Have you seen many adolescents with eating disorders?"
"What do you recommend in terms of treatment (both medical
    and psychological)?"
"Whom do you refer your patients to and why?"
"How successful do you think your patients have been with
    treatment?"

If your pediatrician proves not to be an expert, you can take
steps to find one. We should note that pediatricians are sometimes
reluctant to make referrals to such specialists because they are
unsure whether changes in eating behaviors are due to emotional
problems or just developmentally normal adolescent experimentation. In addition, because an adolescent with an eating disorder
often denies or minimizes symptoms, physicians sometimes don't
get the whole story from the adolescent. It might be helpful to go
over the lists of warning signs presented earlier to encourage your
pediatrician to make a referral if you have observed any of the
behaviors on the "Act Now" list in your child.

A referral from your primary care physician or pediatrician
often permits full insurance coverage for your child's psychiatric
evaluation, so getting this referral rather than seeking an expert on
your own is important for this reason as well. Scheduling such an
evaluation may, unfortunately, be more complicated than it should
be because of insurance processes and the limited availability of
experts in eating disorders. Still, these obstacles can usually be

overcome with persistence and a referral from a pediatrician speci-fying the need for the consultation.

Consult the Resources section at the end of this book for guid-ance on where to begin your search for help. One caveat, however: Many clinicians who treat adults with eating disorders are not pre-pared to evaluate younger patients. They are neither trained to look for the ways these younger patients' symptoms develop nor trained in ways to engage them or their parents to evaluate them effectively. There are many exceptions to this rule, of course, but the wise parent will inquire about the clinician's experience with younger patients before scheduling an appointment.

WHAT TO DO TO GET HELP

Most adolescents with eating disorders do not want help—at least initially. They see themselves as choosing to manage a problem with weight, and even if they recognize some problems with their diet-ing, they generally prefer to be left alone to sort it out themselves. Unfortunately, case descriptions like those you've just read make it pretty clear that many adolescents do not figure a way out soon enough to prevent serious problems from setting in. That leaves it up to parents to get the ball rolling sooner. This is easier said than done. So parents immediately face at least two problems in trying to help their child with an eating disorder: (1) how to get their child to have an evaluation for an eating disorder and (2) whom and what to look for in terms of evaluation.

How to Get Your Child to Have an Evaluation

Before you delve into the challenge of getting your child to agree to an evaluation, make sure that you and your spouse (if there are two parents) agree that there is a problem that demands an evaluation. The importance of parents working together is a major theme of this book that is discussed in more detail later, particularly in Chap-ter 9. But even in agreeing that there is a problem, many parents

differ on what to do about it. Using the guidelines provided in our lists of warning signs may help the two of you see things the same way. And even if one parent is reluctant to move forward, the more concerned parent may have to take the lead initially to get things started. As long as the other parent doesn't manifest active opposition, this may be where some families have to start.

Once you're in agreement that your child needs a professional evaluation, it's important to let your child know you're planning to seek one. Springing the evaluation on her, which may be tempting inasmuch as you know she may resist going, can backfire because it makes it more likely that she will refuse to cooperate with the interviewer. Moreover, we feel it is important to be honest and up-front with your concerns. Deceiving your child about what you're doing makes it harder to develop trust, and ultimately you'll need that trust if you're going to be successful. Still, telling your child you're planning to seek professional help often leads to an uproar. Be prepared for your child to try to dissuade you from undertaking the consultation. Your child may object to missing school for the appointment or point out that you'll have to take time away from work, but you need to stand firm. The importance you place on this appointment sends a message that will be key to your continuing to be active in getting your child's problem under control. Certainly we have had parents "drag" their child in for an evaluation with us, but this is not the norm. Instead, a clear message that the pediatrician has made this referral, that you are concerned, and that this visit will help to clarify the situation is usually enough to get the child to the expert's clinic. Then it's up to the experts to do their job in providing a helpful assessment and set of treatment recommendations.

Whom and What to Look for in an Evaluation

Actually, in our experience, the second problem—getting a good evaluation for an eating disorder in a child or adolescent—is in some ways the greater problem of the two you face once you've decided you need help. Many communities don't have resources to assist with diagnosing and treating children and adolescents with

eating disorders, particularly professionals who are up to date on the best techniques and approaches. It is clear that we cannot solve this problem with this book, but we hope that from the outset, by emphasizing the seriousness of the problems that eating disorders cause, we can encourage parents to make an effort to seek out regional expertise in the area, even if it is not available at the community level. We liken eating disorders to any other serious medical problem—such as leukemia or heart disease—for which it is often necessary to travel a bit farther to specialty centers for consultation and initial evaluation and treatment to achieve the best outcomes. In the Resources section of this book, we provide a guide to regional centers of expertise that we hope will help parents locate experts closer to them. At the same time, the following paragraphs provide a description of our evaluation process to help you know what to anticipate when you do have an expert consultation, based on processes at our treatment centers.

Once a referral has been made and an appropriate expert has agreed to meet with the patient and parents, an evaluation will probably begin with the clinician meeting alone with the adolescent. This provides a developmentally appropriate entry into the family that respects the adolescent's developing autonomy. The adolescent should expect to be interviewed with support and warmth, with the clinician minimizing presumptions of understanding. Open-ended questions about family, schoolwork, interests, and activities are used to break the ice with reluctant adolescents. Open-ended questions also provide an opportunity for the adolescent, when willing, to offer her own perspective on what's happening to her and what's motivating her and to express whatever level of discomfort she experiences with eating. This open-ended approach is also important because not presuming an understanding of what's happening, but still being clear about what needs to be explored, is the most objective way to gather information in a clinical interview.

It's important, of course, that the interview focus on eating behaviors and problems, but most clinicians will find that they need to collect a significant amount of other relevant information. This other information includes such things as medical problems, other behavioral issues (with adolescents this includes drug and alcohol

use), perspectives on other family members, and any history of traumas or abuse. The interview identifies any history of concern about weight and shape or health that preceded the onset of dieting or other behavioral efforts to change weight and shape. Adolescents will be asked about their exposure to common triggers for dieting and weight concerns such as those mentioned earlier: hearing comments (positive or negative) on their weight, experiencing the onset of menses, dating, being involved in or exposed to family conflicts, starting middle school or high school, breaking up with a romantic partner, observing others beginning to diet at home or in their social circle, and so forth. The clinician should compile a detailed history about your child's efforts to lose weight. Examples of such behaviors include counting calories, restricting fat intake, fasting, skipping meals, restricting fluid intake, restricting meat and protein intake, increased or excessive exercising, binge eating, purging behaviors (exercise, use of laxatives or diuretics), and using stimulants and diet pills (over-the-counter items, health food products, and illegal products). Adolescents who binge eat and purge usually go through a cycle leading to increasing frequency of dieting, followed by binge eating and compensatory purgation. Persons with either anorexia or bulimia nervosa can binge eat and purge. However, those who are at extremely low weights because they are restricting their eating are more likely to call a much smaller quantity of food a "binge" than normal-weight adolescents who binge eat and purge.

Health consequences of these behaviors should also be evaluated. Adolescents with eating disorders commonly report chest pain, dizziness, headaches, fainting spells, weakness, poor concentration, stomach and abdominal pain, and cessation of menses. For those with bulimia nervosa, throat pain, involuntary regurgitation, broken blood vessels in the eye, and swollen neck glands are also common. Because eating disorders are often accompanied by anxiety disorders, depression, personality disorders, or obsessive–compulsive disorder, the interviewer will ask about symptoms of these disorders as well.

In addition to those areas specific to eating problems, interviews will include an evaluation of other possible contributors to the development of the disorder, including physical and sexual abuse,

traumas, and emotional and physical loss. Some elements of this aspect of the interview will be necessarily private, and the contents will not be shared with you as parents unless warranted.

After the interview with the adolescent, you will usually be interviewed without your child present. If there are two of you, both of you need to be present. Your respective perspectives on your child and family are otherwise unavailable. You will be asked about the general development of your child—complications during pregnancy, early feeding, developmental milestones, transitions to preschool and elementary school, aspects of attachment (such as problems with separation when you dropped your child off at preschool, excessive clinging or irritable behavior when you were separated from your child, refusal to spend the night with friends because of fear of separation from you), early temperament and personality traits, family problems during childhood, and peer and sibling relationships. Your perspective on who your child is and how she may have come to have this problem creates an atmosphere of shared understanding and often makes it easier for the clinician to proceed to the specific history of the eating and weight problems that have brought you to the practitioner's office.

Next you will be asked how you saw the problem developing: When did you first perceive a problem? What have you tried to do to help? Do you see other kinds of emotional or developmental problems, such as depression or anxiety, peer problems, or other changes in behavior in your child? It's likely that the evaluation will compare information obtained during the interview with the adolescent with the parents' version of events and will explore commonalities as well as differences. Together, these differing perspectives help generate a more comprehensive narrative of the events leading up to and sustaining the current eating problems.

> Susan agreed to meet with the psychiatrist reluctantly. She did not want to miss school, and she said she was eating well. In the interview, Susan said she had lost weight because her stomach was bothering her—she had had the flu a few weeks ago, and her stomach was still recovering. She denied having any desire to lose weight and said she had eaten a muffin and juice for breakfast; a sandwich, chips, and cookies for lunch; and pasta

with chicken and cheese sauce for dinner the day before. She said she exercised for only half an hour a day. She denied any lightheadedness, weakness, or headaches. She did admit to having skipped her menstrual period for the last 2 months.

When the clinician met with Susan's parents, they reported a very different version of events. Susan had begun losing weight about 5 months earlier. She did have the flu, but she had already lost 20 pounds by then and had lost another 5 pounds during that illness, which she had failed to gain back. Her parents reported that Susan had eaten about two bites of a muffin the morning before and drunk about 4 ounces of juice. They also said they had regularly found Susan's lunches in the trash. Susan also exercised for at least an hour a day and hardly ever sat down anymore.

Sometimes clinicians who treat eating disorders ask for consultation from a dietitian with expertise in working with eating disorders. Sometimes dietitians calculate ideal body weight (IBW), which is derived from norms of weight for height in the patient's age group. Alternately, they may calculate the body mass index (BMI), defined as (weight in kilograms ÷ height in meters^2). Either way, these weights serve as a general guide to determine a reasonable weight range for recovery. This can be helpful in clarifying the degree of weight loss or weight gain your child has experienced and how far off he is from expected growth and weight norms for his age, maturity, and height. Dietitians can also provide educational advice to you, your teenager, and your doctors about the need for proper nutrition for health.

THE CHALLENGES OF DIAGNOSING AN EATING DISORDER

At the end of a proper consultation, if warranted, your child will likely receive a diagnosis of one of the major types of eating disorders. However, it is possible that the assessment will lead to a diagnosis of another problem that initially resembled, but is not, an eating disorder. Sometimes a fear of choking can lead to refusal to

eat, and this may also look like anorexia. In this case, appropriate treatments would be for other conditions—depression and anxiety—rather than for an eating disorder.

Diagnoses are made to help clinicians decide on the best treatment recommendations for specific problems. So that you understand what the evaluating clinician means when rendering a diagnosis of your child, we think it is important that you know how eating disorders are described in the American Psychiatric Association's *Diagnostic and Statistical Manual of Mental Disorders*, the standard reference for diagnosing psychiatric problems in the United States, which was just revised in 2013 (see full reference on page 34).

Carlos had been overweight his entire life. Both his mother and his older sister were overweight as well. When Carlos started eighth grade, he decided he would go on a diet. His parents supported this idea, because they felt it would improve his health and self-esteem. Carlos was determined in his dieting and lost 10 pounds in a little more than 2 weeks by eating and drinking very little and beginning an exercise program of walking and jogging. Over the next 2 weeks, Carlos increased his exercise and continued to eat very little. He lost another 5 pounds. He became increasingly focused on his dieting. He got up early in the morning to go for a run and stayed up late doing "crunches" and leg lifts. Over the next month, Carlos lost another 5 pounds. He was now at a normal weight for his height, but his parents noticed that he was not satisfied. Carlos said he wanted to lose another 20 pounds. Teachers reported that Carlos was having trouble paying attention in class. Carlos said he was just going over the calories he had eaten during that day. He was still getting good grades, but he no longer had time for friends because of his exercise program. His parents tried to get Carlos to eat more, but he refused.

When Carlos went to see a psychologist, he was told he had an eating disorder. Carlos protested that he wasn't too thin and he wasn't throwing up his food. The psychologist pointed out that Carlos was totally preoccupied with losing weight, food, counting calories, and excessive exercise. Carlos countered that he was just "getting healthy" and that he was tired of being fat. Carlos began to cry when told he needed help.

When reading about Carlos, it is not clear whether Carlos is in the early stages of anorexia, may be at risk for developing bulimia, or will develop binge-eating disorder. What is clear is that Carlos has an eating disorder and needs help.

Although you will be faced with the dilemma of how to get started, as we've described here, you should be less uncertain about when to act. Now is the time. The one thing you can be certain of is that once eating disorders become established, they do not give up their firm emotional and physical grip on your child. We know that for both anorexia and bulimia nervosa the longer someone has the illness, the more difficult it is to treat. For anorexia, for example, we have little evidence of any effective treatments after someone has been ill for several years. In the case of bulimia we know that a chronic course, in which symptoms come and go for periods of several years, is a common pattern when the illness goes untreated. A delay in taking action only facilitates increased habituation to these illnesses, making it harder for you to succeed in helping your child. So act now!

FOR MORE INFORMATION

American Psychiatric Association, *Diagnostic and Statistical Manual of Mental Disorders, Fifth Edition*, 2013. Washington, DC: American Psychiatric Association.

Fairburn, C. G., and K. D. Brownell, Editors, *Eating Disorders and Obesity: A Comprehensive Handbook, Second Edition*, 2002. New York: Guilford Press.

Garner, D. M., and P. E. Garfinkel, Editors, *Handbook of Treatment for Eating Disorders, Second Edition*, 1997. New York: Guilford Press.

Le Grange, D., and J. Lock, Editors, *Eating Disorders in Children and Adolescents: A Clinical Handbook*, 2011. New York: Guilford Press.

Lock, J., *The Oxford Handbook of Child and Adolescent Eating Disorders: Developmental Perspectives*, 2012. New York: Oxford University Press.

Thompson, J. K., *Handbook of Eating Disorders and Obesity*, 2004. Hoboken, NJ: Wiley.

CHAPTER 2

Get Together

Everyone is confused.

Bridget refused to eat with her family. Her mother told her father that Bridget was going through a phase. She just needed time to make her own decisions. Bridget's father disagreed. He felt she was stonewalling the family and shouldn't be treated differently from anyone else. Bridget's sister was mad that she still had to eat dinner with her parents and little brother. Bridget's little brother said he missed Bridget and asked how come she didn't eat with them now.

No one knows what to do.

Bella has had anorexia nervosa for 2 years now. She meets with her therapist twice a week and her nutritionist once a week. Bella says her therapist tells her that she needs to decide to eat and get better and that her parents should stay out of it. The therapist said as much to her parents as well. The nutritionist advises Bella on what to eat and how much. Bella's parents aren't sure what Bella's weight is or what the nutritionist is recommending, but Bella remains very thin and her food choices are still quite limited.

You are frightened and angry.

For the third time this week, Sam is making a trip to the bathroom just after eating dinner. Sam's father follows him to the bathroom at a safe distance. Through the closed door Sam's father hears the shower being turned on, and a few minutes later he hears a coughing and choking sound. Sam's father stands outside the door and begins to cry silently.

You are helpless.

You've just left the pediatrician's office. Laila has gained another 5 pounds since her visit a month ago. You have found the fast-food wrappers under her bed and in her closet. You hear her creeping down the stairs at night and wake up in the morning to see the wastebasket full of discarded cartons and packages.

You've been told by therapists and friends and you've read in books and on the Internet that if your child has an eating disorder, you should stay out of it and let the therapist help your child work on the issue. You're told that this hands-off approach is the correct one because a salient feature of eating disorders is the need to control something. Adolescents with eating disorders reportedly feel "out of control," and it follows that this makes them feel anxious, so they seek to control the one thing they think they can control—what they eat. You also may have been told that these feelings of being out of control probably arise from things you did as a parent. You may have been told you were either too intrusive and overinvolved and controlling, or too distant, underinvolved, and abusive. Either way, it seems you could be the source of the problem, and therefore how can you be part of the solution? In fact, the farther away you are, the better.

You've heard all these things, but they don't feel right to you. How can you stand by and watch your daughter starve herself or listen outside the bathroom door while your son throws up his dinner? How do you explain to your other children that you know their brother or sister is not eating or is binge eating or is throwing up, but that you're trying to help by letting their sibling "manage" it alone? They don't buy it. Your other children are already trying to get your son to eat more and to quit throwing up. These things

don't feel right to you because your gut sense as a parent is that it is somehow wrong to stand by and do nothing when one of your children is suffering. It also doesn't make sense to you because you know that you should be able to help. You *need* to help.

Why is it so hard to find a way to help with eating disorders? You would know what to do if your child had another kind of problem, even a very serious one like cancer—you'd take him or her to the hospital, get the best doctors, support your son or daughter during radiation therapy, surgery, or chemotherapy by being with the child. You would make sure that you understood the medicines, and you would make sure your child took them. You would make sure your daughter or son got to all scheduled appointments for follow-up visits, and you'd be on the lookout for signs of relapse or problems.

In other words, you would be a part of helping, no matter what. You would take off work or quit work if needed. You would borrow money to pay for treatment. You would question the doctors, and you would carefully evaluate all of their recommendations. You would not leave all decisions up to your child, because you know that your child wouldn't or couldn't fully appreciate the repercussions of complicated decisions and options. You would do these things because you are a parent.

In contrast, when your child has an eating disorder, you are often left to your own devices. You don't know what's being done in terms of treatment. You're not sure about what options there are. You are told not to interfere with the therapist's and nutritionist's recommendations. You are told to butt out.

> After her third hospitalization in 5 months for a low heart rate and blood pressure due to starvation, 13-year-old Sarah's parents were fed up. Each time Sarah came home she had promised to eat more. There were always excuses. Sarah's therapist felt she wasn't trying in therapy. Sarah's nutritionist said she wouldn't see her anymore unless she agreed to eat more and gained weight. Sarah's pediatrician felt she should be sent to a residential treatment center, where she would get 24-hour-a-day care, individual therapy, group therapy, dance therapy, pet therapy, recreational therapy, medications, and art therapy. Her parents would be 500 miles away. Sarah didn't want to be sent away. She was trying her best.

Seventeen-year-old Tony is throwing up every day at school
after lunch. The boys hear him doing it and have told the guidance counselor. She has now called you. Tony says he's got the
flu one day, ate something that didn't agree with him another,
or just doesn't answer at all. He says he's quitting school if you
send him to a shrink.

You wonder why eating disorders are so different from other illnesses. Why shouldn't you be able to help? Isn't there a way to help?
There *must* be a way to help.
    There *is* a way to help.

HOW THE NATURE OF EATING DISORDERS
PITS PARENTS AGAINST THEIR CHILDREN

You know that your son or daughter has changed since developing
an eating disorder. You've observed that your child is more distant,
seems depressed or moody or irritable, is obsessive about food (and
probably other things). In some cases the teen's already pronounced
tendencies toward perfectionism are further accentuated. Actually,
your child's driven nature is more pronounced, period, whether in
a good way or a bad way. What has happened?
    We like to use a Venn diagram to describe what has happened
(see Figure 2.1). One circle (white) represents your child before the
eating disorder started. The other (black) represents the eating disorder. Over time, the eating disorder circle increasingly overlays the

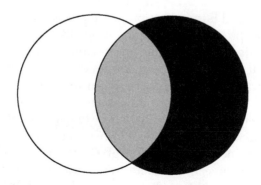

FIGURE 2.1. How an eating disorder overshadows your child's true self.

circle that represents your child. Her circle pattern is still there and recognizable but is now being altered by the eating disorder. So, many of her traits, though still present, are colored by the eating disorder. Say, for example, she tends to be perfectionistic. This trait is still present, but now it is particularly evident in connection with food—precise calorie counting, exact measuring, obsessive label reading, and so forth. Or perhaps she is anxious. Now her anxiety is increased at mealtime, and she refuses to eat around family or friends. Driven qualities can also be redirected. She now exercises for 3 or 4 hours a day at increasingly intense levels. We like to say that the eating disorder is using your child's characteristics (often great strengths) against her. That's one of the reasons it's so hard for your child to battle the illness on her own—she's fighting herself and her own determination, drive, perfectionism, and obsessiveness. This combination of your child's characteristics and those of the eating disorder is confusing. You recognize your child's personality traits, and yet there are these major changes in focus—about food, weight, and exercise. This makes it difficult to know how to proceed. Some of the very things you may value in your child now stand in the way of your being able to help her. Here's an example: Your child is an exceptionally talented ballet dancer. She develops anorexia nervosa. You see her losing weight, but she gets a principal role in the dance company's production. Her talent, persistence, and ambition are paying off, but they are also being used to further the physical and emotional devastation of anorexia nervosa. As a parent you're torn between supporting your child's talent and allowing anorexia nervosa to become further entrenched.

Maybe that example is too easy. Suppose your daughter is a high school marathon runner. She is likely to be one of the best in the state. However, she has started throwing up and not eating so as to improve her performance. Her performance does improve. Still, she exercises more and more. Her performance begins to deteriorate. You know she has an eating disorder and should quit the team, but your daughter cries that without running she will get depressed and will kill herself. That's all she cares about.

Here's yet another example: Your child is preparing for the SAT. She's gotten straight As and is taking AP (advanced placement) courses. Her SAT scores, though, are not as high as they need to

be to clinch her admission to the prestigious college she aspires to. In addition to having anorexia, she has become an overdedicated student—staying up very late at night and getting up very early—in preparation for retaking the SAT, which is about 8 months away. You see that her focus on schoolwork is actually helping to prevent her from eating normally, and you hear her exercising late at night when she's taking a break. She tells you she has to study for the SAT and needs to exercise to keep awake. You want her to get into the college she wishes to attend, but you also see her becoming thinner, with darker circles under her eyes, and increasingly withdrawn from friends and family.

All of the preceding examples demonstrate how the nature of eating disorders is confusing for parents and can pit them against their child. However, there are other ways that eating disorder symptoms lead to conflicts between parents and children. One of the most bedeviling problems is the timing of these illnesses. They usually occur just when adolescents are both more able to be independent and certainly very interested in being so. Thus, you are battling both the symptoms of the illness and the developmentally appropriate stage of increasing independence. In other words, sometimes you don't know if you're struggling with an eating disorder or with typical adolescent strivings for autonomy. When your child says to you, "I'm old enough to make my own decisions about what I eat," there is a ring of truth to it. The only problem is that often when adolescents make decisions because they have an eating disorder, and battle for them, the fight is "fixed"—the eating disorder wins, and both you and your child lose.

> Lidia had always been fiercely independent. When she was a preschooler, she spent hours learning to tie her shoes rather than let someone help her. Her parents had always respected Lidia's spirit and supported her when she struggled with the task, because they could understand what she was trying to accomplish on her own. As a young teenager, Lidia had chosen her own classes, decided who her friends would be, and chosen her own clothes. Not surprisingly, when she began losing weight and her parents tried to step in to help her, Lidia was strident in her opposition. She fought over every morsel, filled herself

up with water, and refused to eat anything her mother cooked for fear that her mother had put butter in it. At first her parents chalked this up to normal teenage rebellion and delayed taking any definite action about treatment. Lidia continued to lose weight and then began binge eating and purging. Now they realized that the things they were fighting Lidia about were not normal teenage issues, nor were they rational problems. They were evidence that Lidia's thinking had gone awry and that an eating disorder had developed.

Along with this striving for independence, with adolescence come increased wishes for privacy. This too helps eating disorders along. Eating disorders tend to increase secretive behaviors to avoid detection and thereby prevent intervention. So, because of others' respect for these adolescent needs for privacy, eating disorders can go on for months and even years without anyone really appreciating their presence. This is true despite the fact that adolescents themselves often leave abundant clues. Some save all the packages from the food they consume in boxes under their beds. Others vomit into plastic containers and save them in their closets. Still others lose a great deal of weight and hide under sweatshirts and baggy clothes. Even if you've noticed some of these behaviors, it feels like prying to ask about them. Such is the power of an adolescent's need for privacy.

It's pretty clear that the symptoms of eating disorders, your child's personality traits, and the expectations for autonomy and privacy during adolescence make it difficult to know how to take this problem on. How can you?

HOW CURRENT APPROACHES TO TREATMENT CAN REINFORCE CONFUSION ABOUT THE FAMILY'S ROLE

The main approaches to treating adolescents with eating disorders are family therapy, individual psychodynamic therapy, cognitive-behavioral therapy, and dialectical behavioral therapy. These approaches are important clinical interventions that undoubtedly

help many adolescents with eating disorders. At the same time, some of the ways these approaches conceive of parental involvement can be problematic both for your child and for you as a parent.

There are long-standing debates about the role of parents in the treatment of eating disorders, particularly anorexia nervosa. The earliest physicians to describe the treatment of anorexia nervosa disagreed about this. In the late 19th century, Charles Lasègue in France felt parents were essential to treatment, whereas Sir William Gull, just across the English Channel, proposed that parents were the "worst attendants." Many current approaches either exclude or blame parents, explicitly or implicitly, causing parents to be confused about whether and how they can help their child with an eating disorder. In addition, because of the severity of both the psychiatric and medical problems of anorexia nervosa, hospitalization or residential care is often recommended. This requires separating the child with anorexia nervosa from you and other family members. "Parentectomy" is seen as desirable and is still common in Europe, though the costs of these types of long-term hospitalization have become very burdensome in the United States.

Short of a parentectomy, some individual approaches to the treatment of adolescents with eating disorders in the outpatient setting also advise strongly against parental involvement. These approaches view the young adolescent with anorexia nervosa as having an inadequate sense of self resulting from a problematic relationship with her parents, usually her mother. This inadequate sense of self is supposedly due to insufficient nurture and respect for the child's needs and failure to sufficiently separate maternal needs from those of the developing child. These developmental failures lead to the child's developing an identity based on overcompliance with parents' and other authorities' expectations, with little sense of her own needs and wishes. During adolescence this compliant strategy falters, but because of fear of parental rejection, feelings of powerlessness, and little sense of her real wishes, the teenager turns to extreme dieting and an irrational pursuit of thinness as a way of expressing her internal anxieties about separation and individuation. She feels "out of control" because she does not have the internal resources to cope with the independent thought and action required

during adolescence and adulthood. A focus on what she can control, her weight and food intake, provides reassurance that she has some identity—albeit one devoted to the sole pursuit of thinness. In this way anorexia nervosa becomes intricately bound up with the developing sense of identity, making it difficult to challenge.

Certainly, many adolescents with anorexia nervosa do seem to struggle with the typical adolescent issues. Nonetheless, the implication that treatment should be focused only on the adolescent through her relationship with a therapist to "re-parent" her is questionable on several grounds. First, there is little scientific evidence supporting the notion that parents, and mothers in particular, of children with anorexia nervosa, systematically differ from others in how they have parented their children. Most parents of children who develop anorexia nervosa have other kids who do not develop the disorder but were generally parented similarly. Studies of the feeding practices of mothers whose children later develop anorexia nervosa show that they don't appear to differ substantially from typical feeding practices. For example, although one researcher found that "picky eating and early introduction of solid foods" predicted more eating disorders in adolescence, the same practices when used with siblings did not lead to eating difficulties. Further, studies of parental psychopathology as an indicator of overinvolvement with children don't provide clear evidence that these parents truly differ from others. The studies suggesting that this is the case evaluated families who were in crisis about their child's starving, making it impossible to draw conclusions about their functioning without this stress. In other words, even those studies that find evidence of intrusiveness and overinvolvement in families in which a child has an eating disorder can only say that these differences were present once an eating disorder had developed, but not before. This is important, because it is this presumption—that parents, in particular mothers, have *caused* the problem of anorexia nervosa in their children—that supports the clinical notion that they should be excluded from treatment.

Jamal was always good at school, though he was somewhat shy. He didn't really like rough sports, but he excelled at tennis and

swimming. When he developed anorexia nervosa at age 14, his parents took him to a psychiatrist who said he believed that Jamal was struggling with being independent and was confused emotionally and sexually. The psychiatrist suggested psychoanalysis as a way to help Jamal address these problems instead of avoiding them by starving himself. His parents wanted only the best for their son, and they had the resources to pay for intensive psychotherapy—anything to help him.

Jamal was happy enough at first to go to therapy. He was never a disobedient child. Even as a teenager, he seldom mouthed off or complained about his parents' requests. However, over time Jamal complained about time away from his homework (he was in an honors class in all subjects) and from his workout schedule, which included a 2-hour swim in the morning and a run in the afternoon. He said he liked this therapist. They talked about his friends and his parents, but not much about eating or weight.

His parents dutifully took Jamal to therapy four afternoons a week. However, after a few months, they didn't see any improvement. In fact, they felt Jamal was getting worse. He was still losing weight and he was eating even less. His therapist had told them to let Jamal decide what to eat and when to exercise, and they deferred to this recommendation, though they were constantly worried. Things came to a head when Jamal began to refuse to go to therapy. He said that he didn't see any reason to go and that he was better. His parents could see that he wasn't.

Other adherents of individual therapy have excluded parents for developmental reasons. Developmental theorists have suggested that to support adolescent autonomy, parents should be, in the main, left out of treatment. To support age-appropriate autonomy, some clinicians contend that it is the adolescent herself who must take on the challenge of anorexia nervosa, more or less as a preamble to beginning to emerge as an adolescent once again. Parents, according to this school of thought, will simply reinforce the preadolescent stance, furthering anorexia nervosa's regressive hold on their child.

Gary was on his high school's rowing crew and had developed anorexia nervosa initially while trying to be as fit and as lean

as possible to better succeed at this sport. When Gary's parents took him to a therapist, she suggested that Gary was struggling with a wish to be more independent but was frightened of the responsibilities of work and relationships that being more grown up would entail. She suggested that Gary needed help with being more self-assertive and that he should be given more control over his life as was appropriate for a 16-year-old boy. Gary's parents agreed that he should be independent, but they thought that at this point he was too ill to make good decisions and were worried about the consequences to his health if he made poorer ones. Risk taking and exploration are a part of adolescence, the therapist explained, and it was necessary to trust Gary more and let him make mistakes if need be.

Gary competed avidly on crew and his team did well, but by midseason he was no longer able to participate because he had lost additional muscle mass and wasn't strong enough to row even short distances. Gary said he understood that he had made a mistake and would now eat more to gain his muscle back. He did this for a while but became anxious about getting out of shape and once again cut back on eating and increased his exercise. Gary's parents wanted to step in to help their son, but because they wished to respect his adolescent need for independence, they held back.

You only have to think about the behavior of children with anorexia nervosa to see that the illness effectively stops adolescent development. It throws children off the normal trajectory of physical maturation (ceasing menstruation, for example), encourages them to isolate themselves from the peers with whom they need to start to align to acquire independence, and leads to their being more involved with their parents and family, because of being ill, than would be usual for a teenager. But why would this necessarily lead to a conclusion that adolescents with anorexia nervosa should face the challenge of battling this illness without a great deal of parental involvement? After all, kids don't generally face the challenges of adolescence without parents. In fact, the presumption that having a stormy, conflict-ridden relationship with their parents is a necessary rite of passage for all teenagers no longer has much support. We now know that the teenagers who function best are

those who continue to make productive use of their parents during adolescence—whose parents develop skills that enhance and support their adolescent children's progress through this stage of burgeoning autonomy. This may be even truer for adolescents who have difficulties of one kind or another. That is, teenagers who not only face the predictable challenges of adolescence but also have a physical or emotional problem are likely to need to rely even more on parental resources to ensure their ultimate success with and mastery of the tasks of adolescence. Thus, it may be all the more important for teenagers who develop anorexia nervosa to be able to garner the support of their parents in their struggles with the illness.

Many believe that the fundamental issues driving the development and maintenance of eating disorders should be addressed in individual therapy rather than through parental management. Eating disorders are often described as illnesses of "control," and so it is assumed that "taking control" away from the adolescent with regard to eating and dieting will exacerbate the problem. It's true that eating disorders lead to high levels of anxiety about food and weight, and indeed this anxiety decreases, relatively but briefly, when patients feel they are controlling these parts of their lives. Nonetheless, the anxiety returns rapidly and with renewed insistence, leading to even greater restriction and control, resulting in a cascade of increasing weight loss and worry. Patients report their mind-numbing preoccupations with counting calories, reading recipes, counting fat grams, weighing, measuring, special cookware, plates, and so on. The misery that accompanies these preoccupations is tolerable only because of the relief from the anxiety, which occurs intermittently, that reinforces these behaviors.

If, however, eating disorders are diseases of control, the sense of control is quite illusory. Patients do not feel in control; rather, they feel a *need to* feel in control. This difference is crucial. The pursuit of thinness, weight loss, dieting, and so forth, is a search for control, not true evidence of control. In this sense, contending that the adolescent needs to remain in control of her eating and diet is a fabrication because when she has an eating disorder she does not have this control to begin with; instead, she is constantly trying to reassure herself that she will get such control. In this sense, the

adolescent with an eating disorder is in need of someone to take control or at least help her take control, rather than leave her with an ever-shrinking ability to meet the behavioral and psychological demands of her illness.

Ironically, treatment modalities that advocate parentectomy to a greater or lesser extent, in the name of giving the adolescent control over food and weight, actually take most of the control away. Hospital programs regularly insist on consumption of set amounts of food or liquid supplements over which the patient exercises no control. Dietitians regularly prescribe dietary regimens for patients to follow. Some refeeding programs (professionally administered programs designed to rapidly restore weight) simply resort to nasogastric refeeding rather than involve the patient in even the activity of chewing and swallowing. Still, upon discharge, parents are told to let the child manage her food choices on her own. What is interesting, though, is that most younger patients experience a brief period of relief of anxiety when they are treated in such programs. That is, when someone else takes control of their eating and weight, they can often allow themselves to let go of the anxiety about these concerns. This accounts to no small degree for the success of these inpatient refeeding programs in treating the acute weight loss and malnutrition associated with anorexia nervosa. If most people with an eating disorder simply rejected these interventions, these programs would not succeed.

Why don't people with eating disorders rebel against these intrusive procedures as they do at home? It could be argued that it is against their nature to be confrontational and directly rebellious. Others report that these people have supreme (and somewhat justifiable) confidence that they can undo this weight gain rather quickly once they are allowed to be in charge again. Both of these perspectives are likely true, but certainly the latter point is not contested. Though most refeeding programs succeed in helping people with anorexia to eat more in the hospital (or other intensive settings), many lose the weight gained and revert to their restrictive behaviors when left to their own devices upon discharge. The question then is how best to build on the progress accomplished in these programs.

Lilly was a precocious 10-year-old who developed anorexia after
she lost weight at summer camp. She was hospitalized for severe
starvation. In the hospital, Lilly at first protested against eating and yelled and cried for her mother. She complained about
missing her family and her friends. She hated missing school.
Members of the nursing staff, who were quite experienced with
these behaviors, provided a consistent presence at mealtimes
and quietly insisted that Lilly eat her meals. They waited with
her, encouraged her when needed, and set a limit on how long
she had to complete her meals. Meals were provided at regular
intervals, and snacks were also served routinely. Lilly gained
weight and seemed less troubled by her eating symptoms, and
after 3 weeks was discharged home.

Lilly almost immediately began to restrict her eating again.
Her parents were unsure what to do, although they now knew
more about anorexia nervosa than they had before. Lilly said
that she and the nutritionist had worked out a meal plan that
she was supposed to follow. Her parents didn't really understand it. Meanwhile, Lilly started school immediately and threw
herself into the work with her usual vigor. As she studied more
and once again became preoccupied with her grades, she ate
even less. Within 2 months Lilly was back in the hospital, weighing even less than she had when she was first admitted.

Another reason parents have been excluded from individual
treatment is the assumption that parents of adolescents with eating
disorders are unduly focused on weight and dieting. The theory is,
somewhat reasonably, that parents are the vehicle through which
children and adolescents learn about and filter their experiences of
the culturally informed thin ideal. Parents who emphasize extreme
concerns about weight in themselves, others, or their children are
seen as likely to promote body dissatisfaction in their children, who
internalize the thin ideal as communicated by their parents. For
this reason, treatments focused on helping with body image dissatisfaction or, more important, body image distortion, exclude parents, who are seen as the likely suspects in causing this increased
reliance on the thin ideal as a source of self-evaluation. Although
it is undoubtedly true that parents can influence dieting concerns
and behaviors, few support the distortions associated with eating

disorders even if they have the illness themselves. Instead, parents can and often do serve as a reality check on these distortions and thereby likely mediate the influence of other social and cultural pressures such as the use of alcohol and drugs, sexual activity, and social role performance.

Yet another reason that parents may be excluded from treatment is that many therapists believe that it is the parents who have caused the illness or are doing things to make it worse. Families themselves have been implicated in the etiology and maintenance of anorexia nervosa. The most famous formulation of the family as the cause of anorexia nervosa is based on the psychosomatic family process as observed by Salvador Minuchin and colleagues. These clinical investigators characterized psychosomatic families (including families with a child with anorexia nervosa) as enmeshed, overprotective, conflict avoidant, and rigid and said that each characteristic led to difficulties for the adolescent in negotiating the transition to adolescence:

1. In enmeshed families, the needs of the individual were unclear and difficult to assert.
2. Overprotective families prevented adolescents from the necessary social and psychological risk taking crucial for developing autonomy.
3. Families that tended to avoid conflict thwarted the necessary strivings for independent thinking and behavior.
4. Rigid families had difficulty adapting to the necessary change in role and function associated with having an adolescent whose needs were different from those of younger children.

In addition to these problems in family process, psychosomatic families were said to have structural problems, such as where children take up the role of a parental figure and/or where the parents, facing the developmental challenges of adolescence, abdicate responsibility. Other researchers have suggested that there may be problems in how parents are emotionally connected (attached) to their children with anorexia nervosa. Some feel these parents

promote a kind of false independence by not relating sincerely and deeply to their children. If children develop this "false independence," it tends not to hold up during adolescence, and problems such as eating disorders may ensue.

Lan and her family came to family therapy for anorexia nervosa after they had read that problems in families were often the reason children developed eating disorders. Lan's parents were professionals who had accomplished a lot in their respective careers. Her father was an accountant who traveled a great deal, and her mother was a physician. There were no other children. Lan had been a somewhat anxious child, but over time she had gained increasing confidence and had, to all appearances, sailed through elementary school both academically and socially. When she developed anorexia nervosa in eighth grade, it was the parents' first sign that there were problems.

The family met with the therapist, who determined that Lan was too close to her parents, particularly her mother. Being too close to her mother interfered with Lan's need to be more independent as a teenager. In addition, and in part because Lan and her mother were so close, Lan's father and mother, it was suggested, weren't acting together, and instead Lan was usurping her father's role. Finally, the therapist said, the family needed to address their suppressed anger. They needed to acknowledge their disagreements with one another. The family agreed to try.

For several weeks the therapist asked the family to describe their conflicts, which were at this point all about Lan's not eating. The therapist accepted that not eating was the subject of their arguments but suggested that not eating was just a symptom of other conflicts they weren't describing. The family was increasingly perplexed but tried hard to identify problems. Lan's parents spent more time together, as the therapist directed. Lan was encouraged to spend time outside the family, which she did, mostly by going on runs or going to the gym. Meanwhile, Lan continued to lose weight and had gone on to her eighth month without a menstrual period. Lan's parents asked the therapist when they could expect Lan to get better.

The research literature on the pathology of parents and families of adolescents with anorexia nervosa is fraught with difficulties,

and conclusions are far from clear. Many researchers and clinicians argue that it is not the family that is causing some of the problematic behaviors seen in teens with anorexia nervosa, but rather the illness and the family's experiences of the illness. In other words, families become overprotective *because* their children are ill. They become enmeshed *because* they're trying to understand what's happening to their child and therefore appear intrusive and overinvolved. They want to avoid conflicts *because* they fear making things worse. They become more rigid *in reaction* to the stress the illness imposes on them. Although this debate is not resolved, the position taken by many clinicians is to presume the parents and family are guilty until proven innocent, thereby justifying the limitation of parental involvement in treatment.

Despite this stance by many clinicians, the notion that parents are unnecessary to treatment has been challenged increasingly over the years. Family therapists view the families of patients with anorexia nervosa as not only necessary to involve in treatment but essential to the recovery process. However, many still arrive at that conclusion because they see families as the "problem" in anorexia nervosa, and therefore neglecting to treat them would mean leaving the essential core of the illness to fester. It is only recently that parents and families of adolescents with anorexia nervosa have been perceived as being likely to exert a *positive influence* on bringing about recovery of anorexia nervosa but *not* being perceived as the likely cause of the problem to begin with.

HOW FAMILIES CAN COME TOGETHER TO FIGHT EATING DISORDERS

As we've said, many current therapies exclude parents and families, pay them only lip service, or blame them for causing or worsening the illness. However, family-based treatment, or FBT, is a therapeutic approach that takes a different view. The basic tenets of this approach were first developed at the Maudsley Hospital in London in the 1980s. This form of family therapy doesn't blame the family but encourages its members to support their child actively by taking

responsibility for helping their child eat normally, restore weight if malnourished, and normalize activity. This treatment, unlike many of the other currently used approaches, has been actually studied in a series of trials that provide evidence that it is helpful. Indeed, it's the only therapy for anorexia nervosa that has any substantive empirical support (see Chapter 6).

The basics of FBT are as follows. First, parents and the family as a whole are helped to understand how serious eating disorders are. To do this, the therapist reviews just how much the adolescent has changed, as well as the trajectory of serious problems (medical and psychological) that follow if the eating disorder goes unchecked. Next, the therapist helps family members to see how important they are in changing the outcome, while reminding them of their abilities and previous successes in solving other family problems. The therapist also reminds parents that unless they are prepared to send their child away, it will be they who will have the ultimate responsibility for setting up an environment that supports improved behaviors related to eating and weight. This responsibility can feel overwhelming, and so parents are assured that the therapist will help them, not by telling them what to do, but rather by reviewing with them their successes and dilemmas and problem solving with them, using the resources that parents and siblings bring to help.

With this as an impetus, the therapist, using his or her expertise and experience, consults with parents in their efforts to change maladaptive eating behaviors. When working together with a therapist, most parents are able to make dramatic changes in such behaviors relatively quickly. When these behaviors have ceased to be the main concern, the therapist encourages the parents to help their adolescent manage eating independently, but with some guidance. Once the adolescent is managing eating and weight on her own, the therapist concludes treatment by strategizing with the family members about how they might address more general issues of adolescence. This helps to prepare the family to leave therapy ready to proceed in the normal course of things.

We've been using this therapy in our centers for eating disorders in adolescents for over 15 years now. We have been involved in

research, as well as in clinical work using this approach that doesn't blame parents, but helps them better help their children with the symptoms of eating disorders and provides ample opportunity for education and support. Consequently, we've seen adolescents with eating disorders improve dramatically. Not only do their symptoms abate, but, on the whole, the family also feels better able to negotiate adolescent issues in other areas.

Even if this form of family therapy is not available to your child, adopting its principles, described in the following paragraphs, can help you find a way to be involved in your child's treatment, to the child's ultimate benefit.

1. **Parents bring important resources to their child's recovery and can be involved in whatever type of treatment the child receives.** It's the purpose of this book, in fact, to demonstrate how you can adopt this perspective to your child's benefit in a variety of clinical settings.

2. **It's important for parents to take eating disorders seriously.** One insight that FBT highlights is the importance of realizing that eating disorders are serious medical and psychiatric illnesses. They are so serious, in fact, that as a parent you need to be highly aware of their potential for killing or severely damaging your child. Bulimia nervosa, anorexia nervosa, and binge-eating disorder are not just instances of taking dieting too far; they are truly *illnesses*. By emphasizing this principle, as we began to do in Chapter 1, we hope to help motivate you to take more immediate and definite action to help your child.

3. **You need to know what you're up against.** As a parent, you need to become sufficiently informed about the eating disorders that you know how to evaluate to a reasonable degree whether your child is getting better or not doing well. Parents are prepared for many difficulties that adolescents may develop, but they are understandably not expected to know very much about eating disorders. The work by the Maudsley group, as well as that in our own centers, demonstrates that educating parents about how people with eating

disorders think and behave, and why they do the odd things they do, helps parents to be more sympathetic, supportive, and effective in helping their children.

4. **It's not your fault.** Our approach includes a nonblaming attitude toward parents. If you feel guilty and responsible for causing the eating disorder, you likely also feel hopeless and inadequate when facing the task of trying to help your child change her eating behaviors. As we've said, though, we believe you are a key ingredient in your child's success in fighting the eating disorder. So it's our job, both in our practice and in this book, to alleviate any anxiety or guilt that is keeping you from contributing to your child's return to health.

5. **You need to be empowered to take up your parental role effectively.** Leveraging your love and abilities as parents in the service of fighting an eating disorder is crucial. This is fairly easy to see in the case of anorexia nervosa, where the adolescent seldom has any motivation to recover. Without your strength, your child is left to the devices of the disorder and the downward spiral of weight loss and obsessional thoughts about food and calories. However, the same holds true for bulimia nervosa, where the shame of the illness holds your daughter or son captive. When you are able to be a part of the process, the element of shame actually diminishes as you support your child through these dilemmas.

6. **"Getting together" involves the whole family.** It's not just you who are a resource for your child. In fact, your whole family is able to help, in distinct but definite ways. Everyone in the family is affected when a child has an eating disorder. Everyone is worried or angry or both. Your other children see the effects on you and on their sibling. They are often most articulate about how much their brother or sister has been changed by the disorder. They also have clear memories of activities and qualities that are no longer present in their sibling with an eating disorder. Siblings can provide an avenue of support for their sister or brother who is ill, especially when your child may be angry at you for being firm about requirements for attending therapy or setting a limit on a behavior such

as throwing up or not eating. They are also excellent sources of distraction and fun, which are needed when someone is fighting an eating disorder.

7. **The therapist is your consultant, not the boss.** In this sense, all therapy with children and adolescents must acknowledge the importance of family relationships. Therapists may be experts in particular areas, but they are not going home with you and do not routinely have to confront the problems in your home—they do not have to eat meals with your family regularly, clean up the bathrooms, and so on. That's what you do as parents. Therapists can help you think through problems and sometimes may even work independently with your child, with your approval, support, and understanding, when needed. But, ultimately, you are the parent and they are advisers to you as you try to navigate the difficult problems that eating disorders present for you, your child, and your family.

So, there is a way you and your family can help your child who is suffering with an eating disorder. It involves, to start with, discarding the notion that you caused the problem. This idea is unproven and will cripple you in your efforts to help. Next, you need to learn all you can about how people with eating disorders think and behave, what motivates them to do what they do. When you do this, you are better prepared to counter them instead of being surprised and taken for a ride. Any therapist you find, regardless of his or her approach, should want to involve you. You should ask about how you will be involved and how you can help. According to some approaches, the therapist sees his or her job as helping you help your child, whereas other therapists that you may find attractive might see you in a more supportive role. In any case, you need to know what the treatment is, what its goals are, and what you will be doing to support it and your child. You should not sit back, but should instead take responsibility for your child. Don't let an eating disorder "de-skill" you as a parent; don't assume that you no longer know anything. Instead, assume you have a right to know what treatment your child is receiving, a right to look for ways you

can help, and a responsibility to ensure that your child is getting the best treatment.

The rest of this book is designed to help you grow more confident in playing an active role in your child's (and your) struggle with an eating disorder. We hope to educate you more about what eating disorders are and how they can affect your child and family. We will review the kinds of treatment options you are likely to find and help you determine how you can be a part of each of these types of treatments. We also will provide you with examples of the kinds of problems you may face and how you might negotiate them. We hope this will help to make you feel more empowered and, with that, even more capable and responsible as, with your help, your son or daughter combats an eating disorder.

FOR MORE INFORMATION

Bruch, H., *Eating Disorders: Obesity, Anorexia Nervosa, and the Person Within*, 1973. New York: Basic Books.

Bruch, H., *The Golden Cage: The Enigma of Anorexia Nervosa*, 1978. Cambridge, MA: Harvard University Press.

Crisp, A., *Anorexia Nervosa: Let Me Be*, 1995. Hove, UK: Erlbaum.

Dare, C., and I. Eisler, Family Therapy for Anorexia Nervosa, in D. M. Garner and P. E. Garfinkel, Editors, *Handbook of Treatment for Eating Disorders, Second Edition*, 1997. New York: Guilford Press, pp. 307–324.

Le Grange, D., and J. Lock. *Treating Bulimia in Adolescents: A Family-Based Approach*, 2007. New York: Guilford Press.

Le Grange, D., J. Lock, K. Loeb, et al., An Academy for Eating Disorders Position Paper: The Role of the Family in Eating Disorders, *International Journal of Eating Disorders*, 2010, *43*, 1–5.

Lock, J., and D. Le Grange, *Treatment Manual for Anorexia Nervosa: A Family-Based Approach, Second Edition*, 2013. New York: Guilford Press.

Minuchin, S., B. Rosman, and I. Baker, *Psychosomatic Families: Anorexia Nervosa in Context*, 1978. Cambridge, MA: Harvard University Press.

CHAPTER 3

Don't Waste Time on "Why?"

Is this my fault?

> Mike woke up at 3:00 in the morning again. His wife, Ariana, was already awake. They were worrying about their daughter Julie, who had anorexia. Mike was lamenting the time he had spent talking to his children about the importance of regular exercise. Now Julie wouldn't stop exercising. Ariana blamed herself for focusing attention on good nutrition. Now Julie could tell you every food's calorie content and fat grams. Ariana was also berating herself for having fashion magazines at home. Now Julie spent an inordinate amount of time looking at herself in the mirror, pinching nonexistent fat on her stomach and thighs. Mike and Ariana were sure they had somehow caused Julie's illness. They felt sick with guilt and overwhelmed with doubt about how to proceed.

Perhaps the biggest hurdle you face in trying to figure out how to help your child is the message, both covert and overt, that you must have caused this problem. Something you did as a parent, some failure on your part, some trauma you unconsciously inflicted on your child, resulted in the development of an eating disorder.

As we'll discuss, however, the causes of eating disorders remain unknown, and your possible role is at best uncertain. There may be things we do as parents that increase the risk to our children of a variety of problems, both emotional and physical. However, none of those things we might do—for example, worrying about weight, being vegetarians, or eating unhealthily—appear to be specific enough to warrant being labeled a cause of eating disorders.

The truth is that causes of illnesses, especially psychological illnesses, are not easily discoverable. Remember, it took several thousand years to discover the bacterial and viral causes of illnesses like smallpox and pneumonia, and for infectious illnesses the line of causation is direct: Exposure to these bacteria or viruses will ultimately lead to the development of an infectious illness. (Although some attempts have been made to explain anorexia nervosa as a result of exposure to streptococcus, there is no evidence that this is the usual cause of this illness.) An explanation for how psychological illnesses arise, including those with a very clear genetic basis, relies on a much more complex theory of causation that is both indirect and interactive. It is fairly easy to show that by ridding the environment of certain bacteria, pneumonia won't develop. But it's impossible to rid the environment of genetics or vice versa (in fact, they evolve together and inform one another).

Despite the complexity involved in uncovering causation for psychological illnesses, and for eating disorders specifically, theorists have tended to support their recommendations for treatment on the basis of presumed causes. This is confusing and at times misleading. Psychological treatments clearly do not depend on specific knowledge of causation. If they did, we would have little hope of finding helpful interventions. This means that you don't need to understand what has caused your daughter's or son's eating disorder in order for them to recover. In fact, dwelling on what may have caused the problem often diverts parents' energies from helping their child. And like Mike and Ariana, many parents who get mired in the question "Why?" end up with nowhere to point the finger of blame but at themselves and then become paralyzed by guilt.

Although eating disorders have been around for a long time (some have cited evidence of eating disorders going back as far as

ancient Egypt), modern recognition of these illnesses dates from the first descriptions of anorexia nervosa in the 1600s by Richard Morton and then in the late 19th century by Sir William Gull in England and Charles Lasègue in France. Since it was first described, theories about the etiology of anorexia nervosa have ranged from viewing it as a purely physical disease to seeing it as the result of societal forces and not a disease at all. In contrast, bulimia nervosa is a much more recent phenomenon and was first described by Gerald Russell only in 1979 and was initially seen as "an ominous variant of anorexia nervosa." Bulimia nervosa as a distinct disorder has emerged over the ensuing years. Its cause is also unknown, but it is usually described as having biological, social, and psychological roots. Binge-eating disorder has been studied as a separate disorder from bulimia nervosa for about a decade but became a separate diagnosis only in 2013 with the publication of DSM-5. Avoidant/restrictive food intake disorder was included for the first time in this most recent version of DSM-5. The causes of these disorders are unknown.

A CLOSER LOOK AT INDIVIDUAL FACTORS IN CAUSATION

At this point in the evolution of our understanding, eating disorders overall appear to be multifactorial—that is, caused by the interaction of many factors. In the following pages we review some of the factors that theoretically contribute to causing anorexia, bulimia, and binge-eating disorder to help you understand (1) how little we actually know about the causes of eating disorders and (2) how assuming we know the cause can lead us down paths of treatment that may not be helpful.

Although it's certainly not a bad thing to have some theoretical ideas about the cause of an illness, when these ideas remain untested but still become gospel for therapists—as has happened for eating disorders, particularly anorexia nervosa—treatments that aren't based on these ideas often remain unexplored as well. And when these ideas center on parents' contribution to cause, they

can remove parents as a key ingredient in recovery by disabling them through guilt and creating counterproductive therapist bias against them. The mental health field saw the same thing happen with schizophrenia and autism: The development of these severe psychiatric disorders was typically laid at the parents' doorstep until a deeper understanding of the biological causes of these illnesses was gained. By explaining what we do know about various potential causes for the eating disorders covered in this chapter, we hope to convince you that you are not to blame any more than parents of children with schizophrenia or autism are ever at fault. Putting self-blame behind you will restore your confidence in your ability to help with the problems that eating disorders present for your child. As you're reading about the *theorized* causes of eating disorders, remember that your goal is to go beyond these theories to embrace the need for change and begin to take action.

It's Biology!

Some interesting and important research is actually being done on the biological and genetic aspects of eating disorders. For example, studies show that anorexia and bulimia nervosa tend to aggregate in families, especially among first-degree female relatives. Eating disorders are three to five times more common in families in which a person is found to have such a disorder than in families in which no one has had an eating disorder. Still, of course, the vast majority of family members, male and female, do not have an eating disorder. One way researchers have tried to refine these observations about family clustering of eating disorders is by determining whether identical twins raised separately have similar rates of illness. Identical twins have exactly the same genetic makeup (or nearly so), so any differences in the occurrence of eating disorders between identical twins who are raised in different families are likely to be due to different environmental factors. Investigators have found that there's a significantly increased risk in twins that appears to be genetic rather than environmental. So, vulnerability to eating disorders appears to be inherited. Because, at least for now, we can't do

much about our genes, we can't entirely blame parents, families, or society for the problem.

Not only do eating disorders appear to be heritable, but it's possible that certain personality traits and susceptibility to different behaviors may also be inherited. Traits such as perfectionism, obsessionality, anxiety, feeding behaviors, and negative mood states, which are associated with eating disorders, may also be heritable and thereby constitute particular vulnerability for developing eating problems. So far, researchers haven't figured out very much about this issue, but the idea is that eating disorders are caused indirectly, at least in part, by these inherited personality characteristics. It seems likely that this is true. The problem is that the Hiroe characteristics may lead to very healthy outcomes. We've observed this many times. For instance, a young boy with anorexia has a mother who is a CEO and a father who is a doctor. They share many personality traits such as perfectionism, drive, and obsessionality, but the outcomes are totally different, because in the parents these traits are applied to work, whereas in the boy they are focused on a preoccupation with dieting and weight.

Other research suggests that certain neurotransmitters are involved in vulnerability to developing eating disorders. Neurotransmitters are chemicals in the brain that affect a variety of brain functions such as sleep, appetite, mood, and attention. When something goes awry with these chemicals, problems in any of these areas may result. Many neurotransmitters have been implicated in eating disorders (e.g., dopamine, norepinephrine, and serotonin). Probably the most important neurotransmitters currently being studied are dopamine and serotonin. It appears that problems with regulating these brain chemicals are related to both anorexia and bulimia. Recent studies suggest that people with anorexia do not respond the same way to rewarding experiences (such as eating). Instead of experiencing pleasure, they are overwhelmed and anxious. It is suggested that being oversensitive to dopamine may be at the heart of this kind of anxious response. Studies using neuroimaging are trying to sort out these neurobiological aspects of eating disorders in more detail, and perhaps we will someday better

understand the role of dopamine and other neurotransmitters in eating disorders.

For now, however, the exact nature of what goes wrong isn't clear, and, unfortunately, medications that aim to fix the problem (and that are effective for depression and anxiety problems) don't work as well with eating disorders. They do, however, help somewhat with bulimia and binge-eating disorder. So, the argument goes that for some reason (inheritance, environmental stress, nutrition) something goes wrong with one or more of these neurotransmitters (or others not yet identified), which increases the likelihood that an eating disorder will start. Again, this may indeed be true, and medications may someday be of more help in treatment than they are now. However, focusing on neurotransmitters alone is unlikely to be enough because the attendant behaviors and thoughts appear to have a life of their own that is reinforced through habit and time. Unless those thought processes and behaviors are addressed directly, targeting neurotransmitters through medications isn't likely to "cure" the disorder.

It's All in the Head!

Dora was 13 when she began restricting her foods in an attempt to lower her weight. She had always been small and thin and did not like the idea of growing bigger. Dora was a bit of a loner. She could socialize with others when she had to, but she clearly preferred to read or study. She showed no romantic interest and shared none of her friends' enthusiasm for boy–girl parties. She was very close to her mother, who had seen Dora from an early age as a shy and vulnerable girl who needed her help to negotiate social challenges.

Gull and Lasègue's early descriptions of anorexia dovetailed with the emerging psychoanalytic movement in psychiatry and psychology that was to have profound influence on psychiatric treatment for half a century. Psychoanalysis is fundamentally a dyadic treatment (that is, one therapist meets with one patient). It also contends that psychological problems stem from early deprivations,

traumas, and fantasies related to parents. The approach is basically designed to be used with adult patients (though Sigmund Freud occasionally treated children, and his daughter, Anna Freud, designed treatments for adolescents and children), whose fantasy life is explored through free association and dream interpretation. Patients with anorexia nervosa were seen as reasonable candidates for the psychoanalytic method, and their symptoms of self-starvation were interpreted in various ways. The early theoreticians relied heavily on Freud's understanding of sexual repression as the origin of all mental illness, and as a result, their theories of anorexia coincide with this idea. Thus, early psychoanalytic theory focused on guilt and oral impregnation fantasies, with weight loss seen as a defense mechanism—that is, "not eating" was a way of avoiding sexual thoughts and feelings. Although it has been observed that patients with anorexia are often sexually avoidant and may struggle with interpersonal intimacy, it's not clear whether this is more a result of the disease (starvation, for example, leads to lower sexual hormone levels, and this in turn leads to lowered sexual desire) than the cause.

Later, but still based in the psychoanalytic tradition, Hilde Bruch suggested that the person with anorexia is suffering from an "inadequate sense of self." By this she meant that the patient was socially immature and psychologically underdeveloped. As a result of not feeling confident and assertive, such adolescents turn to other ways of expressing their feelings, especially their anger. Thus, restrictive eating and related disturbed eating patterns are seen as forms of "acting out" the frustration and feelings of inadequacy that these adolescents experience. To assist with these problems, psychoanalytic treatment aims at helping to "find a voice" for this deficient self that substitutes psychological understanding and expression as opposed to disturbed eating as a way of communicating. Indeed, these adolescents often seem immature, naïve, and not particularly assertive as compared with their peers. In fact, the theoretical idea that adolescents with anorexia need help with finding a sense of identity makes a great deal of sense. How to help them best accomplish that task in the context of a serious illness such as anorexia is less clear.

Other recent research has suggested that some of the problems people with eating disorders may have could be related to *how* they think. Studies suggest that adults with eating disorders show problems in being flexible in their thinking style, which makes it difficult for them to consider alternatives and to use therapy. Other studies have found that people with eating disorders struggle with not seeing the forest for the trees and get lost in too much detail. An overfocus on details makes it easier to perseverate and obsess rather than see the consequences of ongoing problems. It is unclear how these problems in "thinking style" may relate to the risk for an eating disorder or whether they can be addressed in treatment, but all of this is under study.

It's All in the Family!

Hiro's parents did not get along. His father was a busy surgeon, and his mother participated in many charity events and social activities. They seldom had overt conflicts, but they also were seldom together. Hiro's father left for work at four thirty in the morning and returned after dinner. Hiro's mother was often out in the evening at fund-raising planning meetings. When Hiro stopped eating, no one noticed for quite some time. By the time his father finally asked Hiro if he was losing weight and arranged for a physical exam, he had lost almost 25 pounds. When the family sat down together for therapy, it was the first time they could remember having been together for several weeks.

Heather's mother had sent her to live with her father when she was 12 because she and Heather were fighting all the time. This arrangement went all right until Heather's father remarried. Heather and her stepmother did not get along well. Heather felt picked on, and her stepmother felt she wasn't respected. Heather moved back with her mother. During this period, Heather began to diet and throw up. She said she felt fat and ugly and no one liked her. She had few friends and was very isolated. Her mother was also quite busy with her own work and social life.

When family therapy arrived on the scene in the 1960s and 1970s, it was developed from a psychoanalytic base. Like

practitioners of psychoanalysis, many family therapists see anorexia nervosa as a symptom of underlying pathology, this time located in the family as a whole. Therefore, conventional family intervention tries to modify perceived problems within the family or, if this fails, to remove the child from the family. Yet another form of family therapy, so-called structural family therapy for anorexia (probably the best-known approach), was devised based on clinical observations of families by Salvador Minuchin (a pioneer in family therapy for anorexia nervosa). Because the child played a critical role in the family's overall avoidance of conflict, self-starvation was seen as powerfully supported by the family, though its members were not aware of this. Structural family therapy tries to alter family organization by identifying and challenging what are believed to be inappropriate alliances between parents and children, encouraging the development of stronger sibling support of one another, and promoting open communication. The aim is to reduce the child's emotional involvement with parents and to improve the effectiveness of the parents. So this approach also strongly supported the idea that families, and particularly parents, are in some way the cause of anorexia nervosa and without help will only perpetuate the problem. Data on the idea that families of patients are truly "pathological" are surprisingly conflicting. Some studies suggest that these families do have unique problems of the type that Minuchin described, whereas others don't appear to detect differences between these families and so-called normal families. Even if there are such differences, though, it isn't clear how they relate to the development of an eating disorder. In other words, a family can have many problems (as in Heather's case), but the direct link between such problems and their causing an eating disorder is a *leap* that cannot and really should not be made.

It's a Stage. She'll Outgrow It!

Mimi has always been a good student but "slow to warm" socially. When her family moved to another city at the beginning of her sixth grade, it was not very surprising that she struggled to make new friends. She complained about the new school and

about being lonely. She fantasized about going back to her own town, where she was happier and felt more accepted. Just after the winter holiday, Mimi had her first menstrual period. She told her mother that it hurt and she didn't like it. Although her mother tried to be supportive, Mimi remained very upset. Not long afterward, Mimi began to diet. She told her mother that she had an upset stomach or was too nervous to eat. Over time she ate less and less, and her parents became increasingly concerned. When the gym teacher called to ask Mimi's parents to meet with her about Mimi's weight, they were not surprised, but they didn't know what to do either.

Eating disorders generally begin during adolescence. It is principally for this reason that many theorists have viewed the disorders as related to issues of this developmental period, specifically with struggles for autonomy. A model for the cause of anorexia was developed by Arthur Crisp, a London psychiatrist, who speculated in the 1970s and 1980s that anorexia was the result of phobic avoidance of adolescence. That is, Crisp suggested that adolescents who develop anorexia were anxious about the physical changes associated with puberty, about establishing a more socially independent identity, and about entering social relations as sexually mature beings. The weight loss that resulted from excessive dieting and exercise restored the body shape and hormonal status of preadolescence, and the medical and psychological secondary effects returned the adolescent to the more dependent status of a younger child. Therefore, the child apparently accomplished her goal of avoiding adolescent struggles. This theory, which is said to apply to adolescents with an eating disorder, shows a healthy respect for the normal processes of adolescents and families and provides a very good context for thinking about therapy for teenagers. Still, it is unclear how best to employ the insight that developmental issues are key to understanding eating disorders. Moreover, in a certain sense the theory raises the question of causation: After all, the developmental challenges associated with adolescence are common to everyone, so why do only some teenagers develop eating disorders in response? No one knows for sure.

It's Hollywood!

Darnell spent hours studying himself in the mirror. He compared himself with the male models and athletes he saw in magazines. He felt his arms were too flabby and undefined. He wanted to be "cut" and lean. He wanted a "six-pack" of abdominal muscles. He began with lifting weights and cutting down on desserts and fast foods, but soon he was counting calories and throwing up to make sure he would lose weight. His friends noticed that he was looking very muscular and trim. Several girls talked to him and flirted. Darnell was sure he was on the right track.

Yet another approach to determining the cause of eating disorders focuses on the social and cultural forces on developing adolescents that may lead to increased problems with eating behaviors, body image concerns, and poor self-esteem. Although these forces have been influencing adolescent girls for some time, it's now clear that the same forces are acting on boys more than they used to. Several forces are considered likely culprits: notably, media images, Western cultural ideals, and wealth.

Media

The forces imposed by the media influence children at a fairly early age. For girls, Barbie dolls and similar toys set very early standards for unrealistic expectations with regard to body shape and size. For boys, male images of unrealistic body mass and musculature are increasing as well. When the Han Solo action figure based on the *Star Wars* movies first came out in the 1970s, he had human proportions, but the more recent action figure is unrealistically muscled. In addition, studies of *Playboy* and *Playgirl* centerfolds document a continuing trend toward ever-decreasing body fat and greater leanness in the male and female models represented. Even a cursory look at a fashion magazine or television program yields a host of examples of very thin women and men with extremely lean and muscular bodies modeling the latest styles. The basic difficulty is that these toys, images, and models set an unhealthy standard for

beauty that vulnerable children and young adolescent males and females then aspire to.

> Lia wanted to be a model when she grew up. She bought all the fashion magazines she could find. She shopped at every opportunity and spent a lot of time getting dressed for school and outings. During her second year of high school, Lia went to a modeling agency. She was told that she had a good face but she needed to lose 15 pounds if she wanted to be considered. Lia was not overweight, but she decided that becoming a model would be worth losing those pounds. Lia began dieting, exercising, and taking diet pills to curb her appetite and laxatives to "cleanse" her system. She lost about 8 pounds, and her friends and family said she looked great. However, Lia felt she could be thinner. She continued to restrict her intake, but when she did eat, even a normal meal, she would throw it up.

Western Cultural Ideals of Beauty

That the popular media have a great influence on all of our lives, especially the lives of adolescents, is obvious. Social values surrounding food and weight have long influenced our behavior. In the 16th century, for example, being overweight was "in," which made eating in abundance desirable, whereas being unduly thin was a mark of social inferiority and even sickness. In the Pacific islands of Tonga, eating disorders were unknown and overeating and corpulence were considered desirable until television was introduced in the early 1990s, after which eating disorders started to appear and young girls and women began to worry about their weight and to diet.

Western ideas of beauty and body shape are permeating other cultures all over the world, particularly in Asia. In the last several years, eating disorders have apparently been developing rapidly in Japan, Taiwan, Singapore, and Hong Kong. Studies of immigrants suggest that young women who move from a non-Western culture to a Western culture are at increased risk for eating disturbances.

> Indira's parents, both engineers, moved to the United States from India when Indira was about 2 years old. She had done

very well in school, excelling in both academics and athletics. However, at the beginning of high school, Indira began to lose weight and to complain about her skin color. She asked her parents for blue-tinted contact lenses. Indira explained her desire to lose weight and wear blue contact lenses as a way to fit in better with her mostly white friends in the private school she attended. Her parents were concerned about Indira's developing identity and saw her anorexia nervosa as a manifestation of her conflicts about being a minority person in a white majority group.

Indira's description of her experience is in line with some cross-cultural studies suggesting that immigrants, especially nonwhite immigrants, are experiencing increasing problems with eating disorders. Among these adolescents there seems to be an increased cultural strain, that is, an increased need to "fit in" and be "acceptable" relative to the white cultural thin ideal. To accomplish this, some teenagers try to change their appearance, particularly their weight, to become more desirable and to compete more successfully. Becoming psychologically and emotionally invested in meeting Western standards of beauty regarding thinness causes some of these young people to pursue unhealthy weight-loss strategies to the point where they develop eating disorders.

Related to the problems inherent in the Western idea of beauty are feminist perspectives on eating disorders and their development. The basic idea is that Western ideas of beauty, in their focus on thin body ideals, are part of a large cultural attack on women and women's bodies that is designed to keep women disempowered. This is accomplished by setting unrealistic standards of attractiveness. When women feel they don't meet these standards, the result is low self-esteem, poor self-worth, and less ability to perform in the culture. In addition, of course, these feelings and perceptions lead to eating disorders—an effect of this larger attack on women.

The feminist perspective on the development of eating disorders is instructive in several ways. First, it integrates the ideas of beauty, power, and gender, which are common themes in eating-disordered patients. It also synthesizes the roles of culture and media in the development of eating problems. Further, it suggests

that even women in the wealthier classes (see the next section) are not immune. Although not usually articulated, the feminist perspective also provides a partial rationale for why and how eating disorders might be more common among gay men. However, it has less to say about eating disorders among heterosexual men, athletes, and religious persons, who are less likely to be victims of media and other mainstream social forces identified in the feminist literature in the same way.

Wealth

Eating disorders, especially anorexia, have long been associated with higher socioeconomic status. The maxim "You can never be too rich or too thin" captures the essence of this association. There are several possible origins of this relationship. The first is rather concrete: The wealthy no longer have to worry about basic survival, and being thin manifests this freedom. The second is more subtle: That is, wealth confers a special status—a superior status—such that one doesn't need to eat. Of course, the confluence of wealth and fashion fuels the fantasy that to be rich is to be thin and vice versa. In fact, it appears that anorexia does seem to cluster more commonly among wealthier families. This is not to say it doesn't occur in the less wealthy because it certainly does.

However, it is less clear that wealth itself is the risk factor. It may be that some families are wealthier in part, as we have suggested earlier, because of some temperamental or personality traits that when applied to business lead to work and success, but when applied to dieting lead to anorexia. Thus, it may be a tautology to see wealth per se as the cause of anorexia. On the other hand, other eating disorders such as bulimia and binge-eating disorder don't appear to cluster to the same extent according to socioeconomic status. Instead, they are more widely distributed socioeconomically, culturally, and racially. Yet it may be that patients with bulimia are more sensitive to the influences of culture, media, or status (wealth), and this sensitivity may contribute to the development or maintenance of their eating-disordered behaviors, but how much or how specifically is speculative.

It's Due to Trauma!

There is a long-standing association between mental illness in general and sexual abuse and trauma. Researchers have been particularly interested in sexual abuse and eating disorders because many young women with eating disorders reported experiences of this kind to their doctors or therapists. Most studies have found that sexual or physical abuse is, in fact, a risk factor for eating problems, particularly bulimia, but no specific link between eating disorders and abuse has been established. The basic theory is that sexual trauma may heighten anxieties about the body, exacerbating an already exaggerated emphasis on weight and shape and leading to the development of eating-disordered thoughts and behaviors. Although certainly reasonable, this theory is not applicable to everyone, inasmuch as most people with eating disorders have not been abused or traumatized. And just as with targeting neurotransmitters, focusing solely on abuse or trauma seems unlikely to alleviate eating disorder symptoms, which take on a "life of their own" over time and need to be addressed specifically. The dilemma for therapists seems to be that it's easy to make sexual abuse or other trauma the sole focus of treatment because abuse is such a devastating event. Yet doing so, in our opinion, might make it more difficult to treat the eating disorder.

The role of trauma in the etiology of some children and adolescents with avoidant/restrictive food intake disorder appears to be important. Many report that the precipitant event to avoiding food was a choking incident. After this kind of event, some children become worried that they will choke and perhaps die and they are therefore afraid to eat.

DON'T GET STUCK ON "WHY?"

If it now seems that all of the reasons proposed for developing an eating disorder make sense—or that none of them do—rest assured that both of these statements are true. It's a matter of perspective. It is also true that focusing on why your child has developed or

maintains an eating disorder may not be very helpful. Imagine your child does not have an eating disorder, but cancer. No one knows exactly why she developed cancer, and the treatment prescribed does not aim at the cause of the cancer but instead targets the effects—removal of the malignancy and treatment with radiation and chemotherapy to prevent the growth of new cancerous lesions. Treatment for many childhood cancers is remarkably effective, even though the cause is often unknown and the treatment doesn't necessarily aim for it. For many of the diseases we treat in medicine, this is also the case. With diabetes, for example, we often don't really know why the body stops making adequate insulin, but we can control the disease with medications. Another example includes some types of seizures. We can generally identify the part of the brain in which the electrical impulses have gone awry, and sometimes we can perform surgery to resect that part. Usually, however, more conservatively but just as effectively, we treat the disorder with medications and the seizures are controlled. The list could go on. The point is that for most illnesses we have to treat symptoms—and in many cases we end up doing away with the disease in the process—but for mental illnesses we expect treatment to focus on eradicating the cause. This is largely because psychological and psychiatric research has been so interested in psychological explanations and conflicts, and this applies particularly to eating disorders. As we've seen, though, we seldom *know* what the cause is. How can we hope to eradicate the illness if we treat it by trying to eliminate what we can only guess is the cause?

It's understandable for you to want to know why your child has developed an eating disorder. It seems a random and unfair event, causing worry, hazard, and difficulty for your child and family. It's also understandable that psychologists and psychiatrists find investigating cause fascinating. Unfortunately, although research into why eating disorders occur may eventually help us prevent them from developing, we think the subject of cause just lures practitioners off course. Dwelling on cause in treatment keeps therapists and parents from dedicating their efforts to the problem at hand— keeping the starving teenager before them alive and restoring her

to health. With your child starving or throwing up in front of you, a discussion of her genetic vulnerability for anxiety and eating problems, how controlling you were as parents, how immature she is psychologically, and the problems of society's standards for beauty will likely be distracting and probably take you off track, at least initially. This is time you may not be able to afford to waste. In fact, such meditations and preoccupations sometimes play directly into the hands of the eating disorder by allowing the behaviors and thoughts to persist without confrontation and redirection, for longer periods and with more success. (More on this phenomenon is presented in Chapter 5.) We know that the longer a person loses weight, maintains low weight, purges, and binges (in other words, the more chronically ill she is), the less likely we will be successful in getting rid of the eating disorder. This is true for any illness. The longer you have diabetes before you are treated, the more difficult it is to control and the more problematic are the long-term effects. The same is true for cancer, heart disease, and other debilitating illnesses. That being the case, it's important to take action quickly and decisively rather than just ponder why.

Setting aside the question of "Why?" may be easier said than done. We would prefer that the question be deferred or bracketed while the disordered eating behaviors and weight problems remain unresolved. We see these problems as leading to a kind of thinking that is similar to trying to do therapy with someone who is inebriated: You just can't do it because that person can't process what you're saying. You've got to wait until she is sober, or at least somewhat sober, before you can hope to communicate with her. In the meantime, you have to get her sober. That means getting the alcohol out of her system and trying to keep her from drinking again. With eating disorders, at least at the beginning, we think you have to do the same thing. Stop the behaviors that are leading to the problem and keep them from recurring long enough that discussions about the problems associated with the disorder can be approached.

Perhaps the most important reason not to get stuck on "Why?" is that your child needs your help. By setting the problem of "Why?" to the side, we hope that you will feel less ashamed and guilty, see

yourself as an excellent candidate to help your child get the treatment and support he or she needs, and involve yourself in that treatment with confidence and commitment.

FOR MORE INFORMATION

Anderson-Fye, E. P., and A. E. Becker, Sociocultural Aspects of Eating Disorders, in J. K. Thompson, Editor, *Handbook of Eating Disorders and Obesity*, 2004. Hoboken, NJ: Wiley, pp. 565–589.

Bulik, C. M., Genetic and Biological Risk Factors, in J. K. Thompson, Editor, *Handbook of Eating Disorders and Obesity*, 2004. Hoboken, NJ: Wiley, pp. 3–16.

Crisp, A. H., *Anorexia Nervosa: Let Me Be*, 1980. London: Academic Press.

Field, A., Risk Factors for Eating Disorders: An Evaluation of the Evidence, in J. K. Thompson, Editor, *Handbook of Eating Disorders and Obesity*, 2004. Hoboken, NJ: Wiley, pp. 17–32.

Kaye, W., J. Fudge, and M. Paulus, New insights into symptoms and neurocircuit function in anorexia nervosa, *Nature Reviews Neuroscience*, 2009, *10*, 573–584.

Klump, K. L., S. A. Burt, A. Spanos, et al., Age Differences in Genetic and Environmental Influences on Weight and Shape Concerns, *International Journal of Eating Disorders*, 2010, *43*, 679–688.

Klump, K., and K. Gobrogge, A Review and Primer of Molecular Genetic Studies of Anorexia Nervosa, *International Journal of Eating Disorders*, 2005, *37*(Suppl.), S43–S48.

Levine, M., and K. Harrison, Media's Role in the Perpetuation and Prevention of Negative Body Image and Disordered Eating, in J. K. Thompson, Editor, *Handbook of Eating Disorders and Obesity*, 2004. Hoboken, NJ: Wiley, pp. 695–717.

Morton, R., *Phthisiologia: Or, a Treatise of Consumptions*, 1694. London: Smith and Walford.

Nasser, M., *Culture and Weight Consciousness*, 1997. London: Routledge.

Nasser, M., M. Katzman, and R. Gordon, Editors, *Eating Disorders and Cultures in Transition*, 2001. New York: Brunner-Routledge.

Vandereycken, W., Families of Patients with Eating Disorders, in C. G. Fairburn and K. D. Brownell, Editors, *Eating Disorders and Obesity: A Comprehensive Handbook, Second Edition*, 2002. New York: Guilford Press, pp. 215–220.

Wonderlich, S., Personality and Eating Disorders, in C. G. Fairburn and K. D. Brownell, Editors, *Eating Disorders and Obesity: A Comprehensive Handbook, Second Edition*, 2002. New York: Guilford Press, pp. 204–209.

Wonderlich, S., R. Crosby, J. Mitchell, et al., Eating Disturbance and Sexual Trauma in Childhood and Adulthood, *International Journal of Eating Disorders*, 2001, *30*, 401–412.

PART II

UNDERSTANDING EATING DISORDERS

CHAPTER 4

Know What You're Dealing With

The Complexity of Eating Disorders

We probably don't have to tell you that you can't solve a problem unless you know what you're dealing with. Every day, at home and at work, you take steps to figure out what you're up against before devising a strategy for attacking a particular challenge. Whether it's getting the car to run or your checkbook to balance, getting your assistant to be more productive or your sales force to exceed last year's gross, you decide on a solution based on your understanding of the problem. Helping your child overcome an eating disorder is no different.

As you now know, having read Part I of this book, eating disorders are enigmatic and idiosyncratic. There are lots of gaps in our scientific understanding of anorexia, bulimia, and binge-eating disorder. What we do know sets eating disorders apart from other psychiatric problems affecting children and adolescents, which has made treating them an ongoing challenge. The gaps in our understanding of these disorders stem from the fact that there is a comparative dearth of research on eating disorders in children and adolescents. For instance, as of the writing of this book, only

five published psychological treatment studies have been conducted for anorexia and none for bulimia. To heighten our challenge in the treatment of eating disorders, myths and misconceptions about these disorders abound in the popular media.

It's essential that you know what you're dealing with if you're to help a child who has an eating disorder. In this chapter we give you up-to-date, scientifically based information on these disorders. With this foundation, your quest to help your child will gain the greatest possible chance for success.

We can't state this too often: Know the facts. It could save your child's life.

EATING DISORDERS ARE PSYCHOLOGICAL ILLNESSES WITH SERIOUS MEDICAL CONSEQUENCES

Talk about complicated: No other psychological illnesses affecting children and adolescents involve pathological thoughts, behaviors, and emotions that lead to such serious short- and long-term medical complications. Because these disturbances in the way individuals think, feel, and act, in turn, bring about a dramatic change in food consumption, eating disorders can cause physical illness perhaps more than any other mental illness currently known. This means that parents and health care providers must not only understand the psychological workings of these disorders and apply psychological treatments, but also be alert to what's happening to the child's physical health. In fact, it is fair to say that in most cases you should deal first and foremost with your child's medical status. Starvation poses several medical risks, as we elaborate on in the following pages. Moreover, many of the psychological symptoms you may have noted in your child are the direct consequence of these medical problems. Therefore, it is of paramount importance that your child enter a treatment regimen, whether outpatient, inpatient, or residential, that will attend to her medical status and provide a supportive environment in which the psychological workings of her disorder can begin to be explored.

How Are Eating Disorders Defined?

Eating disorders, as we explained in Chapter 1, are of four main types: anorexia nervosa, bulimia nervosa, binge-eating disorder, and avoidant/restrictive food intake disorder. There are differences between them, but they also share many features. We have to consider both the similarities and the differences when we ask the question "What is an eating disorder?" It's sometimes difficult to know at the outset which of the four eating disorder diagnoses will be the most accurate because over time as many as one-third to one-half of patients can eventually be diagnosed with two or more of the different types of eating disorders. Although we mentioned the specific challenges of making an accurate diagnosis of an eating disorder in children and adolescents in Chapter 1, it's important to revisit these issues, with an emphasis on helping you identify the overlapping as well as distinguishing characteristics of the particular disorder type.

> Annette, now 16, has been ill with an eating disorder since she was 12 years old. She has spent most of the past 4 years in and out of the hospital. As a result, it has been very hard for her to spend significant periods of time at home with her parents and siblings, to make and keep friends at school, and to have an opportunity to build and learn from meaningful relationships outside her family. In addition, she has fallen seriously behind in her schoolwork even though the hospital unit to which she is usually admitted provides schooling for the adolescents in its program.
>
> Every time Annette is admitted, she is severely emaciated, which requires her doctors to put her on strict bed rest with frequent visits by the nursing and medical staff. Eventually, her weight begins to approach healthy levels again and she is prepared to be discharged to her parents' care. At this time, however, her parents are always told to "back off" as Annette should now take care of her own eating. Unfortunately, every time she tries to eat on her own, she promptly runs to the bathroom to induce vomiting because she "cannot stand" feeling so "full."
>
> The nurses in the hospital would have prevented Annette from vomiting, but at home, following the doctor's advice, her parents are backing off. Consequently, Annette's weight, time

and again, spirals downward as she checks in every week with her outpatient pediatrician. Her pediatrician is concerned about the speed with which Annette always manages to lose weight once she is discharged, and he is also very worried because her daily vomiting after every meal has caused her electrolyte levels to drop well within dangerous levels. Every couple of weeks, Annette gets herself admitted to a medical ward to restore her electrolytes to normal levels. Although this is a life-saving necessity, it again takes Annette away from her home environment, her friends, and school. This cycle—going to an eating disorder inpatient unit, back home, and then in and out of the medical unit—as well as receiving a multitude of different medications, has been a sad routine for Annette and her family for many years now.

According to DSM-5, the criteria for anorexia nervosa are as follows[1]:

A. Restriction of energy intake relative to requirements, leading to a significantly low body weight in the context of age, sex, developmental trajectory, and physical health. Significantly low weight is defined as a weight that is less than minimally normal or, for children and adolescents, less than normal or, for children and adolescents, less than that minimally expected.
B. Intense fear of gaining weight or of becoming fat, or persistent behavior that interferes with weight gain, even though at a significantly low weight.
C. Disturbance in the way in which one's body weight or shape is experienced, undue influence of body weight or shape on self-evaluation, or persistent lack of recognition of the seriousness of the current low body weight.

Denial of the seriousness of malnutrition is also a common symptom, especially in younger patients. There are two subtypes of anorexia nervosa, a restricting type and a binge eating–purging

[1]Reprinted with permission from the *Diagnostic and Statistical Manual of Mental Disorders, Fifth Edition* (pp. 338–339). Copyright 2013 by the American Psychiatric Association.

type. In DSM-5, amenorrhea (loss of regular periods) is no longer required to meet diagnostic criteria. The level of severity (mild to extreme) in adults is based on current body mass index (BMI); in children and adolescents, severity is based on age and gender norms according to BMI percentiles. A BMI below the 10th percentile is considered to be consistent with the degree of malnutrition associated with anorexia nervosa. Alternatively, if longitudinal growth charts are available, deviations from individual growth trajectories can be observed.

In terms of the subtypes, some people with anorexia nervosa use only extreme dieting techniques by limiting their intake (called the *restricting subtype*), and others engage in binge eating and purging (use of vomiting, laxatives, other purgatives) behaviors (called the *binge–purge subtype*). But among the diagnostic criteria for anorexia, there is the suggestion that failure to grow, an event specific to childhood and adolescence, will substitute for meeting the usual weight-loss criteria.

Bulimia nervosa is also defined as having both behavioral and psychological components. Behavioral components include intermittent severe dieting strategies that lead to weight fluctuations while the person maintains an overall weight within the normal range. The specific DSM-5 criteria for bulimia nervosa include[2]:

A. Recurrent episodes of binge eating. An episode of binge eating is characterized by both of the following:
   1. Eating, in a discrete period of time (e.g., within any 2-hour period), an amount of food that is definitely more than what most individuals would eat in a similar period of time under similar circumstances.
   2. A sense of lack of control over eating during the episode (e.g., a feeling that one cannot stop eating or control what or how much one is eating).
B. Recurrent inappropriate compensatory behaviors in order to prevent weight gain, such as self-induced vomiting, misuse of

---

[2]Reprinted with permission from the *Diagnostic and Statistical Manual of Mental Disorders, Fifth Edition* (p. 345). Copyright 2013 by the American Psychiatric Association.

laxatives, diuretics, or other medications; fasting; or excessive exercise.

C. The binge eating and inappropriate behaviors both occur, on average, at least once a week for 3 months.

D. Self-evaluation is unduly included by body shape and weight.

E. The disturbance does not occur exclusively during episodes of anorexia nervosa.

The severity of bulimia nervosa (mild to extreme) is based on the frequency of compensatory behaviors. In addition, for someone to be diagnosed with bulimia nervosa, these behaviors should be accompanied by extreme beliefs and attitudes that overemphasize control of shape and weight as the sole or major way to maintain self-worth and self-esteem. Children and adolescents developing bulimia may not necessarily meet these frequency criteria (the number of binges and purges per week), as the illness is not so well established yet.

Binge-eating disorder is recognized as a diagnosis in DSM-5. It is characterized as follows[3]:

A. Recurrent episodes of binge eating. An episode of binge eating is characterized by both of the following:
   1. Eating, in a discrete period of time (e.g., within any 2-hour period), an amount of food that is definitely more than what most individuals would eat in a similar period of time under similar circumstances.
   2. A sense of lack of control over eating during the episode (e.g., a feeling that one cannot stop eating or control what or how much one is eating).

B. The binge-eating episodes are associated with three or more of the following:
   1. Eating much more rapidly than normal.
   2. Eating until feeling uncomfortably full.
   3. Eating large amounts of food when not feeling physically hungry.

[3]Reprinted with permission from the *Diagnostic and Statistical Manual of Mental Disorders, Fifth Edition* (p. 350). Copyright 2013 by the American Psychiatric Association.

4. Eating alone because of feeling embarrassed about how much one is eating.
5. Feeling disgusted with oneself, depressed, or very guilty afterward.

C. Marked distress regarding binge eating is present.

D. The binge eating occurs, on average, at least once a week for 3 months.

E. The binge eating is not associated with the recurrent use of inappropriate compensatory behaviors as in bulimia nervosa and does not occur exclusively during the course of bulimia nervosa or anorexia nervosa.

In younger patients with binge-eating disorder, these criteria are sometimes hard to apply because binge eating may occur only when parents are absent, so the frequency may be lower. In addition, because children and adolescents often don't buy the food available to them, the ability to binge eat depends in part on food being in the home. For these reasons, some have argued that if your child reports feeling out of control when eating, this is a strong indication that a problem with binge eating is developing.

As noted in the introduction, there is another new diagnosis in DSM-5, called avoidant/restrictive food intake disorder (ARFID). Little is known about this disorder, but the diagnostic criteria in DSM-5 for ARFID are as follows[4]:

A. An eating or feeding disturbance (e.g., apparent lack of interest in eating or food; avoidance based on the sensory characteristics of food; concern about the aversive consequences of eating) as manifested by persistent failure to meet appropriate nutritional and/or energy needs associated with one (or more) of the following:
1. Significant weight loss (or failure to achieve expected weight gain or faltering growth in children).
2. Significant nutritional deficiency.

---

[4]Reprinted with permission from the *Diagnostic and Statistical Manual of Mental Disorders, Fifth Edition* (p. 334). Copyright 2013 by the American Psychiatric Association.

3. Dependence on enteral feeding or oral nutritional supplement.
4. Marked interference with psychosocial functioning.
B. The disturbance is not better explained by lack of available food or by an associated culturally sanctioned practice.
C. The eating disturbance does not occur exclusively during the course of anorexia nervosa or bulimia nervosa, and there is no evidence of a disturbance in the way in which one's body weight or shape is experienced.
D. The eating disturbance is not attributable to a concurrent medical condition or is not better explained by another mental disorder. When the eating disturbance occurs in the context of another condition or disorder, the severity of the eating disturbance exceeds that routinely associated with the condition or disorder and warrants additional clinical attention.

This disorder is associated with disturbances in psychological development and functioning. Some patients are very picky eaters who also display a particular fear of different or new foods. They are sometimes excessively sensitive to food texture, appearance, and taste. For the patients with a swallowing or choking event or fear that contributes to food avoidance, a specific event can sometimes be identified as having caused that fear. The ARFID diagnosis is also used for children who simply have a lack of interest in eating or who have low appetite. For many reasons ARFID can be confused with anorexia, but the main differences are that, unlike adolescents with anorexia, these children are not afraid of weight gain, have no shape and weight concerns, and make no efforts to lose weight. In fact, children are usually aware that they are underweight and may say they wish they could eat more and gain weight but are afraid to actually eat enough to do so.

Medical Complications of Anorexia Nervosa

In Chapter 2 we exhorted you to view yourselves as part of the solution to your child's eating disorder—advice that's difficult to take

when your son or daughter is treating you as if you're crazy at best, an enemy at worst. In truth, living with a child who has developed anorexia can make you feel as if you *are* insane. The illness is publicly quite visible—the fact that your child is emaciated is plain for all to see (if she hasn't shrouded herself in baggy clothing to hide the skeletal frame that you have been pointing to), yet she very likely will insist that nothing is wrong. This view of an illness as nonproblematic or "perfectly normal" makes anorexia a disorder that we call *ego-syntonic*. The adolescent with anorexia may very well view her illness with a sense of pride or achievement and protect the illness through denial. As a consequence, your child may not willingly seek or accept treatment. In fact, this peculiar characteristic of anorexia tends to make your job as a parent more difficult overall when it comes to the medical complications of the illness. Adolescents without anorexia may notice a particular physical ailment, such as stomach pain or a headache, and be more than likely to bring that knowledge or awareness to their parents' attention. In contrast, adolescents with anorexia will almost certainly not appreciate the potential seriousness of any of their symptoms and, consequently, will not bring up the issue with you, their parents. Likewise, if you should note anything that worries you about your adolescent's health, you will experience the uphill and frustrating battle of trying to convince your adolescent that something serious might be wrong and that there is a need to check with your family pediatrician.

Let's say that you're Linda's mother. Linda is 17 and has always been slender. You weren't particularly concerned about this; after all, she appears to be happy, does well at school, and seems to get along with her friends. All the women in your family have been "slow starters" in regard to the onset of menses, and you haven't been very concerned about the fact that Linda has never had a period at age 17. Your concerns were also brushed aside a year ago when you took Linda for a visit with her pediatrician and the doctor said not to worry and put Linda on the birth control pill. The reasoning behind the doctor's intervention was that the medication would start her periods and thus "take care of things." In the last year, though, you have noticed that Linda

has become increasingly withdrawn, even looking depressed at times. She remains picky about her food and doesn't eat as much as you think she should, and you've begun to wonder whether her frequent running could be making things worse. You decide to ignore your pediatrician's words of comfort and take Linda to see someone who specializes in eating disorders.

After you, your spouse, and Linda have talked to a team of specialists, you all learn that Linda's health has been compromised to a much greater extent than anyone has imagined. It turns out that she meets the criteria for anorexia. In addition to your worries about her mood and the fact that she's much more isolated socially and not as confident as you thought your 17-year-old would be, Linda's physical symptoms have alarmed the specialty team greatly. The medical examination revealed that in addition to Linda's low weight, which has persisted for several years now, she suffers from osteoporosis (a condition of brittle bones that fracture easily, which is quite common in postmenopausal females but very uncommon in someone who is healthy and of Linda's age). Making things worse, it turns out that Linda is no longer 67 inches tall as her medical records have always confirmed. Now she has lost a full inch in height (losing height is, again, quite common in older females who suffer from osteoporosis, but highly unlikely in someone as young as Linda). You learn from the psychiatric team that treatment for Linda is going to be very complex, for it will not only address her weight loss, which is something she dreads, but will also help her with mood and social isolation. At the same time, the medical part of the treatment team will have to address the lack of menses (being maintained artificially by the birth control pill) and figure out how best to make sure that further loss in bone density can be prevented.

There's no denying that all of these health problems are disturbing, especially when the child herself is denying there's anything wrong. Parents can get so caught up in the battle over eating, however, that some miss the early signs that life-threatening starvation has begun. Once the adolescent has reached an obvious state of emaciation, one of the first telling signs that starvation has reached serious proportions is the loss of menstruation, in postmenarcheal girls and women, as body fat declines. What can be confusing is

that, for some, amenorrhea sets in after relatively little weight loss, but for others, only very low weight triggers the loss of periods. As noted earlier, this may be especially true for adolescents who do not have firmly established menstrual cycles. For many reasons, it also becomes a confusing issue in the case of boys with an eating disorder, as there is no clear equivalent to loss of menses. If you're worried about a son who may have an eating disorder, you'll have to be alert to the signs of other medical complications such as low heart rate, low energy, and low testosterone levels.

In addition to causing loss of menses, severe malnutrition usually leads to a variety of serious medical consequences. Several systems are impacted by self-starvation: the central nervous system and the cardiovascular, renal, hematologic, gastrointestinal, metabolic, and endocrine systems. The most significant acute problems are bradycardia, hypothermia, and dehydration. All of these complications can become life threatening. The most important chronic medical problems for adolescents with anorexia are the potential for significant growth retardation (your adolescent with anorexia may not maximize her growth spurt and may consequently fail to achieve optimal height); pubertal delay or interruption, which can have serious consequences in terms of menses and fertility; and peak bone mass reduction, which can lead to osteoporosis or osteopenia (an increased porosity of the bone associated with frequent fractures). In addition, many other side effects of malnutrition are often noted:

1. **Hypothermia:** Lower than normal body temperature. You may notice that your adolescent wears extra layers of clothing to try to stay warm even when it is warm outside.

2. **Hypotension:** Decreased blood pressure (a systolic blood pressure of less than 90 millimeters of mercury for adults). Low blood pressure generally has no clinical symptoms, so you might not notice that anything is amiss with your child. However, if it is associated with decreased tissue perfusion (e.g., poor circulation causing cold hands and feet, or slow healing of cuts), your child may have increased heart rate, sweating, lightheadedness, and pallor. This is called *shock*, and it is deadly.

3. **Bradycardia:** Decreased heart rate (for adults, fewer than 60 beats per minute) or a slow pulse. In someone with anorexia, this correlates with the severity of the illness but can be seen only by taking a pulse or performing an electrocardiogram.

4. **Changes in skin and hair texture:** Skin becomes dry and flaky, and hair becomes brittle and can thin out quite dramatically. This is perhaps one of the few consequences of starvation that you, as a parent, may begin to notice.

5. **Lanugo:** There is often a development of fine, downy body hair, most noticeable on your adolescent's face and the back of her neck. This is another way in which the body is attempting to accommodate to the slowdown in metabolism, essentially trying to maintain core body temperature. As with the other skin and hair changes, you might actually notice this growth of fine hair on your child's face or neck.

6. **Growth hormone changes:** There is often an increase in growth hormone secretion, which can be detected only through laboratory tests.

7. **Hypothalamic hypogonadism:** This describes a decrease in sex hormones, which causes an absence of menses and leads to infertility. Blood tests can reveal this condition.

8. **Bone marrow hypoplasia:** Decreased blood cell production, including a low count of red blood cells, white blood cells, and platelets, which leads to anemia. The anemia may contribute to your noticing your child being a bit more fatigued than usual. The lowered white cell counts have not been found to be associated with decreased immune functioning in the case of anorexia.

9. **Structural abnormalities of the brain, generalized atrophy of the brain, and occasional regional atrophy:** This describes a decreased size of the brain or parts of the brain. There are no clear clinical signs of this happening in your child; it can be detected only if you specifically request a neuropsychological evaluation.

10. **Additional changes in electrical brain activity:** The electroencephalograms (EEGs, which show brain activity with electrodes placed on the head) of children with anorexia are often abnormal.

You will not be able to see these abnormalities just by looking at your child.

11. **Cardiac dysfunction:** This may include peripheral edema, decreased cardiac diameter, narrowed left ventricular wall, decreased response to exercise demand, pericardial effusion, and superior mesenteric artery syndrome. Your adolescent may describe fatigue, decreased ability to exert himself, and a swelling of his legs. Cardiac complications are often lethal and can be confirmed only with the help of an electrocardiogram.

12. **Gastrointestinal difficulties:** Delayed gastric emptying, gastric dilatation, or decreased intestinal lipase and lactase, for example, may manifest itself in your child as abdominal discomfort; your child may complain about a sense of stomach fullness after eating very little. Again, only sophisticated tests will help you confirm the true nature of your child's gastrointestinal problems.

Although these complications are most typical for adolescents with anorexia, restricting subtype, several other complications that are related to binge eating and purging behaviors in particular should also be considered. These complications will be clearer once we've discussed the medical issues associated with bulimia nervosa.

Medical Complications of Bulimia Nervosa

Nora, now 17, had been binge eating and purging since she was 15 years old. Over the past several months, as she neared her graduation, she felt increasing pressure to excel in school. Unfortunately, she was also being pressured by her boyfriend to become sexually intimate, something she was afraid to do because she was ashamed of her "thunder thighs" and her "fat stomach." She began to purge more frequently, resulting in blood appearing in her vomitus. She was increasingly dizzy when she stood up, and her heart would race. One afternoon, as she went to her car from school, she fainted. Her friends called 911, and she was taken to the emergency room, where she was found to be dehydrated and anemic; she also had a low potassium level.

Bulimia is a more secretive illness than anorexia, making it easier for your adolescent to hide her symptoms. The medical complications are also not as evident as might be the case with anorexia, for most adolescents with bulimia usually have a healthy appearance. In contrast to anorexia, bulimia is described as *ego-alien*, which implies that the sufferer is embarrassed or ashamed about her symptoms and is therefore hesitant to seek treatment.

Children and teenagers with bulimia nervosa rarely approach the low weights associated with anorexia. In fact, although some patients with bulimia are quite underweight and others quite overweight, most fall within normal weight limits. Unfortunately, we don't have much research data on teenagers with bulimia. We do, however, know that doctors who see such cases find the same signs and symptoms that are typical of adults with bulimia. We can then assume that the medical complications of bulimia will be about the same for your teenage daughter or son as for adult patients. We don't have any mortality figures for bulimia in either adults or teenagers, but certainly the medical complications that sometimes require hospitalization—hypokalemia, esophageal tears, gastric disturbances, dehydration, and orthostatic blood pressure changes—can result in death. There are indeed case examples of adults with bulimia nervosa who died because of esophageal tears, with extensive internal bleeding. Because many teenagers with bulimia nervosa have periods of starvation similar to those of teenagers with anorexia, many medical complications of bulimia are the same as those of anorexia. However, because bulimia nervosa is mostly characterized by binge-eating and purging episodes, there are some unique medical complications that are more common in bulimia. These are:

1. **Hypokalemic alkalosis or acidosis:** Low potassium level (less than 3.5 milliequivalents per liter in adults) and acid/base imbalance go hand in hand, because changes in the acid/base balance affect the functional potassium levels. With low potassium, you may notice general weakness and malaise in your child. The most catastrophic effect of a low potassium level, however, may

be abnormal electrical conduction in the heart, which can lead to death.

2. **Hypochloremia:** This condition describes low serum chloride levels resulting from the body's attempt to retain electroneutrality in the presence of an acid/base imbalance. The lack of chloride increases serum bicarbonate levels, which then leads to metabolic alkalosis. What this means is that the body has accumulated too much of an alkaline substance (e.g., bicarbonate) and does not have enough acid to effectively neutralize the effects of the alkali. This can be detected only with blood tests.

3. **Dehydration:** Because of decreased body fluid, your child may have dry skin and complain of fatigue or lightheadedness upon standing.

4. **Renal problems:** These can include prerenal azotemia—acute and chronic renal failure. *Azotemia* describes increased nitrogenous wastes in the blood (urea and creatinine), which are a sign of kidney dysfunction. Azotemia may be associated with generalized fatigue, paleness, anorexia (loss of appetite), and swelling. *Prerenal* indicates that the cause for this condition is not within but before the kidney, such as reduced fluid volume associated with the dehydration of eating disorders. *Acute and chronic renal failure* describes kidney malfunction or failure.

5. **Seizures:** Seizures are abnormal, sudden, excessive discharges of brain neurons. During a generalized seizure, the type of seizure generally relevant here, your child may experience a loss of consciousness, muscle jerking, tongue biting, and urinary incontinence.

6. **Cardiac arrhythmias:** These are irregular heartbeats. Many adolescents with arrhythmias don't have any clinical signs or symptoms, although some might notice palpitations (most commonly), shortness of breath, chest pain, lightheadedness, and loss of consciousness. Arrhythmias can be lethal.

7. **Myocardial toxicity caused by emetine** (using ipecac syrup to purge): Cardiac muscle poisoning by ipecac may cause

cardiomyopathy, which may manifest itself in your child as loss of consciousness, fatigue, and arrhythmia. It too can be lethal.

8. **Enamel loss and multiple caries:** As a result of the tooth damage often caused by bulimia, your child may report frequent toothaches, or you may notice that the general status of her dental health (and appearance) has deteriorated. In cases of frequent vomiting over time, some patients have lost almost all their teeth.

9. **Swollen parotid glands, elevated serum amylase levels, and gastric distention:** Your child with swollen parotid glands may look as if she has "chipmunk cheeks."

10. **Cramps and tetany:** Tetany describes intermittent paroxysmal muscle spasms. Tetany may also be associated with nervousness, numbness, and tingling of the arms and legs.

A vital aspect in the care of eating-disordered patients is an appreciation for the medical complications of such illnesses. It is often too easy for both parents and clinicians to underestimate the severity of these illnesses. It is only when a comprehensive evaluation of the adolescent's medical status has been completed and medical follow-up has been established that the psychiatrist or psychologist can focus on appropriate treatment to address the eating disorder symptoms and the concomitant psychosocial issues. So, always make 100% sure that your child has received a thorough medical workup by a pediatrician who understands eating disorders. In addition, make sure you're present for much of this examination so that you can add information the physician will need to reach a complete understanding of your child's medical status. Too often we find that the illness, whether it's anorexia, bulimia, or binge eating, prevents the teenager from sharing all the vital facts with the doctor.

Medical Complications of Binge-Eating Disorder

The main medical risks associated with binge-eating disorder are those related to the development of obesity as a result of chronic binge eating. Obesity is a severe health problem for the United

States as well as many other countries because it leads to diabetes, hypertension, ischemic heart disease, stroke, and probably mortality.

EATING DISORDERS ARE OFTEN ACCOMPANIED BY OTHER PSYCHOLOGICAL ILLNESSES

It's not uncommon for eating disorders to be accompanied by other types of mental illness, at least in adults. We have less information in this area regarding teenagers, but you should be aware of this possibility. Other disorders that occur at the same time as the eating disorder—a condition referred to as *comorbidity*—can complicate your child's treatment and possibly reduce the success of treatment if the comorbid illness(es) isn't (aren't) managed well.

Maria was first brought in for treatment when she was only 12 years old. She was away on vacation with her parents for a few months prior to her first treatment visit. It was during this family trip that her parents noticed she was looking very frail, and they became concerned about her increasing "fussiness" over eating and her insistence on exercising at least once every day. At the time Maria's parents first brought her in for treatment, there were also some early signs that this prepubertal young girl was a very determined, hardworking, fastidious, and even overorganized person. In addition to being supportive and understanding toward members of the family, given the crisis they were all facing, one of the first goals of treatment was to guide the parents in helping Maria get her weight back on track. Without this weight gain, Maria would not have a fair chance of entering her anticipated growth spurt as she approached menarche. Moreover, without weight recovery (and continued weight gain, given that she was only 12 and needed to gain weight throughout adolescence), her body wouldn't be healthy enough to receive the trigger that will start her first period.

Although weight gain was proceeding well, it became evident that there was another difficulty at hand that might seriously complicate the family's ability to remain focused (for now)

on the job of getting Maria's physiological and psychological development back on track. Maria was becoming increasingly ritualistic in almost all of her behaviors. What this meant in terms of her day-to-day life was that the mere act of walking to school became an ordeal, for she couldn't step on cracks in the sidewalk. At school, she could look only at some kids but not at others. At home, she had to arrange and rearrange her room several times a day to get it "just right." Most of these rituals, together with the repeated thoughts that "I must think 'good' things," kept her from any weight gain, or at least Maria was convinced this was true.

Of course, all these activities made a routine day very hard for everyone in the family and left Maria very little time to enjoy being with her parents and siblings, visiting with friends, or doing any homework. At this point, understanding these thoughts and rituals better so that appropriate treatment could be started had to be added to an already stressful treatment regimen of weight restoration and medical follow-up.

Several more assessments were added to everyone's busy schedule, including more visits to the pediatrician and even a neurologist. A brain scan was completed to make sure that nothing was overlooked in trying to make sense of the increasingly debilitating obsessive–compulsive symptoms. Different combinations of powerful drugs, with potentially serious side effects, were started, all in the attempt to help Maria gain some control over the intrusive thoughts and tiring rituals. All in all, her treatment became very complicated, and Maria, her parents, and even the treatment team had trouble managing all the different components.

Obsessive–compulsive disorder, as in Maria's case, seems to be a common occurrence with eating disorders, especially anorexia, in just over one-third of patients with chronic anorexia, according to one report. Because addressing these debilitating symptoms involves a great deal of extra attention from the treatment team, such as additional interventions—cognitive-behavioral therapy, and often several medications—it is easy to see how the focus could be diverted from Maria's self-starvation. The challenge here is to address the comorbid illness but not lose track of the primary job: taking care of the eating disorder.

Depression is another psychiatric illness that's quite likely to occur in combination with a child's eating disorder. According to one study, as many as 63% of all patients with eating disorders have a lifetime history of depression. It's important, however, to determine whether the co-occurring depression is a primary (independent) diagnosis or the result (side effect) of self-starvation—a question best sorted out by your teen's psychiatrist or psychologist. Although it will not always be easy for your child's doctor to distinguish between these two forms of mood disturbance, effective treatment of your adolescent will depend on a careful and accurate evaluation of her mood.

Clinical depression and low mood because of an eating disorder are two different things, even though they may look very similar to you. If your child, in addition to her eating disorder, suffers from clinical depression, the depression may respond to medication, or it may persist even when the eating disorder has responded to treatment. Keep in mind, though, that many eating-disordered adolescents appear dysphoric and demoralized. This form of "depression" may certainly be the result of the eating disorder, inasmuch as poor mood is a frequent side effect of starvation. The same is true when your child engages in binge eating and purging: She could very well feel "blue," guilty, disgusted, demoralized, sad, and so forth, because of these symptoms.

For clinical depression, you should make sure your child's psychiatrist considers psychotherapy specifically for the depression, and in some instances psychotherapy plus an antidepressant, as the primary treatment. If you and your child's doctor are convinced that her low mood is secondary to her eating disorder symptoms, you should monitor her mood closely to be sure it also improves as her eating disorder is getting better. If that doesn't happen, additional treatment for the depressed mood might be in order.

Some researchers in this field argue that, in addition to obsessive–compulsive disorder and depression, there is a higher than expected comorbidity between **personality traits** and eating disorders. For instance, avoidant traits (characterizing someone who is overcautious when it comes to interpersonal relationships, who finds it extremely difficult to make friends and is very shy, etc.)

and anorexia often co-occur, and a significant number of individuals with bulimia have borderline personality traits (they are very impulsive in their behaviors and have changeable moods as well as great instability in relationships). Although this may be the case for adults with eating disorders, it's unclear whether personality traits *and* an eating disorder are applicable to adolescents or children.

Nonetheless, many researchers from a number of theoretical backgrounds have reported differences in personality makeup among teens with various eating disorders. What many of them show is that anorexic girls are often very anxious, inhibited, and regimented, whereas bulimic adolescents can be all of these, but some also tend to be more emotionally volatile, impulsive, and/or uninhibited.

You should, however, keep two things in mind when trying to get an idea of how likely it is that your child—or any child—has other psychological problems along with an eating disorder. First, we'd be oversimplifying the eating disorders if we were to see each disorder as clearly demarcated by eating disorder symptoms alone because both anxiety and depressive states often accompany these symptoms. Second, it is also possible that current studies overestimate comorbid illness among individuals with an eating disorder. It may be that many eating-disordered patients who are included in research projects come from specialized eating disorder clinics, and therefore the more seriously compromised individuals may be overrepresented among those studied. In reality, children and adolescents with eating disorders are quite varied, and although many of them have comorbid illnesses, many do not. For you as a parent, the important point is to be aware of the possibility and alert to signs that something else may need the attention of your child's mental health care team.

Finally, **alcohol and drug abuse** are also commonly diagnosed in adults with bulimia, though no studies have documented this in younger patients. Many teens, however, start experimenting with alcohol and drugs, and your child may not be different. If your child has both bulimia and substance use difficulties, treatment can be considerably complicated. We have mentioned that bulimia can be quite a secretive illness, which already complicates your involvement

in trying to help your child. When the eating disorder coexists with another secretive problem such as drug taking, your adolescent child will be very reluctant to have you "interfere" with any of these behaviors. You will have to approach your child very carefully under these circumstances, for you might have to follow a narrow line between convincing your teen that you want to help and antagonizing your child because she perceives you as interfering.

Notwithstanding the sparse information about comorbid psychiatric illness among adolescents with eating disorders, if we borrow from the adult literature as well as from our own clinical experience, it seems clear that the eating disorders are indeed becoming more heterogeneous. That means there is not a "typical" eating-disordered adolescent, and these illnesses often appear along with other psychiatric illnesses. Certainly, this makes our understanding of eating disorders more complex, and, as we've demonstrated, it inevitably complicates treatment further. A final example demonstrates this point well:

> Tina had had bulimia since she was 13 and rapidly exhibited a range of other psychiatric problems. First she became increasingly confrontational and difficult with her parents, then she began skipping school to meet boys in the park, where she smoked marijuana and drank shots. At first these activities, like her bulimia, were kept secret from her family, but over time her parents caught on. However, by that point Tina was already drinking heavily and experimenting with crack cocaine. She needed treatment in a substance abuse program before directing attention to her bulimia was even considered.

At this point there should be no doubt in your mind that eating disorders are serious illnesses that require serious attention. Think of the title of Chapter 1 as your clarion call. Go back to the warning signs and "act-now" signs listed on page 24. If your child fits these descriptions, take action before an eating disorder does any more damage to your child's health. If you're concerned that your child may suffer from something other than an eating disorder, seek treatment so that these problems are prevented from doing additional harm.

It won't be easy. As you probably already know, the nature of eating disorders pits you against your child, because the eating disorder wants to stay in control. If you're to have the best possible chance of setting your child on the road to recovery quickly, you'll have to get into your child's head to get an idea of how your son or daughter actually experiences the eating disorder. Knowing how an eating disorder changes your teenager's thinking, attitudes, and behaviors will help you fight for your child's life.

FOR MORE INFORMATION

Golden, N., D. Katzman, R. Kreipe, et al., Eating Disorders in Adolescents: Position Paper of the Society for Adolescent Medicine: Medical Indications for Hospitalization in an Adolescent with an Eating Disorder, *Journal of Adolescent Health*, 2003, *33*, 496–503.

Le Grange, D., and J. Lock, Editors, *Eating Disorders in Children and Adolescents: A Clinical Handbook*, 2011. New York: Guilford Press.

Lock, J., *The Oxford Handbook of Child and Adolescent Eating Disorders: Developmental Perspectives*, 2012. New York: Oxford University Press.

Palmer, B., *Helping People with Eating Disorders: A Clinical Guide to Assessment and Treatment*, 2000. Chichester, UK: Wiley.

Zipfel, S., B. Lowe, and W. Herzog, Medical Complications, in J. Treasure, U. Schmidt, and E. van Furth, Editors, *Handbook of Eating Disorders*, 2003. Chichester, UK: Wiley, pp. 169–190.

CHAPTER 5

Get Into Your Child's Head

The Distorted Thinking Behind
Your Teenager's Behavior

If your daughter or son has an eating disorder or seems to be developing one, you've probably already been told many times, "You don't understand me" or, in fact, "Nobody understands me." This feeling is very real for someone who is struggling with an eating disorder, and it's possible that you've become very frustrated trying to understand your daughter or son. Trying to communicate your position to your troubled child can be even more problematic.

The fact is that you may *not* understand what your child is experiencing. Children and adolescents with eating disorders see their behavior—especially behavior related to food, eating, weight, exercise, and health—quite differently from the way it looks from the outside. Eating disorders alter logical ways of thinking about food and body image. They distort what your son or daughter sees in the mirror. They implant in your child's mind irrational expectations about the consequences of eating and not eating, exercising and not exercising.

Unless you begin to understand how your teenager's thinking has been affected by the eating disorder, your efforts to be supportive of your child's struggle against the illness will be handicapped.

You may be reading your child's behavior as nonsensical or defiant, when she sees perfect sense in it and is not trying to make you feel bad but hoping to make herself feel good. It may seem irrefutably clear to you that your child is emaciated and dangerously ill, but how can you hope to get her to change her behavior if you don't realize that she still sees a fat person in the mirror and feels proud of herself for sticking to her "diet"?

Your child sees herself and all things food-related through a lens imposed by the eating disorder. We call the thoughts that emerge through this lens *cognitive distortions*. In this chapter we explore the cognitive distortions that are driving your child's behavior so you can see things the way she does and thus know better how to respond constructively.

A SHIFT IN ATTITUDE, A NEW APPROACH

Before delving into specific cognitive distortions that you may be trying to deal with every day, think for a minute about the strategy you've been using in trying to resolve your teenager's disordered eating. Have you been trying to "talk some sense" into your daughter? Or are you assuming that your adolescent thinks the same way you and everyone else does when informed by common sense and reason? Now is the time to recognize that helping a child recover from an eating disorder requires, first and foremost, a new set of assumptions and a new strategy.

Understanding exactly how your child with an eating disorder is thinking is a challenge. In fact, it is often quite tricky for doctors to fully understand just how the mind of an adolescent with anorexia or bulimia works with regard to the issues of eating, weight, and dieting. Yes, you should try to develop an understanding of the ways of thinking that guide your child's behavior. But you won't always be able to fathom what makes her do what she does or feel how she feels. So the safest strategy for you as the parents to adopt is to *assume*, as hard as this may be for you, that your adolescent's thinking with respect to weight and shape issues is probably almost always distorted. This is especially true with anorexia.

It will also be helpful in coping with your child's illness not to underestimate just how firmly lodged these mental distortions are. It's easy to underestimate the intransigence of these distortions, and you will often be tempted to talk some sense into your child. After all, it all seems so clear to you. Watching your child struggle to eat what appears to be a perfectly reasonable portion of food, for example, could certainly lead you to think or say, "Why not just eat it? It's so easy." Likewise, parents with a teen suffering from anorexia find themselves exhausted after lengthy, and fruitless, arguments, having tried to convince their child that a salad with dressing won't be harmful. The parents of an adolescent with bulimia may discover that their child has made herself sick in the bathroom and might very well be tempted to advise her to "just stop doing it," adding, "It'll be easy: Just get some self-control." It is, of course, not easy at all—not for you or for your child. Both anorexia and bulimia exert such a firm grip on your child's thinking that most of your pleading or arguing will be in vain.

We like to refer to such discussions as "anorexic debate" or "bulimic debate"—parents trying, in a very rational way, to convince the child that eating is good for her or that she needs the salad or that the meal the parent so painstakingly prepared won't be harmful. Most of the time, parents lose these debates. The thinking of someone with an eating disorder is so firmly lodged in cognitive distortions that there is no way you are going to argue your child out of her eating disorder. Someone with anorexia won't understand your perfectly logical argument about why this or that food item should be eaten. The beans, rice, or chicken you know will be nutritious for your child simply fills her with horror, because the food is "bad," "fattening," "unnecessary," "not the right food group," "scary," or deemed unacceptable in some other way.

When you find yourself tempted to try to reason with your child in these debates, it may help to keep one fact firmly in mind: *These cognitive distortions are usually the side effects of starvation, and dislodging such beliefs through rational debate is all but fruitless.* No doubt you were shocked by the long list of medical consequences of starvation that you read in Chapter 4. Cognitive distortions are another serious consequence, possibly the most ominous of all, because this is the

one that keeps the eating disorder going. Restoring weight will certainly help in this matter, but we'll get to how that happens later on.

Teenagers with bulimia have many of the same concerns about what food may "do to them" as those with anorexia. Some subtle differences may center on "forbidden foods." This is not to say that someone with anorexia would not have a long list of "forbidden foods"—quite the opposite—it's just that for those with bulimia, there are very definite foods they believe are "forbidden" because they know eating these in particular will set off a binge that will be followed by purging. Because this chain of events is all too familiar to your child with bulimia, these particular foods are avoided at all costs!

COGNITIVE DISTORTIONS: HOW THINGS LOOK TO YOUR CHILD AS COMPARED WITH HOW THEY LOOK TO YOU

Accepting the fact that the eating disorder itself is making it impossible for your child to grasp reality and embrace logic in food-related matters confers a couple of important benefits:

1. It helps you separate the illness from your teenager and thereby remain as compassionate and empathetic as possible as you guide your child toward recovery. Interpreting refusal to eat, or denial of what the mirror declares, as defiance or some other willful negative behavior is counterproductive, only reinforcing the adversarial relationship on which the eating disorder thrives. We discuss this topic further a little later in this chapter and in Chapter 7 as well.

2. It allows you to shift your attention to exploring the specific ways in which your child thinks differently from you, which in turn will give you ideas for fighting the eating disorder in everyday situations. The rest of this chapter is devoted to the common cognitive distortions that come with eating disorders, with general suggestions for how to respond constructively. Part III of this book

goes into more detail on applying this knowledge to individual situations.

It's killing her, but your daughter feels good about refusing to eat, because it's something she does well.

Adolescents who have eating disorders, especially those with anorexia nervosa, are usually quite driven in nature. You can't just get "a little" anorexia; you have to be "perfect" at having anorexia. In fact, you have to be better at having anorexia than any other adolescent with this illness. We often see girls with anorexia who, when told they need inpatient care, burst into tears in our office, saying, "But I will be the 'fattest' anorexic on the ward!" or "I can't go there—I won't be as 'good' as the others."

Adolescents with anorexia have usually been praised for being "determined," "focused," and "energetic," not for their anorexia, of course, but for their performance at math, cross-country, or just about anything they put their minds to. Many parents describe their teen with anorexia this way: "Once he's decided to do anything, there's no way you're going to deter him," or, "When he goes for something, he gives it all he has." This quality usually leads to numerous healthy achievements in school, sports, and other extracurricular activities. The difficulty arises when everyone other than your child—you, his teachers, and his peers—recognizes these achievements, but he does not. For someone with anorexia, achievements are soon forgotten, but failures (real or perceived—getting an A- as opposed to an A+) are mulled over and quickly blot out any prior accomplishments.

This all-or-nothing thinking can be devastating. Susan works very hard at being the perfect student, does her work meticulously every day, has no time to go out in the evenings or even on weekends, and has an "unblemished" report card that is a strong reminder to her that she is a "good" person and that others will like her. Without that, she'll be "nothing," "worthless," and an "utter failure." So when she was given a B in calculus, her first B ever, she was devastated. She came home sobbing, telling her parents that "things will

never be the same again," "no one will ever speak to me again," and she was a "miserable failure," "dumb, stupid," and "useless!"

Often a young person with anorexia really thinks she is in fact a "loser," "good at nothing," "unattractive," and so on, when she doesn't achieve just as much as she has set out to achieve. The bar is always set high and is constantly being raised, all in an effort to convince herself that she is indeed worthy. Hilde Bruch, a famous psychiatrist who wrote extensively about issues such as self-esteem in persons with anorexia (see Chapter 3), talked about this focus on one's failures as an "overwhelming sense of ineffectiveness."

As a result, and for reasons we don't fully understand, dieting may seem an attractive solution to your child—something she thinks will "really help me feel better about myself." This may especially be the route she is attracted to when she thinks she's good at nothing else, and she thinks she's overweight, or someone at school made a derogatory comment about her weight, or so many other teens are on diets and it seems like a good thing to do. Because your child has this ability to do whatever she does well, or to go all out, if she sets her mind on dieting or exercising, she will likely do these well too. Unfortunately, when she starts succeeding at dieting and/ or exercise and begins losing weight, she may be encouraged by the way she looks, by the positive reinforcement she may be getting from peers, from her family, by her improved performance at cross-country running, and so on. It seems easy then for this achievement to supplant most other achievements, and it soon becomes the only thing your child thinks she does well.

In fact, anorexia nervosa is often associated with an immense sense of pride: "I can say no to food when everyone else does not have such will power" or "I can lose weight successfully when all of you are struggling just to shed a pound" or "I can run this extra mile even though I have not eaten much all day—none of you would be able to do that." This sense of "better than you" might be subtle, but if it's the only thing your teen thinks she's good at, she will do everything to defend it. Thus, soon this ability to go without food is seen as her only sense of accomplishment, and anyone who attempts to persuade her to gain weight is seen as ignorant at best, but most likely as cruel and insensitive. It therefore feels incongruous when

others criticize the teenager for being such a successful dieter (something many peers and parents have failed at) or try to "derail" his twice-daily routine of 200 crunches, 200 push-ups, 200 sit-ups, and so on. Your child feels that others simply envy him or her.

Again, the struggle for most parents is tackling this relentlessness that is so characteristic of eating disorders, without feeling as if they are taking something perceived to be so precious away from their child. Indeed, most teens with anorexia nervosa will make parents feel as if they're being most unkind in getting them to gain weight, while the parents will have to find a way to persevere in their efforts to help their child redirect her ability to be a "good anorexic" into another, much more fruitful and healthier endeavor.

Your child's behavior demonstrates that she's out of control, but she sees it as a way to stay in charge and express her independence.

In the usual pursuit of autonomy, there are many ways in which adolescents seek control of their own lives: choosing their own friends, driving themselves where they need to go, setting their own standards of performance, and so on. However, when adolescents' choices indicate they are not in control—binge drinking, serious risk-taking behavior, *and* anorexia and bulimia nervosa, to name just a few examples—the issue for parents is clearly how to set appropriate limits on independence and control. When dieting leads to anorexia, the adolescent needs help to reestablish normal adolescent autonomy processes and experimentation, and the options available do not include food restriction. The same is true when food restriction leads to bouts of binge eating, followed by purging, as is the case with bulimia: Parents often have to assist the adolescent in normalizing eating (three healthy meals per day) so that other aspects of adolescent experimentation do not also suffer as a consequence of the lack of control over eating.

The challenge for most parents, though, is that although the child's behavior demonstrates that she is out of control, your teenager will more than likely see the eating disorder as the only way to stay in charge and express some independence. Your teenager will

vigorously fend off any attempts you might make to help. There will be little you can do that won't be perceived as "you're always telling me what to do" or "you always want to control my every move."

Anorexia may look somewhat different from bulimia here. Adolescents with anorexia will probably come across as quite "together" or "in control" of their lives. In fact, the illness is often associated with a great sense of order, neatness, and discipline. Grades in school continue to be high. All of this serves to confuse most parents as they contemplate the fact that their child is perhaps not in charge of things. We've often heard parents say, "Yes, she's 17 and weighs 82 pounds, but her grades are excellent, she's really working hard, and she's doing so well." The dilemma is made even more difficult by the fact that your daughter with anorexia will assert, repeatedly, that she is fine, that she is in control, and that she can make her own decisions in a rational way. Your daughter will be so persuasive in her arguments that you will find it hard not to believe her. The irony is that the illness also has the ability to convince the adolescent that she is indeed in charge of her eating and weight management and that she can stop dieting and losing weight anytime she wants—"just not now!"

"I can take care of this myself" is also very persuasive to most parents, frightened about what they think might happen to their child but desperate in their willingness to believe that she can get better by herself, as she's repeatedly assured them she can. However, the way the physiology and psychology of starvation work is that at a certain point, usually once weight loss has clearly begun, the adolescent loses control over this process and cannot stop dieting, or get herself to eat a decent amount of food, even if she *wants* to. The anorexia has firmly established its own control over the thinking and behavior of your adolescent.

This is a critical point to remember at all times: *Once your child has reached the point of significant weight loss, she usually cannot get better by herself, even if she proclaims that she can.* As a parent, it's important for you to realize that this doesn't necessarily mean she does not want to get better. It's just that the anorexia is more powerful as an illness than your child's solo efforts at defeating the illness. Remember your new set of assumptions when you're tempted to fall

back into the attitude that your child is just being obstinate and all it will take for her to start eating normally again is for you to talk some sense into her.

Again, the only way to get your child out of this dilemma is for you and her treatment team to help her restore her weight. *It is only with weight restoration that she will think in healthy and rational ways, and it is only with weight restoration that she will have a chance to get back on track with adolescent development and achieve healthy and appropriate control over her individuation and budding independence.*

Bulimia and binge-eating disorder are not altogether different, but with these illnesses it may be easier for you to notice that your adolescent is indeed out of control. You can probably think of many times that you've missed a box of cookies from the pantry: You knew it was there just this morning, and now it's gone. You remember putting last night's leftover chicken in the fridge, and now it's missing. You've noticed the candy wrappers in the trash in Maggie's room every day! And in the case of bulimia, you've also spotted the remnants of her purging in the bathroom, week after week now.

Many adolescents with bulimia or binge-eating disorder may feel ambivalent about anyone interfering with their attempts to control their weight, their eating, and even their purging, but are in fact quite relieved when a parent helps them succeed in breaking the shameful pattern of binge eating and purging. Another difference in bulimia and binge-eating disorder, as compared with anorexia, is that your teenager with bulimia will not so stridently insist that she is in control of her eating. In fact, every time she has a binge-eating or purging episode, your daughter feels more and more out of control: "I feel disgusted with myself every time I do this, but I just don't know how to stop." In the case of bulimia, this is followed by thoughts such as "I am so afraid that I will gain weight if I don't make myself sick, and that's why I just can't stop doing this." However, some teens may deny feeling out of control, especially as they'll probably make every effort to reestablish control over eating *after* a binge/purge episode. Unlike that of a teen with anorexia, this sense of control seldom lasts for more than a couple of days, only to be followed by binge eating and, in the case of bulimia, purging again. Nevertheless, your daughter with bulimia or binge-eating disorder

is probably more likely to assert that she is, in fact, in control of her behavior and that it isn't up to you to tell her what to do about her difficulties. This is particularly confusing to you as a parent, as you've seen your child acting quite independently in so many other areas of her adolescence. Helping her with her bulimia or binge-eating disorder now seems almost counterintuitive!

Whether your child has anorexia, bulimia, or binge-eating disorder, it is highly likely that he won't think he is out of control and will probably resent you for trying to help. The challenge for you is how you will delicately balance your understanding of your teenager's developmental needs for independence with your understanding of his dilemma and find a way to help him assert healthy control over his life at a time he might resent you for your "interference." What is clear, though, is that you don't really have a choice. You have to help your child as the eating disorder continues to cloud his judgment.

To you, this is a deadly disease; to your child with anorexia, it's "just a perfectly healthy diet."

You now realize just how devastating an eating disorder is, but to see your child being flippant about her low heart rate, anemia, blood in her vomit, and swollen parotid glands is to come face to face with one of the most alarming aspects of anorexia and bulimia—the inability of the person with the eating disorder to appreciate just how deadly these illnesses can be. This denial of the seriousness of the severe malnutrition associated with anorexia nervosa is a core symptom of the illness. Teens with bulimia nervosa or binge-eating disorder will not necessarily understand the seriousness of their symptoms either, especially the long-term serious health consequences. Someone with anorexia does not appreciate how lethal severe emaciation can be, and similarly, someone with bulimia does not understand that low potassium, due to frequent vomiting, for instance, can cause death. For those with binge-eating disorder the risk of obesity and diabetes and hypertension may seem remote. Still, it's fair to say that this denial is more pronounced in anorexia.

In Chapter 4 we explained that anorexia is an ego-syntonic illness. What this means is that, unlike those with many other mental

disorders, the patient with anorexia "likes" or "cherishes" the illness or "takes comfort" in it. Someone with anorexia doesn't appreciate its dangers and will do almost anything to protect it, that is, prevent you from "taking it away." Although parents and doctors alike find this aspect of anorexia very difficult to understand, it helps to think of anorexia in comparison with other mental disorders: The patient who is depressed wants to feel better, the person who is anxious wants to relax, but the person with anorexia still wants to be thinner. This denial is actually reinforced through constant dieting and further weight loss, as well as focusing on these issues (dieting and weight) all the time to the exclusion of other, healthier perspectives. Thus, her diet is still normal to your daughter, even though everyone else sees it for what it is. Therefore, it's not uncommon for someone with anorexia to take pride in brushes with death: "Wow, I got my potassium down to 1.8, and I made it" (showing up in the emergency room with a potassium level that low is considered most critical, and few people can be revived).

What makes this illness so incredibly dangerous is that no matter how much you argue this very point with your teenager with anorexia—"You could have died. . . . We are so lucky they managed to revive you at the hospital. . . . We were so, so scared. . . . Do you understand how serious this is?"—these facts usually will have little impact on your son or daughter. Quietly, your teen will perceive this "crisis" as another achievement in his or her quest for that ideal weight.

By comparison, bulimia and binge-eating disorders are more ego-dystonic. What this means is that although an adolescent with bulimia or binge-eating disorder exhibits many of the aspects of denial of her illness that are common in anorexia, there is less pride involved in her symptoms. Rather, great discomfort and shame are associated with binge eating and purging. Nevertheless, this doesn't mean that your son or daughter will be forthcoming and ask for help as an adolescent who is depressed or anxious might. Quite the opposite is true. Because thinness is highly valued and the seriousness of the illness is not appreciated, *and* because of the guilt and shame associated with binge eating, most adolescents will do their best to binge eat without your knowledge. For those with bulimia,

the anxiety that the food they ate will make them gain 5 pounds overnight is so overwhelming that they absolutely "have to" get rid of it and will make every effort to make sure there's a way to purge after the binge-eating episodes. It certainly is not uncommon for a teenager with bulimia to evaluate an invitation for a movie and a meal with his or her friends, based not on what movie they'll see or what kind of food (Asian, Italian, etc.) they'll eat, but rather on the answers to questions such as "Will I be able to purge at that restaurant?" or "Can I slip away at that movie house to use the bathroom to throw up?"

As has probably become clear by now, gaining a better understanding of how the eating disorder leads your child to think and behave in very fixed ways concerning weight, shape, and eating issues will be helpful to you in finding the right way to help your adolescent overcome this struggle. That doesn't mean this understanding will automatically suggest an instantly effective strategy; it's just that without this understanding you're unlikely even to know why your efforts fail. Chapters 7 and 8 offer various ideas for helping your child, based on your understanding of these cognitive distortions.

You're the enemy, even though you're trying to save your son's life, because you're "forcing" him to do the one thing he is trying to avoid: eat.

The cognitive distortions born of eating disorders, by their very nature, create an adversarial relationship between you and your child. You want the child to eat appropriately to regain his health; he is firmly committed to continuing to lose weight or to hide the truth that he is binge eating and purging. The fact that you can't "talk some sense into him" means that any attempt you make to confront your child's false beliefs and consequent denial only makes you seem like a greater enemy.

The rift between you may seem to widen from your own perspective too when you try to confront your teenager about irrational beliefs surrounding food and weight. You may very well have come to count on the rational discussion and sharing of decision making

that are among the beneficial developments of life with an adolescent. In fact, you may feel today that you have a perfectly rational adolescent around the house most of the time—"We can talk about homework, our vacation plans, or the music she likes to listen to"— but when it comes to food and weight issues, "it's as if a switch was turned off: She makes no sense, and the worst is, she doesn't see the difference." The fact that your teenager is no longer meeting your expectations for rationality may make you feel as if it's the child who is creating the adversarial situation. With this kind of standoff, who wins?

The eating disorder wins.

That's because the real—and only—enemy is the anorexia, bulimia, or binge-eating disorder. Recognizing this is the key to responding constructively to this particular cognitive distortion.

The thought distortions associated with eating disorders can be so severe that rational discussion and decision sharing about your child's health are no longer possible. Parents have to be prepared to accept the idea that in the area of food, eating, and weight, they are no longer dealing with a child who is rational. It is the *illness* they are dealing with.

We've seen many parents in distress when their usually kind adolescent lashes out when his parents make any attempt to intervene in the illness: "I don't want to eat that! You're killing me. Can't you see how unhappy you make me?" or "I hate you, I want nothing to do with you, don't even talk to me!" or "Leave me alone! You are making me *so* miserable." Desperate utterances from your adolescent sounding anything like these are obviously distressing to any parent. What the adolescent with an eating disorder wants is for you to back off in your efforts to help. As tempting as this might be for many parents, acquiescing only means allowing the illness to triumph.

What can you do? Negotiating with your adolescent under these circumstances is a great challenge and one that you are most likely to lose. In defense of his illness, your son will try to make sure that your efforts fail, whether you are trying to get him to eat more or to keep him from purging the food that he has consumed. Knowing that there is little you can do to rationally argue, discuss,

or convince your son about the perils of his illness and that the behaviors he is manifesting are illness related as opposed to those of "your child" (separating the illness from your adolescent) will help you when you're trying to help him. Knowing that getting involved in "eating disorder debates" will be fruitless and that you will probably lose the argument and end up being convinced, against your own better judgment, that an apple is better than a pasta dish with a cream sauce for a starving teenager, it's best not to argue. Instead, you will want to find a way to let your child know that you understand his dilemma, that the illness doesn't allow him to be rational about food and weight right now, that you understand that for the time being he sees you as the enemy, but that none of this can deter you from doing what you know will save his life—to get him to eat what he should eat or to keep him from binge eating and purging.

Earlier we mentioned the concept of separating the illness from your adolescent. This is an important principle in dealing with a teenager with an eating disorder, just as it is in helping someone of any age with any psychiatric disorder. Understanding how the illness is "separate" from your teenager will be crucial in helping you understand your child's troubled behaviors and deal with the illness effectively. We discuss this principle in more detail in Chapter 7.

"Not eating" is not just the most important thing in the life of your daughter with anorexia: It's "the only thing."

For parents, it is often very difficult to understand just how important eating or not eating, weight loss, or feeling the "right" size is to their daughter. In fact, for someone with anorexia, nothing can be more important than focusing on that next pound that she should lose or making sure that she doesn't eat at all until 5:00 P.M. every day of the next week. For someone with bulimia, nothing can be more important than how she can get rid of the food she has just eaten, believing it's going to make her fat. Indeed, managing to adhere to all these "rules" and "regulations" around eating or not eating eventually eclipses the importance of school, family, and friends, or at least it appears to do so, especially if the eating

disorder behaviors are allowed to continue unchecked. It is especially hard for parents to witness their kind child appear completely oblivious to other crises in the family—it's not uncommon for an adolescent with anorexia to show little concern for a parent who was just diagnosed with a severe illness, because the adolescent is so preoccupied with her quest for thinness. This adolescent is, of course, not heartless; it's just that anorexia or bulimia has a way of overtaking the sufferer, leaving little room for anything else.

Paradoxically, when someone with anorexia continues to starve himself, it actually becomes easier and easier not to eat. At the onset of the illness the adolescent has to work very hard to keep his appetite "in check," making sure he doesn't "give in" to these "horrible urges" to eat, always feeling that he cannot let his guard down for a moment. With increasing weight loss, though, it becomes easier to feel a sense of mastery over these urges, and with time the teenager no longer feels any hunger. However, with increased starvation, the adolescent also becomes more preoccupied with thoughts about food and weight. In fact, some young women and men find themselves in the unenviable position where they can think of virtually nothing else but "What is that half bagel from this morning going to do to my weight?" or "What can I do to avoid having lunch with my friends?" or "How can I make sure that I have no more than a salad without dressing for dinner?" and so on. It's hard to imagine just how much of one's time, on a daily basis, will be taken up by such thoughts. Some teens with anorexia will say, "I can think of nothing else but my weight—literally nothing else!"

Much of what happens with the dieting adolescent, especially when starvation has set in, also happens to people who lose extreme amounts of weight because of a variety of medical illnesses. In fact, much of what we know about the effects of starvation on the human mind and on human behavior is derived from what we have learned from individuals without an eating disorder. Ancel Keys and his colleagues, in a landmark study in Minnesota in the early 1950s, published their results of a semi-starvation study of World War II conscientious objectors. The physical and psychological changes in these healthy men who were starved for several months were the same as those we typically observe in our patients with an eating

disorder—the men became increasingly preoccupied with their weight and with food once they had lost a substantial amount of weight. It's almost as if the part of the brain that controls hunger and satiety will not let you forget about the one thing you need most when you're starved—food! The good news is that once these starved study participants were allowed to eat normally again, their weights were restored and the symptoms of starvation also disappeared. These observations reveal exactly what we also witness in many patients with anorexia when they return to a healthy weight.

Your daughter with anorexia has consumed mere crumbs of food, but she thinks she's telling the truth when she says she's eaten a huge amount of food today.

When your adolescent has consumed only a few bites of her sandwich and proclaims to have eaten "tons" or "too much" or a "huge amount," there are at least two ways in which her account is accurate from her perspective. First, she sees eating anything at all as a failure and a sign of weakness. So, psychologically, even a small amount is the same as a large amount to her. The anxiety and guilt she experiences after eating half a bagel are the same as if she had eaten a whole sandwich. Second, and in reality, the stomach of someone with anorexia usually decreases in capacity, and as a consequence, the rate at which the stomach empties has been slowed. It's therefore quite likely that your child will feel full and stay feeling that way longer after eating even a relatively small amount of food. Moreover, prolonged starvation has allowed your teenager's hunger cues to have been stilled, making eating even more difficult when she states that she's not hungry. So, when she does eat, even what are in fact mere crumbs, your daughter will feel that she has overeaten on both accounts. "I will get fat if I eat that bagel (half an apple/three carrots/etc.)," she will say, or "I just can't eat that much, I've already had enough," in reference to the small bowl of salad without dressing that sits half eaten. These incidents are, in fact, experienced by your child as really having eaten too much or really finding it hard to eat the "whole" salad.

The situation is further complicated when parents want to believe their adolescent's account of what was eaten when they (the parents) weren't around to supervise a meal. And parents can become increasingly despondent when their child doesn't gain weight despite "all the food" she claims to be eating on a regular basis. It is very important for you to remember that eating even half an apple at school lunch, when your adolescent son has promised himself not to eat at all, is seen by him as a calamitous transgression of his own food rules and that the half apple was a huge amount of food—"huge" because it "should not have been eaten." Likewise, asking your adolescent daughter to tell you what she ate for lunch at school might get you a response along these lines: "A yogurt and an apple and a milkshake." That may sound like enough, but if you inquire carefully, it may in fact mean that in reality she ate a scoop of yogurt, a bite of an apple, and a sip of a milkshake. As has become clear to you by now, even when your child protests about "too much food" or says, "I can't possibly have more to eat," recovery from anorexia can really come about only when sufficiently healthy amounts of food are consumed to return your child's thinking about these issues to normal and, of course, to restore gut functioning to normal.

The same scenario may be true for an adolescent with bulimia, but it will take a slightly different form. Whereas your teen with bulimia will also try to restrict her food intake and may also consider mere crumbs of food "a lot," many teens with bulimia are very scared that if they eat "one more crumb" than their self-imposed food rules allow, they will "just go ahead and eat the whole cake." Sadly, that is what happens for many teens with bulimia, and that's why your child will so rigidly try to hang on to these beliefs.

**No matter how emaciated she becomes,
what your daughter with anorexia sees in the mirror
is a fat person.**

This is called *body image distortion*, which is a result of an overfocus on weight and shape that eventually leads to misapprehension of realities. Many teenagers with anorexia overestimate their own body

size, and quite paradoxically, the thinner they become, the more they may see themselves as fat. Body image distortion is much less common among those with bulimia, binge-eating disorder, or avoidant/restrictive food intake disorder. Some teenagers may go so far as to cover all mirrors in their homes so that they can never catch a glimpse of themselves. There are sophisticated methods whereby body image distortion can be evaluated. However, you only need to hear your child referring to herself as fat, or have her tell you what she sees when she looks in the mirror, to know that she actually sees someone who is much larger than she actually is.

Unfortunately, the only "solution" your son or daughter can think of to escape this agonizing dilemma is to lose yet another pound, thereby establishing a cycle of further weight loss and further distortion of reality. One insightful teenage patient described her experience like this: "I thought I was fat when I wore these pants. Now that I have gained weight I can't see any difference (I still look as fat), but the pants are the same. I guess I can't see things the way they really are. My fear of being fat makes me look fat no matter what."

Many teenagers, though, know they are thin and don't actually see themselves as fat, yet they still cannot escape "feeling fat." Someone might say, "I know I'm not fat, but every morning I wake up feeling fat, and I know there's only one way to tackle my problem and that's to lose more weight. Perhaps then I won't feel fat." What may be happening here for some teenagers who are predisposed to developing an eating disorder is that it's "easier" to wake up in the morning and focus on their weight than to think about "that issue at school" or "the breakup with my boyfriend." Many teenagers with eating disorders may not know how to tackle or resolve the issues that cause them to feel depressed, but it's a little "easier" to go on a diet and lose weight. So, instead of waking up saying "I am depressed" and then having to figure out how to deal with that feeling, it seems somewhat more manageable to "replace" the depression with "I feel fat," because at least "I have a plan to cut back on my food intake some more and lose another pound. Maybe then I'll feel okay." Obviously, losing that extra pound does not help with the feeling of fatness. But even with that evidence before her—that losing an

extra pound doesn't eliminate her feeling of being fat—you will find it very difficult, if not impossible, to convince your daughter that she isn't fat. As long as that "feeling" persists, she will stay on the cycle of trying to lose weight, and not eating will continue to cause the body image distortion that tells her loud and clear that she is fat.

Ironically, body image distortion usually, but not always, improves or even normalizes when weight is restored for a period of a few months in an outpatient setting. (Not surprisingly, those whose thoughts about eating and weight are still distorted even after their weight is normalized usually have a poorer prognosis than those whose thought processes improve along with their weight.)

Your son with bulimia continues to vomit even though his weight is clearly increasing.

One of the ironies of bulimia is that the weight-control strategy of purging is quite ineffective. It is impossible to vomit up the full amount one has eaten during an hour-long binge-eating episode— too much food has already entered the intestinal tract. Thus, a hefty percentage of these high-calorie foods remains in the system and adds weight. Over time, then, instead of losing weight, patients with bulimia tend to gain weight. However, this only adds to the urgency of their efforts to control their weight, which leads to increasing self-starvation, binge eating, and then purging. Still, they keep on doing it. Why?

The answer is, in part, that over time binge eating and purging are experienced as a coping strategy for other of life's problems. Over time, adolescents report feeling tremendous relief after purging. This reinforces the purging behaviors whether or not they lead to weight loss. Many adolescents who have been ill for a while readily admit that they know the purging does little to help them with weight control: "It's just that I have to do it. I feel much better afterward, even if that feeling doesn't last very long." So, when your son feels he didn't perform well at a wrestling meet, he may binge eat and purge. The same is true when your daughter breaks up with her boyfriend or is having academic trouble. In other words, binge eating and purging are no longer efforts at weight control alone; they

are used more generally in an effort to cope with other problems of adolescence. When a behavior like binge eating and purging is being used to manage any number of types of problems, it's harder to let go of, and the "logic" that it doesn't control weight doesn't pertain.

Your daughter seems prideful about her self-starvation but miserable at the same time.

One of the hardest things to appreciate about severe dieting is that although your teen appears to be reveling in the accomplishment of lower and lower weights, she is also quite miserable. Anorexia nervosa is a really tough taskmaster. Whenever your child eats even a small amount, she experiences severe harassing and critical thoughts about failure and worthlessness. These thoughts are unrelenting and merciless. In addition, the preoccupation with eating, obsessive and repetitive thinking about how much was eaten, how many calories, how much weight gain, and so forth, disrupt usual thinking, making it sometimes difficult to focus in school or during social gatherings. The point is, however determined and steadfast your child appears, she is really suffering, physically and psychologically, as a result of the punitive thinking experienced.

Adolescents with bulimia are usually filled with shame and feelings of failure because they "give in" to eating and "purge" even though it's disgusting. These adolescents experience a combination of guilt, shame, recrimination, and anxiety about gaining weight. It helps to have a sympathetic view of this experience, because as a parent, when your child is suffering, you want to relieve that suffering, even if the illness behaviors are themselves frustrating and provoke anger in you.

Your son weighs himself 10 times a day and is constantly pinching himself to see if he has any fat despite his obvious severe weight loss.

Body checking and repeated weighing appear irrational to us because we know that weights do not vary much during a day and

that pinching or repeatedly checking our appearance in the mirror will not provide new information. However, the anxiety about weight gain and a concomitant hyperfocus on body fat are pervasive in adolescents with anorexia or bulimia. To combat perceived weight gain or imagined weight gain, those with an eating disorder look for reassurance in these constant "checking" activities, whether it's pinching the stomach or thighs a hundred times a day or standing in front of the mirror for what seems like hours at a time, checking and rechecking to see whether any weight was put on. Unfortunately, the reassurance is only momentary (if at all), and they quickly need to check again. If you remember that these behaviors also reinforce the hyperfocus on shape and weight concerns, you will see why it's often necessary to find ways to help your child reduce his dependence on such strategies so as to reduce the child's anxiety about weight and shape. For instance, you might make this struggle a great deal easier for your child if you remove your bathroom scale. You can reassure your child that he will be weighed at regular intervals at the doctor's office, and it is at the doctor's office that these concerns can be addressed.

Your daughter promises to stop binge eating, but every day you find missing food cartons and potato chip bags under her bed.

Your daughter's intentions to stop binge eating are sincere and genuine. She wishes she could follow through on them. It is not a loss of will power or a character problem or just wanting to be spiteful. Rather, it is that she has learned to use food to manage her emotions, conflicts, and self-esteem. Food is very reinforcing for most of us because it is immediately rewarding on a physical and neurochemical level. Food has also been used to soothe, comfort, and reward in socially condoned ways throughout history and currently. Your daughter may not care about the long-term effects of binge eating on her weight or health, but the short-term rewards are hard to ignore, especially when she is feeling overwhelmed and doesn't have an alternative strategy to help her cope.

WHAT'S A PARENT SUPPOSED TO DO?

When you understand your child's thinking with regard to these issues, you've laid the foundation for whatever practical interventions you will implement to help fight your child's eating disorder. By separating the illness from your child (also called *externalizing the illness*), you support your child as a developing adolescent while insisting that she fight the eating disorder.

As we've shown, eating disorders are clearly very complicated illnesses, both in terms of the effects of starvation on the mind and the body and in terms of how coexisting psychiatric illnesses further complicate the picture. In addition, as we've seen in this chapter, how your child experiences them makes her thinking and behaviors appear irrational and confusing, though there is a kind of logic to them when you understand them better.

Treatment for eating disorders must respond to these complicated thoughts, behaviors, and, at times, medical problems. What this usually means is that good treatment pays attention to all aspects of these illnesses—psychological, psychiatric, medical, and nutritional. Good treatment also means that you, the parent, play an active role in helping your daughter or son receive care and that you actively participate in this care. Your involvement in treatment is particularly helpful here, as these cognitive distortions are so persistent and so powerful that someone has to be on hand to help counteract them, and, obviously, the parents (and the rest of the family) are usually the only ones routinely in the position to do this.

In the following chapter, we outline what research to date has been able to tell us about the effectiveness of the best-studied treatments for eating disorders. If you choose to have family therapy along the lines of the FBT (see Chapter 7), it will help you to use everything you now know about how your child thinks to enhance your success in taking charge of the problematic eating behavior. If you choose among other types of treatment, you can still use what you know about cognitive distortions to support the treatment team's efforts, as described in Chapter 8.

FOR MORE INFORMATION

Garner, D. M., Psychoeducational Principles in Treatment, in D. M. Garner and P. E. Garfinkel, Editors, *Handbook of Treatment for Eating Disorders, Second Edition*, 1997. New York: Guilford Press, pp. 145–177.

Le Grange, D., and J. Lock, Editors, *Eating Disorders: Children and Adolescents: A Clinical Handbook*, 2011. New York: Guilford Press.

Lock, J., *The Oxford Handbook of Child and Adolescent Eating Disorders: Developmental Perspectives*, 2012. New York: Oxford University Press.

Treasure, J., and B. Bauer, Assessment and Motivation, in J. Treasure, U. Schmidt, and E. van Furth, Editors, *Handbook of Eating Disorders*, 2003. Chichester, UK: Wiley, pp. 219–232.

CHAPTER 6

Understand Your Options

*What the Research Says about the Best Ways
to Treat Anorexia, Bulimia, Binge-Eating Disorder,
and Avoidant/Restrictive Food Intake Disorder*

Having a better understanding of your adolescent's difficulties involving self-esteem, body weight, shape, and eating habits enables you to take the next step: finding help. Identifying the most appropriate treatment for your child can be a challenge, however, because researchers and the clinical community still struggle with many unknowns. Fortunately, we know more today than ever before about treatments that reverse self-starvation or binge eating and purging, that assist you and your adolescent in understanding some of the psychological makeup of his or her difficulties, and that can help get your daughter or son back on track with adolescent development.

In this chapter we present what we know about the different treatments for eating disorders. Before we get into the specifics, however, it's important to understand that most treatment studies providing evidence for the effectiveness of these therapies have focused exclusively on people who meet the full criteria for either anorexia or bulimia. This does not mean that no treatment is available if your child does not meet the full criteria for an eating disorder. Clinical

experience has shown that in most settings a child whose symptoms resemble anorexia or bulimia, for instance, should be treated the same way teenagers who meet the full criteria for these disorders are treated. And in some ways, the outcome might be more favorable for your child if she has been ill for only a few months or a year and does not qualify for the full diagnosis of anorexia or bulimia. *An important point to remember as you read about the available treatment options is that early and good treatment usually bodes well for your child's recovery from an eating disorder.* We start by discussing studies that evaluate outpatient approaches, and we then turn to more intensive therapies such as inpatient, day-hospital, or residential treatments.

OUTPATIENT TREATMENTS

In this section we explain what the latest research has shown about the effectiveness of the main psychological treatments for eating disorders (family therapy, psychodynamic individual therapy, cognitive-behavioral therapy, interpersonal psychotherapy, and nutritional counseling) and medication treatments.

Psychological Treatments

Only a few treatments for adolescents with anorexia have been studied systematically using valid scientific methods. Psychological treatments for anorexia that have been studied include family-based treatment (FBT), adolescent-focused treatment (AFT), and cognitive-behavioral therapy (CBT). Six randomized clinical trials with a total of 323 adolescent participants have evaluated FBT. In these studies, FBT was either as effective as or superior to comparison therapies. These studies also found that FBT worked more quickly in promoting weight gain and decreased the need for hospitalization. While AFT (an individual therapy aimed at addressing adolescent self-efficacy and autonomy) was not as effective as family therapy in these studies, this approach was helpful for many patients, especially those with less severe symptoms. CBT was

used in one study and found to be the most cost-effective approach compared to treatment as usual or hospitalization. A recent study using an enhanced version of CBT (CBT-E) suggests that this new approach may also be useful for adolescents with anorexia.

Although there have been a number of treatment studies for the treatment of adults with bulimia, only two randomized clinical trials, with a total of 165 patients, have looked at treatments for adolescents. One study compared a version of FBT to a therapist-supported self-help version of CBT. It found that adolescents did about the same in both treatments. The other study compared FBT to an individual supportive therapy and found that those in family therapy improved more quickly and did better overall. While there are no other studies of adolescents with bulimia, studies of adults have been done on interpersonal psychotherapy (IPT), a treatment that focuses on the role of difficulties in relationships in eating disorder symptoms, and dialectical behavior therapy (DBT), a treatment that focuses on learning how to manage emotions. A study that compared IPT to CBT found that CBT worked more quickly, but over time there were no differences in outcome between the two treatments. DBT is effective for adults with bulimia nervosa and adolescents with problems with suicidal ideation and self-injury. Some therapists are using DBT with adolescent patients who have bulimia and suicidal ideation or self-injury, but how effective this treatment will be is not yet known.

Many studies have been done on the treatment of binge-eating disorder in adults. These studies suggest that binge-eating disorder responds to many treatments, including CBT, IPT, and DBT. For adolescents with binge-eating disorders, IPT has been used in a number of patients, but no randomized clinical trials have been reported.

There are no scientific studies of treatments for those children and adolescents with avoidant/restrictive food intake disorder (ARFID). In clinical practice, therapists develop behavior plans that provide rewards for changes in behavior, usually by gradually increasing food intake in terms of both types of food and amounts. Parents are often included in these behavioral plans.

Family-Based Treatment in More Detail

Because eating disorders often occur in adolescents, working with the family was identified as a possible avenue of treatment. Family therapy generally emphasizes the family system as a potential solution for the dilemmas of the eating disorder in a teenager. Although some important differences have been found between early attempts to involve parents in the treatment of adolescents with eating disorders and more recent work, the groundwork has been laid to bring parents directly into the treatment process because parents are seen as most helpful in resolving the eating disorder in their adolescent. Therefore, family therapy for eating disorders has been seen as a valuable treatment since the mid-1970s.

In general family therapy, the therapist focuses on how family members communicate, how they relate to one another, and how they solve problems. The notion is that in families in which a member has an eating disorder, certain predictable problem areas become evident, such as parents allowing a child to function as an authority figure in the family, avoidance of addressing problems in the interest of keeping the peace, and anxiety about allowing an adolescent child to be independent. The focus of this form of family therapy is not on symptoms or symptom management as in FBT, but instead on these more general family process concerns.

Several noncontrolled trials of family therapy (in which a series of patients receive the same treatment without any comparison treatment) suggest that involving families in treatment is effective at least for younger patients with anorexia nervosa. Child psychiatrist Salvador Minuchin, who spent most of his professional life at the Child Guidance Clinic in Philadelphia, conducted the most important of these studies. He and his team reported good outcomes (recovery) in more than 85% of their patients in a case series of 53 adolescents with anorexia. All these patients were treated with family therapy. The most influential systematic research into psychological treatments for eating disorders so far, however, has been the FBT studies conducted at the Maudsley Hospital in London that focused on anorexia. We introduced FBT in Chapter 2. Comparable work has been conducted, or is currently under way,

in various centers in the United States, Europe, Asia, and Australia. Most of these studies, in both the United Kingdom and the United States, have shown that FBT can be very effective for adolescents with anorexia, especially for those who have been ill for less than 2 years. A main difference for you to remember here is that FBT, unlike some other family therapies for eating disorders, does not assume that there is something "wrong" with families or that this "something wrong" with you or your family is the reason you should be involved in your child's treatment. On the contrary, FBT regards families as the best resource in treatment. Recovery of the teenager can be accelerated by successfully getting the family on board in treatment, helping the therapist to resolve the eating disorder symptoms (the starvation), and getting the adolescent back on track with adolescent development.

Seven randomized clinical trials have examined FBT. These studies produced a number of important findings. First, patients and their families did not drop out of treatment when using FBT treatment. The adolescents in these studies were typical of the type of teens who come for treatment for anorexia. Most important, FBT was as good as or better than any of the treatments that it has been compared to so far. In the first study, published in 1987, adolescents with anorexia recovered at a higher rate than those in individual therapy. In a study comparing FBT to AFT, adolescents in family therapy had greater and faster weight restoration and menstrual return and showed no differences in other measures of psychological functioning. Two forms of FBT—one in which parents were seen separately from their child with anorexia and the other in which the whole family was seen—found that the approaches were equally helpful, except for families where parents were more critical of their child. In those cases, separated family therapy was more effective. Another study compared a short 6-month course of FBT to a longer course lasting one year. There were no differences overall, suggesting that FBT could be effective in a short time. However, for families where there was a single parent or divorced parents, longer treatment was better. Adolescents who had very high levels of obsessive features also did better with longer treatment. In the largest outpatient study of anorexia in adolescents published to date, FBT

was better than AFT because it led to faster weight gain, decreased hospitalization use, and higher recovery rates by a margin of two to one. Several studies have followed the adolescents who were treated with FBT and found that most continued to do well. The most recent study of adolescents with anorexia conducted by Stewart Agras and colleagues compared FBT to a more general family therapy targeting family processes rather than weight restoration. This study found no differences in clinical outcomes between the two treatments, but FBT was more efficient in promoting weight restoration, used less hospitalization during treatment, and was more acceptable to parents than more general family therapy. Thus, FBT appears to be the most effective treatment for adolescent anorexia in either the short term or the long term.

Although anorexia, bulimia, and binge-eating disorder are distinct illnesses, many adolescents with any of these types of eating disorders report similar symptoms. Therefore, in the absence of many treatment studies for adolescents with bulimia or binge-eating disorder, it makes sense that FBT that has proven effective for teenagers with anorexia may also be beneficial to your adolescent with bulimia or binge-eating disorder. Although you should view these results with some caution, FBT for adolescent bulimia and binge-eating disorder has considerable potential and should be considered among your treatment options.

Individual Psychodynamic Psychotherapy

As mentioned in Chapter 2, a variety of individual psychotherapies are available, but the kind of therapy your child is most likely to receive at this time is psychodynamic therapy. This means the treatment will focus more on "underlying issues" than on weight and shape concerns and how to restore healthy body weight. This form of treatment addresses the perceived psychological problems that may cause eating disorders. Specifically, adolescents with eating disorders are believed to be immature and highly anxious about a variety of adolescent issues, including assuming independent roles as adults in a responsible manner. Therapy using this model focuses on the symptoms of disordered eating only insofar as they represent

an ineffective and dangerous strategy that keeps the adolescent from addressing her real concerns and issues. Psychodynamic therapy for eating disorders is often relatively unstructured in nature and is not time limited, with treatment goals that are not necessarily very specific. Nevertheless, there is some evidence to support this treatment. In two trials, Arthur Crisp and his colleagues at St. George's Hospital in London reported substantial improvements in their patient groups (these included both adolescents and adults) in terms of both medical/nutritional recovery and psychological improvement, using individual therapy approaches. Many colleagues who practice this approach are mindful of the fact that it may be difficult to do intensive psychotherapy early in treatment when someone is very starved and, consequently, they will adapt their treatments to reflect this reality.

An exception to these general comments about the nonspecificity of individual psychodynamic therapy is the approach developed by Arthur Robin and colleagues at Wayne State University in Detroit, originally called ego-oriented individual therapy and now called AFT for anorexia. Derived from the psychodynamic tradition, AFT aims at maturational issues associated with puberty and adolescence. AFT devised for adolescents posits that individuals with anorexia are immature and unaware of their emotions, particularly strong emotions such as anger and depression. These adolescents do not want to face such problems, so they turn to controlling food and weight as a way to keep their feelings and conflicts from surfacing. Thus, according to these theories, eating disorders disrupt normal psychological and physical maturity during adolescence. To develop better ability to manage the challenges of adolescence, they must first learn to identify, define, and tolerate their emotions. In addition, a primary goal of AFT is to foster the adolescent's separation and individuation from the family.

Robin and colleagues used AFT in a randomized clinical trial comparing it with family therapy. The comparison revealed that at the end of treatment family therapy resulted in greater improvements, but at 1-year follow-up there were no significant differences between the two approaches in how patients did. About two-thirds of the adolescents did better overall. This study suggests that AFT

is effective, though slower in achieving results than family therapy. What may distinguish AFT from other psychodynamic therapies is the degree to which parents are involved in the treatment, though they specifically did not directly manage eating or other compensatory behaviors like binge eating or purging. Other recent studies suggest that AFT is almost as helpful as FBT in adolescents with anorexia who are not as severely ill, specifically those adolescents who say they have fewer eating disorder thoughts, are less obsessed with those thoughts, and do not also binge eat and/or purge in the context of anorexia.

As we noted, there are only two published randomized clinical trials for adolescents with bulimia. These studies suggest that either FBT or CBT may be helpful for adolescents with bulimia. In adults, CBT is the treatment that has the best evidence of being helpful.

The cognitive-behavioral model of bulimia assumes that the main factors involved in the maintenance of bulimia are problematic *attitudes* toward body shape and weight. Such attitudes lead to an overvaluation of thinness, to dissatisfaction with the body, and to attempts to control shape and weight through excessive dieting. This restrictive pattern of eating then results in both psychological and physiological deprivation, which are often associated with a depressed mood. As a result of the dietary restriction, hunger is increased, leading to an enhanced probability of binge eating, particularly in the presence of depressed mood. Because binge eating raises concerns about gaining weight, it is eventually followed by purging in an attempt to compensate for calories consumed during the binge. Based on this model, treatment for bulimia using CBT focuses first on helping to change eating patterns to make them more normal (i.e., three meals and snacks without long periods of fasting between them) so that the urge to binge eat (and therefore purge as well) is decreased. Next, the treatment focuses on the effect of overvaluation of shape and weight on self-esteem and other related thoughts that support an excessive preoccupation with these matters and lead to disordered eating behaviors. Finally, the treatment focuses on what might be expected to lead to a return of eating problems in the future and helps to determine what might be done to prevent a relapse.

Different groups of investigators in several countries have completed a number of randomized controlled trials of CBT for bulimia in adults. Almost all of these studies have demonstrated that CBT is the treatment of choice for adults with bulimia. More specifically, these studies have shown that CBT produces a mean reduction in binge eating and purging of about 70% and a mean abstinence rate from these symptoms approaching 50%. Dietary restraint is also lessened significantly, and the disturbed attitudes toward body weight and shape are greatly reduced. Several studies have shown good maintenance of change at follow-up, ranging from 6 months to 6 years.

Another effective treatment for adults with bulimia is IPT. IPT was initially developed as a brief treatment for depression and anxiety problems in adults. It is based on the idea that emotional problems are best conceived of as a result of interpersonal problems, particularly current ones. Treatment for bulimia using IPT also focuses on the interpersonal context within which the eating disorder developed and is maintained, with the aim of helping the patient make specific changes in identified interpersonal problem areas. So, in direct distinction from CBT, the focus is not on changing behaviors or cognitions related directly to bulimia. In fact, little attention is paid to eating habits or attitudes toward weight and shape. Several studies now provide empirical support for the use of IPT to treat bulimia, though none have shown it to be superior to CBT.

Both CBT and IPT can probably be helpful to adolescents with bulimia, but we have found it important to include parents in these treatments. When parents are included in treatment, they can provide support and encouragement as well as direct assistance in helping to change bulimic behaviors and attitudes.

Nutritional Counseling

Another approach commonly used for treating eating disorders is nutritional counseling. Nutritionists have long played a role in this treatment, on the assumption that their expertise in diets and health can help patients reevaluate their choices along more

reasonable guidelines. Usual nutritional counseling consists of providing meal plans, caloric recommendations, discussion of alternative food choices to meet nutritional requirements, and support for continued progress in making healthier food choices. To date, however, the few studies that have examined this treatment have been conducted with adult patients and have found that other psychological treatments (family therapy and individual therapy) are superior to nutritional counseling. However, it may be helpful at times to consult with a nutritionist for guidance on specific nutritional requirements or difficulties.

In summary, the research literature suggests that two forms of outpatient psychotherapy may be effective for anorexia: FBT and AFT as developed by Robin and colleagues. Up to this point, family treatment has received greater attention and has more evidence to support it. However, the tradition of psychodynamic psychotherapy lends additional credibility to AFT. For bulimia nervosa, although no treatment studies for adolescents have been completed, the best evidence suggests that CBT is the treatment of choice, but FBT is also effective. As noted, it is likely that CBT needs to be modified for adolescents to account for developmental variables in the younger group, specifically, with the inclusion of a family component. IPT is also a likely effective treatment for bulimia, and as it has been shown to be helpful for teenagers with depression, it's a reasonable option. Again, though, family involvement is usually crucial to work with adolescents in IPT. The role of nutritional counseling remains uncertain from a research perspective, though this treatment alone appears to be inadequate for most patients. Integrated into other psychological interventions, however, nutritional counseling may still have a role.

Psychiatric Medications

In addition to psychological outpatient treatments, a variety of medications have been studied to see if they are of benefit for eating disorders. Although psychotropic medications—medications that are exclusively developed for the treatment of psychiatric illnesses—can

be helpful for some, it's important to appreciate how little we know about the efficacy of medications in the treatment of eating disorders.

Antidepressant and antianxiety medications have been examined in adults with anorexia and found to be of limited help, especially during periods when these patients were acutely medically compromised. Many earlier, smaller studies have demonstrated few significant improvements in patients as a result of psychopharmacological intervention. The role of medications in adolescents with anorexia has received almost no attention. Among adult patients, medications that have been prescribed most frequently include antidepressants, designed to help patients with mood problems, and low-dose neuroleptics, used to address severe obsessional thinking, psychotic-like thinking, and severe anxiety. There is little research evidence that such medications produce any benefit for those with anorexia; moreover, these medications have been shown to pose problems in that some patients report binge eating while taking them.

Studies over the last few decades have explored the role of selective serotonin reuptake inhibitors (SSRIs, such as Prozac) in the treatment of anorexia. Prozac has been tried in inpatient and outpatient settings as a means of preventing relapse in patients who have made progress in treatment. So far, findings are mostly inconclusive, and large systematic studies are not yet available. Overall, the conclusion you should draw from this limited work is that the benefits of medication in the treatment of anorexia remain quite uncertain. In fact, most clinicians will agree that *the best medicine for anorexia remains food at a dose of three meals and three snacks per day!*

Yet, please keep in mind that several other psychiatric illnesses, such as depression and anxiety, may co-occur with anorexia, as discussed in Chapter 4. If your child has such a co-occurring disorder, she may very well benefit from a course of antidepressant or antianxiety medication, as long as the medication is prescribed for the depression or the anxiety. In addition, there are a host of medical complications for anorexia, as we have elaborated on earlier, and many patients benefit from several nonpsychotropic medications

that your pediatrician can prescribe to deal with abdominal discomfort or any other medical complication associated with your child's illness.

In contrast to these discouraging findings about the help medications might offer for anorexia, most studies show convincing evidence that supports the use of antidepressant medications for adults with bulimia and binge-eating disorder. Researchers were prompted to pursue the use of these medications precisely because so many patients with bulimia also prove to be suffering from depression when they consult their doctors. Inasmuch as antidepressant medications are helpful in depression, they may also be helpful in bulimia and binge-eating disorder. These observations led to a series of double-blind, placebo-controlled trials of antidepressants among adult patients with bulimia and binge-eating disorder. In such a trial, neither the researchers nor the study participants know whether they are taking the medication under investigation or the placebo (sugar pill). Most classes of antidepressant medications have been tested in these studies, including the tricyclics, monoamine oxidase inhibitors (MAOIs), SSRIs, and atypical antidepressants such as bupropion and trazodone. In almost all these studies, both tricyclics and fluoxetine (the SSRI most commonly known by the trade name Prozac) have proven to be better than the placebo in terms of the reduction in binge frequency. Generally, depression and preoccupation with shape and weight also show greater improvement with medication as opposed to placebo pills. Overall response to medication treatment alone for bulimia nervosa is less than for psychological treatment alone.

Perhaps the most important finding is that there is little evidence for the long-term effect of pharmacological treatment. Only one group of researchers has shown that 6 months of treatment with desipramine, an antidepressant, produced lasting improvement even after the medication was withdrawn.

Several controlled studies have looked at medication *and* psychotherapy treatments for bulimia in adults. These studies evaluated the relative (medication vs. psychotherapy) as well as the combined (medication plus psychotherapy) effectiveness of CBT and

antidepressant drug treatment. These studies indicate that (1) CBT is superior to medication alone, (2) combining CBT with medication is significantly more effective than medication alone, and (3) combining CBT and medication provides only modest incremental benefits over CBT alone. The result is that patients who receive CBT versus medication are often less likely to drop out of treatment. A recent meta-analysis (combining data from several studies to increase statistical significance) of psychosocial and pharmacological treatment studies for adult bulimia confirmed CBT as the treatment of choice. Taken together, these outcomes mean that *just* receiving antidepressant medication is seldom sufficient for bulimia. So when medications are used, other psychological treatments (e.g., CBT) should almost always be included. Another finding that favors CBT is that psychotherapies are usually more acceptable to patients as compared with medication. The benefits of medication treatment for binge-eating disorder are not as clear. Medications alone appear to be helpful for many. Studies of medication treatments for ARFID do not yet exist. However, antidepressants are sometimes used to decrease anxiety about eating and swallowing as well as stimulate appetite.

In summary, recent studies of treatment for adults with bulimia and binge-eating disorder have demonstrated that CBT and antidepressant medications (especially SSRIs such as Prozac) are potentially effective treatments. No treatment study that exclusively involves adolescents with bulimia or binge-eating disorders has been published, however. Until adolescents are studied, whether treatments that have shown to be helpful for adults can be applied to adolescents will remain speculative. However, many adolescents do benefit from the same medications that have been tested in adult populations. As a parent, you might want to make sure that your doctor appreciates this fact and exercises the necessary caution when prescribing medications. Even if these treatments can be applied to adolescents, we do not know whether they are as effective for adolescents as for adults. You should therefore carefully question your doctor in terms of how she might apply these findings gathered from adults with bulimia to your adolescent.

INTENSIVE TREATMENTS

Unfortunately, a significant minority of those with anorexia, and many with bulimia, who are critically ill may require a period of inpatient treatment. Inpatient, day-patient, and residential treatments all have one thing in common: Your child receives treatment at a health care facility, either full time or for a large portion of each day. This usually means that you will not be involved in the day-to-day management of your child's eating problems, although the treatment team may work with you to varying degrees, depending on the therapeutic approach of the facility. In this section, we discuss the scientific support available suggesting that intensive treatments such as inpatient hospital programs are helpful for eating disorders.

Many parents we've counseled have expressed confusion about the differences between inpatient, day-patient, and residential treatments. Inpatient treatment is usually indicated when someone is in urgent need of weight restoration or has other acute medical problems associated with an eating disorder. Once these problems are addressed, many patients are transferred to a day-patient program. Here the patient is further encouraged to gain weight and eliminate other disordered eating behaviors, but gets to go home every evening and weekend. Finally, residential treatment looks a lot like an inpatient program but usually serves the purpose of accommodating those patients who may have "failed" other treatments and require quite a lengthy stay (up to several months) to help them get back on track. In essence, though, there are perhaps more similarities than differences between these three intensive treatment approaches.

All three forms of intensive treatment attempt to, first, restore weight and stop or significantly decrease binge eating and purging, if these are concerns. Second, the programs aim to help the patients learn to manage continuing health on their own and assist the patients through a variety of forms of psychotherapy to reach an improved understanding of why they developed an eating disorder or are maintaining one. All the while, the patients are supported

and encouraged through psychotherapeutic meetings in a group format and, often, in family therapy settings as well.

However, in addition to providing psychological insight-oriented therapies, it's fair to say that many such programs follow a behavioral approach. What this means (again, whether in an inpatient, day-patient, or residential setting) is that a primary focus of day-to-day activity will be on eating and disordered eating behaviors. In practice, this means that for those who are severely underweight, independence will initially be restricted so as to conserve energy; as they gain weight, they will also be released from the restriction of bed rest or may start participating in a supervised but limited exercise program. For those with unremitting binge eating or purging or overexercising, close observation by professional staff is designed to prevent those behaviors, with the idea that disrupting the chronic practice of these behaviors will help to reduce their recurrence. Overall, these prohibitions and observations by professional staff are decreased as the patient demonstrates improvement. The idea is that you gain greater freedom, in terms of both independence and food decisions, as you return to normal weight and eating behaviors. These activities take place in all three of these treatment settings, with the difference often being the length of stay and the number of hours spent in the treatment setting from day to day, as well as the extent to which and the speed at which independence is encouraged and permitted.

Several investigators have published reports on the effectiveness of hospitalization in the treatment of anorexia, but there are no comparable studies for bulimia. In most cases, specialist units are quite successful at refeeding patients and restoring a healthy body weight. For example, one study found overall clinical improvement in the 16 participating patients after an average of 3 months of inpatient treatment using a behavioral approach, whereby the patient gains more freedom/rewards as weight increases. Also, using a behavioral approach, another researcher found that 70% of patients showed continued improvement at 3-year follow-up when treated for a period of 6 months as inpatients. However, a large study conducted in the United Kingdom of 167 adolescents with anorexia who were randomly treated with a 16-week hospital stay or

two forms of outpatient therapy found no differences in outcomes between the groups, except that the cost of treatment was much greater in those who were treated in the hospital. This means that for most adolescents with anorexia, an inpatient treatment program is not more helpful than outpatient treatment. This does not mean hospital treatment is not needed for some adolescents with anorexia. That is, those who are medically unstable and those who struggle to make weight gains in outpatient treatment should be in the hospital. However, the study strongly suggests that inpatient treatment is not necessarily the first step parents should consider in treating their child. In another recent study, Sloane Madden and colleagues in Sydney, Australia randomized adolescents with anorexia nervosa to receive a short medical hospitalization for stabilization of low heart rates and low blood pressure or a longer medical hospitalization aimed at weight restoration. At discharge, all participants received FBT. At the end of one year of treatment and one year of follow-up, there were no differences in clinical outcomes, rates of readmission to hospital, or use of other therapies between the two groups. These authors conclude that a short medical hospitalization followed by FBT is as effective clinically as restoring adolescents to near normal weight before starting FBT. However, overall, the costs of treatment were much lower for the group that received the shorter hospital treatment.

These studies together indicate that inpatient treatment is likely to result in short-term clinical improvement, but the longer-term benefits are uncertain. It's important to keep in mind, though, that what happens in study settings is often very different from what happens in reality. For instance, a study protocol may allow for relatively lengthy treatment stays, whereas in practice you may find that your insurance company will pay for only a few weeks of treatment.

One of the discouraging aspects of inpatient treatment is that within a few short weeks of discharge many patients promptly lose the weight they painstakingly gained, even when they have had months of intensive treatment. For instance, one researcher who reviewed inpatient treatments reported that at least 40% of hospitalized patients are readmitted at least once. Further, this report

indicates that eating-disordered patients spent *more* time in the hospital with each succeeding admission than any other patient group with nonorganic disorders. In other words, many patients, especially those with anorexia, seem to spend an inordinate amount of their young lives in hospitals. We've pointed out that for many patients inpatient stays are, unfortunately, necessary. Several recent studies have found that adolescents who are treated with FBT typically require fewer admissions and have shorter stays than those who received other therapies. To us this finding suggests that for adolescents, in particular, it is likely best to try to help them at home, with their family and friends available to support them.

WHAT CONCLUSIONS SHOULD YOU DRAW ABOUT THE TREATMENTS AVAILABLE FOR EATING DISORDERS?

The results from the empirical data so far available about all the treatments reviewed in this chapter fall within the modest-to-moderate range, and treatment studies to date are few. Still, several clear guidelines have emerged from these studies, as well as from our own experience with patients.

First, it's of paramount importance that you act early when your child shows signs of an eating disorder. Please don't hesitate or worry that you'll be seen as overreacting or interfering. Detecting and treating any illness in its early stages is invariably more favorable than waiting for the symptoms to set in and become more intractable.

Second, your involvement, especially in outpatient treatments, should be the rule and not the exception. Although you may feel ill equipped to tackle an illness as severe as an eating disorder, this concern is usually unfounded. Eating disorders are complex illnesses, and successful treatment often requires the dedicated efforts of a team of professionals (psychologists, psychiatrists, pediatricians, and nutritionists). Each of these professionals will help with your adolescent's treatment program, and each will address an important part of the problem. You should be able to count on the

expertise of these professionals, but they should also recognize the important contribution you can make. No matter how your child came to have an eating disorder, as a parent you know your child best and you spend more time with your son or daughter than any of the professionals on the treatment team. You not only have a lot to offer; your participation is critical because your teenager will be under your supervision more than anyone else's.

Third, early and careful attention to medical problems associated with eating disorders is critical. Too often, energetic attempts at addressing the causes of the illness are pursued prior to taking care of the life-threatening symptoms of an eating disorder. If your parental instinct tells you your child is in trouble, but the professional you consult wants to explore why your daughter won't eat or why your son is throwing up his dinner every night, insist on immediate attention to the urgent problem at hand: restoring your child's health. If you and the practitioner can't agree on that course of action, you need to find another expert (see Chapter 10). Most clinicians will, of course, have your teenager's best interests at heart and should be willing to work with you in returning your child to health. In the next two chapters, we discuss just how you can make sure that you're productively involved in your child's treatment, regardless of the specific treatment received.

FOR MORE INFORMATION

Agras, W. S., J. Lock, H. Brandt, et al., Comparison of 2 Family Therapies for Adolescent Anorexia Nervosa: A Randomized Trial, *JAMA Psychiatry, 71*(11), 1279–1286.

Andersen, A., W. Bowers, and K. Evans, Inpatient Treatment of Anorexia Nervosa, in D. M. Garner and P. E. Garfinkel, Editors, *Handbook of Treatment for Eating Disorders, Second Edition,* 1997. New York: Guilford Press, pp. 327–353.

Attia, E., C. Haiman, B. T. Walsh, et al., Does Fluoxetine Augment the Inpatient Treatment of Anorexia Nervosa?, *American Journal of Psychiatry,* 1998, *152,* 1070–1072.

Beumont, P., C. Beumont, S. Touyz, et al., Nutritional Counseling and Supervised Exercise, in D. M. Garner and P. E. Garfinkel, Editors,

Handbook of Treatment for Eating Disorders, Second Edition, 1997. New York: Guilford Press, pp. 178–187.

Garfinkel, P., and B. T. Walsh, Drug Therapies, in D. M. Garner and P. E. Garfinkel, Editors, *Handbook of Treatment for Eating Disorders, Second Edition*, 1997. New York: Guilford Press, pp. 372–382.

Gowers, S. G., A. Clark, C. Roberts, et al., Clinical Effectiveness of Treatments for Anorexia Nervosa in Adolescents: Randomised Controlled Trial, *British Journal of Psychiatry*, 2007, *191*, 427–435.

Hagman, J., J. Gralla, E. Sigel, et al., A Double-Blind, Placebo-Controlled Study of Risperidone for the Treatment of Adolescents and Young Adults with Anorexia Nervosa: A Pilot Study, *American Journal of Child and Adolescent Psychiatry*, 2011, *50*, 915–924.

Kaplan, A., and M. Olmsted, Partial Hospitalization, in D. M. Garner and P. E. Garfinkel, Editors, *Handbook of Treatment for Eating Disorders, Second Edition*, 1997. New York: Guilford Press, pp. 354–360.

Madden, S., J. Miskovic-Wheatley, A. Wallis, et al., A Randomized Controlled Trial of Inpatient Hospitalization for Anorexia Nervosa in Medically Unstable Adolescents, *Psychological Medicine*, 2014, *44*, 1053–1064.

Robinson, P., Day Treatments, in J. Treasure, U. Schmidt, and E. van Furth, Editors, *Handbook of Eating Disorders*, 2003. Chichester, UK: Wiley, pp. 333–348.

Touyz, S., and P. Beumont, Behavioral Treatment to Promote Weight Gain in Anorexia Nervosa, in D. M. Garner and P. E. Garfinkel, Editors, *Handbook of Treatment for Eating Disorders, Second Edition*, 1997. New York: Guilford Press, pp. 361–371.

MAKING TREATMENT WORK

How to Solve Everyday Problems
to Help Your Child Recover

CHAPTER 7

Taking Charge of Change

How to Apply Family-Based Treatment
to Help with Eating Disorders

"We've tried everything. We tried letting her decide. We tried to force her to eat. We threatened her. We've punished her. Nothing works."

This is what we typically hear from parents who have just been told they will be taking direct responsibility for getting their child to return to normal eating patterns. If you're involved in a form of treatment that asks you to take charge of normalizing eating behavior for your adolescent—such as FBT—you may initially be perplexed and doubtful and perhaps even frustrated by the request. Parents tell us they don't know *how* to get their son or daughter to eat—either enough or regularly. Naturally, this is a source of exasperation and increasing frustration for them. It can also feel as if the situation is creating a great rift between the parents and the child who doesn't want to eat or who wants to purge. Many parents end up feeling as if they're fighting not just this illness but the child they're trying desperately to help as well.

In this chapter and the next, we discuss the range of ways you can become practically involved in helping your adolescent with

various problems related to eating disorders. This chapter focuses on the FBT approach, which informs much of this book's basic premise, wherein you are asked to be *directly responsible* for changing eating-related behaviors at home. If your daughter or son is receiving a different kind of treatment that does not ask you to take this responsibility—or even discourages it—you can and should still be involved in your child's return to health; you'll find suggestions on how to do so within the other forms of therapy used for eating disorders (described in Chapter 6) in Chapter 8.

Whether the abnormal eating pattern is related to anorexia or bulimia, you will be surprised by how successful you can be in helping your child without resorting to threats, punishments, or berating. The leverage you have as parents that no one else has is your love and commitment to your children. This is powerful leverage.

You are naturally anxious about your child's health and welfare, and this may make you unsure about what to do. A certain degree of anxiety is a good thing—it helps propel you to action—but too much anxiety can overwhelm and immobilize you. There is no denying that finding ways to help your child eat normally is challenging. You may try things that don't work well. For example, some parents try to "sneak" butter or other fat into foods. This sounds like a good idea from a nutritional perspective, but it usually leads to the child's distrusting you. We have found it better to be very clear and specific about expectations as well as very direct in stating them. This is just one example of the principles we can offer to guide you in coming up with your own ways to help your teenager begin to eat healthily again. Throughout this chapter our goal will be to help you gain confidence in your ability to handle this problem, as you have handled so many other dilemmas of parenthood, thereby alleviating anxiety.

Excessive anxiety only makes parents hesitant, which leads to another problem. Your lack of confidence and uncertainty will often be perceived as a lack of resolve. This encourages your child to resist you even more because of the hold the eating disorder has on her. As we said in Chapter 1, don't hesitate. Act now.

A FEW FUNDAMENTAL PRINCIPLES

As with many behavioral problems in children, some fundamental guidelines will apply here. First, come up with an approach to helping your child eat normally that you can carry out. It's not much help to say you will eat all meals with your son if you're working all day and can't possibly be there. Second, be reasonable in your expectations of both yourself and your child for making behavior changes. Changing behaviors will take some time; prepare to be patient. Third, use strategies that respect your child, but guard against succumbing to pressures to let up on your expectations. This means remembering that your child has an illness and is not fully in control of her thinking and actions. In addition, it means being sympathetic and caring rather than critical and punishing. Fourth, make sure you have support, both from other family members and friends and from professionals, because this is going to be difficult at times. If the challenge were not difficult, this kind of action on your part would not be warranted to begin with. Finally, make sure you don't give up too soon. Sometimes early success leads to lowering your guard too soon, allowing the eating problem to resurface.

When you're involved in FBT, the following specific principles will apply:

1. Work with experts who know how to help you.
2. Work together as a family.
3. Don't blame your child or yourself for the problems you're having. Blame the illness.
4. Focus on the problem before you.
5. Don't debate with your child about eating- or weight-related concerns.
6. Know when to begin backing off.
7. Take care of yourself. You are your child's best hope.

The rest of this chapter is dedicated to examining each of these principles in turn. To illustrate, throughout the chapter we describe the experiences of many of the families we've helped treat,

in addition to following 15-year-old Cindy, as she and her family take up the challenge of fighting anorexia nervosa together.

> Cindy was a very focused teenager. Her father, Jorge, was an accountant, and her mother, Susan, was a real estate agent. She also had a 17-year-old brother, Todd, who attended the same high school. Cindy had always been an excellent student, though she was also somewhat shy socially. She began dieting when she was a freshman because she felt she could "improve" herself if she was more fit and healthy. As she lost weight, some girlfriends commented that she looked "really good," and this made Cindy feel more accepted and liked. However, in a few months Cindy's parents became alarmed at her weight loss. She now weighed 80 pounds at a height of 5 feet even. When her parents took her to her pediatrician, she referred Cindy and her parents to a family therapist, who used family treatment that asked Jorge and Susan to take initial responsibility for refeeding Cindy.

WORK WITH EXPERTS WHO KNOW
HOW TO HELP YOU

We discussed the importance of expert evaluation and treatment in Chapter 1. This is particularly important if you're going to be in charge of directly changing eating-disordered behaviors in your home. By now you know that understanding eating disorders is not a simple matter. So, the more experience your expert has had in helping families with these problems, the deeper his understanding of the complexities of these disorders. And the deeper the expert's understanding, the more assistance you're likely to receive in refining your own understanding of why you may be having difficulty changing your child's eating-related behavior.

Although we strongly believe you have the skills to help your son or daughter with an eating disorder, applying those skills effectively usually requires help. An expert consults with you about what you're doing and advises you to examine what works and doesn't work. An expert with a great deal of experience can offer advice on

how to improve your current efforts or what to consider when you feel you've hit a brick wall.

At the same time, an expert can help you better understand your child's thinking. This is important, because at first it will appear to your child that the therapist is "on your side" and against the teen. By helping you better understand the illness, the therapist demonstrates an understanding of your child's experience to the child, inspiring greater trust and cooperation with treatment over time.

The expert therapist will also understand that every family is different and has its own style of self-management and problem solving. An experienced therapist will be able to identify the common threads that tie together all families struggling with eating disorders without imposing one-size-fits-all recommendations. The details regarding a therapist's former patients and the examples we offer in this chapter won't necessarily be completely transferable to your own family. That's where your therapist comes in. The therapist is there to help you make these principles pertinent and particular to your family.

WORK TOGETHER AS A FAMILY

In our experience, parents have indeed tried many things in their efforts to help their son or daughter change the self-destructive eating patterns of anorexia or bulimia; usually, however, they haven't tried any tactic consistently, confidently, and with clear commitment from both parents (see Chapter 9).

> After their first family therapy meeting, Jorge and Susan, parents of Cindy, felt overwhelmed and bewildered. The therapist had told them to find a way to make Cindy eat. Jorge sat down with Cindy and asked her what she would eat. Cindy said she would eat her rice and steamed vegetables. Susan said she wanted her to eat a piece of chicken. Cindy refused. Susan told her she must eat it. This led to a shouting match that ended when Cindy left the table without eating anything.

When Cindy's therapist met with the family next, she listened carefully to what had happened. First, she asked her parents if the two of them agreed that Cindy needed to eat the chicken as well as the rice and vegetables. They agreed about that. However, Jorge said he couldn't stand all the yelling that went on and was happy to see Cindy eat anything. It was apparent to the therapist that although Jorge and Susan agreed about what should be done, they did not have the same threshold for what that meant. The therapist explained that it was just this kind of "gap" in the plan that allowed the eating disorder to slip through and reduce their effectiveness. The therapist suggested that Susan and Jorge work together to refine their plan to include what the threshold for eating enough would be and what they would do to enforce it.

The next day Jorge and Susan went out for coffee. They agreed that Cindy had to eat chicken in addition to rice and vegetables. They also agreed that she would need to eat one breast, but they would allow her to choose how it should be prepared. They, not she, would prepare it, however.

What Jorge and Susan did was take a *first step* toward identifying a solution to breaking the hold anorexia had on Cindy. There would be many more steps in their struggle. There are many ways that parents can *seem* to be working together, but when push comes to shove, they are not. Often they can even be working at cross-purposes. This scenario is so common we've devoted an entire chapter to it (Chapter 9). For now, though, it's important to realize how critical it is that you and your child's other parent or any other adult in the household present a united front in trying to reestablish normal eating behavior.

Dinah's mother diligently made her eat her meals, but her father, who believed that allowing Dinah to exercise would help motivate her to eat, took her running or to the gym most nights, effectively undermining any weight gain as she used up more calories with this exercise than she took in.

Neither of Dinah's parents was "wrong," but because they didn't connect the two parts of the plan, they were not successful in working together.

Haddiyah's mother resented doing any direct refeeding and was angry about it, though she professed to her husband that she was behind the effort. Haddiyah's mother would "be around" during mealtimes but did not really observe to see if Haddiyah was actually eating. Haddiyah knew this and easily slipped most of her food into the trash. Thus, it appeared to everyone that Haddiyah's lack of progress was inexplicable.

Again, neither of Haddiyah's parents was wrong. They just hadn't really agreed to the treatment approach. It turned out that Haddiyah's mother felt that her husband had bullied her into this kind of treatment and she had not wished to confront him directly.

Tammy's father had abandoned the family when she was just a baby. There was no other extended family nearby either, so Tammy and her mother were very close. In the case of Tammy's mother, the conflict was with herself. On one hand, she felt she had to keep her daughter from purging every day, but on the other, she felt so terrible about "watching and controlling" her teenage daughter that she found herself giving in and "ignoring" the obvious signs that Tammy was purging.

Tammy's mother's mixed impulses are very understandable. As we've discussed, the person with an eating disorder often demonstrates perfectly normal thinking in most settings—except where food and weight are concerned. Parents have described mealtimes as similar to watching a "fog" roll over their child's personality and thinking. The teenager appears perfectly normal, but when expected to consume food the parents have designated as appropriate, anger, resentment, and bizarre behaviors emerge. It's very confusing to see your child thinking and acting rationally and then becoming irrational, highly emotional, or withdrawn at mealtime. This confusion may lead to uncertainty and ambivalence about your efforts to refeed your child or prevent binge eating and purging. Like Tammy's mother, you may end up hesitant to do what you need to do. Unfortunately, hesitancy leaves room for eating-disordered thinking to slip through and establish a firmer foothold, as we mentioned earlier. Feelings like those Tammy's mother experienced undermine the success of either taking control and intervening or

identifying a different treatment approach (see the next chapter) that might be more consistent with a strong dislike of monitoring the child with the eating disorder.

Don't Exclude Siblings

Your other children are another resource that can help defeat eating disorders. Your own brothers and sisters are the people with whom you will likely have the longest relationship in your life, and this is just as true for your child. Whether or not they show it, siblings are usually affected when one of their own has an eating disorder. They are sometimes aware of the problem before you are. However, they often feel confused, burdened by a mixed obligation to both protect and help their sibling. They can also be angry at the brother or sister with an eating disorder for "causing all these problems" for the family.

In therapy, siblings can help *support* your son or daughter with an eating disorder. First, just by coming to treatment, siblings express their interest and concern. True, at first they may come only because you force them to. However, over time they also benefit from seeing how the family together can be a resource in overcoming a problem, in this case an eating disorder. Younger siblings, ages 5–6, may not understand all that is going on, but the therapist will ask them to do something kind for their sister or brother—such as make a card or do a chore that would ordinarily be done by that sibling. Older siblings may take their brother or sister on an outing to help distract their sibling from feeling miserable about eating and gaining weight or to prevent the sibling from purging. In these ways, and many others, siblings can help make the process of changing problematic eating behaviors in the home easier.

Of course, at times siblings can be unhelpful. Monica and Delphine were twins who had always competed with one another. When Monica began to diet and lost a little weight, Delphine had to take it further. When Delphine developed anorexia, Monica was anything but supportive. She felt she had to be an "even better anorexic" than her sister. In this instance, the continued competition over weight and appearance made it impossible to see the whole family together.

Instead, the therapist worked with just the parents and supported each daughter separately while the parents worked to help both of them. Sometimes, brothers can continue to be insulting about weight and ridicule their sisters, though they usually learn to stop. It's helpful to understand what really lies behind these behaviors. Is it jealousy? Fear or worry? Or is it evidence of an unsalvageable relationship? Your therapist should help you figure out what's behind the behavior and how best to deal with it. In any event, as a parent, you need to act to stop this type of behavior because it will undermine your success.

DON'T BLAME YOUR CHILD OR YOURSELF

It's very difficult not to hold your son or daughter responsible when what you see before you is a child who appears to be obstinately refusing to eat. However, just as we know it's not helpful for you to feel blamed for causing an eating disorder (see Chapter 3), it is clearly also not helpful to blame your child. Remembering that your child has a life-threatening illness that distorts her thinking and experience about her weight and shape can sometimes keep your own thinking clearer about the situation. Still, this is tricky because, of course, your child is there in front of you, and it is her voice saying "no" and her refusal to adhere to reasonable eating behaviors that is causing the problem. However, she is also clearly miserable and cannot please you or herself in this dilemma. To explain this further, let's return to Cindy's family.

> At their next meeting Cindy's parents complained to the therapist about how much resistance to eating Cindy was putting up and how angry they were at her. The therapist expressed sympathy for the difficulty they were having but, by drawing on the board a Venn diagram of intersecting circles, like the one presented in Chapter 2, reminded them just how differently Cindy was seeing the world through the lens of anorexia nervosa. Then she reminded them that it usually wasn't helpful to blame Cindy for her preoccupation with weight loss. She had an illness that kept her from seeing things the same way others did. The

therapist helped the family see how much her anorexia was over-shadowing who Cindy really was—she couldn't participate in her school or social life, all her time was spent on worrying about her weight and food, and she had completely lost her sense of humor. However, the therapist noted that understanding her plight was one thing, but allowing starvation to continue was another. She once again charged them with finding a way to help Cindy eat and fight anorexia. Keeping the illness separate from Cindy was more difficult than it seemed. This was hard on Susan, who still struggled to stop seeing Cindy's eating disorder as "willful," but she would try. Jorge also agreed that no matter how hard it was to listen to Cindy's wailing, he would not leave the room.

When dinnertime came, Susan and Jorge put the meat they expected Cindy to eat on her plate. Cindy immediately got up and left the table. Calmly, they followed her to her room, brought her dinner with them, and sat next to her on the bed. They gently explained that they knew this was hard on her, they loved her, and they would be there to help her. They sat there for about an hour, and Cindy still refused to eat. Susan began to get angry, and Jorge asked if perhaps she might want to take a break and come back in a minute. Susan thought this was a good idea and did so. Cindy now began to cry and claimed that her dinner was ruined. Jorge explained that he would heat it up and she could eat it. Cindy ate a few bites and climbed into bed. Her parents explained that they would not give up on her and were happy she had eaten some of her dinner with them. Her mother said, "I know how hard it was for you to eat that because anorexia is so powerful. We'll keep trying."

It's important to understand that Cindy and her family were just beginning to work on her anorexia together. At this point, Jorge and Susan had determined that their support and encouragement were the correct response to Cindy's minimal consumption *at this meal*. This does not mean they would allow Cindy to continue to eat too little food to regain weight or even sustain her. An important aspect of fighting an eating disorder is establishing consequences for not eating, as discussed later in this chapter. Setting consequences not only serves as an incentive for the child to eat but also gives parents another way to respond to not eating other than getting angry and falling prey to the instinct to blame the child for the illness.

It makes perfect sense to hold a healthy teenager responsible for her own behavior. It even makes sense to hold an eating-disordered adolescent responsible for behavior that has nothing to do with weight or food. But when it comes to eating and exercise patterns in a child with an eating disorder, it's critical to remember to *separate the illness from the child*. No matter how rational she may sound, no matter how committed she is to her beliefs about eating and weight, your child is not really responsible for what she says and does with regard to food if she has an eating disorder. When you talk to her about these subjects, it's the eating disorder that answers you. And it's the eating disorder you should designate as your foe, never your son or daughter. Many parents naturally have trouble remembering that "No, I won't eat" is not coming from the same source as "No, I don't think I should have to have a curfew." A thorough understanding of the cognitive distortions described in Chapter 5 can, however, help you keep it clear in your mind that you're struggling with an illness rather than with your son or daughter.

> Mike's father went into a tirade whenever he found evidence that his son was still throwing up. When Mike's dad got angry, he became critical and hostile and Mike felt as though he were being attacked. This led to Mike's increased efforts to hide the fact that he still hadn't completely stopped purging. This made it hard for his family to see the progress he was making or to see just where he was having continued difficulties. This meant they couldn't help him as effectively.

Anger can throw you off and make it harder for you to know that the illness is the problem and not your child. When helping your child eat, anger will definitely interfere with your success.

Another way you can separate the illness from the child is to keep in mind that your child does not really choose to be ill, even if it appears that way. The child with anorexia nervosa may have little motivation to recover, but it's the illness that is so recalcitrant, rather than your child. Certainly, purging is frustrating because it appears to many people as wasteful and dirty. However, most children who purge their food feel trapped into doing so by their worries and anxieties about weight and have become caught in a chronic cycle

that they don't know how to break out of. Keeping these facts in mind may help you contain your anger. It may also help if you try to remember that it's hard for your child to perceive that your anger is directed at the illness and not at her for being willful, ungrateful, difficult, and frustrating.

Still, your anger about having to take on this problem is understandable. You certainly don't deserve this—and neither does your child. To keep your anger from either overwhelming you or being vented on your child, it's important to recognize the signs that this may be happening. You may notice that your patience is short, that you're jittery, that your tone of voice is tinged with sarcasm, or that you're irritated by things that you usually would let pass. When you find this is so, take a break. Find someone to talk to. Get away. Otherwise, your anger can undo much of the good work you've done.

As we've pointed out, there's not much evidence that you're to blame for your child's eating disorder. However, there is growing evidence that you can be part of the solution, regardless of the cause of the eating disorder, but only if you aren't feeling guilty and powerless. Feeling guilty is especially problematic when you're trying to get started. Blaming yourself leads to a lot of second guessing and hesitation on your part, which gives the eating disorder room to maneuver and slip through.

> Keshia felt sure that her own weight struggles and dieting were the cause of the bulimia that her 15-year-old daughter was struggling with. She felt that it was duplicitous to ask her daughter to eat regularly when she herself had for so many years dieted while her weight yo-yoed.

Keshia had a point—it probably wouldn't help for her to be dieting or worrying about her own weight when her daughter was struggling. But there was a difference. Keshia had never developed an eating disorder, whereas her daughter had. By blaming herself and holding back on doing what she could to help her daughter, Keshia was actually allowing bulimia to get a firmer grip on her child. Their family therapist pointed out that Keshia was hesitating and not following through on monitoring her daughter because of guilt. This was ultimately more harmful than anything she might have

done before, because now her daughter needed her help. Keshia decided that even if she felt guilty, she would not let it interfere with helping her daughter. She found that helping her daughter actually lessened her guilt, especially as her daughter also began to respond.

FOCUS ON THE PROBLEM BEFORE YOU

As we suggested in Chapter 3, it's easy to become distracted and to be led down the primrose path if you spend a lot of time trying to figure out *why* your child developed an eating disorder. But there are many other ways to lose your way as well. Staying focused on what the problem is—disordered eating behaviors and beliefs—is challenging. To stay focused, it's imperative that you make changing disordered eating *the* priority, be available to intervene to change behaviors, establish a regular pattern of eating, and figure out ways to expand food choices, whether your child has anorexia or bulimia. At the same time, it's important to determine when it's reasonable to allow exercise, to prevent binge eating and purging, and to know when things are going well enough that you can begin to step back and hand control over eating back to your child. Let's examine each of these in turn to see how to stay focused.

Make Changing Disordered Eating Your Top Priority

To make changing disordered eating *the* priority sounds easy enough, but in practice families find this is harder than expected. In most families, plenty of distractions can and do interfere. The demands of work, household chores, needs of other family members, and so forth, frequently command attention. For example, Laura's family was torn between her needs and those of her two siblings. As parents, they felt it was unfair to pay such disproportionate attention to Laura and her problems. Well, it was unfair, but Laura was so malnourished that her life and future hung in the balance. Their therapist helped Laura's parents to accept the fact that this extra focus on Laura was necessary, but also to see that it was *time limited*.

Thirteen-year-old Danny's father was torn between his son's needs and his demanding job. As CEO of a large corporation, Danny's father traveled out of state almost weekly. Perhaps because Danny's mother was free to stay home and help their son fight anorexia, his father continued to make work his first priority. The family's therapist quickly stepped in and made a persuasive case for the need for the whole family to make changing Danny's disordered eating the number-one priority. Danny's father was able to reschedule many of his upcoming trips and delegate his role to others in the company.

The demands of many professions can be compelling. And unlike Danny's family, many families will suffer financially when the parents take time off to help their child eat normally again. But for the sake of a child's continued survival and return to health, parents who take responsibility for their child's eating behaviors have to put that goal above all others. In addition, making this kind of intensive effort may appear costly at first, but in the long run it can prevent the need for even more expensive services like hospital or residential treatment.

It's your therapist's task to help you keep this priority in focus and in your sights. You may be tempted to stray off into other "interesting issues," such as why the eating disorder arose in the first place, or to find "unavoidable obstacles" to taking charge, but these diversions will only keep you from the work you need to do at this point—getting your child to eat normally.

Be Available

By now you're undoubtedly getting the picture: You and/or your spouse will likely need to *be available* for all mealtimes and snacks to monitor eating at least for several weeks. This is a big adjustment for many parents, who have not been present for breakfast and lunch, or even dinner in some cases, sometimes for many years, because of work or school schedules. Accepting this requirement means that you will need to make adjustments to your personal and occupational lives. If the demands on your schedule seem onerous, go back to Chapter 1 and remind yourself that just because an eating

disorder is a psychiatric illness does not mean that it is not serious. As we've shown, we see these illnesses as being on a par with any physical illness. They deserve to be given the same attention you would provide for a child after surgery, an accident, or another serious medical problem.

> Although it was a difficult decision, Jorge and Susan both took several weeks off from work to help Cindy. They discussed the pros and cons of this measure but ultimately decided that using sick leave and vacation time this way was necessary, as they now recognized how seriously ill Cindy was. Jorge had a harder time at first, and his boss was less sympathetic than Susan's. Jorge took some information about eating disorders and the treatment they were using to his boss. This helped her appreciate the gravity of Cindy's illness and Jorge's concern, as well as his need to be away from work more.

Don't assume you won't be able to negotiate a fair arrangement with your employer. Taking a brief medical leave is a good idea, because presenting a unified front at all meals is potentially most powerful, but in practical terms you may have to compromise. Figure out how you can adjust your schedule to allow you to be present at as many meals as possible. Maybe you can both plan to be on hand at breakfast and dinner but will have to alternate days off work to be present for lunch and snack times. A common solution in two-parent families is to divide up mealtimes, but this does leave each of you to battle the problem alone at different meals. As we discuss in Chapter 9, this can create a lot of opportunities for parents to drift into doing things differently at their respective mealtimes with the child, with the result that the eating disorder spots a chance to slip through the crack in the unified front. This is why we strongly encourage you to try to figure out from the start how both of you can be there at all meals, at least for the first few weeks.

If you have to split up the task, consider things such as whether one of you is more of a "morning person" than the other; in that case the early riser could be assigned the job of making sure that breakfast is eaten. If only one of you can be available during the day, that one could go to school at snack and lunch times. Some parents

have arranged for a school counselor or nurse to have lunch with their son or daughter, but this is usually appropriate only after some time has passed, once you have a plan that is generally working and you are getting sufficient cooperation from your child to try this (there is more on figuring out when you can step back at the end of this chapter).

If you don't have a spouse, it may be important to enlist the help of another adult relative. This can be effective even when two parents are available, as it was with Sarah, whose parents both worked but whose grandmother—who was the main cook in the house in any event—was available at all mealtimes.

It may seem that your just being present won't make a big difference in terms of your child's eating, but it will. Being there provides both emotional and structural support as well as encouragement to eat. Of course, your child won't benefit from this support and encouragement unless she too is present for all mealtimes. This sometimes means a leave from school or home study for several weeks, taken as a medical leave. This is often the preferred strategy, as it was in Cindy's case.

> Susan asked Cindy's pediatrician to write a note that would excuse Cindy from school for several weeks because of her medical and psychiatric fragility. Because this was clearly appropriate, the pediatrician provided the note and Cindy's schoolwork was brought to her by a home teacher on a weekly basis. Cindy fought this arrangement at first, claiming she would miss too much work. Her parents pointed out that at this point her health, not her schoolwork, was the priority. Although they also supported Cindy's academic achievements, they said good grades would be irrelevant if she did not recover from anorexia nervosa. This plan allowed Cindy and the family to focus on eating rather than on the social and academic pressures at school.

As noted earlier, sometimes parents are able to attend school during the lunch hour or work with the school to develop a flexible schedule for a few weeks to permit eating to take place at home. Understandably, most adolescents don't like their parents showing

up at school to eat with them. It is, however, a reminder of the cost of the illness to them that they readily appreciate, so sometimes it's an additional motivation to the child to return to normal eating. Yet being at home for all meals can send a clear message about the importance of your child's health relative to academic work at this point in time, making it clear what the first priority is. You'll have to decide which will be a more powerful incentive for your child and help her make the needed changes.

Although this example focuses on the need for monitoring eating in the case of anorexia, it's just as important that regular eating occur for children with bulimia or binge-eating disorder, as we have stressed; otherwise, they will be more likely to binge eat and then purge. So, your help in making sure that eating is monitored throughout the day is important for anorexia, bulimia, and binge-eating disorder.

Besides both parents and the eating-disordered teenager, siblings and other family members living at home need to be available for meals too. Having the whole family eat together as much as possible definitely makes a difference, because that way your son or daughter knows that everyone is trying to help her. As parents, you help by making sure the right foods and the right amounts of food are prepared and eaten. Siblings help to alleviate the tension and stress of trying to eat and contribute to making mealtimes more normal. They also distract the eating-disordered child, to some extent, from thinking only about what she has to eat. They can also support her if she becomes angry or upset about your demands that she eat.

Seventeen-year-old Todd had had a relatively close relationship with his sister Cindy when they were younger, but he was pretty busy with his own life now. He resented having to be home for dinner at first. His coach told him he might have to leave his basketball team if he missed too many practices, which often stretched into the dinner hour. Jorge and Susan worked hard to accommodate Todd's schedule because they thought he was important to helping Cindy. At first Cindy ignored Todd, but when she saw that he made such a big effort to be there, she turned to him more often for support when she felt overwhelmed by fighting with her parents.

Ballet lessons, soccer, and friends, among many other distractions, are likely to beckon and take your other children away from the table at mealtimes, so you will have to make a strong case for why everyone needs to be present and call on the assistance of the therapist to support your request. We stress that this need to be together for most meals will not last forever, but that it's important now because a member of the family is ill and needs everyone's help. Usually, when brothers and sisters realize the urgency of getting their sibling to start eating normally or to stop purging, they acquiesce. But you should still be prepared to find ways to accommodate their needs too. One family excused their other children from family dinners two nights during the week and in this way helped them be more supportive and less resentful of helping their sister with anorexia. It will be up to you to determine what's possible, keeping in mind the option of leaving a sibling out of the plan for a while if that child is so resentful about giving up the time or certain activities that his being at the table is completely counterproductive. Even in this case, though, you should continue to encourage all other siblings to participate. Many eventually do come around. For example, Darren, a 10-year-old boy whose sister Terry had anorexia, persisted in teasing and calling her names, but he started to change his tune after his parents recognized how jealous he was of the time they were spending with Terry and made an effort to address his needs as well.

This is a common problem, especially with younger siblings, who initially feel anxious and slighted because of the focus on a sibling with an eating disorder. It can be tough on parents to find a way to take care of all the needs of their children at once, but often, just spending a little focused time with the unaffected siblings helps to reduce tension and jealousy.

Also be prepared for the fact that many siblings don't want to be involved because they simply feel they don't know how to help at first. Over time, if encouraged, they usually find ways to help that fit their relationships with their sibling.

At first, Todd was at a loss about what he could do to help. However, it soon became clearer that he didn't need to do anything

dramatic. So, each week he would find something "nice" to do for Cindy. For example, he would ask her to play a video game (one of her choosing) after dinner or watch a video with her. As Cindy improved, he volunteered to go places with her and asked her to his games. This was enough for both Cindy and Todd. By being at the meals, Todd served as a comforting presence for his sister and a reminder that she had a relationship with someone, other than with her eating disorder.

Establish a Regular Pattern of Eating

Once you, your child with the eating disorder, and the rest of your family are able to be present during most meals, the next challenge is to structure those mealtimes throughout the day. Whether the disorder is anorexia nervosa or bulimia nervosa, regular mealtimes are imperative. Again, this practice may diverge widely from what you were doing before the eating disorder developed. In our busy lives, meals are increasingly quick, eaten alone and at haphazard times. In our experience of interviewing families, it is not uncommon at the beginning of treatment for families to have no set pattern for eating. What was pretty normal for many of these families when their children were quite young—three meals and two or three snacks—is no longer the case. So it may be a struggle at first to set up this mealtime structure again, but it is essential. In the case of anorexia nervosa, the body needs regular feeding to sustain itself physically. However, in addition, as many of those with the illness will tell you, if they skip eating for several hours, the desire to continue fasting increases. For those with bulimia nervosa and binge-eating disorder, skipping meals entails another hazard—increasing the risk of binge eating because of increased hunger—so in both cases structured eating times promote normalizing eating patterns. In Cindy's case, Susan and Jorge established regular mealtimes. Breakfast was at about 7:00 A.M., morning snack at about 10:00 A.M., lunch at noon, afternoon snack at 3:00 P.M., dinner at 6:00 P.M., and nighttime snack at 9:30 P.M.

You may face some difficulties in trying to structure eating. The main obstacles are usually conflicting schedules for work, school, and other activities of siblings or parents. One mother, a

nurse who worked the night shift, requested a change of schedule for several months. A father who had a long morning commute prepared breakfast for his wife and son and then left it for them. In this way he could contribute to the morning meal even though he wasn't there. To understand the importance of a regular meal schedule, it may be helpful to remember when your child was an infant and you had to feed her at regular and close intervals to ensure her health and growth. For most parents that was an exhausting and demanding time, but it lasted for only a year or so in most cases. That's what has to happen again here. The difference is that back then she probably cried to let you know she was hungry. Now her illness keeps her from crying out.

Related to the difficulty in setting up a schedule, a common impediment is travel. Travel during the early part of treatment is not usually a good idea. Travel means a change of schedules, eating in restaurants, and often stressful social situations for your child, who may not be ready for it, as was the case with Tamara.

> Tamara wanted to go to New York to visit relatives. She knew this would be hard, and she promised to eat, but when she got to New York she found that she couldn't. She didn't trust the restaurants, and she was not yet ready to eat with anyone other than her mother and father. When she returned, she had lost 6 pounds and was close to needing to be hospitalized because her heart rate had dropped perilously low.

Even a trip to Disneyland designed as a reward for progress can cause problems because such a reward, if it occurs too early, can backfire. The success that earned the trip can quickly disappear because of the limited availability of "safe foods" and "safe situations" for someone who is still early in recovery. Nonetheless, some travel may be necessary. When it is, parents have discovered that they need to be prepared by taking along a range of foods in case they find themselves in situations where the choices are not good or restaurants are too challenging. Sometimes this means an extra suitcase, but being prepared is well worth the inconvenience overall.

Once your child is starting to recover, brief trips can be a way of evaluating progress and promoting new experiments with eating

that challenge the distorted assumptions about eating, food, and weight common to both anorexia and bulimia. Often a good way to start is to visit "safe" or "comfortable" local restaurants to see how eating goes in these environments.

In rare instances, though, traveling can be helpful even early in treatment. One family that had enormous difficulty being together because of work and school found that when they spent 2 weeks in Hawaii, they could actually be available and support their daughter for the first time. They didn't eat out much. Still, when they returned to the mainland, they saw the progress that had been made, and this helped motivate them to keep at it even when they were home.

Help Your Child with Anorexia or Avoidant/Restrictive Food Intake Disorder to Eat More

When recovering from anorexia nervosa or malnutrition related to ARFID, in contrast to bulimia nervosa or binge-eating disorder, one has to eat not only regularly but also a lot. This is usually the next challenge after you've established a pattern of eating: how to increase the amount your child is eating.

> Using their schedule, Jorge and Susan tried to determine what they thought Cindy should eat at each meal and snack. At first they asked the therapist to "tell us" what she should eat. The therapist said she was confident they would figure out how to feed Cindy. She pointed out that Cindy's older brother, Todd, was a healthy high school senior. The therapist explained that the reason she could not "tell them" what to do was that Jorge and Susan were the ones who had to carry out whatever plan they came up with. The therapist said she would be happy to advise them, based on her experience. She said sometimes parents didn't at first appreciate how much more their child with anorexia needed to eat. It was important to remember that gaining weight takes more eating than just maintaining weight.

Like Cindy's parents, you may find it a challenge to decide how much food to provide to your child with anorexia at each meal. Parents typically find themselves underestimating how much their

son or daughter needs to eat. We've often heard, "How can she not be gaining weight? She's eating more than I do!" But what parents sometimes fail to see is that a person with anorexia nervosa is actually burning food extremely rapidly, and not until rather large quantities are consumed is it possible to make headway.

Getting your child to eat more when she thinks she doesn't want to is at the heart of the challenge of recovering from anorexia. There are lots of ways parents succeed, but first they must set *clear expectations*. Veronica's parents set out her complete meals and snacks, based on the amounts they thought she needed to eat to recover her weight loss. They would put the food she was to eat on her plate. She had absolutely no choice in what she ate or the amount. Her parents knew from experience that offering Veronica a choice put her in a predicament she couldn't yet resolve: to give up anorexia or keep it. Veronica did not like this, of course, but another part of her was somewhat relieved that she didn't have to decide. If they make me eat, she thought, I can't be held responsible. This would temporarily relieve the anxiety and stress she felt about eating and gaining weight. Sarah's parents did it a little differently. They felt that Sarah could fill her plate and choose what to eat, but they also made it clear that if they thought what she chose was insufficient, they would add to it.

For some parents, offering limited choices works well, as long as they are the ones who decide whether the amount is sufficient. Of course, if just setting the right expectations and filling plates were enough, we probably would not need to write this book. In addition to providing enough food, you have to establish *clear consequences* for not eating.

> Veronica knew that if she did not eat, she would have to stay in her room on her bed, where she could read or do homework, but no other distractions would be permitted. She also knew that if she persisted in not eating, her parents would take her to the pediatrician, who would ultimately admit her to the hospital if her heart rate or her body temperature was too low, where she would have to stay until she was better. She knew that if that happened she would be made to eat there.

As we mentioned earlier when we talked about blame, setting consequences can help you avoid the trap of responding angrily to food refusal. This is why consequences should be established well ahead of time, certainly before the plate is on the table. Again, each family must decide on the best way to impose consequences.

> Sarah's parents decided not to impose consequences for failure to eat a certain amount at an individual meal. Instead, they would praise Sarah for what she did eat, ignore what she did not, but make it clear that they hoped she would do better. It was at the end of the day that they would make it clear to Sarah that if she didn't continue to gain weight, they would need to become stricter. This meant that they would offer fewer choices and allow less freedom.

An important factor to keep in mind about consequences is that for most families these are really protections for the child. Viewing them this way may make it easier for you to impose them and for your child to accept them. When your child is malnourished, it may sound and feel like punishment to your daughter to have to stay in bed and rest, but when she is malnourished it is also *necessary*, to make sure she doesn't lose more weight through exertion. Similarly, keeping your son out of school may seem unfair and counterproductive, but school, though a source of accomplishment for many, is often actually stressful and adds to the burden of trying to fight the disordered thinking associated with an eating disorder.

Reasonable, productive consequences may also help you avoid harsher punishments, which are rarely helpful. Parents sometimes entertain the idea of imposing harsh punishments for not eating because eating disorders can be such frustrating illnesses. Most parents avoid resorting to such measures because they already, correctly, see their child as sensitive and generally responsive to gentler correctives—at least in everything except eating. In most cases, even those who try harsher punishments quickly find them counterproductive, leading to a hardening of their child's resolve against their efforts to gain the child's cooperation.

After being clear about both what you expect and what will happen if your expectations aren't met, the next challenge is *sticking with it* and being doggedly persistent. This is where you must outlast the willful hold the eating disorder has on your child. Remember, you have several advantages. First, in situations where there are two parents, at least when you are working together, your combined energy can thwart the eating disorder more effectively. In this instance, two against one (when the one is anorexia or bulimia) is fair play. Next, you are older and wiser and more experienced. You know your child and what makes her tick. You can use that information to slowly build motivation to fight anorexia within her. Moreover, even if your child is an adolescent, you continue to have both legal and parental authority to count on. These are no small advantages, inasmuch as they can allow you to make decisions on behalf of your child even when the teenager, because of her illness, refuses to cooperate with interventions like going to therapy or being admitted to a hospital. You also love your child, and your dedication to her welfare supplies a powerful reservoir of energy for you to call on when you're struggling.

Regardless of these advantages, you still will need to outlast, outmaneuver, and overcome the eating disorder. Like any plan, it is only a plan until and if it is *carried out*. This is where parents usually have the most difficulty. They want it to be easier, they want it be shorter, and sometimes they want someone else to do it. Carrying out the plan and consequences is the *work* that must be done, and there's no getting around it. Your patience, energy, and determination will all be tried. We like to remind parents that eating disorders don't develop overnight; instead, they begin, as we described in Chapter 1, insidiously and slyly. We like to remind parents that eating disorders must be defeated *one bite at a time*.

It might help if you think of carrying out the plan like weeding an overgrown garden. If at the beginning of the day you focus on how many weeds there are and how long it will take and how tiring the job is, you will have trouble getting past the first few feet. Instead, just starting to weed, pulling out weeds one by one, and focusing on that single weed that's rooted deeply, then moving on to the next, slowly but perceptibly, you will make progress. So,

Julia's parents felt dismayed and defeated when they had only gotten Julia to eat two or three more bites of bland fish than she had the day before. They wanted to give up. They felt incompetent and angry. The therapist working with them encouraged them to see it another way. He said, "You have succeeded in helping Julia eat three bites she otherwise would not have. That is a great start. If she eats six bites tomorrow, that's better still. Hang in there." Treading the line between being clear about expectations and being flexible enough to find alternatives, while also not giving in to the eating disorder, is tricky business. While not completely overwhelming your child, you have to make it impossible for the eating disorder to slip through.

> Over the next several days, every meal Cindy ate was an ordeal. Susan and Jorge talked together after each attempt and tried to identify new ways to encourage their daughter. First they tried to bribe her: "If you eat this, we'll get you that new laptop." Cindy did eat, but she stopped again at the next meal. "It wasn't worth it," she said. Next they tried making her feel guilty. "Look how upset everyone is. Your mother can't sleep nights. We are all a wreck!" This made Cindy cry, and she tried to eat but ended up just feeling worse. What did appear to work was saying very little about eating or food. Just encouraging her to keep trying and making sure she rested and had little other stress or distractions seemed to be helpful. Little by little their patience and persistence began to show results. Cindy's resolve not to eat slowly began to crumble in the face of their loving determination. First it was a mouthful of chicken, then a half cup of milk, but the progress was steady, and when the family met with the therapist and saw that Cindy was gaining weight, albeit slowly at first, they had their first taste of hope for many months.

You will often be told by your child that she's "too full" or her "stomach hurts" or she's "not hungry" and that she's "just eaten." In a way, each of these statements may contain a grain of truth, but they miss the point. For anorexia nervosa, eating more than usual is necessary. In the case of anorexia, food is literally medicine. Parents can, however, help their child with these complaints to a

limited extent. One set of parents found that it helped their son to drink a liquid supplement rich in nutrition (proteins and essential fatty acids) as a regular part of his meals because it made him feel less full as well as reduced his discomfort after eating. It was also a rich source of calories. Other parents have found it helpful to make sure enough is eaten early in the day so they can be a little more flexible later on. Sometimes, something as simple as a heating pad or hot water bottle, a gentle neck rub, or another soothing activity helps, because it is really not the physical problem that is causing discomfort (though it seems to your child that it is), but more the emotional discomfort she feels about eating and the anxiety she has about gaining weight that's at the root of her complaints.

We often use the metaphor of "climbing a sand hill" to describe how one must proceed in this refeeding effort. When climbing a sand hill, you have to keep moving up the hill, or the loose sand will cause you to slip back down. If you keep moving up the hill at a sufficiently quick pace, you will find you can proceed, with effort, toward your destination. However, if you pause to rest, you begin to slide and may find yourself back where you started. Only when you've reached the top of the hill can you rest.

Help Your Child with Anorexia or Avoidant/Restrictive Food Intake Disorder to Expand Food Choices

In addition to structuring eating times and helping your child eat more, it's important to help your child expand the types of foods she will eat. Children with eating disorders have often developed a very specific list of foods they feel comfortable eating. Often these foods are very low-calorie, non- or low-fat, and low-density foods. Or, as is the case with bulimia nervosa and binge-eating disorder, there are foods that they crave (often candies, starches, breads), but they allow themselves only small amounts—until a binge epi-sode occurs. In either case, the children's preoccupations with food choices are also further delimited by calorie counting, fat gram counting, weighing and measuring food, demands that they pre-pare all food for themselves (and sometimes others), and sometimes the use of specific cooking pots, plates, bowls, or utensils.

You will have to decide whether you want to approach this range of behaviors as one big problem area—in which case you might just decide what and how your child should eat—as you did when he was much younger. This means that you wouldn't permit calorie counting (or at least not base what was being eaten on a specific caloric amount); you would insist on fat consumption and require that a range of food be eaten. You see, unless challenged, each of these behaviors encourages the persistence of eating-disordered thinking. Counting calories means setting a constant measure (one that the "dieting" teenager will always wish to be lower) by which to evaluate eating. The same goes for fat grams, as well as measuring and weighing portions. In other words, this obsessiveness about food measurement reinforces disordered thinking about food. This is true of all food rules in general. The rules that the person with an eating disorder sets up appear at first to protect him from overeating and gaining weight, but such rules ultimately backfire and become a cage of regulations that prevent normal eating. So, when you challenge these rules, you are challenging the disordered thinking about food that underlies the disorders.

It can be argued that a full-scale assault on this disordered thinking is the best way to proceed, and it is the basis of many hospital and residential refeeding programs. Yet you might feel, as many parents do, that you want to take a more gradual approach to changing these behaviors. Thus, you may want to start by allowing some of the food rules to persist if eating improves and weight gain is appropriate in the case of anorexia or ARFID. If you take this approach, you may experience a bit less early resistance about eating from your child at first, but you will be in for a longer haul.

> Gia's parents decided they would ask her to eat one new food a week. The *amount* she ate would be what she needed to continue to make progress on her weight gain, but in addition, she could choose one new food to add to her diet—usually a food that was one she was struggling with but in the past enjoyed. In Gia's case the first food to be added was cheese. She had always liked cheese but had become completely unwilling to eat it over the last 6 months because she was afraid of the fat it contained. Gia's parents gave her a choice about *what* cheese

she was going to start with, *but she had to choose one.* Gia chose Parmesan cheese. She felt more comfortable with that because it was shredded and seemed less threatening (or fattening) as a result. She sprinkled only a little on her salad, but she tried it. Again, the process was slow at first, but gradually she became used to eating Parmesan cheese and was more willing to try other cheeses as well.

Another challenge, also involving a dairy product, that arises fairly frequently is drinking whole milk. Most adolescents who are malnourished refuse to drink whole milk. "Too much fat," they say. But fat is what many of them need, so getting them to switch from nonfat milk to whole milk (even if just for a time) can provide an important source of nutrition. "Pick your battles" is our usual advice to parents about food choices. Don't argue over a lettuce leaf. Argue over something that counts—fettuccine with cream sauce or steak and mashed potatoes. Whole milk may or may not be worth fighting for if your child's diet already contains enough calcium and fat. Dora's parents thought it was worth the battle, and they simply didn't buy nonfat or low-fat milk. This was a switch for the family (and one that was only temporary, until Dora was better nourished). At first Dora balked, but when her parents gently but relentlessly prodded her, she gave in. In the beginning she took only a little milk on cereal, then a half cup with a snack, but in the end the part of Dora that knew she needed to drink milk to get better began to submit, and she actually slowly agreed that it was a good idea—at least until she was at a healthy weight.

Help Your Child Use Exercise Appropriately

Exercise is a wonderful thing. However, in the minds of those with eating disorders, it can become an opportunity to express a great deal of pathology. In those with anorexia nervosa, exercise is an effective way to lose weight and to keep from gaining weight. In those with bulimia nervosa, exercise is sometimes used as a way of purging by making sure that any calories consumed are balanced by calories exercised away on a treadmill or bike.

It's often challenging to know how and when to intervene in relation to exercise. Certainly, if your child has anorexia nervosa and is underweight, exercise should generally be prohibited. This means letters to school (sometimes requiring a physician's note as well) exempting your child from physical education. Sometimes it means monitoring in-room exercising (sit-ups, jumping jacks, etc.). Again, your involvement is aimed at promoting the physical health of your child rather than allowing continued deterioration. So, as soon as your child is eating normally and out of medical danger, it's usually a good idea to allow exercising, in moderation, once again. As with eating, however, you may at first have to be scrupulous about this reintroduction, as it's very easy for your child to get carried away. Hence, it's helpful to lay out a careful plan. For example, you could allow 15 minutes of exercise a day to begin with, and if weight continues to improve, this can be increased to 30 minutes, where it should probably remain until all signs of the disorder are gone. In some cases it's helpful to allow exercise a bit earlier. Some parents have found this helps to improve appetite, support cooperation, and increase motivation for recovery. We think that this approach can indeed be helpful, but only if you and the medical professionals you are working with feel comfortable with it. Practically, this usually means that your child is continuing to show progress in regard to her eating and weight.

For those with bulimia nervosa and binge-eating disorder, reasonable exercise, not in relation to overeating or binge eating, can help minimize frustration and increase tolerance for not purging. Often, the child may resort to purging in lieu of exercise because exercising is perceived as being more work and taking more time. Helping your child with bulimia nervosa develop a reasonable, structured approach to exercise, very similar to that taken in structuring meals, can offset this perception. Sometimes joining a health club or a structured exercise program (kickboxing, karate, etc.) in which thinness is not a virtue works well (some types of dance classes, in which a slim appearance seems to matter, can backfire). You may want to help your child identify a friend to exercise with so she'll be more likely to stick with it. Depending on the nature of your

relationship with your child, you may even be able to act as your child's exercise partner. Either way, your encouragement about this way of attaining and maintaining a healthy weight and body can be very beneficial for those with bulimia.

Help Your Child to Prevent Binge Eating and Purging

In addition to everything we've already said about normalizing eating, you'll need to prevent binge eating and purging when your child's problem includes these behaviors. In the case of binge eating, for example, you are primarily responsible for what foods are available and when they are available to be consumed in your home. Therefore, it helps a great deal for you to understand more about *what* foods are likely to lead to your child's binge eating. These foods vary from person to person, but it is usually pretty evident from what's missing from your cabinets which foods your child is likely to binge eat. Common examples are cereal (by the box), ice cream (by the half-gallon), and whole packages of cookies, potato chips, cheese, and jars of peanut butter. A general rule is that binge foods are typically high-calorie, high-fat, and often sweet foods— foods that dieters try hard to limit severely and that therefore represent an indulgence.

One teenager reported that her mother routinely baked a cake for dessert on Sunday. Each member of the family of four had a piece, leaving half a cake. This cake was a consistently available and desirable food to binge on each Sunday evening. Another child reported that the "stock" of large bags of potato chips and ice cream containers bought at wholesale food markets and stored in the pantry and refrigerator were a constant source of binge foods. It's perfectly understandable that you'll sometimes bake cakes or that you might be in the habit of buying food in quantity to economize. Until your child is in better control of binge eating, however, you may need to change these and similar ways of cooking and shopping. There are likely other ways in which you're supplying food that lend themselves to binge eating that you might curtail for the time being.

In addition to making tempting foods available, you may be unwittingly supporting binge eating by not being present to prevent it. Many binge eaters will do so only in private because they're ashamed of the behavior. So, many teenagers who binge eat figure out the times when no one is likely to be around or when their activities will go undetected. There are usually several such times each day. One is after school between 3:00 and 6:00 P.M., and other times are late at night or very early in the morning. These times also fit nicely into the distorted eating pattern that usually accompanies bulimia, because long periods of "restricting"—all day or all night, for example—produce increased hunger and feelings of deprivation, leading, in response, to overeating during a binge. So it is very important that you become aware of the most likely periods when your child will binge eat and that you make an effort to be available during those times to help prevent the behavior.

With bulimia nervosa, most purging follows the consumption of a lot of food, precipitated by guilt, shame, and anxiety about overeating and fear of gaining weight. Purging, like binge eating, is usually a secretive behavior. Because purging is effective only in emptying undigested food (to the limited degree that it is) only fairly soon (usually within 30 minutes) after eating, it is a considerably predictable behavior. So, if you know *when* your child has eaten, or particularly when he has binge eaten, you are in a position to know when he will try to purge. Thus, as in the case of binge eating, knowing the time purging is likely to occur will help you know when to be on the lookout and to implement strategies to prevent it.

It's also helpful to know *where* your child purges. This is not always so straightforward. Most, of course, purge into the toilet, but many also purge in the shower, into garbage bags, or into shrubbery. Purging is often governed by very specific rules—and can be done only under those conditions. For example, some people can purge only at home, others can purge only when no one is around, and others have rules about where they cannot purge, such as at school or at church. When these conditions are understood, it is much easier to prevent them from being met and thereby disallow the opportunity for purging. If your child purges only at home (which is

not uncommon in the early stages of the illness), you have an advantage because you have a specific limited environment to monitor. Nonetheless, the conditions can change, and it's important to keep abreast of any changes in locations for purging because any change opens a potential loophole to allow the behavior to continue.

It is also important to learn about *how* your child purges. Most often this simply involves putting one's finger down the throat, stimulating a gag reflex. However, sometimes this is ineffective and other instruments, such as spoons, toothbrushes, nail files, and so forth, are used. Some adolescents learn about syrup of ipecac, which is used to cause emesis after poisoning. When used routinely to purge, however, it is associated with cardiac problems and even death. Over time, some people learn to purge without any direct stimulation. This means that it's possible to purge at any time and very surreptitiously, making the behavior more difficult to detect and disrupt. Nonetheless, knowledge of the means your child uses to purge will help you intervene, because you can look for the signs of continued purging activity (e.g., broken nails, scratches on the back of the hand resulting from teeth scratching them). If your child uses syrup of ipecac, it's essential that you remove this substance from your home or lock it up because of the danger it poses.

Remember, your child will feel compelled to purge if she believes she's overeaten (and in this sense, she has little choice about her wish). Further, she feels tremendous relief if she purges. Thus, purging is a very reinforcing behavior, even if it is shameful and sometimes painful. Your job is to help her tolerate the discomfort of not purging while supplying other positive reinforcements instead of purging, such as attention, distractions, or opportunities for other positive things to do. *To provide these alternatives, you need to talk to your child about what she thinks would be helpful.* Some parents have found playing a video game, watching a movie, taking a walk, or going shopping may help to prevent purging when a period of binge eating has occurred.

Laxative abuse is another common way that some adolescents attempt to purge their foods. As we noted in Chapter 4, taking laxatives is a very dangerous way to go about this and is very ineffective in addition. The use of laxatives over the long term leads to a variety

of medical problems, including severe abdominal pain, bloating, and intestinal plasticity. To be effective, doses have to be increased, which can result in toxicity in some cases. Many who use laxatives report that they wish to feel "empty" and to "flatten their stomachs" rather than just get rid of food. Psychologically, emptying the gut feels like a relief as well. To help your child stop taking laxatives, keep several things in mind. Certain laxatives can be detected in blood or stool samples, and your pediatrician can test for those, helping you to know whether your child is using them without your knowledge. In addition, laxatives can be expensive if used frequently, so if your child has a ready supply of cash, you should monitor spending to make sure it isn't being used to purchase laxatives. However, many adolescents also steal laxatives because of their cost. It is not uncommon for bulimic persons to be caught shoplifting laxatives.

Purging can also take the form of extreme exercise. After binge eating, your child may try to estimate the number of calories she consumed and try to "run it off" on a treadmill or through other strenuous activities. This pattern of exercise purging may not appear to be as harmful as taking laxatives or vomiting, but because of the stress it places on the body as well as the anxiety about "not getting all the calories worked off" and the time it takes, trying to compensate for a binge through exercise can exact a great toll. Your role in such a situation is to help your child exercise as a usual activity for health, not weight control per se, and especially not to compensate for abnormal binge eating, which results from unduly restrictive dieting.

DON'T DEBATE WITH YOUR CHILD ABOUT EATING- OR WEIGHT-RELATED CONCERNS

One of the most common problems parents face, and you probably will too, is the distorted thinking of the child with an eating disorder. You may believe that you should be able to get your child to "see reason," "be reasonable," or "see the light" or that she "will just get over it." At the start, this just doesn't happen very often (if at all). Instead, what happens is that you are often drawn into

a variety of debates and struggles that are illogical from start to finish, except from the perspective of someone whose thinking is distorted with overconcern, unrealistic investment in, and anxiety about food, weight, and shape. We discussed in detail what this thinking is like in Chapter 5. However, when you're in the trenches, up against anorexia or bulimia, the problems that this thinking can cause you are no longer abstract; they are quite specific, and it's not always clear how to proceed. Examples of the difficulties you will face include obsessive weighing, food shopping, clothes shopping, the influence of friends, and the influence of the media and fashion.

Don't Permit Obsessive Weighing

Constant weighing is a common problem in many people with eating disorders. There is an obsessional quality to it, so much so that over time weighing becomes a way of assessing one's emotional state (feeling good or bad), one's self-worth (successful or a failure), and one's desirability (being likable or unlikable). Of course, a person's weight does not really define these attributes, but their association with weighing over time makes it seem so. In addition, weighing at really frequent intervals is deceptive and inaccurate. Too many other factors (what one is wearing, when one ate, time of day, recent activity, recent fluid intake) can change weight by 1–3 pounds. You will notice that your child may be momentarily reassured by a low weight, only to come crashing down a few hours later because of a "high" weight. You know her weight has not changed substantially, but that's not how it feels to your child. At the same time, it's important that weights be taken at regular intervals so that everyone knows how things are progressing. For all of these reasons, we recommend that during treatment weight be taken only once or twice a week. This may mean throwing out the bathroom scale (or hiding it). It is also useful if the professionals you work with agree on when weights will be taken and who will take them. There's nothing helpful about a child's weight going up in the pediatrician's office, down in the nutritionist's office, and being unchanged in the therapist's office. Having too many scales just leaves everyone confused.

Decide When It Is a Good Idea to Take
Your Adolescent Grocery Shopping

Shopping for food when your child has an eating disorder can be a very difficult proposition. There will be a lot of rules you're supposed to follow, and these rules tend to change a lot. Still, some parents elect to take their child with them when shopping to help them buy foods that the child will agree to eat. In our experience, this is often counterproductive. The child wanders the grocery store aisles looking for something acceptable to eat (but finding very little) if she has anorexia nervosa, and feeling guilty and tempted if she has bulimia nervosa or binge-eating disorder. So, early in treatment, though it is good to understand your child's likes and dislikes, it is often better to shop alone. Later, once recovery has started, involving your child in these excursions is useful as it allows you and the child to better see the progress being made in terms of comfort with food and more flexibility in her choices.

Hold Off Clothes Shopping Until Symptoms Are Decreased

Shopping for clothes, another common activity for teenagers, is best limited during the early part of treatment as well. Often, like weight, clothing sizes will serve as "markers" for emotional and social worth. A child's pride in being size 0 is as distorted as the shame in being size 20 in the context of an eating disorder. Overall, though, because the size that fits an adolescent with anorexia nervosa will be increasing, it just makes sense to wait until full (or nearly full) weight recovery before shopping for clothes. For those with bulimia nervosa, the issue is often one of sizes going up and down during the period of early treatment, meaning that here too it's better to wait.

One shopping trip you may not be able to avoid is the one for a special outfit for a dance, particularly a dress for a girl. Such dresses and occasions often stimulate much anxiety on everyone's part. Be sure to evaluate your own investment in this process inasmuch as fashion and appearance affect us all. Try to avoid dresses that are too form fitting, regardless of how stylish, because they tend to

emphasize many of the characteristics, for good or ill, that your child worries so much about.

Allow Supportive Friendships

Parents often worry about whether a friend who has an eating disorder will have a negative impact on their child's progress. There is no simple answer to this question because so much depends on the friend and your child. A great number of teenagers have eating disorders, so it is likely you won't be able to avoid them. If, however, your child's friend is not being treated and also appears to be encouraging eating-disordered behaviors in your child, it would be wise to limit this friendship as much as possible, at least during the early period of treatment. This is a delicate problem, though, because teenagers' friends are very important to them. If you feel it is absolutely necessary to limit contact with a particular friend, be clear about your reasons and about your intention to reevaluate the situation as your child continues to make progress. Certainly, it is important to discuss this important issue with your child's therapist to get further guidance.

Limit the Influence of Media-Related Values
Regarding Weight

A number of influences beyond your home and family will affect how your child thinks about herself. Some of these influences are general and touch all of us in one way or another (e.g., media, fashion, and culture); others are peculiar to the adolescent world (adolescent peer groups and values), and some to the world of eating disorders (pro-eating disorder websites). How can you limit the negative aspects of these external influences insofar as they may keep your child from fully recovering from an eating disorder?

Adolescents are particularly vulnerable to the influences of media productions. They are still developing a sense of who they are and are seeking outside confirmation for their emerging identities. Ironically, in a sense, adolescents often seek to conform to a set of norms as defined by the media rather than finding their own

niches. This decision to conform has to do with the need to "fit in" with a peer group. Fitting in with a peer group is important for several reasons. First, as social animals, humans naturally seek out others. During adolescence, relationships outside the family constitute the vehicle whereby social learning, including dating, takes place. As a result, adolescents invest heavily in their peer groups. They want to be liked, and this may take on a very simple and concrete meaning for them: Being thin (or thinner) will make them more likable. It's easy to understand why adolescents see things this way—there's a certain degree of truth to this perception. However, they often fail to see that this is hardly the sole basis for being valued. Someone is more often liked because of being funny, smart, or kind. In addition, adolescents are still developing a sense of perspective. They turn to the media and their various products to help them see things outside their smaller world. Unfortunately, the popular media, on the whole, do not provide a real perspective, but instead a highly distorted one, where beauty and attractiveness define success, happiness, and accomplishment.

As a parent, it's your responsibility to help to reestablish other values. When we talk to adolescents with eating disorders, we sometimes ask them to rank the relative importance of their weight or shape as compared with other attributes or concerns. Those with eating disorders substantially overvalue their weight and shape as compared with their intelligence, personality, friends, family, and even religious beliefs. Of course, weight is important for both health and attractiveness, but when it is *so* important that it substantially outranks all these other important qualities and relationships, it becomes a problem. It's more difficult for your child to see these other values, particularly in the visual media. The media cannot place values on these other factors—for one thing, they're harder to capture in a picture—and even if they did, these things wouldn't "sell" because they are unfortunately not perceived as "rare" or "special" the way beauty is.

As a parent of an adolescent, you are in a difficult position. You are an adult, and as such you are "out of touch," as it were (or as it seems), with the world of your teenager. If you directly question particulars in fashion (leggings, ripped jeans, spandex tops, etc.), you

will likely be dismissed. Therefore, it's important to approach the matter with more of a questioning attitude than a critical one. This means that if you want to help your child consider heroes or heroines outside the celebrity group, it's important to try to understand what other values your child holds that you might be able to tap into to encourage her in those directions. For example, if your child values academic or athletic achievement, these can be supported as alternatives to physical beauty in terms of value. It's also often possible to tap into the altruistic sentiments of many adolescents by identifying ways in which social values are opportunities for balancing the relative merits of physical attractiveness and other sources of self-esteem and self-worth, such as volunteering, tutoring, conservation programs, and religious and church groups.

The need for parents to respond to a child's overvaluing of appearance and attractiveness is not unique to parents whose children have eating disorders. However, you have a special task because your child has developed specific problems that play into the worst aspects of the physical ideals set up to be admired. Your mandate is to monitor and limit the influence of the values being promoted, at the same time identifying alternative sources and supporting your child in turning to them for the development of self-esteem and values.

Sometimes the media communicating health issues are even more problematic than the media promoting fashion and celebrity. This is the case, in part, because it is difficult to see health as a problematic value. What is problematic is the way health is defined. For example, there is frequent emphasis on vegetarianism, low-fat/nonfat foods, dieting, and certain kinds of intensive exercise regimens. In the hands (and head) of someone with an eating disorder, the worth of these things is exaggerated way out of reasonable proportion. We stress that most of these choices, when made in pursuit of health, lead to good outcomes, but when they are desired in order to diet or maintain an extremely low body weight, they do not.

Among the most insidious forces that now encroach on the health of adolescents with eating disorders are pro-eating disorder websites. These websites, cleverly labeled to be misleading, provide chat groups, information, and strategies that encourage adolescents

to develop eating disorders, refuse intervention, and oppose parental involvement in their treatment. There is no easy solution. Free speech is guaranteed. However, as a parent you do have some options. It may seem draconian, but for the period of time that your child is in treatment, it may be necessary to disconnect his or her tablet, laptop, and smart phone from the Internet or to allow it to be used only under very close supervision. You can learn techniques for detecting your adolescent's use of such sites—tracking "cookies"—but as is often the case, your child may be more savvy about digital media than you. Still, the perniciousness of these sites is so strong that we recommend taking a firm stance against accessing them by whatever means you have at your disposal. Of course, your adolescent may be able to access these sites from other venues (school, library, or friends), but the time he has will be more limited.

KNOW WHEN TO BEGIN BACKING OFF

As hard as it may be to imagine now, there will come a time when you will need to figure out how to begin backing off from being so involved in the day-to-day management of your child's eating disorder symptoms and behaviors. In fact, that is the ultimate goal of your getting so involved in the first place. You will know you're approaching that point when your child is at or very near her normal weight, is eating reasonable amounts on a reasonable schedule, is not compulsive in exercising, is not binge eating or purging, and is generally more like her old self. If your daughter lost her menstrual period, its return is also a very good indicator of physical health.

It can be difficult to let go after you have struggled so hard to get a hold on this problem. It's a frightening experience to see someone whose life you treasure veer off in a dangerous direction. Studies of childhood cancer survivors have shown that the kids who went through all the chemotherapy, radiation, and surgeries were, at a later point, not particularly preoccupied with those events. Yet their parents still had many worries, intrusive thoughts, dreams,

and continued anxieties about what their child went through long before. So keep in mind that your child may move on and feel out of danger (and may even be right about this) before you feel comfortable again.

With regard to your starting to hand control back to your child, we often use the analogy of how you might manage letting your child drive again after a traffic infraction. You might start by allowing him to drive only to and from school, then later allowing him to drive in the daytime on weekends, and so on, until full privileges have been earned. With respect to eating, you might start with allowing your teenager to eat snacks unmonitored, then lunches, and so on, until you are confident that eating is going well without your supervision. This may take several months to accomplish fully. Usually, by this time, you are more comfortable and know what to look for and how to help if problems arise.

We strongly encourage you, though, to try to allow as many other social activities as possible as your child is beginning to recover. We suggest that you do this—in part, because such engagements permit more normal development—while also ensuring that eating takes place. This may mean having to schedule activities after or before mealtimes when you're first getting started. Still, by encouraging these activities, you will be able to help your child see you as controlling only her eating behaviors and not interfering as much with other age-appropriate activities. Such an approach may also help your child tolerate your involvement in the area of eating.

We like to say that the ultimate goal in treating an eating disorder is to have *life* replace the obsessional behaviors and the thoughts about food and weight associated with them. For your adolescent, this means returning to school, taking up the challenge of explaining to her friends where she's been, and slowly entering a more normal adolescent social life. Returning to school is a worry, as the need to perform at high levels is so common to many with eating disorders. Because they've been ill, they feel they are behind, less well prepared, and perhaps will never achieve what they hope to. Helping a child get back to school requires, in part, accepting the idea that some of this concern is okay. The thought to convey is "You can still be a good student, catch up, and be successful even if you don't take

five AP [advanced placement] classes in your junior year." It requires a bit more tact or judgment to decide how much information about why the child has been out of school is appropriate to share. Most teenagers just say they had "heart problems" or "stomach problems" or something to that effect. Others, like Cindy, decide they want to help others through their experience. They become peer health aides who try to help other people with eating problems.

You may find that you need to help get your adolescent back on track by encouraging him more actively than you might have expected to. You may sometimes even have to take the lead in arranging visits with friends and encouraging attendance at school functions. Many children with eating disorders have some degree of social anxiety. This may have to be addressed even after the eating-disordered behavior and thinking have subsided. Treatment for these problems, as for other psychiatric difficulties such as depression or obsessive–compulsive disorder, may require separate treatment with medications, therapy, or both.

TAKE CARE OF YOURSELF

It was probably evident to you as you read this chapter that helping your child will be a lot of work. So it's important that while you're doing this crucial job you take care of yourself as much as possible. If you're not able to continue to support your child, she will lose her most important asset in her fight against her eating disorder. To take care of yourself, you must recognize that you will need more rest, regular exercise, and good nutrition. You should also plan on sharing the burden with your spouse and with other family members when you need a break. If you find yourself feeling depressed or overanxious, consider seeking additional personal therapy for support. In our experience, it has not been at all unusual for parents to seek such support. You may also find support through your family, friends, or spiritual community. Making use of your own support system will help both you and your child.

At the end of all this work, though, will be the great satisfaction that you have helped your child with a life-threatening problem.

Although we cannot guarantee the outcome, as we have stated before, there's very good reason to be optimistic about your chances.

FOR MORE INFORMATION

Dare, C., and I. Eisler, Family Therapy for Anorexia Nervosa, in D. M. Garner and P. E. Garfinkel, Editors, *Handbook of Treatment for Eating Disorders, Second Edition*, 1997. New York: Guilford Press, pp. 307–324.

Dare, C., I. Eisler, G. Russell, et al., Family Therapy for Anorexia Nervosa: Implications from the Results of a Controlled Trial of Family and Individual Therapy, *Journal of Marital and Family Therapy*, 1990, *16*, 39–57.

Eisler, I., D. Le Grange, and E. Asen, Family Interventions, in J. Treasure, U. Schmidt, and E. van Furth, Editors, *Handbook of Eating Disorders*, 2003. Chichester, UK: Wiley, pp. 291–310.

Krautter, T., and J. Lock, Is Manualized Family- Based Treatment for Adolescent Anorexia Nervosa Acceptable to Patients?: Patient Satisfaction at End of Treatment, *Journal of Family Therapy*, 2004, *26*, 65–81.

Le Grange, D., and J. Lock, Bulimia Nervosa in Adolescents: Treatment, Eating Pathology, and Comorbidity, *South African Psychiatry Review*, 2002, *5*, 19–22.

Le Grange, D., and J. Lock, *Treating Bulimia in Adolescents: A Family-Based Approach*, 2007. New York: Guilford Press.

Le Grange, D., J. Lock, and M. Dymek, Family-Based Therapy for Adolescents with Bulimia Nervosa, *American Journal of Psychotherapy*, 2003, *67*, 237–251.

Le Grange, D., K. L. Loeb, S. Van Orman, et al., Bulimia Nervosa in Adolescents: A Disorder in Evolution?, *Archives of Pediatrics and Adolescent Medicine*, 2004, *158*, 478–482.

Lock, J., Treating Adolescents with Eating Disorders in the Family Context: Empirical and Theoretical Considerations, *Child and Adolescent Psychiatric Clinics of North America*, 2002, *11*, 331–342.

Lock, J., and D. Le Grange, *Treatment Manual for Anorexia Nervosa: A Family-Based Approach, Second Edition*, 2013. New York: Guilford Press.

CHAPTER 8

Playing a Supporting Role

*Other Ways You Can Be a Part
of Your Child's Recovery*

In Chapter 7 we focused on ways you can be involved in *directly* changing disordered eating and related behaviors through family-based treatment (FBT). In this chapter we illustrate how you can be involved in other types of treatment as well. The treatments discussed in this chapter were not developed with the tenets used in FBT in mind, and they vary in their adaptability to parental involvement. How much you are permitted and encouraged to participate may also vary from practitioner to practitioner within the same form of therapy. But all of these therapies can be delivered in ways that do not exclude you, that show respect and support for your role as parents, that educate you about what is being done to help your child, and that specify how you *can* help. Your involvement in these other therapies is just as important as in family treatment, though your role in changing behaviors is usually more *indirect*.

In earlier chapters we emphasized that the importance of parents in supporting adolescent development has been underestimated. Increasingly, it is clear that involved parents make a real difference in how successfully children and teenagers negotiate their lives. So, whether you take a direct or an indirect role in helping your child, your involvement will likely make a significant contribution to your child's recovery.

PRINCIPLES FOR PLAYING A SUPPORTING ROLE

In the following pages, we discuss how you might be involved in intensive treatments (such as inpatient programs, residential programs, and day programs) as well as in outpatient psychotherapies, especially individual approaches. Your involvement in any of these forms of treatment will vary in the particulars, but there are some general principles that apply to all of them.

1. Agree on the Approach You Will Try.

As we've stressed from the outset, one of the biggest obstacles to helping your child recover is disagreement between parents about how to help. How you can address these difficulties is detailed in Chapter 9. However, even before you make the first appointment, try to get your heads together to see if you can determine where the differences are and identify the treatment that makes the most sense for your child and family.

See Chapter 6 for information on the data available on the effectiveness of each type of therapy. If you don't find the therapy you're considering in that chapter, ask the referring doctor why he believes that type of treatment may help and why it might be a better choice than the therapies that show the greatest effectiveness in recent, reliable research. If the doctor does not have an answer that satisfies you, and the therapy does not fall into any of the categories discussed in Chapter 6, you can be fairly sure that there is no reason to expect it to be effective in improving your child's symptoms, which means that wasting time on it could endanger your child's health needlessly. Ask for another referral, and if you don't get one, see the Resources section of this book for other ideas on finding a good source of help.

When we advise you to come to agreement on which approach to try, we mean that you should include only you and your child's other parent or guardian. Don't make your child part of this decision. It's counterproductive to allow your child to have too much say in which steps will be taken to eliminate an eating disorder because, before your child begins to recover, when you talk to her

about the problem, you'll end up hearing from the disorder more than from your daughter. This doesn't mean that you cannot ask your child's opinions, but the decision remains in your hands as parents. By reading this book, you are preparing yourself to make a decision on how to help your child with an eating disorder. Your child may have opinions and strong feelings about what treatment is desirable, but as you now know, motivation for recovery is not high in many adolescents with eating disorders. Ultimately, then, it will be up to you to assess the treatment options and to decide how best to proceed.

2. Learn All You Can about Any Treatment You Choose.

The introduction to the various treatment approaches for eating disorders we provide in this book is limited in scope and detail. So, as you consider the different options in more detail, you should seek out additional resources and information. Chapter 6 contains information on research evidence as of the publication of this book, but data from ongoing studies are always accumulating, so you may want to stay abreast of any results published in the interim. The Resources and Further Reading sections of this book will give you sources to consult for both types of information. Your child's pediatrician, too, may be able to tell you where you'll find reliable sources of up-to-date research, and if you are already working with a therapist, she may be able to provide you with handouts about various treatment approaches.

3. Share Your Perspectives on Your Child and the Child's Treatment from the Start.

As we've said, anyone who is treating your child should ask you to describe your child's development and to give your observations of the child's current behaviors and symptoms. However, you should also take the opportunity to share as much as you can about what you think are contributing problems and conflicts, as well as any strengths and abilities that may be called on in both your child and your family as a whole. Providing this information and sharing your

perspectives with your therapist will allow you to begin to forge a relationship in which you are working together from the start. If you have trouble in continuing to work together, Chapter 10 has ideas for improving your teamwork.

4. Keep in Frequent Contact with Any Therapists or Physicians Involved in Providing Treatment.

Sometimes parents feel that once a professional is involved, their responsibility is over. Other parents feel they cannot or should not ask a therapist questions or get feedback on how their child is doing. Neither of these is a sound perspective. Although there are some areas in which confidentiality between a teenager and his individual therapist should and must be respected (sexual behaviors, intimate feelings, social activities), you still need to be involved. Regardless of the approach, your perspectives on why the disorder developed, how symptoms are currently being expressed, and how you and your family are being affected by your teen's ongoing struggles are all appropriate areas for regular discussions with the therapist.

5. Determine How You Will Assess Progress.

One thing that is helpful to ask the therapist at the beginning of treatment is what to expect in terms of improvement of symptoms and over what time period. This way everyone has an agreed-upon benchmark to use that, though not ironclad, will likely help everyone see the trajectory of recovery. If you also agree on how and when you'll be updated on how things are going, you'll go a long way toward ensuring that your child is getting the treatment needed at this time. This updating should be negotiated between you, the therapist, and your child to allow you to evaluate how things are going at reasonable intervals. For example, with a teen who suffers from anorexia, never knowing for sure whether your child is gaining weight will make it difficult for you to assess your child's progress. Also, if your child purges, but does so surreptitiously, you might not know when she's doing better or worse.

6. Have a Backup Plan.

Although one of the biggest mistakes we see parents make is to keep changing therapists and treatment approaches, we nonetheless feel that you should keep your options open in case the approach you take doesn't work for your child. No treatment for any condition works 100% of the time for everyone, so it's best to be prepared with an alternate plan should progress not be as you, your child, and the therapist had hoped. Having a backup plan is not the same as undercutting a current therapy, but rather a way of making sure you aren't caught without alternatives—because, as we've said many times throughout this book, the longer these problems persist, the harder they are to change. To make a backup plan, work together as parents with your therapist and physician to see what would be the best next step as soon as progress is definitively stalled. The treatments described in Chapter 6 should provide a good start for you in evaluating your options.

7. Keep Your Child in Treatment.

Although your role in most forms of individual therapy is somewhat circumscribed, it's still very important, partly because your child's motivation to be treated for eating problems is initially apt to be low. So you can expect that you will need to encourage, support, and even insist on your adolescent's attending treatment sessions. This may mean that you will have to work with your child's school to excuse him from classes so he can attend treatment, inasmuch as it is usually impossible for all therapy sessions to take place outside of school hours. This issue can cause another struggle with your child, who may not want to miss classes or time with friends. In addition, you will likely be asked to participate in some treatment sessions. The content of these sessions will vary, depending on the type of therapy your child is being provided. Regardless, make it a priority to attend these sessions. Your attendance helps to send a message that you support the treatment even if you're not the main player.

HOW YOU CAN STAY INVOLVED EVEN WHEN YOU'RE NOT IN CHARGE

Throughout this book we have acknowledged how difficult it can be to be excluded from your child's treatment, whether you're just left uninformed or told directly to stay out of it. It's especially tough when this catches you off guard. If you don't know how you *can* participate, you'll feel pretty powerless to find a role in your child's recovery. The rest of this chapter shows specific ways you can remain involved in various forms of therapy. Even though inpatient treatment is neither the most common nor the best-studied treatment setting, it serves as a paradigm for parental participation when you're not directly in charge of treatment, as you would be in FBT, so we'll start there.

What is your role in intensive treatments (hospitals, residential programs, and day treatment programs)?

Unfortunately, many children with eating disorders need intensive treatment provided in some type of institutional setting. Depending on the goals of these programs, the term of inpatient treatment may be as short as a few days or as long as 12 weeks. When inpatient treatment is used purely to stabilize an adolescent's acute medical problems, such as when the patient needs rehydration, the stay will likely be only a few days long and probably in a pediatric medical unit rather than an eating disorders unit. When the primary goal for inpatient treatment is to restore weight and give treatment-resistant patients with life-threatening weight loss a real chance at recovery, inpatient treatment might last between 10 and 12 weeks. However, for some programs the main treatment goal is to halt rapid weight loss and just jump-start weight restoration. In these instances, rather than providing several weeks of treatment, the stay might be only 10–14 days.

What you should take from this information is that you need to be sure inpatient treatment is recommended at the right time and for the right reasons. Too often, we meet parents who have felt pressured

to admit their child when they were not considered in the decision-making process. Specifically, they did not receive an adequate explanation of the necessity for this particular course of action, the goals of the admission, the anticipated length of hospitalization, and why an outpatient treatment was not considered. At other times, the converse is true, when there is pressure to keep patients out of the hospital when it is, in fact, required. Instead, the child is kept in inadequate outpatient treatment because of costs. Some parents, with the help of their doctors and considerable amounts of lobbying, have succeeded in convincing their insurance companies of the dire need for hospitalization. This route, however, is not only frustrating but also very time-consuming, especially when inpatient care is urgently required. It is best to discuss your options with your child's doctor when you are concerned about your child's weight loss.

The criteria used to recommend that your child be admitted for an eating disorder will vary from one inpatient treatment team to another, but the differences should be in nuance as opposed to substance. Both you and your child's treatment team should generally adhere to most of the following guidelines when deciding whether your child should become an inpatient for acute medical reasons (a couple of days in the case of rehydration, for instance) or for a longer-term admission for weight restoration (several weeks, as discussed earlier). General guidelines for medical hospitalization have been published by the Society for Adolescent Medicine and the American Academy of Pediatrics. The precise guidelines will have to be established by your child's pediatrician, but in general they should resemble the following:

- Severe malnutrition (less than 75% of expected body weight)
- Pulse rate less than 50 beats per minute in the day, less than 46 beats per minute at night
- Temperature less than 36.4 degrees Celsius during the day, 36.0 degrees Celsius at night
- Orthostatic (lying to standing) systolic blood pressure greater than 10 millimeters of mercury, or pulse change greater than 35 beats per minute

- Irregular or slow pulse
- Abnormal electrolytes (usually potassium less than 3.0 milliequivalents per liter)

The need for a child to be hospitalized almost always causes considerable worry. Parents often approach inpatient treatment with just about as much trepidation as their adolescent child. Their uncertainty is further increased because the child, wanting to stay out of the hospital, exerts pressure on them. Although parent and child may have different reasons for feeling ambivalent about inpatient treatment, it's important to keep in mind that hospitalization reflects a crisis and is therefore often experienced as traumatic and certainly disruptive.

The only way to limit the impact of hospitalization is to keep the hospitalization brief, but this decision may be entirely out of your hands. So, taking your child for inpatient treatment is no easy decision. However, even if your child is in need of longer-term inpatient treatment, but it is possible to have her admitted for only a short stay, this could be a life-saving step you might have to take.

When you're weighing the possible effectiveness of inpatient treatment for your child against that of other treatment modes, be sure to consider what kind of follow-up treatment to the inpatient stay will be available. Without proper follow-up, it's often very difficult to maintain the improvements that have been achieved while the child was an inpatient. If the specialist unit at which your child may become an inpatient is near your home, regular follow-up appointments with your child's doctors may not be very complicated. If the facility is not close by, however, is another source of follow-up care on an outpatient or day-patient basis accessible? Making sure that your child's inpatient care is complemented by good follow-up treatment should be a combined effort between you and the discharging inpatient team. Make sure the team is willing and able to help in this way before making a decision on inpatient care.

Yet perhaps the most important issue at stake is your involvement in your child's inpatient treatment. How much and in what ways you're permitted to be involved while your child is an inpatient

will vary with the treatment approach taken by the team, but it's important that you avail yourself of every opportunity offered to you. This is another reason that location is important. If the specialist unit at which your child will be an inpatient is far away, participating day by day may be logistically difficult for you. Yet this participation will help lay the groundwork for you to be active in maintaining your child's gains during the follow-up period after discharge. We have already alluded to the fact that many teenagers end up returning to the hospital because they don't sustain the weight gains they have made during their hospitalizations, as Brenda's case illustrates.

> Brenda was only 12 when she was first admitted to a very-well-known inpatient unit a couple of states away from where her family lived. There was no such facility within Brenda's home state. She progressed well in the hospital and was sent home after several weeks to "take care" of her eating by herself. Unfortunately, her parents, bewildered on the sidelines and against their own better judgment, watched Brenda promptly lose weight, and they had to make the trip across state lines once again. As with the first admission, Brenda settled down in the unit and started gaining weight. Her parents were not involved in the hospital's refeeding efforts and weren't given much feedback about how they might be able to help Brenda once she was discharged again. As before, with the encouragement of the nursing staff, Brenda did really well in terms of her eating. She was discharged after several weeks at a healthy weight, and again her parents were told that it was now "up to Brenda to take care of herself." Thirteen-year-old Brenda tried hard to cope with her anxieties about eating, but again her parents remained on the sidelines as they were instructed. Consequently, she lost all the weight she had gained in the hospital just a few weeks after returning home. By now, Brenda's parents knew the road to the inpatient unit all too well. The same scenario was repeated once more.

Obviously, everyone interested in Brenda's well-being would have liked to prevent this type of cycle. To avoid the same trap with your own child, we encourage you to learn as much as you can from

the inpatient team while your child is there. Here are the kinds of opportunities to look for:

1. **Parent education meetings:** These meetings are common in most inpatient settings. They provide you with an opportunity to ask questions about anorexia and bulimia and to learn more about these illnesses from experts, who will also have some specific knowledge about your child and the situation.

2. **Observation of nursing and other professional staff:** If you observe experienced staff members doing their jobs, you may learn why and how they are successful at getting your child to eat and gain weight when you haven't been. You will likely notice that they don't argue about what should be eaten or when—these expectations are clearly established.

3. **Opportunities to try helping your child eat while she's in the hospital:** Some programs encourage parents to come in for some meals to allow them to see what their child is eating and to allow them to attempt to monitor a meal themselves.

4. **Discussions with the nutritionist:** A meeting with a nutritionist while your child is in the hospital can be helpful. A nutritionist can help you understand better how much food and what types might be most helpful for your child.

5. **Parent support groups and therapy:** Many inpatient programs have support groups for parents. These groups will help you see that your struggles are not unique and can provide a useful tonic for the feelings of isolation and shame that are common to families when they first struggle with a child with an eating disorder.

Unfortunately, too often parents are excluded, or exclude themselves, from inpatient programs. This can result in a cycle of weight gain in the inpatient setting, followed by rapid weight loss at home. Eventually the patient is "blamed" for not wanting to change, the parents' skills are not capitalized on, and the result is that the teenager is sent away to spend several months at a residential facility, which is often hundreds of miles from her family and friends.

In addition to short-stay admissions, intensive day treatment programs may be an effective alternative to longer-term, intensive inpatient treatment for some patients with eating disorders. Day treatment is sometimes recommended for those patients who have completed intensive inpatient treatment; they then "graduate" to this step-down treatment prior to being discharged from the hospital altogether. Sometimes day treatment will be deemed appropriate for a patient without the patient's having spent time in an inpatient facility. This poses a difficult decision, for essentially the doctors are telling you and your child that she is very sick but not "sick enough" to spend 24 hours a day as an inpatient—a fine line to draw.

Day treatment is a good alternative to inpatient treatment in that there is a little less disruption of regular family life and it is easier for parents to be involved in treatment. For instance, parents get to oversee an evening snack as well as all meals on the weekend. If the day program can really involve parents in the treatment, this is a good way in which parents and program staff can learn from each other, so that by the time the teen graduates from the day program, his parents are more confident that they can continue to help their child, independent of the institution.

A limitation of many residential and some inpatient and day programs is that they often do not treat younger patients (under age 14) or boys. In some instances, rightly or wrongly, residential treatment is considered a treatment of last resort. When an adolescent has spent a great deal of time in outpatient treatment, and may also have had several stays in an inpatient facility, and yet her illness has not responded to these treatment efforts, residential treatment is often recommended. This is not to say that every patient at such a facility has failed at prior treatments; for many patients, residential treatment is the first type of program in which they participate. But it's fair to say that, as a rule, several other treatment options are explored before most doctors (or parents, for that matter) consider residential treatment. At many residential centers a program for educating parents and parent support groups are part of the overall treatment. However, by necessity, because of distance and the cost of travel, both the scope and scale of these programs are limited.

Nonetheless, if your child does need to be treated in a residential facility, try to find one that involves you as much as possible and that can provide help for you when your child is discharged home.

What is your role in general family therapy for eating disorders?

FBT does not focus on general family problems or processes; instead, the main focus is on how the family can help change specific symptoms of anorexia, bulimia, binge-eating disorder, or ARFID. In contrast, many therapists use other forms of family therapy that do not directly and specifically focus on your changing or managing your child's eating disorder symptoms. Instead, these types of family therapy try to address more general family problems because they believe that these general issues contribute to either the development or maintenance of an eating disorder. As we pointed out in Chapter 6 and elsewhere, the evidence that this idea is valid is very limited, but this type of family treatment is both common and considered effective by many clinicians, so you may encounter it among the options available to your child.

In these forms of family therapy, the therapist tries to change a variety of general family processes. Specifically, the therapist wishes to identify and correct inappropriate alliances within the family, communication problems, avoidance of conflict, and suppression of individuation and separation among family members, particularly the adolescent with an eating disorder. When family therapists discuss "inappropriate alliances," what they mean is that from their perspective families work best when parents work together and have clear authority. Sometimes, though, a child may end up getting closer to one of the parents than the other. This kind of alliance can happen, for example, when a child is very ill, requiring a parent to focus almost all of his or her energy on the child. Such an alliance can also be encouraged if there are significant problems between the parents themselves. Regardless of their origin, these alliances can interfere with parents working together, especially in terms of getting rid of an eating disorder. A therapist will attempt to help a family redress the problems created by such alliances by first

identifying them and then illustrating how they are interfering with the parents' working together.

Family therapists address "communication problems" by opening the lines of dialogue. Unfortunately, many family members lose the capacity even to talk to one another. This can result from many factors, among the most common of which are parental preoccupation with work or responsibilities, parental anxiety or depression, and marital discord. A specific form of communication problem is *avoidance of conflict*. Conflict avoidance goes beyond the general problems of communication to a reluctance to take on significant problems in order to "keep the peace" and "avoid fighting." Avoidance of conflict is held as a higher good than solving the problem. Avoiding conflict can, unfortunately, backfire and allow problems such as eating disorders to fester and grow. Therapists help families to determine when and how and sometimes why they prefer to avoid conflict over approaching a problem directly even if it means a period of hostility.

Finally, some families appear to struggle with supporting the evolution of their child's independence during adolescence. Because of worry about what might happen to their child or what the family would be like if their child were more independent, some families appear to send a covert, and sometimes overt, message that they don't support their child's growing up and leaving the family. Addressing this problem means that families have to explore why it might be hard to have a family member grow up and leave them. Common reasons that have been identified by family therapists include fear that without the child present the family will disintegrate, that parents will be lonely, and an unrealistic fear that the child is too immature to leave home.

Your role in these forms of family treatment is to make yourselves as open and available as possible to the examination of the kinds of problems discussed here. This may be easier said than done. It's challenging for all of us to open ourselves to this kind of scrutiny. In addition, remember the principles offered at the beginning of this chapter: Make sure you understand how progress will be measured and that you have a backup plan in case you can honestly say that you've given the treatment a chance and are not

satisfied that it's helping—or, always, if you see your child continue to lose weight or suffer other debilitating medical consequences of the eating disorder.

What is your role in individual psychodynamic approaches?

Clearly, the main argument of this book is that parents need to actively take charge of helping their children with eating disorders. We have stressed repeatedly that eating disorders distort thinking and behavior to such a degree that, as a parent, you are your child's best hope for making significant progress. Nonetheless, other approaches based on psychodynamic therapy have been shown to be helpful in addressing the developmental and emotional problems associated with eating disorders, even if not in addressing the behaviors themselves. In this way they share some similarities with the general family treatments we just discussed. Many clinicians have practiced these types of therapy for years with a sense of clinical success. There are many individual schools of thought that can loosely be grouped as psychodynamic, but adolescent-focused therapy (AFT) has been shown to be effective in treating anorexia in adolescents (see Chapter 6). We'll use it in our example of how you can be involved in individual psychodynamic psychotherapy. AFT grew out of ideas derived from a type of psychodynamic theory called *self psychology*. AFT is a psychodynamic therapy that tries to resolve developmental problems to leave the child with a strong sense of self and sustained feelings of confidence and efficacy. As it pertains to anorexia, the theory suggests that children with this disorder have difficulty with feeling assertive and independent and, as a result, confuse control over eating and weight with other psychological and emotional needs related to independence and confidence. As such, it uses the therapeutic relationship with the individual therapist as the primary vehicle for promoting change.

According to this therapeutic approach, anorexia is a self-destructive attempt to manage problems with emotional immaturity, fear, anxiety, and depression by restrictive dieting and weight loss. To find alternatives to the self-destructive strategies associated

with severe dieting, patients must first learn to identify and define their emotions, both positive and negative, rather than avoid awareness of these feelings through starvation. Recovery also entails increasing their sense of effectiveness in managing problems common to adolescence, including learning to successfully separate and individuate from their family of origin. Other goals of treatment are to help the adolescent develop a healthier sense of self, her family, and the challenges of adolescence and young adulthood so that she feels stronger and more capable.

Even though the main focus of AFT is on the child, parents are routinely involved. At the beginning of AFT, parents are oriented to the rationale for and nature of this form of therapy. Therapists meet with parents in separate (collateral) meetings where they try to assess parental functioning and family dynamics and begin to provide parents with information on how they can help their child manage the developmental challenges that are affecting the anorexia. The therapist should explain that these sessions are designed to support the parents. Parents are educated about separation and individuation being a part of normal adolescent developmental processes and are helped to better understand that what might be regarded as normal and desirable (perfectionism, compliance) are, from the theoretical perspective of adolescent-focused therapy, likely part of the underlying pathology of anorexia. Parents are told that improvement may lead to increasing noncompliance and disagreements with them, as testing limits in these ways is seen as normal in the quest for greater appropriate autonomy during adolescence. At the same time, a teenager's withdrawal may seem problematic to some parents, but the therapist helps them understand that during the course of recovery, this should be expected because it too is normal adolescent behavior.

Over the course of AFT, the therapist will meet with you to assess the degree to which you are handling your child's difficulties appropriately and offer suggestions accordingly. This may be especially necessary for the welfare of younger or less assertive patients. In addition, you will be asked about how you are handling stresses in your child's life and respecting her need for confidentiality; again, the therapist may offer suggestions to help you in these tasks. For

example, the therapist can help you limit the number of extracurricular activities or tutors the child has if the child feels that either is a problem. In short, the therapist serves as your child's advocate in these collateral sessions.

To help you appreciate your child's underlying dilemmas, the therapist will try to help you by suggesting ways to understand your child's behavior and thought processes (especially as they relate to the etiology and maintenance of anorexia) without violating the confidential trust between the therapist and your child. In this regard, it's sometimes helpful for the therapist to ask you for more information about any significant life events that your child has disclosed. The therapist will explain to your child the value of sharing this information. For example, it may provide an opportunity for parents to help or to create a better support system for the child. Moreover, in the process of talking with you, the therapist may discover information (for example, that there is severe marital discord or that one parent has an eating disorder) that, with your permission, will be useful to take back to individual therapy with your child. The therapist's conveying this information may help your child take your limitations less personally and feel less devastated by them. This may be particularly the case with adolescents who are especially self-critical and who have trouble viewing their parents as imperfect.

Thus, with AFT, your role is fundamentally to support the individual therapy designed to enhance your child's capacities for mastering her dilemmas with regard to adolescence and eating. However, as you can see, you are important in the process because you provide information, support the treatment, and open yourself to changing your own attitudes and beliefs if they interfere with your child's needs.

> Sixteen-year-old Sarah had been seeing her therapist in individual treatment, and she had gradually gained weight and stopped binge eating, though she still occasionally purged when she felt she went off her diet. However, she was increasingly surly with her mother and steadfastly ignored her father whenever he spoke to her. Sarah and her therapist discussed these

issues and framed them as having to do with Sarah's wish that her parents would treat her more like her 18-year-old brother.

The therapist asked to meet with Sarah's parents to discuss their view of adolescence. Sarah's mother felt that Sarah was struggling with her because they were too much alike. Sarah's father felt that Sarah was angry because they placed restrictions on whom she could date (no one older than 17) and had a curfew (no later than 10:00 P.M. on Fridays and Saturdays and no going out on school nights).

The therapist served as an educator and advocate for Sarah in the meeting with Sarah's parents. She strove to help them understand the importance of allowing some risk taking (without going overboard) to help Sarah develop more confidence in her own judgment and ability to make appropriate choices. Specifically, they agreed to allow Sarah a trial period of dating whom she chose as long as they could meet him and to allow her to be in charge of her curfew as long as she behaved responsibly.

After several weeks, the parents were asked to return to see how things were going. Although there had been some missteps (on one occasion Sarah had stayed out very late without calling), overall her parents felt that Sarah had demonstrated to them that she was capable of being more responsible than they had expected. Further, the conflicts they had been experiencing had diminished. Over time, Sarah gave up purging on a regular basis. Her conflicts with her parents were fewer and, gradually, she was less preoccupied with her weight as she became interested in her plans for college.

What is your role in supporting cognitive-behavioral therapy for bulimia and binge-eating disorder?

Although cognitive-behavioral therapy (CBT) for bulimia and binge-eating disorder is primarily a treatment involving your child and her therapist, it is reasonable and appropriate to be involved in this treatment as well. That is, you can help improve motivation, support the attempts by the therapist and your child to change behaviors and thinking, and in many cases (though not all) be involved in meal planning and monitoring for and assisting with efforts to

decrease binge-eating and purging episodes. Your involvement in CBT for bulimia nervosa and binge-eating disorder capitalizes on your abilities to alter your home environment to support a change in binge eating and purging, similar to what you may do in family treatment, as described in Chapter 7. However, as CBT is primarily an individual therapy, your role is somewhat different and is further delineated by the various stages of CBT.

At the start of CBT treatment, your child's therapist should explain the CBT model of bulimia and binge-eating disorder and how the specific interventions (e.g., self-monitoring, behavioral experiments, problem solving, and cognitive restructuring) are helpful treatments. This helps you understand what your child will be doing and may help you determine how you can be helpful. The first task in the first stage of CBT is to regularize the eating pattern to prevent binge-eating episodes. You may be asked to assist with providing mealtime structure (three meals and two snacks) and to help prevent binge eating by limiting access to trigger foods and prevent purging by staying with your child for a certain period of time after meals.

> Sixteen-year-old Tanika's pattern of eating was to restrict her intake all morning and through the early afternoon. Then, when she got home from school, she would begin to eat a snack, but this quickly escalated into a binge-eating episode, followed by purging. The therapist discussed with Tanika various strategies for changing her eating pattern. The one that appealed to her most was to ask her mother to eat breakfast with her and to be home after school so that she could help her avoid binge eating. This meant that her mother had to leave work early for several weeks, but her support helped to change Tanika's eating patterns enough that, after several weeks, binge eating was reduced significantly.

Self-monitoring by keeping records of foods consumed and weight is a key component of CBT, although it is sometimes challenging for adolescents because it involves both the ability to self-observe and the effort of writing down these observations. Because adolescents are typically less skillful at self-monitoring than adults,

you can support your child's efforts in CBT by helping her understand the importance of completing the food records. This may
mean something as simple as asking if your child has a food log
sheet or just gently reminding her to complete it. These records
are usually private entries that your child makes to discuss with
her therapist, but sometimes, especially with younger adolescents,
it may be helpful to ask if you can help the child complete these
records, at least at first. Moreover, parents sometimes keep logs
of their own observations of their child's behaviors and apparent
emotional states. These can be used as comparison documents for
discussion with the therapist and adolescent as well. In addition,
mobile phone applications for self-monitoring are being developed.
These applications can be appealing to tech-savvy adolescents and
may improve self-monitoring compliance.

> Maureen was a 14-year-old with bulimia nervosa who repeat-
> edly denied she engaged in binge eating or purging. However,
> the therapist routinely checked with Maureen's parents about
> her behaviors, and they reported that although she had had
> a period without binge eating, they had once again noticed a
> large amount of food missing and evidence in the bathrooms
> that purging had resumed. The therapist asked the parents to
> join Maureen in a session. In this session, the therapist asked the
> parents to share their observations and concerns. The session
> was not confrontational, but aimed instead at helping Maureen
> see that although she was minimizing her symptoms, they were
> still a significant problem. Maureen's mother described discov-
> ering that several boxes of cookies and pints of ice cream were
> missing, with no explanation for their disappearance, but said
> she was worried that they were too tempting for Maureen to
> resist. Her father, who did the cleaning in the house, reported
> finding evidence that Maureen had recently been throwing
> up in the guest bathroom and wondered how he could help
> her. Maureen was initially tearful and angry that her parents
> had "snooped" on her. However, she eventually acknowledged
> that it was true that she was again struggling with binge eat-
> ing and purging. Her parents were not critical of her and said
> they understood how difficult it was to stop these behaviors.
> They asked what more they could do to help. Maureen and her

therapist decided to meet independently of Maureen's parents to come up with some suggestions to consider.

A primary aim of the second stage of CBT for bulimia nervosa and binge-eating disorder is to continue to monitor your child and if necessary to extend progress toward or maintenance of a regular pattern of eating. The next aim is to help your child delineate the nature of feared and avoided foods and to gradually reintroduce, often with your help, some of these foods into her diet. You can be helpful in these activities by contributing your own observations of your child's behaviors. For example, a feared food—one that is likely to induce binge eating—may be ice cream. You can volunteer to go with your child to get ice cream so that you can be available to support him in eating only one cone and to help him by discussing how he feels about this challenge.

You will probably not be directly involved in the specific activities of problem solving or cognitive restructuring, wherein your child tries to identify strategies to prevent binge eating and purging, as well as problems in her thoughts and beliefs about food and weight. However, you may be a part of some of the solutions that your child and her therapist devise. For example, your child may decide that she has a problem with binge eating when she's alone after school. You may be asked to be available during that time to help prevent binge eating. Or your child's beliefs about attractiveness may overemphasize weight as a focus, in which case you can provide insight and assistance in thinking about these issues in the context of your family.

The final stage of CBT is concerned primarily with the maintenance of improvement following treatment. Progress is reviewed, and realistic expectations are established. Relapse-prevention strategies are used to prepare for future setbacks. You can be helpful by identifying upcoming situations that may be stressful and by establishing yourselves as a resource for your adolescent to turn to if things become difficult again. Your involvement in CBT helps to acknowledge the illness and to ultimately reduce shame in your child, so that help (and particularly your help), should it be needed, can be asked for sooner rather than later.

What is your role in interpersonal psychotherapy for bulimia and binge-eating disorder?

Although adults treated with interpersonal psychotherapy (IPT) are often seen alone, therapists who treat adolescents using this approach would generally include you in the treatment because you play such an important role in the interpersonal dilemmas of your child. Remember that IPT approaches changing disordered eating behaviors related to bulimia nervosa very indirectly. However, IPT is still a very focused treatment, and your importance to the specific tasks is highlighted in the examples that follow.

As is the case with CBT, motivation of the child to attend sessions may be the initial point of entry for parents:

> Sixteen-year-old Felicity eagerly began treatment for bulimia nervosa because she was interested in working on her problems with friends. However, Felicity tended to either forget appointments or show up half an hour late. The therapist discussed how she could improve Felicity's attendance and suggested that her parents could remind her when sessions were scheduled by calling her on her cell phone in advance. Felicity agreed that this would help. Her parents were happy to assist in Felicity's treatment, and this involvement seemed to them and to Felicity to be supportive but not intrusive. In addition, Felicity's therapist had only daytime appointments, and so it was necessary to contact her school (with Felicity's parents' permission) to ask that she be excused from classes for treatment. Contact with the school's counselor helped the school administration to support treatment as well.

In IPT for adolescents there are five main problem areas: grief, role disputes, role transitions, interpersonal deficits, and single-parent families. You are likely to play a role in working on some aspect of each of these areas. The most pertinent for working with adolescents with eating disorders are role disputes, role transitions, and the impact of having only one parent.

Role disputes are differences of opinion about the readiness to take up certain adult roles or behaviors (e.g., dating, jobs). Adolescents frequently act out their role disputes with parents through

disruptive, antisocial, or self-punishing behaviors. What differs in helping with conflicts and role disputes with adolescents is the nature of the problem and your involvement as parents. Your child's therapist will attempt to preserve workable family relationships and to provide alternatives to the disruptive behavior. To do this, it is often useful if you come to some sessions to facilitate the negotiation of these disputes, with the therapist present to help you.

Mandy was a 14-year-old who had recently developed bulimia nervosa. She began to skip school, was caught drinking alcohol, and on two occasions met a male friend late at night in a park. Her parents were furious at her behaviors and confused by them, as Mandy had previously been a straight-A student and model child. The therapist helped the parents and Mandy realize that Mandy was struggling to assert herself and develop a sense of independence from her mother, in particular, who tended to be controlling and intrusive (mostly out of love and interest).

Nonetheless, both the therapist and Mandy's parents were worried about the seriousness of the risks that Mandy was taking. Mandy's parents were considering sending her to a residential treatment setting, where someone "could keep a better eye on her." Mandy had a good relationship with her therapist and trusted him to help her. She admitted that at times she too was worried about her behaviors and didn't really understand why she did such things. She reported that she enjoyed drinking because it took her mind off her problems but that she felt vulnerable and a bit stupid for going out late at night to a park where she might get hurt. Her therapist discussed with Mandy what was happening with her parents and wondered with her if she was deliberately using these behaviors to "fight" with them. Mandy agreed that she was angry at her parents, particularly her mother, who still made her lunch and bought her clothes for her. She couldn't quite see how this made her do the things she was doing, but she did know that her relationship with her parents was stressful to her.

When the therapist invited Mandy's parents to a session, the aim was to help Mandy describe how her relationship with her parents was stressful to her and to help them to think about how things might change. The therapist explained that

the conflict they were having among themselves was increasing Mandy's discomfort and that she herself recognized problems with what she was doing. During the session the therapist encouraged further discussion of Mandy's anger at her mother, and Mandy expressed her wish for more age-appropriate freedoms. Her mother agreed to try expanding Mandy's freedoms, though it would be difficult for her, if Mandy also promised to refrain from drinking and sneaking out at night. This initial session was followed by several others specifically examining the changes the parents and Mandy were making and the effects of those changes on their relationships with one another. Over the next few months, disputes and conflicts diminished, and Mandy was more responsible in terms of her risk-taking behaviors.

Both adolescents and adults experience role transitions. Normal role transitions for adolescents include passage into puberty, shift from group to dyadic relationships, initiation of sexual desires and relationships, separation from parents and family, work, college, and career planning. The strategies for addressing role transitions in adolescents do not differ significantly from those used with adults, but therapists will often want and need you, the adolescent's parents, to be included in treatment sessions. The therapist would particularly include you to support the adolescent's giving up a role and to help the family adjust to normative role transitions.

Eighteen-year-old Tanya was preparing to leave for college when her mother discovered Tanya had bulimia. Tanya's parents were anxious for her safety while she was in college and told her that their payment of tuition was dependent on her seeking treatment. The therapist helped to focus Tanya and her family on the importance of the impending role transition that would occur when she went to college. This required that the parents attend several sessions, but the major focus was on Tanya's guilt about leaving home and her anxiety about going to college. To address these issues, the therapist had to help the family acknowledge to one another that this was a significant shift in their relationships and that this change entailed a loss, in the sense that the previous relationship based on cohabitation and day-to-day meetings would be forgone. They were also asked

to focus on the opportunity to forge a new relationship with one another based on a more adult way of being together. The parents said that they were worried about how Tanya would do without them. They had questions for her about how she would manage the temptations of drug and alcohol use, boyfriends, and commitment to study. Tanya, for her part, listened patiently to her parents' questions and reminded them that she had some experience with all of these issues and that she had thus far managed them well. She admitted, however, to also feeling worry about what it would be like to be alone more. Tanya's parents described their own experiences of going off to college and were supportive.

Single-parent families (whether resulting from divorce, death, or parental choice) are an added interpersonal focus for adolescent IPT. Not only is the child's relationship with the absent parent affected, but also her relationship with the remaining parent. Interpersonal tasks associated with this problem area include (1) acknowledging that having a single-parent family is a problem to the adolescent; (2) addressing any feelings of loss, rejection, abandonment, and/or punishment; (3) clarifying expectations for how to relate to the absent parent; (4) negotiating a working relationship with the remaining parent; (5) establishing a relationship with the removed parent if possible; and (6) accepting the permanence of the situation.

Fifteen-year-old Monica developed binge-eating disorder approximately 2 years ago when her father gained sole custody of her. Her mother suffered from a substance abuse disorder. Monica had not lived with her father since she was 5 years old. She says her binge-eating symptoms have worsened since living with him. The therapist working with Monica helped her assess the importance of her life with her single father as it related to (1) her guilty feelings about having been abandoned by her mother, (2) her anger at her father for not being in her life previously and for failing to protect her from her mother's behaviors while she (her mother) was intoxicated, (3) her wish for a female figure with whom she could discuss her romantic relationships, and (4) her wish to reconcile her parents so they would both be available to her.

As we've said, the treatments discussed in this chapter are focused on helping your adolescent make changes in his own behavior while you take a supporting role. In many cases, the targeted behaviors are not the eating-related behaviors that are causing your child's health to deteriorate. This means that you should be vigilant in monitoring your child's progress, as well as supportive of the efforts made in therapy. If a child with anorexia continues to lose weight, or if a child with bulimia or binge-eating disorder continues to binge eat—and especially if these behaviors worsen—you need to take action to get your child medical help quickly and put into effect the backup plan recommended at the beginning of this chapter.

What is your role in dialectical behavior therapy for bulimia and binge-eating disorder?

Dialectical behavior therapy (DBT) is designed to help adolescents with eating disorders by teaching a range of skills in emotion regulation, interpersonal effectiveness, distress tolerance, and mindfulness that are flexibly applied in contexts where dysfunctional behaviors (e.g., binge eating, cutting, substance use) would be used to regulate these negative emotions. These skills can be taught in an individual or group format. In individually based DBT, therapists try to help adolescents by scaffolding skill acquisition through practice in joint sessions with parents. An alternative model for involving parents in DBT is through multifamily groups where a group of five or six adolescents learn skills side by side with their parents. In the individual DBT model, the specific issues of each adolescent receive greater focus, while in the multifamily group adolescents and parents get support and learn from one another. In either form, DBT tries to support the emerging autonomy of adolescents in a family context.

What is your role in cognitive remediation therapy for eating disorders?

Cognitive remediation therapy (CRT) is a treatment that tries to change the style of thinking found in many patients with eating

disorders. In particular, it uses cognitive exercises to improve flexibility and big-picture thinking. There is no direct focus on weight, eating, or eating-related psychopathology, and for this reason CRT is best used only in the context of more focused treatment of the eating disorder. CRT encourages the adolescent to consider how his thinking style affects other situations in his life. During the sessions, feedback focuses on skills to challenge these thinking styles and how these skills can be used and maintained outside of the sessions. The content of the sessions is tailored to the patient's progress. Sessions usually include eight to ten tasks, followed by a conversation between therapist and adolescent about their experience and thoughts about the exercise. Parents are not involved in CRT but can provide support for the child's attendance.

Only time will produce additional data to reveal which types of therapy are most effective in saving lives being damaged by eating disorders. For now, remember that you have a right and a responsibility to be involved in your child's care. In the next two chapters we turn to possible impediments to your success in finding ways to help your child, particularly if you are taking direct charge of changing behaviors.

The next chapter focuses on working together as parents and the dilemmas with seeing eye to eye on treatment choices and the management of eating-related behaviors. However, even when you overcome your own disagreements as parents, you may encounter problems in working with your treatment team. So in our final chapter we turn to the difficulties you may face in working with professionals and with staying empowered and effective as parents fighting against your child's eating disorder.

FOR MORE INFORMATION

Agras, W. S., and R. F. Apple, *Overcoming Eating Disorders: A Cognitive-Behavioral Therapy Approach for Bulimia Nervosa and Binge-Eating Disorder: Therapist Guide, Second Edition*, 2008. New York: Oxford University Press.

Fairburn, C. G., A Cognitive Behavioural Approach to the Treatment of Bulimia, *Psychological Medicine*, 1981, *11*(4), 707–711.

Fairburn, C. G., Interpersonal Psychotherapy for Bulimia Nervosa, in D. M. Garner and P. E. Garfinkel, Editors, *Handbook of Treatment for Eating Disorders, Second Edition*, 1997. New York: Guilford Press, pp. 278–294.

Fitzpatrick, K., A. Moye, R. Hoste, et al., Adolescent-Focused Psychotherapy for Adolescents with Anorexia Nervosa, *Journal of Contemporary Psychotherapy*, 2010, *40*, 31–39.

Le Grange, D., J. Lock, and M. Dymek, Family-Based Therapy for Adolescents with Bulimia Nervosa, *American Journal of Psychotherapy*, 2003, *57*, 237–251.

Lock, J., Treating Adolescents with Eating Disorders in the Family Context: Empirical and Theoretical Considerations, *Child and Adolescent Psychiatric Clinics of North America*, 2002, *11*, 331–342.

Lock, J., S. Agras, D. Le Grange, et al., Randomized Clinical Trial Comparing Family-Based Treatment to Adolescent-Focused Individual Therapy for Adolescents with Anorexia Nervosa, *Archives of General Psychiatry*, 2010, *67*, 1025–1032.

Mufson, L., K. P. Dorta, D. Moreau, et al., *Interpersonal Psychotherapy for Depressed Adolescents, Second Edition*, 2004. New York: Guilford Press.

Robin, A. L., P. T. Siegel, A. W. Moye, et al., A Controlled Comparison of Family versus Individual Therapy for Adolescents with Anorexia Nervosa, *Journal of the American Academy of Child and Adolescent Psychiatry*, 1999, *38*(12), 1482–1489.

Safer, D., J. Couturier, and J. Lock, Dialectical Behavior Therapy Modified for Adolescent Binge Eating Disorders: A Case Report, *Cognitive and Behavioral Practice*, 2007, *14*, 157–167.

Safer, D., C. F. Telch, and E. Chen, *Dialectical Behavior Therapy for Binge Eating and Bulimia*, 2009. New York: Guilford Press.

Tanofsky-Kraff, M., D. Wilfley, J. Young, et al., A Pilot Study of Interpersonal Psychotherapy for Preventing Excess Weight Gain in Adolescent Girls At-Risk for Obesity, *International Journal of Eating Disorders*, 2010, *43*, 701–706.

CHAPTER 9

Harnessing the Power of Unity

How to Stay on the Same Page in Your Fight against Eating Disorders

A good specialist inpatient unit often succeeds in helping children eat normally and, in the case of anorexia, gain weight in part because a nursing team is on hand 24 hours a day to tackle the problem consistently and persistently. This is what you need to do within your family unit if you're to succeed in helping your child conquer anorexia or bulimia: Unite as a family and stay on the same page, all the time. As we've said before, the fact that children tend to relapse after hospitalization underscores the inability of many families to present the same united front. And with outpatient care being the dominant form of treatment today, it's obvious that parents (with backup from siblings wherever possible) need to learn to come to agreement on exactly how they will participate in their child's fight for health and how they'll stick with it for as long as it takes.

If your daughter is anorexic, you have to figure out how you can develop a united front in getting her to eat. If your son is bulimic, you need to find a consistent path toward helping him eat normal amounts of food and not purge. In Chapters 7 and 8 we showed you what your role might involve if your therapist is using a family approach or another type of treatment to help your child. But even

if you adhere to our principles and guidelines, you'll be surprised by how quickly any positive achievements will crumble if you don't spend as much effort on building a united front.

Developing a united front may seem straightforward. You may even feel you don't need this chapter. After all, you know that you and your child's other parent are already in agreement on wanting your son or daughter to get better. Unfortunately, where there's a will, there's not necessarily a way, unless it's exactly the same way and it's well thought out in advance. Wanting to see your child get better is not the same as both of you doing exactly the same thing to make that recovery happen. You and your child's other parent have to "be on the same page" regarding the urgency of the problem, when and how to pursue professional help, what to do at home—deciding what to say to your child to get him or her to eat or to avoid purging, how much food is appropriate, what consequences should be established for lack of progress, how the other kids in the family should be involved, what family sacrifices will be made to facilitate change for the child, and even details such as whether the child has to drink whole milk or skim milk. And you have to stay on the same page every minute of every day.

If you're a typical couple, you may find the idea of being in such constant agreement laughably unrealistic. Most couples have disagreements, some more than others. That's not the issue here. Despite these everyday conflicts, most parents are 100% in agreement that they want their child to recover. The issue here is to figure out how you can work together so that there is no room for the eating disorder to slip through, as evidenced in many of our illustrations in Chapter 7. Only then will your efforts to help your child really bear fruit. So, resolve to set your other disagreements aside; on this life-and-death matter, you can agree to agree.

DIVIDE AND CONQUER: HOW EATING DISORDERS SLIP THROUGH

If it's still hard for you to picture your child's eating disorder slipping through your defenses when both parents are so committed to

the recovery process, imagine a fishing net. If the holes in the net are too big, the fish will just slip through. Your family, too, must be tightly woven if you're to keep your child's eating disorder from slipping through. In fact, just like a fisherman, you'll need to check the integrity of your net regularly. Holes have a way of appearing where you least expect them. For instance, you may think you and your child's other parent are saying the same thing while your teenager with an eating disorder hears two different messages.

> Samantha's mother, Jill, says in a strident voice, "For goodness' sake, Samantha, eat now!" Her father, John, rebuffs his spouse by saying, "Don't be so hard on Samantha" before turning to Samantha and saying, "Come on, Sammy dear, just one more bite." Jill and John believe they're on the same page—they've both told Samantha to eat. But clearly the messages are different on the receiving end. Samantha's mother is issuing a command and already sounds angry. John is making a request and treating his daughter with kid gloves, in addition to criticizing his wife.

In cases like this one, which are quite common, the parents are more successful at battling each other than at finding a common strategy to battle their daughter's eating disorder. While Mom and Dad are quibbling about how to get Samantha to eat more, Samantha doesn't have to eat, and the eating disorder is given time to catch its breath, so to speak, or to "slip through." The best way for these parents to get Samantha to eat the amount they want her to eat is for them to really get on the same page. In fact, not just on *the same page*, but *the same line, the same word*, and *the same letter*. This will enable them to speak with one voice and say exactly the same thing: "We know it's hard for you, but we want you to eat more, and we have no choice but to find a way to help you beat this eating disorder."

In the following pages we illustrate a variety of typical disagreements between parents and how you can head them off. We hope that being aware of the insidious ways in which your child's eating disorder will try to divide and conquer the two of you will help you avoid as many of them as possible and quickly resolve those you

can't. These examples will also remind you, as parents, to continue to work together in forging a path toward helping your child.

If your child has only one parent, you can still gain insight from these scenarios. As we've already shown, you may be getting help from another adult—the child's grandparent or another relative, a partner who lives with you, or even a close family friend—and that person also needs to stay on the same page as you. But even if you're going it alone, you may experience ambivalence over many of the same issues, as Tammy's mother did (see Chapter 7) when she was trying to keep her daughter from purging. Her internal conflict over how much she should control her daughter gave bulimia the loophole it needed to slip through and emerge victorious in the fight for this teenager's health. So, in the following pages, when we refer to your spouse or your child's other parent, we mean to include any other adult who is helping you in this effort.

TYPICAL DIVIDE-AND-CONQUER SCENARIOS AND HOW TO AVOID THEM

1. Only one of the child's parents is convinced that this is the time for action and that they ought to be involved in treatment.

Even though everyone in the family showed up for the evaluation, Mom and Dad argued in the office about whether they should be there. "I'm not sure we should do this right now," Mom said, turning to her daughter, soliciting her agreement. Dad, fuming, said, "I'm tired of pretending that nothing's wrong. When do you think it will be time for us to do something about Rachel's not eating?"

As we've stated several times, most patients do well when their illness has been recognized relatively early on and when both parents realize the need for them to become active participants in their child's recovery. Unfortunately, several factors often work against this potential scenario. Many parents end up immobilized because they feel they are blamed for having caused their daughter's illness. They may feel guilty and therefore think their involvement will only

make things worse, or their adolescent is pleading with them not to take her for treatment because she can "handle it" on her own. In that case it's not uncommon for one parent to give in to the pleading of the teenager, to express discomfort with "pushing" her into treatment when she so clearly doesn't want to go, or to try to convince the other parent that the adolescent isn't ready yet—"she doesn't want to change." The eating disorder is quite good at spotting this kind of opportunity, where rallying the ambivalent parent is often enough to delay any meaningful action, while the adolescent continues to starve herself and the grip of the eating disorder tightens.

This scenario is even more likely to take shape when the adolescent has bulimia. With anorexia, parents can see that their anorexic child looks so obviously unwell. In the case of bulimia, binge-eating disorder, and even avoidant/restrictive food intake disorder (ARFID), however, it's quite likely that parents will not be aware or will only suspect that food is disappearing or that frequent bathroom trips after mealtimes have nothing to do with "freshening up" but more with their child making herself sick to continue managing her anxiety about weight gain. Unfortunately, all these different possibilities result in the same situation—the parents feel immobilized for one reason or another, the eating disorder is good at taking advantage of this gap, and the adolescent goes without helpful treatment.

If this is the case in your family, what should you do? Try to keep your adolescent out of discussions concerning her health care as much as possible! This may seem unfair to you—after all, she's 16 and you've included her in almost all recent decisions involving her. Unfortunately, anorexia, as well as bulimia to a lesser degree, doesn't allow your teen to think rationally about her need for treatment. Inform your child of your decision, but refrain from seeking her opinion about health care measures. That is what you and your spouse should be talking about. When you two have a private moment, try to sit down to discuss the pros and cons of your child's remaining untreated. It's important to be in agreement, even if this means deciding to "give it another 10 days, but at the end of that time, we will do X, Y, or Z," as opposed to continuing to disagree while your child languishes with an eating disorder.

2. One parent's denial is actively colluding with the adolescent's illness.

> Debra's parents have been told that there is little doubt that the diagnosis is anorexia. Dad almost seemed relieved: "I knew it. I was always convinced that this was the problem. We had her visit so many doctors, from the endo guys to the GI docs and back. They couldn't find a thing wrong." Mom was less comfortable with the news: "I think we should go back to Dr. A in the GI clinic. I'm not convinced her regurgitating her food is in her head; there must be something wrong with her intestinal tract. It has to be something with her stomach or such."

Realizing that their child is seriously ill is devastating for almost all parents, so a certain amount of denial is understandable. Some parents, however, find that a diagnosis of an eating disorder remains too uncomfortable to deal with even after they finally come to terms with the fact that their child is unwell. This discomfort often results from the fact that anorexia and bulimia are psychiatric diagnoses. Unfortunately, we still live in a society in which a psychiatric illness carries a certain stigma for some, and perhaps one or both parents will find the thought of their son or daughter's being mentally ill intolerable. In that case it's understandable that parents might prefer to settle for a more acceptable diagnosis such as a gastrointestinal or endocrine disorder or another medical condition. An accurate diagnosis, however, usually leads to the right treatment, which in turn provides the best opportunity for a favorable outcome. It therefore becomes a real treatment dilemma when one or both parents are unable to accept the diagnosis of an eating disorder for their adolescent.

Just as worrisome is the fact that this scenario provides the adolescent's eating disorder with the ideal opportunity to thrive. Earlier in this book we characterized anorexia as ego-syntonic, meaning that the sufferer will often be unable to appreciate the severity of the disorder. In fact, we've known many patients who don't think they are ill at all! Having a parent question the validity of the eating disorder diagnosis only feeds that delusion. In the case of bulimia, the sufferer knows that binge eating and purging are abnormal but is ashamed of the behavior and often tries to hide it. A parent's

denial that a problem exists, which often happens, may only make it easier for the child to keep the problem under cover. In both cases, the family is left with a stalemate. With Mom and Dad sitting in opposite camps, the illness remains untreated (or the child is treated for the side effects of her eating disorder rather than the eating disorder itself), perhaps with precious time being lost while the child is dragged from one medical test to the next in futile pursuit of some nonexistent gastrointestinal ailment.

Once again, the crucial issue here is for Mom and Dad to look at the facts together and try to reach an understanding of what the next step in treatment should be. That may be difficult, though, if the adolescent is closely aligned with one parent in such a way that this alliance opposes or excludes the other parent, as is often the case when this scenario develops. The adolescent is "recruited" as an active "consultant" to at least one of the parents, leaving the other parent on the outside and quite frustrated as a result.

Debra's parents need to consult one another, not their adolescent, on these particular health concerns. If you and your child's other parent find yourself mired in disagreement about what's wrong, your child's therapist should be able to help. It's not unusual for us to devote an entire therapy session to getting a parent in denial to see the light.

3. Each parent thinks the other one is not doing enough or doing the right thing to make sure the eating disorder is addressed.

Becky is not gaining weight. Her parents are beside themselves with worry. Instead of focusing on how they can succeed at helping her next time, Dad starts in on Mom: "I told you to give her whole milk. Why do you keep insisting on skim?" Mom then feels humiliated and lashes out at Dad to remind him that he isn't doing "his job": "I asked you to have Becky eat three pancakes at breakfast, but you always seem too busy to wait around till she's done. That's no good either!"

Here the parents have indeed taken action to get their adolescent into treatment and to encourage her to eat more. These parents are also heeding the clinician's call that they work as a united team

to be most effective in helping to combat their child's eating disorder. However, many couples have disagreements about a variety of issues, including how they should raise their children. So, instead of just being on the same page about how they will manage their daughter's illness, these parents are trying to outdo each other. Helping their son or daughter becomes yet another way in which they battle each other instead of battling the illness. Most adolescents with an eating disorder are quite astute at realizing that Mom and Dad are not quite on the same page, even though on the surface it might appear that way. These parents are making it relatively easy for their adolescent to criticize one parent—"You give me all these foods that you know I don't like"—just to have the other parent join the adolescent in criticizing that parent for not trying harder or being more creative in finding different foods that the child will eat. Needless to say, the eating disorder's strategy to divide and conquer works well in this family. Next time the adolescent criticizes the other parent, the remaining parent joins in the criticism, and so the cycle continues.

If you find that this happens in your family, you and your spouse should remind yourselves that disagreeing in this way is not going to help your child recover from anorexia. Although you're both trying to get her to eat more (which is good and will help her gain those much needed pounds), you won't be nearly as successful as you could be unless you can remind yourself that on the issue of how much food, when, or how, you cannot disagree with your spouse at all! Try not to disagree in front of your child. When your spouse says something about food type or amount in front of your child and you don't agree, go along with your spouse for the moment. When the two of you have some private time, discuss your differences frankly and make sure you come to an agreement about how to handle the situation when it comes up again. Always agree in front of your child!

4. One parent blames the other for being too critical of the child with an eating disorder.

Sasha didn't gain weight this week. Her mother seems really upset and says, "I wish you'd tried harder. I just knew yesterday

that there's no way you were going to be 'up' at weigh-in today, I just knew it." Sasha looks distraught, and Dad quickly jumps to her rescue: "I wish you wouldn't always focus on the negative. You know this isn't easy for Sasha!"

In some families, there is tremendous acrimony between the parents, which is a reflection of the nature of their relationship well before the onset of the eating disorder. This does not mean that these parents will not be able to help their adolescent. But their challenge will be to find a way to agree to disagree on many other issues and work out how they are to battle their child's eating disorder as a united team. It's very easy, however, for the adolescent to use these circumstances of acrimony between parents to "protect" the eating disorder. If one can accuse one's parent of being horrible, bad, unreasonable, too strict, or critical, it may be easy to get the other parent to take sides by accusing the spouse of never seeing progress, of always expecting the worst, and so on. The end result is that although both parents want their adolescent to get healthy again, they constantly get caught up in three-way struggles.

If you find yourself in this dilemma, you'll have to put your marital issues aside until your teenager is well again. We realize this is easier said than done. Some parents in these circumstances continually remind themselves that arguments between child and parent often lead to arguments between the parents, and that's how they remain vigilant to the eating disorder trying to slip through. But if marital discord continues to get in the way of your helping with your child's eating disorder, you should consider asking the therapist to help you address some of the crucial issues that make it so hard for you two to agree.

Although it seems fairly typical for one parent to "spoil" a child more than the other, in part because of differences in parenting style (one's permissive, one's not) and maybe also because of favoritism toward one child over the others in the family, you should attempt to find a way to avoid getting into whose approach is right. Instead, agree, as a general rule, that you'll hash out the acceptable responses to your child's food refusal—what tone of voice is appropriate, what words are okay and which are not, how you will remind each other, without being accusatory, when one of you goes beyond

those parameters. As we said earlier, you should at least agree not to criticize each other at all in front of your child, but talk about these things only afterward, when alone. The best way to demonstrate your united front is for one parent to say, "Sasha, I want you to eat this plate of pasta," and the other parent to immediately respond with, "Sasha, your mother and I want you to eat this plate of pasta." In other words, parents should repeat each other's instructions and always try to reiterate that the request for further food intake comes from both of them.

5. **One parent addresses the eating disorder with relative harshness, whereas the other constantly tries to soften the verbal blows of the first parent.**

> "Kate, you have to eat that piece of chicken on your plate," Dad says adamantly. "I hate it when you tell me what to do," Kate retorts. Then she turns to her mother and says, "Tell him not to yell at me. You know I don't like chicken. Tell him, Mom, tell him." Kate's mother knows that it's Kate's anorexia that's trying to divert her attention to quarreling with Kate's father so that the anorexia can have its way. So she doesn't "tell him" as her daughter pushes her to do. Instead, she says, "We both know you don't like chicken, honey. No one's trying to make you eat food you don't like. Maybe you can skip your meat, just this once."

In this variation on the preceding scenario, the child's eating disorder is again trying to gain a foothold by training the parents' attention on each other and away from the illness that's causing their child to waste away. Here, however, the parents seem to be on the same page, because Kate's mother is on to anorexia's tricks. But not quite. Kate's parents may be on the same page, but they're not on the same line, the same word, and the same letter, as they need to be. They may not have gotten engaged in a dispute with each other, but anorexia did win.

Kate's mother doesn't know what else she could have done. Both parents are trying very hard to get Kate to eat more healthy meals. But if Kate's mother insists that Kate eat what's in front of her, she'll have refused to protect her daughter from her father's "bullying"

and will be seen as a bully herself. If she gives in to her daughter's wishes, she'll be opposing her husband's efforts to get their daughter to eat healthier quantities of food. Kate's mother chose to bargain with the eating disorder and let Kate have a compromise meal—in this case, as is typical, a salad with fat-free dressing or no dressing at all. This scenario leaves Kate satisfied, Dad frustrated with his wife *and* daughter, and Mom embattled for trying to please both her husband and *her daughter* (read *the eating disorder*). The winner, of course, is the eating disorder.

When parents disagree about how to help their child, as these two parents have, they should always discuss their differences in private. Acting out these differences in front of the adolescent at mealtimes will only serve to blow more steam into the already invigorated illness. Even though Kate's mother would have felt uncomfortable with how this meal was proceeding, supporting her husband's effort (demand for eating X, Y, or Z), would keep them on the same page. Once these parents have a private moment, they should discuss what's just happened at the table and figure out how to deal with it when this scenario presents itself again.

6. After some progress, one parent gets nervous about the child's weight gain and begins to criticize the other parent's efforts.

Juanita's mom and dad did a lot of homework together, reading as much as possible about her anorexia, investigating every treatment option, and pursuing the goal of getting their child back on track with remarkable determination. The therapist had few difficulties in convincing them of what needed to be done to make sure that Juanita started eating what she needed to gain the 25 pounds she had lost in the preceding 3 months. Things went well from the treatment perspective, and every week the parents would tell their doctor how they had managed, under difficult circumstances, to make decisions together about how much their child should eat. Juanita's weight responded likewise and made good progress, with a pound or so gained every week.

However, as her weight started to approach a healthy level, Juanita became increasingly uncomfortable and anxious and

accused her parents of feeding her too much and making her fat. Although this was not the case, Dad started undermining Mom's efforts at helping Juanita eat sufficient amounts of food at regular intervals. "I don't think she needs to eat quite that much anymore," he'd say. It turns out that Dad was also getting anxious about Juanita's weight gain. Mother, in an outburst, accused Dad of being afraid that his daughter would, in fact, become overweight: "I always suspected that you wanted her to be thin. I always knew it."

Some parents appear to be able to work well together from the start, and Juanita's parents certainly began on the same page. However, Juanita's constant pleading, especially with Dad, not to make her eat eventually convinced him that perhaps they were, in fact, "making her fat." For Juanita to reach a healthy weight, Dad needed a great deal of assurance from the therapist that he and his wife were doing the "right thing."

All parents know well what to feed their child when he or she is starving—it's just that the eating disorder trips them up, getting them to doubt themselves. Therefore, the challenge for Juanita's parents, especially her dad, is to remind themselves and one another that they usually do know best and should follow their gut instincts, hang in there, and listen to one another when it comes to their child's health status. If unsure, they should consult with a professional and not allow their child to counsel them on her health care needs—after all, she is only 12! Juanita, on the other hand, obviously needs her parents' assurance that they are helping her, that they only want her to be healthy and happy again. They must repeat this message jointly to her as often as needed.

What happened in this family is actually quite common. The adolescent manages to gain weight in the beginning, as parents have put up a united front in their efforts to help their child recover. However, in many instances the adolescent "goes along" in the beginning, only to find himself getting very anxious at reaching a certain level in weight gain, at which point he "slams on the brakes." The parents' challenge is to continue in their efforts even beyond this point. Their task is not only complicated at this juncture, as perhaps they are tired after a long struggle, but when one parent "agrees" with

the adolescent that "perhaps this is enough weight gain," the family has a real challenge at hand. It's not uncommon for one parent to be quite anxious about the child's weight gain, as is the case for Juanita's father. In such situations, parents need to check with one another about their goals for their child. And, as with everything else in recovery, they need to agree on what weight will be acceptable. You have to discuss such disagreements and not allow your own possible anxieties about weight gain to get the better of you.

7. Divorce or other circumstances have created a parental triangle that makes staying on the same page almost impossible.

> Diane and Lou's divorce was not amicable, and the two have a hard time speaking, much less spending time together with 16-year-old John, who has anorexia. Diane is the custodial parent, but she works the 7:00–3:00 shift at a hospital an hour's drive away. So her mother, who has her own home about 5 miles away, comes over at 7:30 to make John's breakfast before he goes to school and to see that he eats it. It's not very convenient, but John desperately needs to gain weight, and she's willing to make this sacrifice. John then has lunch on his own at school and goes to his father's house after school, where he has his afternoon snack under Dad's supervision. He then returns home for the evening and has dinner with Mom. This array of adult caregivers involved in John's eating makes coordination of their refeeding effort extremely difficult, and John's progress has been slow. "I'm sorry," his mother has said repeatedly when their therapist expresses concern about this arrangement. "I love my son, and I'm trying to do the best I can. But I have to go to work early, and there is no way I can get time off. We're already understaffed. If I ask for a leave, I'll lose my job permanently. Yes, of course, I'm worried about John, but his dad and grandmother will just have to help out."

Everyone in this family wants to be involved in the care of the teenage boy they love, but getting all three interested parties on the same page is quite a challenge. When such family members don't necessarily talk with one another (as is the case between Mom and her ex-husband) or live in the same home, their refeeding program

is vulnerable to failure no matter how well intentioned everyone is. Because there are so many loopholes in this regimen, it's very easy for the eating disorder to find an escape route and slip through. For instance, John can easily convince Grandma that he doesn't have to have "that much" for breakfast, because "Mom already gave me so much to eat for dinner last night." John does not have to have any lunch at school because there is no one to supervise him there. When he goes to his dad's for his afternoon snack, he can announce that he doesn't feel like eating much "since I had tons of food for lunch at school." In keeping with what we have tried to make clear in previous chapters, it's not that John wants to lie to his parents, but, rather, the eating disorder is being given an ideal opportunity to slip through the cracks of this very "porous" system the adults have put in place. This family system is supposed to help John restore his weight to within a normal range for his age and height.

What needs to happen here to remedy the situation? There are many differences that may have brought on the divorce between John's parents, and Mom may have issues with her own mother because her mother has had to step in to help with child care. If John stands any chance of recovering from his anorexia, these adults will have to find a way to talk with one another, set their personal differences aside, and figure out how they can work together more successfully in John's refeeding. Their therapist should be able to help them work this out.

One possible solution is for each member of this family, after the meal for which he or she is responsible, to report by phone to the next person in line. Grandma calls Dad and leaves a message telling him what John ate and what John's response was to eating; Dad then decides what is an appropriate snack. Dad likewise makes a call, leaving a message for Mom so she can decide how to handle dinner. That way they don't have to talk to each other in person. Moreover, a school counselor, for instance, could be assigned the task of checking up on John discreetly at lunch to see what he's eating and maybe even offer a couple of words of encouragement. In that case, Grandma could call the counselor directly or could leave a message for Mom and Mom could make the call. Then the counselor could report to Dad.

If this schedule does not work out as planned, and all parties cannot put their differences aside, they may have to return to the therapist, who can serve as a mediator to help them communicate about how best to help John. The therapist could, for instance, designate one of the three as the "point person" who is responsible for communicating with the others and keeping track of what John is eating. In John's case, it could be his mom inasmuch as she's the custodial parent and the obvious choice, or it could be the grandmother because she may find it easier to talk to both of the others than it is for them to talk to each other.

8. One parent is very effective while the other feels defeated.

> "I feel I have to do everything to help Karen get better. I know her dad agrees with me that she's really sick, but he's given up and doesn't want to fight this illness anymore. I resent that, because I end up being the one who has to make all the milkshakes. I'm the one who sits with Karen until she has finished her meal. I'm the one who gets up early and makes her breakfast. I think she really hates me, and all the while he gets to be the good guy."

Karen's mother understands the predicament her child is in, and she is taking appropriate steps to get their child into treatment. But she can't take much satisfaction in her accomplishments, because Karen's dad is leaving his wife to feel like "bad cop," on top of suffering the exhaustion and resentment of handling all the food preparation and meal monitoring. Mom is, in effect, battling both Karen's illness and her husband, as the illness has been able to obtain "refuge" in Dad's abdication. This is most unfortunate, for in every setup outlined here so far, one issue is the same—while frustration and despair mount in the family, the eating disorder flourishes.

One parent can be successful in refeeding the child or making sure she doesn't binge or purge, as long as this parent has the emotional support and understanding of the other parent. Some couples, whether because of personality, temperament, or mere

logistics, opt to have one parent do the work. However, the important prerequisites are their agreement on the fact that their child has a serious illness and their willingness to support each other, even if this support means only emotional or psychological comfort.

Every family has its own unique set of circumstances that will determine how it responds in the face of a crisis. The important point is that regardless of this set of circumstances, the parents always have to agree on the seriousness of their child's illness and always have to agree to support each other in addressing the problem. Karen's father seems to agree that his daughter has a terrible illness, but his willingness to give up on fighting it may be his way of denying the full urgency of the problem. Or maybe it's just that he really has exhausted his personal resources for fighting the illness. Like overcoming most potentially fatal or chronic illnesses, battling anorexia or bulimia requires quite a bit of stamina on the part of the parents. That is why it's so crucial for parents to be able to put their differences aside and figure out a way to present a united front. It's all too easy for the adolescent with an eating disorder to spot the differences between parents and capitalize on these differences to allow the eating disorder to persevere. If the "hardworking" parent runs out of steam, there won't be another parent to provide backup.

It is therefore imperative that Karen's parents work out an agreement whereby they can be supportive of one another. Even if Karen's mother ends up doing all the hard work of refeeding, the chances are greater that she'll be able to persevere *if* she feels Dad supports her efforts in spirit if not in body. If he feels he cannot do what his wife is doing, he should verbally support his spouse and make her feel that he is 100% behind her efforts. And he should do so in his daughter's presence so that her eating disorder knows in no uncertain terms that there is no opportunity to slip through. Being "bad cop" on top of doing all the work will leave anyone depleted.

9. Parents take turns in siding with the adolescent (the eating disorder) against the other parent.

When parents take turns in siding with their child, the eating disorder has an ally in both parents but not at the same time. When

parents are not used to working together, they may, in fact, find it a little awkward when they do agree. This may be because they aren't used to it, or they don't really want to because they are so used to taking opposing viewpoints. When they're confronted with the prospect of figuring out together how to address their child's eating disorder, they have a real dilemma on their hands. Unfortunately, as in every scenario sketched so far, it's the adolescent's eating disorder that comes out on top. Because the parents in this example cannot see eye to eye, they will instinctively oppose each other, even when there has been progress in defeating the eating disorder. How does this look in practice?

> Dad has been quite successful at working out a schedule whereby he or his wife spends time with Linda after every meal, whether it's watching television together, reading together, or making sure she doesn't throw up the meal she just had. Dad feels quite pleased that he has been able to help Linda not throw up every time he's spent time with her after a meal, perhaps even to Linda's relief. Because of Mom and Dad's long-standing inability to work together, however, even when it might mean helping their adolescent, Mom accuses Dad of being too rigid or too strict with Linda and says, "How can you be supervising her like that? She's not 3 years old." Dad backs off to allow Mom to take the lead in helping Linda. He then finds himself in a position to challenge Mom about doing something wrong when it comes to Linda's care: "I think you made her eat that rice too fast," Dad says. "That's why she wanted to purge right after the meal. I think you should give her more time."

In the preceding scenario of endless back-and-forth bickering, Linda's eating disorder doesn't have to do too much to render her parents' efforts relatively futile. This again points to our now familiar argument: It is absolutely essential for parents to find common ground in whatever strategy they feel most comfortable with when they address their adolescent's illness. Think of a well-oiled nursing team in a specialist inpatient unit and how the success of the team members' work is attributed mostly to their ability to speak with one voice and never to second-guess each other when it comes to addressing the eating disorder. If you and your spouse disagree,

don't display this division in front of your teen. Instead, go along with the spouse who took the first step at normalizing your child's eating. Only later, perhaps after a meal and when you are on your own, let your spouse know that you disagree and discuss a compromise strategy.

STAYING ON THE *RIGHT* PAGE

Sometimes parents are on the same page, but it's the wrong page. They're unified in their efforts and their attitudes, but because they're headed in the wrong direction, the eating disorder is going to emerge victorious.

1. The parents are united, but in fighting their child, not the eating disorder.

> "I don't know when to believe John anymore. He tells lies all the time. He says he doesn't vomit, and then I find all the evidence in the bathroom," John's mother says. "Yes, he is really difficult. He's come to be such a negative influence in our family," his dad adds.

We discussed the importance of separating the illness from the adolescent in Chapter 7. For parents to be effective in helping their child through an eating disorder, and for the adolescent to know that his parents and the doctors aren't fighting him, it's very helpful to see the eating disorder as something that has overtaken the adolescent. The eating disorder should be perceived as an illness that has taken over his life, something he hasn't brought on himself, and something that's most certainly not within his control. Understanding an eating disorder this way helps parents in their struggle—they are not fighting their adolescent but are battling the illness. So, when your teenager finds a way to hide food, dispose of food, eat an entire cake and not tell the truth about it, or get rid of the food by throwing up, you should remind yourself that he isn't a "bad" person and is not willfully trying to deceive you. Rather, his illness gets your child to do this because he is so dreadfully anxious that

weight gain will result if he doesn't throw the food away or throw up after a binge.

Naturally, then, when we propose that parents need to present a united front, we mean a united front against the illness, not against their adolescent. In the preceding brief example, John's parents are indeed on the same page, but unfortunately they are united in their disapproval of their son (because *he* lies, *he* hides food, *he* throws up, and so on). In this scenario where the parents do not separate John from his eating disorder, the adolescent is left vulnerable to be overtaken by an illness that controls the way he thinks about himself, his weight, and his shape and that powerfully influences how he behaves in response to these thoughts. He also has his parents thinking that he's a bad kid for "doing all this." The more these parents fight their child, the more they'll probably feel frustrated and be convinced that "he's doing this to spite us" or keep asking themselves and each other, "Why doesn't he just snap out of it?" The adolescent ends up feeling alone in his predicament and will have a very hard time convincing his parents that he isn't a bad person. All the while, the chances are good that his symptoms will flourish, further heightening the parents' disgust with him for throwing up, for instance, and his despair for being so utterly misunderstood.

These parents' shared inability to separate the illness from their adolescent has made it very difficult for them to help their son through this ordeal. John's parents should constantly remind themselves that an eating disorder is no different from any other illness—an adolescent with cancer didn't choose to have the illness, nor is he responsible for feeling miserable, tired, in pain, or for having other illness-related feelings and behaviors.

2. The parents check with the adolescent about important health-related decisions.

Sharon is just not gaining much weight from week to week, and her parents can't quite understand why. It turns out that Sharon is very much involved in her own treatment planning. "Yes," her mother explains, "we always ask Sharon whether she's okay with our meal plan." "It's a good thing," Dad adds, "that she has to help us make these decisions because she has to feel she's

part of the process. Otherwise, she'll feel left out and won't eat anything."

In commonsense terms, these parents sound as though they're doing the right thing. Their daughter does eventually have to make the right decisions about what to eat on her own, and so it sounds smart to get her involved now. Unfortunately, she's not yet ready. These parents have been checking with their adolescent regarding her views or thoughts on a variety of subjects. Giving your adolescent an opportunity to voice her own views and develop her own ability to make important decisions or choices is part of normal adolescent development. You'd want that to happen for your child, and you've spent many years cultivating a very democratic style of parenting. But when an eating disorder comes along, and *only* in terms of managing the eating disorder, you may temporarily have to take back control, at least until your child is ready to be independent again in her eating patterns.

If your child is not yet an adolescent, habitually involving the child in decision making is more a matter of parenting style than of making a natural transition to the child's evolving independence. In this case, you may temporarily have to alter your parenting style. How you will manage your child's eating disorder by changing your parenting style will be a personal decision and will depend on the unique circumstances in each family.

> Sharon's parents know that Sharon should have ice cream for dessert. After all, she is terribly underweight, she had very little of her dinner, and she needs more calories to stave off further weight loss. They both know that and agree with one another about the course of action. Still, they can't resist asking Sharon whether she wants the ice cream. This is, after all, a reasonable thing to ask any healthy adolescent, and accepting her answer if she declined would be reasonable as well.

What Sharon's parents are forgetting is that when they talk to Sharon about food, they are not talking to a daughter who has reached the level of maturity expected of a typical 15-year-old, but to anorexia nervosa. And anorexia nervosa will always answer "no." Sharon may

very well want the ice cream, but when someone is overtaken by the symptoms of anorexia, she will certainly refuse it—"It's bad for me, it'll make me fat" or "You know I don't like ice cream" are typical responses. The result is that the parents find themselves in an awkward dilemma. They may feel that the alternative to continuing to ask such questions of their daughter is to be unacceptably "mean" or disrespectful of the kind of person she has proven herself to be. "We always let her have what she wants," said Sharon's mother. "She's such a careful and thoughtful child, and we know she'll make the right decision." This may indeed be true for every aspect other than eating, and it may have been true for all aspects of Sharon's adolescence before the eating disorder overtook her thoughts and feelings about food, weight, and shape. But it's not true now, because Sharon is not the one making the decisions about food.

What should Sharon's parents do? They have to *temporarily* find a way to avoid giving Sharon much of a choice when it comes to the foods she eats. If they feel that contradicts their parenting style and they feel they *have* to introduce choices, these choices should be between chocolate and strawberry ice cream, as opposed to ice cream or no ice cream. Although our proposal may seem somewhat dogmatic, chances for the recovery of your adolescent are accelerated when her weight goes up, when she manages to refrain from binge eating or purging her food, and when getting stuck in an endless "eating disorder debate" is avoided.

CAN PARENTS AGREE? THEY MUST.

We've presented several typical disagreements in parents' approach to an eating disorder, each time pointing out how these disagreements can hamper your child's recovery and how your child might try to steer you away from ultimately helping her with her eating dilemma, by dividing your efforts or by simply distracting you from the task at hand—her recovery. In each example, we've also pointed out what to look for in your own behavior that may, in fact, complicate the steps you've already taken to help your child. Finally, we've shown specifically how you, as parents, can work together in a way

that's productive for your child, even if you and your spouse have to agree to disagree for now. We hope you'll use these examples as inspiration in your efforts to find a way to agree on how to help your child, from meal to meal, from minute to minute.

FOR MORE INFORMATION

Le Grange, D., Family Therapy for Adolescent Anorexia Nervosa, *Journal of Clinical Psychology*, 1999, 5, 727–740.

Le Grange, D., and J. Lock, *Treating Bulimia in Adolescents: A Family-Based Approach*, 2007. New York: Guilford Press.

Le Grange, D., and J. Lock, Editors, *Eating Disorders in Children and Adolescents: A Clinical Handbook*, 2011. New York: Guilford Press.

Le Grange, D., J. Lock, and M. Dymek, Family-Based Therapy for Adolescents with Bulimia Nervosa, *American Journal of Psychotherapy*, 2003, 57, 237–251.

Lock, J., *The Oxford Handbook of Child and Adolescent Eating Disorders: Developmental Perspectives*, 2012. New York: Oxford University Press.

Lock, J., and D. Le Grange, *Treatment Manual for Anorexia Nervosa: A Family-Based Approach, Second Edition*, 2013. New York: Guilford Press.

CHAPTER 10

Staying Empowered and Informed

*How to Work with Professionals
Who Are Trying to Help Your Child*

Professionals who are trying to help your child will always have your child's best interest at heart. That does not mean, however, that you'll always find yourself in agreement with the doctors when it comes to their treatment plan for your adolescent. You may have to struggle to see eye to eye with your child's pediatrician, psychologist, psychiatrist, or therapist because in many cases parents are still viewed more as part of the problem than as a key to the solution. So, as much as we would like to believe that you can become a full member of your child's treatment team just by being willing and able to participate, that's not yet the case in all treatment settings. Fortunately, the mindset that resists parental involvement in the care of teenagers with eating disorders is shifting as research data supporting the importance of parents' contribution continue to accumulate. Just be aware that you may have to make a greater effort to stay informed and empowered than you might expect, which is why we've devoted a chapter to suggestions for handling the dilemmas you may encounter during your child's diagnosis and treatment.

Throughout this book we've emphasized the critical need to *stay on the same page* during your child's treatment. In Chapter 9 we looked at what that demands of two parents or other adults raising a child who has an eating disorder. But the concept applies equally to everyone involved and in contact with your child while she is recovering from an eating disorder. Not only must you and your child's other parent be on the same page; so should the members of the treatment team be in full agreement with one another and with you and your child's other parent. Obviously, this condition can't be met unless you feel your treatment team is on the right course. The value of this *agreement* among all parties should not be underestimated—it is all too easy for the adults (you and the professionals) to become confused about the right course of action to pursue, while your child's treatment suffers as a result. In the last chapter we talked about how the eating disorder can exploit disagreements to derail the efforts to get your child back to health. An eating disorder can also easily find cracks in the front established by the *entire* alliance formed to help your child—both parents and all the professionals involved. In the next several pages, we detail some potential pitfalls that might make it difficult for you to agree with your child's treatment team, as well as what you can do about such a situation so that you can remain a vital part of the solution. Although it is not possible to advise you on the specific makeup of the treatment facilities or treatment teams in your area, we hope you will read this chapter in conjunction with the information provided in the Resources section that follows and that this can help you come up with a strategy that will support your efforts to help your adolescent. Finding the best treatment facility for your child will be a challenge, but we hope that having reached this point in this book will equip you with sufficient knowledge to make an informed decision and play a constructive role in your child's recovery.

In addition to the difficulties of parents that are discussed in Chapter 9, the following are common dilemmas that parents encounter, not only in trying to stay on the same page with the practitioners treating their child but also in retaining an active role in the child's recovery. Keep in mind that the central question is not whether the professionals on your child's team are dedicated

to helping her get better, but whether their treatment philosophy allows you to be fully involved. If it does not, preparing yourself to stand your ground in a constructive manner will go a long way toward enabling you to play an active part in your adolescent's treatment.

A professional you've consulted says your child's problem "cannot be an eating disorder."

There are many reasons that your child's pediatrician or other doctor might make this pronouncement. If you've agonized over the decision to seek help, your child has resisted, and you're sick with worry, this conclusion may initially provide some relief. But relief can quickly turn to increased anxiety when you know that something is wrong and the doctor has left you with no explanation or course of action, especially if, like many parents, you've been doing some research on your own and are pretty well convinced that your child has an eating disorder. What do you do?

To start, consider why the doctor has reached this conclusion. Knowing this can lead you to a next step that will get you on the path to helping your child. Is it likely that this doctor is simply not very psychologically minded and would not ordinarily consider a psychiatric diagnosis? If you have prior experience with the practitioner, what does that history tell you? Has the doctor ever suggested considering psychological factors when your child has had a problem in the past? If not, and he has said something like "I've examined Rachel very carefully, and I have given this a lot of thought. Although I can't find any medical reason for her weight loss, I just don't think it is an eating disorder," obviously, you'll need to ask him why he doesn't think this is an eating disorder and what you should do now inasmuch as your child continues to resist eating or to binge eat and purge. If the doctor suggests a "wait-and-see" course, you'll have to make it clear that you've already waited and that you are far too concerned about your daughter's health to allow any more time to pass before taking action. This statement can be firm without being abrasive: "Doctor, I appreciate the care you've taken to consider all the medical causes of Rachel's behavior, but

I'm really worried and don't know what to do. Can you refer us to someone who has experience with eating disorders so we can be sure that ruling this out is the right thing to do?"

Another possibility is that, despite her best intentions, the pediatrician you have consulted has not based her view on all the available evidence, both medical and psychological/psychiatric. Again, you can ascertain this by asking exactly what the doctor has taken into account—"Doctor, are you satisfied that you've done all the tests to rule out a medical illness that can explain my child's weight loss? We want to be sure that every angle has been considered"—and making your own judgment about how certain the doctor seems and how thorough her assessment appears to have been. Does she respond cryptically, vaguely, or defensively? If so, it may simply be an indication that she is not very comfortable in this area. In most cases, a tactful question along these lines will give the doctor an opening to admit that she's not satisfied with her own finding and will refer you to someone else who can do more.

It's also possible that the doctor has taken into account *only* what the tests and office exam can show—not the behaviors you have observed at home or that have been reported to you by your child's school. Your child's eating habits are not going to be evident in the doctor's office, so what you and others who are around your child much of the day see her doing is critical to a diagnosis of an eating disorder. If you think the doctor has not taken your reports seriously, reiterate them. Many parents benefit from bringing a written log of the behaviors they've observed (what their child has eaten and not eaten at various times during the day, what she has said about food and eating, notable changes in behavior, exercise habits, and so forth) to the doctor's office. If you haven't already done this, and the doctor can assure you that your child is in no imminent danger (see the warning signs on page 24), you might offer to construct such a log for the week ahead and then meet with the doctor again.

Although making a diagnosis of an eating disorder may be straightforward for those who work with these illnesses on a daily basis, many pediatricians and other general practitioners don't have this background. If they've seen very few cases of an eating disorder, they may be somewhat cautious to make this diagnosis. If your

child is between 9 and 11 years old, it will be difficult for the doctor to recognize such a disorder even if he has been dealing with adolescents with eating disorders, because eating disorders are quite rare among young children and the manifestation of the illness in them may be atypical. Similarly, eating disorders are not as common among boys or among some ethnic minorities, and again, the pediatrician may not be inclined to consider an eating disorder as a potential diagnosis because your child is male or a member of an ethnic minority.

Unfortunately, diagnoses of eating disorders are overlooked from time to time because it's simply not the first diagnosis that medical professionals will think of—or even consider—if they haven't seen these disorders before. If your instinct and your knowledge of your child tell you that she indeed has anorexia or bulimia, for instance, you should ask for a second opinion from someone such as a child and adolescent psychiatrist or a psychologist who specializes in the treatment of eating disorders. You may be hesitant if you feel intimidated by medical professionals, or you may fear that your pediatrician will somehow be offended, that you don't trust her. But once you have put your reluctance aside, getting a referral from your child's pediatrician ought to be a relatively straightforward request and procedure. Most doctors would welcome you to explore this option, for they could also learn from the outcome of such an evaluation. If it turns out that a diagnosis of an eating disorder is confirmed, then you should consult your pediatrician about how he would like to continue to be involved in your child's medical care. Most pediatricians would want to stay involved in your child's care and would probably be quite happy to consult with your child's psychologist or psychiatrist.

A professional tells you to stay out of, or on the sidelines of, your own child's treatment.

Parents can experience a variety of forms of exclusion, such as not being part of the core assessment and planning phase of the treatment, not being made a part of the solution by meeting with their child's doctor on a regular basis to discuss the progress in treatment,

or worse still, being excluded from the treatment altogether. This approach is in stark contrast to most available evidence that supports parental involvement in the treatment of an adolescent with an eating disorder, as we have stated throughout this book. It is, therefore, quite inconceivable that treatment can be successful without the parents' constructive involvement in one form or another. If you need a reminder of the research findings in favor of parental involvement, see Chapter 6.

Many professionals, however, will follow a treatment path that mostly (or only) addresses your adolescent's concerns and worries, while attempting to keep you at bay. Some professionals may even think of many parents as "overinvolved" and "interfering" in the treatment process. It is, therefore, not uncommon to hear parents report that their child's therapist would not meet with them or even (fortunately, more rarely) take their calls. Any of these types of exclusion can be difficult to overcome.

Although there is no "one right way" for parents to be involved in their child's treatment, you should not be excluded from being a part of making these crucial decisions at the outset of treatment. If you are not to be a part of the treatment process, you should still ask the professionals about the balance between addressing the eating disorder symptoms on one hand and exploring the "underlying issues" on the other. It should be quite acceptable to ask your child's therapist, "Can you explain your reasoning for not including us in the treatment process?" and "Can you let us know how Sandy's medical status will be monitored throughout this process, who will weigh her and how regularly, and how we can be kept informed about her progress, in psychological as well as medical terms?"

Your aim is to make sure that the dire consequences of starvation or binge eating and purging are addressed urgently and consistently. You should be allowed to question the treatment team regarding your child's progress, in terms of both the improvement in eating disorder symptoms and the role of and emphasis on psychological treatment. If the medical aspects of your child's illness are not addressed, or if you are not informed about the progress in weight gain or cessation in bulimic symptoms, you should insist on being informed in the same way an oncologist would diligently

keep parents abreast of how their child's tumor was responding to treatment.

You are given advice you don't agree with.

Regardless of the exact treatment approach, parents often feel uncomfortable about the advice given by the treatment team but don't know whether they can or even have the right to disagree. You may be told that your child's eating disorder can "be treated only in an inpatient setting" or that "the medications we have prescribed are standard for adolescents with anorexia" or that "residential treatment (in another state) is really your only option." You might be surprised to know that many other parents intuitively feel uneasy about such advice but don't think they can second-guess the professional team. "Who am I to question the doctor?" is the reaction that still pops into parents' minds when they don't feel completely comfortable with professional advice; after all, most of us have been brought up to believe that the professionals "know best." Although our advice is not aimed at setting you on a collision course with your child's treatment team, or encouraging you to immediately oppose or question every decision, you should feel comfortable, as a matter of routine, about asking your child's therapist *why* course X as opposed to Y was chosen. You should feel confident in asking your child's doctor why she has decided on medication to treat your child's bulimia and why medication A was chosen as opposed to B. Many doctors want to go into detail about their decisions but are prevented from doing so simply because of time constraints. To make sure this doesn't stand in the way of your being fully informed, you can always ask if another appointment, just to talk through all the important issues, would be wise, or you may be able to set up a regular time when you and the doctor can touch base by phone.

Most important, and perhaps more difficult for you to do, you should feel that you can tell the doctor when you disagree with the chosen treatment course. You should, of course, have a good rationale for this approach after you've done your research thoroughly. How you approach this situation is crucial, as you don't want to be seen as antagonistic and you don't want to invite your doctor to react

defensively. You may start by saying, "Can you help me understand why you recommend a residential treatment program as opposed to an intensive outpatient regimen?" or "I don't understand the mechanism of the medication you have recommended. Can you explain how this works and why you've chosen this particular path?" With this approach, even though your questioning might be motivated by your disagreement with the doctor's recommendation, you've phrased your disagreement as a question for clarification. This gives your child's doctor an opportunity to provide a satisfactory rationale that may help convince you, or unfortunately, may confirm that you really cannot agree with the chosen treatment path. Most important, you should be prepared to discuss your differences with your child's doctor in an atmosphere of trying *together* to find the best course of care for your child. The likelihood that treatment will be successful is usually enhanced when everyone is in agreement and can enthusiastically endorse the route of care chosen.

Incidentally, when you have doubts about the advice you're being given, be sure to examine your reasons for feeling this way. For all the reasons discussed in Chapter 5 and elsewhere, your adolescent may try to get you to doubt the professionals. Remember, because her thinking and judgment are severely distorted as a result of her eating disorder, she will try to find ways to perpetuate it. So, when the eating disorder speaks for your child, the effort will be to convince you that the doctor who made the diagnosis was wrong and that the treatment team's attempts to curtail the symptoms are ineffective. After all, if you buy into this claim, you might withdraw your teenager from treatment, in which case the eating disorder wins! Treatment is in serious trouble when your adolescent succeeds in getting you to question the treatment and leads you to either seek "alternative" treatment or, worse still, abandon treatment altogether.

You may start out with full faith in your child's treatment team, but the cognitive distortions that mark an eating disorder can make your teenager very persistent in trying to undermine the treatment and the professionals providing it. So, when you find yourself experiencing growing dissatisfaction with your child's treatment, ask yourself whether you have concrete reasons for doubting its

effectiveness. If not, and you realize you're being swayed by your child, gently but firmly remind him that you, as parents, are in the best position to make treatment decisions, not your child—not just because your child is still under age, but mostly because the eating disorder does not allow him to make rational health care decisions. Also, remind your adolescent that everyone (parents and professionals) must be united in fighting the illness and that it's your goal to stay that way to give your child the best possible chance at recovery.

Your adolescent may still feel that you're fighting him. In this case, remind yourself to separate the illness from the adolescent: You are battling the *illness*, not your *child*. This thinking will help you stay on course, even when your adolescent puts forward "logical" arguments as to why you should question the interventions prescribed by the professionals.

If, after examining the source of your doubts, you still aren't convinced that the advice you're getting is right, remember that professionals can't always back up their treatment decisions with hard data, especially considering that the research studies on eating disorders are still so sparse, but they should nevertheless attempt to provide you with the reasons behind their decisions. It is *your* child's treatment; *asking* will make you a part of the treatment effort, and *knowing* enables you to pursue a particular treatment choice with greater conviction. In fact, you might be pleasantly surprised to find that most therapists will be all too happy to take a few extra minutes and have you think with them about the chosen route for treatment.

You've been given conflicting advice.

Because there's no uniform treatment for adolescents with eating disorders, it's relatively common for parents to be told one thing by doctor *A* at hospital *A* and another by doctor *B* at clinic *B*. Your dilemma, of course, is "What do I do now?" You obviously want to do what's best for your child, but your job is made considerably more difficult with two opposing viewpoints from professionals. If you find yourself in this dilemma, we can only offer some guidelines about finding the right course of action. First, and as we have suggested earlier in this chapter, ask the respective professionals:

- How they've arrived at their particular advice
- Which guidelines they consult as a basis for their decisions
- How many patients they have treated this way
- What the response has been
- Whether this is standard practice among other professionals in this field
- Whether there are published data to support this approach

Although this may seem unnecessary to some, think of the questions you asked when your child was fitted with her first set of braces; think of the detail the orthodontist went into in explaining "why," "what," and "when." It's quite acceptable to follow the same approach here, even if your child's psychiatrist appears a little reluctant to engage in this kind of discussion. Remember, it's your child's life at stake, and you want to be assured that you are following the right course of action. Second, and again, as we've mentioned earlier, it's important for you to feel comfortable with the advice so that you can endorse the actions necessary to help return your adolescent to a healthy state. This will happen only if the doctor takes some time walking you through the decision-making process. So, trust your gut instinct when you feel this might not be the right treatment for your child, especially in the absence of research or clinical data. *Parents are usually on target!* Pursue your concerns (within reason) until you are satisfied that you can endorse a specific treatment route.

The professionals are not on the same page.

Whereas the preceding dilemma refers to your having made visits to two different clinicians about your child's eating disorder, the difficulty presented here refers to members of your child's treatment team (two professionals under the same roof) not being in sync with one another. We've already mentioned that treatment of an eating disorder is complex, and several professionals should ideally be involved in your child's care (e.g., a pediatrician, a psychiatrist, and a therapist). These doctors could inadvertently confuse you and your child by providing guidance that might differ subtly at

times. Possibly the most common issue that arises concerns target weight. Doctor A may say, "She should probably weigh somewhere in the high teens," when your daughter's weight is just over 100 pounds at the time. Another team member (doctor B), in an effort to sound encouraging, may say "We're almost there" in response to the adolescent's begging to know how much more weight she'll have to gain, as she is just over 100 pounds now. Both doctors have the same goal in sight (a healthy weight, given the patient's height and age), but your adolescent will most likely opt to hear from doctor B, "Just 1 or 2 more pounds." You may be confused as well and not quite sure what the "real" message is. Without having to walk on eggshells all the time, doctors who treat patients with eating disorders need to be exquisitely careful about how they phrase information on weight gain issues. Anorexia not only speaks for the adolescent when food issues arise, it also hears for her. So the girl who is told "we're almost there" not only will prefer that message to "we have another 10 pounds to go" because it allows her to delude herself that she doesn't have to gain much more weight; she may also become very upset at the implication. This vague statement of encouragement can set off an alarm—"I must have gained *so* much weight!"—and send her out of the office in tears. It's important that goals be clear and specific and that all the members of the team agree on them.

Unfortunately, you won't be in a position to control much of these kinds of occurrences. However, it's important to understand how the eating disorder gets your child to think and respond to these events and how important it is for you to be able to check with your child's doctor when these misunderstandings arise. Discussing the distress felt by a girl or boy who is very sensitive to any news about weight gain can only further your collective efforts to speak to your child productively. Moreover, understanding this illness can help you notice when the professionals inadvertently confuse you. Your job is to let the professionals know when this happens.

Although unintentional miscommunication is, unfortunately, a common occurrence, the team members have an obligation to make sure that they "speak with one voice." You, on the other hand, should let your team know when they confuse you about their

messages or treatment goals so that ultimately everyone can stay on the same page. This will, we hope, be easy enough. Go back and tell doctors A and B that you're confused, tell them why, and have them clarify the situation. This way the doctors will be reminded of their oversight and will probably try harder to prevent this from happening again. You should definitely let them know; otherwise, they'll be unaware of the confusion they've caused.

The various professionals involved are not staying in communication when your child has several psychiatric problems requiring multiple treatments.

Treatment of an eating disorder is especially complicated and often involves a couple of professionals at the same time when other psychiatric illnesses coexist with the eating disorder. Having an anxiety disorder or depression in addition to an eating disorder will further complicate your child's treatment. This is a difficult process to manage, whether the professionals who treat your child are all part of the same team at the same institution or are located at different facilities/practices and are collectively involved in your child's treatment. In either case, the treatment team's responsibility is to stay on the same page with one another, even though they represent different professions and may approach treatment from slightly different perspectives. You need to make sure that these professionals all speak to one another *and* to you, the child's parents.

> Fifteen-year-old Darlene loves ballet. She has lost so much weight over the last few months that her pediatrician recommended she not be allowed to dance while her parents are trying to help her gain weight. Darlene is also quite depressed and meets with a psychiatrist on a regular basis. The psychiatrist treats her with antidepressant medication. So far so good. However, the psychiatrist thinks it's a good idea for Darlene to continue to dance because this makes her happy and may also help with her depression. Both of these doctors are obviously trying what they think is best for Darlene. But Darlene has latched on to what the psychiatrist had to say about her dancing, making it very hard for her parents and her pediatrician to keep her from

dancing. These two doctors should have been in touch with one another first, to make sure that they were on the same page before verbalizing their treatment plan to the family.

Although you don't want to be put into the position of having to check on the team to make sure it's doing its job, you want to be reassured that the various professionals involved in your child's care do, in fact, share notes with one another. You will have a clear sign that this is not happening when you hear different directives from two or more members of the treatment team, as in the example of Darlene. If this is the case, you should point out to the person who is ultimately in charge of your child's care that you are confused, as you've been hearing different directives. It's the responsibility of the team leader to clarify such inconsistencies and make sure there is a united front in the battle against your child's illness. Go back to the team leader after a while and check with him or her to see whether the team members have conferred with one another. In that way, you can be reassured that the dilemma has been resolved—at least for now.

Also be aware that there will be times when it is up to you to decide which of two conflicting approaches you feel is best and to steer the entire team in that direction. For example, a medical team may be quite worried about the potential for bone loss and may stress weight gain above normal to ensure that bone loss doesn't occur. The psychiatric team may see this additional weight gain at that particular point as risky because it could lead to an intensified preoccupation with weight and a relapse. You may need to study these conflicts for yourselves, to a certain extent, to determine what you believe is the current priority. Similarly, a nutritionist may recommend a particular diet plan, whereas the psychiatric team may see any prescribed "diet" as leading to a preoccupation with food that increases obsessional concerns about eating. It's often up to parents to consider the pros and cons of these professional options and sometimes force the team in a single direction. When that is the case, you can ask the professional with whom you agree for advice on how to speak tactfully to the disagreeing team member.

Too many cooks in the kitchen?

In Chapter 9 we mentioned that you want, at most, only two cooks in your kitchen (you and your spouse, *not* your adolescent) while you're attempting to normalize your child's eating habits. Likewise, you also don't want too many professionals involved in your child's care. It's incredibly confusing for everyone when a treatment team tries to address every possible angle of the eating disorder at the same time (group therapy, family therapy, individual therapy, medication, refeeding, occupational therapy, exercise therapy). Such a multifaceted approach invariably involves a pediatrician to take care of the medical issues, a psychiatrist for medication management, an individual therapist for psychotherapy, a family therapist to meet with the family, a nutritionist to consult with either you or your child, and so on. There is no research evidence that this catch-all strategy will necessarily provide the results you desire. In fact, it can be very confusing and taxing for your child (who may have diminished resources, given his health status), as well as for you. Our advice here is no different from that offered for every scenario described before: You should feel that you can talk to the doctor who is ultimately in charge of your child's care and ask her why another professional has been added to the team, what the rationale is for this practitioner's involvement, what the timing of the other practitioner's interventions will be, and what goals the other professional hopes to achieve.

The treatment team tells you they've done everything they could and can't be of further help.

There are very few, if any, circumstances in which a treatment team should give up on an adolescent's treatment for an eating disorder. No doubt, hearing from your doctors that they have "tried everything" will be distressing to you and will put you, as parents, in the awkward position of disagreeing with your treatment team. You will have to try to persuade them not to give up, or you may have to go ahead and look (yet again, perhaps) for a team of professionals who will make another effort to help your child in his struggle.

Remember, the outcome for most adolescents, if they receive good treatment, is positive. The available data show that when properly treated, we can expect most adolescents to recover from their illness. Therefore, you should question the professionals if you're told that "nothing more can be done," "your child is not ready yet," or "she's not motivated to change." Patients with an eating disorder, as a rule, don't want to get better and will not want to work with you and the treatment team in an effort to overcome this illness. Perseverance is of utmost importance if treatment is to be successful. You *and* the professionals must find a way to persist if you want to help your child overcome this illness.

If worse comes to worst, and the team just can't seem to work together, or you have disagreements with the team that you just can't seem to resolve after diligent efforts to do so, it may be time to make some changes. How do you know when you've reached that point? If you've truly lost your confidence in the team, and your child is getting worse or making no improvement, it's time to consider a change. Your child's welfare is the reason you're in treatment to begin with, and the effectiveness of treatment should be the priority. Remember, though, that it's hardly ever constructive to suddenly jump from one group of professionals to another, denying any team the chance to make headway with your teenager.

You are sent from pillar to post.

Not every family with an eating-disordered teen lives in a city or state where a multidisciplinary team of specialists is available to help with the child's treatment. Consequently, you may find yourself being sent from one specialist to another, and these professionals are often in another city or even in another state. You may also have been told to have your child admitted to either a residential or inpatient facility hundreds of miles away in another state. Going back and forth like this can be confusing, and you are often left not quite knowing which avenue to pursue or even which of the available options will result in the best outcome for your adolescent.

No doubt, this is a very difficult position for you to be in—either shopping around your own city or having to think of sending your

14-year-old away to another state. The important issue here is to feel comfortable with the decision that you will be making and confident that you'll be able to stick with the course you have opted for. This sense of comfort won't be possible unless you feel you have done a fair amount of homework regarding the options available and, consequently, that you've made an informed decision. It's critical that you find a facility and group of professionals that have true expertise in treating adolescents with eating disorders. The Resources section of this book can help get you started on finding such a team, but you can also rely on referrals, track records, years of experience, board certifications, and any other criteria you would normally apply to choosing the best possible health care practitioners for any problem your child has.

So, invest in the time to shop around, because when you've made your difficult decision, it's going to be important for you to show the perseverance we just referred to. As we said at the outset of this chapter, this book should help you be better informed about your child's eating disorder and the treatment options available. When you are in the position of having to shop around or having to send your child away to a treatment facility in another state, you will now feel, with some certainty, that you have taken the best available step.

We've pointed out several times in this book that treatment will probably be most helpful if you're involved in every step of your child's care. Sending your child away to another state for a month or more for the professionals to get her weight back on track or normalize her eating behaviors may be helpful to your child, but she will eventually return home. You will then have to figure out a way to make sure that she doesn't relapse. To do so, you need to be involved in the treatment, and you will have to find a way to communicate this to your treatment team. As we said earlier in this chapter, some professionals would like to keep you out of treatment to a large extent. Your challenge will be either to find a team that recognizes the tremendous value parents bring to treatment or to convince a team of the resources you bring that can help ensure that your child gets back on the road toward recovery. Ask the team members how they usually involve families who travel long distances in their treatment approach.

In this chapter we presented several typical challenges that parents of our patients have experienced with professionals who are trying to help their children. These dilemmas have often resulted in the parents feeling confused and disempowered. There is no doubt that such struggles can hamper your child's recovery. In each example, we have pointed out what the source of confusion between you and your child's treatment team might be. In each case, we have encouraged you to find your voice, make sure you remain informed, and remain a part of the solution. We have also pointed out specifically how you, as parents, can work together with your treatment team in a way that will be productive in your child's recovery. In the next section of this book, you'll find resources for getting the best treatment for eating disorders in the United States and other countries.

FOR MORE INFORMATION

Le Grange, D., and J. Lock, *Treating Bulimia in Adolescents: A Family-Based Approach*, 2007. New York: Guilford Press.

Le Grange, D., and J. Lock, Editors, *Eating Disorders in Children and Adolescents: A Clinical Handbook*, 2011. New York: Guilford Press.

Lock, J., *The Oxford Handbook of Child and Adolescent Eating Disorders: Developmental Perspectives*, 2012. New York: Oxford University Press.

Lock, J., and D. Le Grange, *Treatment Manual for Anorexia Nervosa: A Family-Based Approach, Second Edition*, 2013. New York: Guilford Press.

Resources

The resources in this section are not comprehensive or exhaustive, but should provide guidance in identifying programs and treatment centers in your region. Every effort has been made to ensure that the information we have provided is up to date, but contact information may have changed after publication.

For individual listings and general information about eating disorders please visit:

Maudsley Parents
www.maudsleyparents.org

Families Empowered and Supporting Treatment of Eating Disorders (F.E.A.S.T)
http://members.feast-ed.org

DIAGNOSIS AND TREATMENT

United States

Northeast

NEW YORK

New York State Psychiatric Institute/
Columbia Center for Eating Disorders
1051 Riverside Drive, Unit 98
New York, NY 10032
Phone: 212-543-5739
E-mail: *EDRU@pi.cpmc.columbia.edu*
Website: *http://cumc.columbia.edu/dept/eatingdisorders*

The Columbia Center for Eating Disorders is part of the New York State Psychiatric Institute at Columbia Presbyterian Medical Center. The Center offers free treatment to eligible women who suffer from anorexia nervosa or bulimia nervosa and to men and women who suffer from binge-eating disorder. Both inpatient and outpatient facilities are available. Adolescents welcome for treatment.

Mount Sinai Eating and Weight Disorders Program
Department of Psychiatry
The Mount Sinai Hospital
1425 Madison Avenue, Icahn Building, Floor 6, Room 32
New York, NY 10029
Phone: 212-659-8724
Website: *www.mountsinai.org/patient-care/service-areas/psychiatry/*
areas-of-care/eating-and-weight-disorders-program

The Eating Disorders Program provides medical, nutritional, and mental health assessment and treatment for adolescents with anorexia nervosa, bulimia nervosa, female athlete triad, binge-eating disorder, and other types of disordered eating patterns.

Unity Health System/Eating Disorders Program
Department of Psychiatry
Mental Health Clinic
835 Main Street
Rochester, NY 14611
Phone: 585-368-3709
Website: *www.unityhealth.org/mentalhealth/services_mental_eatingdisorder.*
aspx

This program offers outpatient and inpatient services for adolescents and adults who suffer from anorexia nervosa, bulimia nervosa, and binge-eating disorder.

NEW JERSEY

Eating Disorders Treatment Centers
Michael Pertschuk, MD, Medical Director
750 South Route 73, Suite 104
Marlton, NJ 08053
Phone: 856-810-0100

Eating Disorders Treatment Centers provide comprehensive services for patients with eating disorders. Ages 13 and over.

WASHINGTON, DC

National Medical Center/Eating Disorders Program
Darlene Atkins, PhD, Director
Adolescent Medicine/Eating Disorders Program
Children's Hospital
111 Michigan Avenue NW
Washington, DC 20010
Phone: 202-745-8860 (for Dr. Atkins); or 202-476-3000
    (for general information)
Website: *http://childrensnational.org/departmentsandprograms/
    default.aspx?Id=267&Type=Program&Name=
    Eating%20Disorders%20Clinic*

The Eating Disorders Program sees preadolescent and adolescent (ages 10–21 years) patients with suspected eating disorders such as anorexia nervosa, bulimia nervosa, binge-eating disorder, or obesity. Patients are typically evaluated by the multidisciplinary team, consisting of a psychologist, an adolescent medicine physician, and a nutritionist.

PENNSYLVANIA

Renfrew Center Foundation
475 Spring Lane
Philadelphia, PA 19128
Phone: 877-367-3383
Fax: 215-482-2695
E-mail: *info@renfrew.org*
Website: *www.renfrew.org*

The Renfrew Center Foundation is a tax-exempt, nonprofit organization advancing the education, prevention, research, and treatment of eating disorders. Ages 14 and up.

Center for Overcoming Problem Eating
Western Psychiatric Institute and Clinic
University of Pittsburgh Medical Center
3811 O'Hara Street

Pittsburgh, PA 15213

Phone: 412-647-9329

Website: *www.upmc.com/Services/behavioral-health/cope-eating-disorders*

The COPE program provides services for patients with eating disorders, including comprehensive assessments for individuals (including adolescents 18 and under) and treatment designed to address the specific needs of patients requiring different levels of care.

Children's Hospital of Philadelphia/Eating Disorder Services
Craig Dalsimer Division of Adolescent Medicine
Department of Pediatrics
Perelman School of Medicine at the University of Pennsylvania
34th and Civic Center Boulevard, 11NW, Room 19
Philadelphia, PA 19104
Phone: 215-590-6864
E-mail: *peeblesr@email.chop.edu*

CONNECTICUT

Renfrew Center Foundation
1445 East Putnam Avenue
Old Greenwich, CT 06870
Phone: 800-RENFREW
Website: *www.renfrew.org*

The Renfrew Center Foundation is a tax-exempt, nonprofit organization advancing the education, prevention, research, and treatment of eating disorders. Ages 14 and up.

MASSACHUSETTS

Massachusetts General Hospital/Eating Disorders Clinical and Research Program
2 Longfellow Place, Suite 200
Boston, MA 02114
Phone: 617-726-8470
Website: *www.massgeneral.org/psychiatry/services/eating_disorders_home.aspx*

The Eating Disorders Clinical and Research Program is dedicated to research and education. It seeks to expand knowledge about eating

disorders, their detection, treatment, and prevention and to share that knowledge with the community at large. At the heart of the Center's program is a commitment to promote the healthy development of children, young women, and all at risk.

MARYLAND

Center for Eating Disorders at Sheppard Pratt
Harry Brandt, MD, Director
Steven Crawford, MD, Associate Director
Physicians Pavilion North
6535 North Charles Street, Suite 300
Baltimore, MD 21204
Phone: 410-938-5252
Fax: 410-938-5250
E-mail: *EatingDisorderInfo@sheppardpratt.org*
Website: *http://eatingdisorder.org*

A range of eating disorder services is offered.

NEW HAMPSHIRE

Center for Eating Disorders Management, Inc.
Kathleen Corkery, LICSW, Clinical Director (trained in FBT)
360 Route 101, Unit 10
Bedford, NH 03110
Phone: 603-472-2846
Fax: 603-472-2872

South

NORTH CAROLINA

Duke Center for Eating Disorders
Department of Psychiatry
Duke University
Pavilion East at Lakeview
2608 Erwin Road, Suite 300
Durham, NC 27705
Phone: 919-668-0398
Website: *www.dukehealth.org/services/eating_disorders*

The Duke Center for Eating Disorders emphasizes the implementation of empirically validated treatments for eating disorders. The program serves patients with anorexia nervosa, bulimia nervosa, binge eating, childhood feeding disorders, food avoidance, and obesity. It offers family, individual, and group therapy; a skills-based group program for parents; nutrition services; medical management; and a variety of educational workshops.

**University of North Carolina at Chapel Hill/
Eating Disorders Program**
Neurosciences Hospital
101 Manning Drive, CB #7160
Chapel Hill, NC 27599
Phone: 919-966-7012
Website: *www.psychiatry.unc.edu/eatingdisorders*

The Eating Disorders Program offers a comprehensive and specialized approach to the treatment of anorexia nervosa, bulimia nervosa, and related conditions. It provides the most current and state-of-the-art evidence-based treatments to help individuals suffering from eating disorders achieve a lasting recovery, through intensive inpatient, day treatment, and outpatient services.

LOUISIANA

River Oaks Hospital/Eating Disorders Treatment Center
1525 River Oaks Road West
New Orleans, LA 70123
Phone: 800-366-1740 or 504-734-1740
Fax: 504-733-7020
Website: *http://riveroakshospital.com/programs/the-eating-disorders-treatment-center*

The Eating Disorders Treatment Center provides comprehensive inpatient and partial hospitalization programs for anorexia, bulimia, and related eating disorders, as well as specialized care for males, females, adolescents, and adults.

Midwest

ILLINOIS

Alexian Brothers Behavioral Health Hospital
1650 Moon Lake Boulevard
Hoffman Estates, IL 60194
Phone: 800-432-5005 or 847-882-1600
Website: *www.alexianbrothershealth.org/abbhh/ourservices/eating-disorders*

Alexian Brothers offers outpatient and inpatient services for adolescents and adults with eating disorders.

University of Chicago Medicine/Eating Disorders Program
Andrea Goldschmidt, PhD, Director
Department of Psychiatry
University of Chicago
5841 South Maryland Avenue, MC 3077
Chicago, IL 60637
Phone: 773-834-5677
Website: *www.eatingdisorders.uchicago.edu*
Facebook: *www.facebook.com/UofCEatingDisordersProgram*

To ensure the best possible outcome for each patient, the University of Chicago Eating Disorders program adheres to treatment based on prior research. The program provides comprehensive outpatient services for the assessment, treatment, and follow-up of adolescents with eating disorders. This includes adolescent anorexia nervosa, bulimia nervosa, binge-eating disorder, and related disorders.

Insight Behavioral Health Center
333 North Michigan Avenue, Suite 1900
Chicago, IL 60601
Phone: 312-540-9955
Website: *www.insightbhc.com/stories/about*

The Insight Behavioral Health Center provides outpatient and intensive outpatient services for adolescents and adults with a range of eating disorders.

MISSOURI

McCallum Place
Kimberli McCallum, MD, CEO, Founder and Medical Director
Lynn Stark, APRN, MSN, COO, Co-Founder, Clinical Nurse Specialist,
    and Program Director
Eating Disorders Treatment Center
231 West Lockwood Avenue, Suite 201
St. Louis, MO 63119
Phone: 314-968-1900
Fax: 314-968-1901
Website: *www.mccallumplace.com*

This program consists of outpatient, day treatment, residential, and sub-acute care treatments for adolescents and adults with eating disorders and related conditions.

MINNESOTA

Emily Program
Website: *www.emilyprogram.com*

Anna Westin House
1449 Cleveland Avenue North
St. Paul, MN 55108
Phone: 651-645-5323
Fax: 651-328-8254

St. Louis Park Location
1660 South Highway 100, Suite 260
St. Louis Park, MN 55416
Phone: 952-746-5774
Fax: 952-746-5962

Stillwater Location
Chestnut Building
200 East Chestnut Street, Suite 202
Stillwater, MN 55082
Phone: 651-645-5323
Fax: 651-439-1098

The Emily Program is an outpatient treatment program that provides comprehensive psychological, nutritional, and medical care for individuals with eating disorders. See website for other locations.

Children's Hospitals and Clinics of Minnesota/
Center for the Treatment of Eating Disorders
2525 Chicago Avenue South
Minneapolis, MN 55404
Phone: 612-813-6000
Website: *www.childrensmn.org/services/other-programs-and-services/other-*
programs-and-services-e-l/eating-disorders

Children's inpatient programs and outpatient programs are family-centered and specifically tailored for children, adolescents, and adults.

Park Nicollet Melrose Center
3525 Monterey Drive
St. Louis Park, MN 55416
Phone: 952-993-6200
Website: *www.parknicollet.com*

The program consists of inpatient, partial hospitalization, intensive outpatient, and outpatient treatments for eating disorders.

NEBRASKA

Children's Hospital and Medical Center/Eating Disorder Program
1000 North 90th Street
Omaha, NE 68114
Phone: 402-955-6190
Website: *www.childrensomaha.org/TheEatingDisordersProgram*

The program consists of an inpatient program, partial hospitalization, and outpatient treatments specializing in children and adolescents with eating disorders.

NORTH DAKOTA

The Eating Disorders Institute
100 4th Street South, Suite 204
Fargo, ND 58103
Phone: 701-234-4111
Website: *www.sanfordhealth.org* or *www.med.und.nodak.edu* or *www.nrifargo.*
com/edi.asp

The Eating Disorders Institute is a cooperative program between Sanford Health, the Neuropsychiatric Research Institute, and the University of North Dakota School of Medicine and the Health Sciences Center. The group evaluates, treats, and conducts research on eating disorders and obesity. Adults and adolescents 12 and up.

OKLAHOMA

Laureate
6655 South Yale
Tulsa, OK 74136
Phone: 918-481-4000
Website: *www.laureate.com*

Laureate's program incorporates the 12-step philosophy with other treatment modalities.

WISCONSIN

Rogers Memorial Hospital/Eating Disorder Services
34700 Valley Road
Oconomowoc, WI 53066
Phone: 800-767-4411
Fax: 262-646-3158
Website: *www.rogershospital.org*

Eating Disorder Services provides men and women with comprehensive treatment for eating disorders—inpatient, outpatient, residential, and partial hospitalization using multidisciplinary team and individualized treatment plans.

IOWA

University of Iowa Hospitals and Clinics/
Eating and Weight Disorder Program
200 Hawkins Drive
Iowa City, IA 52242
Phone: 319-356-2263
Fax: 319-356-2587
Website: *www.uihealthcare.org/EatingDisorders*

This program provides diagnosis and comprehensive treatment of eating disorders.

Southwest

TEXAS

Menninger Clinic
2801 Gessner Drive
P.O. Box 809045
Houston, TX 77280-9045
Phone: 800-351-9058
Website: *www.menningerclinic.com*

The Menninger Clinic offers services for individuals (including adolescents) and a structured, 4-week, comprehensive program.

University of Texas, Southwestern Medical Center/
Eating Disorders Services Program
Children's Medical Center
1935 Motor Street, 5th Floor
Dallas, TX 75235
Phone: 214-456-5900
Website: *www.utswmedicine.org/conditions-specialties/mental-health/eating*

This program offers comprehensive diagnostic evaluation and treatment of anorexia nervosa, bulimia, and related disorders. It uses a multidisciplinary treatment approach, with an emphasis on intensive outpatient group treatment where possible to minimize the need for more restrictive levels of care.

University of Texas at Austin/Eating Disorder Services
Department of Educational Psychology
Texas Child Study Center at Dell Children's Medical Center
1600 W 38th Street, Suite 212
Austin, TX 78731
Phone: 512-324-9999, ext. 15852
Fax: 512-324-3314
E-mail: *jeblack@seton.org*

West

WASHINGTON

Eating and Weight Disorders Program of Seattle
1200 5th Avenue, Suite 800
Seattle, WA 98101
Phone: 206-374-0109
E-mail: *info@ebtseattle.com*
Website: *http://ewdcseattle.com/ewdc.html*

This program offers treatment that is guided by research for eating disorders, while at the same time tailoring treatment plans to the individual's unique situation. The treatment team includes psychologists, physicians, dietitians, and psychiatrists who work collaboratively to address the eating disorder and to manage medical complications. Clinicians in the program have received extensive training in evidence-based treatments for eating disorders, including CBT, FBT, IPT, dialectical behavioral skills, AFT, and specialist supportive clinical management.

**Children's Hospital and Regional Medical Center/
Eating Disorders Program**
Department of Child and Adolescent Psychiatry and Behavioral Health
4540 Sand Point Way NE, Building 1, Suite 200
Seattle, WA 98105
Phone: 206-987-2028
Website: *www.seattlechildrens.org*

The Children's Hospital Eating Disorders Program is a multidisciplinary program for the comprehensive treatment of anorexia nervosa, bulimia nervosa, and obesity. The program provides a continuum of care with available inpatient, outpatient, and day treatment services, depending on the level of care needed by an individual.

CALIFORNIA

Center for Discovery
4281 Katella Avenue, Suite 111
Los Alamitos, CA 90720
Phone: 866-458-5441
Website: *www.centerfordiscovery.com/index.html*

This is a comprehensive residential treatment program dedicated to treatment of children, adolescents, and women with eating disorders.

University of California, Los Angeles/Eating Disorders Program
Resnick Neuropsychiatric Hospital at UCLA
150 Medical Plaza
Los Angeles, CA 90095
Phone: 310-825-5730
Website: *http://eatingdisorders.ucla.edu*

This program offers comprehensive services to adults and adolescents, using dynamic, expressive, and CBTs. Inpatient and outpatient services are available.

Stanford University School of Medicine/Eating Disorders Clinic
James Lock, MD, PhD, Director
Child and Adolescent Psychiatry Clinic
Department of Psychiatry and Behavioral Sciences
Stanford University School of Medicine
401 Quarry Road, Room 1326
Stanford, CA 94305
Phone: 650-723-5511
Website: *www.med/stanford.edu/school/psychiatry/eatdisorders*

This clinic offers thorough diagnostic evaluations as well as treatment plans. Treatment plans are based on current scientific research and reflect the values, needs, and resources of the child and family. They often include the following therapeutic approaches: individual therapy, family therapy, group therapy, behavioral therapy, parent counseling, and medication therapy.

University of California, San Diego, School of Medicine/
Eating Disorders Center for Treatment and Research
Walter Kaye, MD, Director
4510 Executive Drive, Suite 315
San Diego, CA 92121
Phone: 858-534-8019
Website: *http://eatingdisorders.ucsd.edu/index.shtml*

The UCSD Eating Disorders Treatment and Research Program offers a range of treatment options for teens and adults with anorexia nervosa and

bulimia nervosa. The multidisciplinary team offers intensive outpatient therapy, day treatment, adolescent day treatment, and intensive multifamily therapy.

University of California, San Francisco/Eating Disorders Program

Daniel Le Grange, PhD, Director
UCSF Division of Adolescent and Young Adult Medicine,
    Department of Pediatrics
Department of Psychiatry, Benioff's Children's Hospital
3333 California Street, Suite 245
San Francisco, CA 94118
Phone: 415-353-2002
Website: *http://eatingdisorderprogram.ucsf.edu*

The Eating Disorders Program offers comprehensive services to children, adolescents, and young adults using evidence-based therapies. Inpatient and outpatient services are provided.

Eating Recovery Center of California

3610 American River Drive, Suite 140
Sacramento, CA 95864
Phone: 916-574-1000
Fax: 916-574-1001
Website: *www.sedop.org*

Formerly known as Summit Eating Disorders and Outreach Program, the Eating Recovery Center of California is a medically supervised treatment program serving female and male adults and adolescents with anorexia, bulimia, binge-eating disorder, ARFID, and co-occurring disorders.

Canada

BC Children's Hospital/Provincial Specialized Eating Disorders Program for Children and Adolescents

P3—Mental Health Building
4500 Oak Street
Vancouver, British Columbia V6H 3N1, Canada
Phone: 604-875-2200
Fax: 604-875-2099
Website: *http://keltyeatingdisorders.ca/provincial-specialized-eating-disorders-program-children-and-adolescents-bc-children-s-hospital*

The Provincial Specialized Eating Disorders Program provides multidisciplinary assessment and treatment for children and youth with anorexia or bulimia. It offers inpatient services, day treatment, and outpatient care.

Dalhousie University Medical School/Eating Disorders Clinic
Department of Psychiatry
IWK Health Centre Child and Adolescent Mental Health Program
5850/5980 University Avenue
P.O. Box 9700
Halifax, Nova Scotia B3K 6R8, Canada
Phone: 902-470-8375
E-mail (for general queries): *psychiatry@dal.ca*
Website: *http://psychiatry.medicine.dal.ca*

A multidisciplinary team helps its young clients deal with the physical and psychological consequences of anorexia nervosa and bulimia. The team is involved with direct clinical services and consultation and with development of education programs.

Hospital for Sick Children/Eating Disorder Program
555 University Avenue
Toronto, Ontario M5G 1X8, Canada
Phone: 416-813-1500
Website: *www.sickkids.ca/Psychiatry/What-we-do/Clinical-care/Eating-disorders-program*

The Eating Disorder Program is an interdisciplinary program for the evaluation and treatment of children and adolescents with eating disorders. It evaluates and treats young people who have anorexia nervosa, bulimia nervosa, or an unspecified eating disorder. Inpatient, outpatient, and consultative services are available.

University of Western Ontario/Child and Adolescent Mental Health Care Eating Disorders Program
London Health Sciences Centre (Victoria Hospital)
800 Commissioners Road East
London, Ontario N6C 2V5, Canada
Phone: 519-667-6640

Children's Hospital of Eastern Ontario/Eating Disorders Program
401 Smyth Road
Ottawa, Ontario K1H 8L1, Canada

Phone: 613-737-7600
Website: *www.cheo.on.ca*

The CHEO Eating Disorders Program requires a doctor's referral and includes outpatient services, day treatment programs, inpatient services, and a parent support group.

Bellwood Health Services, Inc.
1020 McNicoll Avenue
Toronto, Ontario M1W 2J6, Canada
Phone: 800-387-6198 or 416-495-0926
E-mail: *info@bellwood.ca*
Website: *www.bellwood.ca*

Bellwood Health Services provides treatment for people with eating disorders and a variety of compulsive or problematic behaviors. Although its premier treatment center is in Toronto, it has helped clients from all provinces across Canada, the United States, and other countries.

McMaster Children's Hospital Eating Disorder Program
Hamilton Health Sciences
Hamilton, Ontario, Canada
Phone: 905-521-2100, ext. 73497

North York General Eating Disorders Program
North York General Hospital
4001 Leslie Street
Toronto, ON M2K 1E1
Phone: 416-756-6750
Website*: www.nygh.on.ca/Default.aspx?cid=1230&lang=1*

Eating disorder services are available for adolescents and adults with anorexia nervosa, bulimia nervosa, and related disorders.

Westwind Eating Disorder Recovery Centre
1605 Victoria Avenue
Brandon, Manitoba R7A 1C1, Canada
Phone: 888-353-3372 (toll free in North America) *or* (204) 728-2499
E-mail: *info@westwind.mb.ca*
Website: *www.westwind.mb.ca*

The Westwind Eating Disorder Recovery Centre is a private residential program for women 16 years of age and older. It provides counseling and

treatment for individuals suffering from anorexia, bulimia, and related disorders in a home-like atmosphere, significantly different from the institutional format of traditional hospitals and clinics. Treatment is collaborative rather than imposed, various interactive techniques are used, and care is individualized and personal.

United Kingdom

Great Ormond Street Hospital for Children NHS Trust
Great Ormond Street
London WC1N 3JH, United Kingdom
Phone: 7405 9200
Fax: 7829 8657
Website: *www.ich.ucl.ac.uk*

The eating disorders team at Great Ormond Street Hospital includes medical and nursing staff, family therapists, psychotherapists, and psychologists. Its approach to treatment is to help the young person reach a healthy weight and to eat healthily, to correct any medical problems that may occur as a result of the eating disorder, and to help the young person talk about his or her feelings and learn healthier ways of coping with problems.

University of London/Eating Disorders Unit
Maudsley Hospital Institute of Psychiatry
Kings College, Box PO59
De Crespigny Park
London SE5 8AF, United Kingdom
Phone: 7836 5454
E-mail: *edu@iop.kcl.ac.uk*
Website: *www.iop.kcl.ac.uk*

The Institute of Psychiatry's Eating Disorders Unit provides a range of high-quality services for patients of all ages and across the spectrum of eating disorders.

Royal Free Hospital
Pond Street
London NW3 2QG, United Kingdom
Phone: 7794 0500
Fax: 7830 2468
Website: *www.royalfree.nhs.uk*

The hospital has a multidisciplinary child and adolescent service. Comprehensive services are provided for the whole range of child and adolescent problems. The service also has an eating disorders team.

St. Mary's Hospital
Dr. Matthew Hodes, Contact
Praed Street
London W2 1NY, United Kingdom
Phone: 3312 6666
Website: *www.imperial.nhs.uk/stmarys*

Guy's Hospital
Great Maze Road
London SE1 9RT, United Kingdom
Phone: 7188 7188
Website: *www.guysandstthomas.nhs.uk*

South West London and St. George's Eating Disorders Service
Child and Adolescent Service
Harewood House
Springfield University Hospital
61 Glenburnie Road
Tooting SW17 7DJ, United Kingdom
Phone: 8682 6683
Fax: 8862 6724
Website: *www.swlstg-tr.nhs.uk*

Treatment is provided on an outpatient, day-patient, or inpatient basis, depending on need, for ages 11 and up.

Leicester University/Eating Disorders Service
Division of Psychiatry
University Road
Leicester LE1 7RH, United Kingdom
Phone: 6252 2522
Fax: 6252 2200
Website: *www.le.ac.uk*

The Eating Disorders Service is one of the few national and international centers of excellence for these conditions. The department supports research into all aspects of eating disorders, including trials of treatment.

Connect-ED Eating Disorders Specialist Children's Services
NHS Greater Glasgow and Clyde
Glasgow, Scotland
Phone: 0141 277 7406

AUSTRALIA

Wesley Eating Disorders Centre
Wesley Private Hospital
91 Milton Street
Ashfield, New South Wales 2131, Australia
Phone: 9716 1400
Fax: 9799 6585
Website: *www.wesleymission.org.au/centres/wesprivate*

Wesley Eating Disorders Centre offers an inpatient program and day-patient program for eating disorders.

Children's Hospital at Westmead
Dr. Michael Kohn, Contact
Locked Bag 4001
Westmead 2145
Sydney, New South Wales, Australia
Phone: 9845 0000
Fax: 9845 3489
Website: *www.chw.edu.au*

Children's Hospital at Westmead offers eating disorder and weight management programs. Intensive family therapy is provided for families whose adolescent has been in the eating disorder inpatient program upon discharge.

Centre for Adolescent Health/Eating Disorders Program
Royal Children's Hospital Melbourne
Centre for Adolescent Health
50 Flemington Road
Parkville, Victoria 3052, Australia
Phone: 03 9345 4738
Website: *www.rch.org.au/cah/health_services/Eating_Disorders_Program*

The Royal Children's Hospital (RCH) Eating Disorders Program is a collaboration between the RCH Centre Adolescent Health, RCH Integrated Mental Health Programs, the University of Melbourne, and the University

of Chicago. The program has three main components: (1) assessment clinic, (2) outpatient FBT, and (3) inpatient program.

Centre for Clinical Interventions
Dr. Anthea Fursland, Principal Clinical Psychologist
223 James Street
Northbridge, Western Australia 6003
Phone: 08 9227-4399; 08 9328-5911
E-mail: *Info.cci@health.wa.gov.au*

Family Based Eating Disorders Team Clinic
Richard Litster, Senior Social Worker
Child and Youth Mental Health Service
North West Community Health Centre
49–59 Corrigan Street
Keperra, Queensland 4054, Australia
Phone: 07 3335 8888

Interdisciplinary Family Based Treatment Clinic
Ingrid Wagner, Associate Professor
Queensland University of Technology Health Clinics
44 Musk Avenue
Kelvin Grove, Queensland 4059, Australia
Website: *www.healthclinics.qut.edu.au*
Phone: 07 3138 9777

Eating Disorder Program
Kim Hurst, Senior Psychologist
Child and Youth Mental Health Service
Robina Health Precinct
Level 3, 2 Campus Drive
Robina, Queensland 4226, Australia
Phone: 07 56356392

Mater Child and Youth Mental Health Service
Mater Children's Hospital
South Brisbane, Queensland 4101, Australia
Phone: 07 3163 1640 (Eating Disorders Coordinator)
Website: *www.kidsinmind.org.au*

New Zealand

Regional Eating Disorders Service
Auckland District Health Board
Level 2, Building 14
Greenlane Clinical Centre
Auckland, New Zealand
Phone: 623 4650, Ext. 27970
Fax: 623 4656
E-mail: *pmasfen@adhb.govt.nz*

EDUCATION/ADVOCACY/REFERRAL

United States

Academy for Eating Disorders
111 Deer Lake Road, Suite 100
Deerfield, IL 60015
Phone: 847-498-4274
Fax: 847-480-9282
E-mail: *info@aedweb.org*
Website: *www.aedweb.org*

The Academy for Eating Disorders is an international transdisciplinary professional organization that promotes excellence in research, treatment, and prevention of eating disorders. Provides education, training, and a forum for collaboration and professional dialogue.

Alliance for Eating Disorders Awareness
P.O. Box 2562
West Palm Beach, FL 33402
Phone: 561-841-0900
Fax: 561-653-0043
E-mail: *info@eatingdisorderinfo.org*
Website: *www.eatingdisorderinfo.org*

The Alliance for Eating Disorders Awareness disseminates educational information to parents and caregivers about the warning signs, dangers, and consequences of anorexia, bulimia, and related disorders.

American Academy of Child and Adolescent Psychiatry
3615 Wisconsin Avenue NW
Washington, DC 20016-3007
Phone: 202-966-7300
Fax: 202-966-2891
Website: *www.aacap.org*

The mission of AACAP is to promote mentally healthy children, adolescents, and families through research, training, advocacy, prevention, comprehensive diagnosis and treatment, peer support, and collaboration.

American Anorexia/Bulimia Association of Philadelphia
P.O. Box 1287
Langhorne, PA 19047
Phone: 215-221-1864 (24-hour information helpline)
Fax: 215-702-8944
Website: *www.aabaphila.org*

This nonprofit provides services and programs for anyone interested in or affected by anorexia, bulimia, and/or related disorders. Its purpose is to aid in the education and prevention of these life-threatening disorders. In addition, referral programs and support groups assist in the treatment and recovery process.

Eating Disorders Coalition
720 7th Street NW, Suite 300
Washington, DC 20001
Phone or fax: 202-543-9570
Website: *www.eatingdisorderscoalition.org*

The Eating Disorders Coalition for Research, Policy, and Action is a cooperative of professional and advocacy-based organizations committed to federal advocacy on behalf of people with eating disorders, their families, and professionals working with these populations.

Eating Disorder Referral and Information Center
Website: *www.edreferral.com*

The Eating Disorder Referral and Information Center provides referrals to eating disorder practitioners, treatment facilities, and support groups. Referrals to eating disorder specialists are offered at no charge as a community service.

National Association of Anorexia Nervosa and Associated Disorders
P.O. Box 640
Naperville, IL 60566
Helpline: 630-577-1330
E-mail: *anadhelp@anad.org*
Website: *www.anad.org*

ANAD provides hotline counseling, a national network of free support groups, referrals to health care professionals, and education and prevention programs to promote self-acceptance and healthy lifestyles. All services are free of charge. ANAD also lobbies for state and national health insurance parity and both undertakes and encourages research.

National Eating Disorders Association
165 West 46th Street
New York, NY 10036
Phone: 212-575-6200
E-mail: *info@NationalEatingDisorders.org*
Website: *www.nationaleatingdisorders.org*

The National Eating Disorders Association is the largest not-for-profit organization in the United States working to prevent eating disorders and provide treatment referrals to those suffering from anorexia, bulimia, and binge-eating disorder and those concerned with body image and weight issues.

National Institutes of Health
9000 Rockville Pike
Bethesda, MD 20892
Phone: 301-496-4000
Website: *www.nih.gov*

The NIH is the steward of medical and behavioral research in the United States. It is an agency of the U.S. Department of Health and Human Services.

Society for Adolescent Health and Medicine
111 Deer Lake Road, Suite 100
Deerfield, IL 60015
Phone: 847-753-5226
Website: *www.adolescenthealth.org*

A multidisciplinary organization of professionals committed to improving the physical and psychosocial health and well-being of all adolescents.

Something Fishy Website on Eating Disorders
Website: *www.somethingfishy.org*

This website is dedicated to raising awareness with bulletin boards, online chats and support, information, and referral.

Canada

ANEB (Anorexia and Bulimia Quebec)
114 Donegani Boulevard
Pointe Claire, Quebec H9R 2W3, Canada
Phone: 514-630-0907
Website: *www.anebquebec.com*

Hope's Garden Eating Disorders Support and Resource Centre
478 Waterloo Street
London, Ontario N6B 2P4, Canada
Phone: 519-434-7721
E-mail: *info@hopesgarden.org*
Website: *www.hopesgarden.org*

The resource center provides a library, support groups, a speaker's bureau, educational workshops, outreach, information and referral about treatment centers, therapists, and nutritionists, as well as drop-in support.

Hopewell/Eating Disorders Support Centre of Ottawa
Heartwood House
153 Chapel Street, Suite 202
Ottawa, Ontario K1N 1H5, Canada
Phone: 613-241-3428
Fax: 613-241-0850
E-mail: *info@hopewell.ca*
Website: *www.hopewell.ca*

The Eating Disorders Support Centre of Ottawa provides persons affected by eating disorders with support and resources they need throughout the treatment and recovery process.

National Eating Disorder Information Centre
200 Elizabeth Street, ES 7-421t
Toronto, Ontario M5G 2C4, Canada
Phone: 866-NEDIC-20 (toll free) or 416-340-4156

Fax: 416-340-4736
E-mail: *nedic@uhn.on.ca*
Website: *www.nedic.ca*

This Toronto-based nonprofit organization provides information and resources on eating disorders and weight preoccupation.

United Kingdom

British Association for Counseling and Psychotherapy
BACP House
15 St. John's Business Park
Lutterworth LE17 4HB, United Kingdom
Phone: 01455 883300
Fax: 01455 550243
E-mail: *bacp@bacp.co.uk*
Website: *www.bacp.co.uk*

The British Association for Counseling and Psychotherapy provides lists of counselors in local areas.

Eating Disorders Association
Wensum House, First Floor,
103 Prince of Wales Road
Norwich NR1 1DW, United Kingdom
Phone: 1603 619 090
Fax: 1603 664 915
E-mail: *info@b-eat.co.uk*
Website: *www.b-eat.co.uk/Home*

National Centre for Eating Disorders
54 New Road, Esher
Surrey KT10 9NU, United Kingdom
Phone: 8458 382 040
Website: *www.eating-disorders.org.uk*

The National Centre for Eating Disorders is an independent organization set up to provide solutions for all eating problems, including binge eating, bulimia, and anorexia. Services include counseling, professional training, and information for students, journalists, and carers. It is the leading organization providing information, help, and support across the United Kingdom, targeted for people whose lives are affected by eating disorders. It aims to positively influence public understanding and policy.

Somerset and Wessex Eating Disorders Association
Strode House
10 Leigh Road Street
Somerset BA16 0HA, United Kingdom
Phone: 1458 448 600
Website: *www.swedauk.org/index.htm*

The Somerset and Wessex Eating Disorders Association provides resources and informal, nonstigmatizing services that reflect the needs of the community. It offers a telephone helpline, drop-in, community support workers, and library services.

Australia

ACEDA
(incorporating Panic and Anxiety, Obsessive Compulsive,
    and Eating Disorder Associations)
Everard House
589 South Road
Everard Park, South Australia 5035, Australia
Phone: 8297 4011
Fax: 8297 7587
E-mail: *ed@aceda.org.au*
Website: *www.aceda.org.au*

ACEDA offers counseling, assistance, and support to families, partners, and friends. It promotes community awareness.

Eating Disorders Foundation of Victoria Inc.
1513 High Street
Glen Iris, Victoria 3146, Australia
Phone: 9885 0318
Fax: 9885 1153
Website: *www.eatingdisorders.org.au*

A nonprofit organization that aims to support those affected by eating disorders and to better inform the community about disordered eating.

National Eating Disorders Collaboration
103 Alexander Street
Crows Nest, New South Wales 2065, Australia

Phone: (02) 9412 4499
E-mail: *info@nedc.com.au*
Website: *www.nedc.com.au*

The NEDC aims to improve the health outcomes of people with, or at risk of developing, an eating disorder in Australia, recognizing the need to take a long-term approach to promotion, prevention, and early intervention for eating disorders. The NEDC website brings research, expertise, and opinion from leaders in the field together in one place. It's a one-stop portal to make eating disorders more accessible for everyone.

Psychotherapy and Counselling Federation of Australia
290 Park Street, Fitzroy North
Victoria 3068, Australia
Phone: 9486 3077
Fax: 9486 3933
E-mail: *admin@pacfa.org.au*
Website: *www.pacfa.org.au*

PACFA is an "umbrella" association composed of affiliated professional associations that represent various modalities within the disciplines of psychotherapy and counseling in the Australian community.

Eating Disorder Outreach Service
Information and Referral Service for Queensland
Phone: 07 3114 0809
E-mail: *EDOS@health.qld.gov.au*

New Zealand

Canterbury Mental Health Education and Resource Centre Trust (MHERC)
P.O. Box 13 167
Christchurch, New Zealand
Phone: 365 5344 or 424 399 (toll free)
Fax: 03 366 7720
Website: *www.mherc.org.nz*

Eating Difficulties Education Network
1 Garnet Road
Westmere, Auckland, New Zealand

Phone: 378 9039
Fax: 378 9393
Website: *www.eden.org.nz*

New Zealand Association of Counselors

Federated Farmers Building, 3rd Floor
169 London Street
Hamilton 2015, New Zealand
Phone: 834 0220
Fax: 834 0221
E-mail: *execofficer@nzac.org.nz*
Website: *www.nzac.org.nz*

NZAC now represents approximately 2,500 counselors who work in education, health, justice, and social welfare government agencies, community-based social service agencies, Iwi Social Services, Pacific Island Organizations, private practice, and a range of ethnicity-specific helping agencies.

Other International

IAEDP—The International Association of Eating Disorders Professionals

P.O. Box 1295
Pekin, IL 61555-1295
Phone: 800-800-8126
Fax: 800-800-8126
Website: *www.iaedp.com*

The IAEDP aims to provide a high level of professionalism among practitioners who treat those suffering from eating disorders by emphasizing ethical and professional standards, offering education and training in the field, and certifying those who have met professional requirements.

International Eating Disorder Referral Organization

Website: *www.edreferral.com*

This organization provides information and treatment resources for all forms of eating disorders.

Further Reading

GENERAL

Adan, R., and W. H. Kaye, Editors, *Behavioral Neurobiology of Eating Disorders*, 2010. Berlin: Springer-Verlag.

Agras, W. S., Editor, *The Oxford Handbook of Eating Disorders*, 2010. Oxford, UK: Oxford University Press.

Agras, W. S., J. Lock, H. Brandt, et al., Comparison of 2 Family Therapies for Adolescent Anorexia Nervosa: A Randomized Parallel Trial, *JAMA Psychiatry*, 2014, *71*(11), 1279–1286.

American Psychiatric Association, Practice Guideline for the Treatment of Patients with Eating Disorders (Revision), *American Journal of Psychiatry*, 2000, *157*(Suppl.), 1–39.

American Psychiatric Association, *Diagnostic and Statistical Manual of Mental Disorders, Fifth Edition*, 2013. Washington, DC: American Psychiatric Association.

Bulik, C. M., N. Berkman, A. Kimberly, et al., Anorexia Nervosa: A Systematic Review of Randomized Clinical Trials, *International Journal of Eating Disorders*, 2007, *40*, 310–320.

Cooper, Z., and C. G. Fairburn, The Eating Disorder Examination: A Semi-Structured Interview for the Assessment of the Specific Psychopathology of Eating Disorders, *International Journal of Eating Disorders*, 1987, *6*, 1–8.

Dalle Grave, R., S. Calugi, H. Doll, et al., Enhanced Cognitive Behavioral Therapy for Adolescents with Anorexia Nervosa: An Alternative to Family Therapy? *Behaviour Research and Therapy*, 2013, *51*, R9–R12.

Fairburn, C. G., *Cognitive Behavior Therapy and Eating Disorders*, 2008. New York: Guilford Press.

Fairburn, C. G., and K. D. Brownell, Editors, *Eating Disorders and Obesity: A Comprehensive Handbook, Second Edition*, 2002. New York: Guilford Press.

Fairburn, C. G., Z. Cooper, and R. Shafran, Enhanced Cognitive Behavior Therapy for Eating Disorders ("CBT-E"): An Overview, in C. G. Fairburn, *Cognitive Behavioral Therapy and Eating Disorders*, 2008. New York: Guilford Press, pp. 23–34.

Fitzpatrick, K., J. Lock, A. Darcy, et al., Set-Shifting among Adolescents with Anorexia Nervosa, *International Journal of Eating Disorders*, 2012, *45*(7), 909–912.

Fitzpatrick, K., A. Moye, R. Hoste, et al., Adolescent Focused Therapy for Adolescent Anorexia Nervosa, *Journal of Contemporary Psychotherapy*, 2010, *40*, 31–39.

Flament, M., S. Ledoux, P. Jeammet, et al., A Population Study of Bulimia Nervosa and Subclinical Eating Disorders in Adolescence, in H. Steinhausen, Editor, *Eating Disorders in Adolescence: Anorexia and Bulimia Nervosa*, 1995. New York: Brunner/Mazel, pp. 21–36.

Gull, W., Anorexia Nervosa (*Apepsia Hysterica, Anorexia Hysterica*), *Transactions of the Clinical Society of London*, 1874, *7*, 222–228.

Hoek, H., and D. van Hoeken, Review of Prevalence and Incidence of Eating Disorders, *International Journal of Eating Disorders*, 2003, *34*, 383–396.

Keys, A., J. Brozek, and A. Henschel, *The Biology of Human Starvation*, 1950. Minneapolis: University of Minnesota Press.

Kreipe, R., and A. Palomaki, Beyond Picky Rating: Avoidant/Restrictive Food Intake Disorder, *Current Psychiatry Reports*, 2012, *14*, 421–431.

Lasègue, E., De l'Anorexie Hystérique, *Archives Générales de Médecine*, 1883, *21*, 384–403.

Lask, B., and R. Bryant-Waugh, Editors, *Eating Disorders in Childhood and Adolescence, Fourth Edition*, 2013. London: Routledge.

Le Grange, D., R. Crosby, and J. Lock, Predictors and Moderators of Outcome in Family-Based Treatment for Adolescent Bulimia Nervosa, *Journal of the American Academy of Child and Adolescent Psychiatry*, 2008, *47*, 464–470.

Le Grange, D., R. Crosby, P. Rathouz, et al., A Randomized Controlled

Comparison of Family-Based Treatment and Supportive Psychotherapy for Adolescent Bulimia Nervosa, *Archives of General Psychiatry*, 2007, *64*, 1049–1056.

Le Grange, D., P. Doyle, S. Swanson, et al., Calculation of Expected Body Weight in Adolescents with Eating Disorders, *Pediatrics*, 2012, *129*, e438–e446.

Le Grange, D., and J. Lock, *Treating Bulimia in Adolescents: A Family-Based Approach*, 2007. New York: Guilford Press.

Le Grange, D., and J. Lock, Editors, *Eating Disorders in Children and Adolescents*, 2011. New York: Guilford Press.

Le Grange, D., J. Lock, W. S. Agras, et al., Moderators and Mediators of Remission in Family-Based Treatment and Adolescent Focused Therapy for Anorexia Nervosa, *Behaviour Research and Therapy*, 2012, *50*, 85–92.

Le Grange, D., J. Lock, K. Loeb, et al., An Academy for Eating Disorders Position Paper: The Role of the Family in Eating Disorders, *International Journal of Eating Disorders*, 2010, *43*, 1–5.

Lock, J., Adjusting Cognitive Behavioral Therapy for Adolescent Bulimia Nervosa: Results of a Case Series, *American Journal of Psychotherapy*. 2005, *59*, 267–281.

Lock, J., Fitting Square Pegs into Round Holes: Males with Eating Disorders, *Journal of Adolescent Health*, 2008, *44*, 99–100.

Lock, J., *The Oxford Handbook of Child and Adolescent Eating Disorders: Developmental Perspectives*, 2012. New York: Oxford University Press.

Lock, J., W. S. Agras, S. Bryson, et al., A Comparison of Short- and Long-Term Family Therapy for Adolescent Anorexia Nervosa, *Journal of the American Academy of Child and Adolescent Psychiatry*, 2005, *44*, 632–639.

Lock, J., A. Garrett, J. Beenhaker, et al., Aberrant Brain Activation during a Response Inhibition Task in Adolescent Eating Disorder Subtypes, *American Journal of Psychiatry*, 2011, *168*, 55–64.

Lock, J., D. Le Grange, W. S. Agras, et al., A Randomized Clinical Trial Comparing Family Based Treatment to Adolescent Focused Individual Therapy for Adolescents with Anorexia Nervosa, *Archives of General Psychiatry*, 2010, *67*, 1025–1032.

Loeb, K., D. Le Grange, T. Hildebrandt, et al., Eating Disorders in Youth: Diagnostic Variability and Predictive Validity, *International Journal of Eating Disorders*, 2011, *44*, 692–702.

Loeb, K., J. Lock, R. Greif, et al., Transdiagnostic Theory and Application of Family-Based Treatment for Youth with Eating Disorders, *Cognitive and Behavioral Practice*, 2012, *19*(1), 17–30.

Madden, S., J. Miskovic-Wheatley, A. Wallis, et al., A Randomized Controlled Trial of Inpatient Hospitalization for Anorexia Nervosa in Medically Unstable Adolescents, *Psychological Medicine*, 2014, *44*, 1053–1064.

Nicholls, D., R. Lynn, and R. Viner, Childhoood Eating Disorders: British National Surveillance Study, *British Journal of Psychiatry*, 2011, *198*, 295–301.

Norris, M., M. Apsimon, M. Harrison, et al., An Examination of Medical and Psychological Morbidity in Adolescent Males with Eating Disorders, *Eating Disorders*, 2012, *20*, 405–415.

Safer, D., J. Couturier, and J. Lock, Dialectical Behavior Therapy Modified for Adolescent Binge Eating Disorders: A Case Report, *Cognitive Behavioral Practice*, 2007, *14*, 157–167.

Saraf, M., Holy Anorexia and Anorexia Nervosa: Society and Concept of Disease, *The Pharos*, 1998, *61*, 2–4.

Silverman, J., Charcot's Comments on the Therapeutic Role of Isolation in the Treatment of Anorexia Nervosa, *International Journal of Eating Disorders*, 1997, *21*, 295–298.

Striegel-Moore, R. H., D. Leslie, S. A. Petrill, et al., One-Year Use and Cost of Inpatient and Outpatient Services among Female and Male Patients with an Eating Disorder: Evidence from a National Database of Health Insurance Claims, *International Journal of Eating Disorders*, 2000, *27*, 381–389.

Swanson, J, S. Crow, D. Le Grange, et al., Prevalence and Correlates of Eating Disorders in Adolescents, *Archives of General Psychiatry*, 2011, *68*, 714–723.

Tchanturia, K., and J. Lock, Cognitive Remediation Therapy for Eating Disorders: Development, Refinement, and Future Directions, in R. Adan and W. H. Kaye, Editors, *Behavioral Neruobiology of Eating Disorders*, 2010. Berlin: Springer-Verlag.

Thompson, J. K., Editor, *Handbook of Eating Disorders and Obesity*, 2004. Hoboken, NJ: Wiley.

Treasure, J., *Anorexia Nervosa: A Survival Guide for Families, Friends, and Sufferers*, 1997. East Sussex, UK: Psychology Press.

Treasure, J., U. Schmidt, and P. MacDonald, *The Clinician's Guide to Collaborative Caring in Eating Disorders: The New Maudsley Method*, 2010. London: Routledge.

Vandereycken, W., Families of Patients with Eating Disorders, in C. G. Fairburn and K. Brownell, Editors, *Eating Disorders and Obesity: A Comprehensive Handbook, Second Edition*, 2002. New York: Guilford Press, pp. 215–220.

Wilson, G. T., and C. G. Fairburn, Treatments for Eating Disorders, in P. Nathan and J. Gorman, Editors, *A Guide to Treatments That Work*, 2002. New York: Oxford University Press, pp. 559–592.

Zucker, N., Emotion, Attention, and Relationship: A Developmental Model of Self-Regulation in Anorexia Nervosa and Related Disordered Eating Behaviors, in J. Lock, Editor, *Oxford Handbook of Child and Adolescent Eating Disorders: Developmental Perspectives*, 2013. New York: Oxford University Press, pp. 67–87.

RISKS FOR EATING DISORDERS

Agras, W. S., H. C. Kraemer, R. I. Berkowitz, et al., Does a Vigorous Feeding Style Influence Early Development of Adiposity?, *Journal of Pediatrics*, 1987, *110*(5), 799–804.

Attie, I., and J. Brooks-Gunn, Development of Eating Problems in Adolescent Girls: A Longitudinal Study. *Developmental Psychology*, 1989, *25*, 70–79.

Beren, S., H. A. Hayden, D. Wilfley, et al., Body-Dissatisfaction among Lesbian College Students: The Conflict of Straddling Mainstream and Lesbian Cultures, *Psychology of Women Quarterly*, 1997, *21*, 431–445.

Braun, D., S. R. Sunday, A. Huang, et al., More Males Seek Treatment for Eating Disorders, *International Journal of Eating Disorders*, 1999, *25*, 415–424.

Bravender, T., L. Roberston, E. R. Woods, et al., Is There an Increased Clinical Severity of Patients with Eating Disorders under Managed Care?, *Journal of Adolescent Health*, 1999, *24*, 422–426.

Bulik, C. M., Genetic and Biological Risk Factors, in J. K. Thompson, Editor, *Handbook of Eating Disorders and Obesity*, 2004. Hoboken, NJ: Wiley, pp. 3–16.

Bulik, C. M., J. Fear, and A. Pickering, Predictors of the Development of Bulimia Nervosa in Women with Anorexia Nervosa, *Journal of Nervous and Mental Disease*, 1997, *185*, 704–707.

Bulik, C., M. Slof-Op't Landt, E. van Furth, et al., The Genetics of Anorexia Nervosa, *Annual Review of Nutrition*, 2007, *27*, 263–275.

Carlat, D. J., C. A. Camargo, Jr., and D. B. Herzog, Eating Disorders in Males: A Report on 135 Patients, *American Journal of Psychiatry*, 1997, *154*(8), 1127–1132.

Davis, C., and M. Katzman, Perfectionism as Acculturation: Psychological Correlates of Eating Problems in Chinese Male and Female Students

Living in the United States, *International Journal of Eating Disorders*, 1999, *25*, 65–70.

Fairburn, C. G., Z. Cooper, H. A. Doll, et al., Risk Factors for Anorexia Nervosa: Three Integrated Case–Control Comparisons, *Archives of General Psychiatry*, 1999, *56*, 468–476.

Fairburn, C. G., P. J. Cowen, and P. J. Harrison, Twin Studies and the Etiology of Eating Disorders, *International Journal of Eating Disorders*, 1999, *26*, 349–358.

Fairburn, C. G., H. A. Doll, S. L. Welch, et al., Risk Factors for Binge Eating Disorder: A Community-Based, Case–Control Study, *Archives of General Psychiatry*, 1998, *55*(5), 425–432.

Fairburn, C. G., S. L. Welch, H. A. Doll, et al., Risk Factors for Bulimia Nervosa: A Community-Based Case–Control Study, *Archives of General Psychiatry*, 1997, *54*(6), 509–517.

Field, A., Risk Factors for Eating Disorders: An Evaluation of the Evidence, in J. K. Thompson, Editor, *Handbook of Eating Disorders and Obesity*, 2004. Hoboken, NJ: Wiley, pp. 17–32.

Fouts, G., and K. Burggraf, Television Situation Comedies: Female Body Images and Verbal Reinforcements, *Sex Roles*, 1999, *40*, 473–481.

Frank, G., W. H. Kaye, C. C. Meltzer, et al., Reduced 5-HT2A Receptor Binding after Recovery from Anorexia Nervosa, *Biological Psychiatry*, 2002, *52*, 896–906.

Franko, D., and M. Omori, Subclinical Eating Disorders in Adolescent Women: A Test of the Continuity Hypothesis and Its Psychological Correlates, *Journal of Adolescence*, 1999, *22*, 389–398.

French, S. A., N. Leffert, M. Story, et al., Adolescent Binge/Purge and Weight Loss Behaviors: Associations with Developmental Assets, *Journal of Adolescent Health*, 2001, *28*, 211–221.

Gowen, L., C. Hayward, J. D. Killen, et al., Acculturation and Eating Disorder Symptoms in Adolescent Girls, *Journal of Research on Adolescence*, 1999, *9*, 67–83.

Gunewardene, A., G. Huon, and R. Zheng, Exposure to Westernization and Dieting: A Cross-Cultural Study, *International Journal of Eating Disorders*, 2001, *29*, 289–293.

Hill, A., and R. Bhatti, Body Shape Perception and Dieting in Pre-Adolescent British Asian Girls: Links with Eating Disorders, *International Journal of Eating Disorders*, 1995, *17*, 175–183.

Humphrey, L., Structural Analysis of Parent–Child Relationships in Eating Disorders, *Journal of Abnormal Psychology*, 1986, *95*, 395–402.

Humphrey, L., Comparison of Bulimic-Anorexic and Nondistressed

Families Using Structural Analysis of Behavior, *Journal of the American Academy of Child and Adolescent Psychiatry*, 1987, *26*, 248–255.

Killen, J. D., C. B. Taylor, and C. Hayward, Weight Concerns Influence the Development of Eating Disorders, *Journal of Consulting and Clinical Psychology*, 1996, *64*, 936–940.

Killen, J. D., C. B. Taylor, M. J. Telch, et al., Self-Induced Vomiting and Laxative Use among Teenagers: Precursors of the Binge–Purge Syndrome?, *Journal of the American Medical Association*, 1986, *255*, 1447–1449.

Lake, A., P. Staiger, and H. Glowinski, Effects of Western Culture on Women's Attitudes to Eating and Perceptions of Body Shape, *International Journal of Eating Disorders*, 2000, *27*, 83–89.

Lee, S., Self-Starvation in Context: Towards a Culturally Sensitive Understanding of Anorexia Nervosa, *Social Science and Medicine*, 1995, *41*, 25–36.

Levine, M., and K. Harrison, Media's Role in the Perpetuation and Prevention of Negative Body Image and Disordered Eating, in J. K. Thompson, Editor, *Handbook of Eating Disorders and Obesity*, 2004. Hoboken, NJ: Wiley, pp. 695–717.

Marchi, M., and P. Cohen, Early Childhood Eating Behaviors and Adolescent Eating Disorders, *Journal of the American Academy of Child and Adolescent Psychiatry*, 1990, *29*, 112–117.

McClelland, L., and A. H. Crisp, Anorexia Nervosa and Social Class, *International Journal of Eating Disorders*, 2001, *29*, 150–156.

Patton, G. C., R. Selzer, C. Coffey, et al., Onset of Adolescent Eating Disorders: Population Based Cohort Study over 3 Years, *British Medical Journal*, 1999, *318*, 765–768.

Pope, H. G., R. Olivardia, A. Gruber, et al., Evolving Ideals of Male Body Image as Seen through Action Toys, *International Journal of Eating Disorders*, 1999, *26*, 65–72.

Steiner, H., W. Kwan, T. G. Schaffer, et al., Risk and Protective Factors for Juvenile Eating Disorders, *European Child and Adolescent Psychiatry*, 2003, *12*(Suppl. 1), 38–46.

Stice, E., and W. S. Agras, Predicting Onset and Cessation of Bulimic Behaviors during Adolescence, *Behavior Therapy*, 1998, *29*, 257–276.

Strober, M., R. Freeman, C. Lampert, et al., Controlled Family Study of Anorexia Nervosa and Bulimia Nervosa: Evidence of Shared Liability and Transmission of Partial Syndromes, *American Journal of Psychiatry*, 2000, *157*, 393–401.

Strober, M., and L. Humphrey, Family Contributions to the Etiology and

Course of Anorexia and Bulimia, *Journal of Clinical Psychology*, 1987, *55*, 654–659.

Welch, S. L., H. A. Doll, and C. G. Fairburn, Life Events and the Onset of Bulimia Nervosa: A Controlled Study, *Psychological Medicine*, 1997, *27*(3), 515–522.

Welch, S. L., and C. G. Fairburn, Sexual Abuse and Bulimia Nervosa: Three Integrated Case Control Comparisons, *American Journal of Psychiatry*, 1994, *151*(3), 402–407.

Welch, S. L., and C. G. Fairburn, Childhood Sexual and Physical Abuse as Risk Factors for the Development of Bulimia Nervosa: A Community-Based Case Control Study [See Comments], *Child Abuse and Neglect*, 1996, *20*(7), 633–642.

Whelan, E., and P. J. Cooper, The Association between Childhood Feeding Problems and Maternal Eating Disorder: A Community Study, *Psychological Medicine*, 2000, *30*, 69–77.

Wonderlich, S. A., R. D. Crosby, J. E. Mitchell, et al., Eating Disturbance and Sexual Trauma in Childhood and Adulthood, *International Journal of Eating Disorders*, 2001, *30*, 401–412.

Woodside, D. B., C. M. Bulik, K. A. Halmi, et al., Personality, Perfectionism, and Attitudes toward Eating in Parents of Individuals with Eating Disorders, *International Journal of Eating Disorders*, 2002, *31*, 290–299.

MEDICAL PROBLEMS ASSOCIATED WITH EATING DISORDERS

American Academy of Pediatrics, Policy Statement: Identifying and Treating Eating Disorders, *Pediatrics*, 2003, *111*, 204–211.

Andres-Perpina, S., E. Lozanno-Serra, O. Puig, et al., Clinical and Biological Correlates of Adolescent Anorexia Nervosa with Impaired Cognitive Profile, *European Child and Adolescent Psychiatry*, 2011, *50*, 541–549.

Arcelus, J., A. Mitchell, J. Wales, et al., Mortality Rates in Patients with Anorexia Nervosa and Other Eating Disorders, *Archives of General Psychiatry*, 2011, *68*, 724–731.

Crow, S., C. Peterson, S. Swanson, et al., Increased Mortality in Bulimia Nervosa and Other Eating Disorders, *American Journal of Psychiatry*, 2009, *166*, 1342–1346.

Eddy, K., and S. Rauch, Neuroimaging in Eating Disorders: Coming of Age, *American Journal of Psychiatry*, 2011, *168*, 1139–1141.

Faust, J., A. Goldschmidt, K. Anderson, et al., Resumption of Menses in Anorexia Nervosa During a Course of Family-Based Treatment, *Journal of Eating Disorders*, 2013, *1*, 12.

Fisher, M., N. H. Golden, D. K. Katzman, et al., Eating Disorders in Adolescents: A Background Paper, *Journal of Adolescent Health*, 1995, *16*, 420–437.

Franko, D., A. Keshaviah, K. T. Eddy, et al., A Longitudinal Investigation of Mortality in Anorexia Nervosa and Bulimia Nervosa. *American Journal of Psychiatry*, 2013, *170*, 917–925.

Friederich, H., M. Wu, J. Simon, et al., Neurocircuit Function in Eating Disorders, *International Journal of Eating Disorders*, 2013, *46*, 425–432.

Garfinkel, P., E. Lin, and P. Goering, Should Amenorrhoea Be Necessary for the Diagnosis of Anorexia Nervosa?: Evidence from a Canadian Community Sample, *British Journal of Psychiatry*, 1996, *168*, 500–506.

Golden, N. H., D. K. Katzman, R. E. Kreipe, et al., Eating Disorders in Adolescents: Position Paper of the Society for Adolescent Medicine, *Journal of Adolescent Health*, 2003, *33*, 496–503.

Herzog, D. B., D. N. Greenwood, D. J. Dorer, et al., Mortality in Eating Disorders: A Descriptive Study, *International Journal of Eating Disorders*, 2000, *28*, 20–26.

Mitchell, J., H. C. Seim, and E. Colon, Medical Complications and Medical Management of Bulimia, *Annals of Internal Medicine*, 1987, *107*, 71–77.

Patton, G. C., Mortality in Eating Disorders, *Psychological Medicine*, 1988, *18*, 947–951.

Rome, E., and S. Ammerman, Medical Complications of Eating Disorders: An Update, *Journal of Adolescent Health*, 2003, *33*, 418–426.

Sullivan, P. F., Mortality in Anorexia Nervosa, *American Journal of Psychiatry*, 1995, *152*, 1073–1074.

Swenne, I., Heart Risk Associated with Weight Loss in Anorexia Nervosa and Eating Disorders: Electrocardiographic Changes during the Early Phase of Refeeding, *Acta Pediatrica*, 2000, *89*, 447–452.

PSYCHOLOGICAL TREATMENTS FOR EATING DISORDERS

Agras, W. S., and R. F. Apple, *Overcoming Eating Disorders: A Cognitive-Behavioral Therapy Approach for Bulimia Nervosa and Binge-Eating Disorder: Therapist Guide, Second Edition*, 2008. New York: Oxford University Press.

Agras, W. S., T. Walsh, C. G. Fairburn, et al., A Multicenter Comparison of Cognitive-Behavioral Therapy and Interpersonal Psychotherapy for Bulimia Nervosa, *Archives of General Psychiatry*, 2000, *57*, 459–466.

Alexander, J., and D. Le Grange, *My Kid Is Back: Empowering Parents to Beat Anorexia Nervosa*, 2009. Melbourne: Melbourne University Press.

Apple, R. F., and W. S. Agras, *Overcoming Your Eating Disorder: A Cognitive-Behavioral Therapy Approach for Bulimia Nervosa and Binge-Eating Disorder: Workbook, Second Edition*, 2008. New York: Oxford University Press.

Bowers, W. A., K. Evans, D. Le Grange, et al., Treatment of Adolescent Eating Disorders, in M. Reinecke, F. Couturier, M. Kimbler, et al., Editors, Efficacy of Family-Based Treatment for Adolescents with Eating Disorders: A Systematic Review, *International Journal of Eating Disorders*, 2013, *46*, 3–11.

Bruch, H., *Eating Disorders: Obesity, Anorexia Nervosa, and the Person Within*, 1973. New York: Basic Books.

Bruch, H., *The Golden Cage: The Enigma of Anorexia Nervosa*, 1978. Cambridge, MA: Harvard University Press.

Channon, S., P. de Silva, D. Hemsley, et al., A Controlled Trial of Cognitive-Behavioural and Behavioural Treatment of Anorexia Nervosa, *Behaviour Research and Therapy*, 1989, *27*(5), 529–535.

Cooper, P. J., and J. Steere, A Comparison of Two Psychological Treatments for Bulimia Nervosa: Implications for Models of Maintenance, *Behaviour Research and Therapy*, 1995, *33*, 875–885.

Crisp, A. H., *Anorexia Nervosa: Let Me Be*, 1980. London: Academic Press.

Crisp, A. H., Anorexia Nervosa as Flight from Growth: Assessment and Treatment Based on the Model, in D. M. Garner and P. E. Garfinkel, Editors, *Handbook of Treatment for Eating Disorders, Second Edition*, 1997. New York: Guilford Press, pp. 248–277.

Crisp, A. H., K. Norton, S. Gowers, et al., A Controlled Study of the Effect of Therapies Aimed at Adolescent and Family Psychopathology in Anorexia Nervosa, *British Journal of Psychiatry*, 1991, *159*, 325–333.

Dare, C., and I. Eisler, Family Therapy for Anorexia Nervosa, in P. J. Cooper and A. Stein, Editors, *Feeding Problems and Eating Disorders in Children and Adolescents*, 1992. New York: Harwood Academic, pp. 147–160.

Dare, C., and I. Eisler, Family Therapy for Anorexia Nervosa, in D. M. Garner and P. Garfinkel, Editors, *Handbook of Treatment for Eating Disorders, Second Edition*, 1997. New York: Guilford Press, pp. 307–324.

Dare, C., and I. Eisler, A Multi-Family Group Day Treatment Programme

for Adolescent Eating Disorders, *European Eating Disorders Review*, 2000, *8*, 4–18.

Dare, C., I. Eisler, G. Russell, et al., Psychological Therapies for Adults with Anorexia Nervosa: Randomised Controlled Trial of Outpatient Treatments, *British Journal of Psychiatry*, 2001, *178*, 216–221.

Dattilio, F. M., and A. Freeman, Editors, *Cognitive Therapy with Children and Adolescents: A Casebook for Clinical Practice, Second Edition*, 2003. New York: Guilford Press, pp. 247–280.

Dodge, E., M. Hodes, I. Eisler, et al., Family Therapy for Bulimia Nervosa in Adolescents: An Exploratory Study, *Journal of Family Therapy*, 1995, *17*, 59–77.

Eisler, I., C. Dare, M. Hodes, et al., Family Therapy for Adolescent Anorexia Nervosa: The Results of a Controlled Comparison of Two Family Interventions, *Journal of Child Psychology and Psychiatry*, 2000, *41*(6), 727–736.

Eisler, I., C. Dare, G. F. Russell, et al., Family and Individual Therapy in Anorexia Nervosa: A Five-Year Follow-Up, *Archives of General Psychiatry*, 1997, *54*, 1025–1030.

Fairburn, C., A Cognitive-Behavioral Approach to the Treatment of Bulimia, *Psychological Medicine*, 1981, *11*(4), 707–711.

Fairburn, C. G., *Overcoming Binge Eating*, 1995. New York: Guilford Press.

Fairburn, C. G., Interpersonal Psychotherapy for Bulimia Nervosa, in D. M. Garner and P. E. Garfinkel, Editors, *Handbook of Treatment for Eating Disorders, Second Edition*, 1997. New York: Guilford Press, pp. 278–294.

Fairburn, C. G., R. Jones, R. C. Peveler, et al., Three Psychological Treatments for Bulimia Nervosa: A Comparative Trial, *Archives of General Psychiatry*, 1991, *48*(5), 463–469.

Fairburn, C. G., J. Kirk, M. O'Connor, et al., A Comparison of Two Psychological Treatments for Bulimia Nervosa, *Behaviour Research and Therapy*, 1986, *24*(6), 629–643.

Fairburn, C. G., R. Shafran, and Z. Cooper, A Cognitive Behavioural Theory of Anorexia Nervosa, *Behaviour Research and Therapy*, 1999, *37*(1), 1–13.

Federici, A., L. Wisniewski, and D. Ben-Porath, Description of an Intensive Dialectical Behavior Therapy Program for Multidiagnostic Clients with Eating Disorders, *Journal of Counseling and Development*, 2012, *90*, 330–338.

Le Grange, D., and J. Lock, *Treating Bulimia in Adolescents: A Family-Based Approach*, 2007. New York: Guilford Press.

Liebman, R., J. Sargent, and M. Silver, A Family Systems Approach to the Treatment of Anorexia Nervosa, *Journal of the American Academy of Child and Adolescent Psychiatry*, 1983, *22*, 128–133.

Lock, J., and D. Le Grange, *Treatment Manual for Anorexia Nervosa: A Family-Based Approach, Second Edition*, 2013. New York: Guilford Press.

Madanes, C., *Strategic Family Therapy*, 1981. San Francisco: Jossey-Bass.

Minuchin, S., B. Rosman, and I. Baker, *Psychosomatic Families: Anorexia Nervosa in Context*, 1978. Cambridge, MA: Harvard University Press.

Palazzoli, M., *Self-Starvation: From the Intrapsychic to the Transpersonal Approach to Anorexia Nervosa*, 1974. London: Chaucer.

Pike, K. M., B. T. Walsh, K. Vitousek, et al., Cognitive Behavior Therapy in the Posthospitalization Treatment of Anorexia Nervosa, *American Journal of Psychiatry*, 2004, *160*, 2046–2049.

Robin, A. L., P. T. Siegel, A. W. Moye, et al., A Controlled Comparison of Family versus Individual Therapy for Adolescents with Anorexia Nervosa, *Journal of the American Academy of Child and Adolescent Psychiatry*, 1999, *38*(12), 1482–1489.

Russell, G. F., G. I. Szmukler, C. Dare, et al., An Evaluation of Family Therapy in Anorexia Nervosa and Bulimia Nervosa, *Archives of General Psychiatry*, 1987, *44*(12), 1047–1056.

Safer, D. L., C. F. Telch, and W. S. Agras, Dialectical Behavior Therapy for Bulimia Nervosa, *American Journal of Psychiatry*, 2001, *158*, 632–634.

Scholz, M., and K. E. Asen, Multiple Family Therapy with Eating Disordered Adolescents, *European Eating Disorders Review*, 2001, *9*, 33–42.

Stierlin, H., and G. Weber, *Unlocking the Family Door: A Systemic Approach to the Understanding and Treatment of Anorexia Nervosa*, 1989. New York: Brunner/Mazel.

Tchanturia, K., S. Lloyd, and K. Lange, Cognitive Remediation Therapy for Anorexia Nervosa: Current Evidence and Future Research Directions, *International Journal of Eating Disorders*, 2013, *46*, 492–495.

Treasure, J., G. Todd, M. Brolly, et al., A Pilot Study of a Randomised Trial of Cognitive Analytical Therapy vs. Educational Behavioral Therapy for Adult Anorexia Nervosa, *Behaviour Research and Therapy*, 1995, *33*, 363–367.

Watson, H., and C. Bulik, Update on the Treatment of Anorexia Nervosa: Review of Clinical Trials, Practice Guidelines and Emerging Interventions, *Psychological Medicine*, 2013, *43*(12), 2477–2500.

White, M., and D. Epston, *Narrative Means to Therapeutic Ends*, 1990. New York: Norton.

Wilson, G. T., C. G. Fairburn, W. S. Agras, et al., Cognitive Behavioral Therapy for Bulimia Nervosa: Time Course and Mechanisms of Change, *Journal of Consulting and Clinical Psychology*, 2002, *70*, 267–274.

PHARMACOLOGICAL TREATMENTS
FOR EATING DISORDERS

Attia, E., C. Haiman, B. T. Walsh, et al., Does Fluoxetine Augment the Inpatient Treatment of Anorexia Nervosa?, *American Journal of Psychiatry*, 1998, *155*(4), 548–551.

Attia, E., L. Mayer, and E. Killory, Medication Response in the Treatment of Patients with Anorexia Nervosa, *Journal of Psychiatric Practice*, 2001, 7, 157–162.

Fluoexetine Bulimia Nervosa Group, Fluoxetine in the Treatment of Bulimia Nervosa, *Archives of General Psychiatry*, 1992, *49*, 139–147.

Hagman, J., J. Grallam, E. Sigel, et al. A Double-Blind, Placebo-Controlled Study of Risperidone for the Treatment of Adolescents and Young Adults with Anorexia Nervosa: A Pilot Study. *American Journal of Child and Adolescent Psychiatry*, 2011, *50*, 915–924.

Halmi, C. A., E. D. Eckert, and T. J. Ladu, Treatment Efficacy of Cyproheptadine and Amitryptiline, *Archives of General Psychiatry*, 1986, *43*, 177–181.

Kaye, W. H., An Open Trial of Fluoxetine in Patients with Anorexia Nervosa, *Journal of Clinical Psychiatry*, 1991, *52*, 464–471.

Kaye, W. H., K. Grendall, and M. Strober, Serotonin Neuronal Function and Selective Serotonin Reuptake Inhibitor Treatment in Anorexia Nervosa, *Biological Psychiatry*, 1998, *44*, 825–838.

Malina, A., J. Gaskill, C. McConaha, et al., Olanzapine Treatment of Anorexia Nervosa: A Retrospective Study, *International Journal of Eating Disorders*, 2003, *33*, 234–237.

Walsh, B. T., A. S. Kaplan, E. Attia, et al., Fluoxetine after Weight Restoration in Anorexia Nervosa: A Randomized Clinical Trial. *Journal of the American Medical Association*, 2006, *295*, 2605–2612.

Walsh, B. T., G. T. Wilson, K. L. Loeb, et al., Medication and Psychotherapy in the Treatment of Bulimia Nervosa, *American Journal of Psychiatry*, 1997, *154*(4), 523–531.

COMORBID PSYCHIATRIC PROBLEMS
WITH EATING DISORDERS

Casper, R., D. Hedeker, and J. McClough, Personality Dimensions in Eating Disorders and Their Relevance for Subtyping, *Journal of the American Academy of Child and Adolescent Psychiatry*, 1992, *31*, 830–840.

Fischer, S., and D. Le Grange, Co-morbidity and High-Risk Behaviors in Treatment Seeking Adolescents with Bulimia Nervosa, *International Journal of Eating Disorders*, 2007, 40, 751–753.

Godart, N. T., M. F. Flament, Y. Lecrubier, et al., Anxiety Disorders in Anorexia Nervosa and Bulimia Nervosa: Comorbidity and Chronology of Appearance, *European Psychiatry*, 2000, *15*, 38–45.

Godart, N., M. F. Flament, F. Perdereau, et al., Comorbidity between Eating Disorders and Anxiety Disorders: A Review, *International Journal of Eating Disorders*, 2002, *32*, 253–270.

Herzog, D. B., M. B. Keller, N. R. Sacks, et al., Psychiatric Comorbidity in Treatment-Seeking Anorexics and Bulimics, *Journal of the American Academy of Child and Adolescent Psychiatry*, 1992, *31*(5), 810–818.

Herzog, D. B., K. M. Nussbaum, and A. K. Marmor, Comorbidity and Outcome in Eating Disorders, *Psychiatric Clinics of North America*, 1996, *19*(4), 843–859.

Hildebrandt, T., T. Bascow, M. Markella, et al., Anxiety in Anorexia Nervosa and Its Management Using Family-Based Treatment, *European Eating Disorders Review*, 2012, *20*, e1–e20.

Hughes, E., A. Goldschmidt, Z. Labuschagne, et al., Eating Disorders with and without Comorbid Depression and Anxiety: Similarities and Differences in a Clinical Sample of Children and Adolescents, *European Eating Disorders Review*, 2013, *21*, 386–394.

Klump, K., C. M. Bulik, C. Pollice, et al., Temperament and Character in Women with Anorexia Nervosa, *Journal of Nervous and Mental Disease*, 2000, *188*, 559–567.

Telch, C. F., and E. Stice, Psychiatric Comorbidity in Women with Binge Eating Disorder: Prevalence Rates from a Non-Treatment-Seeking Sample, *Journal of Consulting and Clinical Psychology*, 1998, *66*(5), 768–776.

Vitousek, K., and F. Manke, Personality Variables and Disorders in Anorexia Nervosa and Bulimia Nervosa, *Journal of Abnormal Psychology*, 1994, *103*, 137–147.

Wonderlich, S., Personality and Eating Disorders, in C. G. Fairburn and K. Brownell, Editors, *Eating Disorders and Obesity: A Comprehensive*

Handbook, Second Edition, 2002. New York: Guilford Press, pp. 204–209.

RECOVERY FROM AND OUTCOME OF EATING DISORDERS

Agras, W. S., S. J. Crow, K. A. Halmi, et al., Outcome Predictors for the Cognitive Behavioral Treatment of Bulimia Nervosa: Data from a Multisite Study, *American Journal of Psychiatry,* 2000, *157,* 1302–1308.

Bardone-Cone, A., M. Harney, C. Maldonado, et al., Defining Recovery from an Eating Disorder: Conceptualization, Validation, and Examination of Psychosocial Functioning and Psychiatric Comorbidity. *Behavioral Research Therapy,* 2010, *48,* 194–202.

Bryant-Waugh, R., J. Knibbs, A. Fosson, et al., Long-Term Follow-Up of Patients with Early Onset Anorexia Nervosa, *Archives of Diseases of Childhood,* 1988, *63,* 5–9.

Cachelin, F. M., R. H. Striegel-Moore, K. A. Elder, et al., Natural Course of a Community Sample of Women with Binge Eating Disorder, *International Journal of Eating Disorders,* 1999, *25*(1), 45–54.

Collings, S., and M. King, Ten-Year Follow-Up of 50 Patients with Bulimia Nervosa, *British Journal of Psychiatry,* 1994, *164,* 80–87.

Couturier, J., and J. Lock, What Is Recovery in Adolescent Anorexia Nervosa? *International Journal of Eating Disorders,* 2006, *39,* 550–555.

Deter, J., and W. Herzog, Anorexia Nervosa in a Long-Term Perspective: Results of the Heidelberg–Mannheim Study, *Psychosomatic Medicine,* 1994, *56,* 20–27.

Deter, J., W. Herzog, and E. Petzold, The Heidelberg–Mannheim Study: Long-Term Follow-Up of Anorexia Nervosa Patients at the University Medical Center—Background and Preliminary Results, in W. Herzog and W. Vandereycken, Editors, *The Course of Eating Disorders,* 1992. Berlin: Springer-Verlag, pp. 71–84.

Eckert, E. D., K. A. Halmi, P. Marchi, et al., Ten-Year Follow-Up of Anorexia Nervosa: Clinical Course and Outcome, *Psychological Medicine,* 1995, *25,* 143–156.

Eddy, K., P. K. Keel, D. J. Dorer, et al., Longitundinal Comparison of Anorexia Nervosa Subtypes, *International Journal of Eating Disorders,* 2002, *31,* 191–202.

Engel, K., A. E. Meyer, M. Henze, et al., Long-Term Outcome in Anorexia Nervosa Inpatients, in W. Herzog and W. Vandereycken,

Editors, *The Course of Eating Disorders*, 1992. Berlin: Springer-Verlag, pp. 167–181.

Fairburn, C. G., Z. Cooper, H. A. Doll, et al., The Natural Course of Bulimia Nervosa and Binge Eating Disorder in Young Women, *Archives of General Psychiary*, 2000, *57*, 659–665.

George, D., S. R. Weiss, H. E. Gwirtzman, et al., Anorexia Nervosa: A 25 Year Retrospective Study from 1958–1982, *International Journal of Eating Disorders*, 1987, *6*, 321–330.

Gillberg, I., M. Rastam, and L. Gillberg, Anorexia Nervosa Outcome: Six-Year Controlled Longitudinal Study of 51 Cases Including a Population Cohort, *Journal of the American Academy of Child and Adolescent Psychiatry*, 1994, *33*, 729–739.

Hawley, R., The Outcome of Anorexia Nervosa in Younger Subjects, *British Journal of Psychiatry*, 1985, *146*, 657–660.

Herzog, D. B., D. J. Dorer, P. K. Keel, et al., Recovery and Relapse in Anorexia and Bulimia Nervosa: A 7.5-Year Follow-Up Study, *Journal of the American Academy of Child and Adolescent Psychiatry*, 1999, *38*(7), 829–837.

Jenkins, M., An Outcome Study of Anorexia Nervosa in an Adolescent Unit, *Journal of Adolescence*, 1987, *10*, 71–81.

Jones, L., Long-Term Outcome of Anorexia Nervosa, *Behavioral Change*, 1993, *10*, 835–842.

Keel, P. K., J. E. Mitchell, K. B. Miller, et al., Long-Term Outcome of Bulimia Nervosa, *Archives of General Psychiatry*, 1999, *56*(1), 63–69.

Keel, P. K., J. E. Mitchell, K. B. Miller, et al., Social Adjustment over 10 Years Following Diagnosis with Bulimia Nervosa, *International Journal of Eating Disorders*, 2000, *27*(1), 21–28.

Krentz, A., J. Chew, and N. Arthur, Recovery from Binge Eating Disorder, *Canadian Journal of Counselling and Psychotherapy*, 2005, *39*, 118–136.

Olmsted, M. P., A. S. Kaplan, and W. Rockert, Rate and Prediction of Relapse in Bulimia Nervosa, *American Journal of Psychiatry*, 1994, *151*, 738–743.

Srinivasagam, N. M., W. H. Kaye, K. H. Plotnicov, et al., Persistent Perfectionism, Symmetry, and Exactness after Steinhausen H. Outcome of eating disorders. *Child and Adolescent Psychiatric Clinics of North America*, 2009, *18*, 225–242.

Zipfel, S., B. Lowe, D. L. Reas, et al., Long-Term Prognosis in Anorexia Nervosa: Lessons from a 21-Year Follow-Up Study, *Lancet*, 2000, *355*, 721–722.

Index

Abuse, 30–31, 71
Accomplishment, sense of, 19
Acidosis, 92–93
Adolescent-focused treatment (AFT).
    See also Individual psychodynamic
    psychotherapy
  compared to family-based treatment
    (FBT), 128–129
  overview, 125–126, 130–131
  supporting role of parents and,
    200–203
Advocacy, resources for, 272–280
Alcohol abuse, 98–99
All-or-nothing thinking, 105–107. *See
    also* Cognitive distortions
Amenorrhea, 83, 88–89. *See also*
    Menstruation changes
Anger, 19, 155–156
Anorexia nervosa
  adolescent-focused treatment (AFT),
    200–201
  approach to treatment and, 218

body image distortion and, 117–119
cognitive distortions and, 104–121
control, sense of, 107–110, 108
defining, 81–86
development of, 16–19
diagnosing, 84–85
exercise and, 172–174
expanding food choices and,
    170–172
family-based treatment (FBT) and,
    127–129
identifying problems and, 15
increasing the amount your child is
    eating, 165–170
medical complications associated
    with, 86–91
medications and, 133–136
minimizing the seriousness of the
    disease, 110–112
overview, 7
taking seriously, 53
treatment and, 124–125

Antianxiety medications, 134–135. *See also* Medications
Antidepressants, 134–135. *See also* Medications
Anxiety
    causation and, 61
    eating and, 19
    medications and, 134–135
    nature of eating disorders and, 39–40
Anxiety disorders, 30, 33
Autism, 60
Avoidance of conflict, 199
Avoidant personality disorder, 97–98
Avoidant/restrictive food intake disorder (ARFID)
    approach to treatment and, 218
    defining, 81–86
    diagnosing, 85–86
    expanding food choices and, 170–172
    increasing the amount your child is eating, 165–170
    medications and, 136
    overview, 7
    treatment and, 126

B

Bathroom visits after eating, 24
Beauty, cultural ideas of, 68–70
Behavioral experiments, 204
Behavioral treatment approach, 138
Binge-eating behaviors. *See also* Binge-eating disorder
    cognitive distortions and, 121
    development of bulimia nervosa and, 20–23
    helping your child to prevent, 174–177
    intensive treatments and, 138
    overview, 7

as a warning sign, 24
    whom and what to look for in an evaluation and, 30
Binge eating–purging type of anorexia nervosa, 82–83. *See also* Anorexia nervosa
Binge-eating disorder
    body image distortion and, 118
    control, sense of, 109–110
    defining, 81–86
    development of, 23
    diagnosing, 84–85
    exercise and, 173–174
    family-based treatment (FBT) and, 129
    identifying problems and, 15
    medical complications associated with, 94–95
    medications and, 136
    minimizing the seriousness of the disease, 111–112
    overview, 7
    taking seriously, 53
    treatment and, 126
Biological factors, 60–62
Blaming the child, 153–157, 196
Blaming the parents. *See also* Causation; Parents working together
    avoiding, 153–157
    current approaches to treatment and, 36–38, 41–51, 49–51
    family-based treatment (FBT) and, 51–52, 54
Blood pressure, 15
Body checking, 120–121
Body image distortion, 117–119. *See also* Cognitive distortions
Body mass index (BMI), 32
Body temperatures, 15
Bone marrow hypoplasia, 90
Borderline personality, 98
Bradycardia, 90

Brain structure and functioning, 90–91

Bulimia nervosa
approach to treatment and, 218
body image distortion and, 118
control, sense of, 108, 109–110
defining, 81–86
development of, 20–23
diagnosing, 83–84
exercise and, 172–174
family-based treatment (FBT) and, 129
identifying problems and, 15
individual psychodynamic psychotherapy and, 131–132
medical complications associated with, 91–94
medications and, 135, 136
minimizing the seriousness of the disease, 111–112
overview, 7
taking seriously, 53
treatment and, 124–125

BUN (blood urea nitrogen), 25–26

C

Calorie counting, 24, 170–172
Cancer, 25–26
Cardiac arrhythmias, 93
Cardiac dysfunction, 91
Cardiac mass, 15
Caries, 94
Causation. See also Blaming the parents
biological factors, 60–62
individual factors in, 59–71
overview, 58–59, 71–74

Changing disordered eating
being available to monitor eating and, 158–163
establishing a pattern of eating, 163–165
expanding food choices and, 170–172
increasing the amount your child is eating, 165–170
as the priority, 157–158

Charge, taking. See Parental involvement in treatment
Choice, 166–167
Clothes shopping with your child, 179–180
Cognitive-behavioral therapy (CBT). See also Treatment
bulimia nervosa and, 131–132
medications and, 135–136
overview, 41–42, 125–126
supporting role of parents and, 203–206

Cognitive distortions. See also Thought processes
advice from treatment providers you don't agree with and, 243–244
all-or-nothing thinking, 105–107
body image distortion, 117–119
conflict between you and your child as a result of, 112–114
control, sense of, 107–110
focus on food and "rules," 114–116
lying and, 116–117
minimizing the seriousness of the disease, 110–112
overview, 7, 101–102, 103–104, 122
parental involvement in treatment and, 177–178
pride, 120
promises and intentions of your child, 121
purging and, 119–120
understanding in your child, 104–121
weighing and body checking and, 120–121

Cognitive remediation therapy (CRT), 211–212
Cognitive restructuring, 204

Communicating with your child. *See
also* Families working together
about eating- or weight-related
concerns, 177–183
family therapy and, 199
seeking out professional help and,
28
Communication between treatment
providers, 244–249. *See also*
Working with treatment
providers
Comorbidity, 95–100, 134–135
Complete blood count, 25–26
Complications. *See also* Symptoms;
individual disorders
anorexia nervosa, 86–91
bulimia nervosa, 91–94
evaluations and, 30–31
importance of seeking help and,
15–16
laxative abuse and, 176–177
medical consequences associated
with eating disorders, 80–95
medications and, 134–135
Conflicts between parents and
children
cognitive distortions and, 112–114
divide-and-conquer scenarios,
217–231
family therapy and, 199
nature of eating disorders and,
38–41, 38*f*
parental involvement in treatment
and, 177–183
thought processes and, 101–104
Consequences for not eating, 154,
166–170
Control. *See also* Parental involvement
in treatment
blaming the parents and, 36–37
cognitive distortions and, 107–110
excluding parents from treatment
and, 46–47

focusing on the problem and,
157–177
knowing when to back off,
183–185
Cramps, 94
Creatinine, 25–26
Cultural factors, 67, 68–70

D

Day-patient treatment, 137–141,
192–198
Death, risk of
bulimia nervosa and, 92
importance of seeking help and,
15–16
taking seriously, 53
Dedication, 39–40
Dehydration, 93
Denial, 219–220
Depressed moods, 22
Depression
diagnosis and, 33
evaluations and, 30
medications and, 134–135
overview, 97
Development of an eating disorder
anorexia nervosa, 16–19
binge-eating disorder, 23
bulimia nervosa, 20–23
warning signs, 23–27
Developmental factors
adolescent-focused treatment (AFT),
201–202
causation and, 65–66
*Diagnostic and Statistical Manual of
Mental Disorders* (DSM-5) and,
4–5
evaluations and, 31
excluding parents from treatment
and, 44–46
Diabetes, 25–26

Diagnosis
    anorexia nervosa, 82–83
    avoidant/restrictive food intake
        disorder, 85–86
    binge-eating disorder, 84–85
    bulimia nervosa, 83–84
    challenges in, 32–34
    overview, 4–5, 81–86
    resources for, 253–272
    whom and what to look for in an
        evaluation and, 28–32
    working with treatment providers
        and, 236
*Diagnostic and Statistical Manual of
    Mental Disorders* (DSM-5)
    anorexia nervosa, 82–83
    avoidant/restrictive food intake
        disorder, 85–86
    binge-eating disorder, 84–85
    bulimia nervosa, 83–84
    causation and, 59
    overview, 4–5
Dialectical behavioral therapy (DBT),
    41–42, 126, 211. *See also* Treatment
Diet books, 24
Diet pills, 24
Dieticians, 32
Dieting. *See also* Extreme dieting; Food
        restriction
    development of anorexia nervosa
        and, 16–19
    as a warning sign, 24
    whom and what to look for in an
        evaluation and, 29–30
Distorted thinking. *See* Cognitive
        distortions
Divide-and-conquer scenarios,
    217–218, 217–231
Divorce
    being available to monitor eating
        and, 160
    family-based treatment (FBT) and,
        128–129

interpersonal psychotherapy (IPT)
    and, 207, 210–211
parental agreement and, 226–228
Dopamine, 61–62
Driven qualities, 39–40
Drug abuse, 98–99
Duration of treatment, 128–129

E

Eating. *See* Food refusal; Monitoring
        eating; Refeeding; Weight
        restoration
Eating disorders in general. *See also
        individual disorders*
    defining, 81–86
    development of anorexia nervosa,
        16–19
    development of binge-eating
        disorder, 23
    development of bulimia nervosa,
        20–23
    diagnosis and, 32–34
    identifying problems and, 15–16
    medical consequences associated
        with, 80–95
    nature of, 38–41, 38*f*
    overview, 7, 79–80
    taking seriously, 53
Eating with the family, 24. *See also*
        Refusing to eat
Education, 272–280
Ego-dystonic illness, 111–112
Ego-oriented individual therapy,
        130. *See also* Adolescent-focused
        treatment (AFT)
Ego-syntonic illness, 110–111
Electrocardiogram, 25–26
Electrolytes, 25–26
Emotion regulation, 23
Emotional loss, 30–31
Empowerment of parents, 54

Enamel loss. *See* Tooth enamel erosion
Esophageal tears, 92
Esophagus lining, 15
Evaluations, 27–32. *See also*
    Professional help
Exercise, 24, 138, 172–174
Expectations, 166–167, 168
Experts, working with. *See* Working
    with treatment providers
Externalizing the illness. *See*
    Separating the illness from the
    child
Extreme dieting, 16–19. *See also*
    Dieting; Food restriction

F

Families working together. *See also*
    Communicating with your
    child; Parental involvement
    in treatment; Parents working
    together
divide-and-conquer scenarios, 217–231
family-based treatment (FBT) and,
    54–55, 147–148
how to get professional help and, 28
monitoring eating and, 161–163
nature of eating disorders and,
    38–41, 38*f*
overview, 149–153, 214–215
roles in treatment, 41–51
Family-based treatment (FBT). *See*
    also Parental involvement in
    treatment; Treatment
cognitive distortions and, 122
overview, 3, 51–56, 125–126, 127–129
supporting role of parents and, 187
taking charge and, 145–146
Family factors, 64–65
Family therapy. *See also* Treatment
causation and, 64–65
overview, 41–42

supporting role of parents and,
    198–200
Fasting, 24
Fat checking. *See* Body checking
Fatigue, 15
Feeding behaviors, 61
Feminist perspective, 69–70
Focus on food, 114–116
Focusing on the problem
being available to monitor eating,
    158–163
changing disordered eating as the
    priority, 157–158
debating about eating- or weight-
    related concerns with your child,
    177–183
establishing a pattern of eating,
    163–165
exercise and, 172–174
expanding food choices and,
    170–172
helping your child to prevent binge
    eating and purging, 174–177
increasing the amount your child is
    eating, 165–170
knowing when to back off, 183–185
overview, 157
Food logs, 204–206
Food refusal, 24, 220–226
Food restriction, 16–19. *See also*
    Dieting
Food rituals, 19, 114–116
Friendships, 180, 184–185

G

Gastric distention, 94
Gastrointestinal difficulties, 91
Genetic factors, 60–62
Grief, 207
Grocery shopping with your child,
    179

Growth hormone changes, 90
Guilt, 19

H

Hair loss, 15
Hair texture, 90
Health complications of eating
    disorders. *See* Complications
Heart rate, 15
Hospitalization
    bulimia nervosa and, 92
    overview, 137–141
    supporting role of parents and,
        192–198
Hypochloremia, 93
Hypokalemia, 15
Hypokalemic alkalosis, 92–93
Hypotension, 89
Hypothalamic hypogonadism, 90
Hypothermia, 89

I

Ideal body weight (IBW), 32
Identifying problems. *See also* Symptoms
    development of anorexia nervosa
        and, 16–19
    development of bulimia nervosa
        and, 20–23
    list of things to look for, 24
    overview, 15–16, 23–27
Increasing the amount your child
    is eating, 165–170. *See also*
    Monitoring eating
Independence
    cognitive distortions and, 107–110
    conflicts between parents and
        children and, 40–41
    family therapy and, 199
    intensive treatments and, 138

Individual psychodynamic
    psychotherapy. *See also*
    Adolescent-focused treatment
    (AFT); Treatment
    excluding parents from, 42–51
    overview, 41–42, 129–132
    supporting role of parents and,
        200–203
Inpatient treatment. *See also* Treatment
    bulimia nervosa and, 92
    overview, 137–141
    supporting role of parents and,
        192–198
Intensive treatments. *See also*
    Treatment
    bulimia nervosa and, 92
    overview, 137–141
    supporting role of parents and,
        192–198
Intentions, 121
Internal bleeding, 92
Internet use, 182–183
Interpersonal deficits, 207
Interpersonal psychotherapy (IPT)
    nutritional counseling and, 133
    overview, 126
    supporting role of parents and,
        207–211
Irritability, 22

L

Lanugo, 90
Laxative abuse
    helping your child to prevent binge
        eating and purging and, 176–177
    importance of seeking help and, 15
    as a warning sign, 24
Liquid supplements, 170
Loss, 30–31
Lying, 116–117, 227. *See also* Separating
    the illness from the child

M

Malnutrition, 82–83
Media
    causation and, 67–68
    parental involvement in treatment
        and, 180–183
Medical complications. *See*
        Complications
Medical problems, 25–26
Medications, 25–26, 62, 133–136. *See
        also* Professional help
Menstruation changes
    diagnosing anorexia nervosa and,
        83
    importance of seeking help and, 15
    overview, 88–89
    as a warning sign, 24
Mental illness, 95–100
Milk, 172
Minimizing the seriousness of
        the disease, 110–112. *See also*
        Cognitive distortions
Missing food, 24
Monitoring eating. *See also* Refeeding;
        Weight restoration
    being available for, 158–163
    establishing a pattern of eating,
        163–165
    helping your child to prevent binge
        eating and purging and, 174–177
    increasing the amount your child is
        eating, 165–170
    parental agreement regarding how
        to handle, 220–226
Mood, 61
Mortality rate. *See also* Death, risk of
    bulimia nervosa and, 92
    importance of seeking help and, 15
    taking seriously, 53
Myocardial toxicity caused by emetine,
        93–94

N

Negative mood states, 61
Neurobiological factors, 61–62
Neurotransmitters, 61–62
Norepinephrine, 61–62
Nutritional counseling, 132–133

O

Obesity, 94–95
Observing staff members, 196
Obsessionality, 61
Obsessive-compulsive disorder, 30,
        96
Osteoporosis, 15
Outpatient treatments, 125–136. *See
        also* Treatment
Overeating, 20–23. *See also* Binge-
        eating behaviors

P

Parent education meetings, 196
Parent support groups and therapy,
        196
Parental agreement. *See also* Parents
        working together
    divorce and, 226–228
    effectiveness of each parent,
        228–229
    overview, 234–235
    regarding disease management,
        220–226, 231–234
    regarding the approach to
        treatment, 217–218
    regarding the illness and its
        seriousness, 219–220
    separating the illness from the child
        and, 231–232

siding with the adolescent and,
229–231

when one parent does all the work,
228–229

Parental involvement in treatment.
See also Family-based treatment
(FBT); Supporting role of parents;
Working with treatment providers

being available to monitor eating
and, 158–163

current approaches to treatment
and, 35–38, 41–51

debating about eating- or weight-
related concerns with your child,
177–183

establishing a pattern of eating,
163–165

exclusion of parents from treatment
and, 240–242

exercise and, 172–174

expanding food choices and,
170–172

focusing on the problem and,
157–177

helping your child to prevent binge
eating and purging, 174–177

how to get professional help, 27–32

increasing the amount your child is
eating, 165–170

individual psychodynamic
psychotherapy and, 130–132

knowing when to back off, 183–185

overview, 1–6, 140–141, 145–148

taking care of yourself and, 185–186

Parents working together. *See also*
Families working together;
Parental agreement; Parental
involvement in treatment

agreeing on treatment approach,
188–189

being available to monitor eating
and, 158–163

current approaches to treatment
and, 41–51

denial of one parent and, 219–220

divide-and-conquer scenarios,
217–231

effectiveness of each parent,
228–229

family-based treatment (FBT) and,
54–55

how to get professional help and,
27–28

one parent doing all the work,
228–229

overview, 149–153, 214–215

separating the illness from the child
and, 231–232

siding with the adolescent and,
229–231

Parotid glands, 94

Pediatricians, 25, 238–240

Peer relationships, 180, 184–185

Perfectionism

all-or-nothing thinking and,
105–107

causation and, 61

nature of eating disorders and,
39–40

Personality disorders, 30

Personality traits, 61, 70, 97–98

Phone apps, 205. *See also* Self-
monitoring

Physical abuse, 30–31, 71

Physical examination, 25–26,
238–240

Physical loss, 30–31

Physician, 25

Picky eating, 24, 86

Portion control, 24

Potassium depletion, 15

Power, 19, 107–110

Praise, 167

Preoccupation with food, 19, 33–34

Presenting a united front. *See* Parental agreement; Parents working together
Prevention, 72–73
Privacy, 41
Pro-anorexia or pro-eating disorder websites, 24
Problem solving, 204
Pro-eating disorder websites, 24, 182–183
Professional help. *See also* Working with treatment providers
  how to obtain, 27–32
  overview, 6–7
  when to seek out, 14–16, 23–27
Progress assessment, 190
Promises, 121
Psychiatric medications. *See* Medications
Psychoanalysis, 62–64
Psychoanalytic tradition, 62–64
Psychological aspect, 80–95
Psychological treatments, 125–126. *See also* Treatment
Psychosomatic family process, 49–51
Punishments, 167. *See also* Consequences for not eating
Purgative use, 15
Purging
  avoiding blame and, 155–156
  cognitive distortions and, 119–120
  development of bulimia nervosa and, 20–23
  exercise and, 173–174
  helping your child to prevent, 174–177
  identifying problems and, 15
  intensive treatments and, 138
  overview, 7, 175–176
  as a warning sign, 24

R

Recording food intake, 204–206
Refeeding, 47, 165–170, 220–226. *See also* Monitoring eating; Weight restoration
Refusing to eat, 24, 220–226. *See also* Eating with the family
Relationship with your child, 38–41, 38*f*, 101–104. *See also* Conflicts between parents and children
Renal problems, 93
Residential treatment
  bulimia nervosa and, 92
  overview, 137–141
  supporting role of parents and, 192–198
Responsibility, 155
Restricting type of anorexia nervosa, 82–83. *See also* Anorexia nervosa
Rituals around food. *See* Food rituals
Role disputes, 207–209
Role transitions, 207, 209–210
Routines, 163–165, 174–177
Rules, 175–176

S

Scheduling meals, 163–165
Schizophrenia, 60
School
  knowing when to back off and, 184–185
  monitoring eating and, 160–161, 227
  school work and the development of bulimia and, 22
  treatment and, 191
Seizures, 93

Selective serotonin reuptake inhibitors
(SSRIs), 134. *See also* Medications
Self-blame by parents, 57–59. *See also*
Blaming the parents
Self-care, 185–186
Self-esteem, 106, 131–132
Self-management, 149
Self-monitoring, 204–206
Self psychology, 200–201
Separating the illness from the child
advice from treatment providers you
don't agree with and, 243–244
avoiding blame and, 153–157
cognitive distortions and, 114, 122
increasing the amount your child is
eating and, 168–169
parental agreement and, 231–232
Serotonin, 61–62
Serum amylase levels, 94
Sexual abuse, 30–31, 71
Shame, 22
Showering, 24
Siblings, 152–153, 161–163. *See also*
Families working together
Single-parent households
being available to monitor eating
and, 160
family-based treatment (FBT) and,
128–129
interpersonal psychotherapy (IPT)
and, 207, 210–211
parental agreement and, 226–228
working with treatment providers
and, 217
Skin changes, 15, 90
Skipping meals, 24
Social activities, 184–185
Social difficulties, 23
Social factors, 67, 68–70
Socioeconomic status, 70
Spouses working together. *See* Parents
working together

Starvation
identifying problems and, 15
medical complications associated
with, 88–89, 92
overview, 7
seeking out professional help and,
25–26
Stomach flu, 24
Stomach lining, 15
Strength, 19
Structural family therapy, 65
Structuring eating, 163–165
Substance abuse, 98–99
Support groups, 196
Supporting role of parents. *See also*
Parental involvement in
treatment
cognitive-behavioral therapy (CBT)
and, 203–206
cognitive remediation therapy (CRT)
and, 211–212
dialectical behavioral therapy (DBT)
and, 211
family therapy and, 198–200
individual psychodynamic
psychotherapy and, 200–203
intensive treatments and, 192–198
interpersonal psychotherapy (IPT)
and, 207–211
overview, 187–191
staying involved when you aren't in
charge, 192–212
Symptoms. *See also* Complications;
individual disorders
conflicts between parents and
children and, 38–41, 38*f*
defining eating disorders and,
80–95
identifying problems and, 15–16
warning signs, 23–27
what to expect in terms of progress
and, 190

T

Taking care of yourself, 185–186
Taking charge. *See* Parental
    involvement in treatment
Temperamental traits, 70. *See also*
    Personality traits
Tetany, 94
Therapist role, 55
Therapists, 191, 240–242. *See also*
    Treatment; Working with
    treatment providers
Therapy for parents, 196
Thinking style, 62–64
Thought processes. *See also* Cognitive
    distortions
  causation and, 62–64
  overview, 7, 101–104
  working with experts and, 149
Thyroid disease, 25–26
Tooth enamel erosion, 15, 94
Trauma, 30–31, 71
Traveling, 164–165
Treatment. *See also* Cognitive-
    behavioral therapy (CBT);
    Dialectical behavioral
    therapy (DBT); Family-based
    treatment (FBT); Family
    therapy; Parental involvement
    in treatment; Supporting
    role of parents; Working with
    treatment providers; Individual
    psychodynamic therapy
  agreeing on, 188–189
  attendance, 191
  bulimia nervosa and, 94
  choosing, 188–189
  communication between treatment
    providers and, 244–249
  current approaches to treatment
    and, 41–51
  family's role in, 41–51
  intensive treatments, 92, 137–141,
    192–198
  outpatient treatments, 125–136
  overview, 124–125, 140–141
  resources for, 253–272
  what to expect in terms of progress
    and, 190
Trust, 149

U

Urine specific gravity, 25–26

V

Values regarding weight, 180–183
Vegetarianism, 24
Vomiting, 15. *See also* Purging

W

Warning signs, 23–27. *See also*
    Identifying problems
Weakness, 15
Wealth, 70
Websites that are pro-anorexia or pro-
    eating disorder, 24, 182–183
Weighing frequently, 120–121, 178
Weight loss, 24, 25–26
Weight restoration. *See also* Monitoring
    eating; Refeeding
  increasing the amount your child is
    eating, 165–170
  intensive treatments and, 137–141
  parental agreement regarding how
    to handle, 220–226
Western ideals of beauty, 68–70
Whole milk, 172
Withdrawal from family and friends, 22

Working together with a spouse. *See* Parents working together
Working with treatment providers. *See also* Parental involvement in treatment; Professional help; Therapists; Treatment
advice you don't agree with, 242–244
exclusion of parents from treatment and, 240–242
family-based treatment (FBT) and, 147–148
giving up by the providers, 249–250
increasing the amount your child is eating and, 165
multiple providers and, 244–249
overview, 8, 148–149, 214–215, 236–238, 250–252
supporting role of parents and, 187–191
when the treatment provider denies existence of an eating disorder, 238–240

About the Authors

James Lock, MD, PhD, is Professor of Child Psychiatry and Pediatrics at Stanford University and Director of the Stanford Child and Adolescent Eating Disorders Program. Dr. Lock has received numerous awards for his research on eating disorders and has published several books for professionals in collaboration with Daniel Le Grange. He is committed to providing evidence-based treatments to children, adolescents, and their families.

Daniel Le Grange, PhD, is the Benioff UCSF Professor in Children's Health in the Departments of Psychiatry and Pediatrics and Joint Director of the Eating Disorders Program at the University of California, San Francisco. He is Emeritus Professor at the University of Chicago, where he was Director of the Eating Disorders Program until 2014. An award-winning researcher, Dr. Le Grange was a member of the team at the Maudsley Hospital in London that developed family-based treatment for anorexia nervosa. Over his career, he has treated numerous adolescents and families struggling with eating disorders.